FOUNDATION PRESS

PRESIDENTIAL POWER STORIES

Edited By

CHRISTOPHER H. SCHROEDER
Professor of Law
Duke University

CURTIS A. BRADLEY
Professor of Law
Duke University

FOUNDATION PRESS
2009

© 2009 By THOMSON REUTERS/FOUNDATION PRESS
        195 Broadway, 9th Floor
        New York, NY 10007
        Phone Toll Free 1–877–888–1330
        Fax (212) 367–6799
        foundation–press.com
Printed in the United States of America

ISBN 978–1–59941–373–0

 TEXT IS PRINTED ON 10% POST CONSUMER RECYCLED PAPER

This book is dedicated to our families:
Kate, Emily, Ted, and Lily, and
Kathy, David, and Liana.

*

PRESIDENTIAL POWER STORIES

FOUNDATION PRESS

PRESIDENTIAL POWER STORIES

*

Introduction

Christopher H. Schroeder
Curtis A. Bradley

The Story of Presidential Power

To the drafters of the Constitution, achieving their objective of a central government both strong enough to handle national domestic problems and the nation's security while also controlled enough to avoid the abuse of power depended crucially on a proper allocation of authority among the separate branches of the federal government, as well as between state and federal authorities. They therefore devoted considerable attention to defining and dividing the powers of the new federal government between Congress and the President.

Many of their countrymen did not entirely share their faith that structuring government power would adequately protect individual liberties from government excess, and insisted that explicit protections of certain individual liberties be added. The addition of the Bill of Rights, however, ought not to change our understanding of the important role the separation of powers plays in protecting individual liberties. Many of the chapters of this book present judicial decisions in which individuals challenge a claimed infringement on their rights or liberties. In most of these cases, there is no question that the federal government taken as a whole possesses the authority to act. Instead, the challengers claim the action cannot stand because the President's unilateral power under the Constitution does not give him the legal authority to act without congressional authorization, or in the face of congressional opposition. By dividing government authority so that the political branches of government must often act jointly before rights or liberties can be limited, the Constitution creates an additional layer of potential legal protection. Determining when existing presidential authority is sufficient to justify an action thus becomes a matter of great importance.

Individuals are not always in a position to challenge assertions of presidential authority, sometimes because those actions affect individual rights only in indiscernible or attenuated ways (think of a dispute between Congress and the President over whether one of his aides must give testimony to Congress), and sometimes because limitations on the power of the judiciary prevent claims from being brought (think of challenges to the Vietnam War based on claims that it lacked the necessary congressional authorization). Nor can members of Congress typically take the President to court.[1] Numerically, disagreements about presidential authority that end without any litigation at all far outnumber those that end up in court, let alone those few cases that make their way to the Supreme Court. This would hardly have surprised the Framers, who thought that the primary mechanism through which the elected branches of government would be kept within their proper spheres of action would come from each branch jealously guarding its own powers.

By focusing on notable occasions of judicial resolution of presidential power questions, then, this book concentrates on the atypical rather than the typical situations in which questions of presidential power arise. In studying presidential power, however, the litigated instances have some distinct advantages as the initial objects of study compared to any comparable number of instances that ended without litigation. Almost all arguments solely between Congress and the President over the President's powers end inconclusively, without any sense that the rival parties have reached a shared view on the extent of either branch's powers. By and large, the parties fight until they achieve a modus vivendi enabling them to navigate past the current controversy, retiring to their corners to fight another day.

Beyond the problem of a lack of agreement between the two parties, it can frequently be difficult even to determine the position of Congress at all, particularly when binding votes are lacking. Has Congress acquiesced in some presidential action, for instance, because it recognizes the legitimate assertion of presidential authority, or because the action has proven in some sense successful in achieving an objective agreeable to Congress, which therefore decides that it will desist in challenging a desired fait accompli? In comparison, judicial decisions, while often rife with ambiguities of their own, at least confront the arguments and counterarguments and result in a decision with a rationale that can be analyzed and dissected. In addition, each judicial decision usually surveys a body of prior disagreements, drawing together the historical background as well as the dispute's more immediate context to provide a larger perspective on the nature of these disagreements and their possible resolutions. Finally, the relatively few occasions in which the Supreme Court has decided a presidential powers issue themselves consti-

---

[1] *See* Raines v. Byrd, 521 U.S. 811 (1997).

tute significant markers in debating the boundaries of those powers by virtue of the respect such judgments are accorded.

Cumulatively, the cases demonstrate just how much material outside of the constitutional text the Court must draw upon to resolve the questions presented. Despite the considerable importance of separated powers and the attention originally given to the allocation of authority under the Constitution, the actual workings of our government have generated far more allocation questions than the Constitution's text answers. Such was perhaps inevitable, because by building the potential for friction and disputes between the branches into the very heart of the government's structure, the Constitution practically guarantees that the day to day operations of government will produce disagreements over the extent of any one branch's powers, and yet the document's text, while attending to some important issues quite directly, is nonetheless extremely sparse in its details. Frequently, the document is content to rely on quite broad concepts. Critical terms such as the President's "executive power," his status as "commander-in-chief," and Congress's power to "declare war" and to provide for the "regulation of the land and naval forces" are entirely undefined, their ramifications and implications unstated. Still other concepts, such as executive privilege, are not mentioned at all. Once the two elected branches of government began jostling with each other over their respective roles in the actual operation of government, they have encountered numerous questions whose answers require supplementing the text.

The incidents and controversies described in the chapters of this book illustrate the range of questions that have arisen: may the President interpret treaties and announce that interpretation as the position of the United States when doing so may affect Congress' authority to declare war; may the President make criminal a violation of international law when Congress has not enacted a criminal statute that does so; may the President decide when a state of war exists notwithstanding Congress' authority to declare war; may the President create military commissions to try persons detained during times of war and charged with violations of the laws of war; may the President employ force to protect judicial officers of the United States; may the President be compelled to gain approval of the Senate in removing those officers for whom senatorial advice and consent is required; may the President take control of critical privately-owned production facilities in the name of national security; may the President authorize wiretaps without congressional authorization; may the President withhold information from Congress in the name of preserving the confidentiality of presidential communications; may Congress create a federal prosecutor over whom the President can exercise only limited control?[2]

When the Supreme Court has attempted to answer questions such as these, it has supplemented the constitutional text in a variety of ways. Even more than the outcome of any specific dispute, the Court's reasoning about which supplements it finds useful and why they deserve to be accorded weight helps us to frame our own thinking about the relevance and implications of the various factors that might be brought to bear on these disputes. The Justices have drawn guidance from the overall structure of the Constitution and the government it establishes, from the actions of the early Presidents and Congresses, from subsequent patterns of behavior of later Presidents and Congresses, from the needs of operating an effective government, from the demands of emergency and exigent circumstances, from the appropriateness of deferring to executive judgment, especially in matters of foreign affairs and national security, and from principles of international law. Their judgments are also frequently complicated by the broader political, social, and legal context in which these disputes come to the Court.

This volume is premised on the belief that tracing the narrative of these disputes, with attention both to the trajectory of the litigation itself and to the pertinent features of the larger context, can improve our appreciation of the decisions and thus can advance our understanding of presidential powers.

The first chapter presents the only incident in the volume that did not produce a Supreme Court ruling. In it, Martin Flaherty addresses the Neutrality Controversy of 1793.[3] With the commencement of the French–English War of the 1790s, President Washington viewed the national interest to be best served by a policy of neutrality toward the two protagonists. Wishing to articulate that stance for both international and domestic purposes, Washington needed to decide how far he was entitled to go in interpreting existing treaties as well as in articulating the foreign policy of the United States as it related to the questions of neutrality. His eventual "Proclamation" was cautious, stating the American stance to be one of neutrality, but declining to use the precise term "neutrality" for fear that it might be taken to be a term of art having

---

[2] We have tried to select cases that are both interesting and significant, after seeking advice from other scholars, including the contributors. We ended up with a collection that is particularly focused on the President's foreign affairs and commander-in-chief authorities, although some significant domestic authority cases are also included here. As is inevitable in a selective treatment, some important issues are not addressed. For a recent assessment of the president's domestic authorities set within a comprehensive analysis of the Constitution's system of separated powers, *see* Harold H. Bruff, *Balance of Forces: Separation of Powers in the Administrative State* (2006).

[3] Martin S. Flaherty, The Story of the Neutrality Controversy: Struggling Over Presidential Power Outside the Courts, Chapter 1.

implications properly determined by Congress. Despite the caution, some saw Washington's declaration as overreaching. That reaction prompted a famous defense of Washington's actions by Alexander Hamilton, writing under the pseudonym Pacificus, based on two possible conceptions of presidential authority, one broader than the other. To this James Madison, writing as Helvidius, responded in the name of a still narrower conception.

The Pacificus–Helvidius debate articulated visions of presidential authority that are debated still, but the dispute over the propriety of Washington's declaration of the United States' foreign policy position passed without judicial involvement. In fact, Washington's attempt to enlist the advice of the Court by propounding a list of 29 questions concerning United States policy was rebuffed by the Court as calling for an advisory opinion, thereby laying down a limit on judicial authority to which the Supreme Court has adhered ever since. Once Congress convened after Washington's Proclamation, both Houses passed resolutions praising Washington's handling of the situation, but having no need to weigh in on the competing conceptions of presidential authority put forth by Pacificus and Helvidius, Congress did not do so.

The remaining eleven chapters address Supreme Court decisions. Most of the cases exhibit the same characteristic pattern: some executive branch action that has infringed or threatens to infringe an individual's claim of right is challenged not because the Constitution prohibits the federal government from taking the action, but rather because the President acting alone, or in the face of congressional opposition, is argued to lack sufficient authority to do so.[4] The chapters proceed in chronological order.

The Prize Cases may, as Thomas Lee and Michael Ramsey state, involve circumstances and a question of the law of war that are "opaque" to modern readers.[5] In these Civil War cases, the owners of cargo seized by Union ships maintaining a blockade challenged the lawfulness of the seizures. In April 1861, after Fort Sumter had fallen but prior to the outbreak of any further armed hostilities, President Lincoln had ordered the blockade in advance of any declaration of war or authorization of force by Congress. Under international war, the right to blockade and the attendant rights to seize a ship's cargo depended upon

---

[4] In *Ex parte Milligan*, trial by military commission was challenged as both unconstitutional and as unauthorized by Congress, and a majority of the Supreme Court ruled on the constitutional issue, saying that the commissions would be invalid even if authorized by Congress. In *Morrison v. Olson*, the petitioner challenged the actions of the independent counsel on the ground that that office was too far removed from direct control by the President, not because the President was exercising power that he did not have.

[5] Thomas H. Lee & Michael D. Ramsey, The Story of the *Prize* Cases: Executive Action and Judicial Review in Wartime, Chapter 2.

whether a state of war existed. Did the President have the authority to make his own determination that a state of war existed—and, just as importantly, did that unilateral determination then legitimize the block-ade—or did respecting Congress' power to declare war under the separa-tion of powers require that Congress act before the United States could avail itself of the rights of blockade?

In a 5–4 decision, the Supreme Court upheld the seizures. The Court's decision depended heavily upon questions of international law regarding the necessary preconditions for triggering a nation's right to blockade, but a decision adverse to Lincoln's action could also have had far reaching ramifications outside of that context. Not only would all other seizures made prior to Congress' official sanctioning of military action against the Confederacy have been subject to challenge, such a ruling might have cast doubt on other unilateral actions by the Presi-dent, including the Emancipation Proclamation. The Justices were un-doubtedly aware of the potential downstream consequences of such a ruling, just as they were aware that they were being asked to rule against the President while the Civil War still raged, and to cast judgment on presidential actions that Congress had swiftly ratified once it came into session in July 1861. On the crucial question of whether an actual state of war existed in April 1861, the majority seemed to defer to the President's judgment, although the majority also referenced objective facts that made the existence of hostilities seem obvious. Each of these elements in the case—the level of national security threat present when the decision was handed down, the legal implications for other decisions that already had been made, the propriety of deference to the executive, and the role of international law in defining the president's war pow-ers—is a recurring theme in many presidential powers decisions.

The next chapter involves another Civil War-era decision, this time with an extremely contemporary ring to it. After the attacks of Septem-ber 11, 2001, President Bush announced that he intended to use military commissions to try foreign nationals accused of participating in those attacks or aiding the groups responsible for them. This prompted many people to consult *Ex parte Milligan*,[6] the seminal decision of the Supreme Court to address the use of military commissions. *Milligan*, which arrived at the Supreme Court after the Civil War had ended, ruled that President Lincoln lacked the authority to try the petitioners before military commissions. Curtis Bradley's account of the decision reveals some inconsistencies between the Court's discussion of the status of the

---

[6] 71 U.S. (4 Wall.) 2 (1866).

petitioners as well as of the charges brought against them, compared to the facts and charges as revealed by the evidence below and the historical record.[7]

Bradley also sets the case in the context of the widespread use of military commissions during the Civil War, noting that it is unclear how much of this larger practice the Supreme Court meant to repudiate. These complications make the decision a difficult one to interpret and apply to contemporary circumstances. The immediate reaction to the opinion, furthermore, contrasts sharply with *Milligan's* treatment today as a landmark civil liberties decision. At the time, it was widely criticized as potentially undermining Reconstruction efforts by calling into doubt the exercise of military jurisdiction in the South. Notwithstanding *Milligan*, commissions continued to be used in the South, often to try white Southerners for acts of violence against blacks, unionists, and federal officials. In order to prevent the Supreme Court from hearing further habeas challenges from these commission trials, brought by persons charged with acts aimed at slowing progress toward racial equality, Congress restricted the Supreme Court's appellate jurisdiction, an action that was upheld by the Court in *Ex parte McCardle*.[8]

Bradley sounds a cautious note regarding how much light *Milligan* sheds on contemporary military commission issues in the context of the war on terror, suggesting that a study of the case's context and aftermath "reveal[] the limitations of judicial precedent," and suggest the desirability of a politically-accountable Congress regulating the use of commissions.[9]

In re Neagle,[10] the case discussed by John Harrison, is the first case in the volume that did not involve foreign affairs.[11] This case arose after Attorney General Miller authorized the United States Marshal in northern California to hire a deputy to protect Justice Stephen Field when Field was riding circuit in the state. Concerns for Field's safety were occasioned by threats that a litigant, David Terry, had made against Field in open court, in a case in which the circuit court's decision was adverse to Terry. So far, this hardly seems a likely circumstance to test the outer limits of some aspect of presidential power. Events became more complicated when the hired deputy, David Neagle, shot and killed

---

[7] Curtis A. Bradley, The Story of *Ex parte Milligan*: Military Trials, Enemy Combatants, and Congressional Authorization, Chapter 3.

[8] 74 U.S. (7 Wall.) 506 (1868).

[9] Prompted by the Supreme Court's decision in *Hamdan v. Rumsfeld*, Congress enacted commission-enabling legislation to regulate the use of commissions in the war on terror. *Hamdan* and the Military Commissions Act are discussed in Chapter 12.

[10] 135 U.S. 1 (1890).

[11] John Harrison, The Story of *In re Neagle*: Sex, Money, Politics, Perjury, Homicide, Federalism, and Executive Power, Chapter 4.

Terry when Terry later approached Justice Field in a public place. The sheriff of the city of Stockton then arrested Neagle for murder, and when Neagle sought a writ of habeas corpus in federal court, issue was joined on whether Neagle had available to him defenses that would normally be available to a law enforcement officer. The answer to that question turned on whether or not Neagle had been lawfully hired, there being no federal statute on the books clearly providing for the protection of federal judges when they were not conducting official duties in a federal courthouse.

Asserting executive authority to protect a federal judge in the absence of a federal statute clearly authorizing that protection became necessary in order to satisfy the jurisdictional requirements of the federal habeas statute as it then was written and thus to secure a federal forum to weigh the disputed self-defense evidence. A federal forum seemed essential to Neagle's defenders because they believed such a forum would be much more hospitable to the claims of a federal deputy than would a state court jury. Here, Harrison describes a larger legal context of Supreme Court decisions affirming the ability of the federal government to protect its functions, without reliance upon state authorities. These prior decisions were embedded in a historical pattern of state hostility to federal law enforcement that made the assertion of self-protection by the federal government essential to its full and effective operation. *In re Neagle* wrestled with the consequences of Congress failing to have provided by statute for one dimension of that self-protection, and concluded that the President possessed the interstitial authority to provide it without statutory authorization.

The Supreme Court's understanding of the functional demands of maintaining an effective government seem very much at the forefront of this presidential powers decision. As Justice Miller wrote, "it would be a great reproach to the system of government of the United States, declared to be within its sphere sovereign and supreme, if there is to be found within the domain of its powers no means of protecting the judges in the conscientious and faithful discharge of their duties from the malice and hatred of those upon whom their judgments may operate unfavorably."[12]

Functional demands are also prominent in the next chapter's case, *Myers v. United States*.[13] Under an 1876 statute, the President was required to obtain the Senate's advice and consent to remove a postmaster. Practice in the Senate appeared to give great deference to the President's removals: Sai Prakash reports in this chapter that the Senate routinely acquiesced in removal decisions simply by giving its

---

[12] 135 U.S. at 59.

[13] Myers v. United States, 272 U.S. 52 (1926).

consent to the individual chosen by the President to replace a current occupant of the office.[14] Events proceeded differently, however, in the case of Portland, Oregon's first class postmaster, Frank Myers. Criticized for his abrasive management of the office, and having offended some local Democratic politicians, Myers was discharged by the Postmaster General, but the President never obtained Senate approval for the discharge, and did not submit a replacement to that body, either. When the term for which Myers had been appointed expired, he sued for backpay to which he claimed to be entitled because he had remained ready and willing to work and because he argued that his discharge was ineffective under the statute.

The First Congress had debated the role of the Senate in the removal of cabinet officials when it was enacting laws establishing the first executive departments. When Chief Justice Taft, our only former President to serve on the Supreme Court, wrote the decision for the Court upholding the President's power to discharge Myers notwithstanding the 1876 statute, his opinion was notable for its extended discussion of and reliance upon this early congressional history. In so relying, the opinion discounted the significance of the impressive list of subsequent legislation in which removal restrictions had been placed on the President. *Myers'* dissenters in effect reversed the priority of these two factors, placing more weight on a long pattern of such legislation.

While the discussion in the First Congress obviously lent weight to Taft's judgment and influenced his thinking, Taft wrote that he was drawn to this history, "not because a congressional conclusion on a constitutional issue is conclusive, but first because of our agreement with the reasons upon which it was avowedly based."[15] The debate in the First Congress invoked quite varied reasons, including essentialist arguments about what the concept of "executive power" must necessarily include, but also functional arguments claiming that the power to remove is important to the executive in order to give him sufficient disciplinary authority over subordinates to manage effectively. Later on, Taft was reported as saying that he "never wrote an opinion that I felt to be so important in its effects."[16]

Whereas in *Myers* Congress had attempted to restrict the President's powers, *Curtiss-Wright*[17] arose after Congress sought to augment

---

[14] Saikrishna Prakash, The Story of *Myers* and its Wayward Successors: Going Postal on the Removal Power, Chapter 5.

[15] Myers v. United States, 272 U.S. at, 136.

[16] 2 Henry Pringle, *The Life and Times of William Howard Taft* 1025 (1939). In subsequent decisions, the Court has declined to embrace some of the broader potential implications of *Myers*, as Kevin Stack discusses in his chapter on *Morrison v. Olson*.

[17] United States v. Curtiss–Wright Export Corporation, 299 U.S. 304 (1936).

those powers. In order to control the shipment of American arms to Paraguay and Bolivia during the Chaco War between these two countries, Congress enacted a Joint Resolution authorizing the President to make arms sales to those countries illegal, subjecting violators to imprisonment and fines. Principal officers of Curtiss–Wright were indicted for violating the arms sales ban.

As Jeff Powell explains, *Curtiss-Wright* tells several different stories.[18] The most remembered of these stories focuses on the broad rhetoric of the decision, extolling the President's role as "sole organ of the nation in its external relations," vested by the Constitution with "delicate, plenary and exclusive power" in the field of foreign relations. As such, the opinion has become a frequent reference point for advocates of extensive and exclusive presidential powers in foreign relations.

Interestingly, had the events giving rise to the case occurred even a few years later, the narrower story of the specific legal challenge that the petitioners brought against their indictments would never have had to be written. Events were such, however, that Congress' and the President's actions to prevent American arms from further fueling the Chaco War took place in the mid–1930s, thereby raising a potentially fatal nondelegation challenge. The Joint Resolution's grant of discretionary authority to the President to decide whether to criminalize arms sales quite arguably ran counter to the Court's recent precedent in *Schechter Poultry* and *Panama Refining* interpreting the Constitution to constrain Congress in granting discretionary powers to the President. Because these cases made reliance on a grant of congressional authority questionable, the only other justification for sustaining the charges against Curtiss-Wright's officers had to rest on some authority the President derived directly from other sources. Drawing a distinction between the government's domestic powers, where anything not clearly authorized is prohibited, and the government's foreign affairs authority derived from its status as a sovereign nation, Sutherland's opinion sustained the President's proclamation.

The government's lawyers had not sought to argue the case on such broad grounds as Sutherland invoked. Instead, they pointed to the long historical practice of giving the President broad delegations to conduct foreign policy, using this plus a careful construction of the Joint Resolution to argue that the Resolution satisfied the limitations on congressional delegation of authority even as they had recently been construed by the Supreme Court. In so doing they sought to avoid having the Court place even further restrictions on the ability of Congress to enact New Deal legislation aimed at economic recovery, for it was the potentially negative impact of the case on the President's domestic agenda that

---

[18] H. Jefferson Powell, The Story of *Curtiss-Wright Export Corporation*, Chapter 6.

worried them the most. The Court's 1937 shift in its standards for reviewing domestic economic legislation removed that concern, but the decision has had broader significance because of its rhetoric about presidential foreign affairs authority. Powell examines the nature of the decision's continued use in presidential powers debates.

Youngstown Sheet & Tube Co. v. Sawyer is the next case.[19] Probably the most familiar decision in the volume, the case was brought by steel manufacturers after President Truman had seized their facilities and placed them under government control in order to ensure a steady supply of steel for military purposes during the Korean War. As Patricia Bellia's account shows, Truman acted because a labor management dispute over wages threatened to devolve into a strike, shutting down the steel mills.[20] The company owners had refused to grant the unions a pay increase that the government's Wage Stabilization Board determined to be warranted unless the companies also received the right to raise prices in an amount that Truman thought to be excessive.

Previous presidents had occasionally seized industries, but under circumstances that were not identical to those facing Truman. Congress had also recently enacted the Taft–Hartley Act, which employed a regime of court-injunction and cooling off period to address labor-management disputes in critical industries. Prior legislation that authorized presidential seizures had expired or been replaced by legislation lacking such explicit authorization, and seizure authority had been debated but not included in Taft–Hartley.

During hearings in the trial court on whether the steel companies were entitled to an injunction against the government's takeover of the mills, the government's lawyers had advanced a strong claim that the President's authority in a time of emergency was essentially unlimited, save by the exercise by Congress of its impeachment authority or by the people of their ballot box authority. By the time the case reached the Supreme Court, however, the government had trimmed its claim considerably, relying heavily on what it considered a convincing past practice of presidential seizures, typically but not always combined with clear congressional endorsement, as substantiating this particular action.

Justice Black wrote for the Court in declaring the seizure to be beyond the President's authority, although the case is most widely remembered for Justice Jackson's concurrence and its familiar tripartite approach for evaluating the extent of presidential power depending upon whether it is exercised with congressional concurrence, silence, or opposition. Black's opinion along with the multiple concurrences and dissent

---

[19] 343 U.S. 579 (1952).

[20] Patricia L. Bellia, The Story of the *Steel Seizure* Case, Chapter 7.

provide a rich set of differing perspectives on the law and facts presented. The conference notes of several Justices indicate that several of those
in the majority were skeptical about the seriousness of the emergency
facing the country and unwilling to defer simply to the President's
assertion that one existed—and hence give rise to the speculation that
the case might have been decided differently had the emergency been
more palpable—while the dissenters were much more willing to treat the
emergency as genuine. The opinions also draw different implications
from the past seizures as well as from the legislation that Congress had
enacted. In their concurrences, Justices Frankfurter and Jackson focused
on Congress's activity aimed directly at creating a legal framework to
address labor-management disputes, which taken cumulatively led them
to conclude that Congress had prohibited unilateral presidential action
in favor of alternative mechanisms. The dissenters saw a larger legislative landscape. For them, the landscape included the legislation Congress
had enacted authorizing troop expansions and appropriations for the
Korean War effort, which in their view created a presidential obligation
to carry forward the war effort successfully. In their eyes, then, the
President was legitimately discharging his take care responsibilities in a
complex environment of multiple legislative instructions.

The presidency of Richard Nixon, which generated the next two
cases, saw unprecedented assertions of unilateral presidential authority
across a wide range of presidential conduct. Nixon articulated his conception of the presidency in 1977, in the first interview he gave after
resigning from office. In that interview, David Frost asked him, "So,
what in a sense you're saying is that there are certain situations, and the
Huston Plan . . . was one of them, where the president can decide that
it's in the best interests of the nation or something, and do something
illegal." To which former President Nixon replied: "Well, when the
president does it that means that it is not illegal. . . . If the president, for
example, approves something because of the national security, or in this
case because of a threat to internal peace and order of significant
magnitude, then the president's decision in that instance is one that
enables those who carry it out, to carry it out without violating a law.
Otherwise they're in an impossible situation."[21]

The Huston Plan, authored by Deputy White House Counsel Tom
Huston, had set forth a program of surveillance, infiltration, and disruption of anti-war and other dissident protest groups. Initially approved by
President Nixon, it was soon withdrawn after FBI Director J. Edgar
Hoover expressed opposition to it. The withdrawal of this specific document did not signal any change in the conception of presidential power
that accompanied the President's initial endorsement of it, however.

---

[21] Available at http://www.landmarkcases.org/nixon/nixonview.html.

That conception came to be tested in court, in circumstances quite close to those contemplated by the Plan, namely the surveillance of dissident groups. The case was *United States v. United States District Court for the Eastern District of Michigan, Southern Division*, often referred to simply as the *Keith* case, after Damon Keith, the judge of the Eastern District of Michigan who presided over the criminal trial from which the Supreme Court litigation arose.[22]

As Trevor Morrison tells the story, *Keith* occurred after federal agents arrested and brought to trial several members of the White Panther Party, accusing them of having detonated a bomb in front of a CIA recruitment office in Ann Arbor, Michigan.[23] In response to a pre-trial defense motion, the government disclosed that one of the defendants had participated in telephone conversations that had been monitored by government agents gathering intelligence about threats to national security from domestic organizations, under written authorization by the Attorney General but without a court wiretap order. Whether such surveillance could be conducted without prior judicial approval was a question that had been left open by *Katz v. United States*, the case in which the Supreme Court had extended the Fourth Amendment's warrant requirements to electronic surveillance.[24]

In the district court, the government took the position that surveillance ordered by the President in furtherance of the nation's security was exempt from the warrant requirement of the Fourth Amendment—a position quite close to that expressed by Nixon during the Frost interview. When Judge Keith rejected that position and ordered the government to disclose the contents of the monitored conversations, the United States sought a writ of mandamus against the judge and his order. In the Supreme Court, the government modified its position, conceding that presidential surveillance remained subject to the Fourth Amendment, but insisting that the fundamental requirement of the Fourth Amendment, the requirement that searches be "reasonable," was satisfied in this case because surveillance ordered by the president in the name of national security was *per se* reasonable. This was not much of a modification, of course, and was insufficient to satisfy the Justices. In a decision with no dissents, *Keith* held that protecting the country from domestic threats created no exception to the warrant requirement. Cases of threats from abroad were expressly reserved for another day.

---

[22] 407 U.S. 297 (1972).

[23] Trevor W. Morrison, The Story of *United States v. United States District Court (Keith)*: The Surveillance Power, Chapter 8.

[24] 389 U.S. 347 (1967).

The decision, authored by Justice Powell, traversed several of the contextual elements that have come to mark presidential power decisions. Justice Powell noted the historical practice of presidentially ordered surveillance for national security purposes beginning with President Roosevelt and extending "more or less continuously," but ended up not according it dispositive weight. *Keith* also dealt with the question of deference to the president, and ended up showing very little. Contrary to the government's argument that judges were incapable of assessing the needs of national security, Justice Powell concluded instead that judges would be quite capable of evaluating such claims and were, in fact, in a better position to weigh those claims properly against personal liberty than was the executive.

Keith did open one door with regard to treating national security surveillance differently from standard criminal surveillance by announcing the idea that Congress could establish a separate set of procedures and standards for obtaining prior judicial approval of electronic surveillance for national security purposes. Congress and Presidents Ford and Carter took advantage of the opening to negotiate and enact into law in 1978 the Foreign Intelligence Surveillance Act (FISA). For nearly twenty-five years, FISA seemed a satisfactory and stable compromise of the national security and constitutional interests involved. That changed after 9/11, as President Bush determined that the National Security Agency needed to undertake warrantless surveillance aimed at gathering intelligence against Al Qaeda because the FISA process was, in the President's assessment, inadequate to the needs of national security. The surveillance program became the subject of substantial legal and political debate after it was revealed by the New York Times in December 2005.[25]

Just three days before *Keith* ruled against the president on warrantless surveillance of the White Panther Party, more such surveillance was under way, this time of the Democratic Party in its Watergate headquarters. This, along with the breaking and entering required to plant the eavesdropping equipment, set in motion the events that would lead to the second Nixon-era decision, *United States v. Nixon*.[26] As Chris Schroeder recounts, although Presidents from George Washington forward had asserted some presidential authority to withhold presidential documents and communications from disclosure to Congress or the public, *Nixon*

---

[25] *See generally* Eric Lichtblau, *Bush's Law: The Remaking of American Justice* (2008); James Risen, *State of War: The Secret History of the CIA and the Bush Administration* (2006).

[26] 418 U.S. 683 (1974).

marked the first time the Supreme Court ruled on this question of executive privilege.[27]

The challenge to the President's assertion of executive privilege grew out of the criminal prosecution, first of those who took part in the Watergate break in, and subsequently of those accused of obstruction of justice for their role in trying to thwart the first prosecution and the further investigation of the matter. While these criminal proceedings were pending, congressional inquiries into the 1972 presidential campaign and election—those involved in the break in were thought to have been looking for information that would aid President Nixon's re-election bid—turned up the existence of a taping system in the Oval Office. Some of the conversations between the President, his aides, and other close advisors were relevant to the obstruction of justice charges, and the special prosecutor issued a subpoena to obtain them. To this, the President interposed an assertion of executive privilege, and the issue was ultimately brought before the Supreme Court. In a unanimous decision, the Court first held that the President did indeed enjoy an executive privilege to withhold presidential communications, something that had theretofore been disputed, but then, second, held that the privilege was a qualified one that could be overcome by a sufficient showing of need by those seeking disclosure. On the facts of *Nixon* itself, where the President was asserting a bare interest in confidentiality, unaided by any additional public need for confidentiality, such as the maintenance of military or national security secrets, his privilege had to give way to the legitimate needs of the criminal justice system to obtain information germane to questions of guilt or innocence.

Nixon reached the Supreme Court as impeachment proceedings were gaining momentum in the House, and at a time when the people of the nation seemed deeply troubled by allegations of presidential involvement in the obstruction of justice but still highly ambivalent about using the mechanism of impeachment to oust him from office. Schroeder argues that the Justices were acutely aware that the political environment surrounding the case was tense and anxious for a resolution, an awareness that manifested itself in the Court's unusual decision to hear the case before it had been argued to the court of appeals, and then in the structure of the opinion itself.

One of the most tense and dramatic weekends of the entire Watergate affair began with President Nixon's firing of the original special prosecutor, Archibald Cox. Before President Nixon could find someone in the Department of Justice to carry out his order, the two top officials in the Department, Elliot Richardson and William Ruckelshaus, had resigned because each felt that firing Cox violated pledges each had made

---

[27] Christopher H. Schroeder, The Story of *United States v. Nixon*: The President and the Tapes, Chapter 9.

to the Senate Judiciary Committee during confirmation hearings. The firings and resignations became known as the Saturday Night Massacre. Even though public pressure on the President resulted in his appointing a successor to Cox, Leon Jaworski, and even though Jaworski was able to prosecute the cases he was investigating to his satisfaction, the Massacre dramatized for many the importance of creating a special prosecutor's office, with someone who would be able to prosecute high government officials, secure from dismissal by restrictions on the President's ability to fire. After President Nixon resigned, Congress created such an office by statute.

In debating this statute, defenders of presidential authority argued that nothing could be more central to the president's obligation to take care that the laws be faithfully executed than to have full control over the very prosecution of those laws. On that basis, they reasoned that the power to prosecute must be the President's alone. Some fifteen years after the Saturday Night Massacre, the question of the constitutionality of a statute insulating a federal prosecutor from full presidential control reached the Supreme Court in *Morrison v. Olson*.[28]

Morrison arose out of a dispute between the House of Representatives and the Reagan Administration when President Reagan claimed executive privilege with respect to documents relating to settlements reached by the Environmental Protection Agency and the Department of Justice in litigation against industrial firms over liability for the costs of cleaning up hazardous waste sites. Theodore Olson was Assistant Attorney General for the Office of Legal Counsel at the time (and later became Solicitor General under President George W. Bush), and in that capacity he gave legal advice on the propriety of asserting the presidential privilege. The dispute over documents was eventually settled, but not before it became acrimonious, leading to a congressional contempt citation, litigation brought by the House to enforce its subpoena and, ultimately, a charge that Olson had given false testimony to a congressional committee that had questioned him about his role in the assertion of executive privilege. All this led to the appointment of Alexia Morrison to investigate perjury charges against Olson.

Kevin Stack's account shows how recollections of the Watergate affair and the Saturday Night Massacre, with the accompanying sense that there simply had to be some insulation between the President and a prosecutor in order for the latter to function effectively when investigating the wrongdoing of high government officials, hung over the case as it was litigated.[29] There were other even larger shadows over the indepen-

---

[28] 487 U.S. 654 (1988).

[29] Kevin M. Stack, The Story of *Morrison v. Olson*: The Independent Counsel and Independent Agencies in Watergate's Wake, Chapter 11.

dent counsel litigation as well. The Reagan Administration had been pursuing various ways for the President to acquire firmer control of executive branch agencies, believing that the Constitution vests substantially more authority to control directly the actions of subordinates than various federal laws on the books seemed to acknowledge. The practical problems of lack of full presidential control were felt most acutely with respect to the so-called independent agencies, which were frequently headed by multi-person commissions whose members were appointed to staggered terms in order to distance the agency leadership from full presidential control and whose members also enjoyed tenure in office protections similar to the independent counsel's tenure protections. As the *Morrison* dispute made its way to the Supreme Court, it was widely anticipated that the Court could rule in a manner affecting not only the independent counsel statute, but that could also place the constitutionality of the independent agencies into doubt. As it turned out, the Supreme Court upheld the independent counsel statute, with a lone, impassioned dissent from Justice Scalia, putting an end to jurisprudential efforts to assert firmer presidential control over either the independent counsel or the independent agencies.

The political environment after *Morrison* has been less kind to the independent counsel than to the independent agencies. After a series of independent counsel investigations, including high visibility investigations of Republican President Reagan after the Iran–Contra affair and of Democratic President Clinton after the Whitewater and Monica Lewinski affairs, the valence of political opinion regarding the value of the independent counsel function shifted, and in 1999 the statute was permitted to expire. As for Ted Olson, he was eventually cleared of all charges, but was left with a substantial liability for legal expenses incurred in his defense.

Sandwiched in between the Nixon-era cases and *Morrison* came a 1981 decision that grew out of a crisis produced when youthful supporters of Iran's new revolutionary government took American embassy personnel hostage in the fall of 1979. In the waning days of President Carter's administration, United States negotiators reached an agreement for the release of the hostages, who had been held by Iran for over a year. The President concluded the United States part of the deal through an executive agreement, without the participation of Congress. The deal included transferring claims by Americans against the Iranian government to an international claims settlement tribunal, along with placing in escrow $1 billion of Iranian assets seized by the President soon after the hostages were taken, to provide a fund from which awards by the tribunal could be paid. The seizure of Iranian assets had a firm statutory basis, but the transfer of claims and the accompanying bar on any proceedings in United States courts to collect on those claims did not.

Dames & Moore claimed Iran owed it millions of dollars for design work done on a nuclear reactor, and had obtained a judgment in federal district court while the hostages were being held. When the settlement with Iran threatened to cut off its ability to recover on its judgment, Dames and Moore challenged the executive agreement as exceeding the president's authority.[30]

The hostage settlement required that the United States return all seized Iranian funds (amounting to about $12 billion in all) by July 19, 1981, but in early June a district court entered an injunction preventing the United States from transferring any assets that were subject to judgment liens in favor of Dames & Moore. Aware of the urgent need for resolution, the Supreme Court granted review directly from the district court on June 11. The parties briefed the case and it was argued on June 24. The decision upholding the executive agreement and the funds transfer came eight days later.

In Harold Bruff's recounting of the *Dames & Moore* story,[31] Justice Rehnquist's decision reflects both the immediate context as well as a modification of the tripartite approach to presidential power issues enunciated by Justice Jackson in his *Youngstown* concurrence, which Rehnquist helped draft while clerking for Jackson. For Rehnquist, the involvement of Congress in adding to or detracting from authority that the President might otherwise possess could better be characterized as falling somewhere along a continuum, rather than being forced into one of three distinct boxes. With that modification in hand, Rehnquist's opinion found a sufficient basis to indicate "congressional acceptance of a broad scope for executive action in circumstances such as those presented in this case,"[32] a qualification that the opinion lets stand without fully elucidating what the relevant circumstances might be.

Justice Jackson's framework from *Youngstown* also plays an important role in the last chapter on *Hamdan v. Rumsfeld*.[33] In that decision, the Court found that, in establishing military commissions after 9/11 to try alleged terrorists, President George Bush violated procedural requirements imposed by Congress for the use of such commissions. His actions therefore fell within the lowest tier of the Jackson framework, in which presidential actions will not be upheld unless they fall within an area of exclusive presidential authority. Because the Court concluded

---

[30] Dames & Moore v. Regan, 453 U.S. 654 (1981).

[31] Harold H. Bruff, The Story of *Dames & Moore*: Resolution of an International Crisis by Executive Agreement, Chapter 10.

[32] 453 U.S. at 677.

[33] 548 U.S. 557 (2006).

that Congress had concurrent authority with the President to regulate military commissions, it held that the military commissions were invalid.

Dawn Johnsen situates the *Hamdan* decision against the backdrop of the strong claims of presidential power asserted by the Bush administration after the 9/11 attacks. In response to the attacks, President Bush declared that the nation was engaged in a war on terror, and he often referenced his responsibilities as commander-in-chief. Invoking precedent from more traditional wars, the President claimed, among other things, a right to detain and subject to military trial individuals determined by the administration to be members of the enemy, which was defined to include the Al Qaeda terrorist organization and affiliated groups.

When the President sought congressional support for his actions in the war on terror, he generally received it. In the immediate aftermath of 9/11, Congress quickly enacted an Authorization for the Use of Military Force (AUMF), approving the use of "all necessary and appropriate force" to pursue those responsible for the 9/11 attacks. Shortly thereafter, Congress also enacted the USA PATRIOT Act, granting the administration a broad array of augmented law enforcement, surveillance, and detention authorities. At the same time, administration lawyers claimed that the President's actions in the war on terror stemmed from the Constitution and thus did not require congressional authorization. Indeed, as reflected in a number of legal memoranda from the Office of Legal Counsel in the Department of Justice, the claim was made that the President's commander-in-chief authority allowed him even to disregard federal statutes that might prohibit such actions.

Johnsen describes *Hamdan* as one of a series of setbacks for this conception of presidential authority. In 2004, in a case involving an American citizen who was captured in Afghanistan and then detained in the United States, the Supreme Court declined to accept the administration's assertion that as commander in chief the President could hold such an enemy combatant until the war ended simply on the President's authority. Instead, the Court ruled that, while the AUMF authorized such detention, such individuals were also entitled to notice of the grounds for their detention and an opportunity to be heard.[34] In another case from the same Term involving foreign nationals being held at the Guantanamo Bay Naval Base in Cuba, the Court rejected a claim of unilateral presidential authority to hold detainees without access to the courts.[35] *Hamdan* reached the Supreme Court two years later. Johnsen argues that the result in the case, and in the *Boumediene* decision in

---

[34] *See* Hamdi v. Rumsfeld, 542 U.S. 507 (2004).

[35] *See* Rasul v. Bush, 542 U.S. 466 (2004).

2008,[36] reflects a continuing belief among a majority of the Justices that unilateral presidential authority to determine how individuals are to be treated is inconsistent with our system of separated powers.

* * *

The United States has changed considerably in the more than two hundred years since the Neutrality Controversy. What started as a vulnerable set of former colonies hugging the eastern seaboard is now a military superpower with global interests and challenges. The powers of the presidency, and even the nature of the office, have inevitably evolved with changes to the nation. At the same time, modern disputes over presidential power, such as the disputes in the war on terror, demonstrate that the connection envisioned by the Framers between separation of powers and the protection of individual liberty remains as relevant as ever.

---

[36] *See* Boumediene v. Bush, 128 S.Ct. 2229 (2008).

1

Martin S. Flaherty

The Story of the Neutrality Controversy: Struggling Over Presidential Power Outside the Courts

The nation's first important presidential powers dispute, its first important foreign relations battle—its first major constitutional controversy of any sort—was not referred to by the Supreme Court until 159 years after it was resolved. Since known as the "Neutrality Controversy," the struggle centered on how the still young and fragile United States should best stay out of war between two superpowers: its former master, the United Kingdom; and its formal ally, revolutionary France. The dilemma raised epic issues about the proper role of the President, Congress, and international law; pitted Alexander Hamilton against Thomas Jefferson and James Madison; and made President Washington the initial arbiter of constitutional meaning.

When the Court finally did mention the Neutrality Controversy, it was only in passing, and then largely to dismiss its relevance. In *Youngstown Sheet & Tube Co. v. Sawyer*, the Justices considered the scope of presidential authority in a conflict in which the United States was decidedly not neutral, the undeclared Korean War. There Justice Robert Jackson lamented: "Just what our forefathers envisioned, or would have envisioned had they foreseen modern conditions, must be divined from sources almost as enigmatic as the dreams Joseph was called upon to interpret for Pharaoh."[1] He continued, "[a] century and a half of partisan debate and scholarly speculation yields no net result but only supplies more or less apt quotations from respected sources on each

---

[1] Youngstown Sheet & Tube Co. v. Sawyer, 343 U.S. 579, 634 (1952) (Jackson, J., concurring).

side of any question. They largely cancel each other."[2] Exhibit One: "A Hamilton may be matched against a Madison."[3] The subsequent citation referred to the two "forefathers'" famous debate as "Pacificus" and "Helvidius" during the Neutrality Controversy.

Yet Jackson dismissed the Neutrality Controversy—and history more generally—too quickly. History, especially an early constitutional struggle, may cast light on possible "original" understandings of the Constitution, an approach to constitutional interpretation that had wide though by no means universal currency even in the early Republic. In this instance, Jackson rightly concluded that at least aspects of the dispute pitted too many prominent Founders against one another to have much use for originalists. But he also went too far in suggesting that the Founding generation never agreed on anything, such as who exercises the War Power.[4] It requires consulting history in the first place, moreover, to figure out which situation is which. Second, Jackson's opinion itself places great weight on constitutional "custom"—how American political institutions worked out dealing with one another over the years once the Constitution was in place.[5] Had he looked more deeply, he would have understood that the Neutrality Controversy provides a case study of how all three branches worked out practical solutions in the absence of clear constitutional rules, some of which have endured. Finally, understanding the Neutrality Controversy as well as later cases helps us appreciate the ways in which the U.S. foreign relations law issues of the past were utterly different in some ways, and yet surprisingly similar in others, to the issues we face today. We either ignore or obey history at our peril.

Had the Neutrality Controversy landed in court when it took place, the lawyers' briefs would have focused on two principal issues. The one that endures marks the Constitution's separation of powers. Does the Executive have the sole authority to fix a policy in which the nation refuses to take sides in a global conflict? That is, can the President alone "make peace"? The second issue that generated more concern at the time involved international law. What were the United States' ongoing treaty obligations with France in light of both the Revolution and the

---

[2] *Id.* at 634–35.

[3] *Id.* at 635 n.1.

[4] *See* Louis Fisher, *Presidential War Power* (1995); William Michael Treanor, *Fame, the Founding, and the Power to Declare War*, 82 Cornell L. Rev. 69 (1996–1997); Charles A. Lofgren, *War-Making Under the Constitution: The Original Understanding*, 81 Yale L.J. 672 (1972). *But see* John C. Yoo, *The Constitution of Politics by Other Means: The Original Understanding of War Powers*, 84 Cal. L. Rev. 167 (1996).

[5] *Youngstown*, 343 U.S. at 637 (Jackson, J., concurring); *id.* at 579, 610–11 (Frankfurter, J., concurring).

war? One further question arose as the controversy unfolded that tied the first two together. Did either the President's policy or the nation's international law obligations provide a basis to criminally prosecute Americans who supported the war effort of either side?

But the Neutrality Controversy was not resolved in the courts. When no less than President Washington requested its guidance, the Supreme Court turned away. As with other disputes, Washington in effect acted as a Justice more than anyone sitting on the bench, making judgments amidst some of the most cogent constitutional arguments ever made by some of the country's most original constitutional minds. Congress played a part as well, though mainly to confirm rather than confront the President's conclusions. So too, did France and Britain, at least with regard to international law.

All of which raises an even larger issue which has special relevance to presidential power disputes in the realm of foreign relations. What is, has been, and should be the role of the courts in resolving disputes concerning the country's relations with other nations? Did the judiciary play a minimal role because the times were different and the Supreme Court less well-established? Or, as some argue, are foreign relations matters simply less suited for judicial resolution?[6] Or, as still others contend, have we simply lost the ability to appreciate how constitutional law gets made "outside the courts"?[7] Precisely because the Justices did not settle it, the nation's first major foreign affairs story has much to offer on these more fundamental questions as well.

Conflict Abroad and at Home

In the closing days of the first Washington Administration, on February 1, 1793, the French Republic declared war on Great Britain and Holland. Just a week earlier, it had publicly executed King Louis XVI for treason. The timing was no coincidence. The war reflected the radicalization of the French Revolution and with it the determination of Europe's monarchies to fend off the specter of republicanism that France now sought to spread. When viewed looking outward, as a foreign policy matter, the conflict left the United States with only one option. Given its weakness as a young republic caught between two superpowers, the nation had to remain neutral. The view of the war all but reversed, however, when seen looking inward, with an eye to its domestic implica-

---

[6] *See, e.g.*, Baker v. Carr, 369 U.S. 186, 211 (1962) ("Not only does the resolution of [foreign relations] issues frequently turn on standards that defy judicial application or involve the exercise of a discretion demonstrably committed to the executive or legislature; but many such questions uniquely demand single-voiced statement of the Government's views."). *But see id.* ("Yet it is error to suppose that every case or controversy which touches foreign relations lies beyond judicial cognizance.").

[7] *See, e.g.*, Mark V. Tushnet, *Taking the Constitution Away from the Courts* (1999).

tions. Through this lens of internal politics, the war exacerbated the tensions between new and rival visions of the nation's future. Domestically, the distant war made these visions appear vast, explosive, and potentially irreconcilable.

A war between France and Britain meant only bad news for America. Though the United States had won the Revolution, that struggle had been defensive, for survival, and had left certain regions devastated. The United States in 1789 remained a nation heavily dependent on foreign trade, without a standing army or navy, and proceeding with an unproven constitution. John Jay's remarks during ratification still held: "If foreign nations find us either destitute of an effectual government ... or split into three or four independent and probably discordant republics or confederacies, one inclining to Britain, one inclining to France, and a third inclining to Spain, and perhaps played off against each other by the three, what a poor pitiful figure America will make in their eyes!"[8] Jay's line of argument had helped get the Constitution ratified, a success that for the moment averted any regional split. But it still remained to be seen whether the new framework would insure "that our national government is efficient and well administered, our trade prudently regulated, our militia properly organized and disciplined...."[9] As it was, the country could not risk joining a war against either power. Still less could it hazard choosing the losing side.

A policy of neutrality also brought affirmative benefits. Under the law of nations, a neutral state could not be attacked by one warring nation for trading with its opponent. Belligerents could not attack neutral shipping.[10] Nor could they impress into their own service the sailors of a neutral state unless the particular seaman had some connection to the belligerent nation. As it conferred rights, the law of nations imposed duties as well. A neutral could not permit its citizens to join one warring side or the other. It could not authorize its citizens or ships to operate as privateers against belligerents. A neutral further could not permit a belligerent to authorize the neutral's citizens or ships to operate as privateers in the conflict. It cold not permit a belligerent to operate prize courts on its soil to liquidate the value of any ship the warring power captured in the conflict. Complicating matters, the United States and pre-revolutionary France had entered into treaties of friendship and alliance dating from American's own revolution. These

---

[8] *The Federalist* No. 4, at 49 (John Jay) (Clinton Rossiter, ed., 1961).

[9] *Id.*

[10] For discussion of international law of war rules with respect to shipping, see Chapter 2 in this volume, discussing *The Prize Cases*.

treaties would make the path to neutrality more difficult, but not any less desirable.[11]

No one appreciated the situation better than George Washington. Not long after the news of the war reached America, the President convened the Cabinet to consider the nation's options. In preparation, he circulated nineteen questions ranging from potential political responses to international law obligations. The most pressing issues, which book-ended the list, produced immediate and unanimous agreement. On the last question, Washington's advisors agreed that "it was not necessary or advisable to call together the two Houses of Congress with a view to the present posture in European affairs." On the more important first question, the Cabinet concluded that the President should issue a proclamation "for the purpose of preventing interferences of the Citizens of the United States in the War between France and Great Britain & ca."[12]

Washington issued the Proclamation on April 22. The statement addressed two matters. First, the proclamation announced the national policy of neutrality—or to use the document's precise term, "impartiality": "the duty and interest of the United States require, that they should with sincerity and good faith adopt and pursue a conduct friendly and impartial to the belligerent powers." Second, Washington cautioned Americans from taking part in the hostilities, warning "citizens of the United States carefully to avoid all acts and proceedings whatsoever, who may in any manner tend to contravene such disposition." The President further addressed the consequences for those who would ignore this warning. "And I do hereby also make known," the President continued, "that whosoever of the citizens of the United States shall render himself liable to punishment or forfeiture under the law of nations, [by helping the belligerents will not receive protection] will not receive the protection of the United States against such punishment or forfeiture." Washington concluded with the additional possibility of criminal consequences: "further . . . I have given instructions to those officers to whom it belongs, to cause prosecutions to be instituted against all persons, who shall, within the cognizance of the Courts of the United States, violate the law of nations, with respect to the powers at war, or any of them."[13]

---

[11] *See* 3 Emmerich de Vattel, "Of Neutrality and Passage of Troops Through a Neutral Country," *The Law of Nations or Principles of Nature Applied to the Conduct and Affairs of Nations and Sovereigns* 398–429 (Northampton, Mass., Simeon Butler 4th Am. ed. 1820) (1758).

[12] Questions Submitted to the Cabinet by the President (April 18, 1793) *in* 32 *The Writings of George Washington* 419–20 (John C. Fitzpatrick ed., 1939).

[13] Proclamation of Neutrality (April 22, 1793), *in id.* at 430–31.

The Cabinet's unanimity had been made easier thanks to the ever more radical course that the French Revolution then pursued. Louis XVI's execution in particular dampened American enthusiasm for its sibling's uprising. Substantial pro-French enthusiasm flourished nonetheless, mainly in popular opinion, but even within the government itself. One of revolutionary France's best friends, in fact, was none other than the Secretary of State, Thomas Jefferson. Jefferson knew that the United States had no realistic option other than to stay out of any war between Europe's major powers. But even at this stage he signaled his unease over appearing to abandon our French allies or worse, supporting the British. Thanks to Jefferson, the "Neutrality Proclamation" never actually used the term "neutral." The Secretary of State also privately indicated his displeasure with the general tone of the document as drafted by fellow Virginian, Attorney General Edmund Randolph. Anticipating battles to come, Jefferson—also privately—noted with concern that even though the questions submitted to the Cabinet were in the President's handwriting, "it was palpable from their style, their ingenious tissue and suite that they were not the President's, that they were raised upon a prepared chain of argument, in short that the language was Hamilton's, and the doubts his alone."[14] As Jefferson well knew, any doubts that Hamilton had about American policy would be resolved in favor of Great Britain.

These tensions would detonate to make the "Neutrality Controversy" controversial. Along the way they did much to produce the ancestors of American political parties. Not least, they gave the nation its first foreign relations "case." The irony is that little of what followed resulted from fundamental foreign policy determinations, about which Hamilton and Jefferson largely agreed. Neither Anglophiles nor, which was more likely, Francophiles advocated American entry into the war on one side or the other. What fueled this foreign relations dispute was growing ideological divisions about the character of the United States domestically. This split had already begun to drive apart friends who together had campaigned for the new Constitution. The "present posture in European affairs" turned the split into a chasm, but not over how the United States should project itself abroad. The controversy instead resulted mainly from how France and Britain projected themselves into American politics at home.

Even before the war, Europe served as sort of a looking glass into which Americans gazed to see what they wanted in themselves and their government. Some, above all Hamilton, preferred to look one way and see the United States as an eventual successor to the United Kingdom.

---

[14] Notes on Washington's Questions on Neutrality and the Alliance with France *in* 25 *The Papers of Thomas Jefferson* 665 (John Catanzariti ed., 1992).

This reflection among other things meant a strong central government, a powerful executive, particularly in foreign affairs, and a strong national system of banking and credit that would foster manufacturing and trade. Others, notably Jefferson, Madison, and Monroe, looked slightly south and saw America reflected in revolutionary France. This reflection included some features that the new French republic appeared to embrace early on, including commitments to a strong legislature and to individual liberty. But even more than this, the French Revolution in its early stages appeared to validate America's own Revolution, and with it, America's rejection of Britain. Both sides had every incentive to replicate the European conflict for domestic political advantage. For Hamilton, advocating policies that would hamper or embarrass France had less to do with any actual threat France posed than it did with embarrassing his ideological opponents. Exactly the same considerations applied in mirror image to Jefferson and Britain. Each side, moreover, believed that the most important battlefields in this domesticated European conflict would be legal.[15]

The first clash involved the law of nations. The United States may have wanted to be neutral in the conflict, and international law at once created incentives, but hurdles as well. The law of nations almost literally provided the nation a safe harbor assuming it could qualify as a neutral. What was not entirely clear was whether and to what extent the nation could sail into this safe harbor given its treaty obligations with France. As Washington—or in truth Hamilton—provocatively asked, was the United States obliged "to consider the treaties heretofore made with France as applying to the present situation?" If the United States has an option, "would it be considered a breach of Neutrality to consider the Treaties still in operation?" Is the Treaty of Alliance in particular "applicable to a defensive war only," and is that the type of war France was waging? Should the President even receive a minister from the French Republic and appear to validate both treaties and the regime to begin with? On these questions, domestic political orientations would produce brilliant briefs on either side.

The second conflict, more epic and enduring, was over constitutional law. The policy of neutrality that Americans generally desired had been declared by the President alone. He had done so, moreover, not as an interim matter pending the convening of Congress, but after deciding not to call Congress into session at all. All within the Cabinet agreed he could do this, including Jefferson, who knew that even "impartiality" would be seen to pro-French Americans as effectively abandoning an ally

---

[15] For what remains perhaps the best political account of the Neutrality Controversy, *see* Stanley Elkins & Eric McKittrick, *The Age of Federalism, 1788–1800*, 303–73 (1993). *See also* David P. Currie, *The Constitution in Congress: The Federalist Period, 1789–1801*, 174–88 (1999).

in the cause of liberty. Once more, domestic orientations led to radical disagreement as to why, and ultimately, even as to whether the President could do so. This too would lead to historic arguments on either side.

The Arguments

Until John Marshall, no American played a greater role resolving fundamental legal and constitutional questions facing the new republic than George Washington. The President, however, was neither well-suited for this role, nor had he sought it. In contrast to his fellow Founders, Washington had a comparatively limited formal education and lacked legal training of any sort. Famous for not seeking power, Washington found himself in the position of initially resolving basic legal questions facing the new government almost by default. Congress for much of the next century met only a few months a year. Nor had the Supreme Court assumed anything like the role it would assume during Marshall's tenure. Nor was it presented with a clear opportunity to intervene. No case presenting the relevant issues came before it. The Justices, moreover, felt compelled to turn down the President's express request to weigh in on the issues in an advisory fashion. It therefore fell to Washington to make at least the initial decisions concerning matters such as corresponding with foreign nations, establishing consulates, and in seeking the Senate's advice (or not) during treaty negotiations. Under these circumstances, the President's decisions tended to effectively become precedent.[16]

Washington was fully mindful of his power and his limitations as a legal officer. He also fully appreciated that notoriously fragile republics found stability in the rule of law, a trait he had shown even as commander of the Continental Army. If not exactly judicial, he was nothing short of judicious in considering whether his policies comported with the Constitution and other relevant laws. In this task, the President benefited immeasurably from his cabinet. Unlike him, men like Hamilton, Jefferson, and Randolph were trained lawyers, at times brilliant ones. They were also independently-minded. Modern party politics tends to make a President and his advisors like-minded, the better to deal with the opposition. During Washington's presidency, the idea of a party system was only just taking shape.[17] The best way to influence policy was not yet to go into opposition, but instead to plead one's case before the President.

---

[16] *See* Glenn A. Phelps, *George Washington and American Constitutionalism* (1993).

[17] For a classic account, *see* Richard Hofstadter, *The Idea of a Party System: The Rise of Legitimate Opposition in the United States, 1780–1840* (1969).

Treaties and the Law of Nations

The Anglo–French War showed the process at its most judicious. After the April 18 meeting, the President determined that written opinions should be submitted to him on the remaining questions concerning the law of nations and U.S. treaty obligations. He had them by May 6. What he received on both sides showed a mastery of international law that would be the envy of even the most accomplished lawyer or official today.

The first set of issues dealt with the United States' obligations and opportunities under international law. The legal question centered on whether the nation was still bound by the treaties it had concluded with the ancient regime of Louis XVI now that this had given way to the French Republic. Related to the legal issue was the question of how the United States should receive the new French Ambassador, Edmond Genet. The Cabinet was agreed that he should be received. If the treaties with France were to remain in full force, then Genet should be admitted without qualification as a matter of course. If, however, the treaties could be suspended as a result of the change in government, the argument followed that Genet should be admitted only provisionally to avoid the claim that the United States had acquiesced in having the treaties carry forward to the new government.

On May 2, Hamilton, joined by Secretary of War Henry Knox, argued the case against France. As was his style, Hamilton did not settle for modest arguments when he could attempt a coup de grace. That coup was the assertion that the United States reserves the right to deem its treaties with France "temporarily and provisionally suspended."[18] Since all of Washington's remaining questions directly or indirectly turned on how the treaties potentially limited U.S. options, once those treaties were deemed suspended, so too were any obstacles to full neutrality, the best possibility that Britain's American sympathizers could expect. Nor did Hamilton leave any doubt about whether the right to suspend the treaties should be exercised. The balance of his briefs pushes the relevant international law principles with vigor and originality.

In fact, Hamilton pressed his international law arguments with perhaps too much vigor and originality. The Treasury Secretary set out several bases for suspension, each of which was more compelling as rhetoric than as law. First and foremost, Hamilton contended that the treaties were made "with his most Christian majesty," Louis XVI, "his heirs and successors." But Louis had been executed perhaps unjustifiably, and he and his heirs replaced with violent and perhaps illegitimate

---

[18] Letter and Enclosed Answer from Alexander Hamilton and Henry Knox to George Washington (May 2, 1793), *in* 14 *The Papers of Alexander Hamilton* 367, 367–96 (Harold C. Syrett et al. eds., 1969).

regime. Hamilton knew full well that the law of nations permitted a nation "to change its form of government," and that "real treaties" bind nations "notwithstanding any changes which happen in their forms of government." Yet Hamilton asserted these principles had certain reasonable limits. France's change of government could not lawfully render the treaty obligations of its partner dangerous. Moreover, France's revolutionary forces could not lawfully insist on the benefits of the treaty made by the king they executed until the ongoing civil war over the Revolution was decided one way or the other. For these propositions, Hamilton cited Grotius, Vattel, and Puffendorf, the leading international law authorities of the day. As with any aggressive lawyer, artful quotations and partial emphasis implied that these writers supported his position far more than they did.[19]

Hamilton's second major legal argument, contained in a companion letter, assumed that the treaties were in force but inapplicable in light of revolutionary French aggression. Here the key was the Treaty of Alliance in particular, which called for U.S. assistance should the French West Indies be attacked, a real possibility. The title of the treaty, however, was the "Traite d'Alliance *eventuelle* et *defensive*"—contingent and defensive. Should France be engaged in an offensive war, all bets were off. Hamilton therefore first set out to show that the usual authorities drew a general distinction between offensive and defensive wars. That done, Hamilton almost took relish in proving one of the many reasons he abhorred the ever more radical French Republic. Even before the war, it had decreed nothing less than "the total subversion of all the ancient establishments of every country into which the arms of France should be carried," and therefore "an outrage little short of a declaration of war against every government of Europe, and ... a violent attack upon the *freedom of opinion of mankind.*"[20]

To these legal positions, Hamilton folded in advice that sounded purely in foreign policy. Only by suspending the treaties, he urged, could the United States avoid the potential disaster of being seen to side with revolutionary France, especially should the French Revolution fail. For Hamilton, law and policy pointed to but one remedy the President should prescribe. The new Minister from France, Edmond Genet, should be received, but with the qualification of making plain the right to consider the treaties suspended pending the outcome of the war and with it, the French Revolution itself.[21]

---

[19] *Id.* at 386–89.

[20] Letter of Alexander Hamilton to George Washington (May 2, 1793), *in id.* at 398, 398–408 (emphasis in the original).

[21] Letter and Enclosed Answer from Alexander Hamilton and Henry Knox to George Washington (May 2, 1793), *in id.* at 387–96.

Jefferson responded with the case for the French Republic in late April. Contrary to form, Jefferson's opinion concentrated on the law, bypassed ideology, and left little room for response by the Secretary of the Treasury, usually the far more rigorous legal mind. As his effort showed, Jefferson could do this because the law of nations was more or less clearly on his side. The Secretary of State began by stating he could not admit the soundness of Hamilton's reasoning, but he could subscribe "most fully to its ingenuity." Ingenuity, however, could not overcome settled legal principles. Those principles held that "[c]ompacts between nation & nation are obligatory on them" in much the same way contracts are obligatory between individuals, subject to certain and few narrow exceptions. First, a nation could be absolved from a treaty only if "performance becomes *'impossible'* or *'self-destructive.'*" Second, a nation facing such could release itself only "from so much of the treaties only as is bringing great & inevitable danger on us & not from the residue, allowing to the other party a right at the same time to determine . . . they will consider the whole void." Third, even when a nation justifiably withholds compliance from a treaty, "it is bound to make compensation."[22]

Jefferson delighted in cornering Hamilton, the cosmopolitan New York lawyer, on the law. He devoted almost a third of his brief to a sort of internal appendix in which he quoted Grotius, Puffendorf, and Wolf more precisely than Hamilton and at greater length. Yet Jefferson took special pleasure in taking Hamilton to school on Vattel, the source on which the Treasury Secretary placed his greatest reliance. Jefferson conceded that Vattel did say that performance was not due when treaties became "useless" or "disagreeable." He argued nonetheless that Vattel could not have meant that a nation did not have to live up to its end of a treaty merely when the obligation became unpleasant. To prove this point, Jefferson appealed "to Vattel himself, in those parts of his book where he cannot be misunderstood & too his known character," with citation after quotation after citation.[23] As with any aggressive and thorough lawyer, his brief turned his opponent's strongest assertion against itself.

Jefferson gave no quarter on the facts either. Having established that the "danger which absolves us" of our treaty obligations "must be great, inevitable, and imminent" he showed that any possible danger was just that, merely possible and no more. The French Republic's ostensible despotism was no worse than the perfect despotism of the French monarchy. France's republicanism "is the hope of the mass of

---

[22] Letter and Enclosed Answer from Thomas Jefferson to George Washington (April 28, 1793), *in* 25 *The Papers of Thomas Jefferson* 607, 607–18 (John Catanzariti ed., 1992).

[23] *Id.* at 609–10, 613–18.

our constituents, and not their dread." True, the outcome of the Revolution may be in doubt, but the possibility of a dangerous outcome is not danger in itself. France might call on the United States should the West Indies be attacked, but the chances of such a call were remote. The treaties may permit French ships, privateers and prizes to enter U.S. ports, but so too do U.S. treaties with Britain. The treaty may deny France's enemies the right of outfitting privateers in U.S. ports, but Britain could hardly complain on this score since the United States could likewise deny that right to France. Any danger from adhering to the French treaties was no more than speculation.[24] By any measure, moreover, the United States did adhere to the treaties. The French made no call for the defense of the West Indies. Washington adopted a policy denying French and British privateers and prizes access to American ports. So too did the President deny either side permission to outfit privateers. The President in fact would adhere to these prohibitions despite vigorous attempts to get around them by none other than the French ambassador that the Administration decided to receive.

Jefferson demonstrated that at least on this occasion the law complemented his ideology. He addressed the issue of whether the President should consider the treaties to be in full effect far more rigorously than Hamilton. He likewise asserted more convincingly that Washington should not merely receive, but welcome, the man known as "Citizen Genet" as the Ambassador of the French Republic.

Separation of Powers

The second set of "briefs" have proven more enduring. They first of all were argued in public. More importantly, they helped introduce the types of arguments that have framed many of the presidential power controversies, implicating issues ranging far beyond neutrality, that have come later.

The separation of powers debate arose over the great issue that had not caused any dissent in the cabinet—Washington's authority to issue the Neutrality Proclamation in the first place. Yet this initial agreement would soon fall prey to the scheming of Genet, which split Federalist Anglophiles and Jeffersonian Francophiles irrevocably. Genet arrived to a warm popular welcome in Philadelphia on May 16, after which he was duly received by the President. He then overplayed his hand at every opportunity. He asked for advance payment of the United States' debt to France. He sought to have American ports open to France as he announced France's were open to the United States. Ominously, he authorized the commissioning of a captured British ship, *The Little Sarah*, as a French privateer, *La Petite Democrate*, in express violation of

---

[24] *Id.* at 610–13.

Washington's orders. Worse yet, Genet wrote progressively more tendentious missives to the Administration and even sought to appeal over Washington's head directly to the American public though appearances at banquets. By May, an emboldened French sympathizer with the pseudonym "Veritas" (probably Jefferson's overzealous and misguided friend, Philip Freneau) had begun publishing a series of essays that directly questioned Washington's authority to have proclaimed American neutrality. So explosive had Genet and his allies made the situation that even Jefferson, originally a supporter, realized that no one had damaged the French cause in America quite so much as the French minister.[25]

Not surprisingly, Hamilton viewed Genet with similar contempt. The French ambassador and his friends crossed an important line when they attacked Washington and the Proclamation, and the Treasury Secretary leapt at the chance to defend both. On June 29, Hamilton entered the public fray with the first of seven essays under the name, "Pacificus." The pieces, among other things, addressed America's obligations (or lack of obligations) with France, both legal and moral, as well as the wisdom of neutrality. But the one essay most read today deals with, in Hamilton's words, the key "inquiry," which is "what department of the government of the United States is the proper one to make a declaration of Neutrality, in the cases in which the engagements of the Nation and its interests require such a declaration?" Not surprisingly, he answered that a "correct and well-informed mind will discern at once that it can belong neither to the Legislature nor Judicial Department and of course must belong to the Executive."[26]

Yet of far greater significance, "Pacificus" fully articulates, for the first time in American history, the classic "Hamiltonian" position on Executive Power. Sometimes known as "Executive power essentialism" or "the Vesting Clause Thesis,"[27] that position holds that executive authority includes an array of powers that go beyond mere execution of laws, and that these powers are vested in the President subject only to express exceptions that the Constitution may make. As its original setting suggests, the "Hamiltonian" position reaches its zenith in foreign relations. Presidents and their supporters have made the most of both the argument and its pedigree ever since. Chief Justice (and former President) William Howard Taft gave the idea the Supreme Court's imprimatur, at least temporarily, in *Myers v. United States*.[28] More

---

[25] Stanley Elkins & Eric McKittrick, *The Age of Federalism, 1788–1800*, 341–54 (1993).

[26] Alexander Hamilton, Letters of Pacificus No. 1 (June 29, 1793), *reprinted in* 15 *The Papers of Alexander Hamilton* 33–37 (Harold C. Syrett & Jacob E. Cook eds., 1969).

[27] Curtis A. Bradley & Martin S. Flaherty, *Executive Power Essentialism and Foreign Affairs*, 102 Mich. L. Rev. 545, 546 (2004).

[28] 272 U.S. 52, 118 (1926). However, as Justice Jackson noted in *Youngstown Sheet & Tube Co. v. Sawyer*, Taft when a professor had earlier disagreed with the Vesting Clause

recently, the Department of Justice's Office of Legal Counsel relied on it in the so-called "torture memos," arguing that the President was not bound by legislation prohibiting the practice when engaged in prosecuting a war.[29] "Pacificus" therefore deserves close scrutiny. A closer look, however, indicates that Hamilton himself was not as Hamiltonian as he has since been made out.

The first clue is that Hamilton does not start with the argument that has since made him famous. Instead, he starts—and ends—his affirmative case for Washington's power to declare neutrality by relying on specific grants of power. Hamilton asserts that the Neutrality Proclamation "appears to be connected with [the Executive] department in various capacities." Yet each of the powers that underpin these roles more plausibly derives from specific grants rather than some residual general reservoir of Executive power. First, declaring neutrality has a connection to the President's "role as the organ of intercourse between the Nation and foreign nations." This authority in turn was widely understood to rest upon the President's power to appoint and receive ambassadors and other ministers.[30] Second, the Proclamation in part rests upon Washington's role "as the interpreter of the National Treaties" in cases outside the jurisdiction of the courts and so require diplomatic action "between Government and Government." This point likewise hews closely to grants of presidential authority with regard to diplomacy.[31] A further role rests expressly upon the President's authority, through the Executive Power Clause, and duty, via the Take Care Clause, simply to executive laws.[32] As Hamilton puts it, "that Power, which is charged with the Execution of the Laws, of which Treaties form

---

Thesis in his book responding to Theodore Roosevelt's "stewardship" theory of expansive presidential power. 343 U.S. 579, 634, 635 n.1 (1952) (Jackson, J., concurring) (contrasting Taft's *Our Chief Magistrate and His Powers* with Roosevelt's *Autobiography*). For more on *Myers*, see Chapter 5 in this volume.

[29] *See* Draft Memorandum from John Yoo, Deputy Assistant Attorney General, and Robert J. Delahunty, Special Counsel to William J. Haynes II, General Counsel, Department of Defense, "Application of Treaties and Laws to al Qaeda and Taliban Detainees" 14–15 (Jan. 9, 2002); http://www1.umn.edu/humanrts/OathBetrayed/policies-index.html/; Memorandum from Jay S. Bybee, Assistant Attorney General to Alberto R. Gonzales, Counsel to the President, and William J. Haynes II, General Counsel at the Department of Defense, "Standards of Conduct for Interrogation under 18 U.S.C. secs. 2340–2340A" (Aug 2, 2004) *in Torture and Truth: America, Abu Ghraib, and the War on Terror* 115, 147 (Mark Danner ed., 2004).

[30] U.S. Const. art. II, § 2, cl. 3 (The President "shall receive Ambassadors and other public Ministers").

[31] U.S. Const. art. II, § 2, cl. 2. (The President "shall appoint Ambassadors, other public Ministers and Consuls").

[32] U.S. Const. art. II, § 3 (The President "shall take Care that the Laws be faithfully executed").

a part." Finally, Hamilton references the Commander in Chief Clause,[33] additionally resting the authority to proclaim Neutrality on "that Power which is charged with the command and application of the Public Force."[34]

Only then does Hamilton turn to the argument that would resonate with successive Presidents. That argument holds: first, that the Constitution's vesting of "executive Power" entails a range of specific powers that go beyond mere implementation of laws; second, that Article II's more specific enumeration of powers are elaborations rather than limitations; and third, that the President therefore enjoys comprehensive Executive power exclusively unless expressly limited by constitutional text. Hamilton starts his "Vesting Clause Thesis" by quoting the clause itself. Moving to Article II's more specific grants of powers, he asserts that "[i]t would not consist with the rules of sound construction to consider this enumeration of particular authorities as derogating from the more comprehensive grant in the more general clause . . . [and] . . . ought rather to be considered as intended by way of greater caution, to specify and regulate the principle articles implied in the definition of Executive Power." At this point he concludes that "the Executive Power of the Nation is vested in the President; subject only to the *exceptions and qu*[a]*lifications* which are expressed in the [Constitution]"—such as the Senate's role in treaties or appointments. It follows that "issuing of a proclamation of neutrality is merely an Executive Act; since also the general Executive Power of the Union is vested in the President, the conclusion is, that the step, which has been taken by him, is liable to no just exception on the score of authority."[35]

But the Executive Vesting Clause Thesis is neither the only, nor the most important, argument that Hamilton makes. Hamilton had relied previously on an array of specific texts to get to the same place. Moreover, no sooner does Hamilton venture as far as his lawyerly skill will take him with the Vesting Clause, than he retreats to the safer, more conventional ground of specific texts. His final argument does this by brilliantly juxtaposing Congress's enumerated power to "declare War," with a return to the President's duty to faithfully execute the laws. He notes an argument made by opponents of the proclamation that the power to declare war might be seen as an express exception to Executive authority, and that this power necessarily includes the author-

---

[33] U.S. Const. art. II, § 2, cl. 1 ("The President shall be Commander in Chief of the Army and Navy of the United States, and of the Militia of the several States, when called into the actual Service of the United States").

[34] Alexander Hamilton, Letters of Pacificus No. 1 (June 29, 1793), *reprinted in* 15 *The Papers of Alexander Hamilton* 38 (Harold C. Syrett & Jacob E. Cook eds., 1969).

[35] *Id.* at 38–39.

ity to determine whether the nation is under an obligation to go to war. Declaring war, in short, entails the power to declare peace.[36]

This Hamilton denies. To the contrary, it is the "duty of the Executive to preserve Peace till War is declared." That duty in turn requires the President to judge whether the nation's treaty obligations are consistent with maintaining a state of neutrality under "the law of nations," that is, a body binding rules arising out of a consistent, widespread practice among nations which today is known as customary international law. Upon determining that the nation's legal obligations are consistent with the state of neutrality, "it becomes both [the Executive's] province and duty to enforce the laws incident to that state of the Nation." This duty comes directly from the Constitution's specific grant of power, interpreted literally, to implement the laws and specific requirement that it do so:

> The Executive is charged with the execution of all the laws, the laws of Nations as well as the Municipal law, which recognizes and adopts those laws. It is consequently bound, by faithfully executing the laws of neutrality, when that is the state of the Nation, to avoid giving a cause of war to foreign powers.[37]

In his first salvo, Pacificus showed that Hamilton had regained command of the legal skills for which he was known. Among other things, he articulated in detail the Vesting Clause Thesis, almost certainly for the first time in American history. But that argument would resonate mainly in the future. For the present, Pacificus based Washington's unwritten power to proclaim neutrality on a selection of related, written texts. Hamilton's subsequent essays would likewise showcase his more general polemical skills. All told, his efforts represented a high point in his campaign against the excesses of Genet and the incipient opposition to Washington's policies.

Then again, the opposition sensed that Hamilton and his supporters had benefited from a unique set of circumstances, and had nowhere to go but down. No one sensed this more keenly than Jefferson himself. Ironically, both he and Hamilton had been working fairly effectively together to promote neutrality and undercut any appeal that Genet might make directly to the American public.[38] Yet on another level Jefferson knew full well that the Pacificus essays exploited the political weakness of fellow American supporters of France and all that France symbolized to its detractors. Rather than take on Hamilton once more, Jefferson dragooned a friend and ally with palpably better skills as a constitutional analyst than he. On July 7, Jefferson wrote to James

---

[36] *Id.* at 40–41.

[37] *Id.* at 40.

[38] Stanley Elkins & Eric McKittrick, *The Age of Federalism, 1788–1800*, 447 (1993).

Madison imploring him to deal with Pacificus: "Nobody answers him & his doctrines will therefore be taken for confessed. For God's sake, my dear Sir, take up your pen, select the most striking heresies and cut him to pieces in the face of the public. There is nobody else who can & will enter the lists with him."[39]

Madison agreed, but reluctantly. "I am," he wrote, "in hopes of finding that someone else has undertaken it." Later he added, that taking up Jefferson's challenge proved "the most grating [chore] I ever experienced."[40] To counter Pacificus he adopted the comparatively arcane but provocative pseudonym "Helvidius," an allusion to Helvidius Priscus, an ardent advocate of republicanism during the reign of the Emperor Nero.[41] The somewhat clunky name prefigured a somewhat clunky brief. Most observers have concluded that, simply as an exercise in constitutional advocacy, Hamilton easily bested his former *Federalist* co-author. Helvidius's essays betray a number of flaws, not least an absence of pragmatism, which was uncharacteristic of Madison. A closer look, however, reveals an irony. What has arguably made Hamilton's Vesting Clause argument forceful over the years is the simplicity of its categorizing numerous powers in addition to the execution of laws—including the power to declare neutrality—as essentially executive in nature. Yet it is just this type of approach that has opened Madison to subsequent criticism, namely his contention that declaring neutrality is essentially legislative.[42]

Helvidius comes by way of his own formal conception of legislative powers not by directly confronting Hamilton's mirror image formal conception of executive power, but instead by targeting his reliance on the Take Care and Treaty Clauses. He begins his affirmative argument asserting that, "[i]f we consult for a moment, the nature and operation of the two powers to declare war and make treaties, it will be impossible not to see that they can never fall within a proper definition of executive powers." Adopting the plain meaning of the term, Helvidius explains that Executive authority "must presuppose the existence of laws to be executed."[43] A treaty is not "an execution of laws," but rather is itself a

---

[39] Letter of Thomas Jefferson to James Madison (June 29, 1793), *in* 26 *The Papers of Thomas Jefferson* 401, 404 (John C. Catanzariti ed., 1995).

[40] Letter from James Madison to Thomas Jefferson (July 18, 1793), *in* 15 *The Papers of James Madison* 44 (Thomas A. Mason et al. eds., 1985).

[41] *See* Tacitus, 4 *The Histories* 5 (Kenneth Wellesley ed., 1964).

[42] *See e.g.*, Edward S. Corwin, *The President's Control of Foreign Relations* 28 (1917); Saikrishna B. Prakash & Michael D. Ramsey, *The Executive Power over Foreign Affairs*, 111 Yale L.J. 231, 236, 239 (2001).

[43] Letters of Helvidius No. 1 (Aug. 24, 1793), *reprinted in* 15 *The Papers of James Madison* 66, 69 (Thomas A. Mason et. al eds., 1985).

law to be executed. Likewise, a declaration of war cannot be the execution of laws since it is itself a deliberative act "that has the effect of *repealing* all the *laws* operating in a state of peace, so far as they are inconsistent with a state of war." It follows, Madison concludes, "that leaving them to result to their most natural department, the legislature would be without a rival in its claim."[44]

Helvidius confirms this conclusion with a structural argument that borders on the mechanical. Simply put, the power to declare war appears in Article I, "where every other legislative power is declared to be vested." Conversely, the treaty-making power does appear in Article II. But, Helvidius adds, there are reasons to conclude that treaty-making has "more affinity to the legislative than to the executive character." One is the two-thirds requirement for Senate approval, which differs from the mere majority requirement for approval of arguably executive appointments. More importantly, treaties are to have "operation of *laws*, and to be a rule in controversies between man and man, as much as any *other laws*."[45]

Treaty-making, declaring war, and so with them proclaiming neutrality, follow as well from a brief excursion into a sort of original understanding. Madison pointedly wonders where Pacificus could possibly have hit upon the idea that any of these powers are essentially executive. The answer: they are "royal prerogatives in the British government, and are accordingly treated as Executive prerogatives by *British commentators*." But the "arbitrary" British position is what the American Founders rejected. In one of Madison's more deft rhetorical moves in an otherwise fairly leaden display, for proof he quotes at length a passage from *The Federalist* asserting that making treaties, far from an executive function, is entirely legislative.[46] The author of that particular paper was of course the *Federalist* project's chief advocate of executive authority in foreign relations—Alexander Hamilton.[47]

Madison's second main argument asserts that the Constitution does not allow for the concurrent exercise of powers that are purely legislative or purely executive. Here he attempts to use the power to declare war offensively much as Hamilton deployed the responsibility to execute the laws defensively. Pacificus had conceded that Congress's power to declare war entailed a power to determine whether the United States had to make war under its international legal obligations. But these cut against the President enjoying the same power since that would be

---

44 *Id.* at 68–69.

45 *Id.* at 71 (emphasis in original).

46 *Id.* at 72–73 (emphasis in original).

47 *The Federalist* No. 75, at 449, 450 (Alexander Hamilton) (Clinton Rossiter ed., 1961).

"contrary to one of the first and best maxims of a well organized government, and ought never to be founded in a forced construction, much less in opposition to a fair one."[48] In other words, the power to judge whether to go to war rests upon the power to declare war, and each function is at once essentially and exclusively legislative in nature.

Helvidius could have fared better on both constitutional and popular fronts. Had he simply relied on textual analysis, he might simply have argued that the authority to judge the bases for declaring neutrality were so tethered to the power to declare war itself that this connection trumped any authority the President might otherwise have to make similar determinations under the Take Care Clause. As it was, Madison uncharacteristically embraced a view that governmental powers all fell neatly into one of the three basic categories of government function and, contrary to his own masterly essay in *Federalist No. 47*, that these powers were mutually exclusive.[49] Then again, while Hamilton did not fall prey to the exclusivity argument, his Vesting Clause thesis posited the same categorical view no less than Madison. The glaring problem with this approach was that while one Founder contended that the authority to determine neutrality was quintessentially legislative, the other no less confidently asserted that it was executive. Essentialist analysis of this sort all but guarantees a conclusory stalemate. But then, reliance on text, structure, and history do not provide substantially greater guidance. Without specific text on point, even members of the Founding generation could not agree on how to resolve an obviously basic constitutional question no matter the sources or approaches that they invoked. Later separation of powers disputes involving Executive power would prove no different. As one of the first great disputes of this sort, the Neutrality Controversy should therefore remain a cautionary tale.

Washington's Decisions

Resolution of the Neutrality Controversy took place in the Executive Mansion rather than by the Supreme Court. In this way, the dispute is an illustration of a significant portion of constitutional law that gets settled outside the courts. Notwithstanding *INS v. Chadha*, for example, the so-called "legislative veto" flourishes in the form of congressional committees and sub-committees reviewing agency decisions as a condition of funding.[50] Once upon a time disputes over presidential elections

---

[48] Letters of Helvidius No. 2 (Aug. 24, 1793), *reprinted in* 15 *The Papers of James Madison* 80–86, 83 (Thomas A. Mason et al. eds., 1985).

[49] *The Federalist* No. 47, at 300–08 (James Madison) (Clinton Rossiter ed., 1961).

[50] 462 U.S. 919 (1983); *see* Louis Fisher, *Constitutional Conflicts Between the President and Congress* 141–51 (5th ed. 2007).

were settled by Congress, as in 1800, or in congressionally-established commission, as in 1876. Congressional-executive agreements are nowhere mentioned in the Constitution, but they now constitute the vast majority of the international agreements entered into by the United States.

As Justice Jackson intimated, this "constitution outside the courts" phenomenon appears nowhere stronger than in separation of powers disputes, especially in foreign relations. At least today, an important school of thought both within and outside the judiciary believes that the so-called "political branches" should resolve foreign relations matters relatively free from judicial oversight. At times the Court has apparently agreed. Even in cases it does adjudicate, it at least pays lip service to the idea of deferring to the foreign relations expertise of the Executive in particular. It has also found ways not to hear cases on the unconstitutionality of undeclared wars such as Vietnam, or on the President's unilateral termination of treaties, such as the Panama Canal Treaty. As has been seen, the Court declined the President's invitation to weigh in on U.S. treaty obligations to France.

The point should not be overstated. Scholars have recently shown how courts in the early Republic believed that the President was subject to "the law of nations," and that early U.S. courts regularly rejected the Executive's interpretation of treaties. In our own time the Court itself has asserted its authority more aggressively in the post–9/11 context. *Rasul v. Bush* erred on the side of expanding the reach of congressionally-authorized judicial oversight.[51] *Hamdi v. Rumsfeld* noted constitutional checks on Executive detention.[52] *Hamdan v. Rumsfeld* again read congressional intent to check Executive foreign relations authority.[53] *Boumediene v. Bush* bolstered these decisions by holding that the constitutional right of habeas corpus required a meaningful hearing for detainees held at Guantanamo Bay, and that review tribunals instituted by the Executive and later enacted into law by Congress did not provide an adequate substitute.[54] *Boumediene* therefore showed that the Court would restrict the President's attempts to bypass the judiciary even when Congress clearly endorsed such restrictions. Among the key claims that would be preserved for judicial review would derive from international law; in particular, the Geneva Conventions.

It nonetheless remains the case that George Washington resolved more important constitutional matters during his time in office than did

---

[51] 542 U.S. 466 (2004).

[52] 542 U.S. 507 (2004).

[53] 548 U.S. 557 (2006).

[54] 128 S.Ct. 2229 (2008).

the Supreme Court. Washington, for example, at first followed the literal text of the Treaty Clause and appeared before the Senate to get its advice regarding a proposed agreement, only to be so exasperated with the experience that he established the current practice of merely submitting a treaty for approval. He could do this in part because he had to. As the first President, he was confronted with any number of issues great and small before anyone else. Congress itself typically sat for only four months a year. But perhaps most of all, Washington's towering personal prestige insured that his constitutional judgment would prevail.

Each of these factors were on display throughout the Neutrality Controversy. Washington, then, served as the Justice before whom opponents in the Neutrality Controversy pled their case. Yet unlike a Justice, Washington in particular left few clues as to his own way of thinking, apart from his judgments themselves. A Spartan writer, he produced volumes of requests, orders, and decisions, but rarely indulged in significant analysis, least of all legal analysis.

The problem matters less with regard to the international law issues. First, those issues were cleanly defined and bifurcated. Either the treaties with France were still valid or the fact and policies of the French Revolution allowed them to be suspended. Second, the rationale for either result was fairly straightforward. Honoring the treaties meant following conventional international law analysis; suspending them meant taking a leap of faith in Hamilton's legal creativity.

There is, therefore, no reason to suppose that Washington did not fully embrace Jefferson's cogent rationales for honoring the treaties. What does stand out as a result, however, is the President's apparent concern with adhering to accepted norms of international law. The treaties prescribed certain duties. Customary international law, here the presumption of successor state obligations, moreover presumed that these duties remained in force. Comporting with international law, moreover, may not have derived from a constitutional command, but it did reflect a constitutional value evident in writings of such Founders as Jay, Madison, and Hamilton himself. This value in part arose from a general respect owed the rule of law and in part on the belief that following international law would help better keep the United States, still a new an comparatively weak republic, at peace.[55] Not surprisingly,

---

[55] *See* Martin S. Flaherty, *Judicial Globalization in the Service of Self-Government*, 25 Ethics & Int'l Aff. 493–99 (2006). Chief Justice Marshall gave one example of Founding respect for international law in discussing the contemporary rule that alien property within a nation not be immediately confiscated in the event of a war: "The Constitution of the United States was framed at a time when this rule, introduced by commerce in favor of moderation and humanity, was received throughout the civilized world. In expounding that constitution, a construction ought not lightly to be admitted which would give to a

respect for the law of nations also reflected Washington's parallel determination that the best way to keep the United States out of a ruinous conflict was to maintain neutrality since the treaties did not call for any measures that would jeopardize U.S. relations with Britain. Yet Washington's request, and the "briefs" submitted, emphasized a striking commitment to international law.

By contrast, the absence of a Washington "opinion" on the separation of powers question leaves room for wide disagreement down to the present. The President appears to have viewed the scope of the authority he actually exercised narrowly. According to Jefferson, "he never had an idea that he could bind Congress against declaring war, or that anything contained in his proclamation could look beyond the first day of their meeting," Jefferson, moreover, interpreted Washington's position as reflecting his own, which held, "the President, having received the nation at the close of Congress in a state of peace, was bound to preserve them in that state till Congress should again meet, and might proclaim anything that went no further."[56]

But as to the constitutional basis for this power Jefferson left no direct indication. The Cabinet had not only immediately agreed that Washington issue the proclamation, but that he do so without convening Congress. It did so, moreover, without dissent and evidently no discussion of the constitutional basis for the action. There are nonetheless reasons to doubt that Washington embraced Hamilton's Vesting Clause Thesis. For one thing, that argument had virtually never been advanced previously, and even Pacificus sandwiched it between more conventional textual arguments. For another thing, Washington did not need it. As Hamilton himself showed, a number of specific constitutional provisions plausibly served as the basis for the Neutrality power. This same point, moreover, applies to nearly every other assertion of authority made during his tenure. In foreign relations alone, Washington among other things maintained control over the old Department of Foreign Affairs left over from the Confederation period, managed the diplomatic corps, negotiated treaties, and effectively recognized the French Republic. Yet each of these actions can logically rest on an express grant of power in the Constitution. Conversely, at no point did Washington exercise a power for which the only plausible basis could be a general conception of executive power.[57]

---

declaration of war an effect in this country it does not possess elsewhere. . . ." Brown v. United States, 12 U.S. (8 Cranch) 110, 125 (1814).

[56] Thomas Jefferson, Annas, *in* 9 *The Writings of Thomas Jefferson* 177, 178 (H.A. Washington, ed., 1854).

[57] *See* Curtis A. Bradley & Martin S. Flaherty, *Executive Power Essentialism and Foreign Affairs*, 102 Mich. L. Rev. 545, 626–87 (2004). For a contrary view, *see* Saikrishna

Congress likewise relied on specific textual grants. The legislative branch by design remained the other arbiter of constitutional meaning, especially when the judiciary hesitated to intervene. For all of Washington's prestige, Congress had shown that it was up to the task of asserting itself. By the time of the Neutrality Proclamation, those assertions has fallen into a coherent pattern. Congress almost always acceded to Washington's actions without dissent when the President's own assertions could be tied to some express grant of power. When, however, any claim extending executive authority had no such clear basis, or conflicted with a grant of authority to the legislative branch, significant controversy would follow. When, for example, the President received communications from foreign governments, no voice of dissent was heard. By contrast, when it was originally proposed that the Secretary of State be removed at the President's discretion, rather than, as with the appointment, with majority Senate approval, a firestorm erupted since known as the "removal debate."[58]

Neither dissent nor dispute greeted the Neutrality Proclamation. To the contrary, each house praised the President for the measure without recorded objection. Congress finally came back into session in December, seven months after Washington had declared neutrality. A week later, the Senate adopted an address to the President noting that, "As the European powers with whom the United States have the most extensive relations were involved in war, in which we had taken no part, it seemed necessary that the disposition of the nation for peace should be promulgated to the world ... [w]e ... contemplate with pleasure the proclamation you promulgated, and give it our hearty approbation."[59] The House added its own "approbation and pleasure" for Washington's policy. The Representatives nonetheless did make clear where they thought the President's authority came from, namely, that "the maintenance of peace was justly to be regarded as one of the most important duties of the Magistrate charged with the faithful execution of the laws," clearly alluding to the law of nations.[60]

The actions that Congress took, and did not take, further suggest a general view that the President enjoyed the authority to proclaim neutrality. In any number of later separation of powers disputes, Congress would enact a law ratifying a presidential action in part to make clear that the given measure required legislative approval. Congress's

B. Prakash & Michael D. Ramsey, *The Executive Power over Foreign Affairs*, 111 Yale L.J. 231, 298–311 (2001).

[58] *See* Curtis A. Bradley & Martin S. Flaherty, *Executive Power Essentialism and Foreign Affairs*, 102 Mich. L. Rev. 545, 656–64 (2004).

[59] 4 Annals of Cong. 17–18 (Dec. 9, 1793).

[60] *Id.* at 138 (Dec. 6, 1793).

suspension of habeas review during the Civil War, which Lincoln himself requested, would be perhaps the most famous instance of this device. But Congress made no such attempt to preserve any authority to determine neutrality that it might have thought it had after the fact. It would, however, weigh in on one further aspect of the Neutrality Proclamation that went beyond either the Executive's interpretation of international law or its authority to proclaim neutrality: enforcing the policy through criminal prosecution of Americans whose actions threatened to drag the country into war.

The Immediate Impact

The immediate impact of the Neutrality Proclamation followed its own logic and apparent force. In the first instance it clearly issued as a statement by the President in lieu of Congress. This proved to be the least controversial part of the controversy. The action met with no dissent in the Cabinet, even from the pro-French Jefferson. Nor did Congress resist. The only aspect of the separation of powers question that did generate debate centered on the basis for Washington's authority. As noted, that debate arose largely because of Hamilton's attempt to argue for as extensive a conception of executive power as the Republic had yet seen, a polemic that in turn led to overreaction by Madison. Madison's arguments, however, made little impression then or now. And however much the so-called Vesting Clause Thesis has echoed since, it did not resonate at the time.

The Proclamation's first substantive claim addressed the nation's "duty" to remain impartial, an allusion to its commitments under international law.[61] Securing this goal took longer to resolve, albeit through no fault of Washington. Hamilton notwithstanding, Washington's decision in May to receive Citizen Genet on the basis that the United States would honor its treaty obligations received widespread support. Thanks to Genet himself, however, that support did not last the summer. Also as noted, Genet courted American popular opinion in an apparent attempt either to pressure, or worse, bypass, the Administration. He also continued his privateering activities, prompting British protests. As if these actions were not audacious enough, Genet also wrote to Jefferson suggesting that Congress, not President Washington, should be determining U.S. policy toward France.[62] Not for nothing did Hamilton see the opportunity to undermine support for France with his Pacificus essays.

---

[61] Proclamation of Neutrality (April 22, 1793), *in* 32 *The Writings of George Washington* 430 (John C. Fitzpatrick ed., 1939).

[62] Stanley Elkins & Eric McKittrick, *The Age of Federalism, 1788–1800*, 350 (1993).

For America's leading Francophile, it became clear that the problem was not Hamilton but Genet himself. After initially supporting the Ambassador, by early July Jefferson had had enough. "Never, in my opinion," he wrote Madison, "was so calamitous an appointment made as that of the present minister of F[rance] here." He continued, "Hot-headed, all imagination, no judgment, passionate and even indecent to the P[resident] in his written as well as his verbal communications, talking of appeals from him to Congress, from them to the people, urging the most unreasonable and groundless propositions, and in the most dictatorial style. . . ."[63]

With Jefferson's desertion, Genet's days were numbered. But the problem remained of how to get rid of the French Ambassador, who jeopardized peace with Britain, without endangering relations with France. By early August, the Washington and the cabinet decided to send a letter to Gouverneur Morris, the U.S. Ambassador to France, giving a detailed account of Genet's misconduct and asking Morris to request his recall. This Morris did in October, and the French government granted the request three days later. Genet continued to make trouble until the very end, even to the point of demanding that Chief Justice John Jay and Senator Rufus King be prosecuted for libel. News of his recall finally arrived mid-January 1794. The new French Ambassador Jean Fachet, who arrived the next month, was content to abide by the Administration's conception of neutrality and not make further trouble. Genet himself decided to stay in America on the probably correct assumption that he would be executed by the new Jacobin regime if he returned to France. He settled as a gentleman farmer in New York and married the daughter of Governor DeWitt Clinton.[64]

With the Proclamation issued and neutrality preserved, the main remaining issue involved enforcement. Washington devoted the bulk of his statement to making known that, first, American citizens were subject to "punishment or forfeiture under the law of nations" by aiding any belligerents; second, that such persons would not receive the protection of the United States; and finally, that he had instructed relevant officials "to cause prosecutions to be instituted against all persons, who shall, within the cognizance of the courts of the United States, violated the law of nations."[65] Yet the President's formulation, perhaps deliberately, begged significant questions. On what basis were Americans to face criminal liability? The law of nations itself? The President's order?

---

[63] Letter from Thomas Jefferson to James Madison (July 7, 1793) *in* 26 *The Papers of Thomas Jefferson* 443–44 (John C. Catanzariti ed., 1995).

[64] Stanley Elkins & Eric McKittrick, *The Age of Federalism, 1788–1800*, 372–73 (1993).

[65] Proclamation of Neutrality (April 22, 1793), *in* 32 *The Writings of George Washington* 430 (John C. Fitzpatrick ed., 1939).

Judge-made federal common law? In the absence of a clear criminal statute, the answers were unclear. So too was whether any or all of these bases for criminal liability fell within the "cognizance" or jurisdiction of the federal courts.

More than at any other point in its neutrality policy, the Executive Branch pressed its authority up to and beyond the limits that much of the nation was willing to accept. This assertion, however, arose ironically as a result of the President seeking to defer to the judiciary. Contemplating the problems with enforcing the Proclamation's warnings, Washington had Jefferson write a letter to the Justices of the Supreme Court, seeking their guidance on how the nation's treaty and law of nations obligations did or did not bind individuals from involving themselves in the war and to what extent. As Jefferson put it, "These questions depend for their solution on the construction of our treaties, on the laws of nature and nations, and on the laws of the land; and are often presented under circumstances which do not give a cognizance of them to the tribunals of the country." Jefferson continued that, the decision involving these matters was nonetheless "so little analogous to the ordinary function of the Executive as to occasion much embarrassment and difficulty to them." To the letter the Secretary of State appended twenty-nine questions, starting with whether the Franco–American treaties allowed French citizens a right to fit out armed vessels in U.S. ports.[66]

The Supreme Court famously declined the invitation. In response, the Justices declared that the three branches of government "being in certain respects checks on each other, and our being judges of a court in the last resort, are considerations which afford strong arguments against the propriety of our extra-judicially deciding the questions alluded to."[67] In short, the Court would not issue advisory opinions. In consequence, the cabinet drafted detailed "regulations" that constituted the Executive's own interpretation of relevant the relevant international law matters. These regulations would in part serve as guidelines for criminal prosecutions of Americans who took up privateering for France in violation of the Proclamation's injunctions.[68]

Among the first to face prosecution was Gideon Henfield, a U.S. citizen who served as a prize-master aboard the French-commissioned privateer with the all too probable name, *Citoyen Genet*. Authorities had

---

[66] Letter from Thomas Jefferson to the Justices of the Supreme Court (July 18, 1793), *in* 26 *The Papers of Thomas Jefferson* 520 (John C. Catanzariti ed., 1995); Questions for the Supreme Court *in id.* at 534–35.

[67] Letter of the Justices of the Supreme Court to George Washington (Aug. 8, 1793), *in* 33 *Writings of George Washington* 15–19 (John C. Fitzpatrick ed., 1940).

[68] David P. Currie, *The Constitution in Congress: The Federalist Period, 1789–1801*, 180–81 (1999).

arrested Henfield when the ship arrived in Philadelphia with a captured British ship as a prize. Henfield's case became a cause célèbre which put before the public the various questions finessed in the last part of the Proclamation. Both Henfield's attorneys and the pro-French press mainly relied on the same straightforward argument. Under Article I, section 8, the Constitution empowers Congress to "define and punish Offenses against the Law of Nations." Yet Congress had not done so. As John Marshall later noted, the pro-French, pro-Jefferson newspapers "universally asked, 'What law had been offended, and under what statute was the indictment supported? Were the American people already prepared to give the proclamation the force of a legislative act, and to subject themselves to the will of the legislature?' "[69]

The chief articulation of the Executive's case came not from the Administration but from Chief Justice John Jay and Justice James Wilson. Around the time of Henfield's arrest in late May, Jay gave a famous charge to the grand jury for the circuit court in Virginia. The charge did not apply directly to Henfield, but was intended to state the general basis for those prosecuted under the Proclamation. The charge suggested at least two foundations for any prosecution. First, Jay noted that treaties in the United States were self-executing. As "the supreme law of the land," any doubts arising from their interpretation must be settled according to the maxims of international law, and further "every citizen is a party to them." Next, Jay dealt with the law of nations itself, to which he notes forms "a very important part of the laws of our nation," along with treaties. "From these observations" he concludes that the Proclamation correctly stated the obligations that both the nation and its citizens were bound to observe. Following the Proclamation, Jay declared that "they who commit, aid, or abet hostilities against these powers, or either of them, offend against the laws of the United States, and ought to be punished."[70] Wilson, at greater length, echoed these points.[71]

Henfield was acquitted nonetheless. Several explanations could account for why. Jefferson believed that the jury did not want to punish anyone who did not know he was breaking the law. Others attributed the verdict to pro-French sympathies. More to the point, still others thought the jury did not want to convict anyone on the basis of an executive proclamation rather than a statute.[72]

---

[69] John Marshall, 5 *Life of George Washington* 41 (1926 ed.).

[70] Circuit Court for the District of Virginia (May 22, 1793) *in* United States v. Henfield, 11 F.Cas. 1099, 1100–05 (C.C.D. Pa. 1793).

[71] *See id.* at 1105–15.

[72] David P. Currie, *The Constitution in Congress: The Federalist Period, 1789–1801,* 181 (1999).

Washington in any event chose to place the enforcement of neutrality on less controversial ground. When Congress met in December, the President made clear that neutrality was the priority. Congress was willing to accede both because the policy remained popular and because it was happy to assert its perceived constitutional place. As noted, it welcomed the Proclamation itself and made no attempt to assert a concurrent power to declare peace. By contrast, it chose clearly to exercise its authority under its authority to define and punish offenses against the law of nations.[73] Section 1 of the Neutrality Act of 1794 declared that if any U.S. citizen within the United States or its jurisdiction accepted a commission from a foreign sovereign to serve on land or sea, "the person so offending shall be deemed guilty of a high misdemeanor, and shall be fined not more than two thousand dollars, and shall be imprisoned for not exceeding three years...."[74] With each of the branches having marked out their territory, the Neutrality Controversy drew to a close.

The Continuing Importance

The Neutrality Controversy would continue to command attention generally if only because of its characters and plot. Washington, Jefferson, Hamilton, Madison, war, peace, revolution, intrigue, politics—all of these elements make for a compelling chapter in the early history of the nation. But the dispute also still commands the attention of constitutional lawyers. It resolved, or at least pointed toward the resolution, of several critical separation of powers questions, especially in foreign relations. Perhaps more importantly, it offers a useful initial reminder of how, and how much, constitutional law can develop outside the courts.

The issues that the Neutrality Controversy resolved at the time range from quaint to controversial when viewed today. The initial question—whether the President has the authority to declare that the United States remains neutral in light of war between other sovereign states—now appears almost trivially obvious. Given the vast expansion of presidential power in 200 years, including the initiation of countless armed conflicts, a power to announce that the United States will remain at peace generates little if any opposition even among the Executive Branch's most vociferous critics. And apart from Madison's strained attempts, this proposition hardly generated much greater opposition at the time, either in the cabinet or Congress. The basis for this authority remains another matter.

---

[73] U.S. Const. art. I, § 8, cl. 10 (Congress shall have the power "To define and punish Piracies and Felonies committed on the high Seas, and Offenses against the Law of Nations").

[74] Ch. 50, 1 Stat. 381 (1794). A version of this statute is still in use, *see* 18 U.S.C. § 959.

Here the Neutrality Controversy did not so much resolve matters as set the framework for ongoing debate. At the congressional end of the spectrum, Madison's categorical arguments about core legislative powers may not have succeeded then or now, but they did help establish the convention of defending congressional authority based upon specific grants of power. At the presidential end, Hamilton famously introduced the Vesting Clause argument, versions of which have been used by administrations ever since. Yet, as noted, at the time this argument was not only novel, but also prompted a strong reaction from Madison and Jefferson among others. During this period, the far safer basis for executive authority was likewise the Constitution's specific grants of power.

By contrast, the other central question that the Neutrality Controversy raised, the obligation of the United States to comply with international law, at least in recent years has become contested. This is not to say international law failed to prompt debate at the time. Unlike the decision to declare neutrality, determining on what terms to receive France's new ambassador created sharp division within the cabinet and prompted Washington to have the issue thoroughly briefed before he made a decision. Here Jefferson's orthodox analysis won out over Hamilton's more creative efforts, and the President received Genet on the understanding that the United States would honor its treaty obligations as applied under the law of nations.

All sides, however, above all Washington himself, agreed on one point: that the nation in general and the Executive in particular should follow international law. It may or may not be too much to infer that Washington believed he could not violate international law without congressional sanction.[75] As was said in another regard, the concern the Washington administration showed may now appear "quaint."[76] The position of Knox, Randolph, Hamilton, Jefferson, and Washington might nonetheless merit some consideration before the nation's international law commitments are dismissed out of hand.

---

[75] A number of scholars have recently suggested that the Constitution originally meant to place the President under an obligation to follow treaties while in force and the law of nations. *See, e.g.*, Michael D. Ramsey, *The Constitution's Text in Foreign Affairs* 362–76 (2007). The Supreme Court would later suggest that only the "sovereign power" could authorize the President to disregard the law of nations, at least for the purposes of seizing enemy alien property within U.S. territory during war. Brown v. United States, 12 U.S. (8 Cranch) 110, 120 (1814).

[76] Attorney General Alberto Gonzales characterized provisions of the Geneva Conventions of 1949 as "obsolete" and "quaint" in the "new paradigm" of opposing terrorism. Memorandum of Alberto R. Gonzales to the President (Jan. 25, 2002) *in Torture and Truth: America, Abu Ghraib, and the War on Terror* 83, 84 (Mark Danner ed., 2004).

One further substantive issue that the Neutrality Controversy continues to address involves presidential lawmaking. This issue arose not with the issuance of the Proclamation but its enforcement. One basis asserted for the initial prosecution of Henfield and others who aided the European belligerents was that these actions violated the President's say so interpreting the law of nations. That say so, specifically Washington's admonition to Americans who took take part in the war would be in violation of international law, together with the Executive's subsequent regulations, in effect acted like a criminal statute. Nor is this position a historical curiosity. Prior to the Military Commissions Act of 2006, the Bush Administration claimed that the President enjoyed independent authority to articulate what crimes under the laws of war would apply in military commissions to try Guantanamo detainees.[77]

Such arguments reflected a broader conception of executive authority than even Hamilton had fleetingly put forward concerning the President's foreign affairs powers. They also prompted the Controversy's most compelling reaction. Almost certainly one reason the Henfield jury in effect nullified the prosecution had to do with concerns about the executive's ability to impose criminal sanctions in the absence of a statute. In time, the Supreme Court would determine that federal criminal law required an act of Congress against claims that the federal judiciary could exercise its common lawmaking powers to impose criminal sanctions.[78] But the more general question of the President's ability effectively to set rules, especially relating to foreign affairs, endures, and with uneven results. The matter arose in *Youngstown*, where the Court rejected President Truman's attempt to seize the steel mills as unauthorized lawmaking. Conversely, the Court more recently could be read to suggest that policy statements from executive officials could trump contrary state laws, although in that case binding executive agreements also provided evidence of presidential policy.[79] The Neutrality Controversy shows America's Founding generation generally to be profoundly skeptical of steps approaching presidential lawmaking.

Conclusion

The Neutrality Controversy should remain vital regardless of its specific resolutions. The nation's first generation of leaders possessed

---

[77] *See* U.S. Dep't of Defense, Crimes and Elements of Trials by Military Commission, 68 Fed. Reg. 39,381 (July 1, 2003).

[78] *See* United States v. Hudson, 11 U.S. (7 Cranch) 32, 33 (1812) ("The legislative authority of the Union must first make an act a crime, affix a punishment to it, and declare the court shall have jurisdiction of the offence.").

[79] American Ins. Assn. v. Garamendi, 539 U.S. 396, 421 (2003). More recently, the Court has attempted to clarify its language in *Garamendi* by emphasizing the necessity that longstanding congressional acquiescence to a presidential policy concerning claims settlement in international disputes. *See* Medellin v. Texas, 128 S.Ct. 1346 (2008).

unmatched experience in applied political science. Many spent a decade attempting to find a way to go forward within the British Empire, another decade experimenting with state constitutions and a federation of states, followed by conceiving, establishing, and implementing the new Federal Constitution. Historical circumstances also worked to insure that some of the most accomplished persons in the nation's history took part in all these tasks. Certain approaches to the Constitution place even greater weight on how the Founding generation resolved the challenges they faced. Originalists, of course, would view their actions as near conclusive, either as evidence of what those who ratified the Constitution had in mind or in their own right. But according the Founders some measure of deference is by no means confined to originalists. It would be difficult if not impossible to find a theory of constitutional interpretation that did not consider the first chapters of our constitutional history offering presumptive guidance to modern cases. Contrary to Justice Jackson, moreover, the actors in this particular controversy did not simply "cancel each other." Presidential criminal lawmaking met with resistance and defeat. Every relevant player showed a desire to remain faithful to international law. Helvidius notwithstanding, the President's authority to determine neutrality appears to have met with general acceptance.

Yet guidance from the past does not necessarily mean command, especially with regard to executive authority, separation of powers, and foreign relations. Experienced and talented as they were, Madison, Hamilton, Jefferson, and Washington grappled with these early questions even though they arose 200 years ago, in what was a weak, untested, agrarian republic, among persons who could not possibly have envisioned the place or power of the United States today. Moreover, while nearly every theory of constitutional interpretation suggests respect for history, many approaches call for no more than that and instead rely on evolving tradition, political science, or conceptions of fundamental justice. Even for those who would follow the past as a command, too often the exact order is unclear. On close review, the sources for the Neutrality Controversy may not cancel each other. But neither do they conclusively answer such questions, either. At what point do the President's foreign policy declarations infringe upon Congress's war powers? Must the President always respect treaties and customary international law? Can, and if so under what circumstances, may the President make rules in the absence of clear congressional authorization? The Neutrality Controversy may point in certain directions, but not to actual destinations.

Beyond specific questions, the dispute also serves as a reminder of how much of constitutional law did, and still does develop. For all the scrutiny Supreme Court decisions receive, much of the way even epic

constitutional matters get resolved is through individuals and governmental actors working out the meaning of the Constitution's terse
phrases and gaps over time. The Neutrality Controversy suggests that
the process of working through constitutional accommodations is nowhere more central than in questions involving overlapping powers of
the President and Congress, especially when they accept the Constitution's "invitation to struggle" in foreign relations. It also shows that
historical circumstances gave Washington an especially prominent role
in settling constitutional questions.

None of this is to say that the judiciary does not matter. Founding
attitudes may have envisioned a more significant role for the judiciary in
both separation of powers and foreign relations than is sometimes
thought.[80] As one of the three branches of government, the courts
presumptively have their own role to play, where appropriate, in working
out constitutional meaning. And despite his skepticism about the ability
and the power of the judiciary to reverse the flow of authority from one
branch to another, Justice Jackson himself deeply believed in the duty of
the Supreme Court to weigh in on issues of executive authority.[81] The
Supreme Court would answer this call in cases that followed.

---

[80] See William Michael Treanor, *Judicial Review Before* Marbury, 58 Stan. L. Rev. 455
(2005); Thomas H. Lee, *The Supreme Court of the United States as a Quasi–International
Tribunal: Reclaiming the Court's Original and Exclusive Jurisdiction over Treaty–Based
Suits by Foreign States against States*, 104 Colum. L. Rev. 1765, 1838–49 (2004).

[81] Youngstown Sheet & Tube Co. v. Sawyer, 343 U.S. 579, 637 (1952) (Jackson, J.,
concurring).

2

Thomas H. Lee and Michael D. Ramsey

The Story of the *Prize Cases*: Executive Action and Judicial Review in Wartime

The President mobilizes troops and authorizes military force in the face of a national emergency. Among other things, he directs the U.S. Navy to seize ships and cargoes belonging to foreign and American citizens engaged in maritime commerce who have not taken up arms against the United States nor violated any U.S. laws. The President has not consulted Congress nor received legislative authorization for his actions; there was not, he says, time to do so. Critics assail him for exceeding his constitutional powers. A constitutional challenge reaches the U.S. Supreme Court nearly two years after the crisis has ripened into a full-blown war. The Justices must decide: is this challenge something the Court should take up? And if it is, how should they interpret the President's constitutional authority? These questions framed the *Prize Cases*,[1] decided in early 1863 at the height of the Civil War with the outcome of the war still in doubt.

It is surprising that the *Prize Cases* do not figure more prominently in modern debates over the President's authority during emergencies, as judicial pronouncements regarding wartime powers are rare in our constitutional history. This neglect may arise because the Court's decision seems opaque to modern readers and far removed from modern challenges. The cases involved the unique circumstance of a full-scale struggle for the internal unity of the nation. Much of the decision is intertwined with the archaic legalisms of nineteenth-century naval warfare—blockades, the capture of prizes, and the antiquated rules of international maritime law that accompanied them. It seems to belong to another time, a historical curiosity. Yet on closer examination, its underlying questions are timeless: among them, what constitutes war;

---

[1] The Prize Cases, 67 U.S. 635 (1863).

how a constitutional democracy responds to crisis; and what role courts should play in such difficult times.

Political Context

The Secession Crisis

Abraham Lincoln, the Republican Party candidate, won the November 1860 presidential election with a majority of electoral votes in a four-way race. The results underscored the nation's intense sectional divide over slavery. The Democratic Party had split into northern and southern factions over the issue, nominating rival candidates and easing the way for Lincoln's victory. Though the Republican platform called only for prohibiting slavery in the western territories, Lincoln was widely seen as the anti-slavery candidate and was bitterly opposed throughout the slave-holding South. He carried every free state in the North except New Jersey (which divided its votes) but received just under 40 percent of the popular vote and did not win a single electoral vote in any state where slavery was legal; in some of these states his name did not even appear on the ballot.

Many southerners declared before the election that if Lincoln won they would not remain in the Union.[2] Once Lincoln's victory was announced, events moved quickly toward crisis. South Carolina called a convention to consider secession almost immediately. Most states of the deep South seemed poised to follow.

The impending collapse of the Union posed an array of tough legal questions. Was secession constitutional? If not, what could the federal government do to stop it? Could there be such a thing as war against the recalcitrant states? What could be done about federal posts and property within the seceding states? And what branch of the U.S. government could make these decisions? In the election's immediate aftermath, incumbent U.S. President James Buchanan—a northern Democrat and southern sympathizer—referred these and related questions to his Attorney General, Jeremiah Black. Black's response, a formal opinion dated November 20, 1860, found that although secession was unconstitutional,

---

[2] Important general histories of the period include Doris Kearns Goodwin, *Team of Rivals: The Political Genius of Abraham Lincoln* (2006); Michael Green, *Freedom, Union and Power: Lincoln and his Party during the Civil War* (2004); James M. McPherson, *Battle Cry of Freedom: The Civil War Era* (1988); and Phillip Paludan, *The Presidency of Abraham Lincoln* (1994). The classic work on the Civil War's constitutional aspects is J.G. Randall, *Constitutional Problems under Lincoln* (rev. ed. 1963). Other leading accounts from a legal perspective include Daniel A. Farber, *Lincoln's Constitution* (2003); Brian McGinty, *Lincoln and the Court* (2008); Robert Bruce Murray, *Legal Cases of the Civil War* (2003); Mark. E. Neely, Jr., *The Fate of Liberty: Abraham Lincoln and Civil Liberties* (1991); and James F. Simon, *Lincoln and Chief Justice Taney: Slavery, Secession, and the President's War Powers* (2006).

there was not much the federal government could do about it. "The General Government," he wrote,

> may lawfully repel a direct aggression on its property and officers, but cannot carry on an offensive war to punish the people for the political misdeeds of their State Governments, or to prevent threatened violations of the Constitution, or to enforce an acknowledgement that the Government of the United States is supreme.[3]

Though Black's opinion may seem unduly timid today, at the time many southerners—and some northerners—thought Black too aggressive even in his first conclusion that secession was unconstitutional. The Constitution was a compact among the states, they argued; states could withdraw if they chose, and nothing in the Constitution said they could not.[4] If that were true, it followed as a matter of course that the remaining states could not make war on those that wished to depart.

President Buchanan largely adopted Black's conclusions in a message to Congress on December 3.[5] Though he condemned secession as unconstitutional, Buchanan said that not just the President but the entire federal government lacked constitutional authority to prevent it.[6] Thus he gave southerners reason to think that no forceful response would—or could—be forthcoming. Emboldened by Buchanan's apparent paralysis, South Carolina's convention voted to secede on December 20. Six other states—Alabama, Mississippi, Georgia, Florida, Louisiana and Texas—followed South Carolina's lead by the end of January 1861. Together they formed the Confederate States of America, with Jefferson Davis as provisional president, in February.

As southerners surely anticipated, Buchanan failed to mount any meaningful opposition. Indeed, he failed to take firm measures even in the one area Black said he could—the defense of federal posts and property in the South. Owing to Buchanan's inaction, most federal

---

[3] *Power of the President in Executing the Laws*, 9 Op. Att'y Gen. 516, 517, 525–26 (Nov. 20, 1860). *See* Daniel A. Farber, *Lincoln's Constitution* 75–76 (2003); on Buchanan and events leading to war, *see* David Potter, *The Impending Crisis, 1848–1861* (1976).

[4] *See* J.G. Randall, *Constitutional Problems under Lincoln* 12–24 (rev. ed. 1963) (recounting these arguments); Daniel A. Farber, *Lincoln's Constitution* 77–91 (2003) (same). The most elaborate—and massive (two volumes, 1,455 pages)—postbellum articulation of the secessionist position came from the former Vice President of the Confederacy, Alexander H. Stephens. Alexander H. Stephens, *A Constitutional View of the Late War Between the States; Its Causes, Character, Conduct and Results Presented in a Series of Colloquies at Liberty Hall* (1867, 1870).

[5] *Message of the President of the United States*, Cong. Globe, 36th Cong., 2d Sess., App., at 3 (Dec. 3, 1860).

[6] For an especially sharp critique of Buchanan's reasoning and actions, *see* David P. Currie, *The Constitution in Congress: Descent into the Maelstrom, 1829–1861*, at 228–42 (2005). Daniel A. Farber, *Lincoln's Constitution* 75–76 (2003), is only slightly less harsh.

facilities in the South were abandoned or taken over without resistance in the early months of 1861. When Lincoln took office as President in March 1861, seven states had seceded, the independent Confederacy had been organized and had consolidated control of its territory, and the federal government had effectively done nothing. With the allegiance of the remaining eight slave states hanging in the balance, the question was how Lincoln would respond.

Lincoln began cautiously,[7] but events quickly forced his hand. The immediate issue was the fate of the few remaining federal posts in the South under Union control—especially Fort Sumter, guarding the harbor of Charleston, South Carolina. While other federal posts had succumbed to Confederate control in the waning months of Buchanan's administration, Major Robert Anderson, the resolute federal commander in Charleston, consolidated his forces at Sumter, which—thanks to its island location—could be defended in the short run. Confederate forces cut off supplies to the fort and demanded its surrender. Attorney General Black told Buchanan he had the constitutional power to reinforce Sumter, and urged him to do so, but Buchanan dithered even on this modest action (he sent only an unarmed merchant ship, which turned back after shore batteries fired warning shots). By March, after Lincoln's inauguration, Anderson was running low on supplies. Lincoln had to decide whether to attempt a seaborne resupply of the fort that would almost certainly be opposed by Confederate military action.

Despite conflicting and shifting opinions from his cabinet members, Lincoln decided to launch an armed naval expedition to assist Anderson's garrison.[8] That move in turn led Confederate troops in Charleston to open fire on the fort on April 12. After an intense bombardment (albeit without the loss of life),[9] Anderson surrendered. Whether this was the start of a war (a question the Supreme Court later confronted), it was, in any event, open armed conflict.

Lincoln's War Measures

Congress was not in session when Sumter fell, nor was it scheduled to reassemble for some time. Lincoln called Congress to meet for a

---

[7] Daniel A. Farber, *Lincoln's Constitution* 14 (2003) (noting Lincoln's attempt, in his inaugural address, to "uphold unionism without further inflaming the South"); *see First Inaugural Address*, March 4, 1861, 4 *Collected Works of Abraham Lincoln* 262–70 (Roy Basler, ed., 1953).

[8] Doris Kearns Goodwin, *Team of Rivals: The Political Genius of Abraham Lincoln* 334–45 (2006). When Lincoln first posed the question, five members of his cabinet favored surrendering Sumter and only one, Postmaster General Montgomery Blair, unambiguously favored resupply. Lincoln declined to adopt the cabinet's advice and eventually persuaded a majority to support his decision. *Id*. at 336–37, 340–41.

[9] One Union soldier was killed during the surrender by a friendly misfire.

special session[10] on July 4, over three months away.[11] That gave him time to formulate an initial response on his own authority, which he did quickly and forcefully.

First, Lincoln raised an army. On April 15, he called for an initial levy of 75,000 militia from the states. On May 3, he appealed for an additional 42,000 federal volunteers. To be sure, the call-ups could be viewed as purely defensive measures to protect federal property and personnel. But Lincoln's language already suggested a more comprehensive war footing: the state militias were needed, he said on the 15th, to "suppress" those "combinations" who opposed the laws of the United States, and to "cause the laws to be duly executed."[12] The federal volunteers, he similarly said on May 3, were intended for the "suppression of the insurrectionary combinations now existing in the several states opposing the laws of the Union and obstructing the execution thereof."[13] The mention of "suppression" and the scale of the call-ups suggested affirmative military actions beyond the immediate defense of federal property. At the very least Lincoln appeared to have in mind much more than Black and Buchanan had thought constitutionally permissible a few months earlier, although he undertook no major military action on land during this initial period.

Next, on April 19, Lincoln proclaimed a naval blockade of all ports in the seven states that had already seceded.[14] On April 27, he extended the blockade to the ports of Virginia and North Carolina in light of their imminent secessions.[15] On Lincoln's orders, ships failing to respect the blockade would be fired upon if they refused to stop and would be captured and subject to condemnation as prizes (along with their cargoes).

In part, the blockade responded to a Confederate measure extending the conflict to the seas: Davis declared on April 17 that the Confederacy would issue letters of marque to anyone who would attack U.S. ship-

---

[10] See U.S. Const. Art. II, § 3 (giving the President power "on extraordinary Occasions, [to] convene both Houses [of Congress].").

[11] Proclamation Calling Militia and Convening Congress, April 15, 1861, 4 Collected Works of Abraham Lincoln 331–32 (Roy Basler, ed., 1953). See Daniel A. Farber, Lincoln's Constitution 117 (2003) (suggesting that Congress could have assembled earlier and that the delay was calculated to give Lincoln time to set his own course).

[12] Proclamation Calling Militia and Convening Congress, April 15, 1861, 4 Collected Works of Abraham Lincoln 332 (Roy Basler, ed., 1953).

[13] Proclamation Calling for 42,034 Volunteers, May 3, 1861, id. at 353.

[14] Proclamation of a Blockade, April 19, 1861, id. at 338–39.

[15] Proclamation of Blockade, April 27, 1861, id. at 346–47.

ping.[16] But the blockade was no mere defensive measure. It promised violence and deprivation against the seceding states as a whole—not only against those individuals actively fighting in rebellion, but against their populations and economies. Moreover, Lincoln's blockade of North Carolina and Virginia arguably amounted to the preemptive use of military force to interdict maritime trade to and from states that had not yet formally withdrawn from the Union; in Virginia a convention had voted for secession on April 17 but subject to ratification by popular referendum on May 23; the North Carolina secession convention voted on May 20.[17] As important—and by contrast to the call-up of land forces—a blockade meant using armed naval force, possibly in international waters, against the citizens of neutral foreign nations such as Great Britain and France who sought to ship goods to and from ports in states that had seceded or were likely to secede.

Lincoln's objectives were clear enough, and they showed his move to wartime measures. The blockade was designed to disrupt the export-dependent southern economy and to prevent the mostly agrarian South from importing manufactured goods and war materials. The proclamations were, moreover, cast in the language of war: as described more fully below, a "blockade" in international law took place between belligerent nations in wartime to obstruct supplies and funds from reaching the enemy. (Indeed, some members of Lincoln's cabinet, most prominently Secretary of the Navy Gideon Welles, initially opposed declaring a blockade on the ground that it might be taken to recognize the Confederacy as an independent nation with which the United States was at war.)[18]

Together with the call for troops, the blockade signaled that Lincoln saw the firing on Sumter as giving rise to a state of war and that he meant to use armed force not just to defend the North but to prevent secession. That determination, applauded in the North, hardened the commitment of the deep South and drove four more states—Virginia, North Carolina, Tennessee and Arkansas—to join the Confederacy in May and June of 1861.

Congress' Approval

On July 4, 1861, Congress convened—a very different Congress from the body that adjourned indecisively in early 1861. Now dominated by

---

[16] *Proclamation of a Blockade*, April 19, 1861, *id*. at 338–39.

[17] Two of the captures at issue in the *Prize Cases* involved the property of avowedly loyal U.S. citizens resident in Virginia on May 17 and May 20, days before the Virginia referendum had passed.

[18] Doris Kearns Goodwin, *Team of Rivals: The Political Genius of Abraham Lincoln* 351 (2006); Brian McGinty, *Lincoln and the Court* 121–22 (2008).

northerners, Congress approved in just over a week an array of wartime measures, including funding and authorizing an expanded army and navy. Congress also approved continuation of the blockade by giving the President power to declare portions of the country in "insurrection" and to interrupt commence to and from them.[19] With Congress fully behind him, Lincoln directed the first large-scale military offensive against the South, sending 30,000 troops to seize the town of Manassas, Virginia (culminating in the disastrous Union defeat at Bull Run on July 21, 1861, and setting the course for an agonizing fight to the finish).[20]

Congress also took up a proposal to ratify in specific terms Lincoln's prior actions, including building up the army and declaring the blockade.[21] Lincoln defended his unilateral actions in his message to Congress at the beginning of the session,[22] but constitutional doubts remained. Some congressmen protested strongly that Lincoln had transgressed Congress' prerogatives. While the leading objections centered on Lincoln's unilateral suspension of the writ of *habeas corpus* (which he had done in May in response to riots in pro-secessionist Baltimore),[23] the blockade and call-up measures also drew opposition. Congress and not the President, it was said, should decide whether to suppress secession by force; a blockade "cannot be exercised until war has been declared or recognized," argued Representative Clement Vallandigham of Ohio, "and Congress alone can declare or recognize war."[24] Lincoln's congressional defenders responded firmly and appeared to have overwhelming numbers, but for reasons that remain unclear, Congress dropped the specific authorization and on August 6—almost the end of the special session—passed only a vaguely worded approval, tacked on to the end of a measure addressed to military pay. By this provision, "all the acts, proclamations, and orders of the President ... respecting the army and navy of the United States and calling out or relating to the militia or

---

[19] Act of July 13, 1861, §§ 5 & 6, 12 Stat. 255, 257. For the proceedings of Congress' special session, *see* Cong. Globe, 37th Cong., 1st Sess. (1861).

[20] Doris Kearns Goodwin, *Team of Rivals: The Political Genius of Abraham Lincoln* 370–71 (2006).

[21] *See* Cong. Globe, 37th Cong., 1st Sess., at 16.

[22] Message to Congress in Special Session, July 4, 1861, 4 *Collected Works of Abraham Lincoln* 421 (Roy Basler, ed., 1953).

[23] For more on Lincoln's suspension of *habeas corpus*, see Chapter 3 of this volume.

[24] Cong. Globe, 37th Cong., 1st Sess., at 58; *see also id.* at 49 (Senator Trusten Polk of Missouri arguing that the President "has usurped the war powers of the Government"); *id.* at 67 (Senator Lazarus Powell of Kentucky arguing that the President lacked the power of blockade because "blockade is necessarily a war measure").

volunteers from the States are hereby approved and in all respects legalized. . . ."[25]

In the meantime, the blockade had come into operation. At the time of Lincoln's proclamations, it was doubtful whether the blockade could be "effective" as required by international law: the Union Navy had only 42 commissioned ships to patrol more than 3,000 miles of coastline.[26] But Union naval commanders promptly began seizing ships to enforce the blockade. In accordance with the practice of the time, captured ships were brought into Union-held ports and "condemned" in judicial proceedings before federal district judges acting as prize courts. These prize courts, among other things, awarded "prize money" to the crews and officers of the captors and gave the federal government title to the ships and cargoes. The traditional judicial nature of these proceedings provided an opening for constitutional challenges to the blockade—and by implication, to the general course of Lincoln's post-Sumter actions. In defending against forfeiture, the owners of the captured ships and cargoes argued that the blockade, as a war measure, lay beyond the President's unilateral authority. After litigation in the lower courts and a delay in scheduling arguments, the Supreme Court heard the four consolidated "Prize Cases" in February 1863 and published its decision the following month.

Legal and Factual Background

"Blockade" in the nineteenth century was a term of art under the international laws of war, as it continues to be today. It encompassed the use of armed force to interdict seaborne passage to and from the ports and coasts belonging to or occupied by the enemy. The naval forces enforcing a valid blockade had the right to stop and search all ships, whether friendly, enemy or neutral, bound for, or departing from, the enemy's ports or coastline. They could capture vessels and cargoes they identified as "contraband of war," that is, susceptible of military use. They could also capture any vessels and cargoes that attempted to run the blockade, regardless of whether they were contraband. In the nineteenth century, the rules of capture fell under the rubric of the international law of "prize." At the time, it was generally accepted that a blockade could only be asserted in a state of war because it meant the use of coercive force to deny both the enemy and neutral nations the peacetime right of free commercial intercourse, which was often memori-

---

[25] Act of Aug. 6, 1861 ("An Act to increase the pay of the Privates in the Regular Army and in the Volunteers in the Service of the United States, and for other purposes"), § 3, 12 Stat. 326. *See* Phillip Paludan, *The Presidency of Abraham Lincoln* 82 (1994).

[26] *See* Madeline Russell Robinton, *An Introduction to the Papers of the New York Prize Court, 1861–1865*, at 27 (1945).

alized in bilateral treaties of amity, navigation, and commerce ratified among the relevant countries.[27]

To understand the international maritime law aspect of the *Prize Cases*, it is necessary to review some background history of the blockade concept. Predating the twentieth-century Geneva and Hague Conventions on the laws of war, the first multilateral treaty governing war was the Declaration Respecting Maritime Law signed by former belligerents in the Crimean War at Paris on April 16, 1856.[28] Although the Declaration is most famous for its statement abolishing privateering—the practice of issuing letters of marque authorizing private citizens to prey on enemy shipping—three of its four principles touched upon blockade and the rules of capture. First, it asserted that "blockades, in order to be binding, must be effective, that is to say, maintained by a force sufficient really to prevent access to the coast of the enemy." This was to prevent the sort of "paper" blockade attempted during the Napoleonic Wars, when both the French and the British sought to obtain the commerce-deterrence benefit of declaring blockades on the enemy's ports without having to expend the naval resources to enforce them.[29]

The remaining principles concerned the law of prize generally. Neutral goods carried on enemy-flagged ships, and enemy property carried on neutral-flagged ships, were subject to confiscation by a belligerent only if they were contraband of war. Of course, what exactly constituted contraband was not resolved and would prove to be an enduring source of controversy. Technically, a blockade of enemy ports might be viewed as similarly restricted only to interdiction of contraband-of-war cargo or enemy ships, and, in principle, a neutral vessel without any contraband that declared its presence to the blockading force might be allowed to pass. But in practice, the international maritime law doctrine of contamination—any contraband "contaminated" the entire cargo and rendered the whole condemnable—made it unlikely that neutrals could avoid confiscation, and blockading forces routinely understood their power to encompass a comprehensive closure of seaborne commerce to and from the blockaded coastline.

---

[27] This may not be a strict requirement of blockade at customary international law today, as witness the U.S. Navy's "quarantine" of Cuba during the Cuban Missile Crisis—a military operation that in practical terms was indistinguishable from blockade. And modern treaty law—Chapter VII of the United Nations Charter—presumptively authorizes the U.N. Security Council to order a blockade even in the absence of war.

[28] *See Documents on the Laws of War* 47–52 (Adam Roberts & Richard Guelf, eds., 3rd ed. 2001).

[29] *See* Bryan Ranft, *Restraints on War at Sea Before 1945*, in *Restraints on War: Studies in the Limitation of Armed Conflict* 44 (Michael Howard, ed., 1979).

The United States, at least prior to the Civil War, favored maximum protection of neutrals' maritime commerce rights.[30] Indeed, the United States and Spain were the only major maritime nations that did not immediately join the Paris Declaration of 1856. For the United States, this was in part because privateering was considered an essential supplement to a small national navy—the functional equivalent of state militias on land. Another key reason for non-accession concerned the three other Declaration principles. It was against the interests of the United States, as a perennial neutral reliant on maritime trade,[31] to recognize any limitation on the right of neutrals to trade freely with nations at war. Accordingly, the United States favored an "effective" requirement (as a second-best alternative to a no-blockade rule) and a simple rule of full immunity from seizure for all private property—neutral or enemy—carried on enemy or neutral hulls, regardless of the potential for military use; the American proposed rule would have avoided the confounding need to define contraband of war.[32] Despite this ardent antebellum posture, the United States at the beginning of the Civil War was placed in the unaccustomed position of a belligerent seeking to interdict the maritime trade of its enemy. Lincoln quickly brushed away the nation's prior position and announced that the United States would apply the Paris Declaration's more trade-restrictive principles.[33]

In addition to the Declaration's principles, two rules of customary international maritime law also featured prominently in the *Prize Cases*. First, a blockading state had to give notice to neutral governments and local authorities in blockaded areas of: (a) the date the blockade commenced; (b) the geographical area under blockade; and (c) a grace period during which neutral ships could leave blockaded ports without being subject to capture. Second, as touched on above, a ship attempting to run a blockade could be captured and condemned along with its cargo, whether or not it or its cargo would have been protected under the Declaration principles. In the case of a neutral vessel, condemnation arising from violating a blockade required actual or constructive knowledge of the blockade. With respect to shipowners, knowledge was presumed if the ship sailed from a blockaded or neutral port after appropriate notice of the blockade had been given to local or neutral authorities.

---

[30] *See id.* at 44–47; John B. Hattendorf, *Maritime Conflict*, in *The Laws of War: Constraints on Warfare in the Western World* 109 (Michael Howard et al., eds., 1994).

[31] For background on debates about neutrality in the early Republic, see Chapter 1 of this volume.

[32] *See* Bryan Ranft, *Restraints on War at Sea Before 1945*, in *Restraints on War: Studies in the Limitation of Armed Conflict* 44–47 (Michael Howard, ed., 1979).

[33] *See* John B. Hattendorf, *Maritime Conflict*, in *The Laws of War: Constraints on Warfare in the Western World* 109 (Michael Howard et al., eds., 1994).

As to owners of property that was shipped, the cargo could only be condemned if at the time of shipment the cargo owner knew or should have known of the ship owner's or crew's intention to break the blockade.

The *Prize Cases* arose out of the U.S. Navy's capture of four merchant ships—two, the *Amy Warwick* and the *Crenshaw*, owned by allegedly pro-Union Virginians; and two, the *Hiawatha* and the *Brilliante*, owned by nationals of neutral countries (Great Britain and Mexico)—along with their respective cargoes for violations of the blockade. The captures occurred between May 17 and July 10, 1861, prior to Congress' ratification of the President's blockade proclamations. Three of the ships—the *Brilliante*, the *Hiawatha*, and the *Crenshaw*—were captured leaving Southern ports for neutral destinations. The *Crenshaw* and the *Hiawatha* were captured leaving Richmond for Great Britain with cargoes of tobacco on May 17 and May 20, respectively; the vessels and cargoes were condemned in the Southern District of New York. The *Brilliante* was captured anchored in Biloxi Bay on June 23, 1861, allegedly on the verge of breaching the blockade outward to Mexico with a cargo of flour loaded in New Orleans; the vessel and cargo were condemned in the district court for the Southern District of Florida at Key West (which remained in Union hands throughout the war). The fourth merchantman, the *Amy Warwick*, was captured on July 10, 1861, en route to Virginia from Rio de Janeiro; it and its cargo of coffee were condemned in the District of Massachusetts.[34]

Each district court granted a decree of condemnation in favor of the U.S. government and the officers and crews of the captors.[35] As permitted by U.S. law and practice of the time, the former owners appealed the condemnation decrees. At the circuit court level, they were again unsuccessful, although in at least one case the appellate court rendered a perfunctory affirmance to facilitate appeal to the U.S. Supreme Court.[36] Shortly thereafter, the Supreme Court consolidated the four cases and set them for argument in late 1862.

The Supreme Court and the Decision

Despite prevailing in the lower courts, as Lincoln's lawyers approached the Supreme Court they could not have been too confident of a

---

[34] *See* Robert Bruce Murray, *Legal Cases of the Civil War* 3–6 (2003). For background on the practice and procedure of nineteenth-century prize courts, *see* Madeline Russell Robinton, *An Introduction to the Papers of the New York Prize Court, 1861–1865*, at 27–52 (1945).

[35] The Amy Warwick, 1 F.Cas. 799 (D.C. D.Mass. 1862); The Hiawatha and The Crenshaw, 12 F.Cas. 95 (S.D.N.Y. 1861). No opinion has survived in the case of *The Brilliante. See* Robert Bruce Murray, *Legal Cases of the Civil War* 7 (2003).

[36] *See* Robert Bruce Murray, *Legal Cases of the Civil War* 7 (2003).

favorable outcome. Six of the nine Justices had been appointed by prior Democratic Presidents: of these, three (John Catron, James Wayne, and Chief Justice Roger Taney) were from slave states, while the other three (Robert Grier of Pennsylvania, Samuel Nelson of New York, and Nathan Clifford of Maine) had been viewed as sufficiently sympathetic to southern interests to survive the difficult confirmation hurdle in the pre-war Senate. Five of them joined at least part of the Court's infamous pro-slavery *Dred Scott* decision in 1857,[37] which Lincoln and the Republicans denounced and campaigned against in 1860. (The sixth, Clifford, was appointed by Buchanan after the *Dred Scott* decision, but had indicated that he agreed with the majority).[38] Taney, the Chief Justice, had already rebuked Lincoln's exercise of wartime emergency powers in another context: sitting as Circuit Justice in Maryland in 1861, he denied Lincoln's power to suspend *habeas corpus* in *Ex parte Merryman*, and he was no doubt fuming over Lincoln's subsequent refusal to comply with his order.[39] Nelson, early in Lincoln's presidency, sought to play intermediary between Lincoln's cabinet and Confederate negotiators, and in the process he reportedly expressed doubt that the federal government could constitutionally use force against the seceding states.[40] Even assuming

---

[37] Dred Scott v. Sandford, 60 U.S. 393 (1857). Among other things, the Court appeared to hold that Congress could not prohibit slavery in the western territories. Taney, Wayne, Catron and Grier embraced all or most of the majority positions; Nelson would have decided against Scott on narrow grounds.

[38] For more background on the Justices, *see* Carl B. Swisher, *The Taney Period, 1836–1864, in* 5 *The Oliver Wendell Holmes Devise History of the Supreme Court of the United States* 53–54, 59–64, 220–247 (1974); Michael Green, *Freedom, Union and Power: Lincoln and his Party During the Civil War* 191–96 (2004); Brian McGinty, *Lincoln and the Court* 146–63 (2008).

[39] Lincoln authorized suspension when rioters obstructed the movement of troops through Baltimore on their way to Washington. Lincoln to Winfield Scott, April 27, 1861, 4 *Collected Works of Abraham Lincoln* 347 (Roy Basler, ed., 1953). One of the people subsequently detained, John Merryman, sought a writ of *habeas corpus* from Taney. Taney granted the writ, holding that the President lacked unilateral power to suspend it, but Lincoln refused to release Merryman or any other detainees. Ex parte Merryman, 17 F.Cas. 144 (C.C. D.Md. 1861); *see* Carl B. Swisher, *The Taney Period, 1836–1864, in* 5 *The Oliver Wendell Holmes Devise History of the Supreme Court of the United States* 842–54 (1974); Daniel A. Farber, *Lincoln's Constitution* 16–17, 157–63 (2003); and Chapter 3 of this volume.

[40] Carl B. Swisher, *The Taney Period, 1836–1864, in* 5 *The Oliver Wendell Holmes Devise History of the Supreme Court of the United States* 742 (1974). The account comes from Justice John Campbell, a southerner who worked with Nelson on this project and resigned from the Court after Sumter. As Professor Swisher recounts, "According to Justice Campbell's account, Justice Nelson had been for some time engaged in a study of the constitutional power of the executive, and discussing the matter with Chief Justice Taney, had reached the conclusion that coercion could not be used against the seceding states—the position hitherto taken by Buchanan and Black.... Justice Nelson visited three members of Lincoln's cabinet, Seward, Chase and Bates, to state his convictions...."

that Lincoln's three appointees would back the President in the *Prize Cases*, he needed two of the six Democrats on the Court, and none seemed likely to be sympathetic. Perhaps with these concerns in mind, the government requested—and the Court granted—a delay of the arguments until early 1863.[41]

Of course, things could have been worse for Lincoln. He had been in office less than two years and yet had made three appointments to the Court. Lincoln's immediate predecessor, Buchanan, nominated his former Attorney General Black—who had opined that the federal government lacked power to oppose secession—to the Court in February 1861. Black might well have been confirmed had his nomination been sent in earlier when the vacancy first arose in the summer of 1860, but Buchanan (characteristically) hesitated in submitting it, and by the time he did so most southern Senators had resigned and the remaining Senators declined to act on the nomination.[42] (Black went on to become the Court's reporter of decisions, a post he held when the *Prize Cases* were decided.) Further, Justice John Campbell of Alabama left the Court in the aftermath of Sumter to join the Confederacy. Together with the death of Justice McLean in 1861, these events gave Lincoln three appointments, when he quite easily might have had only one—and thus have been faced with eight potentially hostile Justices instead of six.

Lincoln had good reason to be concerned about an adverse decision. True, there were several ways the Court could find for the ship and cargo owners without impugning Lincoln's then-existing wartime measures (which, unlike the initial blockade, had mostly been approved in advance by Congress). But the cases at least offered the possibility of a broader ruling that implicated the legal arguments over secession and the use of coercive force against it. Surely some "Copperheads" (as northerners who opposed the war were called) hoped for a ruling vindicating the secessionists' constitutional arguments.

Further, Lincoln faced growing charges of unconstitutional usurpations in other areas. As noted, soon after Sumter he suspended *habeas corpus* in Maryland, allowing military detention of suspected southern sympathizers despite the Chief Justice's constitutional ruling in *Merryman*. By the end of 1862, military detentions and trials had spread throughout the North, targeting at least some people who apparently had done little more than express opposition to the war. Republicans lost

---

[41] The delay allowed Lincoln's third appointment, David Davis, to take his seat on the Court before the cases were argued. That year the Republican Congress also enacted a bill authorizing a tenth Justice, which Lincoln signed into law the week before the decision was announced.

[42] Carl B. Swisher, *The Taney Period, 1836–1864, in* 5 *The Oliver Wendell Holmes Devise History of the Supreme Court of the United States* 735–36 (1974).

ground in the 1862 off-year elections, and the resurgent northern
Democrats—led by New York governor Horatio Seymour—focused on
the accumulating infringements of civil liberties. In January 1863, just
before the *Prize Cases* argument, the Wisconsin Supreme Court, echoing
Taney's *Merryman* opinion, held that rioters in Wisconsin who faced
military detention and courts martial had a right to *habeas corpus*
despite the purported presidential suspension; Lincoln's Attorney General, uneasy about the sympathies of the U.S. Supreme Court, decided not
to appeal the decision.[43] To be sure, the growing controversy over civil
liberties in the North—ultimately leading to the *Vallandigham* and
Milligan cases in the Supreme Court[44]—did not directly implicate anything in the *Prize Cases*, but with the administration already under
constitutional fire, a rebuke from the Court would surely have further
damaged its position.

Of more direct relevance to the *Prize Cases*, six weeks before the
argument Lincoln on his own authority took perhaps his greatest wartime action, at least symbolically: his Emancipation Proclamation freed
all slaves in areas in rebellion.[45] The Proclamation stands among Lincoln's most revered legacies, but it was highly controversial at the time,
and even today it is the subject of some theoretical debate among
constitutional scholars.[46] Like the blockade, it deprived southerners—
even those not openly in rebellion—of what they viewed as their constitutionally protected property, on the basis of a unilateral presidential
proclamation. Even a narrow ruling against the President in the *Prize
Cases* might call into question the constitutional basis of emancipation.

Finally, in terms of international and foreign-policy ramifications,
the Court might conclude that an insurrection in which one side refused
to recognize the reciprocal sovereign and belligerent rights of its enemy
was not the type of war or "state of war" under international law
sufficient to confer upon the United States the belligerent right to
blockade and thereby to deprive neutral nations of the fruits of free
commerce with the Confederacy. From the outset, Lincoln's administra-

---

[43] In re Kemp, 16 Wis. 359 (1863); on the growing issue of civil liberties generally, *see*
James F. Simon, *Lincoln and Chief Justice Taney: Slavery, Secession, and the President's
War Powers* 233–44 (2006).

[44] Ex parte Vallandigham, 68 U.S. 243 (1863); Ex parte Milligan, 71 U.S. 2 (1866). For
more on these cases, see Chapter 3 of this volume.

[45] *Emancipation Proclamation,* Jan. 1, 1863, 6 *Collected Works of Abraham Lincoln* 28–
30 (Roy Basler, ed., 1953). *See* J.G. Randall, *Constitutional Problems under Lincoln* 342–
404 (rev. ed. 1963); *see also* Daniel A. Farber, *Lincoln's Constitution* 152–57 (2003); *see
generally* Burrus M. Carnahan, *Act of Justice: Lincoln's Emancipation Proclamation and
the Law of War* (2007).

[46] *See* Daniel A. Farber, *Lincoln's Constitution* 152–57 (2003).

tion had struggled to find a way to invoke international law doctrines such as blockade without recognizing the Confederacy as a legally separate nation. If the Court refused to accept the administration's characterization of the conflict, then all captures the U.S. Navy had made and would make in enforcing the blockade—not just those made before Congress' approval—might be unlawful and require compensation or settlement. Such a holding would greatly complicate relations with foreign nations whose citizens' ships and property had been seized.[47] Indeed, on this view, it might be argued that no action of Congress short of a formal declaration of war and recognition of the Confederacy as a separate sovereign nation would be adequate to invoke the belligerent right of blockade under international law.[48] Thus momentous legal and practical issues were potentially before the Court, if it chose to confront them.

Arguments

The Court heard twelve days of oral arguments between February 10 and 25, 1863, and announced its decision two weeks later on March 10. Of the nine lawyers who argued before the Court, two were selected by the Reporter—former Attorney General Black—for substantial summary of their arguments in the official report, ostensibly for reasons of convenience rather than merit.[49] The selection on behalf of the government was U.S. Attorney Richard Henry Dana, Jr. of Massachusetts. He had won the most pro-government lower court decision of the lot in the *Amy Warwick* case before District Judge Sprague in Massachusetts.[50] Dana was not only a leading maritime lawyer of the day but an accomplished sailor and author, having previously achieved national fame with the timeless autobiographical sea travelogue *Two Years Before*

---

[47] Carl B. Swisher, *The Taney Period, 1836–1864, in* 5 *The Oliver Wendell Holmes Devise History of the Supreme Court of the United States* 888 (1974).

[48] The only option for the United States, then, would have been to resort to domestic law to order a closure of the ports, but that required physical control of the land surrounding the port. With the exception of New Orleans, the United States did not control the land approaches to the major southern ports until late in the war; President Lincoln did not declare the southern ports closed until April 11, 1865, after General Robert E. Lee's surrender at Appomattox. Stuart L. Bernath, *Squall Across the Atlantic: American Civil War Prize Cases and Diplomacy* 19 (1970).

[49] The Prize Cases, 67 U.S. 635, 639 (1863). Black indicated in private correspondence, however, that he summarized the arguments he believed to have been the most artfully made. *See* Carl B. Swisher, *The Taney Period, 1836–1864, in* 5 *The Oliver Wendell Holmes Devise History of the Supreme Court of the United States* 893 (1974).

[50] *The Amy Warwick*, 1 F.Cas. 799, 802–07 (1862). *See* William G. Young, *The Amy Warwick Encounters the Quaker City: The District of Massachusetts and the President's War Powers*, 74 Mass. L. Rev. 206 (1989).

the Mast.[51] James Carlisle, a highly regarded lawyer from Washington D.C. and a friend of Chief Justice Taney, was Black's choice among claimants' counsel. Although he was not the maritime expert that Dana was, Carlisle was an experienced and respected member of the Supreme Court bar.[52]

The ship and cargo owners made four main arguments before the federal courts. The owners of the *Amy Warwick* and the *Crenshaw* (and of most of their cargo) were U.S. citizens residing in Virginia. They principally claimed that, as loyal citizens of the United States, the taking of their property was not governed by the international laws of war pertaining to capture of enemy property but rather by the domestic constitutional law protections of the Fifth Amendment. Second, the *Crenshaw* and *Hiawatha* owners argued inadequate notice, as their ships' respective captures on May 17 and May 20 off Virginia came very shortly after Lincoln's April 27 proclamation of blockade. These arguments implicitly presumed the validity of the blockade as a general matter but claimed that the capture and condemnation of their particular property did not comply with the restrictions international and domestic law placed on blockade rights. The Mexican owners of the *Brilliante* and her cargo of flour—ably represented by Carlisle—most directly contested the very validity of the blockade itself, both as a matter of the President's power to declare blockade under U.S. constitutional law and as justified by the prerequisite "state of war" under international law. Carlisle also argued, assuming the validity of the blockade, that the *Brilliante* had no intent to run the blockade but was patiently awaiting the squadron commander's permission to depart (which the law of nations might have allowed, as it was a neutral ship carrying non-contraband neutral property to a neutral port). But it is Carlisle's domestic separation-of-powers argument for which he and the *Prize Cases* are remembered—not surprisingly, given the virtual extinction of the international maritime law of prize.

Condemning ships and cargo belonging to U.S. citizens and foreign neutrals, Carlisle argued, could be justified only as (i) "seizures" authorized by U.S. law, or (ii) "captures" permitted during wartime under

---

[51] Dana's biographer reports that Justice Grier was overheard telling Dana after oral argument: "Well, your little 'Two Years before the Mast' has settled that question; there is nothing more to say about it!" 2 Charles Francis Adams, *Richard Henry Dana: A Biography* 269 (1890).

[52] The unofficial "Lawyer's Edition" reporter, subsequently published in 1884, also included excerpts from the arguments of New York attorney William Evarts for the government in the *Brilliante* case and of Daniel Lord in rebuttal on behalf of the claimants. 17 *Supreme Court Reports, Lawyers Edition* 459, 465–77, 474–76. These arguments generally tracked the descriptions outlined below.

international law.[53] The first category was not implicated, as the condemnations were not done pursuant to any domestic forfeiture statutes or ratified treaties: they rested solely on presidential decrees, and, Carlisle said, the President alone "cannot make, alter, or suspend 'the supreme law of the land.' "[54] Instead, the President's authority to make such decrees supposedly arose from the sovereign right of a belligerent nation to blockade the ports of an enemy (and thus make "captures") under international law. But the right to blockade under international law required the existence of war. Thus, for Carlisle, the critical question was whether war existed at the time the blockade was established. And, in his view, whether war existed in the international legal sense depended on whether the nation's "sovereign power" had recognized it, which depended, in turn, on how the nation's municipal law (*i.e.*, the U.S. Constitution) allocated the relevant sovereign power. The question was, he emphasized,

> was there war? Not, was there '*a state of things*' involving in point of fact all the deadly machinery and all 'the pomp and circumstance' of war; but, had 'the sovereign power of the state' declared war; declared that it should exist, or that, by the act of an enemy, it *did already* exist; war with its legal incidents municipal and international?[55]

In Carlisle's view of the U.S. Constitution, only Congress, not the President, could "declare war" in this sense, and prior to July 1861 Congress plainly had not. Rather, the President, he said (in tones to be echoed in some modern debates) was putting himself above the Constitution through a claim of necessary emergency powers:

> The matter then comes back necessarily to the pure question of the powers of the President under the Constitution. And this is, perhaps, the most extraordinary part of the argument for the United States. It is founded upon a figure of speech, which is repugnant to the genius of republican institutions, and, above all, to our written Constitution. It makes the President, in some sort, the impersonation of the country, and invokes for him the power and right to use all the force he can command to '*save the life of the nation.*' The principle of self-defense is asserted; and all power is claimed for the

---

[53] *Prize Cases*, 67 U.S. at 644.

[54] *Id.* Indeed, Carlisle, on behalf of the *Brilliante* claimants, implied that article 17 of the Treaty of Guadalupe–Hidalgo of 1848, which revived an 1831 Treaty of Amity and Commerce opening the ports of the United States and Mexico to mutual commerce, constituted a treaty commitment to keep U.S. ports open to Mexican ships that was neither "suspended or abrogated by Act of Congress" or "in any degree disturbed by the National Legislature." *Id.*

[55] *Id.* at 646–47.

President. This is to assert that the Constitution contemplated and tacitly provided that the President should be dictator, and all Constitutional Government be at an end, whenever he should think that 'the life of the nation' is in danger....

It comes to the plea of necessity. The Constitution knows no such word.[56]

Carlisle also paraphrased and mocked the executive branch's "very bold and very alarming" objections to the Court hearing the case: one U.S. counsel, he said, expressed "amazement that a judicial tribunal should be called upon to determine whether the political power was authorized to do what it has done. He is astounded that he should be required to 'ask permission of your Honors for the whole political power of the Government to exercise the ordinary right of self-defense.' He pictures to himself how the world will be appalled when it finds that *one of our Courts* has decided that 'the war is at an end.' He tells us that this is merely a Prize Court, and that the Prize Court sits 'by commission of the sovereign' merely as 'an inquest to ascertain whether the capture has been made according to the will and intent of the sovereign.' "[57] And, Carlisle added, another government counsel had gone so far as to claim that if "the pure and simple function of the Prize Court be transcended, then the Court is no longer a Court of the sovereign, but an ally of the enemy."[58] In Carlisle's powerful rhetoric, at least, the President was setting himself above the law and the Court on grounds of national emergency.

Whether the government's lawyers actually made arguments in this tone,[59] Dana's summary of his own presentation indicates a gentler tack.[60] Dana began, not with the separation-of-powers salvo brought home by Carlisle, but with a point raised by the Virginia ship and cargo owners in the *Amy Warwick* case he had won below. They asserted that as loyal U.S. citizens, the condemnation of their private property was governed by the U.S. Constitution and not international law. Dana retorted that it was axiomatic in foreign wars that "enemy" property

---

[56] *Id.* at 648. It is interesting to speculate what Carlisle would have concluded about the President's power to establish a blockade if the existence of war were not a prerequisite to a valid blockade under prevailing international law, as appears to be the customary rule today.

[57] *Id.* at 645.

[58] *Id.* at 646.

[59] The arguments to which Carlisle apparently referred were not preserved. Dana's co-counsel William Evarts reportedly told the Court that Carlisle's separation-of-powers arguments "aid and abet rebellion." 17 L.Ed. at 466.

[60] *Id.* at 652.

could be seized at sea even if the individual owners were not taking part in hostilities (or even opposed them). He asserted that the same rule should apply in "internal wars." This extension—plain, minor, and unexceptionable as it seemed—was Dana's invention. It also cleverly masked a major problem: in an "internal" war, by contrast to a foreign war, loyal citizens of a national government who happened to reside in so-called "enemy" states seeking secession could plausibly claim the protections of not only international law but also the nation's domestic constitution with respect to takings of their private property by governmental force. In other words, Dana assumed—without bothering to justify the assumption—that in a war of domestic complexion implicating the rights of U.S. citizens, the international laws of war displaced (or allowed the President to displace) the ordinary application of the rules of domestic constitutional law that would have protected the private property of U.S. citizens during peacetime, at least as applied to residents of states in insurrection.[61]

Dana then brought his guns to bear on Carlisle's separation-of-powers attack. He challenged Carlisle's contention that the existence of war—then a precondition for a valid blockade under international law—had to be established solely by reference to the legal question whether Congress had " 'declared' war, or at least done some act recognizing that a case exists for the exercise of war powers, and of what powers." To the contrary, Dana argued, "war is a state of things, and not an act of legislative will. If a foreign power springs a war upon us by sea and land, during a recess of Congress, exercising all belligerent rights of capture, the question is, whether the President can repel war with war . . .?"[62]

Dana was careful not to claim more presidential power than he needed. "The question," he said, "is not what would be the result of a conflict between the Executive and the Legislature, during an actual invasion by a foreign enemy, the Legislature refusing to declare war." Further, "[i]t is not as to the right to *initiate a war, as a voluntary act of sovereignty*. That is vested only in Congress." Rather, the question was

---

[61] This was in essence Lincoln's legal argument justifying the Emancipation Proclamation, announced only a few months prior to the argument in the *Prize Cases*. Yet its premise seems in tension with the U.S. government's previous opposition to the Paris Declaration based on the free-seas principle that no private property—enemy or neutral—should be subject to condemnation in war. *See* Bryan Ranft, *Restraints on War at Sea Before 1945*, in *Restraints on War: Studies in the Limitation of Armed Conflict* 44–47 (Michael Howard, ed., 1979).

[62] *Id.* at 659–60. Similarly, according to the Lawyers' Edition reports, Dana's co-counsel William Evarts insisted: "War is, emphatically, a question of actualities. Whenever the situation of opposing hostilities has assumed the proportions, and pursues the methods of war, the peace is driven out, the ordinary authority and administration of law are suspended, and war, in fact and by necessity, is the *status* of the nation. . . ." 17 L.Ed. at 465.

only "as to the power of the President before Congress shall have acted, in case of a war actually existing." Moreover, he emphasized, the President was acting "within the rules of civilized warfare, and subject to established laws of Congress." But within those limits, he said, "overwhelming reasons of necessity" required the President to act and "[t]he function to use the army and navy being in the President, the mode of using them . . . must be subject to his discretion. . . ."[63]

So, on the core separation-of-powers point, the battle lines were clearly drawn. For Dana, there was war on the ground, begun by the other side, and this "state of things" in itself authorized the President to respond with wartime measures without judicial second-guessing. For Carlisle, it was for Congress, not the President, to decide whether the facts on the ground justified a shift from the laws of peace to the laws of war. Until Congress did so, the President could act only under U.S. domestic law, not the international laws of war, and U.S. domestic law did not permit seizing the private property of innocent parties.

With respect to the international maritime law issues, one key disagreement between the two sides mirrored the separation-of-powers debate. The issue was whether the United States possessed the belligerent right to declare a blockade, for which a precondition in international law was the existence of war—Carlisle and Dana agreed up to this point. For Carlisle, resolving the international legal question required consulting the relevant municipal law, and the Constitution ordained that congressional action was a necessary precondition to the existence of war. For Dana, determining the existence of war (in order to assess the legality of the blockade) required an examination of the specific factual circumstances. The second major international law question was whether the property of allegedly loyal U.S. citizens residing in southern States could be condemned as enemies' property. Despite the absence of clear authority on the specific point, Dana concluded that the usual rule of enemy property should also apply in a civil war and that the Court should defer to the executive on the point; counsel for the Virginian claimants asserted that international law did not displace the ordinary operation of domestic constitutional law protections against the taking of their property. The parties further disputed more practical interpretations of international prize law regarding notice, grace periods, and conduct constituting breach by a neutral.

Justice Grier for the Majority

To the administration's relief, Dana and his co-counsel persuaded an unlikely coalition of five: the three Lincoln appointees plus northern Democrat Grier and southern Democrat Wayne. Wayne, the senior

---

[63] *Prize Cases*, 67 U.S. at 660–61.

Justice in the majority, assigned the opinion to Grier. A respected federal district judge in Pennsylvania, Grier was appointed to the Supreme Court by Democratic President James Polk in 1846 after the Senate rejected a series of previous nominees. On the Court, Grier developed some expertise in admiralty, which perhaps accounted for the assignment. Notably, in 1861, as Circuit Justice, he had tried some criminal cases against Confederate privateers for treason and piracy—charges that implied that the Confederacy did not have the belligerent right to issue letters of marque (as Jefferson Davis had purported to do in his April 17 proclamation).[64] But on the whole his career on the Court was, as one modern writer describes it, "notably uninspired."[65] The *Prize Cases* became his moment in the historical spotlight.

Grier formulated the main question as "whether, at the time this blockade was instituted, a state of war existed which would justify a resort to these means of subduing the hostile force."[66] He then embraced Dana's view that this was a commonsense question of the facts on the ground. Grier began the proof by quoting (without attribution) the eighteenth-century treatise-writer Emmerich de Vattel's definition of war as "[t]hat state in which a nation prosecutes its right by force."[67] Although the belligerents in a "public war" were "independent ... sovereign States," Grier added, a war might also exist "where one of the belligerents claims sovereign rights as against the other"—a civil war.[68] True, an "[i]nsurrection against a government" might not rise to the level of a war, but it might ripen into one depending on "the number,

---

[64] J.G. Randall, *Constitutional Problems under Lincoln* 92–93 (rev. ed. 1963). Foreshadowing his decision in the *Prize Cases*, Grier indicated his frustration with these trials when juxtaposed to the government's implicit acquiescence of the Confederacy's belligerent status on land, as signified by the failure to prosecute captured rebel soldiers for like crimes: "But why make a difference between those taken on land and on water? Why not try all those taken on land and hang them? That might do with a mere insurrection but when it comes to civil war, the laws of war must be observed, or you will lay it open to the most horrid reactions that can possibly be thought of; hundreds of thousands of men will be sacrificed upon mere brutal rage." *Id.* at 93.

[65] David P. Currie, *The Constitution in the Supreme Court: The First Hundred Years, 1789–1888, at* 281 (1985). On Grier's background and appointment, *see* Carl B. Swisher, *The Taney Period, 1836–1864, in* 5 *The Oliver Wendell Holmes Devise History of the Supreme Court of the United States* 228–33 (1974).

[66] *Prize Cases*, 67 U.S. at 666.

[67] *Id. See* 3 Emmerich de Vattel, *The Law of Nations*, ch. I, at 1 (London, J. Coote 1759). Vattel was immensely influential among American lawyers and statesmen in the late eighteenth and nineteenth centuries. *See* Thomas H. Lee, *Making Sense of the Eleventh Amendment: International Law and State Sovereignty*, 96 Nw. U. L. Rev. 1027, 1061–68 (2002).

[68] *Prize Cases*, 67 U.S. at 666.

power, and organization of the persons who originate and carry it on."[69] And an insurrection was surely a war "[w]hen the party in rebellion occupy and hold in a hostile manner a certain portion of territory; have declared their independence; have cast off their allegiance; have organized armies; [and] have commenced hostilities against their former sovereign."[70] Because of its creeping, evolutionary nature, a "civil war is never publicly proclaimed,"[71] unlike a declared war, but is rather "a fact in our domestic history which the Court is bound to notice and to know."[72] And, according to "the sages of the common law," the operations of the courts are a particularly important barometer of the existence of civil war: "When the regular course of justice is interrupted by revolt, rebellion, or insurrection, so that the Courts of Justice cannot be kept open, *civil war exists* and hostilities may be prosecuted on the same footing as if those opposing the Government were foreign enemies invading the land."[73] This reality was validated as a legal matter, Grier intimated, in the absence of any explicit constitutional provision for congressional power to declare war against the states.[74] Put this way, it seemed clear enough that (as Dana had argued) the existence of war would—and must—be found from the facts on the ground rather than on the basis of a legislative pronouncement.

Grier next emphasized the President's constitutional powers: "The Constitution confers on the President the whole Executive power. He is bound to take care that the laws be faithfully executed. He is Commander-in-chief of the Army and Navy of the United States and of the militia of the several States when called into the actual service of the United

---

[69] *Id.*

[70] *Id.* at 666–67.

[71] *Id.* at 666.

[72] *Id.* at 667.

[73] *Id.* at 667–68. The point foreshadowed a key reason given by the Court in *Ex parte Milligan* for denying the possibility that the laws of war supplied a source alternative to the U.S. Constitution and congressional enactments for the authority of military commissions: the international laws of war "can never be applied to citizens in states which have upheld the authority of the government, and where the courts are open and their process unobstructed." Ex parte Milligan, 71 U.S. 2, 121 (1866). *See* Chapter 3 of this volume.

[74] Grier wrote: "By the Constitution, Congress alone has the power to declare a national or foreign war. It cannot declare war against a State, or any number of States, by virtue of any clause in the Constitution." *Prize Cases*, 67 U.S. at 668. It is not clear why Grier thought this to be so. There was certainly an important political reason why Congress might not declare war against a state, namely, the implicit recognition of the state's independent sovereign status, and, as the beneficiaries of a successful rebellion and the architects of a fragile union of independently-minded states, the Framers may have been inclined to Grier's position. But the text of the Constitution does not appear to foreclose the possibility of Congress declaring war on a state or states.

States." Like Dana, he acknowledged that Congress "alone has the power to declare a national or foreign war" and thus the President "has no power to initiate or declare a war." But—and here Grier reached the core question—"[i]f a war be made by invasion of a foreign nation, the President is not only authorized but bound to resist force by force. He does not initiate the war, but is bound to accept the challenge without waiting for any special legislative authority." In other words, if the country finds itself in the reality of a war initiated by others—whether foreign invaders or sufficiently organized rebels—the "President was bound to meet it in the shape it presented itself, without waiting for Congress to baptize it with a name; and no name given to it by him or them could change the fact."[75]

Nor, according to Grier, was the present war any "less a civil war" because the Union claimed sovereignty over the seceding states and deemed the insurgents "rebels or traitors." On the contrary, foreign nations had "acknowledge[d] it as war" by their declarations of neutrality, which presumed the presence of "belligerent parties in hostile array." And surely, "[a]fter such an official recognition by the sovereign, a citizen of a foreign State is estopped to deny the existence of a war with all its consequences as regards neutrals. They cannot ask a Court to affect a technical ignorance of the existence of a war, which all the world acknowledges to be the greatest civil war known in the history of the human race, and thus cripple the arm of the Government and paralyze its power by subtle definitions and ingenious sophisms."[76]

Grier also invoked longstanding statutes from 1795 and 1807 authorizing the President to "call[] out the militia and use the military and naval forces of the United States in case of invasion by foreign nations, and to suppress insurrection against the government of a State or of the United States."[77] It is not clear what weight he sought to place upon them, however. These laws presumably supplied a statutory basis for Lincoln's call-up of land and naval forces to apply armed forced against active rebels.[78] They were, however, inapposite to the armed force at issue in the *Prize Cases*. The captures and condemnations were proble-

---

[75] *Id.* at 668–69.

[76] *Id.* at 669–670.

[77] *Id.* at 668. Dana's co-counsel Evarts emphasized these statutes in his argument, *see* 17 L.Ed. at 465, but Dana put less weight on them, perhaps grasping that they could not supply presidential authority to capture ships and cargoes engaged in peaceful commerce owned by foreign neutrals and U.S. citizens from a state that had not yet seceded. Daniel Lord, in rebuttal on behalf of the claimants, effectively undermined reliance on the statutes. *See id.* at 474–76.

[78] *See* Stephen Vladeck, Note, *Emergency Power and the Militia Acts*, 114 Yale L.J. 149 (2004).

matic precisely because they involved using force against individuals who were not actually in rebellion: neutral foreigners and supposedly loyal U.S. citizens residing in Virginia, which, at the time of two of the prize captures, had not even formally seceded. As Grier's reliance on the President's constitutional power indicated, the statutes alone did not seem enough to settle the matter.

Despite the foreign and commonsense support for the existence of war, Grier concluded the first part of the majority opinion with a note of executive deference. On the crucial questions whether the insurrection was sufficiently organized and systematic—of "such alarming proportions"—as to merit its classification as civil war and whether the blockade was the appropriate "degree of force" to meet the threat, Grier found that these were matters to be decided by the President as Commander-in-Chief, and "this Court must be governed by [his] decisions and acts."[79] "The proclamation of blockade," he concluded, "is itself official and conclusive evidence to the Court that a state of war existed which demanded and authorized a recourse to such a measure under the circumstances peculiar to the case."[80]

As a final point, Grier went on to hold, apparently as an alternative ground, that even "[i]f it were necessary to the technical existence of a war, that it should have a legislative sanction," Congress had retroactively approved the blockade in its summer 1861 special session.[81] Notably, although this might be thought a significant factor under modern approaches,[82] for Grier it seemed more of an afterthought, mentioned only briefly at the very end of his constitutional analysis.[83]

Grier then turned to the question whether the property of the allegedly loyal Virginians was subject to capture under international law as "enemies' property." The ships in question had been flying the U.S. flag. The relevant cargo and ship owners asserted that takings of the property of loyal U.S. citizens should be regulated by domestic constitutional law, not international law. Grier concluded that the claimants'

---

[79] *Prize Cases*, 67 U.S. at 670.

[80] *Id.* It is worth remembering that, at the time Lincoln declared the blockade, the only material organized military engagement had been the bombardment of Fort Sumter, in which no lives were lost to hostile fire.

[81] *Id.* at 670–71 (quoting the Act of Aug. 6, 1861).

[82] *See* Chapter 7 of this volume.

[83] It is unclear why Grier did not rely more on Congress' *post hoc* ratification of the President's acts. It may have been the case that he was troubled by the possibility of an *ex post facto* objection. He acknowledged the concern about retroactivity would "have some weight on the trial of an indictment in a criminal Court," but insisted that such "precedents . . . cannot be received as authoritative" in the prize law proceedings at issue. *Id.* at 671.

assertion that "the Constitution and Laws of the United States are still operative over persons in all the States" rested on two dubious propositions "without foundation on the established law of nations."[84] First, it was not true, as the claimants alleged, that just because a civil war exists, "the party belligerent claiming to be sovereign" can only exercise domestic sovereign rights and not any belligerent's rights (including the right of capture of enemy property) over the other party.[85] In a way, this was the flip side of an issue left unaddressed in the first part of Grier's argument: namely, if the Confederate States were entitled to certain belligerent rights as Grier indicated, were they similarly entitled to certain sovereign rights, since routinely both sorts of rights were unified in one government? At the start of the war in 1861, this sort of paradoxical splitting of the bundle of governance rights was viewed as problematic, for reasons related to those undergirding Black's conclusion that secession was unconstitutional but the national government lacked the power to use coercive force to punish or reverse it. But in 1863, with the war in full gear, Grier easily asserted that "it is a proposition never doubted, that the belligerent party who claims to be sovereign [the United States], may exercise both belligerent and sovereign rights."[86]

Second, it was also erroneous of the claimants to assert that "whether property be liable to capture as 'enemies' property' " in a civil war depends on "the personal allegiance of the owner."[87] Grier adopted Dana's underlying assumption of total war and articulated a distinctively positivist outlook. There was "a boundary marked by lines of bayonets, and which can be can be crossed only by force—south of this line is enemies' territory because it is claimed and held in possession by an organized, hostile and belligerent power." Any property belonging to residents of that cordoned-off hostile territory, even allegedly loyal U.S. citizens, was liable to be treated as "enemies' property"—"a technical phrase peculiar to prize courts"—because it "may be used to increase the revenues of the hostile power."[88] In reaching these conclusions, Grier

---

[84] *Id.* at 672–73.

[85] *Id.* at 673.

[86] *Id.*

[87] *Id.* at 674.

[88] *Id.* This rationale tracks a move made a century earlier by Vattel to "submerge the *lex mercatoria*," a body of international law applicable directly to individuals, with "the mercantilist proposition that '[t]he goods even of the individuals in their totality ought to be considered as the goods of the nation, in regard to other states.' " Thomas H. Lee, *International Law, International Relations Theory, and Preemptive War: The Vitality of Sovereign Equality Today*, 67 Law & Contemp. Probs. 147, 152 (Autumn 2004) (quoting Emmerich de Vattel, 2 *The Law of Nations or Principles of the Law of Nature Applied to*

accepted uncritically Dana's theory of enemies' property as applicable to a civil war without considering the ramifications of the displacement of domestic constitutional law protections for residents of seceded or soon-to-secede states by the international laws of war.

After deciding the two main principles, the only task that remained for the majority was to apply them and the other rules of the law of prize to the four cases at bar. The enemies' property principle was enough to defeat the claims of the owners of the *Amy Warwick* and its cargo, who were all residents of Virginia. The *Hiawatha* and its cargo were condemned because the ship had not cleared its Virginia port within the fifteen-day grace period duly noticed by the blockading force. The *Brilliante* and her cargo were condemned for attempting to run the blockade. The *Crenshaw* and the majority of her cargo were owned by Virginians, and so condemned under the enemies' property principle. The Court, however, reversed the district court and ordered that the part of the cargo that had been bought by New Yorkers before the war be restored.[89] These New York claimants were the only successful petitioners.

Justice Nelson for the Dissent

Samuel Nelson wrote for himself, Chief Justice Taney, northern Democrat Clifford and southern Democrat Catron.[90] Like Grier, Nelson was a compromise appointment to the Court following several failed nominations (in his case, an outcome of the feud between the Senate and President John Tyler in the early 1840s). Like Grier, his tenure on the Court was largely unmemorable, with the *Prize Cases* dissent standing far above his other contributions.[91]

---

the Conduct and Affairs of Nations and Sovereigns § 81, 225 (Northampton, Mass. Simeon Butler, 4th Am. Ed. 1820) (1758)).

[89] The lower court held that the New Yorkers were joint owners with the Virginians and the cargo therefore was condemnable in whole as enemies' property. *The Hiawatha; The Crenshaw*, 12 F.Cas. 95, 105 (1861).

[90] One modern commentator, Robert Murray, relying on some ambiguity in the Lawyers' Edition report of the opinions, contends that Nelson's written dissent was a solo opinion in the *Hiawatha* case, and that he and the other three Justices dissented together in the *Brilliante* case without a published opinion. *See* Robert Bruce Murray, *Legal Cases of the Civil War* 17–18 (2003) (citing 17 L.Ed. 459, 481–87). Black's official U.S. reports indicate that the other three Justices joined Nelson's opinion, *see* 67 U.S. at 699, as does contemporaneous reporting by the New York Times. *See The U.S. Supreme Court Decision in the New–Almaden Case—Prize Cases—Close of the Term*, N.Y. Times (March 11, 1863). Modern scholarship follows the official report. *See, e.g.*, David P. Currie, *The Constitution in the Supreme Court: The First Hundred Years, 1789–1888*, at 273–75 (1985); James F. Simon, *Lincoln and Chief Justice Taney: Slavery, Secession, and the President's War Powers* 229–230 (2006); Daniel A. Farber, *Lincoln's Constitution* 138–41 (2003).

[91] Carl B. Swisher, *The Taney Period, 1836–1864, in* 5 *The Oliver Wendell Holmes Devise History of the Supreme Court of the United States* 220–21 (1974). To Professor

Nelson too began cautiously, first arguing in the *Hiawatha* case that the facts did not support a right of capture.[92] "Another objection," he then said, was the lack of legal war, which (adopting the position Carlisle asserted on behalf of the *Brilliante* owners) he thought required an act of Congress to begin.[93] "It is not to be denied," Nelson made clear, "that if a civil war existed ... at the time this vessel and cargo were seized ... she would be a lawful prize of war."[94] That concession indicated that actions taken after Congress' approval of the war—probably including the Emancipation Proclamation—were valid. As Nelson said later in the opinion, "This Act of Congress, we think, recognized a state of civil war...."[95]

Before Congress acted, though, Nelson argued that the President had no constitutional power to act as if war existed. "An idea seemed to be entertained that all that was necessary to constitute war was organized hostility.... Now in one sense, no doubt this is war ... but it is a statement of its existence in a material sense and has no relevancy or weight when the question is what constitutes war in a legal sense...."[96] For the latter, he said "it must be recognized or declared by the war-making power of the Government," which the Constitution gave to Congress.[97]

Unlike Carlisle, Nelson acknowledged the problem of necessity but responded that Congress had provided the President with authority to use the army, navy, and state militias to suppress the insurrection, and this authority "furnishes the most ample means of repelling attacks from abroad or suppressing disturbances at home until the assembling of Congress...." Nelson was not challenging anything central to Lincoln's conduct of hostilities against people actually in rebellion (and in this sense went further in terms of presidential power than had Buchanan,

---

Currie, Nelson was "an unimpressive plodder in the mainstream who wrote little over a long period." David P. Currie, *The Constitution in the Supreme Court: The First Hundred Years, 1789–1888, at* 280 (1985). Professor Swisher, somewhat more charitably, called him "stable, sound, and unspectacular." Carl B. Swisher, *The Taney Period, 1836–1864, in* 5 *The Oliver Wendell Holmes Devise History of the Supreme Court of the United States* 221 (1974).

[92] *Prize Cases*, 67 U.S. at 686–89.

[93] *Id.* at 689.

[94] *Id.* at 689–90.

[95] *Id.* at 694. Nelson referred specifically to the Act of July 13, 1861, which authorized the President to declare parts of the country in a state of insurrection and take steps to suppress it. *See* 12 Stat. 255, 257.

[96] *Prize Cases*, 67 U.S. at 690.

[97] *Id.* at 689.

Attorney General Black, or even Nelson himself in the weeks before Sumter). His main concern seemed to be that the owners of the captured ships and their cargoes were not themselves in rebellion, but were only innocent civilians—either loyal Americans residing in a soon-to-secede state or neutral foreigners—caught up in the conflict. Until Congress acted, he said, "no citizen . . . can be punished in his person or property unless he has committed some offense against the laws of Congress. . . . The penalty of confiscation for the acts of others with whom he had no concern cannot lawfully be inflicted."[98]

In sum, Nelson agreed that the President could respond to force with force as a law enforcement matter, but denied that this would invoke any presidential war powers under international law. In his view, only Congress could create a legal state of war necessary to authorize wartime actions such as blockade. War is a legal condition, not arising from facts on the ground, as the majority maintained, but arising from congressional action. The consequence, in Nelson's view, was that the President could use force, pursuant to his law enforcement powers, only against those persons actually in rebellion; he could not convert this enforcement power (pursuant to U.S. domestic law) into a general war power (under international law) directed against individuals engaged in maritime trade of potential value to the rebellion. The latter required a declaration by Congress to recognize war in a legal sense.

An Initial Assessment of the Decision

On initial inspection, the *Prize Cases* decision is striking in several respects. All nine Justices apparently assumed both that secession was illegal and that the federal government could use force to suppress it. That conclusion was a necessary predicate to Grier's opinion upholding the blockade, but Nelson in dissent also insisted on the President's power to act against what he called an "insurrection." Only two years earlier Black as Attorney General had said that the entire federal government (not just the President) lacked power to coerce the seceding states. Nelson himself had apparently expressed that view in private, and Taney, at least, had likely held it as well. Yet by 1863, that position was not only rejected by all members of the Court, but not even acknowledged. And although Black had denied the legality of secession, others at the time had argued for a constitutional right to secede (so that the southern states, far from participating in an "insurrection," were simply

---

[98] *Id.* at 692–93. Nelson also rejected the idea that Congress could retroactively approve the seizures, apparently in part on *ex post facto* grounds. He objected to the argument that "trade and commerce [by and with the seceding states] authorized at the time by acts of Congress and treaties, may, by *ex post facto* legislation, be changed into illicit trade and commerce. . . . The precedent is one which has not received the approbation of jurists, and is not to be followed." *Id.* at 698.

exercising a legal option to withdraw from the Union). Again, the Court failed even to acknowledge this constitutional position, which commanded a considerable following two years earlier. Of course, in the interim the South had begun the shooting at Fort Sumter (and less notably but of more relevance to the *Prize Cases*, Jefferson Davis had issued a proclamation inviting anyone to attack American shipping). Perhaps these developments would have altered the view of Black and others as to the federal government's right to use force, but it is not obvious that it would have. Nonetheless, almost two years deep into full-scale war, the Court implicitly defined the issues before it so narrowly that it had no need to consider the war's constitutionality.[99]

With these implicit assumptions, the Court reduced the constitutional issue to a narrow conceptual one: whether "war" was something that resulted from facts on the ground (as Dana had said, "a state of things") or was a legal status that depended on formal recognition by Congress. (Under the first position, the President could exercise war powers in response to attack, including enforcement of a blockade by condemnation of property owned by foreign neutrals and allegedly loyal citizens, despite Congress' failure to "declare" war; under the second, he could not.) This focus further drained the opinion of significance, since all the Justices agreed that by ratifying Lincoln's actions in the summer of 1861, Congress had sufficiently acknowledged a state of war from that point forward. At most, had the dissent prevailed, the government would have owed compensation for a relatively small number of captures—those that occurred from April 19 to July 13, 1861.

Further, the Justices seemed untroubled by the issue that had divided Lincoln's cabinet in its initial consideration of the blockade: whether the United States could treat the Confederacy as a belligerent under international law without also recognizing the legality of the Confederacy's independence. At Dana's invitation, Grier addressed the question directly and dismissed it easily on the (supposed) authority of Vattel. But Nelson apparently thought it an unimportant point as well: again, his dissent assumed away potential problems by conceding the legality of the blockade once Congress approved it.

Finally, on the key issue of how to establish the state of war, the Justices relied largely on their own assertions, rather than on persuasive argument. For Grier, war simply was an observable "state of things"; for Nelson, it was a legal status or condition. Neither devoted much space to demonstrating why either proposition was true. Grier quoted a definition from Vattel, without attribution, but it hardly seems conclusive, as the

---

[99] In this regard the Court was assisted by the expert lawyering of the owners' counsel, Carlisle, who carefully avoided claiming any more than his clients needed: his central point was that the blockade was illegal only so long as Congress had not approved it.

passage did not address this particular issue. He also appealed to
necessity, but Nelson's dissent undermined that claim fairly effectively
by showing that the President had ample powers to repel attacks until
Congress could assemble. Nelson provided even less in the way of
reasoning. Thus in the end the Court had less to say than it might have
about what could be quite an interesting and important issue in the
abstract: whether the President has constitutional power to use offensive
force to respond to attacks on the United States.[100]

Immediate Impact

The decision was greeted with relief by the Lincoln Administration.
To be sure, even the dissent had agreed that the blockade was valid after
the summer 1861 congressional enactments. And so, in retrospect, if the
case had gone the other way, the only apparent issue for the administration would have been whether to pay out funds from the U.S. Treasury
to compensate cargo and ship owners for captures made between Lincoln's proclamations of blockade on April 19 and 27 and Congress'
authorization on July 13. But an adverse decision would have had a
strong symbolic effect, putting the Court on the opposite side from
Congress and the President with respect to the propriety of military
actions taken early in the war, and would likely have been perceived as
an implicit endorsement of Taney's *Merryman* opinion.

More important was the avoidance of the most feared outcome. The
Court could have invalidated the blockade *in toto* absent a formal
congressional declaration of war, rendering the blockade unlawful in
1863. "What a position it would have put us in," Dana wrote on the eve
of decision, "before the world whose commerce we have been illegally
prohibiting, whom we unlawfully subjected to a cotton famine, and
domestic dangers and distress for two years! It would end the war, and

---

[100] On the unsatisfactory nature of the opinions' reasoning, *see* David P. Currie, *The
Constitution in the Supreme Court: The First Hundred Years, 1789–1888*, at 273–75 (1985).
Currie argues that James Madison's statement at the 1787 Constitutional Convention—
that the President would have power to "repel sudden attacks"—is near-conclusive support
for Grier's position. *See* 2 *The Records of the Federal Convention of 1787*, at 318 (Max
Farrand ed., rev. ed. 1966) (Madison). But that seems to overstate the point, for it is hardly
clear from the Convention comment alone that Madison thought the President had power
to take offensive actions, or actions against individuals not actively hostile such as allegedly
loyal U.S. citizens or foreign neutrals engaged in trade of possible benefit to the enemy,
even in response to attacks. For debate over the President's response power as matter of
the Constitution's original meaning, and early Presidents' views on the matter, *compare*
Saikrishna B. Prakash, *Unleashing the Dogs of War: What the Constitution Means by
"Declare War,"* 93 Cornell L. Rev. 45 (2007) (finding no presidential power to act
offensively); *with* Michael D. Ramsey, *The President's Power to Respond to Attacks*, 93
Cornell L. Rev. 169 (2007) (finding presidential power to respond offensively to attacks).

where it would leave us with neutral powers, it is fearful to contem-plate!"[101]

The Court's decision also took the wind out of the sails of potential challenges to other unilateral actions of the President, most poignantly the recent Emancipation Proclamation. As the *New York Times* editorial-ized on March 13, 1863: "It is very difficult to see why the very broad language of the Court in respect to the proclamation of the blockade does not involve the constitutional validity of the proclamation against slave property.... It is our firm conviction that the Supreme Court would indorse the constitutional validity of every important act of the Execu-tive or of the Congress thus far in the rebellion."[102] In particular, whether the decision swept so far as the *Times* sought to push it, the Emancipation Proclamation seemed secure. If the President's wartime powers allowed him to confiscate the property of citizens of seceded or soon-to-secede states—and even of neutrals trading with those states—through a blockade at sea, it seemed also to encompass the power to declare the forfeiture of enemy property on land.[103]

The timing of the Court's decision two years into a hard-fought war might have rendered the possibility of any other conclusion by a member of the Court remote, but it was a still a possibility.[104] And the unanimity of both the majority and the minority on the international and constitu-tional legality of the blockade once approved by Congress was a major blow to the Copperheads and Democrats who hoped to find some support in the judiciary branch for a negotiated reconciliation with the South. Had Nelson and Taney sought materially to undermine the President, they surely could have done so (although whether that would have accomplished any useful results from their perspective is another ques-tion). It is important to remember that in early 1863 the war was deeply unpopular in broad segments in the North. Indeed, that circumstance continued, notwithstanding important shifts in momentum in the sum-mer of 1863, into the presidential election year of 1864 (when Lincoln seriously feared that he might lose to the Democrats' anti-war plat-

---

[101] 2 Charles Francis Adams, *Richard Henry Dana: A Biography* 267 (1890) (letter to Charles Francis Adams, March 9, 1863).

[102] *The Copperheads and the Courts*, N.Y. Times (March 13, 1863).

[103] *See* Michael Stokes Paulsen, *The Emancipation Proclamation and the Commander-in-Chief Power*, 40 Ga. L. Rev. 807 (2006) (adopting this view of the *Prize Cases*).

[104] In Dana's words, "such an event is legally possible,—I do not think it probable, hardly possible, in fact. But last year I think there was danger of such a result, when the blockade was new, and before the three new judges were appointed. The bare contempla-tion of such a possibility makes us pause in our boastful assertion that our written Constitution is clearly the best adapted to all exigencies, the last, the best gift to man." 2 Charles Francis Adams, *Richard Henry Dana: A Biography* 267 (1890).

form).[105] A strong holding against the President might well have been politically damaging. Instead, as the contemporaneous *Times* editorial noted, the relative political innocuousness and the studied lawyerliness of even the dissent suggested that the Court was an inhospitable institution for those seeking to vindicate deep and wide-ranging griev-ances against presidential actions in wartime.

Continuing Importance

Does the decision in the *Prize Cases* have continuing importance, or is it lost in the obscurity of nineteenth-century prize law? Although it is a major Supreme Court decision in an area in which decisions are rare, it is not a common citation in modern case law. Indeed, it has not been cited substantively in a Supreme Court majority opinion since World War II. It appeared only in brief competing footnotes in a concurrence and the dissent in the pivotal *Steel Seizure* case in 1952.[106] In the post–9/11 war-on-terrorism cases, it has been mentioned (briefly) only once in a majority opinion, which distinguished it.[107] Even dissents and concur-rences have cited it only occasionally.

As the foregoing sections illustrate, this neglect seems surprising and undeserved, because the issues *The Prizes Cases* confronted—in presidential war power and in international law—have continuing impor-tance. The now-obscure setting in nineteenth-century prize law should not hide its timeless qualities. But *how* the case should bear on modern debates is more difficult to say. Indeed, the two modern Justices who have used it the most, in dissenting and other separate opinions, come from opposing viewpoints and have used it for sharply contrasting purposes. Justice William O. Douglas, in his long and unsuccessful campaign to persuade the Supreme Court to consider the constitutionali-ty of the Vietnam War, repeatedly pointed to the *Prize Cases* for the propositions that the President had limited war power and that the Court could and should decide such questions on the merits.[108] More

---

[105] *See* Doris Kearns Goodwin, *Team of Rivals: The Political Genius of Abraham Lincoln* 653–66 (2006).

[106] Youngstown Sheet & Tube Co. v. Sawyer, 343 U.S. 579 (1952). Justice Clark in concurrence, *id.* at 661 n.3, described the *Prizes Cases*, somewhat incompletely, as turning on retroactive congressional approval; Chief Justice Vinson, in dissent, *id.* at 684 & n.35, described the decision as recognizing presidential emergency power. On the centrality of *Youngstown* to modern analyses of presidential power, see Chapter 7 of this volume.

[107] Hamdan v. Rumsfeld, 548 U.S. 557, 599 n. 31 (2006). For more on *Hamdan*, see Chapter 12 of this volume.

[108] *E.g.,* Holtzman v. Schlesinger, 414 U.S. 1316 (1973) (Douglas, opinion as circuit justice); Da Costa v. Laird, 405 U.S. 979 (1972) (Douglas, dissenting from denial of certiorari); Massachusetts v. Laird, 400 U.S. 886 (1970) (Douglas, dissenting); McArthur v.

recently, Justice Clarence Thomas, dissenting from the Court's (limited) restraint on the President in the post–9/11 war on terrorism, used the *Prize Cases* as authority for the President's broad power to respond to attacks and for substantial judicial deference to the President in such circumstances.[109]

A Strong or Weak View of Presidential Power?

The power Lincoln claimed in the *Prize Cases* was substantial: to authorize military force to capture ships (and their cargoes) that belonged not merely to those involved in insurrection but also to loyal Americans and neutral foreign citizens. In upholding that power, the Court seemed to give significant content to the President's executive and commander-in-chief powers, which Grier's opinion invoked prominently. Specifically, Grier's reasoning at least appeared to endorse a broad view of the President's power to respond to attack, presumably including not just by blockade but through other offensive operations, and perhaps also through other measures beyond strictly military ones. More generally, it seemed to accept a conception of presidential power well beyond merely executing the will of Congress. It is this face of the decision to which Justice Thomas appealed.

Of course, the closeness of the decision, the emergency nature of Lincoln's actions and their prompt ratification by Congress, and the unique circumstances of organized domestic rebellion may somewhat undermine the decision's support for broad independent presidential power. Moreover, the Court and the government's counsel emphasized limits on the President: that the President could not initiate war, and that he was acting in conformity with existing acts of Congress and with international law. Perhaps instead the decision is (as Justice Douglas thought) precedent for weak presidential powers, finding them only in the unusual circumstance of an emergency response to attack, pending submission for approval by Congress. And perhaps the circumstance of domestic rebellion makes the precedent even more narrow, for in that case (but not others) the President might rely on the constitutional direction to "take Care that the Laws be faithfully executed." But in fact none of the broader claims of presidential power was presented in the case (not even the question of war initiation); it is unclear at best whether the Court was relying on the existence of emergency or of domestic rebellion in assessing presidential power. Further, in contrast to much modern debate, the Court was not preoccupied with whether

---

Clifford, 393 U.S. 1002 (1968) (Douglas, dissenting from denial of certiorari); Mora v. McNamara, 389 U.S. 934 (1967) (Douglas, dissenting from denial of certiorari).

[109] Hamdi v. Rumsfeld, 542 U.S. 507, 581, 584, 588 (2004) (Thomas, dissenting); Hamdan v. Rumsfeld, 548 U.S. at 679, 684–87, 725 (Thomas, dissenting).

Congress had approved the President's action. Congress *had* approved it, albeit retroactively and in a vague and somewhat backhanded way, and the Court used that as an alternate holding. But Grier directly denied that the approval was necessary and spent little time on it.[110]

A more nuanced reading might suggest that the decision takes an intermediate position. It surely sees in the President's constitutional powers *some* independent substance; its presidency is far from simply a tool of Congress. But the presidential powers it acknowledges arise only from the particular circumstance of a proportionate reaction by armed forced to a war begun by an opposing side—a stoppage of the Confederacy's maritime trade to reciprocate for the Confederacy's prior invitation to attack Union merchant shipping. It provides little foundation for presidential power to begin war, or to use military force or to take other actions in other circumstances. Thus Justices Douglas and Thomas might both be right—Thomas in thinking that the decision recognized substantive presidential powers in wartime, Douglas in thinking that those powers are limited to particular circumstances.[111]

A Strong or Weak View of Judicial Power?

The most immediately striking aspect of the *Prize Cases* is that the Court considered a constitutional challenge to the President's military actions during wartime and very nearly ruled against the President. And this attention came despite strong arguments by the President's counsel for judicial abstention (including, apparently, the suggestion that deciding the merits would make the Court an "ally of the enemy"). For Justice Douglas, this made it a precedent supporting a strong judicial role.[112]

But although the Court made a show of deciding the cases on their merits, the majority opinion contained language of substantial deference to the executive. The Court was quite willing to accept the President's

---

[110] *See Prize Cases*, 67 U.S. at 670–71; *compare* Youngstown Sheet & Tube Co. v. Sawyer, 343 U.S. 579, 634 (1952) (Jackson, concurring).

[111] The idea that the President has broad substantive powers to respond to attack but is limited in initiating conflict dates at least to Alexander Hamilton's 1801 essay *The Examination*. Alexander Hamilton, *The Examination No. 1*, N.Y. Evening Post, Dec. 17, 1801, *reprinted in* 25 The Papers of Alexander Hamilton 455 (Harold C. Syrett ed., 1974). One of us has argued (without relying on the *Prize Cases*) that the intermediate vision of presidential war powers as substantive but limited is the best reading of the Constitution's original meaning. *See* Michael D. Ramsey, *The Constitution's Text in Foreign Affairs* 218–58 (2007); Michael D. Ramsey, *The President's Power to Respond to Attacks*, 93 Cornell L. Rev. 169, 190–94 (2007).

[112] *E.g.*, *Holtzman*, 414 U.S. at 1318 (Douglas, Circuit Justice) (citing *Prize Cases* for the proposition that, in Vietnam War cases, "[t]he question of justiciability does not seem substantial").

characterization of the situation as war (even though, at the time the blockade was proclaimed, shots had been fired only at a single fort, and no one had been killed by hostile fire). Indeed, Grier asserted that the President's determination on this ground was conclusive on the Court, a point Justice Thomas emphasized in his dissents.[113] And even Nelson's dissent does not go all that far in constraining presidential power, especially as against actual threats as opposed to innocent parties.

On the other hand, notwithstanding the language of deference, on the crucial question whether the insurrection had progressed to the level of a full-blown civil war the Court also referred to contemporaneous recognition of a state of war by foreign nations, the comparatively amorphous and evolving nature of a civil war, the disruption of the courts, and the commonsense obviousness of its conclusion before making the point about deference. Indeed, one could easily argue that the executive deference point (like the alternative rationale of legislative ratification) was a throwaway claim of little consequence placed late in the opinion. Nor, for that matter, did the Court adopt the most pro-government position adopted by a lower court. Judge Sprague, in the federal district court for Massachusetts, appeared to suggest that it was completely discretionary to the Government to claim belligerent and sovereign rights as to Confederates, and to toggle back and forth between one and the other according to what best served its military interests. "The temporary non-us[e] of such [sovereign] rights [by treating rebel privateers as prisoners of war and not traitors and pirates] is not a renunciation of them, but they may be called into practical exercise at pleasure."[114]

---

[113] *E.g.*, *Hamdan*, 548 U.S. at 725 (Thomas, dissenting) (citing *Prize Cases* for the proposition that "The President's findings about the nature of the present conflict with respect to members of al Qaeda operating in Afghanistan represents a core exercise of his commander-in-chief authority that this Court is bound to respect"); *Hamdi*, 542 U.S. at 581 (Thomas, dissenting) (quoting *Prize Cases* statement that "Whether the President in fulfilling his duties, as Commander in-chief, in suppressing an insurrection, has met with such armed hostile resistance [as to warrant a particular measure] ... is a question to be decided *by him*"); *id.* at 584 (Thomas, dissenting) (citing *Prize Cases* for the proposition that the Court's "deference extends to the President's determination of all the factual predicates necessary to conclude that a given action is appropriate"); *id.* at 588 (citing *Prize Cases* for the proposition that Court is "bound by the political branches' determination that the United States is at war"). *See* Harold Hongju Koh, *The National Security Constitution* 85 (1990) (finding in the *Prize Cases* "the Court's hint that the president's decisions could be considered political questions that it ought not review"). In this respect, the Thomas and Douglas readings of the *Prize Cases* decision are not easily reconcilable.

[114] The Amy Warwick, 1 Fed Cas. at 803. The difficulties of classifying hostilities that do not seem to constitute "war" in a conventionally recognized sense, and the tendency of the government to shift among various legal paradigms as convenient, find echoes in more recent war-on-terrorism debates. *See* Hamdan v. Rumsfeld, 548 U.S. 557 (2006) and Chapter 12 of this volume.

On the more immediate level of how the international law of prize applied to the cases at bar, however, the Court was exceedingly deferential to the President. For instance, the owners of the *Brilliante* had argued that the ship had been anchored in Biloxi Bay when captured, awaiting a safe conduct to clear American waters for Mexico. The pass should have been granted as a matter of course under the view of international maritime law that the United States had articulated five years earlier, since it was a private neutral vessel carrying neutral-owned cargo to a neutral port. And the Court, as a prize court of last resort, had the authority to examine the facts of the case *de novo*. But the Court rejected the *Brilliante* claims without discussion. Secondly and more importantly, the majority readily accepted Dana's innovative theory of enemies' property to resolve the *Amy Warwick* and *Crenshaw* cases, despite the absence of support on point for extending the concept to a civil war and the significant concerns voiced by the claimants' counsel against the use of international law to displace domestic constitutional protections for presumptively loyal U.S. citizens. Nor did the Court, in the *Hiawatha* case, consider arguments made by the claimants that they were entitled to equitable tolling of the designated grace period because the *Hiawatha*'s departure had been delayed by circumstances beyond their control. Indeed, an international arbitral tribunal, established by the Washington Treaty of 1871, later expressly disagreed with the Supreme Court's ruling against the *Hiawatha*'s British owners, although it is unclear on what grounds.[115] The extent of executive deference as to prize law questions in these cases stands in stark contrast to the Court's well-known opinion in *The Paquete Habana*, a case arising out of the Spanish–American War three decades later, in which it gave no deference to the executive's litigating position that fishing vessels were lawful prizes under international law.[116]

The Prize Cases and International Law

An under-examined feature of the *Prize Cases* is the Court's treatment of international law. Grier, writing for the majority, accepted that customary international law authorized the wartime confiscation of property from presumptively loyal U.S. citizens in the seceded states as "enemies' property"—and apparently Nelson's dissent would have done so as well if Congress had approved it. (The Justices appear to have assumed without much thought that the same "enemy" could litigate as claimants in the U.S. federal courts.) Grier did not even bother to argue

---

[115] Treaty Claims, Fisheries, Navigation of the St. Lawrence, American Lumber on the River St. John, Boundary, US–Gr. Brit., May 8, 1871, 17 Stat. 853 ("Treaty of Washington"); 1 John Bassett Moore, *History and Digest of the International Arbitrations to which the United States Has Been a Party* 3910–11 (Washington, G.P.O. 1898).

[116] The Paquete Habana, 175 U.S. 677 (1900).

that the captures would have been valid under the domestic Constitution as a back-up argument. At the same time, he seemed to assume—for reasons not entirely articulated—that captures *not* conforming to international law would *not* be valid. In other words, the authorization derived from international law was both necessary and sufficient to uphold the taking of the property of foreigners as well as purportedly loyal U.S. citizens residing in seceded or soon-to-secede states during civil war.

There are at least two ways to look at this result. First, one might say that, not only did the Court assume that the international law was "part of our law," as it famously found three decades later in *The Paquete Habana*,[117] but at least in time of war, the Court thought that customary international law supplied a basis for the President to order the taking of private property at sea in tension with the ordinary constitutional protections of private property rights. (*Paquete Habana* did not involve any claims under the U.S. Constitution.) One difference from today, of course, is that the international law of the time was used to justify governmental action that domestic constitutional law arguably proscribed. By contrast, modern international law is usually deployed to constrain governmental action that would appear permissible under domestic constitutional law. One must also consider that the international maritime law of prize was a special breed of international law, and that the federal courts when they acted as prize courts, realized that they were acting as part of an informal transnational judicial network and not as domestic courts. It is thus not clear that broader conclusions can be drawn about customary international law in general.

A second way to look at the matter is through the lens of separation of powers. The case's crucial separation of powers issue was itself derivative of international law. Lincoln's suspension of *habeas corpus*, for example, did not implicate international law at all. Its legality turned entirely on domestic constitutional and statutory law governing separation of powers. But a blockade had significant adverse effects on foreign neutrals and trade, and the international law of the time limited its deployment to the state of war. Accordingly, the question whether the President had the unilateral right to exercise a war power under the U.S. Constitution was presented. But as the modern blockade rule illustrates, and as might be inferred by reference to the analogue of embargo, one could claim that the power to order the stoppage of trade with another country, even by deployment of naval forces, is not necessarily a "war" power. It was international law that made it a war power, and no one questioned the relevance of the international law rule, for instance, by asserting that the President could—or could not—proclaim

---

[117] *Id.* at 700.

the blockade regardless of whether or not the insurrection was itself a "war" in a qualifying sense under international law. Thus one might say that, for the Court, international law defined and ratcheted up the scope of presidential war power. If so, one might also view the *Prize Cases* as precedent for the proposition that international law can *limit* or ratchet down the scope of presidential war power as well.[118]

Nonetheless, despite the prominence of international law at an abstract level, it is important to remember that, in the application of the specific rules of the international maritime law of prize, the Court was exceedingly deferential to the President. Unlike some of the Court's decisions in War of 1812 prize cases, and Justice Gray's opinion in *Paquete Habana*, Justice Grier's majority opinion did not engage in a lengthy disquisition of specific prize rules, for example, concerning notice, neutral captures, and constructive breach. The majority did not seek to micromanage the Navy Department's decisions on the legality of the captures. Nor, with the exception of the cargo belonging to New Yorkers on the *Crenshaw*, did the Court reverse any condemnation by the courts below. Perhaps most important, the majority did not subject to great scrutiny Dana's provocative enemies' property theory despite its questionable pedigree in international law sources and its domestic constitutional law implications. Thus the robust reliance on international law in the abstract was coupled with very substantial deference on its particular applications.[119]

Finally, it is interesting to note that the Court's decision in the *Prize Cases* was partially rejected by the international arbitral tribunal established under the Washington Treaty of 1871.[120] The three-person panel, with the American member dissenting, ordered compensation for the *Hiawatha* and the part of its cargo owned by British subjects. No rationale was given, but it appears from Professor Moore's account that the panel was swayed by arguments grounded in "justice and equity."[121] To be sure, the arbitration was a state-to-state affair and not a reprise of the suit between the actual parties, but apparently no one objected to an

---

[118] *See* Ingrid B. Wuerth, *International Law and Constitutional Interpretation: The Commander-in-Chief Clause Reconsidered*, 106 Mich. L. Rev. 61 (2007) (suggesting that modern courts should take international law into account in defining presidential powers); Michael D. Ramsey, *The Constitution's Text in Foreign Affairs* 362–67 (2007) (suggesting that under the Constitution's original understanding international law limited presidential power through Article II, Section 3's take-care clause).

[119] *See* Michael D. Ramsey, *The Constitution's Text in Foreign Affairs* 362–76 (2007) (suggesting a similar view of the Constitution's original understanding).

[120] Henry Paul Monaghan, *Article III and Supranational Judicial Review*, 107 Colum. L. Rev. 833, 860–861 (2007).

[121] 1 John Bassett Moore, *History and Digest of the International Arbitrations to which the United States Has Been a Party* 3908 (Washington, G.P.O. 1898).

arbitral award that allowed, in effect, an international tribunal to revisit a decision of the U.S. Supreme Court. At the least, the result of the arbitration indicates that the executive branch's positions on the specifics of international law to which Grier deferred had contestable foundations. It might also seem that this has implications for the modern debate about delegations of Article III adjudication to multilateral courts,[122] although it must be admitted that the unique nature of prize courts might be distinguished as a special case. Indeed, one of the first abortive proposals for a permanent international court involved an international prize court with appellate jurisdiction over the decisions of diverse national prize courts.[123]

Courts and Presidents in Emergencies

Beyond what the majority opinion might be said to have held, one may wish to consider whether the story of the *Prize Cases* provides any broader lessons for the relationship between the judicial and executive branches in times of crisis. Again, here the case seems to point in two directions. On one hand, it might easily have come out the other way. Nelson needed only one more vote to make his dissent a majority, and even assuming that Lincoln's appointees would have held firm, Wayne or Grier might have reached the opposite conclusion, or other circumstances (including a more speedy nomination of Attorney General Black by President Buchanan) might have given Lincoln fewer sympathetic appointees. In this sense, although Lincoln prevailed, the closeness of the decision indicates that Presidents should not assume they will always prevail in emergencies.

On the other hand, the extraordinary narrowness of the legal arguments, given what might have been at stake, is striking. Had Nelson's opinion been the majority, surely Lincoln's position would have suffered, but no fundamental challenge to the conduct of the war would have been issued. Of course, the Court *could* have used the *Prize Cases* to issue a fundamental challenge to the conduct of the war—by considering the constitutionality of secession or the use of offensive force against it, or by questioning the blockade's appeal to international law in the context of domestic insurrection. But notably, no one—not even Taney— showed any inclination to do so. The utter rejection of the more fundamental questions about the war—to the extent that concerns advanced

---

[122] *See* Edward T. Swaine, *The Constitutionality of International Delegations*, 104 Colum. L. Rev. 1492 (2004); Curtis A. Bradley, *The Federal Judicial Power and the International Legal Order*, 2006 Supreme Ct. Rev. 59; Henry Paul Monaghan, *Article III and Supranational Judicial Review*, 107 Colum. L. Rev. 833 (2007).

[123] *Hague Convention (XII) Relative to the Creation of an International Prize Court* (Oct. 18, 1907) in *The Laws of Armed Conflicts* 825–36 (Dietrich Schindler & Jiri Toman, eds., 3rd rev. ed. 1988).

so heatedly two years earlier simply disappeared from the case—surely suggests that courts are willing to go only so far in confronting Presidents in crisis. That may be something to consider for those who look to the Court today for full-throated vindication of challenges to presidential wartime acts.

Conclusion

The *Prize Cases* remains one of the Supreme Court's few statements on the President's war powers and the Court's role in monitoring them. The decision also provides insight into how jurists of the Civil War generation thought about the interaction between international law and the domestic constitutional law of separation of powers. It is, however, not so easy to come to a quick conclusion on what the decision stands for on these enduring questions. For example, the Court appears to acknowledge some robust presidential war powers, but in the specific context of a reaction to a systematic, organized rebellion that has matured into a civil war. With respect to the judicial power, the Court explicitly made a point of deference to the executive and accepted the government's prize-law positions wholesale, despite the blatant reversal of decades-long antebellum positions and the lack of support for Dana's crucial extension of the enemies' property concept to seaborne captures during a civil war. But at the same time the Court did, after all, agree to decide the cases at the height of the war, and it intimated that executive deference did not really mean much, since anyone would have to admit "the existence of a war, which all the world acknowledges to be the greatest civil war known in the history of the human race."[124] Finally, international law plays a very prominent role in the decision, but it is the arcane and specialized maritime law of prize, which may be *sui generis*, a point that often gets forgotten in the homage to the *Paquete Habana*'s venerable pronouncement that "international law is part of our law." Perhaps what the Janus-faced features of the *Prize Cases* indicate, more than anything else, is that there are no easy answers to these enduring and underlying questions.*

---

[124] The Prize Cases, 67 U.S. 635, 669 (1863).

* Our thanks to David Sloss, Stephen Vladek and the participants in the American Society of International Law Interest Group on International Law in Domestic Courts workshop at the University of Texas Law School for helpful comments.

3

Curtis A. Bradley

The Story of *Ex parte Milligan*: Military Trials, Enemy Combatants, and Congressional Authorization

A military commission is a court composed of military officers that is used for various purposes, including the trial of enemy forces for violations of the laws of war. In *Ex parte Milligan*, decided a year after the end of the Civil War, the Supreme Court held that the U.S. military had lacked the constitutional authority during the war to try U.S. citizens living in Indiana before a military commission. A majority of five Justices reasoned that it would have been unconstitutional for the military to conduct the trial even if the trial had been authorized by Congress, whereas four concurring Justices merely concluded that the trial was unlawful because it violated restrictions imposed by Congress. Although the decision was issued after the end of the Civil War, it is often cited as a rare and admirable instance in which the Supreme Court invalidated Executive action during wartime in order to protect civil liberties. There has been a renewed focus on the decision after the September 11, 2001 terrorist attacks and the subsequent detention and proposed military trial by the United States of suspected terrorists.

In this chapter, I will describe the historical and legal context in which *Milligan* was decided and consider its implications for presidential power. These implications, as I will explain, are highly uncertain and probably quite limited, at least at the level of legal doctrine. Part of the uncertainty stems from the decision's unacknowledged inconsistency with widespread military practices during and immediately after the Civil War, including most notably the use of military commissions to try thousands of individuals not formally associated with the Confederate army. Many of these military commission cases involved acts of organized violence or destruction of property that were alleged to violate the customary laws of war. The most famous of these cases was the trial at the end of the War, shortly before the Supreme Court decided *Milligan*, of the individuals implicated in the conspiracy to assassinate President Lincoln. Perhaps because of the particular way in which the government argued the *Milligan* case—focusing on the bounds of martial law rather than on military jurisdiction over violations of the laws of war—the Court in *Milligan* did not discuss this widespread military commission practice, and it is unclear to what extent the Court meant to repudiate it.

The Supreme Court's subsequent treatments of *Milligan* only add to the uncertainty about its scope. The Court has construed *Milligan* as applying only to the military detention and trial of "non-belligerents," but neither *Milligan* nor the subsequent decisions provide a clear line for distinguishing between belligerents and non-belligerents. One possible approach would be to limit military jurisdiction to individuals covered by the international laws of war, but international law is notoriously unclear on the dividing line between belligerency and non-belligerency, and, in any event, the petitioners in *Milligan* were in fact charged with and convicted of violating the laws of war. While the concurring opinion in *Milligan* was able to avoid some of these complications by focusing on the relationship between Congress and the President, it is unclear whether the concurrence thought that the military commission's validity depended on affirmative congressional authorization. More generally, the concurrence raises but does not resolve the important question of the circumstances under which congressional authorization will render valid presidential wartime action that would otherwise be unlawful.

Military Detentions and Commissions in the Civil War

The American Civil War began on April 12, 1861, with the attack by Confederate forces on Fort Sumter.[1] The war would last approximately four years and result in more American casualties than any other war in history, with over 600,000 dead and many hundreds of thousands injured. In attempting to preserve the Union, President Abraham Lincoln often authorized, or acquiesced in, restrictions on individual liberties.[2] These restrictions included the suspension of the writ of habeas corpus, the declaration of martial law, and the military detention and trial of

---

[1] For an excellent one-volume description of the war and its causes, see James M. McPherson, *Battle Cry of Freedom: The Civil War Era* (1988).

[2] For detailed accounts of the Lincoln administration's restrictions on civil liberties, see Mark E. Neely, Jr., *The Fate of Liberty: Abraham Lincoln and Civil Liberties* (1991); William H. Rehnquist, *All the Laws But One: Civil Liberties in Wartime* 3–137 (1998); and Dean Sprague, *Freedom Under Lincoln* (1965).

thousands of individuals not formally associated with the Confederate army.[3] Many of the detentions and trials occurred in Union states that bordered the Confederacy, such as Maryland, Missouri, and Kentucky.

Military commissions are distinct from courts-martial, which have been the usual means of trying U.S. military personnel for criminal offenses. Unlike military commissions, courts-martial have historically been regulated by detailed Articles of War enacted by Congress. In the Revolutionary War period, U.S. armed forces operated under Articles of War enacted by the Continental Congress, and, after the adoption of the Constitution, Congress directed the continued application of these Articles.[4] Congress made modest changes to the Articles in 1806, and it was the 1806 code, with some amendments, that was in place during the Civil War.[5] The Articles of War applied to members of the U.S. armed forces, as well as "[w]hosoever shall relieve the enemy with money, victuals, or ammunition, or shall knowingly harbor or protect an enemy"; "[w]hosoever shall be convicted of holding correspondence with or giving intelligence to the enemy either directly or indirectly"; "[a]ll suttlers and retainers to the camp, and all persons whatsoever, serving with the armies of the United States in the field"; and foreign citizens "who shall be found lurking as spies, in or about the fortifications or encampments of the armies of the United States."[6] These various individuals were therefore subject to trial before military courts-martial.

In contrast with its treatment of courts-martial, Congress has not traditionally regulated the procedural details of military commissions, although the procedures adopted by the military for such commissions have often been similar to those used for courts-martial.[7] Throughout U.S. history, military commissions have been used for three basic purposes: to administer justice in territories occupied by the United States; to replace civilian courts in parts of the United States where martial law has been declared; and to try enemy belligerents for violations of the

---

[3] Until February 1862, the Union's military detention policy was supervised by the Secretary of State, William Seward, and after that it was supervised by the Secretary of War, Edwin Stanton. For an engaging account of Lincoln's cabinet, see Doris Kearns Goodwin, *Team of Rivals: The Political Genius of Abraham Lincoln* (2005).

[4] *See* 1 Stat. 96, § 4 (1789).

[5] *See* Louis Fisher, *Military Tribunals and Presidential Power* 7, 22 (2005).

[6] An Act for Establishing Rules and Articles for the Government of the Armies of the United States, arts. 56, 57, 60, § 2, 2 Stat. 359, 366, 371 (1806).

[7] *See* William E. Birkhimer, *Military Government and Martial Law* 533–34 (3d ed. rev. 1914); William Winthrop, *Military Law and Precedents* 841–42 (2d ed. 1920). Congress adopted detailed rules governing the use of military commissions to try alleged terrorists in the Military Commissions Act of 2006. *See* Pub. L. No. 109–366, 120 Stat. 2600 (2006).

laws of war.[8] The use of these commissions is sometimes traced back to the Revolutionary War, when President George Washington convened a Board of General Officers to advise him about the guilt and punishment of Major John André of the British army, who was charged with spying.[9] The most extensive use of these commissions prior to the Civil War was during the Mexican–American War in the late 1840s. In addition to using military commissions in that war to punish offenses by and against U.S. soldiers in occupied Mexican territory, General Winfield Scott (who was commanding general of the Army and would remain in that post until after the outset of the Civil War) convened what he called "councils of war" to prosecute those engaged in guerilla warfare and attempts to induce U.S. soldiers to desert.[10]

During the Civil War, military commissions were used extensively in the border states, especially in Missouri.[11] The crimes tried before the commissions included guerilla activities involving organized violence or theft of property, as well as sabotage, such as the destruction of railroads, bridges, and telegraph lines—activities that were considered by the military to be violations of the international laws of war.[12] Some of the earliest military commissions in Missouri were authorized by General Henry Halleck, who had published a well-regarded treatise on international law shortly before the outset of the Civil War.[13] In his *General*

---

[8] *See* Hamdan v. Rumsfeld, 548 U.S. 557, 595–96 (2006) (plurality); Madsen v. Kinsella, 343 U.S. 341, 346–47 (1952); *see also* Curtis A. Bradley & Jack L. Goldsmith, *The Constitutional Validity of Military Commissions*, 5 Green Bag 2d 249 (2002). David Glazier points out that military commissions have also been used "when military forces were beyond the jurisdiction of their national courts, but military law did not authorize trying troops for offenses committed against the local population." David Glazier, Note, *Kangaroo Court or Competent Tribunal?: Judging the 21st Century Military Commission*, 89 Va. L. Rev. 2005, 2023 (2003).

[9] *See* George Washington, Letter Order, Head Quarters, Tappan, Sept. 29, 1780, *in* 20 *The Writings of George Washington* 101 (John C. Fitzpatrick ed., 1937); *Proceedings of a Board of General Officers Respecting Major John André, Sept. 29, 1780* (Francis Bailey ed. 1780).

[10] *See* William Winthrop, *Military Law and Precedents* 832–33 (2d ed. 1920). *See also* David Glazier, *Precedents Lost: The Neglected History of the Military Commission*, 46 Va. J. Int'l L. 5, 36–37 (2005).

[11] *See* Mark E. Neely, Jr., *The Fate of Liberty: Abraham Lincoln and Civil Liberties* 168–69 (1991).

[12] *See id.*, at 42–43; J.G. Randall, *Constitutional Problems Under Lincoln* 175 (rev. ed. 1951); *Hamdan*, 126 S.Ct. at 2832 n. 9 (Thomas, J., dissenting). In 1862, the Union military also tried almost 400 members of the Dakota Sioux by military commission for murder, rape, and robbery committed against settlers during an uprising in Minnesota. *See* Carol Chomsky, *The United States–Dakota War Trials: A Study in Military Injustice*, 43 Stan. L. Rev. 13 (1990).

[13] *See* H.W. Halleck, *International Law; or, Rules Regulating the Intercourse of States in Peace and War* (1861). Halleck's predecessor in Missouri, General John Frémont, had

Orders No. 1, Halleck, who at the time was commanding the Department of Missouri, stated that while military commissions were not to be used to try "[c]ivil offenses" when civil courts were operating, "many offenses which in time of peace are civil offenses become in time of war military offenses and are to be tried by a military tribunal even in places where civil tribunals exist."[14] He also stated that although treason was "a distinct offense ... defined by the Constitution and must be tried by courts duly constituted by law," "certain acts of a treasonable character such as conveying information to the enemy, acting as spies, & c, are military offenses triable by military tribunals and punishable by military authority."[15]

Military commissions were also used during the Civil War to try other crimes committed in places where martial law had been declared, most notably but not exclusively in occupied Confederate states and in areas of active combat. Martial law involves the displacement of civilian authority within the United States by military authority. There is no provision in the Constitution for the establishment of martial law, and there was substantial uncertainty during the Civil War about the circumstances under which it could be imposed. General Andrew Jackson had controversially imposed martial law in New Orleans at the end of the War of 1812, and used it as a basis for imprisoning a newspaper editor who criticized his actions, and also a federal judge who issued a writ of habeas corpus in favor of the editor.[16] At the state level, martial law was declared by the Rhode Island legislature in 1842 in response to the Dorr Rebellion (an effort to overthrow Rhode Island's charter

ordered martial law throughout the state and an emancipation of the secessionists' slaves. Concerned at that point that linking the war with emancipation would undermine support for the Union in the border states, President Lincoln overturned this order and had Frémont removed from command. Lincoln of course eventually issued his own Emancipation Proclamation.

[14] *See* General Orders No. 1 (Jan. 1, 1862), *in* 2:1 *The War of the Rebellion: A Compilation of the Official Records of the Union and Confederate Armies* 247, 248 (1894). *See also* S.V. Benét, *A Treatise on Military Law and the Practice of Courts–Martial* 16 (2d ed. 1862) (endorsing this proposition).

[15] 2:1 *The War of the Rebellion: A Compilation of the Official Records of the Union and Confederate Armies* 248 (1894). In some of the early military commission trials in Missouri that pre-dated General Orders No. 1, individuals were prosecuted for "treason," but Halleck overturned the treason convictions on the ground that "such charges were not triable by a military commission." 2:1 *The War of the Rebellion: A Compilation of the Official Records of the Union and Confederate Armies* 405 (1894). *See also* Mark E. Neely, Jr., *The Fate of Liberty: Abraham Lincoln and Civil Liberties* 43 (1991).

[16] *See* Matthew Warshauer, *Andrew Jackson and the Politics of Martial Law: Nationalism, Civil Liberties, and Partisanship* (2006). After the judge was released from custody, he fined Jackson $1,000 for contempt of court, which Jackson paid out of his own pocket. Years later, Congress reimbursed Jackson with interest.

government), and the Supreme Court approvingly stated that "if the government of Rhode Island deemed the armed opposition so formidable, and so ramified throughout the State, as to require the use of its military force and the declaration of martial law, we see no ground upon which this court can question its authority."[17]

Congress passed a number of statutes during the Civil War that were relevant to military detentions and the use of military commissions. The most important statute was probably the 1863 Habeas Act. This statute authorized the President to suspend the writ of habeas corpus "in any case throughout the United States, or any part thereof" "whenever, in his judgment, the public safety may require it."[18] However, the statute also directed the Secretary of State and the Secretary of War to furnish to the federal courts a list of all persons within the courts' jurisdiction who were "citizens of states in which the administration of the laws has continued unimpaired in the said Federal courts" and were being held by the military "otherwise than as prisoners of war."[19] The statute further stated that whenever a grand jury had terminated its session without indicting persons on the list within its jurisdiction, the judge should "make an order that any such prisoner desiring a discharge from said imprisonment be brought before him to be discharged," on the condition that the prisoner take an oath of allegiance to the United States and promise not to give aid and comfort to the rebellion.[20] If the Secretary of State or the Secretary of War refused or failed to furnish the list of such prisoners, the statute provided that a prisoner could nevertheless petition for a discharge on the same grounds—that is, that the grand jury had met and had not indicted him.[21]

There were also several statutes enacted during the Civil War that referred specifically to military commissions. In 1862, for example, Congress authorized the President to appoint, with the advice and consent of the Senate, a Judge Advocate General "to whose office shall be returned, for revision, the records and proceedings of all courts-martial and military commissions, and where a record shall be kept of all proceedings had thereupon."[22] Importantly, the Judge Advocate General would go on to construe the 1863 Habeas Act as inapplicable to individu-

---

[17] Luther v. Borden, 48 U.S. 1, 45 (1849). *See generally* Charles Fairman, *The Law of Martial Rule and the National Emergency*, 55 Harv. L. Rev. 1253 (1942).

[18] An Act Relating to Habeas Corpus, and Regulating Judicial Proceedings in Certain Cases, 12 Stat. 755 (1863).

[19] *Id.*, § 2.

[20] *Id.*

[21] *Id.*, § 3.

[22] 12 Stat. 597, 598, § 5 (1862).

als "triable by court-martial and military commission," such as "prisoners arrested as guerillas or bushwackers or as being connected with or aiding these."[23] In 1864, Congress specifically authorized military commanders to execute the sentences of military commissions "against guerilla marauders for robbery, arson, burglary, rape, assault with intent to commit rape, and for violation of the laws and customs of war, as well as sentences against spies, mutineers, deserters, and murderers."[24]

The influential "Lieber Code," adopted by the Union army in 1863, also had potential relevance to both military detentions and the use of military commissions. Francis Lieber, a German–American scholar who taught at Columbia Law School, assisted the Union War Department during the Civil War by drafting legal guidelines for the army. The most famous of these guidelines, *Instructions for the Government of Armies of the United States in the Field*, also known as the "Lieber Code," was adopted by the army on April 24, 1863 as *General Orders No. 100*.[25] The Lieber Code sets forth detailed rules concerning a variety of topics, including martial law, military jurisdiction, and the treatment of prisoners of war, and it became the foundation for later treaties governing the conduct of troops during wartime, including the Hague Conventions on Land Warfare. It was "the first instance in western history in which the government of a sovereign nation established formal guidelines for its army's conduct toward its enemies."[26]

The Code distinguishes between combatants who are entitled to the privileges of being a prisoner of war, and those who are not. A prisoner of war, according to the Code, is "a public enemy armed or attached to the hostile army for active aid, who has fallen into the hands of the captor, either fighting or wounded, on the field or in the hospital, by individual surrender or by capitulation."[27] Although prisoners of war can be imprisoned, the Code states that "they are to be subjected to no other intentional suffering or indignity."[28] It also states that "the modern law of war permits no longer the use of any violence against prisoners in order to extort ... desired information, or to punish them for having

---

[23] Letter from Judge Advocate General Joseph Holt to Secretary of War Edwin Stanton (June 9, 1863), *in* 2:5 *The War of the Rebellion: A Compilation of the Official Records of the Union and Confederate Armies* 765–66 (1899).

[24] *See* 13 Stat. 356 (1864).

[25] *See* Richard Shelly Hartigan, *Lieber's Code and the Law of War* (1983).

[26] *Id.* at 1–2. *See also* Louis Fisher, *Military Tribunals and Presidential Power* 71, 79–80 (2005).

[27] Richard Shelly Hartigan, *Lieber's Code and the Law of War* 55 (Art. 49) (1983).

[28] *Id.* at 59 (Art. 75).

given false information."[29] Another privilege granted to prisoners of war, the Code explains, is that they cannot be punished for having taken part in hostilities.[30] The Code makes clear that these privileges do not apply, however, to other classes of individuals, such as guerillas, spies, and saboteurs.[31]

As for military trials, the Lieber Code notes that there are two types of military jurisdiction: "First, that which is conferred and defined by statute; second, that which is derived from the common law of war."[32] Within the U.S. army, the Code explains, the first type of jurisdiction is exercised by courts-martial, "while cases which do not come within the Rules and Articles of War, or the jurisdiction conferred by statute on courts-martial, are tried by military commissions."[33] The Code thus expressly recognized the propriety of using military commissions, although it did not discuss the limits of their jurisdiction.

Lieber addressed the subject of military commissions again in 1864. A military commission, headed by General John Dix, had recommended the discharge from military custody of certain individuals who had been involved in running the Union naval blockade. The commission reasoned that blockade-running was not a personal offense against the international laws of war and thus could only result in forfeiture of the ship and cargo. The commission further reasoned that "no persons except such as are in the military or naval service of the United States are subject to trial by military courts, spies only excepted; and that, except in districts under martial law, a military commission cannot try any person whatsoever not in the U.S. military or naval service for any offense whatever."[34] The Judge Advocate General objected to the commission's recommendation of discharge, arguing that the blockade-runners in question were in fact "employés or aiders and abettors of the rebels" and that many of them were also "spies, in rebel employment, of the most repulsive and dangerous character."[35] Dix subsequently indicated that he would like to

---

[29] Id. at 59–60 (Art. 80).

[30] Id. at 56 (Art. 56).

[31] Id. at 60 (Arts. 82–84). Before completing this Code, Lieber had provided the army with an essay entitled Guerrilla Parties Considered with Reference to the Laws and Usages of War, in which he described in more detail the nature of guerilas and other irregular fighters. See id. at 31–44.

[32] Richard Shelly Hartigan, Lieber's Code and the Law of War 47 (Art. 13) (1983).

[33] Id. at 48 (Art. 13).

[34] Letter from Judge Advocate L.C. Turner to Col. James A. Hardie (June 4, 1864), in 2:7 The War of the Rebellion: A Compilation of the Official Records of the Union and Confederate Armies 194 (1899).

[35] Id. at 195.

hear Lieber's answer to the question, "Can any military court or commission, in a department not under martial law, take cognizance of, and try a citizen for, any violation of the law of war, such citizen not being connected in any wise with the military service of the United States?" In response, Lieber maintained that "undoubtedly a citizen under these conditions can, or rather must, be tried by military courts, because there is no other way to try him and repress the crime which may endanger the whole country."[36]

In sum, during the Civil War thousands of individuals not formally associated with the Confederate army were tried by military commissions. This practice was supported to some extent by Congress, and also by the influential Lieber Code. The proper boundaries of military commission jurisdiction, however, were uncertain. Moreover, although Congress's 1863 Habeas Act appeared to provide a basis for judicial release of military detainees who did not qualify as prisoners of war, the Army construed the Act as inapplicable to detainees subject to trial by military commission.

Merryman and Vallandigham

A number of individuals detained or tried by the Union military sought to challenge the legality of the military's action in federal court by filing petitions for writs of habeas corpus. Petitioning for a writ of habeas corpus is a means by which a person held in government custody can seek to have a court examine the legality of their detention, and the Constitution states that "[t]he privilege of the Writ of Habeas Corpus shall not be suspended, unless when in Cases of Rebellion or Invasion the public Safety may require it."[37]

Two cases in particular provide an important backdrop to the *Milligan* case: *Ex parte Merryman*, and *Ex parte Vallandigham*. The events at issue in *Merryman* occurred at the outset of the war. On April 15, 1861, two days after Union forces surrendered at Fort Sumter, and with Congress out of session, President Lincoln issued a proclamation calling 75,000 state militia into national service, and also calling for a special session of Congress to convene on July 4.[38] Two days later, Virginia seceded from the Union, and there was a genuine fear that Maryland would also secede, in which case Washington, D.C. would be surrounded by enemy territory. On April 19, a large mob of Confederate

---

[36] Letter from Francis Lieber to Henry W. Halleck (June 13, 1864), *quoted in The Life and Letters of Francis Lieber* 347–48 (Thomas Sergeant Perry ed., 1882).

[37] U.S. Const. art. I, § 9, cl. 2. *See also* William F. Duker, *A Constitutional History of Habeas Corpus* (1980).

[38] *See* Proclamation Calling Militia and Convening Congress (April 15, 1861), *in* 4 *The Collected Works of Abraham Lincoln* 331–32 (Roy P. Basler, ed. 1953).

sympathizers in Baltimore attacked a group of soldiers from Massachusetts as they were passing through on their way to Washington. Four soldiers and twelve residents of Baltimore were killed in the resulting conflict.[39] Secessionists in Maryland then proceeded to destroy railroad bridges and telegraph lines linking Washington with the North.

On April 27, Lincoln authorized Winfield Scott, the commanding general of the Army, to suspend the writ of habeas corpus along a military supply line between Philadelphia and Washington.[40] Under Lincoln's authorization, the writ could be suspended personally by Scott "or through the officer in command at the point where the resistance occurs." The Army subsequently arrested a number of suspected secessionists and imprisoned them at Fort McHenry in Baltimore. One of them was John Merryman, a lieutenant in a Maryland cavalry unit accused of participating in the burning of railroad bridges after the Baltimore riots.

Merryman filed a petition for a writ of habeas corpus with the U.S. Circuit Court for the District of Maryland in Baltimore. Eighty-four-year-old Chief Justice Taney, the Circuit Justice, granted the writ and directed the commanding officer at Fort McHenry, George Cadwalader, to bring Merryman before the court.[41] When Cadwalader failed to do so, Taney, without hearing argument from counsel, issued an opinion holding that only Congress had the authority to suspend the writ.[42] Taney also suggested in his opinion that, because Merryman was "not subject to the rules and articles of war," he could be detained and tried only by civilian authorities. Taney did not explain, however, why someone who had allegedly engaged in sabotage designed to impede the movement of troops during a war could not be prosecuted by the military for violating the laws of war.

Despite Taney's decision, the military did not immediately release Merryman, although he was eventually released on bail and was never

---

[39] See James M. McPherson, *Battle Cry of Freedom: The Civil War Era* 285 (1988); Dean Sprague, *Freedom Under Lincoln* 9 (1965).

[40] See Message to Winfield Scott (April 27, 1861), *in* 4 *The Collected Works of Abraham Lincoln* 347 (Roy P. Basler, ed. 1953). Using a combination of rail and naval transportation, the military line ran through Annapolis, Maryland, bypassing Baltimore.

[41] For a description of the proceedings in *Merryman*, see Carl B. Swisher, *History of the Supreme Court: The Taney Period 1836–64* 844–50 (1974). Referring to this case, Taney reportedly told the mayor of Baltimore, "I am an old man, a very old man, but perhaps I was preserved for this occasion."

[42] See Ex parte Merryman, 17 F.Cas. 144 (Case No. 9, 487) (C.C.D. Md. 1861). Taney noted that the habeas corpus suspension clause is located in Article I of the Constitution, which "is devoted to the legislative department of the United States, and has not the slightest reference to the executive department." 17 F.Cas. at 148.

tried on any charges, in part because Taney used his authority as Circuit Justice to prevent the case from coming to trial. In his address to the special session of Congress on July 4, 1861, Lincoln implicitly referred to the *Merryman* decision and famously asked, "are all the laws, *but one*, to go unexecuted, and the government itself go to pieces, lest that one be violated?"[43] He also stated that his Attorney General, Edward Bates, was preparing an opinion concerning the President's authority to suspend the writ of habeas corpus, which was in fact completed the following day. In that opinion, Bates sweepingly reasoned that "the President must, of necessity, be the sole judge, both of the exigency which requires him to act, and of the manner in which it is most prudent for him to employ the powers entrusted to him, to enable him to discharge his constitutional and legal duty—that is, to suppress the insurrection and execute the laws," and that, because the judiciary and executive are coordinate branches, "no court or judge can take cognizance of the political acts of the President, or undertake to revise and reverse his political decisions."[44]

After the suspension of the writ of habeas corpus in Maryland, Lincoln subsequently authorized suspension of the writ in parts of Florida, along a military line from New York to Washington, and then along a military line from Bangor, Maine to Washington. In September 1862, he issued a more general proclamation subjecting to martial law "all Rebels and Insurgents, their aiders and abettors within the United States, and all persons discouraging volunteer enlistments, resisting militia drafts, or guilty of any disloyal practice, affording aid and comfort to Rebels against the authority of the United States."[45] The proclamation further suspended the writ of habeas corpus for "all persons arrested, or who are now, or hereafter during the rebellion shall be, imprisoned in any fort, camp, arsenal, military prison, or other place of confinement by any military authority or by the sentence of any Court Martial or Military Commission."[46] As noted above, Congress in 1863 expressly

---

[43] Message to Congress in Special Session of July 4, 1861, *in* 4 *The Collected Works of Abraham Lincoln* 421, 430 (Roy P. Basler, ed. 1953). Of course, Lincoln denied that he had violated even one law, since he maintained that his suspension of the writ of habeas corpus was lawful.

[44] 10 Op. Atty. Gen. 74, 17, 21 (July 5, 1861). Troubles continued in Maryland. In September 1861, fearing that the Maryland legislature would vote to secede, Lincoln had the army arrest thirty-one secessionist members of the legislature as well as the mayor of Baltimore. *See* James M. McPherson, *Battle Cry of Freedom: The Civil War Era* 289 (1988); Mark E. Neely, Jr., *The Fate of Liberty: Abraham Lincoln and Civil Liberties* 14–18 (1991).

[45] *See* Proclamation Suspending the Writ of Habeas Corpus (Sept. 24, 1862), *in* 5 *The Collected Works of Abraham Lincoln* 436–37 (Roy P. Basler, ed. 1953).

[46] *Id.* at 437. In addition to calling up the militia and authorizing suspension of the writ of habeas corpus, another early action by Lincoln was to order a blockade of

authorized Lincoln to suspend the writ, and he soon exercised that
authority throughout the United States with respect to (among other
things) "cases where, by the authority of the President of the United
States, military, naval, and civil officers of the United States, or any of
them, hold persons under their command or in their custody, either as
prisoners of war, spies, or aiders or abettors of the enemy."[47]

A controversial case subsequently arose in Ohio. Clement Vallandigham, a former congressman and vocal opponent of the war, was arrested
by the military in May 1863 after giving an inflammatory anti-war
speech at a rally in Mount Vernon, Ohio. He was tried by a military
commission for violating *General Orders No. 38*, issued by General
Ambrose Burnside (the commander of the military district that included
Ohio), which prohibited "declaring sympathy for the enemy." Vallandigham was convicted by the commission and was sentenced to be imprisoned until the end of the war. He petitioned for a writ of habeas corpus
in the U.S. Circuit Court for the Southern District of Ohio, but the court
denied relief, reasoning that President Lincoln (and, by extension, his
military commanders) had the authority "to arrest persons who, by their
mischievous acts of disloyalty, impede or endanger the military operations of the government."[48] The court apparently did not view the 1863
Habeas Act as providing a basis for relief. President Lincoln subsequently commuted Vallandigham's sentence to banishment to the Confederacy, effectively mooting an appeal of the habeas decision.[49] Counsel for
Vallandigham then tried to appeal directly from the military commission
decision to the Supreme Court. The Court held, however, that it did not
have jurisdiction to hear the case.[50] In doing so, the Court quoted

---

Confederate ports, an action approved after the fact by Congress. *See* Proclamation of a
Blockade (April 19, 1861), *in* 4 *The Collected Works of Abraham Lincoln* 338–39 (Roy P.
Basler, ed. 1953). In an 1863 decision, *The Prize Cases*, the Supreme Court upheld the
President's authority to impose the blockade. *See* 67 U.S. 635 (1863). For discussion of *The
Prize Cases*, see Carl B. Swisher, *History of the Supreme Court: The Taney Period 1836–64*
ch. 34 (1974), and Chapter 2 in this volume.

[47] Proclamation No. 7, *reprinted in* 13 Stat. 734 (Sept. 15, 1863).

[48] *See* Ex parte Vallandigham, 28 F.Cas. 874, 922 (C.C.S.D. Ohio 1863).

[49] In arresting and trying Vallandigham, General Burnside acted without first notify-
ing or obtaining specific authorization from the President, but Lincoln decided not to
repudiate Burnside's actions and instead opted for commutation of the sentence. *See*
Message from Abraham Lincoln to Ambrose E. Burnside (May 29, 1863), *in* 6 *The Collected
Works of Abraham Lincoln* 237 (Roy P. Basler, ed. 1953). In defending the government's
actions in *Vallandigham*, Lincoln asked in a letter, "Must I shoot a simple-minded soldier
boy who deserts, while I must not touch a hair of a wiley agitator who induces him to
desert?" Letter from Abraham Lincoln to Erastus Corning and Others (June 12, 1863), *in* 6
The Collected Works of Abraham Lincoln 266 (Roy P. Basler, ed. 1953).

[50] *See* Ex parte Vallandigham, 68 U.S. 243 (1864). For discussion of the *Vallandigham*
case, see Geoffrey R. Stone, *Perilous Times: Free Speech in Wartime* 94–120 (2004); Carl B.

approvingly from the Lieber Code with respect to the difference between court-martial and military commission jurisdiction, and observed that "[t]hese jurisdictions are applicable, not only to war with foreign nations, but to a rebellion, when a part of a country wages war against its legitimate government, seeking to throw off all allegiance to it, to set up a government of its own."[51]

Whatever one may think of the government's actions in *Merryman*, its actions in *Vallandigham* were more problematic, and they were regarded that way at the time. Unlike John Merryman, Clement Vallandigham was not alleged to have participated in or planned any hostilities against the United States. Instead, he was tried simply for engaging in speech, without any proof that it was likely to cause imminent harm. In addition to raising obvious First Amendment concerns,[52] the government could not argue that such a trial fell within the ostensible jurisdiction of military commissions to try violations of the laws of war and instead had to rely simply on a claim of military necessity. In the subsequent *Milligan* case, with facts falling somewhere between those of *Merryman* and *Vallandigham*, the Supreme Court would finally address the issue of military jurisdiction over individuals who are not formally part of either side's armed forces.

The Military Commission Trial in Milligan

The *Milligan* case arose out of Indiana. While not experiencing the level of insurrection or guerilla activity that occurred in Kentucky and Missouri, Indiana was threatened at times with invasion by Confederate forces, and it was organized into a military district in March 1863. In June and July 1863, Confederate General John Morgan and his cavalry unit made guerilla incursions into Indiana and Ohio, in what became known as "Morgan's Raid." Indiana's powerful governor, Oliver Morton, worked closely with the military commander in addressing threats to the state.[53]

Swisher, *History of the Supreme Court: The Taney Period 1836–64* 925–30 (1974); Michael Kent Curtis, *Lincoln, Vallandigham, and Anti–War Speech in the Civil War*, 7 Wm. & Mary L. Bill Rts. J. 105 (1998).

[51] 68 U.S. at 249. Vallandigham subsequently escaped from the South by running the Union naval blockade and made his way to Canada, where he unsuccessfully campaigned in absentia as the Democratic candidate for governor of Ohio. He returned to the United States in 1864, and, even though that made him subject to arrest, the Lincoln administration decided to ignore him.

[52] It is important to keep in mind, however, that First Amendment doctrine was much less developed during the Civil War than it is today. *See* Daniel A. Farber, *Lincoln's Constitution* 171–72 (2003).

[53] *See* 1 William Dudley Foulke, *Life of Oliver P. Morton* (1899); Kenneth M. Stampp, *Indiana Politics During the Civil War* (1949).

Indiana also had large numbers of Confederate sympathizers, called "Copperheads" or "Butternuts."[54] Some of them joined secret societies, probably the largest of which was the Knights of the Golden Circle, which was reorganized as the Order of American Knights in 1863, and then again in 1864 as the Order of the Sons of Liberty. In addition to elaborate rituals,[55] this organization had a paramilitary structure, and Clement Vallandigham was eventually elected as its figurehead Supreme Commander (while he was still a fugitive in Canada). The Grand Commander in Indiana was a printer by the name of Harrison Dodd. The organization apparently had communications with, and received financial support from, Confederate representatives in Canada.[56]

Union agents had infiltrated the organization, and on August 20, 1864, they raided Dodd's printing shop and discovered thirty-two boxes of arms and ammunition. They subsequently arrested a number of individuals involved in the Sons of Liberty, including Dodd. In September 1864, the newly-appointed military commander for Indiana, General Alvin Hovey, established a military commission of seven officers for the purpose of trying Dodd "and such other prisoners as may be brought before it."[57] Five officers were later added to the commission, for a total of twelve. Trial proceedings were initiated against Dodd on September 17, but during the course of the trial he escaped to Canada. On October 10, he was convicted in absentia and sentenced to death.

Five other individuals were subsequently placed on trial before the military commission: William Bowles, Horace Heffren, Stephen Horsey, Andrew Humphreys, and Lambdin Milligan. The defendants were charged with the following offenses: conspiracy against the government of the United States; giving aid and comfort to rebels against the authority of the United States; inciting insurrection; disloyal practices;

---

[54] The term "Copperhead" was a term of opprobrium adopted by their critics (as in Copperhead snake), although some of them eventually embraced the term by wearing badges made out of copper liberty-head coins. The term "Butternut" refers to the yellow-brown color of one of the common Confederate uniforms.

[55] For a description of the rituals, see 1 William Dudley Foulke, *Life of Oliver P. Morton* 387–90 (1899). One of their key passwords was "Nu-oh-lac," which is "Calhoun" (as in John Calhoun) spelled backwards. *Id.* at 390; *see also The Milligan Case* 277 (Samuel Klaus ed. 1929).

[56] *See The Milligan Case* 32 (Samuel Klaus ed. 1929); 1 William Dudley Foulke, *Life of Oliver P. Morton* 398, 408 (1899). *See also* Oscar A. Kinchen, *Confederate Operations in Canada and the North: A Little–Known Phase of the American Civil War* (1970).

[57] General Henry Carrington, the military commander for Indiana when Dodd and others were apprehended, favored trying them in civilian court, but Governor Morton and Secretary of War Stanton favored a military trial, and Carrington was replaced by General Hovey, who supported the use of a military trial. *See* 1 William Dudley Foulke, *Life of Oliver P. Morton* 419 (1899).

and violation of the laws of war.[58] Among other things, these charges were based on allegations that the defendants were part of a conspiracy to seize federal and state arsenals in several states and release Confederate prisoners in those states and provide them with arms, after which they would join up with Confederate forces in Kentucky and Missouri.[59]

The military commission trial took place from late October through early December 1864. The defendants were tried jointly. Each of them was represented by counsel, and detailed records were kept of the proceedings. In the midst of the trial, Heffren agreed to testify against the other defendants, and the charges against him were withdrawn.

The government presented fourteen witnesses (including Heffren). The evidence showed that the defendants were all active members of the Order of the American Knights a/k/a the Order of the Sons of Liberty. There was also evidence that some members of the organization (most notably Dodd and Joshua Bullitt, a judge in Kentucky) had plans to engage in military activities in support of the Confederacy, including the release of Confederate prisoners. A newspaper editor who had been recruited by the organization testified, for example:

> [Dodd] said that arrangements had been made to release the prisoners on Johnson's Island; at Camp Chase, near Columbus, Ohio; at Camp Morton, and also at Camp Douglas, and that the prisoners at Camp Douglas, after their release, were to go over and release those at Rock Island. At the same time there was to be an uprising at Louisville, at which the Government stores, etc., were to be seized.[60]

In addition, there was at least hearsay evidence that some members of the organization had communicated with, and received support from, representatives of the Confederacy. The former Grand Secretary of the organization testified, for example, that he had heard from Dodd that Dodd had met with Confederate representatives in Canada.[61] A government informant who had infiltrated the organization further testified that, at Bullitt's direction, there were communications between the organization and Confederate guerillas in Kentucky about capturing Louisville.[62]

A number of witnesses specifically tied Bowles to the plans developed by Dodd and Bullitt.[63] There was also some evidence indicating that

---

[58] *See The Milligan Case* 67–73 (Samuel Klaus ed. 1929).

[59] *See id.* at 69.

[60] *Id.* at 293.

[61] *Id.* at 276.

[62] *Id.* at 316.

[63] *See, e.g., id.* at 293, 304, 306, 316–18, 334–35. There was also testimony that Bowles, Dodd, Bullitt, and others worked to develop "Greek fire"—an incendiary device containing

Horsey had been involved in plans to overthrow the state government of Indiana by, among other things, assassinating Governor Morton.[64] The evidence against Humphreys and Milligan was less direct and primarily consisted of testimony that they had both received military titles in the organization and had been present at meetings at which military plans may have been discussed. There was more mitigating evidence, however, with respect to Humphreys. Heffren testified, for example, that Humphreys had advised him to quit the organization and that Humphreys "was for his country right or wrong, and for the Constitution as it was."[65] Another witness testified that Humphreys had "said he had not understood that it was a military organization; and as soon as he learned what were the purposes of the organization, he said he would have nothing more to do with it."[66]

The military commission found each of the defendants guilty on all charges. It sentenced Bowles, Milligan, and Horsey to be hanged, but sentenced Humphreys only to imprisonment with hard labor during the rest of the war. General Hovey approved the sentences, except that he commuted Humphreys' sentence to parole on the ground that "the evidence does not show that the said Andrew Humphreys took any active part or committed any overt acts which were calculated to incite an insurrection or aid the conspiracy."[67] There is some evidence that Lincoln was inclined to commute the death sentences, but he was assassinated before this could occur.[68] President Andrew Johnson subsequently approved the sentences and directed that the executions be carried out on May 19, 1865. As discussed below, Johnson had earlier that month directed that persons implicated in Lincoln's assassination be tried by military commission.

On May 10, 1865, the three prisoners filed petitions for writs of habeas corpus with the Circuit Court for the District of Indiana, in Indianapolis. Their cases were heard by Judge David McDonald, the federal district judge for Indiana, and Justice David Davis of the Su-

---

a highly flammable oil—that would be used for the destruction of government property. *See id.* at 305–07; *see also id.* at 356–58.

[64] *See id.* at 283–85, 286–87.

[65] *Id.* at 348.

[66] *Id.* at 401.

[67] 2:8 *War of the Rebellion: A Compilation of the Official Records of the Union and Confederate Armies* 11 (1899).

[68] *See* Charles Fairman, *History of the Supreme Court: Reconstruction and Reunion, 1864–88* 197 (1971); *The Milligan Case* 39 (Samuel Klaus ed. 1929); Frank Klement, *The Indianapolis Treason Trials and Ex parte Milligan*, in *American Political Trials* 108 (Michael Belknap ed., 1994).

preme Court. The two judges subsequently stated that they had opposing
views on several questions: (1) Should the writs of habeas corpus be
issued? (2) Should the petitioners be discharged? and (3) Did the military
commission have jurisdiction to try them? Pursuant to a jurisdictional
statute in place at the time, the judges certified these three questions to
the Supreme Court.[69] In the meantime, President Johnson (at the urging
of Governor Morton) had commuted the sentences of the three petitioners to life imprisonment with hard labor.

Arguments before the Supreme Court

The *Milligan* case was heard by the Supreme Court in the spring of
1866. There were nine Justices sitting on the Court, although, pursuant
to an 1863 statute, there were ten positions on the Court at the time.
Five of the nine Justices then sitting (Chief Justice Salmon Chase,
Justice David Davis, Justice Stephen Field, Justice Samuel Miller, and
Justice Noah Swayne) had been appointed to the Court by President
Lincoln. Chase, who had served as Secretary of the Treasury under
Lincoln, had replaced Taney, who died in 1864.

The lawyers for the government were James Speed, a Kentucky
lawyer and state legislator whom Lincoln had appointed as Attorney
General in 1864 (replacing Edward Bates); Benjamin Butler, a Massachusetts lawyer and state legislator who had served as an officer in the
army and had engaged in controversial actions in New Orleans that
earned him the nickname "the Beast," and who would later be elected to
the U.S. House of Representatives and become Governor of Massachusetts; and Henry Stanbery, a former Ohio attorney general who would
later serve as Attorney General under President Johnson. The lawyers
for the petitioners were David Dudley Field, a New York lawyer and law
reformer and the older brother of then-sitting Justice Stephen Field;
Jeremiah Black, a Pennsylvania lawyer who had been a judge on the
Pennsylvania Supreme Court and had served as Attorney General under
President Buchanan; and James Garfield, who had served as an officer in
the army and was at the time of the case a member of the House of
Representatives, and who would go on to become President (and, like
Lincoln, be assassinated). According to most accounts, the petitioners
had a stronger team of lawyers than did the government.[70]

By modern standards, the briefs in the Supreme Court are surprisingly short—eight pages for the petitioners and fifteen pages for the
government. At that time, the Court placed much more emphasis on oral

---

[69] *See* 2 Stat. 156, 159, § 6 (1802).

[70] *See, e.g.*, Charles Fairman, *History of the Supreme Court: Reconstruction and
Reunion, 1864–88* 201–04 (1971); William H. Rehnquist, *All the Laws But One: Civil
Liberties in Wartime* 119–20 (1998).

argument than it does today, and it allowed counsel to argue the
Milligan case for more than six days, during the period from March 5–
13, 1866. The arguments were held in what formerly had been the
Senate chamber of the Capitol, which the Supreme Court occupied from
1860 until it moved into its current building in 1935.

In both its brief and oral argument, the government emphasized a
purported link between martial law and the use of military commissions,
asserting that military commissions were proper to try "not offenses
against military law by soldiers and sailors, nor breaches of the common
laws of war by belligerents, but the quality of the acts which are the
proper subject of restraint by martial law."[71] Strangely, given the number of military commission cases in the Civil War based on alleged
violations of the laws of war, the government asserted that "[i]nfractions
of the laws of war can only be punished or remedied by retaliation,
negotiation, or an appeal to the opinion of nations."[72] In addition to
foregoing what was probably its strongest argument for the use of the
commission in this case, the government also made sweeping claims
about Executive authority during wartime. Similar to the argument
made by Edward Bates to justify Lincoln's unilateral suspension of the
writ of habeas corpus, the government argued that, after the start of a
war, the President "is the sole judge of the exigencies, necessities, and
duties of the occasion, their extent and duration," and that "[d]uring the
war his powers must be without limit."[73] In the alternative, however, the
government argued that the petitioners were prisoners of war and thus
were not covered by the 1863 Habeas Act.[74] Finally, the government
contended that even if the petitioners could not be tried in a military
commission, it was at least proper to hold them in military detention
until the end of hostilities.[75]

Counsel for the petitioners argued that the jurisdiction of military
tribunals "extends only to persons mustered into the military service,
and such other classes of persons [such as spies] as are, by express

---

[71] *The Milligan Case* 87 (Samuel Klaus ed. 1929).

[72] *Id.* Although a violation of the laws of war was only one of a number of charges in
Milligan, that was true in many of the military commission cases brought during the Civil
War. *Cf.* Hamdan v. Rumsfeld, 548 U.S. 557, 608 (2006) (Stevens, J., concurring) ("[T]he
military commissions convened during the Civil War functioned at once as martial law or
military government tribunals and as law-of-war commissions.").

[73] *The Milligan Case* 90 (Samuel Klaus ed. 1929).

[74] *Id.* at 91.

[75] *See id.* at 92. Hostilities were over by the time the case was heard by the Supreme
Court, but the government may have been concerned about the possibility of civil damages
for the prior detention.

provisions of law, made subject to the rules and articles of war."[76] They also emphasized that Indiana was neither enemy territory nor a place of active combat, that the civil courts were "open and unobstructed" in Indiana, and that the petitioners could have been tried in those courts for violating various statutes. In answer to the argument that those who assist the rebellion can be considered part of the enemy, petitioners' counsel argued that "[t]his convenient rule would outlaw every citizen the moment he is charged with a political offense[,] [b]ut political offenders are precisely the class of persons who most need the protection of a court and jury, for the prosecutions against them are most likely to be unfounded both in fact and in law."[77] With respect to the argument that, if nothing else, the petitioners could be detained by the military until the end of hostilities, petitioners' counsel argued that "[t]he answer to this is, that the petitioners were never enlisted, commissioned, or mustered in the service of the Confederacy; nor had they been within the Rebel lines, or within any theatre of active military operations; nor had they been in any way recognized by the Rebel authorities as in their service."[78]

The Supreme Court's Decision

On April 3, 1866, Chief Justice Chase announced that the Court had concluded, based on the facts presented in the petitions and exhibits, that writs of habeas corpus should be issued, that the petitioners should be discharged from military custody, and that the military commission had lacked jurisdiction to try them.[79] The Chief Justice also stated that the opinion of the Court explaining these conclusions would be delivered during the Court's next term, "when such of the dissenting judges as see fit to do so will state their ground of dissent."[80] The petitioners were released from military detention a week later, on April 10.

The Court subsequently issued its opinions in the case on December 17, 1866. All nine Justices agreed with the three conclusions set forth in the Court's April 3 announcement, including the conclusion that the military commission had lacked jurisdiction. The Justices disagreed, however, over whether the military commission was inherently unconstitutional or was invalid merely because unauthorized by Congress.

In an opinion by Justice Davis that focused on Milligan's petition, a five-Justice majority concluded that Milligan could not constitutionally

---

[76] *Id.* at 97.

[77] *Id.* at 140.

[78] *Id.* at 118.

[79] *Id.* at 224.

[80] *Id.*

be tried by military commission. After addressing various jurisdictional issues, the majority described the central question as follows:

> Milligan, not a resident of one of the rebellious states, or a prisoner of war, but a citizen of Indiana for twenty years past, and never in the military or naval service is, while at his home, arrested by the military power of the United States, imprisoned, and, on certain criminal charges preferred against him, tried, convicted, and sentenced to be hanged by a military commission, organized under the direction of the military commander of the military district of Indiana. Had this tribunal the legal power and authority to try and punish this man?[81]

The majority observed that "[n]o graver question was ever considered by this court, nor one which more nearly concerns the rights of the whole people; for it is the birthright of every American citizen when charged with crime, to be tried and punished according to law."[82]

After reciting various constitutional rights that apply to criminal trials, the majority asked, "Have any of the rights guaranteed by the Constitution been violated in the case of Milligan? and if so, what are they?"[83] Instead of immediately addressing this question, however, the majority first proceeded to inquire into the military commission's source of authority. The majority reasoned that the commission could not exercise the federal judicial power provided for in Article III of the Constitution because the commission was "not ordained and established by Congress, and not composed of judges appointed during good behavior."[84] The majority also concluded that the laws of war could not serve as the source of the commission's authority because these laws "can never be applied to citizens in states which have upheld the authority of the government, and where the courts are open and their process unobstructed."[85] This would be true, the majority reasoned, even if Congress had purported to authorize the use of military commissions for such citizens: "Congress could grant no such power; and to the honor of our national legislature be it said, it has never been provoked by the state of the country even to attempt its exercise."[86]

The majority further noted that the government had not shown that it was necessary to try Milligan in a military commission. The majority

---

[81] Ex parte Milligan, 71 U.S. 2, 118 (1866).

[82] *Id.* at 118–19.

[83] *Id.* at 121.

[84] *Id.* at 122.

[85] *Id.* at 121.

[86] *Id.* at 122.

explained that Congress had provided for criminal penalties for the offenses in question; that the Circuit Court in Indiana was open and operating peacefully; and that its judges and juries were not unduly biased against prosecution. As a result, "[t]he government had no right to conclude that Milligan, if guilty, would not receive in that court merited punishment; for its records disclose that it was constantly engaged in the trial of similar offences, and was never interrupted in its administration of criminal justice."[87]

At this point, the majority returned to the individual rights protections of the Constitution and reasoned that, in using a military commission to try Milligan, the government had violated his right to a jury trial. The majority expressed the view that "if ideas can be expressed in words, and language has any meaning, this right—one of the most valuable in a free country—is preserved to every one accused of crime who is not attached to the army, or navy, or militia in actual service."[88] The majority further described the jury trial right as "a vital principle, underlying the whole administration of criminal justice; it is not held by sufferance, and cannot be frittered away on any plea of state or political necessity."[89]

The majority next rejected the argument that the use of the commission here could be justified by the imposition of martial law. While acknowledging that martial law could displace civilian law in some circumstances during wartime, the majority rejected the argument that the application of martial law was subject to the complete discretion of the Executive Branch. If this were true, said the majority, "republican government is a failure, and there is an end to liberty regulated by law."[90] The majority reasoned that martial law could not be imposed where the courts are open and unobstructed, and that it must be confined to the "the locality of actual war."[91] It was therefore improper to impose martial law in Indiana, explained the majority, since the courts there were operating effectively, and the state, although it had been invaded in the past and was threatened with invasion, was not actually being invaded at the time of Milligan's arrest.

Finally, the majority concluded that Milligan was entitled to relief from detention pursuant to the terms of the 1863 Habeas Act. Milligan could not be considered a prisoner of war under that Act, reasoned the majority, because "he lived in Indiana for the past twenty years, was

---

[87] *Id.*

[88] *Id.* at 123.

[89] *Id.*

[90] *Id.* at 124.

[91] *Id.* at 127.

arrested there, and had not been, during the late troubles, a resident of any of the states in rebellion."[92] The majority further noted that Milligan "was not engaged in legal acts of hostility against the government, and only such persons, when captured, are prisoners of war."[93] "If he cannot enjoy the immunities attaching to the character of a prisoner of war," the majority asked rhetorically, "how can he be subject to their pains and penalties?"[94]

In a concurring opinion authored by Chief Justice Chase, four Justices agreed that Milligan was entitled to relief under the 1863 Habeas Act, but they disagreed with the majority that the military commission proceeding would have been invalid if authorized by Congress. With respect to the 1863 Habeas Act, the concurrence noted that Milligan was detained under authority of the President, other than as a prisoner of war, when a grand jury met in Indiana, and he was not indicted by the grand jury. Under the terms of the Act, therefore, he was entitled both to petition for habeas corpus relief and to be released from military custody. The military commission's lack of jurisdiction to try Milligan "is an unavoidable inference" from these conclusions, reasoned the concurrence, since "[t]he military commission could not have jurisdiction to try and sentence Milligan, if he could not be detained in prison under his original arrest or under sentence, after the close of a session of the grand jury without indictment or other proceeding against him."[95]

Despite these conclusions, the concurrence expressed the view that "Congress had power, though not exercised, to authorize the military commission which was held in Indiana."[96] The concurrence noted that, at the time of Milligan's arrest, Indiana "was a military district, was the theatre of military operations, had been actually invaded, and was constantly threatened with invasion."[97] It also noted that it appeared that "a powerful secret association, composed of citizens and others, existed within the state, under military organization, conspiring against the draft, and plotting insurrection, the liberation of the prisoners of war at various depots, the seizure of the state and national arsenals, armed cooperation with the enemy, and war against the national government."[98] Under those circumstances, the concurrence did not "doubt

---

[92] *Id.* at 131.

[93] *Id.*

[94] *Id.*

[95] *Id.* at 135, 136 (Chase, J., dissenting).

[96] *Id.* at 137.

[97] *Id.* at 140.

[98] *Id.*

that, in such a time of public danger, Congress had power, under the Constitution, to provide for the organization of a military commission, and for trial by that commission of persons engaged in this conspiracy."[99] The mere fact that the civilian courts were open and functioning did not eliminate this power, the concurrence argued, because the courts "might be open and undisturbed in the execution of their functions, and yet wholly incompetent to avert threatened danger, or to punish, with adequate promptitude and certainty, the guilty conspirators."[100] Finally, the concurrence criticized the majority for potentially foreclosing Congress's ability to indemnify the officers involved in the petitioners' detention and trial.[101]

* * *

There are puzzling aspects to both the majority opinion and the concurrence. Most importantly, it is not clear why the majority chose to opine about whether Congress could have authorized the military commission, since, as the majority itself pointed out, Congress had not done so.[102] One possibility, noted with alarm at the time, was that the Court was signaling to Congress that it would restrict Congress's authority to engage in military reconstruction of the South.[103] In any event, the majority's unnecessary resolution of a constitutional issue, in a case concerning the war powers of the national government, seems questionable by contemporary standards. It is also unclear to what extent the majority opinion is directed to the use of military commissions to try the enemy for violations of the laws of war, as opposed to their use to administer justice under martial law. The government, as discussed above, strangely failed to rely on the law of war argument.

As for the concurrence, it is unclear whether it thought that the invalidity of the military commission stemmed from a violation of congressional restrictions or a lack of affirmative congressional authorization. On the one hand, its reliance on what it construed as congressional restrictions in the 1863 Habeas Act might suggest that it was not addressing whether the commission would be valid in the absence of

---

[99] *Id.*

[100] *Id.* at 140–41.

[101] *Id.* at 136.

[102] *See* William H. Rehnquist, *All the Laws But One: Civil Liberties in Wartime* 137 (1998) (noting that *Milligan* "would have been a sounder decision, and much more widely approved at the time, had it not gone out of its way to declare that Congress had no authority to do that which it never tried to do").

[103] In response to the criticisms of his opinion, however, Justice Davis pointed out in a letter that "[n]ot a word [was] said in the opinion about reconstruction." *See* Charles Fairman, *History of the Supreme Court: Reconstruction and Reunion, 1864–88* 232 (1971).

such restrictions.[104] On the other hand, the concurrence's argument that Congress could authorize the commission might suggest that it thought such authorization was necessary. This distinction between presidential action that violates congressional restrictions and presidential action that lacks congressional authorization is of central importance, as Justice Jackson would point out many years later in his concurrence in the *Youngstown* steel seizure case.[105]

Contemporary Reactions and Subsequent Developments

After being released from military custody, Bowles and Milligan were arrested based on a federal court indictment but were released on their own recognizance. The charges against them were eventually dropped. Milligan subsequently filed a civil suit against General Hovey and the members of the military commission, and he prevailed, although he was awarded only nominal damages because a statute of limitations was found to bar much of his claim.[106] The court allowed the suit to proceed even though Congress had retroactively approved Lincoln's various military actions in the Civil War, including his use of military commissions,[107] concluding that, in light of the constitutional analysis by the majority in *Milligan*, this statute could not bar the suit.[108]

Although *Milligan* is widely praised today as a landmark decision protecting civil liberties, it was highly controversial at the time. As Charles Warren noted in his history of the Supreme Court, "[t]his famous decision has been so long recognized as one of the bulwarks of American liberty that it is difficult to realize now the storm of invective and opprobrium which burst upon the Court at the time when it was

---

[104] The concurrence's conclusion that the commission trial violated the restrictions in the 1863 Habeas Act is debatable, given that the restrictions were directed to the suspension of the writ of habeas corpus rather than the use of military trials. *See* Charles Fairman, *History of the Supreme Court: Reconstruction and Reunion, 1864–88* 210 (1971). David Currie responds that, "[i]n light of the Court's familiar principle of construing statutes if possible to avoid having to find government action unconstitutional ... Chase's position seems entirely reasonable." David P. Currie, *The Constitution in the Supreme Court: The First Hundred Years, 1789–1888* 291 n.25 (1985). The constitutional avoidance principle, however, is usually applied in order to avoid finding that a statute is unconstitutional, not as a basis for construing an otherwise valid statute to prohibit unconstitutional action by the Executive.

[105] *See* Youngstown Sheet & Tube Co. v. Sawyer, 343 U.S. 579, 635–38 (1952) (Jackson, J., concurring). For more on *Youngstown*, see Chapter 7 in this volume.

[106] *See* Milligan v. Hovey, 17 F.Cas. 380 (C.C.D. Ind. 1871).

[107] *See* 14 Stat. 432–33 (1867).

[108] *See* 17 F.Cas. at 381 ("If an act is prohibited by the constitution, and it is beyond the power of congress to authorize it, then it may be said the wrong done by the act is not subject to complete indemnity by congress, because then the prohibition of the constitution to protect private rights would be without effect.").

first made public."[109] Editorials in major Republican newspapers accused the Court of undermining the Union, and they commonly compared the decision to the infamous 1857 *Dred Scott* decision, in which the Supreme Court had held that Congress lacked the constitutional authority to prohibit slavery in the federal territories.[110] The *New York Times*, for example, criticized the majority opinion in *Milligan* for having thrown "the great weight of its influence into the scale of those who assailed the Union, and step after step impugned the constitutionality of nearly every thing that was done to uphold it."[111] The *New York Herald* caustically stated that "[t]his constitutional twaddle of Mr. Justice Davis will no more stand the fire of public opinion than the *Dred Scott* decision."[112] Scholarly opinion was also critical. The new *American Law Review*, while condemning the harsh criticism of the Court as disrespectful to the institution, nevertheless expressed the view that the Justices had "failed in their duty" by discussing an issue that was not presented by the case.[113] Democratic and Southern newspapers, by contrast, generally applauded the decision.[114]

The fears of Radical Republicans that *Milligan* would undermine Reconstruction appeared to have been quickly realized when President Johnson and some lower court judges started relying on *Milligan* to cancel military trials in the South.[115] Concerned that Johnson might appoint Justices who would further limit congressional power, Congress subsequently reduced the number of positions on the Court from ten to seven.[116] It also restricted the Court's appellate jurisdiction, a restriction applied by the Court in *Ex parte McCardle*.[117] In that case, McCardle, a

---

[109] 3 Charles Warren, *The Supreme Court in United States History, 1856–1918* 149–50 (1922) (reprinted in 1999 by Beard Books).

[110] *See* Dred Scott v. Sandford, 60 U.S. 393 (1857). For a detailed discussion of *Dred Scott*, see Carl B. Swisher, *History of the Supreme Court: The Taney Period 1836–64* ch. 24 (1974); Don E. Fehrenbacher, *The Dred Scott Case: Its Significance in American Law and Politics* (2001).

[111] *Trials by Military Commissions—The Supreme Court Decision*, N.Y. Times, Jan. 3, 1867 at 4.

[112] N.Y. Herald, Jan. 2, 8, 1867 (quoted in 3 Charles Warren, *The Supreme Court in United States History, 1856–1918* 154 (1922) (reprinted in 1999 by Beard Books)).

[113] *See* Summary of Events, *Milligan's Case*, 1 Am. L. Rev. 572, 573 (1867).

[114] The Richmond Enquirer, for example, praised the decision. *See* Mark E. Neely, Jr., *The Fate of Liberty: Abraham Lincoln and Civil Liberties* 176 (1991).

[115] *See* 3 Charles Warren, *The Supreme Court in United States History, 1856–1918* 164–65 (1922) (reprinted in 1999 by Beard Books).

[116] *See* 14 Stat. 209, § 1 (1866).

[117] *See* 15 Stat. 44, § 2 (1868); 74 U.S. (7 Wall.) 506 (1868). Charles Fairman observes that "the needless breadth of the language in *Milligan* should be reckoned as the starting

newspaper editor in Mississippi, was arrested by U.S. army officials after writing articles critical of Reconstruction. He brought an action in federal court for habeas corpus relief. Relying on *Milligan,* he argued that the Military Reconstruction Act, which allowed trials of civilians by military courts in the South even though the civil courts were open, was unconstitutional. The Circuit Court denied relief, and McCardle appealed to the Supreme Court. Soon after his case was argued, Congress (over President Johnson's veto) repealed a recent statute that had specifically authorized appeals to the Supreme Court in habeas cases. Because of this repeal, the Supreme Court dismissed the appeal for lack of jurisdiction.[118]

Notwithstanding *Milligan* and Johnson's initial reliance on it, military commissions were used extensively during Reconstruction. Mark Neely reports that "[f]rom the end of April 1865 to January 1, 1869, another 1,435 such [military commission] trials occurred—and still more in 1869 and 1870."[119] These commissions were often used to try what we would today call acts of terrorism—organized violence by groups such as the Ku Klux Klan against blacks, unionists, federal officials, and troops.[120] In fact, the federal commander in Louisiana and Texas during Reconstruction, Philip Sheridan, in looking back on this period, specifically used the word "terrorism."[121] Although some people today consider military commissions inherently antithetical to civil liberties, in the context of Reconstruction they were used to protect civil liberties—in particular, the civil liberties of the newly-freed slaves.

---

point in the sequence of actions and reactions that led to the statute of March 27, 1868, whereby Congress took away the Court's jurisdiction in *Ex parte McCardle*, deliberately to forestall a decision on the constitutionality of the Reconstruction Acts." Charles Fairman, *History of the Supreme Court: Reconstruction and Reunion, 1864–88* 237 (1971).

[118] *See* Charles Fairman, *History of the Supreme Court: Reconstruction and Reunion, 1864–88* ch. 10 (1971). While this case was pending before the Supreme Court, Chief Justice Chase was presiding over congressional impeachment proceedings against President Johnson. In a subsequent decision, the Court held that the repeal of the Court's ability to review habeas cases by appeal had not eliminated the Court's ability to hear habeas cases under a different jurisdictional provision. *See* Ex parte Yerger, 75 U.S. (8 Wall.) 85 (1869).

[119] Mark E. Neely, Jr., *The Fate of Liberty: Abraham Lincoln and Civil Liberties* 176–77 (1991). *See also* Detlev F. Vagts, *Military Commissions: A Concise History*, 101 Am. J. Int'l L. 35, 39–41 (2007).

[120] *See* Detlev F. Vagts, *Military Commissions: The Forgotten Reconstruction Chapter*, 23 Am. U. Int'l L. Rev. 231 (2008).

[121] *See* Philip Sheridan, Personal Memoirs of Philip Sheridan 262 (1881, reprinted 1999) ("Therefore, when outrages and murders grew frequent, and the aid of military power was an absolute necessity for the protection of life, I employed it unhesitatingly, the guilty parties being brought to trial before military commissions and for a time at least, there occurred a halt in the march of terrorism inaugurated by the people whom [President] Johnson had deluded.").

The Lincoln Assassination Trial

The *Milligan* case was decided against the backdrop of a military commission trial of the individuals implicated in the assassination of President Lincoln. Lincoln was shot by John Wilkes Booth on the night of April 14, 1865, while attending a play at Ford's Theatre in Washington, D.C., and died the next morning. That same night, Booth's co-conspirators attempted to assassinate the Secretary of State, William Seward, and they also had plans to assassinate both the Vice–President, Andrew Johnson, and General Ulysses S. Grant, although those plans were not carried out. By the time of these events, Robert E. Lee had already surrendered his forces in Appomattox, and the Confederacy was effectively defeated, although General Joseph Johnston's surrender in North Carolina (with a larger army than Lee's) was still a couple of weeks away and there were also fears that the Confederacy might resort to guerilla warfare. Booth was subsequently killed by Union soldiers after being cornered on a farm in Virginia, but the government arrested eight other individuals in connection with the assassination, including Samuel Mudd, a doctor who knew Booth and had set his broken leg after the assassination, and who had misled authorities when they were searching for Booth.[122]

President Johnson decided to have the Lincoln conspirators tried by a nine-member military commission, and the trial took place during May and June 1865. There was substantial debate among the lawyers involved in the trial over whether the military commission properly had jurisdiction to hear the case.[123] Attorney General James Speed subsequently issued an opinion in support of the commission's jurisdiction.[124] In his opinion, Speed described two types of enemies: "[o]pen, active participants in hostilities," and "[s]ecret, but active participants, as spies, brigands, bushwackers, jayhawkers, war rebels, and assassins."[125] He reasoned that, just as the laws of war allow for the use of military commissions to try open, active enemies, they allow for the use of such

---

[122] For detailed accounts of the assassination and the subsequent search for Booth and his co-conspirators, see Michael W. Kauffman, *American Brutus: John Wilkes Booth and the Lincoln Conspiracies* (2004); Edward Steers, Jr., *Blood on the Moon: The Assassination of Abraham Lincoln* (2001); James L. Swanson, *Manhunt: The 12–Day Chase for Lincoln's Killer* (2006). Another alleged conspirator, John Surratt, was captured in Egypt in 1866 and was tried in a civilian court. The trial ended in a hung jury, and the government eventually dropped all charges against him.

[123] *See The Trial: The Assassination of President Lincoln and the Trial of the Conspirators* 251–67, 351–72 (Edward Steers ed., 2003). During the trial, the government introduced into evidence the Lieber Code. *See id.* at 243–44.

[124] *See* Opinion of Hon. James Speed, *Military Commissions*, 11 Op. Atty. Gen. 297 (July 1865).

[125] *Id.* at 9.

commissions to try secret, active enemies. The mere fact that the civil courts are operating, he further argued, is no barrier to such a trial:

> The civil courts have no more right to prevent the military, in time of war, from trying an offender against the laws of war than they have a right to interfere with and prevent a battle. A battle may be lawfully fought in the very view and presence of a court; so a spy, a bandit, or other offender against the law of war may be tried, and tried lawfully, when and where the civil courts are open and transacting the usual business.[126]

As discussed above, in subsequently arguing the *Milligan* case, for some reason neither Speed nor the other lawyers representing the government made this law of war argument.[127]

All of the Lincoln conspirators were found guilty.[128] Four of them were sentenced to death and were quickly executed. The four others, including Mudd, were sentenced to imprisonment at Fort Jefferson on the Dry Tortugas islands off the coast of Florida. Shortly after *Milligan* was decided, Mudd invoked the decision in petitioning for a writ of habeas corpus. In denying the petition, the federal district court in Florida reasoned that, unlike in *Milligan*, the petitioners in this case had been tried for a military offense.[129] The court observed that the President was assassinated "not from private animosity, nor any other reason than a desire to impair the effectiveness of military operations, and enable the rebellion to establish itself into a Government" and that "the act was committed in a fortified city, which had been invaded during the war, and to the northward as well as the southward of which battles had many times been fought; which was the headquarters of all the armies of the United States, from which daily and hourly went military orders." President Johnson subsequently pardoned Mudd as a result of assistance

---

[126] *Id.* at 31–32.

[127] Benjamin Butler appears to have played a lead role in formulating the government's approach to the merits in *Milligan*. *See The Milligan Case* 84 n.* (Samuel Klaus ed. 1929) (indicating that Stanbery argued only the jurisdictional issues); *id.* at 209 (indicating that Butler presented the reply argument for the government).

[128] For a transcript of the proceedings and discussions of the trial, see *The Trial: The Assassination of President Lincoln and the Trial of the Conspirators* (Edward Steers ed., 2003) (reprinting transcript published by Benn Pitman in 1865).

[129] *See* Ex parte Mudd, 17 F.Cas. 954 (S.D. Fla. 1868), authenticated copy available in Westlaw. More than a century later, Mudd's grandson and great-grandson made an effort to have the military commission decision overturned with respect to Mudd, arguing (based on *Milligan*) that the commission had lacked jurisdiction to try him. The Secretary of the Army rejected this argument, and the federal district court in Washington, D.C. held that the Secretary's decision was not arbitrary, capricious, or not in accordance with law for purposes of the Administrative Procedure Act. *See* Mudd v. Caldera, 134 F. Supp. 2d 138, 145–46 (D.D.C. 2001), *appeal dismissed*, Mudd v. White, 309 F.3d 819 (D.C. Cir. 2002).

he provided to medical officers during an epidemic of yellow fever at the Florida prison.[130]

Subsequent Supreme Court Discussions of Milligan

The Supreme Court did not have occasion to review the *Milligan* precedent in any detail until the *Ex parte Quirin* case decided during World War II.[131] In *Quirin*, eight agents of Nazi Germany, all of whom had previous ties to the United States and two of whom may have been U.S. citizens, had surreptitiously entered the United States with plans to commit acts of sabotage. After they were arrested, the saboteurs were tried by a military commission and a number of them were sentenced to death.[132]

The Court in *Quirin* held that the military commission trial was valid. The Court reasoned that "[a]n important incident to the conduct of war is the adoption of measures by the military command not only to repel and defeat the enemy, but to seize and subject to disciplinary measures those enemies who in their attempt to thwart or impede our military effort have violated the law of war."[133] The Court further reasoned that it was unnecessary in this case to determine the extent to which the President acting alone had the power to create military commissions, because the Court found that, in the 1916 Articles of War, Congress had authorized the establishment of such commissions to try violations of the laws of war.[134]

---

[130] A military commission was also used in 1865 to conduct a war crimes trial of Henry Wirz, the commandant of the prisoner of war camp in Andersonville, Georgia, where over 12,000 Union soldiers died of disease and malnutrition. *See* Lewis L. Laska & James M. Smith, *Hell and the Devil: Andersonville and the Trial of Captain Henry Wirz*, 68 Mil. L. Rev. 77 (1975).

[131] 317 U.S. 1 (1942).

[132] For detailed discussions of this case, see Michael Dobbs, *Saboteurs: The Nazi Raid on America* (2004); Louis Fisher, *Nazi Saboteurs on Trial: A Military Tribunal and American Law* (2003); Michal R. Belknap, *The Supreme Court Goes to War: The Meaning and Implications of the Nazi Saboteur Case*, 89 Mil. L. Rev. 59 (1980); David Danelski, *The Saboteurs' Case*, 1996 J. Sup. Ct. Hist. 61.

[133] 317 U.S. at 28–29.

[134] The Court's conclusion that the Articles of War affirmatively authorized the use of military commissions is questionable. *See* Curtis A. Bradley & Jack L. Goldsmith, *The Constitutional Validity of Military Commissions*, 5 Green Bag 2d 249, 252–53 (2002). Importantly, however, in revising and re-codifying the Articles of War in 1950 as the Uniform Code of Military Justice (UCMJ), Congress used language nearly identical to the language construed by the Court in *Quirin*, and the legislative history of the UCMJ indicates that Congress was attempting to preserve the Supreme Court's interpretation in *Quirin*. *See* Bradley & Goldsmith, *The Constitutional Validity of Military Commissions*, *supra*, at 253.

In explaining the category of individuals who may be tried before a military commission, the Court in *Quirin* (like the Lieber Code during the Civil War) distinguished between lawful and unlawful combatants:

> Lawful combatants are subject to capture and detention as prisoners of war by opposing military forces. Unlawful combatants are likewise subject to capture and detention, but in addition they are subject to trial and punishment by military tribunals for acts which render their belligerency unlawful.[135]

The Court also made clear that the authority to try unlawful combatants before a military commission exists even when the unlawful combatant is a U.S. citizen: "Citizenship in the United States of an enemy belligerent does not relieve him from the consequences of a belligerency which is unlawful because in violation of the law of war."[136]

The petitioners in *Quirin* relied heavily on *Milligan*.[137] In distinguishing *Milligan*, the Court in *Quirin* asserted that the petitioners in *Milligan* were not "part of or associated with the armed forces of the enemy" and were therefore "non-belligerent[s]," and it construed the statement in *Milligan* about the inapplicability of the law of war as limited to the facts of that particular case. By contrast, said the Court in *Quirin,* the petitioners before it were "plainly" within "the ultimate boundaries of the jurisdiction of military tribunals to try persons according to the law of war."[138]

The Court's distinction of *Milligan* is problematic. The petitioners in *Milligan* were in fact alleged to be "associated with" enemy armed forces, and they were specifically charged with (and convicted by a military commission of) violating the laws of war. While the petitioners

---

[135] 317 U.S. at 31. *See also* In re Yamashita, 327 U.S. 1, 11 (1946); Johnson v. Eisentrager, 339 U.S. 763, 786 (1950); Colepaugh v. Looney, 235 F.2d 429, 431–32 (10th Cir. 1956).

[136] 317 U.S. at 37. After the *Quirin* decision, Justice Frankfurter solicited the views of Frederick Bernays Wiener, an expert on military law, about the Court's reasoning. Wiener wrote three letters back to Frankfurter, in which he agreed with the Court's reasoning with respect to the applicability of the laws of war to U.S. citizens and the limited nature of the *Milligan* precedent, but disagreed with the Court's construction of the Articles of War. *See* Louis Fisher, *Nazi Saboteurs on Trial: A Military Tribunal and American Law* 129–33 (2003); Letters from Frederick Bernays Wiener to Justice Felix Frankfurter (Nov. 5, 1942; Aug. 1, 1943; and Jan. 13, 1944) (on file with author). In his letter dated August 1, 1943, Wiener noted approvingly that, with the *Quirin* decision, "[t]he majority opinion in the *Milligan* case, which stated, quite gratuitously, that Congress could never authorize the trial of civilians by military commission in peaceful territory where the courts are open, is limited to the actual facts of the case."

[137] *See* 39 *Landmark Briefs and Arguments of the Supreme Court of the United States: Constitutional Law* 16–18, 55–63 (Philip B. Kurland & Gerhard Casper eds., 1975).

[138] 317 U.S. at 45–46.

in *Milligan* were not formal members of the enemy's armed forces, neither were most of the petitioners in *Quirin*,[139] and historical practice suggests that the laws of war extend beyond such formal membership. In another place in its opinion, the Court in *Quirin* appears to be aware that the petitioners in *Milligan* were charged with violating the laws of war, but it suggests that the conduct at issue in *Milligan* nevertheless did not qualify for trial by military commission:

> We may assume that there are acts regarded in other countries, or by some writers on international law, as offenses against the law of war which would not be triable by military tribunal here, either because they are not recognized by our courts as violations of the law of war or because they are of that class of offenses constitutionally triable only by a jury. *It was upon such grounds that the Court denied the right to proceed by military tribunal in Ex parte Milligan, supra.* But as we shall show, these petitioners were charged with an offense against the law of war which the Constitution does not require to be tried by jury.[140]

This distinction is both cryptic and conclusory, since it does not explain *why* the conduct at issue in *Milligan* either was not recognized by U.S. courts as a violation of the law of war or (relatedly) was triable only by jury.

There are of course other differences between *Milligan* and *Quirin*. Perhaps most notably, the petitioners in *Milligan*, unlike the petitioners in *Quirin*, did not travel from enemy territory into friendly territory.[141] It is unclear, however, how much weight should be given to this distinction of travel, given that enemy agents could be as dangerous, or even more dangerous, if they resided within friendly territory. A better distinction may be that, unlike the petitioners in *Quirin*, the petitioners in *Milligan* were not under the direction and control of the Confederacy and thus may not have been agents of the enemy, although the record on this is not entirely clear, since representatives of the Confederacy appear to have had communications with, and provided financial support to, the

---

[139] Only two of the eight saboteurs were German soldiers. All of the saboteurs were issued German uniforms to wear while coming ashore from the submarines, however, so that they could attempt to claim POW status in the event that they were immediately captured. *See* Louis Fisher, *Nazi Saboteurs on Trial: A Military Tribunal and American Law* 23 (2003).

[140] 317 U.S. at 29 (emphasis added)

[141] Frederick Bernays Wiener emphasized this distinction in one of the letters he sent to Justice Frankfurter concerning the *Quirin* decision. *See* Letter from Frederick Bernays Wiener to Justice Felix Frankfurter (Aug. 1, 1943) (on file with author) ("Milligan, though hostile to the Union, was no invader; he was merely what today we should call a Fifth Columnist.").

petitioners' paramilitary organization. I will return to this point in the conclusion.

Milligan was invoked in another World War II decision, *Duncan v. Kahanamoku*,[142] this time for its reasoning about the proper use of martial law. In that case, the Territorial Governor of Hawaii placed the territory under martial law after the attack on Pearl Harbor, and for several years thereafter military courts tried civilians for ordinary crimes such as assault and embezzlement, even though the territorial courts were open and functioning. In doing so, the Governor relied on the Hawaiian Organic Act, a federal statute that authorized the imposition of martial law "in case of rebellion or invasion, or imminent danger thereof, when the public safety requires it." In concluding that the Act did not authorize the military trials in question, the Court reasoned that "when Congress passed the Hawaiian Organic Act and authorized the establishment of 'martial law' it had in mind and did not wish to exceed the boundaries between military and civilian power, in which our people have always believed, which responsible military and executive officers had heeded, and which had become part of our political philosophy and institutions prior to the time Congress passed the Organic Act."[143] These boundaries, explained the Court, disallow the substitution of military for civilian rule except in narrow circumstances, such as in "occupied enemy territory or territory regained from an enemy where civilian government cannot and does not function."[144] Importantly, because this case involved only the trial of ordinary crimes, not violations of the laws of war, the Court did not address the potential tension between *Milligan* and *Quirin*. Indeed, the Court emphasized that the case before it did not involve "the well-established power of the military to exercise jurisdiction over members of the armed forces, those directly connected with such forces, *or enemy belligerents, prisoners of war, or others charged with violating the laws of war.*"[145]

Even with respect to the treatment of individuals who were indisputably civilians, *Milligan* was not always applied vigorously during World War II. Most notably, it did not stop the Supreme Court from issuing its infamous decision in *Korematsu v. United States*, which upheld the authority of the government to relocate individuals of Japanese ancestry from the West Coast (and prosecute them in federal court if they did not comply).[146] Without mentioning *Milligan*, the Court

---

[142] 327 U.S. 304 (1946).

[143] *Id.* at 324.

[144] *Id.* at 314.

[145] *Id.* at 313–14 (emphasis added).

[146] Korematsu v. United States, 323 U.S. 214 (1944). *See also* Hirabayashi v. United States, 320 U.S. 81 (1943) (upholding criminal enforcement of curfew applied to U.S. citizens of Japanese ancestry).

deferred to the judgment of military authorities that forced relocation was warranted to prevent spying and sabotage. To be sure, the Court in *Ex parte Endo*,[147] decided the same day as *Korematsu*, ordered the release of a concededly loyal Japanese–American citizen from a relocation center, on the ground that there had been no clear authorization of her detention. Importantly, however, the Court distinguished the case before it from both *Milligan* and *Quirin*:

> It should be noted at the outset that we do not have here a question such as was presented in *Ex parte Milligan*, or in *Ex parte Quirin*, where the jurisdiction of military tribunals to try persons according to the law of war was challenged in *habeas corpus* proceedings. Mitsuye Endo is detained by a civilian agency, the War Relocation Authority, not by the military. Moreover, the evacuation program was not left exclusively to the military; the Authority was given a large measure of responsibility for its execution and Congress made its enforcement subject to civil penalties.... Accordingly, no questions of military law are involved.[148]

A plurality of the Court did rely on *Milligan* in a 1957 decision, *Reid v. Covert*.[149] In that case, two wives of U.S. service members stationed overseas were tried by military courts-martial for allegedly killing their husbands, pursuant to authorization from both Congress and an international agreement. In disapproving the use of courts-martial in this situation, a plurality of the Court observed that *"Ex parte Milligan* ... one of the great landmarks in this Court's history, held that military authorities were without power to try civilians not in the military or naval service by declaring martial law in an area where the civil administration was not deposed and the courts were not closed."[150] This invocation of *Milligan* is similar to that in *Duncan*—as a limitation on the use of "martial law" as a basis for having military courts try what are otherwise ordinary crimes committed by civilians. There was little question that the wives in *Reid* were civilians, or that their crimes were ordinary crimes. As noted above, however, the circumstances of *Milligan* are much less clear on these points.

This is where the line of precedent stood with respect to the military trial of U.S. citizens not in the U.S. armed forces prior to the current war on terrorism. The *Milligan* decision generally disallowed the use of military trials for civilian U.S. citizens, but it did not provide a clear test for distinguishing between civilians and combatants. The *Quirin* decision

---

[147] 323 U.S. 283 (1944).

[148] *Id.* at 297–98 (citations omitted).

[149] 354 U.S. 1 (1957).

[150] *Id.* at 30–31.

held that enemy combatants may be tried by military commission for violating the laws of war, even if they happen to be U.S. citizens, but the Court glossed over inconvenient facts in distinguishing *Milligan*. Although the majority in *Milligan* extended its reasoning even to the hypothetical situation in which Congress approves the use of a military commission, that reasoning was heavily criticized at the time and was undercut by the Court's focus on congressional authorization (or the lack thereof) in *Quirin*, *Duncan*, *Korematsu*, and *Endo*.[151]

Milligan and the War on Terrorism

There was a renewed focus on *Milligan* in the wake of the September 11, 2001 attacks, in which members of the al Qaeda terrorist organization hijacked four civilian airliners and crashed them into the World Trade Center in New York, the Pentagon near Washington, D.C., and a field in Pennsylvania. A week after the attacks, Congress enacted an Authorization for Use of Military Force (AUMF) that broadly authorized the President to use "all necessary and appropriate force against those nations, organizations, or persons he determines planned, authorized, committed, or aided the terrorist attacks that occurred on September 11, 2001, or harbored such organizations or persons."[152] Soon thereafter, the United States initiated significant military operations in Afghanistan that ultimately resulted in the overthrow of the ruling Taliban government in that country, which had been harboring leaders of al Qaeda.

In November 2001, after combat operations had begun in Afghanistan, President Bush issued a military order authorizing the detention and trial of individuals where there was reason to believe that the individual either "is or was a member of the organization known as al Qaida," "has engaged in, aided or abetted, or conspired to commit, acts of international terrorism, or acts in preparation therefor, that have caused, threaten to cause, or have as their aim to cause, injury to or adverse effects on the United States, its citizens, national security, foreign policy, or economy," or "has knowingly harbored one or more [of these] individuals."[153] As legal support for this order, the President

---

[151] For discussion of the importance of congressional authorization in the war powers area, see Curtis A. Bradley & Jack L. Goldsmith, *Congressional Authorization and the War on Terrorism*, 118 Harv. L. Rev. 2047, 2050–51 (2005); Samuel Issacharoff & Richard H. Pildes, *Between Civil Libertarianism and Executive Unilateralism: An Institutional Process Approach to Rights During Wartime*, 5 *Theoretical Inquiries in Law* 1 (2004); Cass R. Sunstein, *Minimalism at War*, 2004 Sup. Ct. Rev. 47, 77–93 (2005). *But see* Eric A. Posner & Adrian Vermeule, *Terror in the Balance: Security, Liberty, and the Courts* 46–53, 168–70 (2007).

[152] Pub. L. No. 107–40, § 2(a), 115 Stat. 224 (2001).

[153] Military Order of November 13, 2001, Detention, Treatment, and Trial of Certain Non–Citizens in the War Against Terrorism, 66 Fed. Reg. 57,833 (Nov. 16, 2001).

invoked the AUMF, provisions in the Uniform Code of Military Justice, and his Commander in Chief authority. The U.S. military subsequently detained hundreds of foreign citizens at the Guantánamo naval base in Cuba as "enemy combatants" in the war on terrorism, and it sought to try some of them in military commissions. The government also detained several individuals as enemy combatants within the United States, including two U.S. citizens, Yaser Hamdi and Jose Padilla.

Hamdi was captured while allegedly fighting with Taliban forces in Afghanistan. Although he was initially sent to the Guantánamo naval base, he was transferred to a naval brig in the United States after it was discovered that he was a U.S. citizen. His father filed a petition for a writ of habeas corpus on his behalf, and the case made its way up to the Supreme Court. In *Hamdi v. Rumsfeld*,[154] a four-Justice plurality of the Court, along with Justice Thomas, concluded that the government had the authority to detain Hamdi as an enemy combatant, as long as it gave him notice of the basis for his classification and an opportunity to contest the factual basis for the classification before a neutral decision-maker. The plurality made clear that it was deciding only the government's ability to detain individuals who, like Hamdi, were "part of or supporting forces hostile to the United States or coalition partners in Afghanistan and who engaged in an armed conflict against the United States there."[155]

The *Hamdi* plurality reasoned that, in stating that the President could use "all necessary and appropriate force," the AUMF had authorized the President to engage in the "fundamental incidents of waging war," including detention of the enemy.[156] The plurality also reasoned that individuals fighting with the Taliban "are individuals Congress sought to target in passing the AUMF."[157] Relying heavily on *Quirin*, the plurality concluded that the detention authority extended even to U.S. citizens, since "[a] citizen, no less than an alien, can be 'part of or supporting forces hostile to the United States or coalition partners' and 'engaged in an armed conflict against the United States,' . . .; such a citizen, if released, would pose the same threat of returning to the front during the ongoing conflict."[158]

The plurality distinguished *Milligan* on the ground that "Milligan was not a prisoner of war, but a resident of Indiana arrested while at

---

[154] 542 U.S. 507 (2004).

[155] *Id.* at 516.

[156] *Id.* at 519.

[157] *Id.* at 518.

[158] *Id.* at 519.

home there."[159] It further noted that, "[h]ad Milligan been captured while he was assisting Confederate soldiers by carrying a rifle against Union troops on a Confederate battlefield, the holding of the Court might well have been different."[160] The plurality also reasoned that *Milligan* had to be viewed in light of the decision in *Quirin*, a unanimous opinion that "both postdates and clarifies *Milligan*, providing us with the most apposite precedent that we have on the question of whether citizens may be detained in such circumstances."[161]

By contrast, Justice Scalia argued in dissent that a U.S. citizen who is not serving in the U.S. armed forces could be subjected to military detention only if the writ of habeas corpus were validly suspended, pursuant to the Suspension Clause of the Constitution.[162] Justice Scalia relied heavily on *Milligan*, arguing that "the reasoning and conclusion of *Milligan* logically cover the present case" and that "if the law of war cannot be applied to citizens where courts are open, then Hamdi's imprisonment without criminal trial is no less unlawful than Milligan's trial by military tribunal."[163] He also noted that the petitioners in *Milligan* had been tried "for offenses that included conspiring to overthrow the Government, seize munitions, and liberate prisoners of war," but the Court had nevertheless rejected the government's claim that military jurisdiction was proper.[164] Finally, Justice Scalia argued that the Court in *Quirin* had incorrectly described *Milligan*, which he said stood for the proposition that "[t]hough treason often occurred in wartime, there was, absent provision for special treatment in a congressional suspension of the writ, no exception to the right to trial by jury for citizens who could be called 'belligerents' or 'prisoners of war.' "[165]

The other U.S. citizen to have been detained as an enemy combatant in the war on terrorism was Jose Padilla. Padilla was apprehended by the FBI at Chicago's O'Hare airport after arriving from Pakistan, and it was alleged at that time that he had come to the United States with the intention of developing and detonating a "dirty" (i.e., radiological) bomb. Although originally detained by civilian authorities, Padilla was subsequently deemed an enemy combatant and was transferred to military custody. His case also made its way up to the Supreme Court, but the

---

[159] *Id.* at 522.

[160] *Id.*

[161] *Id.* at 523.

[162] *Id.* at 554–58 (Scalia, J., dissenting).

[163] *Id.* at 567.

[164] *Id.*

[165] *Id.* at 571.

Court concluded that he had filed his habeas corpus petition in the wrong judicial district,[166] so he had to refile it and start over. At this point, the government supplemented its allegations against him, contending that he had received training in al Qaeda camps in Afghanistan, had been there during the post-September 11 fighting, had escaped with other members of al Qaeda into Pakistan, had received further weapons and explosives training in Pakistan, and had come to the United States with the intention of blowing up apartment buildings. Based on these allegations, the U.S. Court of Appeals for the Fourth Circuit held that Padilla could be held as an enemy combatant.[167] The court reasoned that, "[l]ike Hamdi, Padilla associated with forces hostile to the United States in Afghanistan," and that "his detention is no less necessary than was Hamdi's in order to prevent his return to the battlefield."[168] As for *Milligan*, the Fourth Circuit reasoned that *Quirin* had "confirmed that *Milligan* does not extend to enemy combatants," and that, as a result, "*Milligan* is inapposite here because Padilla, unlike Milligan, associated with, and has taken up arms against the forces of the United States on behalf of, an enemy of the United States."[169] The Supreme Court never reviewed this decision because, while Padilla's petition for a writ of certiorari was pending before the Court, the government transferred him back to civilian custody and proceeded to try him on criminal charges.[170]

Subsequently, in *Hamdan v. Rumsfeld*, the Court considered the validity of the military commission system that President Bush had established after September 11.[171] The Court did not have occasion in that case to address the constitutionally permissible scope of military commissions, since it concluded that the system that President Bush had established violated statutory restrictions in the Uniform Code of Military Justice. The Court reasoned, among other things, that Congress had conditioned the use of military commissions on compliance with the international laws of war, and that Common Article 3 of the Geneva Conventions applied to the conflict between the United States and al Qaeda. Common Article 3 prohibits "the passing of sentences and the carrying out of executions without previous judgment pronounced by a

---

[166] *See* Rumsfeld v. Padilla, 542 U.S. 426 (2004).

[167] *See* Padilla v. Hanft, 423 F.3d 386 (4th Cir. 2005).

[168] *Id.* at 391–92.

[169] *Id.* at 396–97.

[170] *See* Padilla v. Hanft, 547 U.S. 1062 (2006) (Kennedy, J., concurring in the denial of certiorari). In August 2007, Padilla was convicted on several counts, including conspiracy to commit violence outside the United States.

[171] *See* 548 U.S. 557 (2006). For more on *Hamdan v. Rumsfeld,* see Chapter 12 in this volume.

regularly constituted court, affording all the judicial guarantees which are recognized as indispensable by civilized peoples,'' and the Court concluded that the military commission system that President Bush had established violated this prohibition because it allowed deviations from the procedures used by the United States in courts-martial proceedings without the showing of a practical need for the deviations. Congress responded to this decision by enacting the Military Commissions Act of 2006, which expressly authorized the use of military commissions in the war on terrorism and prescribed their procedures.[172]

Conclusion

The *Milligan* decision illustrates a fundamental tension in the law governing presidential power that is still with us in the war in terrorism. In light of *Milligan,* as well as *Duncan* and *Reid*, it is settled that, except in narrow circumstances that warrant the temporary imposition of martial law, the military lacks jurisdiction to try civilians for domestic crimes. The extent of military jurisdiction over violations of the laws of war by non-traditional combatants, however, is much less clear. In the Civil War, the boundaries between civilian and military jurisdiction were strained by the existence of guerilla fighters, saboteurs, and paramilitary conspiracies. These boundaries are under even greater strain in the war on terrorism, in light of the non-state character of the principal enemy.

If nothing else, a consideration of *Milligan's* implications for the war on terrorism reveals the limitations of judicial precedent. The extent to which *Milligan* restricted military jurisdiction was unclear even at the time of the decision, a problem exacerbated by the particular way in which the government litigated the appeal. Applying the decision a century and a half later, not to an internal civil war but to a global struggle against Islamic jihadists, in the wake of significant intervening precedent and substantial changes in the nature of the country and of the world, leaves substantial room for judicial discretion. This discretion may in turn suggest the desirability of prompting a politically-accountable Congress to regulate these important policy questions, especially after the immediate crisis has subsided.

Milligan also implicates more general questions about the role of courts during wartime. Is it unrealistic to expect courts to play a meaningful role in policing the Executive during wartime? This view was

---

[172] *See* Pub. L. No. 109–366, 120 Stat. 2600 (2006). In Boumediene v. Bush, 128 S.Ct. 2229 (2008), the Supreme Court held that the war-on-terror detainees at the Guantánamo naval base were constitutionally entitled to seek habeas corpus review of the legality of their detention. In concluding that the military mission at Guantánamo would not be compromised by habeas review, the Court cited *Milligan* and *Duncan* for the proposition that "civilian courts and the Armed Forces have functioned along side each other at various points in our history." *Id.* at 2261.

expressed most famously by Justice Jackson in his dissent in *Korematsu*, in which he asserted that "military decisions are not susceptible of intelligent judicial appraisal" and that "courts can never have any real alternative to accepting the mere declaration of the authority that issued the order that it was reasonably necessary from a military viewpoint."[173] At one level, *Milligan* might seem consistent with this view: the decision was not issued until the war was over, and the majority all but acknowledged that its decision probably would not have been possible during the course of the war.[174] If that is the most that can be hoped for from the courts, it is not much. On the other hand, the judicial progeny of *Milligan*, while hardly confirming a robust role for the judiciary during wartime, also do not show a judiciary completely unwilling to make its own assessments of whether infringements on civil liberties are justified.

Milligan may suggest, however, that courts should generally avoid broad constitutional rulings during wartime. The majority's unnecessary statements in *Milligan* about Congress's constitutional authority were heavily criticized at the time and are probably unrealistic as statements about how the law is likely to be applied by courts in times of crisis. John Burgess, who held the Lieber Chair of Political Science at Columbia University, stated in 1890 that "[i]t is devoutly to be hoped that the decision of the Court [in *Milligan*] may never be subjected to the strain of actual war. If, however, it should be, we may safely predict that it will necessarily be disregarded."[175] Indeed, as discussed, the Supreme Court largely disregarded *Milligan* in *Quirin*, *Korematsu*, and *Hamdi*.[176]

Perhaps the greatest significance of *Milligan* is symbolic rather than doctrinal. It, along with *Youngstown* and *Hamdan*, provides a prece-

---

[173] 323 U.S. at 245 (Jackson, J., dissenting).

[174] *See* 71 U.S. at 109 ("During the late wicked Rebellion, the temper of the times did not allow that calmness in deliberation and discussion so necessary to a correct conclusion of a purely judicial question. Then, considerations of safety were mingled with the exercise of power; and feelings and interests prevailed which are happily terminated.").

[175] 1 John W. Burgess, *Political Science and Comparative Constitutional Law* 251 (1891).

[176] *See also* Edward S. Corwin, *The President: Office and Powers* 165 (1940) ("[*Milligan*] shows, to be sure, that two or three years after a grave emergency has been safely weathered and the country has reaped the benefit of the extraordinary measures which it evoked, a judicial remedy may be forthcoming for some of the individual grievances which these produced, and a few scoundrels like Milligan himself escape a deserved hangman's noose—but it shows little more."); Charles Fairman, *The Law of Martial Rule and the National Emergency*, 55 Harv. L. Rev. 1253, 1287 (1942) ("If the problem were to arise today it seems fair to assume that the Supreme Court would not hold to the letter of Justice Davis' opinion."); Clinton Rossiter, *The Supreme Court and the Commander in Chief* 35, 39 (1951) ("No justice has ever altered his opinion in a case of liberty against authority because counsel for liberty recited *Ex parte Milligan*.... [T]he law of the Constitution is what Lincoln did in the crisis, and not what the Court said later.").

dential counterweight to claims of unlimited government authority in wartime. Its insistence that "[t]he Constitution of the United States is a law for rulers and people, equally in war and in peace,"[177] even if overly idealistic, may provide courts with support, if not for blocking government action, then at least for insisting on procedural limitations or clear congressional authorization.*

---

[177] 71 U.S. at 120.

* I thank David Glazier, Jack Goldsmith, Paul Haagen, Marty Lederman, Eric Posner, Neil Siegel, Scott Silliman, Geof Stone, Amanda Tyler, Detlev Vagts, and Steve Vladeck for their helpful comments and suggestions, and I thank Jonathan Christman for his excellent research assistance.

4

John Harrison

The Story of *In re Neagle*: Sex, Money, Politics, Perjury, Homicide, Federalism, and Executive Power

Lincoln appointee Justice Stephen Field, a War Democrat, was in California to sit on the United States Circuit Court. He was assaulted by David Terry, a Calhounite former judge and Confederate veteran. Deputy United States Marshal David Neagle shot Terry dead and was arrested for murder by a California sheriff. The Supreme Court of the United States delivered Neagle from jail, in an opinion written by Lincoln appointee Samuel Miller, over a dissent by Justice Lamar, former Colonel, C.S.A., joined by Chief Justice Fuller, former copperhead.

What is this federalism case doing in a book about separation of powers?

On learning more of the facts of *In re Neagle*,[1] one may ask, what is this soap opera doing in the *United States Reports*?

This chapter will begin with a review of those often-lurid events, while noting that many crucial questions about what happened were at the time, and remain today, matters of serious dispute. Those facts, and the dispute about them, are part of the background to the Court's decision. A leading theme of this chapter is that much of the background of *Neagle* consists of the long history of state resistance to federal law

---

[1] 135 U.S. 1 (1890). As if to set the theme of uncertainty about even basic facts that will run through this chapter, there is legitimate dispute whether the case in the Supreme Court should be called *In re Neagle*, as it is named in the caption in the *United States Reports*, or *Cunningham* v. *Neagle*, as it is sometimes called and which is closer to its title in the Supreme Court's docket, see *id.* at n.1 ("The docket title of this case is '*Thomas Cunningham, Sheriff of the County of San Joaquin, California, Appellant, v. David Neagle.*' ").

enforcement, and congressional responses thereto. The second section discusses some of the main episodes of such conflict in the nineteenth century. The third section turns to the legal issues and the opinions in *Neagle*. It reviews Justice Miller's opinion for the Court in considerable detail, in order to show that his reasoning was based primarily on federal sovereignty, and hence on considerations of federalism, and not primarily on executive power.

Neagle in its own day was about federalism, or more precisely about the sovereignty of the national government. Yet it is known today for another of its aspects, its approach to the power of the federal executive. Section four seeks to justify *Neagle*'s appearance in this volume, discussing the connections between federalism and presidential authority. *Neagle* is an example of a recurring configuration, in which the affirmation of federal power is therefore an affirmation of executive power, but not for reasons primarily related to the latter. The case is about presidential action in the absence of express legislation, but the main reason the Court endorsed that power was in order to uphold federal sovereignty relative to state power.

Section five treats another issue regarding *Neagle*'s fit into the larger picture of presidential power and especially into contemporary debates about it.[2] It suggests that in that case two questions that are usually separate, presidential power to use federal resources and presidential power to invade private rights, come together. Neagle was a deputy Marshal, and so if he was acting in the line of duty in protecting Justice Field, he was allowed to use deadly force. That confluence is unusual, which has implications for *Neagle*'s meaning with respect to the scope of implicit and inherent presidential power.

The Facts of Neagle, as Far as They Can Be Determined

This volume is a collection of stories, and this is such a story it is hard to know where to begin. As the tale ends in a dispute about judicial federalism, which *In re Neagle* is, one good beginning is an earlier dispute about judicial federalism that pitted Chief Justice David S. Terry against Associate Justice Stephen Field, both of the Supreme Court of California. Terry, born in Kentucky and raised mainly in Texas, went to California in 1849 and brought with him political and legal views derived from John C. Calhoun.[3] After breaking with the California Democracy

---

[2] For further insight into contemporary issues related to the particular question in *Neagle*, which is the President's power to protect federal personnel, assets, and activities, the reader can do no better than to consult Henry P. Monaghan, *The Protective Power of the Presidency*, 93 Colum. L. Rev. 1 (1993). Professor Monaghan's article is fundamental, and all who write on this topic are much indebted to it.

[3] Terry began his California political career as a member of the pro-southern or Chivalry wing of the Democratic Party, supporting the division of California into two

over sectional issues, he was elected to the Supreme Court of California with the support of the Know–Nothing Party.[4] While on that court Terry participated in some decisions that were shocking even for an ante-bellum southerner.[5]

Under the Judiciary Act of 1789, the federal courts had exclusive jurisdiction in admiralty, except with respect to cases that sought common law remedies rather than relying on than the distinctive *in rem* machinery of admiralty. State courts nevertheless decided many cases involving waterborne traffic, and used *in rem* attachment, because the federal admiralty jurisdiction was limited by Supreme Court precedents to the ebb and flow of the tide. Then in *The Propeller Genesee Chief*,[6] the Supreme Court overruled its leading precedent and announced that in America, with its vast network of inland waterways, the admiralty jurisdiction extended to all navigable waters. At a stroke, the exclusive jurisdiction of the federal courts expanded substantially.

Or not in California. Before Terry or Field came to the court, its admiralty cases had adopted an extreme states' rights position. The court had held that California courts could exercise *in rem* admiralty jurisdiction because Congress lacked power to make federal jurisdiction exclusive. After thus defying one part of the Judiciary Act, the court noted that it would defy another if the question came up: Section 25, which provided for Supreme Court review of state court decisions on federal questions, was unconstitutional too. *Martin v. Hunter's Lessee*[7] was wrong, because the federal government, a mere creature of a compact among the states, could not have power over the states.[8]

When Terry joined the court as Chief Justice he continued its Calhounite tradition. He was shortly joined by Stephen Field, who felt about Calhoun's nemesis, Andrew Jackson, the way David Terry felt about Calhoun. Field, born in Connecticut, had practiced law with his brother David Dudley Field in New York before joining the gold rush

---

states, with the southern part recognizing slavery. A. Russell Buchanan, *David S. Terry of California: Dueling Judge* 15 (1956).

[4] In 1853, when the Democratic convention rejected the Chivalry candidate for Governor, Terry left the party. *Id.* at 15. He became a Know–Nothing or American some time around 1855. *Id.* at 17.

[5] The leading work on this subject, on which I have relied heavily, is Charles W. McCurdy, *Prelude to Civil War: A Snapshot of the California Supreme Court at Work in 1858*, The California Supreme Court Historical Society Yearbook 3 (1994).

[6] 53 U.S. 443 (1852).

[7] 14 U.S. 304 (1816).

[8] Johnson v. Gordon, 4 Cal. 368 (1854); Taylor v. Steamer Columbia, 5 Cal. 268, 273–74 (1855).

in '49. In New York he had been a "barnburner" Democrat, a member of the party's wing that defied domination by the southern interest. Field's view of the federal structure was Jackson's, made more explicit and sophisticated. He regarded both the states and the United States as equally sovereign, each within its sphere, and believed that the appellate jurisdiction of the federal Supreme Court played an important role in keeping each government in its proper orbit.

Field became active in California politics as a Democrat almost immediately upon his arrival. He served in the state legislature and probably sought a U.S. Senate seat, but his ambition of organizing a new state's legal system also fitted him for its highest court, to which he was elected in 1857. Not long after Field's election, another admiralty case brought these great questions of federalism before Terry and Field. In *Warner & Wife v. Steamer Uncle Sam,*[9] Terry stood by the doctrine that federal exclusivity in admiralty was unconstitutional and Section 9 of the Judiciary Act of 1789 therefore partly invalid. Field made an extremely strained attempt to recognize the Supreme Court's appellate jurisdiction over his tribunal without holding the California statute invalid. He proposed to follow the statute, so that the Court, on writ of error, could reverse that judgment. It is possible that Field's weird approach was an attempt to obtain the vote of the third Justice. In any event, Field's unionism contrasted sharply with Terry's nullificationist views.

David Terry did not stay on the Supreme Court of California. He lost his seat in the 1859 election, possibly because of opposition from the Free Soil wing of the Democratic Party.[10] Terry seems to have believed that was the cause, and in particular that U.S. Senator David Broderick, a former political ally, was the main reason for his defeat. Terry spoke ill of Broderick, Broderick responded in kind, and the two set out to settle their differences as men of honor did in California in the 1850s.[11] Broderick's pistol went off too early, Terry did not miss, and Broderick died a few days later of the wound.[12] He was said at the time to have pinned the blame on pro-slavery forces with his dying breath, and so became a martyr for slavery's opponents.[13]

That shot ended Terry's political career in California. He continued his adventurous life, practicing law for a bit in the latest mining boom

---

[9] 9 Cal. 697 (1858).

[10] A. Russell Buchanan, *David S. Terry of California: Dueling Judge* 93–94 (1956).

[11] *Id.* at 91–102.

[12] Buchanan describes the duel and discusses the continuing disputes about just what happened. *Id.* at 104–07. Broderick's wound was initially thought not to be mortal, *id.* at 107, so it is possible that Terry was not aiming to kill.

[13] *Id.* at 109–10.

town of Washoe, and then in 1863 circumstances put him in the natural role for a man of southern upbringing, Calhounite principles, physical courage, and a nice sense of personal honor: a cavalry commission with the Confederate States of America.[14] After the Confederacy's fall Terry spent some time in Mexico, then eventually returned to California.[15] By the late 1870s he was once again a successful practitioner, and had regained enough political credibility to play a role in the California constitutional convention of 1878 and 1879.[16]

In March, 1884, Terry associated as counsel in the legal proceedings that would lead to his death, proceedings about events at least as tempestuous as Terry's own life. These proceedings related to William Sharon, a man of great wealth and power. He had made a huge fortune in banking and mining, in California and Nevada, and like all the robber barons had plenty of enemies, possibly for good reason.[17] In 1874 the Nevada legislature elected him to the United States Senate for the 1875–1881 term. Sharon's millions and the Nevada legislature's reputation for corruption, both in general and with respect to Senate seats in particular, suggest that there was a corrupt bargain. On the other hand, Sharon's mining wealth in some ways made him an ideal Senator from Nevada, as he had the means to represent the state lavishly at the national capital, and strong incentives to further the interests of its most important industry.

Sharon's wife died shortly after his term in the Senate began, and he appears to have spent most of the next six years neither in Washington nor in Nevada, but in San Francisco, where he owned hotels and lived in one of them, the Palace.[18] In keeping with the opacity of many of the facts in this connection, it is impossible to say whether Sharon

---

[14] *Id.* at 113–39.

[15] *Id.* at 139–49.

[16] *Id.* at 170–90.

[17] In his biography of Field, Swisher said, delicately, that some of Sharon's activities as a director of the Bank of California "had not been free from what seems to have been well warranted suspicion." Carl Swisher, *Stephen J. Field, Craftsman of the Law* 322–23 (1930).

[18] Sharon's rise to fortune and power is described in Robert H. Kroninger, *Sarah and the Senator* 15–18 (1964). Kroninger seems to me to have become a partisan of the first of the two characters named in his title, so I have been circumspect in relying on his inferences. His account of the basic facts and of the legal proceedings arising from them, however, appears to be reliable.

In addition to his opulent city residence, Sharon owned an estate that he called Belmont in what is now Belmont, California, between San Francisco and Palo Alto. His grand home there, built by and acquired from Sharon's late business partner William Ralston and now called Ralston Hall, is reputed to be the leading example of Steamboat Gothic architecture west of the Mississippi. Now part of Notre Dame de Namur University, it is on the National Register of Historic Places and may be rented for weddings.

regarded the Senate as merely an adornment to his career and Nevada as merely a means to that adornment, or whether the loss of his wife left him with no appetite for the Washington social scene.

Not all his appetites had slackened, however, and Sharon kept a number of mistresses, often putting them up at one of his hotels.[19] In 1880 he came into contact with Sarah Althea Hill, a good-looking young woman of southern origins and either high-class background or pretensions thereto. The exact nature of their relations became a matter of legal dispute between them. According to Sharon, Hill became one of his kept women, with a room at the Grand—the hotel adjoining the Palace—and a monthly allowance.

Hill told a different story after the two later fell out. She said that they had secretly married, and that she was his wife and not his mistress. This disagreement came to light in 1883, after their relationship ended and Hill announced that she was an abandoned wife, with a marriage contract to prove the wife part, and that Sharon, now consorting with other women, was an adulterer.[20] As such, she might sue for divorce on grounds of desertion, for alimony, and for her share of his great wealth under California's community property law.

Sharon sought to get the litigation drop on his estranged wife or mistress by bringing an equity suit in the federal Circuit Court based on diversity jurisdiction, seeking cancellation of the purported marriage contract on the ground that it was forged. Although he resided in San Francisco, Sharon claimed to be a domiciliary of Nevada, and hence a citizen of that state for purposes of diversity.[21] Within a month, Hill brought her divorce proceeding in California court.[22] That case is in the reports as *Sharon v. Sharon*, and as such is emblematic of this entire series of events, as there was a bitter dispute over a fact so basic and seemingly innocuous as the names of the parties: Sharon the defendant maintained that the plaintiff, calling herself Sharon, was his harlot, never his wife.

When the divorce trial began in California Superior Court in March, 1884, counsel for the plaintiff included Terry, who had recently joined

---

[19] *Id.* at 18–19.

[20] *Id.* at 19–21.

[21] Sharon's federal equity suit produced several reported decisions, the first of which was *Sharon v. Hill*, 22 F. 28 (C.C.D. Cal. 1884), which rejected the defendant's then-equivalent of a motion to dismiss. One of the issues at that point was whether Sharon was really a citizen of California, not Nevada, and so not eligible to sue Hill in the diversity jurisdiction.

[22] The first of several decisions of the California Supreme Court in the divorce proceeding was *Sharon v. Sharon*, 67 Cal. 185 (1885), which dealt with the appealability of interlocutory orders granting the divorce and alimony.

the team.[23] Testimony for both sides, and from both parties, told a lurid story, often agreeing on some of the more lurid parts. She described a process in which his blunt offer of money for her favors was rebuffed but led eventually to marriage.[24] He described a process in which his blunt offer of money for her favors was briefly rejected, then accepted within the same evening.[25]

On December 24, 1884, the state court held in favor of the plaintiff, announcing that it would grant the divorce and ordering the appointment of a referee to prepare an order dividing the community property.[26] A few months later, in February 1885, that court issued the divorce decree and ordered Sharon to pay alimony of $2500 per month.[27] Counsel for the Senator noted an appeal and moved for a new trial.

Through 1884 and early 1885, the federal Circuit Court had dealt with a series of preliminary matters, including the propriety of equitable jurisdiction and the citizenship of the parties for diversity purposes. During the summer of 1885 that proceeding turned to substance, and counsel for Sharon took depositions. Hill was often present, and made known her view of those who impugned her integrity. At one point, the court later found, she drew a pistol from her satchel and threatened to shoot one of Sharon's lawyers, former Senator William Stewart of Nevada.[28] That was the occasion when Justice Field, present on the circuit, had his first involvement in the case. He spoke for the Circuit Court in an order directing that Hill be disarmed when she attended depositions and that an officer be appointed to keep her from interrupting the proceedings.[29]

On November 13, 1885, William Sharon died. Sarah Hill was very much on his mind as the end came. Just over a week before his death, he

---

[23] A. Russell Buchanan, *David S. Terry of California: Dueling Judge* 195 (1956).

[24] Sarah Terry's testimony is described in Robert H. Kroninger, *Sarah and the Senator* 53–55 (1964).

[25] According to Sharon, the first evening they had dinner together he offered her $250 a month to sleep with him. She said no and he raised the offer to $500. She said no again and, as the hour was late, accepted his hospitality in the form of a bed of her own for the night. Less than an hour later " 'she came and crawled into my bed. Coming to my bed was an acceptance of the offer, and she continued to demand the five hundred dollars a month, which I paid her and more.' " *Id.* at 120.

[26] *Id.* at 145–46.

[27] *Id.* at 157–58.

[28] Stewart represented Nevada from its admission to the Union in 1864 to 1875, when Sharon replaced him. After practicing law, Stewart later returned to the Senate in 1887, serving three more terms for Nevada.

[29] Sharon v. Hill, 24 F. 726 (C.C.D. Cal. 1885); Carl Swisher, *Stephen J. Field, Craftsman of the Law* 327 (1930).

dictated a statement reiterating that he never offered to marry Miss Hill, that the supporting documents were forged, and that his executors had been instructed to continue resisting her claims.[30] On December 26 of that year the federal Circuit Court, without Circuit Justice Field present, took a step toward fulfilling the Senator's dying wish. In an order made effective retroactively to before Sharon's death, the federal court found that the purported marriage contract was a forgery and that other supporting documents had been forged or altered. It ordered that the contract be turned over to the court so that it could be canceled.[31]

Shortly after the Circuit Court's decision, in January 1886, Sarah Hill resolved the ambiguity regarding her last name by acquiring a new one that was beyond question: Terry. She and her lawyer married.[32]

In the state court, the motion for a new trial involved extensive affidavits calling into question the first decision, and the Superior Court took some time with the issue.[33] Finally, in October 1886, the motion was rejected and defendant's counsel, now representing the Sharon estate, noted an appeal from the denial of the motion (which under California procedure may or may not have been redundant of the appeal from the initial judgment).[34] The Supreme Court of California decided the appeal from the first decree more than a year later. In January, 1888 it affirmed the decree of divorce but substantially reduced the alimony.[35]

Terry had noted an appeal to the Supreme Court of the United States from the Circuit Court's decision of December, 1885, but the appeal was technically defective. Sharon had died by that point, and so the equity proceeding had abated and no action could be taken in it without a bill of revivor. After the appeal time of two years had run, the Sharon heirs sought revivor and an order that the Terrys deliver the marriage contract for cancellation.[36]

---

[30] A. Russell Buchanan, *David S. Terry of California: Dueling Judge* 203 (1956).

[31] Carl Swisher, *Stephen J. Field, Craftsman of the Law* 327–28 (1930); Sharon v. Hill, 26 F. 337 (C.C.D. Cal. 1885).

[32] A. Russell Buchanan, *David S. Terry of California: Dueling Judge* 203–05 (1956). David Terry's wife had died a little more than a year before, *id.* at 194, making him a widower, and his new wife was either single or a widow, so whatever other names she may have been entitled to, her last name became Terry.

[33] Robert H. Kroninger, *Sarah and the Senator* 189 (1964).

[34] *Id.*

[35] Sharon v. Sharon, 75 Cal. 1 (1888).

[36] Carl Swisher, *Stephen J. Field, Craftsman of the Law* 331 (1930). The Supreme Court affirmed the Circuit Court's decision to revive the equity proceeding. Terry v. Sharon, 131 U.S. 40 (1889) (Justice Field did not participate).

This time Justice Field was sitting on the Circuit Court when it heard argument, and he was present to deliver the decision on September 3, 1888. Exactly what happened in the courtroom and outside it that day is, of course, a matter of dispute. All parties agree that there was an altercation, that both Terrys were restrained, and that both were armed.

According to findings later made by the Circuit Court, as the judgment was being read by Justice Field, Mrs. Terry began to scream imprecations, demanding to know how much the Sharon heirs had paid for the decision. When Justice Field directed that Mrs. Terry be removed from the court room, Mr. Terry came between her and U.S. Marshal John Franks, then hit Franks so hard a tooth came out. Terry, though well into his sixties, was a very large and powerfully built man. David Terry was then wrestled to the ground by marshals and bystanders, and removed to the corridor, where he drew a Bowie knife and again was restrained. Mrs. Terry was likewise seized by the Marshals, as was her satchel, which proved to contain a loaded .41 caliber revolver. Her six-shooter had five bullets, suggesting that she was sufficiently sophisticated with hand-guns to know the dangers of carrying one under the hammer.[37]

David Terry's later account described his conduct as less irresponsible, if hardly admirable for a member of the bar. He said that he did come between the Marshal and his wife, but that he had not hit the Marshal until Franks hit him. He also acknowledged that he drew a knife in the corridor, but said that it was a small one and that he did so when he was not allowed into the room where Mrs. Terry was being held. The revolver in Mrs. Terry's satchel he did not deny.[38]

The Terrys were committed to jail for contempt of court—she for three months and he for six.[39] Shortly after the contempt order, while Field was still in California, a federal grand jury indicted them.[40] While in jail and after their release the Terrys made inflammatory statements about Field and what they would do the next time he was in the state.[41]

---

[37] Carl Swisher, *Stephen J. Field, Craftsman of the Law* 332–35 (1930). The Circuit Court's account is found in *In re Terry*, 36 F. 419 (C.C.N.D. Cal. 1888) (Field, Circuit Justice).

[38] Carl Swisher, *Stephen J. Field, Craftsman of the Law* 337–38 (1930); In re Terry, 36 F. 419 (C.C.N.D. Cal. 1888).

[39] These proceedings came before the Supreme Court when Terry sought review of his contempt citation through the so-called original writ, *Ex parte Terry*, 128 U.S. 289 (1888). The facts as found by the Circuit Court are set out in the contempt order, which the Court quoted, *id.* at 297–99. Terry's version is also quoted, *id.* at 299–300.

[40] *See* United States v. Terry, 39 F. 355 (D.C.N.D. Cal. 1889) (motion to dismiss indictment denied).

[41] Carl Swisher, *Stephen J. Field, Craftsman of the Law* 342–43 (1930).

Field, with his own share of pig-headedness, responded by stating that he would not be deterred by threats of violence and would come to ride circuit again in 1889, even though the statutes did not require that he do so until 1890.[42]

Those threats, and that decision, set in motion the final series of events that gave rise to *In re Neagle*. Both Marshal Franks and the United States district attorney for the northern district of California, John T. Carey, were concerned about the possibility of violence, in or out of the court room, should Field and the Terrys encounter one another again. Franks stated that he now took special precautions whenever the Terrys were in the court building, but doubted his authority to act elsewhere. In response, Attorney General Miller authorized him to hire a deputy who would travel with Field and provide security.[43] David Neagle, who had been present at the earlier altercation, was employed for the purpose.[44]

In the spring and summer of 1889 the Sharon litigation continued. In May the Supreme Court of the United States affirmed the Circuit Court's jurisdiction and its decision to revive Sharon's suit against Mrs. Terry.[45] In July the Supreme Court of California changed course and ordered Judge Sullivan to hold a new trial in the Superior Court.[46] The Terrys were also involved in defending themselves from their federal indictments for the events in court the previous year.[47]

Justice Field had arrived in California on June 20, 1889, after having been met by Neagle in Reno. He sat on the Circuit Court in San Francisco, then on August 8 took the train to Los Angeles for a session there. Neagle went with him at the insistence of Marshal Franks.[48] When they returned to San Francisco on August 13, Neagle had in mind that the train would pass through Fresno, where the Terrys lived. Neagle may have been informed that they would be traveling to San Francisco for a court date of their own, or he may simply have been cautious, but in any event he asked the porter to wake him when the train reached Fresno, and where he saw the Terrys board. Neagle informed Field, who by his own later account replied, "I hope they will have a good sleep."

---

[42] *Id.* at 343.

[43] The correspondence between Attorney General Miller and the Marshal and United States Attorney is set out in *In re Neagle*, 135 U.S. 1, 47–51 (1890).

[44] *Id.* at 52.

[45] Terry v. Sharon, 131 U.S. 40 (1889).

[46] Sharon v. Sharon, 79 Cal. 633 (1889).

[47] Carl Swisher, *Stephen J. Field, Craftsman of the Law* 346 (1930).

[48] *Id.* at 346–47.

Neagle asked the porter to wire ahead to Lathrop, where the train would stop for breakfast, and ask for the constable to be present.[49]

No state law enforcement officer was there at Lathrop. According to Field and Neagle, the latter suggested that the judge have breakfast in the buffet car, but Field decided instead to go to the dining room of the station. Maybe that was another instance of Field's refusal to do anything that would look like backing down, or maybe he expected the food to be better. In any event, the judge and his bodyguard sat down together at a table.[50]

Not long after, the Terrys entered. She quickly turned around and went back to the train, possibly because she had noticed Field in the room. David Terry took a seat at another table.[51] Later testimony from the manager of the dining room indicates that he was aware of the presence of the parties and of their mutual acrimony, and that he feared and tried to prevent trouble.[52] His decision not to let Mrs. Terry back into the room (if he had made such a decision and had not invented it afterwards) was not enough. After a while Terry rose and walked back down the aisle of the dining room toward the train, possibly to rejoin his wife. Terry took the aisle along which Field was sitting, so that his path took him behind the Justice.[53]

Exactly what happened next is, as will surprise no one at this point, uncertain. It seems very likely that as he passed Terry struck Field twice. How hard and threatening those blows were was, and is, one of the matters in dispute. Neagle claimed later that the blows were threatening indeed, that he immediately rose from his seat, announced himself as an officer, and shouted at Terry to stop. Neagle said that Terry then made a seemingly familiar move, appearing to reach with his right hand into his left breast pocket for his knife.[54] Whether Neagle's account was correct was also disputed, but there is no dispute that Neagle did draw his revolver and fire two shots, from which Terry quickly died. Some evidence indicates that Neagle was less punctilious than he later made

---

[49] *Id.* at 347.

[50] *Id.*

[51] A. Russell Buchanan, *David S. Terry of California: Dueling Judge* 218–19 (1956); Carl Swisher, *Stephen J. Field, Craftsman of the Law* 347–48 (1930).

[52] *Id.* at 348.

[53] *Id.*

[54] The Court gave Neagle's account, *In re Neagle*, 135 U.S. 1, 53 (1890), in which Terry struck Field two very hard blows, Neagle announced himself as an officer while calling on Terry to stop, and Terry reached into his chest area, apparently for a knife, *id.*

himself out to be, and that he simply drew and fired when Terry touched Field in what may not even have been a violent manner.[55]

Shortly after the fatal shots were fired Mrs. Terry came again into the dining room. She rushed to the dead body of her husband, in great distress. Searches a few moments later found no knife on Terry, but did reveal that Mrs. Terry once again had a revolver in her satchel. At the time and since there has been speculation that she removed her husband's knife from his body, but that remains speculation.[56]

Perhaps Terry's death was a plot gone wrong: maybe he and his wife had intended to provoke Field into an attack on Terry to which Mrs. Terry could respond with deadly force. That is what Justice Miller ultimately concluded.[57] Perhaps there was no plot, Terry gave in to impulse and struck Field two powerful blows and failed to desist upon Neagle's warning. Perhaps the powerful blows were real but the warning was invented afterwards by Neagle, who fired as soon as the attack took place. Or perhaps there really was no attack at all, just light touches intended simply to express contempt for Field or even just get his attention, and Neagle gunned Terry down in over-reaction or cold-blooded murder.[58] Everyone who once knew the truth is long gone and the existing records do not support any confident inference.

No doubts remain, however, about a crucial fact: Neagle shot Terry dead. By some accounts Mrs. Terry immediately attempted to raise a

---

[55] Buchanan points out that the hotel attendant, who was close by, reported that Neagle said nothing before shooting Terry. A. Russell Buchanan, *David S. Terry of California: Dueling Judge* 219 n.5 (1956). Buchanan also notes a possible inconsistency between Field's story and Neagle's: Field said that Terry had raised his hand for a blow, while Neagle said that Terry seemed to be reaching for a knife. *Id.* at n.6. Under the circumstances, it would be easy to mistake one such move for the other, so that whoever was wrong may have been correctly remembering and reporting an incorrect impression from the moment.

[56] *Id.* at 220; Carl Swisher, *Stephen J. Field, Craftsman of the Law* 349 (1930).

[57] *Neagle*, 135 U.S. at 53.

[58] Buchanan canvasses these possibilities, and the evidence supporting them, in a judicious manner. A. Russell Buchanan, *David S. Terry of California: Dueling Judge* 221–25 (1956). He rejects the Court's theory of a plot, *id.* at 221–22, pointing out that despite the Court's conclusion to the contrary, Terry was unarmed: when his body was examined he was found, not only not to have a knife, which his wife might have removed when she rushed to his body, but also to have no sheath in which to carry a knife, *id.* at 222; David Terry was a tough man, but it is unlikely he carried a Bowie knife, unsheathed, in his jacket pocket. Buchanan thinks it most likely that Terry did strike Field, probably not very hard, in order to insult and humiliate him, *id.* at 222. Buchanan also thinks it possible that Terry merely tapped Field with no ill intent at all, and points out that the testimony of the best disinterested witnesses accords with this version. *Id.* at 223–24. Like Buchanan, I am drawn to the theory that a proud man who thought himself grossly insulted and ill-used would strike a contemptuous blow with no intent to inflict serious injury.

mob that would avenge her husband. Neither Field nor Neagle was lynched, but a county sheriff did arrive in time to get on the train with a view to arresting someone. Over Field's objections, the sheriff took Neagle off the train at Tracy and then to the county jail in Stockton.[59] The sheriff of San Joaquin County also wired to a detective in San Francisco, directing him to meet Field at the train station in Oakland and arrest him. That detective was dissuaded by Marshal Franks, and Field arrived in San Francisco, where he stayed at the Palace Hotel, formerly owned by Senator Sharon.[60]

Later that day Sarah Terry swore out a complaint charging Field and Neagle with the murder of her husband. In response a Justice of the Peace issued arrest warrants for both.[61] Neagle continued to be held in the jail, while Thomas Cunningham, Sheriff of San Joaquin County, went to San Francisco to arrest Justice Field. Accompanied by Marshal Franks and the chief of police of San Francisco, Cunningham called on Field at the Palace on the evening of August 15.[62]

The result of that interview was a kabuki-like series of events the next day. Cunningham came to Field's chambers as Circuit Justice, and in the presence of several other judges and a number of lawyers served the arrest warrant. Field accepted it, saying to the sheriff that an officer should always do his duty. Counsel for the Justice at once presented a petition for habeas to Judge Sawyer, who issued the writ, returnable immediately, and gave it to Marshal Franks, who handed it to Sheriff Cunningham, thereby serving him with the process.[63] Cunningham made his return of the writ in the Circuit Court's courtroom, and the matter was adjourned until August 22. Pending the hearing Field was released on his own recognizance.[64]

Field had not forgotten about Neagle, sitting in the Stockton county jail fearing a mob. The Justice apparently arranged for eminent counsel to represent the deputy, and they too obtained a writ of habeas corpus on the 16th of August. Literally observing the command of the writ— have the body of the prisoner brought before the court—Cunningham

---

[59] *Id.* at 350.

[60] *Id.*

[61] *Id.* at 351.

[62] *Id.* at 351–52.

[63] *Id.* at 352. Whether all the participants were in the same room during these proceedings, or just in the same building, I have not been able to determine. Field's petition for habeas was quite harsh in its treatment of the sheriff who had sworn out the warrant on Mrs. Terry's complaint and the Justice of the Peace who had issued it. *Id.* at 353.

[64] *Id.*

fetched Neagle from Stockton to San Francisco, leaving with him in a special railroad car at 4:30 a.m. on the 17th.[65] Cunningham filed his return later that day, explaining why Neagle was in custody, and counsel for Neagle responded with their traverse, arguing that the custody was unlawful. By this point Sheriff Cunningham was represented by the Attorney General of California and the district attorney of San Joaquin County. The Circuit Court likewise adjourned that proceeding until the 22nd.[66]

When that day came counsel for Field, who had not yet traversed Cunningham's return of the writ, did so. Counsel were given five days to brief the case, but that proved unnecessary due to the intervention of the Governor of California. The Governor called Justice Field's arrest a "burning disgrace to the state unless disavowed" in a letter to the Attorney General that urged that the case be dismissed.[67] In response to this pressure, and probably to similar remonstrances from the Attorney General, the San Joaquin County district attorney moved the Justice of the Peace who had issued the warrant to dismiss the case against Field. It was dismissed, along with the federal habeas action, in which Judge Sawyer took the parting shot of denouncing the "shameless proceedings" that had made the writ necessary.[68]

Field's arrest and habeas were over, but Neagle's continued. Pursuant to the federal habeas statute, the Circuit Court took testimony and heard extensive argument.[69] It probably surprised no one when that tribunal held that Neagle was entitled to be discharged from custody.[70] Sheriff Cunningham appealed to the Supreme Court of the United States, before which the Attorneys General of both the nation and California presented argument, along with other notable counsel. With Justice Field recused, the Supreme Court affirmed the judgment below by a vote of six to two.[71]

State Interference With Federal Operations and Law Enforcement

All the foregoing is the background of the events that brought David Neagle before the Circuit Court and then the Supreme Court of the

---

[65] *Id.* at 353–54.

[66] *Id.* at 354.

[67] *Id.* at 354–55.

[68] *Id.* at 355.

[69] Carl Swisher, *Stephen J. Field, Craftsman of the Law* 357–59 (1930).

[70] In re Neagle, 39 F. 833 (C.C.N.D. Cal. 1889).

[71] In re Neagle, 135 U.S. 1 (1890).

United States. In order to understand the Justices' reaction to those facts, it is important also to know the more general background into which Sheriff Cunningham's arrest of Neagle seemed to fit in the view of many at the time: state obstruction of federal law enforcement activities. I will briefly review just a bit of this history.

America has a federal structure, and it is quite common for federal policies to be unpopular in part of the country. The War of 1812—and especially the accompanying embargo—were very unpopular in New England, so much so that some people contemplated secession. No State tried that extreme measure, but lots of people did what they could to thwart the enforcement of federal law. In particular, New Englanders resorted to a familiar tool of Anglo–American public law, personal damages actions against government officers for alleged torts committed while enforcing Congress' statutes. In response, Congress provided for the removal by federal officers of cases against them to federal court, a more sympathetic forum to hear the defense of congressional authorization.[72]

State courts hostile to federal law and policy are a threat to federal supremacy. An even more serious threat is a state legislature that acts to encourage other state institutions to defy federal law. Perhaps the most notorious example took place in South Carolina during the nullification crisis of 1832 and 1833. Maintaining that Congress had enacted unconstitutional protective tariffs, a South Carolina convention in 1832 declared those federal laws to be nullities. The state's legislature acted to implement that principle. It provided for state-court replevin proceedings for imports seized by federal revenue agents, and double damages against agents personally if they took the goods away from the jurisdiction of the state courts. Most ominously, a test oath was imposed on state officials, requiring that the support the ordinance of nullification.

In response Congress adopted an enforcement act, among the more pacific parts of which authorized removal by federal officers sued in state court. Less anodyne parts empowered the President to use military force to collect the tariff, if necessary.[73] Eventually the crisis passed, quite possibly leaving President Jackson disappointed that he had not needed to lead a military force into the Palmetto State and begin summarily hanging traitors, starting with John C. Calhoun. Much of the so-called Force Act expired too, although the removal provision did not.

In subsequent decades the main focus of state resistance to federal enforcement moved north again, as the Fugitive Slave Acts became increasingly aggressive and increasingly obstructed by opponents of

---

[72] Act of Feb. 14, 1815, ch. xxi, § 8.

[73] Act of Mar. 2, 1833.

slavery. *Prigg v. Pennsylvania*[74] was a criminal prosecution by Pennsylvania of a slave-catcher who claimed that he was exercising authority conferred on him by federal law. *Prigg*, and the state-federal confrontation that gave rise to it, were of course well known to the Court that decided *Neagle*.

So was *Ableman v. Booth*[75], which involved not only state resistance to federal law enforcement but the writ of habeas corpus. Booth made himself popular in Wisconsin by aiding fugitive slaves in escaping from slave-catchers. He was charged with violating the federal law forbidding such interference, arrested by a federal commissioner appointed to enforce the acts, and held by Ableman, the United States Marshal. Prior to his trial the Wisconsin courts ordered Booth released from custody on the grounds that the federal statute under which he was being held was unconstitutional, and then after he had been convicted once again ordered him released on similar grounds, notwithstanding the judgment of the federal court. The Supreme Court of the United States disapproved this approach to federal relations, denying the authority of state courts to interfere with prisoners in federal custody.

While the Civil War may have put an end to some of the disputes that had given rise to state resistance, it did not put an end to all of them. In particular, it did not put an end to federal revenue statutes that were locally unpopular. People up in the hills distilling whiskey without a federal license tended to be armed, producing violent encounters after which the local authorities often sympathized with the moonshiners more than with the revenuers. One murder prosecution of a revenue agent came before the Supreme Court in *Tennessee v. Davis*,[76] just ten years before *Neagle*. Relying on the removal provision of the 1833 Force Act, revenue agent Davis removed to federal court and the Supreme Court affirmed, explaining that Congress might find a federal forum necessary because of possible state court prejudice.

Thus when the adequacy of state law to protect Justice Field, and the impartiality of state justice for Deputy Marshal Neagle, came before the Court, there was plenty of history to lead to doubt about bona fides on the state side.

The Legal Issues in Neagle and the Justices' Opinions

With his liberty and quite possibly his life at stake, Neagle faced a problem of judicial federalism. He wanted the most sympathetic fact-

---

[74] 41 U.S. 539 (1842).

[75] 62 U.S. 506 (1859). The principles of *Ableman* were reiterated and expanded shortly after the Civil War in a habeas corpus case involving federal supremacy, Tarble's Case, 80 U.S. 397 (1871), in which Justice Field spoke for the Court in affirming the immunity of federal officers from habeas corpus proceedings in state court.

[76] 100 U.S. 275 (1880).

finder possible, which would be a federal court sitting without a jury. For Neagle everything depended on the facts, as the law was clear. If he had reasonably believed that deadly force was needed to protect Justice Field or himself from violence by Terry, he had a good defense. If not, he had shot a man without justification and was a murderer. While there were different possible sources of the legal rule providing his defense, they all appear to have produced the same substantive principle. Neagle might rely on the general California law governing the use of deadly force in defense of one's self or another, on the California law governing peace officers, or on federal law governing peace officers, if there was any. All three had the same content.

Therefore the facts mattered, and the facts would very much be in dispute. A California jury might well be prejudiced against Neagle. Anti-federal feelings ran high in some quarters, Justice Field and the other federal judges had often offended popular sentiment, and Mrs. Terry had a substantial following who saw her as a victim of a robber baron and of courts that always ruled for the powerful against the people. Indeed, Neagle probably feared that the longer he was in a California jail, the more likely it became that Mrs. Terry's partisans would decide to do justice themselves.

Facing a proceeding before Judge Lynch, or at best before a state court that might be hostile to him, Neagle much preferred his chances before Judge Sawyer and the other federal judges. They were likely to be biased in his favor. Not only had he shot in defense of one of them, but the Circuit Court had determined judicially that Mrs. Terry was a perjurer and that Mr. Terry had violently assaulted a United States Marshal in its courtroom. Moreover, the Circuit Court had found that Terry had tried to draw a Bowie knife in that courtroom, or immediately outside in the corridor. Neagle's defense rested in part on the claim that Terry had appeared to be drawing a Bowie knife.

Neagle thus needed, not just ultimate review in the Supreme Court of the United States, but a federal fact-finder. If he were tried and convicted in state court, the Supreme Court's jurisdiction would be by writ of error and the Court would be bound by the facts found below. Habeas corpus was his only avenue to federal court. Removal was unavailable because the statutes at that time offered it only to federal officers collecting the revenue, not federal officers generally as today (and in any event Neagle had been arrested but not indicted, so there was no proceeding to remove).[77]

---

[77] Removal at the time was governed by R.S. 643, which provided it for revenue officers. Today all federal officers may remove under circumstances like Neagle's. 28 U.S.C. § 1442.

Habeas was governed by R.S. 753, which codified the various habeas corpus statutes Congress had passed from time to time. It authorized federal judges and courts to issue the writ to inquire into the legality of confinement, but imposed significant limitations. For prisoners confined in jail, habeas was to issue only for someone who "is in custody under or by color of the authority of the United States, or is committed for trial before some court thereof; or is in custody for an act done or omitted in pursuance of a law of the United States, or of an order, process, or decree of a court or judge thereof; or is in custody in violation of the constitution or a law or treaty of the United States."[78]

Neagle's central problem was that although he had been authorized to protect Justice Field by the United States Marshal, who in turn had been authorized by the Attorney General, Congress had not empowered the Marshals, or anyone else in the executive branch, to serve as a bodyguard for a judge. Neagle thus had trouble pointing to a law of the United States in pursuance of which he had acted, or in violation of which he was being held.

Argument in the Supreme Court focused on this problem, as did Justice Miller's opinion for the Court and Justice Lamar's dissenting opinion on behalf of himself and Chief Justice Fuller. Miller upheld the Circuit Court's decision to grant Neagle relief through habeas corpus. After describing the facts in considerable detail, and taking the position that the Terrys intended to murder Justice Field, Miller began his argument by emphasizing that Field, while in the dining room in Lathrop, was performing his functions as a federal judge. His job was to sit on the Circuit Courts, and to do that he had to travel from Washington to California and within California, from San Francisco to Los Angeles and back. "We have no doubt that Mr. Justice Field, when attacked by Terry, was engaged in the discharge of his duties as circuit justice of the ninth circuit, and was entitled to all the protection, under those circumstances, which the law could give him."[79]

But how much protection had the laws given him—or authorized Attorney General Miller, the Marshal, and David Neagle to give him? Immediately after confirming that Field was doing his job, Miller turned

---

[78] In re Neagle, 135 U.S. 1, 40–41 (1890).

[79] *Id.* at 58. After recounting Neagle's killing of Terry and the facts leading up to it, Justice Miller said that the record "produces upon us the conviction of a settled purpose on the part of Terry and his wife, amounting to a conspiracy, to murder Justice Field." *Id.* at 53. As I have indicated, the existence of any such conspiracy is highly doubtful. Justice Miller not only endorsed that dubious conclusion as clearly sound, he virtually convicted of conspiracy to commit murder someone who had not been charged with, let alone tried for, that offense. Nearly everyone who learns about Terry's death does so by reading *In re Neagle*. Those who accept the Supreme Court's accounts of the facts in its cases are misled, here and perhaps elsewhere.

to the central objection: "It is urged, however, that there exists no statute authorizing any such protection as that which Neagle was instructed to give Judge Field," and that the habeas corpus statute required "that the act for which Neagle is imprisoned was done by virtue of an act of Congress."[80] Miller agreed that there was no act of Congress authorizing marshals or their deputies to accompany Justices on their circuit travels and act as bodyguards. But the view of the habeas statute that would require such explicit empowerment was "an unwarranted restriction of the meaning of a law designed to extend in a liberal manner the benefit of the writ of *habeas corpus* to persons imprisoned for the performance of their duty; and we are satisfied that if it was the duty of Neagle under the circumstances—a duty which could only arise under the laws of the United States—to defend Mr. Justice Field from a murderous attack upon him, he brings himself within the meaning of the section we have recited."[81]

Fair enough: if Neagle was authorized by the laws of the United States, he was acting pursuant to those laws for purposes of the habeas statute. But how specific did the authorization have to be? For Justice Miller, not very. After again quoting the part of the habeas statute offering relief to anyone imprisoned contrary to the Constitution or laws, he continued: "In the view we take of the Constitution of the United States, any obligation fairly and properly inferrible [sic] from that instrument, or any duty of the marshal to be derived from the general scope of his duties under the laws of the United States, is a 'law,' within the meaning of this phrase."[82] Justice Miller in the next sentence then indicated the approach he would take in fairly and properly interpreting the Constitution and the general scope of the laws. "It would be a great reproach to the system of government of the United States, declared to be within its sphere sovereign and supreme, if there is to be found within the domain of its powers no means of protecting the judges in the conscientious and faithful discharge of their duties from the malice and hatred of those upon whom their judgments may operate unfavorably."[83] The Constitution and laws would be interpreted to uphold complete and effective federal sovereignty.

For Justice Miller, more than for us, an affirmation of the sovereignty of the United States, supreme within its sphere, was very much a statement of independence from state authority. Immediately after stating the functional case for federal authority to protect federal judges,

---

[80] *Id.* at 58.

[81] *Id.*

[82] *Id.* at 59.

[83] *Id.*

Miller turned to leading cases concerning the power of the national government relative to that of the states. First was *Ex parte Siebold*,[84] a then-recent case about congressional power to punish people who interfered with federal elections. *Siebold* had rejected the argument that by providing for such punishment Congress was intruding into the authority of the states to keep the peace, and did so on grounds of inherent federal sovereignty over federal matters like congressional elections. Miller quoted passages to that effect. "We hold it to be an incontrovertible principle that the government of the United States may, by means of physical force, exercised through its official agents, execute on every foot of American soil the powers and functions that belong to it.... Without the concurrent sovereignty referred to, the national government would be nothing but an advisory government. Its executive power would be absolutely nullified."[85]

Miller next relied on a case from the same Term, and raising the same basic questions, as *Siebold*, *Tennessee v. Davis*, discussed above. *Davis* was very similar to *Neagle*, as it had involved the prosecution of a federal officer in state court for murder. In the earlier case the Court had understood the issues as being about federal and state sovereignty. It had relied on one of its master precedents on that topic, *Martin v. Hunter*, for the proposition that the general government could exist only if it could protect its officers.[86] *Davis*, quoted in *Neagle*, made clear that the states were not to be relied on adequately to perform that function: "The legislation of the state may be unfriendly. It may affix penalties to acts done under the immediate direction of the national government and in obedience to its laws. It may deny the authority conferred by those laws. The state courts may administer not only the laws of the state, but equally federal law, in such a manner as to paralyze the operations of the government."[87]

After discussing *Siebold* and *Davis*, recent and applicable decisions, Miller made clear the terms in which he understood the problem: "To cite all the cases in which this principle of the supremacy of the government of the United States in the exercise of all the powers conferred upon it by the constitution is maintained, would be an endless task."[88]

Unless it could protect itself, without relying on the states, the national government was no sovereign government. In *Neagle*, self-

---

[84] 100 U.S. 371 (1880).

[85] *Neagle*, 135 U.S. at 60–61 (quoting *Siebold*, 100 U.S. at 394).

[86] *Id.* at 61–62.

[87] *Id.* at 62.

[88] *Id.*

protection meant action by the executive branch without explicit authorization from Congress. Thus presidential power derived from national
sovereignty. Justice Miller's next step was to emphasize the need, in this
context, for executive and not just judicial action to secure federal
authority. The courts did not have the force needed for that task.
Congress, though it had the power to pass laws to do the job, had not
done so. Who was left? The President has substantial authority under
the Constitution. It gives him the duty to take care that the laws be
faithfully executed, and the power to do so.[89] "Is this duty limited to the
enforcement of acts of Congress or of treaties of the United States
according to their express terms; or does it include the rights, duties, and
obligations growing out of the constitution itself, our international
relations, and all the protection implied by the nature of the government
under the Constitution?"[90]

Justice Miller's answer was of course the latter. He read presidential
power broadly, but did not do so by reading legislative power more
narrowly. His problem, and his solution, were not about separation of
powers in that sense, nor about the relative turf of the different
branches. Rather, they were about the total authority of the United
States, relative to the states, and his expansive view of presidential
authority was designed as an expansive view of overall national authority. In keeping with that way of thinking, Miller then reviewed a series of
instances in which the executive had acted without explicit congressional
authorization to vindicate specifically federal interests. Miller's reasoning was that each such instance involved obviously desirable executive
action, so the lack of specific authority could not have been a problem.

First was the then-famous episode in which a United States warship
threatened to fire upon an Austro–Hungarian vessel where Martin
Koszta, a native of Hungary who had declared his intention of becoming
a United States citizen, was being held. Congress had never stated that
naval vessels were to protect American interests in that fashion, but the
Navy's actions were widely heralded at the time and endorsed by the
Court in *Neagle*.[91] In a domestic case involving self-starting executive
action, the Court had approved steps by the Department of the Interior
to appoint agents who would guard federal lands from timber thieves.[92]
Again, the job needed to be done, and who was to do it but the executive?
Nor were the Court's precedents limited to physical protection of federal
interests in the absence of clear congressional authorization. It had also

---

[89] *Id.* at 63–64.

[90] *Id.* at 64.

[91] *Id.*

[92] *Id.* at 65–66 (discussing Wells v. Nickles, 104 U.S. 444 (1882)).

found that the Attorney General could protect the government against fraud by bringing suit to set aside a land patent that had been obtained by deceit.[93]

The Court thus endorsed what Professor Henry Monaghan has called the protective power of the President.[94] The President can use resources available to him, including the United States Marshals, in order to secure federal interests from physical and legal threats. He does not have to leave that to the states.

Justice Miller then found that there was in fact "positive law investing the marshals and their deputies with powers which not only justify what Marshal Neagle did in this matter, but which imposed it upon him as a duty."[95] Section 788 of the Revised Statutes gave Marshals and deputies "the same powers in exercising the laws of the United States as the sheriffs and their deputies in such state may have, by law, in executing the laws thereof." California sheriffs were charged with keeping the peace, and a California sheriff would have had the power and duty to kill Terry if that had been necessary to protect Justice Field from assault.[96] It is an interesting question whether the federal statute constituted an independent ground of decision or was part of Miller's larger argument concerning executive power. The statute gave federal Marshals state law powers when they were executing the laws of the United States, and so its relevance depended on whether that was what Neagle had been doing, which was the main question in the case. Considered as a free-standing argument, reliance on the statute is question begging. If the prior conclusion about the breadth of the concept of execution of federal laws is accepted, however, the provision confirms what the Court had already found.

Miller was aware that Neagle was asking for a lot in a habeas petition. Neagle had been arrested for murder and was being held pending possible indictment and trial. If the Court was correct he had a federal defense, which he would be able to present to the state court if he were indicted. It was thus difficult to say that Neagle was in custody unlawfully, as there is nothing wrong with arresting on probable cause someone who turns out to be innocent. Nor was *Neagle* a typical case of someone held contrary to the Constitution or a statute or treaty, as no one contended that the California law of murder was unconstitutional.

---

[93] *Id.* at 66–67 (discussing United States v. San Jacinto Tin Co., 125 U.S. 273 (1888)).

[94] Henry P. Monaghan, *The Protective Power of the Presidency*, 93 Colum. L. Rev. 1 (1993).

[95] *Neagle,* 135 U.S. at 68.

[96] *Id.* at 68–69.

Rather, the question was whether Neagle qualified for a defense in a prosecution under that law.

Neagle thus was seeking to use habeas to try part of his case on the merits, and thereby to perform a function normally performed by the state courts. That required an expansive use of the writ, but the Court found support for Neagle's position in the history of the federal habeas statute. That history, discussed above, was one of "a long course of legislation forced upon Congress by the attempt of the states of the Union to exercise the power of imprisonment over officers and other persons asserting rights under the federal government or foreign governments."[97] Habeas, like executive power, was a tool of federal supremacy.

Justice Miller reviewed Congress' extensions of habeas corpus jurisdiction, discussing the nullification crisis, the McLeod affair and its statutory aftermath, and the 1867 statute.[98] He then turned to a series of lower court cases in which habeas corpus had been used to protect federal officers. These included several under the fugitive slave laws "in which the marshal of the United States, while engaged in apprehending the fugitive slave with a view of returning him to his master in another state, was arrested by the authorities of the state." *Id*. at 72. Those federal courts gave relief while explaining that they were engaged in no interference with the state judicial power.

Neagle was just the same to Justice Miller. "[I]f the prisoner is held in the state court to answer for an act which he was authorized to do by the law of the United States, which it was his duty to do as marshal of the United States, and if, in doing that act, he did no more than what was necessary and proper for him to do, he cannot be guilty of a crime under the law of the state of California. When these things are shown, it is established that he is innocent of any crime against the laws of the state, or of any other authority whatever. There is no occasion for any further trial in the state court, or in any court."[99] Sometimes the vindication of federal power required that the federal courts decide a question normally decided by the state courts. Federal supremacy required it, and Neagle was entitled to discharge through habeas corpus.

Justice Lamar, joined by Chief Justice Fuller, dissented. He did not cast the issue as one primarily of federalism, as he agreed that the

---

[97] *Id*. at 70.

[98] *Id*. at 70–72. McLeod was a British officer who led a raid across the border into New York aimed at Canadian insurgents operating out of that State. The British naval action resulted in deaths among the insurgents, and in McLeod's indictment and trial in New York, over the objection of the United States Secretary of State. McLeod was acquitted, but the problem did not go away, and Congress expanded habeas jurisdiction to deal with it.

[99] *Id*. at 75.

federal government was supreme within its sphere.[100] For him the
question was not about federal supremacy, but about the respective
powers of Congress and the executive.[101] In particular, it was about the
power of the executive in the absence of specific legislative authorization.
Justice Lamar quoted at length from Attorney General Miller's statement in oral argument defending implied and indefeasible executive
power.[102]

Implied powers were fine, Justice Lamar maintained, but the Constitution had a particular mode of organizing them: Congress' power under
the Necessary and Proper Clause to carry into execution its own powers
and those of the other branches.[103] Justice Lamar made that point
specifically about the majority's leading precedents, *Siebold* and *Davis*.
In both cases the warrant for federal action, whether of the Marshals or
the courts, was a particular act of Congress. In keeping with this
reasoning, Justice Lamar insisted that the word "law" as used in the
habeas statute referred, as it did almost everywhere else in federal
practice, to a statute of Congress.[104] Because only Congress and not the
President could make law, only Congress could provide the various
enactments, like the Force Act of 1833, that the majority had discussed
as manifestations of federal supremacy. If President Jackson had the
inherent power the majority believed in, why did he need legislation to
put down resistance to federal law? "It is a noteworthy fact in our
history that whenever the exigencies of the country, from time to time,

---

[100] "Nor do we question the general proposition, that the federal government established by the Constitution is absolutely sovereign over every foot of soil, and over every
person, within the national territory, within the sphere of action assigned to it." *Id.* at 77
(Lamar, J., dissenting).

[101] Lamar also objected to the use of habeas to present a substantive defense that
otherwise would arise in the state proceeding. Lamar pointed out that Neagle's claimed
right to discharge on habeas depended on his defense. "Whether his defence is sufficient or
not is for the court which tries him to determine. If, in this determination, errors are
committed, they can only be corrected in an appropriate form of proceeding for that
purpose. The office of the writ of *habeas corpus* is neither to correct such errors, nor to
take the prisoner away from the court which holds him for trial, for fear, if he remains,
they may be committed." *Id.*

[102] Attorney General Miller said that the President is vested by the Constitution "with
necessary and implied executive powers which neither of the other branches of the
government may take away or abridge" and "that many of those powers pertaining to each
branch of the government, are self-executing, and in no way dependent, except as to the
ways and means, upon legislation." *Id.* at 81.

[103] *Id.* at 82–83. Responding specifically to the Attorney General's argument that it was
the duty of the President to protect Justice Field, Lamar maintained, "while it is the
President's duty to take care that the laws be faithfully executed, it is not his duty to *make*
laws or a law of the United States." *Id.* at 83 (emphasis in original).

[104] *Id.* at 92–95.

have required the exercise of executive and judicial power for the enforcement of the supreme authority of the United States government for the protection of its agencies, etc., it was found, in every instance, necessary to invoke the interposition of the power of the national legislature."[105]

So much was Justice Lamar concerned about separation of powers and not federalism that he concluded by specifically disclaiming any comment on "the bearings of this decision upon the autonomy of the states, in divesting them of what was once regarded as their exclusive jurisdiction over crimes committed within their own territory ... We have not entered upon that question because, as arising here, its suggestion is sufficient, and its consideration might involve the extent to which legislation in that direction may constitutionally go, which could only be properly determined when directly presented by the record in a case before the court for adjudication."[106]

Neagle should have remained in state custody, Justice Lamar concluded, in the hands of California officials "competent and willing to do justice." Had he gone to trial on this record, "God and his country would have given him a good deliverance."[107]

Neagle did not have to take that chance, leaving us to wonder whether the Supreme Court of the United States was chosen as the instrument of inscrutable providence.

Federal Supremacy and Executive Power

Justice Miller for the Court presented *Neagle* as a case about the allocation of powers between the states and the national government, and the adequacy of national sovereignty. Justice Lamar in dissent presented it as a case about the relation between legislative and executive power. Both were right, because those sets of questions are closely connected. Because of large-scale features of the American constitutional system, the practical extent of federal authority will depend in large measure on the executive's authority to act in default of explicit congressional authorization. If that executive power is broad, as the majority

---

[105] *Id.* at 96. Lamar also responded to the argument based on the statute giving Marshals the powers of sheriffs, along lines I suggested above. "That section gives to the officers named the same measure of powers when in the discharge of their duties as those possessed by the sheriffs, it is true; but it does not alter the duties themselves." *Id.* at 98. To be entitled to act like a sheriff, a deputy marshal had to be executing federal law, and Justice Lamar could see no federal law that Neagle was executing.

[106] *Id.* at 99. In expressing those doubts Justice Lamar probably was referring to the use of federal habeas as a substitute for the presentation of a defense in state court, and not the authority of Congress to provide a bodyguard for a federal officer.

[107] *Id.*

found it to be, federal power will be broad. If it is restricted, federal power will be restricted. Because of the logic of that relationship, conclusions about one issue have implications for another. A judge like Justice Miller who seeks broad federal power will often find broad executive power in the process. A judge like Justice Lamar who finds limited executive power will often find constricted federal power as a consequence.[108]

The American federal system has two tiers of legislatures, each capable of operating directly on private individuals.[109] Because of the principle of enumerated federal power, the national legislature operates only within specified areas. That is a matter of constitutional compulsion. Problems like that in *Neagle* reflect a distinct but related feature of the system, one that is not mandatory but nevertheless is well established. Even when Congress exercises its powers, it rarely does so comprehensively. Federal statutes often come nowhere close to resolving all the questions that might arise under them, or to providing for all of the practical problems that might come up in their execution. Congress provided that Supreme Court Justices should travel throughout the country, and gave them duties that would make people angry with them, but said not a word about their physical security.

Substantive legal questions that arise in the execution of congressional statutes, and more broadly in the operations of the federal government, present a problem familiar to students of federal jurisdiction. Are those questions to be resolved under state law, under federal law as that concept is used in Articles III and VI of the Constitution, or under a body of principles that is the law neither of the United States per se nor that of any state? Today's doctrine, as adumbrated by the federal courts, combines elements of all three, although the last has become one that dare not speak its name, which is general law.[110]

In finding that there is genuine federal law that governs operations of the United States government, even in the absence of any congressional statute creating or even invoking the applicable principles, the contemporary Supreme Court has explicitly relied on the federal government's independence from the states. Surely the United States cannot be

---

[108] It is possible in Justice Lamar's case that the restriction of federal power was not just a side effect, but from his opinion there is no way to tell. Nothing in Justice Miller's opinion suggests that he cared about presidential power except as a form of national authority.

[109] The most penetrating discussion of these issues remains Henry M. Hart, *The Relations Between State and Federal Law*, 54 Colum. L. Rev. 489 (1954).

[110] The contemporary approaches to this problem, and the indispensability of some form of general law, are fruitfully analyzed in Caleb Nelson, *The Persistence of General Law*, 106 Colum. L. Rev. 503 (2006).

governed by the law of any state, which may be inadequate to its needs or even hostile to its goals. Therefore there must be background principles, including principles of contract, property, and tort, that displace state law under Article VI and give rise to federal jurisdiction under Article III. Thus they must be federal. As those principles must be capable of resolving unforeseen questions, in principle any unforeseen question, and as they are by hypothesis not a comprehensive legislative code, they must comprise a system of common law. Combine those features and there must be federal common law as it has come to be known.[111]

For those who understand common law as judge-made law, to say that there is common law is to say that there are judge-made rules governing unforeseen contingencies. Expanding the role of unwritten federal law relative to state law (written or unwritten) thus expands the role of the judges who make that law, who are mainly, and in the last resort entirely, federal judges.[112] It means that the federal courts will routinely act in default of explicit congressional authorization, and thus has separation of powers implications at the national level, though it is motivated by reasons of federal supremacy.

A close though not exact parallel operates with respect to the executive branch and the performance of functions that seem to be called for in order to make the federal government work but that have not been specifically provided for by Congress. If the United States could not supply Justice Field with a bodyguard, then either he would have to hire one for himself (which Field would never have done) or the State of California would have to supply one. In California in the 1880s, many federal judges, including Stephen Field in particular, would have regarded a California deputy sheriff as a threat rather than as protection. Justice Miller, although he did not specifically contemplate the possibility that a state officer could have been assigned to guard Justice Field, did make a point of the inadequacy of the ordinary California law of homicide for someone facing a specific threat of violence.[113]

This is not to say that questions of the scope of federal power, and of the scope of executive power to make federal programs practically

---

[111] *See, e.g.*, Clearfield Trust Co. v. United States, 318 U.S. 363 (1943) (contracts with the federal government and its agencies are governed by federal, not state, law).

[112] As Professor Bellia explains, under current practice state courts as well as federal courts may be called on to make, or find, federal common law. Anthony J. Bellia, Jr., *State Courts and the Making of Federal Common Law*, 153 U. Pa. L. Rev. 825 (2005). As the contemporary form of federal common law is federal law for purposes of Article III and the Supreme Court's appellate jurisdiction over the state courts, state court decisions concerning federal common law are subject to review in the Supreme Court of the United States.

[113] In re Neagle, 135 U.S. 1, 59 (1890).

effective by dealing with unprovided-for cases, are always about a choice between state and federal authority. Often the choice is between federal authority and nothing, as some federal functions can be performed, or performed effectively, only with federal resources that are not available to the states. If Congress has provided for a substantial number of national park rangers, the extent to which the President can expand their duties will determine whether those additional functions are performed at all in the national parks, simply because the states do not have employees on the ground in those federal enclaves.

Often, however, the choice will be between federal action and state action, and when that is the choice a policy of federal action will be a policy of federal executive action as it was in *Neagle*. When Congress' limited ability to legislate with respect to programs that it creates requires that someone else fill a gap, the choice often will be between the President and the states. A choice in favor of some national actor will, sometimes as a side effect, be a choice in favor of the national executive.

Incomplete legislation by Congress is an inevitable, or nearly inevitable, consequence of the episodic nature of federal action and the limited attention of the federal legislature. A decision maker like Justice Miller who wishes to enhance federal power will thus often advance executive power without having any particular preference for the executive, and without seeking to favor the views of the executive over those of the legislature. That is true, at least, if the absence of federal action reflects limited congressional resources rather than actual congressional policy.

Sometimes, though, a choice between federal and state power will involve a choice between the policy preferences of Congress and those of the executive. It is quite possible that this will happen fairly often, because it is quite possible that Congress is systematically relatively localist, and the President systematically in favor of expanding the range of operation of the federal bureaucracy that he heads and to some extent controls.

Congress is especially responsive to regional minorities, not only because of the Senate but also because of other structures that amount to super-majority requirements. A federal program that is especially unpopular in one part of the country, like the excise on whiskey, may have to be enacted in a weakened form (if it is enacted at all) because of the minority vetoes. One way to weaken a program is to enforce it less than aggressively. It is entirely plausible that the state officers who often sided with the moonshiners had some friends in Congress, and that the federal hand was less heavy in response because of those friends.

Presidents have different political incentives, and while it is too glib to say simply that they tend to be more nationalistic, there is good reason to believe that they will wish the functional power of the national government to be greater than do many in Congress. Although the Court in *Neagle* did not focus on this point, the question there concerned the President's flexibility in using the resources of the federal government. Neagle was hired by the U.S. Marshal, at the direction of the Attorney General, and paid out of the Department of Justice's appropriation. Although Justice Miller referred to the possibility of raising a posse comitatus when force was called for, any serious federal law enforcement action requires the use of professionals paid out of the Treasury, whether they be Marshals or the military. The President is not allowed to raise his own army, despite what President Lincoln may have believed, and he needs congressional authorization in order to call out the state militia. In contexts like *Neagle*, presidential power means the authority to use federal assets, like the Marshals appropriation, in ways not specifically provided for.

Flexibility is power, and politicians often (though not always) want power, not only to advance their policy agendas but also to be able to do good to their friends, and maybe a bit of bad to their adversaries. Congress has many tools for doing so, the President fewer, because he cannot tax and spend on his own. But if he has a great deal of discretion with respect to the functions federal officers perform, then he too controls the means to help his allies and make new ones.

Presidential enthusiasm for federal power, especially in this form, is part of the story of *Neagle*. At argument, the most aggressive position in favor of presidential flexibility was taken by Attorney General William Henry Harrison Miller, who although but a namesake and not a relative of President Harrison's illustrious grandfather Old Tippecanoe, was a former law partner and close friend of the chief executive. President Harrison himself was a strong advocate of federal power, much more so than the Democrat who bracketed him in the White House, Grover Cleveland. Harrison favored increased military spending and had no sympathy with moonshiners who impeded tax collection, nor with states' rights arguments that would protect them.[114] Indeed, after Neagle shot Terry and while the litigation was in progress, Harrison in his State of the Union message recommended that Congress provide specifically for the protection of the federal judiciary. Congress eventually did so, but

---

[114] When he appointed his friend from the Senate, Howell Jackson, to the Supreme Court, President Harrison praised Jackson's nationalistic stance while a circuit judge. Jackson had been firm in dealing with those who impeded federal operations, including whiskey makers prosecuted for killing deputy marshals who were looking for an illicit still. "You were a believer in the nation and did not sympathize with the opinion that a United States marshal was an alien officer, or that election frauds or any other infraction of the federal statutes were deserving of aught but indignant condemnation and punishment." Homer E. Socolofsky & Allan B. Spetter, *The Presidency of Benjamin Harrison* 189 (1987).

that was about a century later, so President Harrison's recommendation probably was not a major factor in the decision.[115]

Neagle was about federalism and about executive power. As the two are closely connected, the case was about executive power because it was about federalism.

Presidential Power, Federal Resources, and Private Rights

Elsewhere in this volume is a discussion of *Youngstown Sheet & Tube*,[116] in which the Supreme Court rejected President Truman's attempt to seize private property in order to further the war effort in Korea. Justice Black's opinion for the majority, with its emphasis on Congress' status as the sole law-maker, reads much like Justice Lamar's dissent in *Neagle*. The executive in *Youngstown*, and Chief Justice Vinson in dissent in that case, relied on *Neagle* for the proposition that the President has authority to achieve the nation's goals, and to protect it from harm, even in the absence of explicit authorization from Congress.[117] But the Court rejected that argument, though it did not purport to question *Neagle*.

It is never obvious how broadly a case should be read, but the majority in *Youngstown* did have a ready ground of distinction, one that is of fundamental importance in understanding executive power. In the unusual practical and legal circumstances of *Neagle*, two issues were closely linked that are normally quite separate. The dispute in that case was not about the existence or even the content of a privilege to use deadly force in defense of another. The key question was whether that privilege came from federal, and not just from state, law. Only if federal marshals had authority under federal law could they qualify for federal habeas, and thereby have the protection of a friendly forum.

Conversely, if Neagle was performing a federal function in protecting Justice Field, then it was quite clear that he had, under R.S. 788, the authority that a state sheriff had to use force. Because Neagle was a peace officer, the question whether he was doing his job and the question

---

[115] It is quite possible that in response to Harrison's recommendation the relevant congressional decision makers temporized, waiting to see whether the courts would take care of the problem and thus remove it from their agenda. When the Supreme Court did so, sighs of relief may well have come from elsewhere in the Capitol. No doubt there were plenty of Senators and Representatives who were not happy with the choice of saying either that federal law enforcement power should be expanded or that federal officers should be sitting ducks for assassins.

[116] Youngstown Sheet & Tube Co. v. Sawyer, 343 U.S. 579 (1952). For more on *Youngstown*, see Chapter 7 in this volume.

[117] Chief Justice Vinson relied on *Neagle* for the proposition that the President is not limited to carrying out the express terms of statutes and treaties, but must provide all the protections implied by the nature of the government. *Youngstown*, 343 U.S. at 687.

whether he had congressional authorization to shoot someone, and thereby invade private rights, went together.

That connection is probably the exception and not the rule when it comes to federal officers, and it is certainly not inevitably the case. In *Johnson v. Maryland*, Justice Holmes concluded that federal mail carriers did not need state driving licenses in order to perform their federally-mandated function.[118] Whether that was a correct reading of Congress' statutes may be doubted, but at least it was clear that in order to deliver the mail the federal officer needed to drive. It is hard to imagine that Justice Holmes would have believed that Congress had implicitly authorized the Post Office to commandeer private vehicles to carry the mail. Congress provides for Post Office delivery vehicles by arranging to purchase them on the market and appropriating funds needed to buy them.

As a general matter, congressional authorization for an agency to carry out its mission is *not* authorization for the agency to invade private rights in order to do so. It is authorization for the agency to use the resources that Congress has provided. Sometimes that empowerment will interlock with existing rules governing and limiting private rights, even if Congress does not explicitly deal with the matter. Federal fire-fighters almost certainly can take advantage of the common law principle of public necessity, which authorizes the destruction of private property in emergencies, with no requirement of compensation. But a federal fire-fighting force would no more have the power to commandeer private vehicles for routine operations than the Postal Service does.

It is thus misleading to say that Congress wants its statutes to be fully carried out, and that any state law obstacles to that goal must yield. On the contrary, Congress usually takes for granted the existence of private rights, such as those of the steel companies in *Youngstown*, and does not displace them without indicating that it has done so. Situations like *Neagle*, in which authorizing the federal function implies authorization to coerce private individuals or otherwise override their legal entitlements, are the exception and not the rule.

While it is possible to say some things about *Neagle* with reasonable confidence, as to others, including whether the version of the facts that appears in the *United States Reports* bears much relation to reality, who knows? And whether that aspect of the case makes it the exception and not the rule, perhaps other chapters in this volume can tell.

---

[118] 254 U.S. 51 (1920).

*

5

Saikrishna Prakash

The Story of *Myers* and its Wayward Successors: Going Postal on the Removal Power

Nobody likes to lose their job. So it was natural that Frank S. Myers, First Class Postmaster of Portland, just wanted to keep his. In 1920, the Postal Service asked Myers to tender his resignation. Myers refused. The Postmaster General subsequently sent Myers a curt letter saying he had been removed at the President's direction. Citing a federal statute that required Senate consent to remove postmasters, Myers denied that he had been removed, sought his salary in the Court of Claims, and thereby set in motion a case that would generate mammoth and scholarly Supreme Court opinions.

Myers' Appointment and Removal

In 1913, President Woodrow Wilson threw out Republican postmasters and replaced them with Democrats.[1] With Senate advice and consent, Wilson appointed Democrat Frank S. Myers as First Class Postmaster of Portland, Oregon, for a term of four years. First class postmasters served throughout the nation, each charged with running one of several hundred large regional post offices. Prior to his appointment, Myers worked for Oregon Senator Harry Lane, first as his campaign manager and later as his legislative aide.[2] Because the Post Office was a rich source of patronage with thousands of offices to fill, it seems likely that Lane recommended Myers to the Wilson Administration. With the office

---

[1] Robert K. Murray, *The Harding Era: Warren G. Harding and His Administration* 305 (1969).

[2] Jonathan Entin, *The Pompous Postmaster and Presidential Power: The Story of Myers v. United States*, Case Research Paper Series in Legal Studies 3–4 (November 2005), http://papers.ssrn.com/sol3/papers.cfm?abstract_id=845026.

came a $6,000 annual salary, worth about $70,000 today when adjusted for inflation.

Myers served his first term without any incident. With the Senate's approval, Wilson reappointed him to a second four-year term in 1917. His second commission authorized him "to hold [his] office with all the rights and emoluments thereunto legally appertaining for and during the terms of four years ... subject to the conditions prescribed by law."[3] Conspicuously absent was any language suggesting that Myers served "during the President's pleasure." Hence Myers' commission lacked the language commonly found in the commissions issued to executive officers in earlier administrations.[4] Presumably, someone within the executive branch concluded that such language was inappropriate given the statute requiring Senate consent for removals.

Myers' second term proved more controversial than his first. Myers clashed with a Senator, a Representative, and the Portland Mayor.[5] Among other things, Myers resisted rehiring postal workers who had left their jobs to fight in the Great War.[6] More momentously, in 1919 Myers became the subject of a postal investigation. Myers had complained about his assistant, perhaps because he suspected the assistant of disloyalty and of having Republican sympathies.[7] Unfortunately, the accusations boomeranged back on Myers because postal investigators turned their attention to him. Apparently, Myers had autocratic tendencies that had antagonized his staff and customers.[8]

In late January of 1920, the investigation culminated in a Postal Service letter to Myers expressing regret that the investigation had not eliminated "the antagonism which existed in the Portland office."[9] Given the animosity, it had "become necessary for the department to take drastic action" and hence "[i]n the interest of the Postal Service,"[10] the Service requested that Myers resign effective at the close of business

---

[3] *Power of the President to Remove Federal Officers*, S. Doc. No. 174, 69th Cong., 2d Sess., at 11 (1926).

[4] Saikrishna Prakash, *Removal and Tenure in Office*, 92 Va. L. Rev. 1779, 1828 (2006).

[5] Jonathan Entin, *The Pompous Postmaster and Presidential Power: The Story of Myers v. United States*, Case Research Paper Series in Legal Studies 4–5 (November 2005), http://papers.ssrn.com/sol3/papers.cfm?abstract_id=845026.

[6] *Id.* at 6–7.

[7] *Id.* at 6.

[8] *Id.*

[9] *Id.* at 7.

[10] Letter from J.C. Koons to Frank S. Myers, reprinted in *Power of the President to Remove Federal Officers*, S. Doc. No. 174, 69th Cong., 2d Sess., at 7 (1926).

January 31, 1920.[11] The letter, presumably routed through Myers' office and delivered by his staff, warned Myers that if he did not resign, the "records will show your separation from the service by removal."[12] Finally, the letter asked Myers to deliver or forward a letter to his assistant, requesting that the latter resign for similar reasons. Even in the midst of rather adverse professional circumstances, Myers was to see the mail delivered.[13]

All parties evidently regarded regular delivery as too slow for subsequent communication. Myers sent a telegram on January 31, 1920, to postal headquarters, declaring that he had not resigned and that his "eminent counsel" had advised that federal statutes "fully protected" him.[14] On the morning of February 2, 1920, the Postmaster General sent a reply telegram to Myers instructing him to "have nothing further to do with the office" as an "order has been issued by direction of the President removing you from office of postmaster at Portland."[15] Myers had been fired . . . or so the Postal Service thought.

The same day, Myers wired a reply to the Postmaster General, saying that he had not resigned and that the attempted removal was not done "according to law."[16] Apparently the rest of the Post Office establishment disagreed, because Myers no longer functioned as First Class Postmaster of Portland, Oregon. Members of the staff were instructed to extend to Myers "no recognition as postmaster and to give no attention to any orders from" Myers.[17] Recognizing that he could no longer effectively serve, Myers vacated his postal offices under protest.[18]

In February, Myers petitioned President Wilson and the Chair of the Senate Committee on Post Offices for a hearing. Michigan Senator Charles E. Townsend responded, seemingly willing to hear from Myers but only after the President nominated a successor. He also cryptically said that the "President, through the Postmaster General, removes postmasters for various statutory offenses, and Congress does not pass

---

[11] Jonathan Entin, *The Pompous Postmaster and Presidential Power: The Story of Myers v. United States*, Case Research Paper Series in Legal Studies 7 (November 2005), http://papers.ssrn.com/sol3/papers.cfm?abstract_id=845026.

[12] Letter from J.C. Koons to Frank S. Myers, reprinted in *Power of the President to Remove Federal Officers*, S. Doc. No. 174, 69th Cong., 2d Sess., at 7 (1926).

[13] Letter from J.C. Koons to Frank S. Myers, reprinted in *id.* at 6–7.

[14] Wire from Frank S. Myers to John C. Koons, reprinted in *id.* at 7.

[15] *Id.* at 7.

[16] Wire from Frank S. Myers to A. S. Burleson, reprinted in *id.* at 7.

[17] *Id.* at 14.

[18] *Id.* at 14–15.

upon his decision in the matter."[19] This seemed to suggest that members of Congress had acquiesced to unilateral removals by the executive branch, at least for certain violations of statutes.

Until his term in office expired in July 1921, Myers consistently claimed that he was the Portland Postmaster. He took no other job nor sought other compensation. Myers rested his claim on an 1876 statute that provided that "postmasters of the first, second, and third classes shall be appointed and may be removed by the President, by and with the advice and consent of the Senate, and shall hold their offices for four years, unless sooner removed or suspended according to law."[20] Because the Senate had not consented to his removal, Myers claimed he had not been removed from office.

The 1876 statute was a remnant of an earlier era, when Democratic President Andrew Johnson and a Republican Congress were at loggerheads over the Reconstruction of the South. A number of statutes from the era limited presidential power to remove federal officers, either by forbidding removal except under certain circumstances or by requiring the Senate's consent to remove. The most famous of such acts was the Tenure in Office Act of 1867, which became law over Johnson's veto.[21] This Act prohibited the removal of any existing or future "civil officer" without the Senate's consent.[22] Some twenty years later, Congress repealed the Tenure in Office Act but not before enacting the 1876 statute that applied the same constraints to the removal of postmasters. Unlike the Tenure in Office Act, Congress never revisited the 1876 statute.

With Myers still claiming to be the Portland Postmaster, President Wilson evidenced his belief to the contrary through the recess appointment of John M. Jones in September of 1920. Though the Senate was in session for much of the period after Myers' supposed removal, President Wilson never presented a nominee to the Committee on Post Offices and the Senate never consented to Myers' removal during the remainder of his four year term. In late 1921, after the expiration of Myers' second term, new President Warren G. Harding nominated Jones. The Senate subsequently confirmed him.[23]

It seems likely that had either Wilson or Harding sought the Senate's approval for the removal of Myers, such approval would have

---

[19] *Id.* at 15–16.

[20] Act of July 12, 1876, 19 Stat. 80.

[21] Tenure of Office Act of March 2, 1867, c. 154, 1, 3, 6, 14 Stat. 430, 431.

[22] 14 Stat. 430.

[23] Myers v. United States, 58 Ct.Cl. 199, 201 (1923).

been forthcoming.[24] Senator Lane, Myers' benefactor, had died in 1917, and Myers had made plenty of political enemies during his second term. One local newspaper reported that veterans had "turned their guns" on Myers for failing to rehire them.[25] Even worse, some of Myers' Democrats longed for his "scalp."[26]

Paralleling Myers' tenure as Portland Postmaster and his fight to reclaim the office was a series of interesting administrative developments. In 1917, the same year that Myers was appointed to a second term, President Wilson partially reversed course from the partisan tack he had taken in his first term. Wilson issued an executive order declaring that all future vacancies in the first three postmaster classes would be filled only by persons standing highest on the Civil Service Commission's eligibility list.[27] So when President Wilson supposedly ousted Myers, his administration must have understood that the new Portland Postmaster would be appointed via the Civil Service and not be a patronage appointee.

Upon assuming office in 1921, President Warren G. Harding might have resumed the spoils system for the some 12,000 postmasters, as some Republicans hoped he would. Instead on May 10, 1921, Harding issued an order that provided that postmasters would be chosen from the three highest eligible names on the Civil Service Commission's eligibility list. This left some room for merit while still allowing candidates to be considered for patronage purposes.[28]

Litigation Over the Removal

In April of 1921, Myers brought a suit in the Court of Claims for his unpaid salary. After the expiration of his second term on July 21, 1921, Myers amended his petition, seeking $8,838.71, the salary that he felt he was entitled to receive as Portland Postmaster. William R. King represented Myers in the lawsuit. King was a Democratic activist who had previously served on the Oregon Supreme Court. Before the Court of Claims, King argued that Myers had not been properly removed from office because the Senate had not consented to his dismissal, as the 1876 statute required. Because the government had improperly prevented him from serving as postmaster, Myers was entitled to back pay.

---

[24] *See* Jonathan Entin, *The Pompous Postmaster and Presidential Power: The Story of Myers v. United States*, Case Research Paper Series in Legal Studies 19 (November 2005), http://papers.ssrn.com/sol3/papers.cfm?abstract_id=845026.

[25] *Id.*

[26] *Id.* at 7.

[27] *See* Robert K. Murray, *The Harding Era* 305 (1969).

[28] *Id.*

With Harding's replacement of Wilson in early March of 1921, it was up to the Harding Administration to decide how to respond to the *Myers* suit. The new Administration might have sought to settle the case with Myers—after all, it was not involved in his supposed firing. Or it might have belatedly sought Senate consent to remove Myers.

The Harding Administration chose none of these options. Instead, its lawyers argued that the President had the constitutional power to remove Myers from office. They further argued that the 1876 statute was unconstitutional because it purported to limit the President's removal power. Because the statute was unconstitutional, it had no bearing on whether Myers was removed or not, the lawyers claimed.

Given Harding's decision to apply a modified version of Wilson's civil service reform to postmaster appointments, it seems clear that the Harding Administration was not arguing for broad presidential power to secure postal spoils for Republican partisans. To the contrary, Harding reappointed John M. Jones, whom Wilson had recess appointed as Myers' successor.[29] Instead, Harding Administration officials evidently thought that the Constitution (and perhaps good government) necessitated unfettered presidential power to remove executive officers, even if civil service rules would be applied to appoint their successors.[30]

In April 1923, almost two years after Myers had filed suit, the Court of Claims denied his monetary claim. The court ended its opinion by tersely claiming Myers had brought his suit too late. It cited Supreme Court cases applying the doctrine of laches to prevent monetary claims from proceeding. One supposes that the Court believed that Myers should have brought his suit as soon as the government stopped paying his salary. Perhaps the Court felt that if the case had been resolved quickly, the public might have derived some benefit from the salary that Myers said the government owed him. Apparently, waiting a little more than a year to bring suit was fatal to his action.

But before dismissing the petition, the Court of Claims leapt at the chance of opining on the constitutional question, thereby making something of a mockery of the doctrine of constitutional avoidance. After citing Supreme Court cases discussing the constitutional power to remove, the Court of Claims, in one quick paragraph, said that doubts "should be resolved by this court in favor of the power of Congress; and this court will not declare a statute unconstitutional."[31] Hence the Court of Claims telegraphed its views that the statute requiring Senate concur-

---

[29] See *Myers*, 58 Ct.Cl. at 201.

[30] Whether Harding was personally involved in the decisions to contest Myers' suit and to argue for a constitutional power to remove is unclear.

[31] *Myers*, 58 Ct.Cl. at 201.

rence for dismissal of first, second, and third class postmasters was constitutional and that the attempted removal of Myers was improper.

Perhaps cheered by the Court of Claims dicta and certain that laches did not properly apply, Myers appealed to the Supreme Court. Unfortunately, Myers passed away in December 1924, before the Court could rule on his appeal. Myers' wife, as administrator of the estate, continued to press his monetary claim before the Court.

Arguments Before the Supreme Court

The Supreme Court set the case for argument on November 17, 1924. Counsel for Myers, William King, did not appear but "submitted the case on his brief." At Solicitor General James M. Beck's suggestion, the case was reassigned for argument in December of 1924, presumably with the hope that King might attend and present an argument at that time. Appointed by President Harding, Beck hailed from Pennsylvania and had served as U.S. Attorney for its Eastern District. The conservative Beck authored several books, the most famous of which, *The Constitution of the United States,* sold some 50,000 copies. He would later serve in Congress representing Pennsylvania.

At the second scheduled oral argument, King once again submitted the case on his brief. Why King declined to make an oral argument twice is unknown. Having served on the Oregon Supreme Court, one would have supposed that he was undaunted and intellectually capable of holding his own during oral argument. Despite the absence of a legal counterpart, Solicitor General Beck made a statement and participated in argument.

Apparently, the Supreme Court was unhappy with the absence of oral arguments defending the constitutionality of the 1876 statute. In January 1925, the Supreme Court scheduled arguments for a third time and invited Senator George Wharton Pepper, a Republican from Pennsylvania, to make an argument on "behalf of Congress" as an amicus curiae. Pepper had attended the University of Pennsylvania Law School, had served as editor and publisher of the precursor to the Pennsylvania Law Review, and was once employed as a law professor at the school.[32] Pepper had come to the Court's attention at the suggestion of his friend, Solicitor General Beck. Apparently unsure whether Myers' counsel would appear for the third argument, the Court had asked Beck to secure a Senator who would defend the constitutionality of the 1876 statute.[33]

---

[32] *See generally*, George Wharton Pepper, *Philadelphia Lawyer* 48, 55, 61, 62 (1944).

[33] Morton Keller, *In Defense of Yesterday: James M. Beck and the Politics of Conservatism*, 1861–1936, 179 (1958).

Leading up to the third scheduled argument, briefs were filed by appellant Myers, the government, and Senator Pepper. These were the second set of briefs filed on behalf of Myers and the government. The brief for appellant Myers argued that laches were inapplicable because Myers had never abandoned his office or accepted that he had been removed from office. Addressing the constitutional question, Myers' brief argued that Congress had the power to decide who would appoint inferior officers, such as first class postmasters. The President had no constitutional power to unilaterally appoint such inferior officers. Because Congress gave the President the ability to appoint first-class postmasters with the Senate's advice and consent, Congress could limit the power of removal over such inferior officers.[34] Finally, Myers' brief noted that the Supreme Court had previously held that Congress could constrain the ability to remove inferior officers. If Congress could limit a department head's ability to remove inferior officers, it could likewise limit the President's ability to remove inferior officers. After all, department heads and the President had authority to unilaterally appoint inferior officers only by virtue of statutes.

In the reply brief, Myers' counsel admitted that the President had the power to remove. But counsel argued that Congress could limit that power. In a deft move, the brief cited Solicitor General Beck's *The Constitution of the United States* for the proposition that the courts ought to declare statutes unconstitutional only when there was an "indubitable repugnancy between the law and the Constitution." Moreover, the brief cited Professor William Howard Taft's book, *Our Chief Magistrate and His Powers*, for the proposition that the President had an "undefined residuum of power" was an unsafe doctrine.

Senator Pepper's amicus brief emphasized the many statutes limited the President's ability to remove various officers.[35] Some statutes granted tenure during good behavior, others required cause for removal, and still others required the Senate's approval for any removal. These statutes covered many types of offices. For instance, Congress had constrained the President's peacetime removal of army and navy officers, had imposed restrictions on the removal of officers pursuant to the civil service laws, and recently had made the Comptroller General removable only by joint congressional resolution.[36] Pepper also emphasized statutes

---

[34] King was wrong to suggest that the Congress had delegated the power to appoint first class postmasters to the President. The President had the power to appoint first class postmasters, with the Senate's consent, under the Constitution itself. *See* U.S. Const. art. II, § 2. As soon as Congress created the office, the President had the power to nominate, and with the Senate's consent, appoint to the office.

[35] To prove his point, Pepper submitted a 12–page supplement listing all the statutes.

[36] Act of June 10, 1921, c. 18, 303, 42 Stat. 20, 24. The Supreme Court considered this act in its case *Bowsher v. Synar*, 478 U.S. 714 (1986).

that constrained the President's ability to appoint officers, arguing that if Congress could regulate his ability to appoint, it could likewise regulate the ability to remove.

Pepper's most notable argument was that the President lacked a constitutional power to remove anyone: Congress had to implicitly or explicitly delegate such a power to the President, or else he would lack it. Pepper also spent a good deal of time canvassing history in a bid to demonstrate that there was no strong sentiment that the President had a power to remove. There was no such view at the Philadelphia Convention or in the states, Pepper argued. The so-called Decision of 1789, where Congress wrote a statute implying that the President had a constitutional power to remove,[37] hardly proved anything because many members of Congress never explained their votes.

This was a crucial argument because prior Supreme Court cases had suggested that the Decision of 1789 represented an early legislative determination that the President had a constitutional power to remove officers.[38] While debating a 1789 bill meant to establish a Department of Foreign Affairs, members of the House rejected text that could be read as a legislative grant of removal power and instead adopted text that assumed that the President had a pre-existing, constitutional power to remove executive officers. Subsequent departmental bills had similar language, thereby confirming the initial Decision of 1789. Finally, early Presidents apparently agreed with the Decision. Each removed many different kinds of officials, even when the statutes creating these officials lacked any language relating to removal. Like the first Congress, early Presidents seemed to believe that the Constitution granted the President a power to remove.[39]

The Solicitor General's brief on behalf of the government argued that by virtue of his executive power and because of his responsibility to execute the law, the President had an absolute power to remove. The power to remove was not based on mere inference. It arose from a fair reading of the Constitution's text. Removal was understood as an executive power and was seen as necessary for the executive to maintain control of his branch. By granting the executive power to the President, the Constitution (and the framers) granted the President a removal power. Besides the grant of executive power, the Solicitor General argued that other pieces of constitutional text also supported a removal

---

[37] For an extended discussion about what, if anything, the Decision of 1789 actually decided, *see* Saikrishna Prakash, *New Light on the Decision of 1789*, 91 Cornell L. Rev. 1021 (2006).

[38] *Id.* at 1027.

[39] *Id.* at 1067–1068.

power, such as the Faithful Execution Clause,[40] the Appointments Clause,[41] and the President's duty to commission officers.[42]

The government's brief also emphasized the Court's historical deference to the Decision of 1789. The government noted that the Supreme Court previously had relied on the Decision and observed that constitutional readings rendered shortly after the Constitution's creation, were entitled to great weight. It also stressed that Presidents had long asserted and exercised the right of removal. In its final argument, the government pointed to practicality, claiming that the government would be paralyzed if Congress required the Senate's concurrence for removal of every federal officer. The President would cease to be the Chief Executive if the Congress regularly conditioned the right of removal on the Senate's consent.

Although most of the Solicitor General's brief was devoted to the claim that the President had an absolute removal power, the government also argued in the alternative: If the Court did not wish to reach that broad question, the Court should still strike down the 1876 statute on narrower grounds. Perhaps Congress could regulate the grounds for presidential removal, say by permitting removals only for neglect of duty, inefficiency, or corruption. What Congress could not do, claimed the government, was take the President's power of removal and share it with the Senate. In other words, while Congress perhaps could limit the President's removal power by requiring certain predicates for dismissals (such as corruption or misbehavior), Congress could not go so far as granting the Senate a check on the President's power to remove. To Solicitor General Beck, this theory deferred the question of whether the President had an absolute power to remove while still securing a victory for the government.

This "middle ground theory" was absent from the first brief filed by the Solicitor General. The theory "never occurred" to Beck prior to reading Pepper's amicus brief and hence the first government brief took the "extreme view."[43] Writing to Pepper, Beck said that he "was so stunned by the powerful reasoning of your brief that I re-arranged my battle lines and tried to take the line of least resistance."[44] According to

---

[40] *See* U.S. Const. art. II, § 3.

[41] *See* U.S. Const. art. II, § 2.

[42] *See* U.S. Const. art. II, § 2.

[43] Morton Keller, *In Defense of Yesterday: James M. Beck and the Politics of Conservatism*, 1861–1936, 180 (1958).

[44] *Id.*

a biography of Beck, the middle ground theory was "close to his personal conviction on the matter."[45]

The Solicitor General's brief ended with a discussion of the recently enacted law providing that the Comptroller General was removable only by a joint resolution of Congress. The government said that the implied bar on presidential removal of the Comptroller General was unconstitutional and that such limits would only multiply if the Court upheld the 1876 statute. Beck noted that though Harding had signed the bill he had done so presumably because he did not want the whole budget law to be defeated merely because of one unconstitutional provision.

On April 13th and 14th, 1925, the case was argued. This time counsel for Myers' estate, William King, participated in oral arguments. The court allowed three hours and forty-five minutes of oral argument. King received 45 minutes, Senator Pepper an hour and 15 minutes, and the government an hour and 45 minutes. Hence the appellant actually received less time than the amicus. This allocation presumably reflected greater confidence in Senator Pepper's ability to engage and edify the Court.

In his recitation of facts, King noted that though the Postmaster General claimed that the President had ordered the removal of Myers, it was the Postmaster who actually removed Myers. He also suggested that it was "doubtful if the President ever heard" of the removal of Myers.[46] King may have been right for President Wilson was likely uninvolved in the removal of a low-level officer like a first-class postmaster. Indeed, because Wilson had suffered a stroke in the fall of 1919 and remained incapacitated at the time of Myers' dismissal,[47] he likely had nothing to do with it.

Perhaps King made these cryptic comments because he thought that the Postmaster General was merely claiming to be acting on the President's behalf without any real authority to do so. If that was so, Myers was not removed under anyone's view of the case, for the Postmaster General clearly had no statutory or constitutional authority to remove anyone. Yet if that was King's point, he never explained it and it seemed wholly lost on the Court. No Justice ever questioned whether President Wilson had removed Myers. Though members of the Wilson and Harding administrations clearly assumed that Myers was no longer the Portland Postmaster, King might have argued that whatever beliefs attributable to members of these Administrations, perhaps no *President* had ordered (or approved of) Myers' ouster.

---

[45] *Id.*

[46] 24 *Landmark Briefs and Arguments of the Supreme Court of the United States, Constitutional Law* 342 (Philip B. Kurland & Gerhard Casper eds.).

[47] Kendrick A. Clements, *The Presidency of Woodrow Wilson* 197–98 (1992).

In any event, King went on to argue that the defense of laches was inapplicable. Myers had consistently and vigorously denied that he had been removed and had offered to perform all duties required of him. He had never conceded that he had been removed. On the constitutional question, counsel argued that to his knowledge, this was the first time that the Department of Justice "questions the constitutionality of its own act–an act of Congress."[48] Whether this was the first time a Department of Justice official had so argued before the Supreme Court is unclear; what is clear is that executive branch officials had long made claims that their own acts were unconstitutional. As early as 1802, President Thomas Jefferson had argued that the Sedition Act was unconstitutional.[49] President Andrew Johnson made similar claims about the 1867 Tenure in Office Act.

Finally, King argued that the Supreme Court had decided an analogous constitutional question in *United States v. Perkins*,[50] and that the Court's rationale should be extended to include the President. In *Perkins*, the Supreme Court curtly adopted the reasoning of the lower court that when Congress delegated the power of appointment to a head of department, Congress simultaneously could limit the department head's ability to remove the individuals he or she had appointed. If Congress could limit the ability of a department head to remove officers appointed unilaterally by the department head, Congress likewise could limit the ability of the President to remove officers appointed by the President with the Senate's consent, or so King claimed. Hence King argued on narrow grounds, hoping that the Court would accept his proposed extension of the *Perkins* rationale. King never argued that the President lacked a removal power or that Congress had broad authority to regulate the removal of all officers. Instead, he defended a limited congressional power to regulate the removal of inferior officers, content to say nothing about the removal of department heads and other non-inferior officers.

As in his brief, Senator Pepper laid great emphasis on the many statutes that limited the President's ability to remove. He also said that the question was in the Constitution's "no-man's land" because the Constitution said nothing about removal of such officers. There were three possibilities: (1) the President had an illimitable power to remove; (2) the President and Senate had a joint power to remove; (3) Congress could decide who might remove and under what circumstances. Pepper favored the third reading, going so far as admitting that Congress might vest the power of removal in the Senate alone. Senator Pepper argued

---

[48] 24 *Landmark Briefs and Arguments of the Supreme Court of the United States, Constitutional Law* 341 (Philip B. Kurland & Gerhard Casper eds.).

[49] *See* Saikrishna Bangalore Prakash, *The Executive's Duty to Disregard Unconstitutional Laws*, 96 Geo. L.J.1613 (2008).

[50] United States v. Perkins, 116 U.S. 483, 485 (1886).

that the President had no constitutional power to remove; but where Congress was silent, it was to be inferred that Congress had implicitly granted the power to remove or that removal was an executive act appropriate for implementing the statutes committed to the officer's care.

Solicitor General Beck argued that the President had a removal power derived from his executive power, the Faithful Execution clause, the appointment power and the duty to commission officers. Nonetheless, Beck limited his argument to executive officers. In response to a question, Beck said that the President could remove the marshal of the Supreme Court only if the underlying office was executive in nature.

Beck focused most of his firepower on Senator Pepper's claim that the President lacked a constitutional power to remove, maintaining that this argument made the Constitution a "house of cards." He also attacked the recent law that made the Comptroller General independent of the executive. Beck argued that if the Comptroller General statute was constitutional, the postal department could be made independent of the executive as well. He went on to repeat the argument in his brief that if Congress could regulate when the President might remove, Congress might make every officer independent of the President.

Trying to win his case rather than advance abstract principles, Beck also emphasized his middle ground theory that perhaps Congress could limit the reasons why the President could remove. This was a way for the Court to side with the government without having to strike down the many statutes that required cause for removals. What Congress could not do, Beck insisted, was transfer the removal power to the Senate, as it supposedly did in the 1876 statute which required the Senate's consent for removal. Judging by the questions, the Court evinced some interest in this alternative claim.

Beck thought his oral argument was "a nice climax to" his "modest career as Solicitor General."[51] An admirer said that Beck's "exceptional" handling of the case hopefully would secure "the entire independence of the executive from any such restraint as Congress is seeking to impose."[52] A newspaper praised Beck's position as "much broader and juster" than the view offered by his friend Pepper.[53]

Supreme Court's Decision

Despite being housed in the Old Senate Chamber, part of the Senate side of the Capitol building, a majority of the Supreme Court sided with

---

[51] Morton Keller, *In Defense of Yesterday: James M. Beck and the Politics of Conservatism*, 1861–1936, 180 (1958).

[52] *Id.*

[53] *Id.*

the President. After the conference, Chief Justice William Howard Taft called a conclave at his house, for those "whose votes can be counted on."[54] He invited six Justices, excluding Justices Louis Brandeis, Oliver W. Holmes, and James McReynolds. At this Sunday afternoon meeting, the six Justices agreed on a conclusion, hoping to secure more votes with a well-crafted opinion. Despite such ambitions, Taft thought it better "not to make any concession" designed to entice more votes.[55]

Taft knew something about presidential administration and the need for some mechanism of control, for he had served as the 27th President of the United States. Taft had been an ambivalent President, all the while hoping to serve on the Court one day.[56] In 1921, Warren Harding appointed Taft to the Court. In 1925, Taft would write that "in my present life [as Chief Justice] I don't remember that I ever was President."[57]

One might have supposed that his ambivalence, coupled with his new position, might have made him skeptical of the constitutional pretensions of Presidents. Indeed, as Professor Taft, he had previously painted something of a whiggish picture of presidential power in his famous book, *Our Chief Magistrate and his Powers*:

> The true view of the executive functions is, as I conceive it, that the President can exercise no power which cannot be fairly and reasonably traced to some specific grant of power or justly implied and included within such express grant as proper and necessary in its exercise.... There is no undefined residuum of power which he can exercise because it seems to him to be in the public interest....[58]

On the precise question of removal, Chief Magistrate Taft seemed quite deferential. Taft tried to remove more than 175 postmasters and sought Senatorial consent each time.[59] He apparently never asserted the right to remove the postmasters unilaterally.

---

[54] Alpheus Thomas Mason, *William Howard Taft: The Chief Justice* 225 (1964).

[55] *Id.*

[56] William Howard Taft, *Our Chief Magistrate and His Powers* ix (H. Jefferson Powell ed. 2002). Taft actually had a chance to serve as a Justice before he was President. He declined Theodore Roosevelt's offer of a Supreme Court appointment. *See* Paolo E. Coletto, *The Presidency of William Howard Taft* 5 (1973).

[57] Stephen Hess, *America's Political Dynasties* 321 (1997).

[58] *Id.* at 139–140.

[59] Jonathan Entin, *The Pompous Postmaster and Presidential Power: The Story of Myers v. United States*, Case Research Paper Series in Legal Studies 20 (November 2005), http://papers.ssrn.com/sol3/papers.cfm?abstract_id=845026.

Yet there were other attitudes that suggested a more robust conception of presidential power, particularly when it came to removal. In the same book, Taft claimed it "was settled, as long as the first Congress . . . [that] the President had absolute power to remove [officers] without consulting the Senate." This decision was based on "the principle that the power of removal was incident to the Executive power and must be untrammeled."[60] Moreover, Taft believed that there were "intimations in the opinions of the Supreme Court that in the tenure of office act Congress exceeded its legislative discretion."[61] While the President lacked an "undefined residuum," it seemed Professor Taft was of the view that the Executive Power Clause of Article II could be (and had been) defined as encompassing a removal power.[62]

Professor Taft's views about removal were of a piece with his earlier beliefs. As Solicitor General for President Benjamin Harrison, Taft seemingly embraced a broad removal power for department heads because "it is impossible to properly conduct a department" where the removal power is limited to cases where specific charges can be proven.[63] He also successfully defended President Grover Cleveland's removal of an Alaskan territorial judge before the Supreme Court.[64]

Taft's opinion was slow in coming. He "said that the case was so important that he would not try to get out an opinion during the 1924 Term, but would work on it during the summer and the following year."[65] Writing in Murray Bay, Canada, the site of the Taft summer home, it took Chief Justice Taft until the fall of 1925 to generate a first draft.[66] At the time, he knew that Brandeis would dissent and that Holmes was likely to, as well. He was unsure of what McReynolds would do.[67]

It would take another year for the opinion to come down. The additional delay stemmed from the need to rework the majority opinion

---

[60] William Howard Taft, *Our Chief Magistrate and His Powers* 56 (H. Jefferson Powell ed. 2002).

[61] *Id.* at 57.

[62] *See* U.S. Const. art. II, § 1.

[63] Alpheus Thomas Mason, *William Howard Taft: The Chief Justice* 254 (1964).

[64] *See* McAllister v. United States, 141 U.S. 174 (1891).

[65] C. Dickerman Williams, *The 1924 Term: Recollections of Chief Justice Taft's Law Clerk*, Supreme Court Historical Society 1989 Yearbook, (1989) http://www.supremecourt history.org/04_library/subs_volumes/04_c11_g.html.

[66] *See* 2 Henry Pringle, *The Life and Times of William Howard Taft* 1024 (1939).

[67] *Id.*

to address the comments of his fellow Justices,[68] particularly McReynolds who only belated decided to write a dissent.[69] Finally, on October 25, 1926, almost seven years after Myers had been removed, and a year and a half after the last set of oral arguments, the Supreme Court, by a vote of six-to-three, affirmed the judgment of the Court of the Claims. Rather than ruling that laches estopped Myers suit, the Court ruled that Myers had been removed after all.

After quickly dismissing the idea that laches barred the suit, Taft's opinion embraced the idea that the Executive Power Clause granted the President a number of executive powers that were constrained and clarified by the remainder of Article II. "The vesting of the executive power in the President was essentially a grant of the power to execute the laws. But the President, alone and unaided, could not execute the laws. He must execute them by the assistance of subordinates." These subordinates, Taft said, must be removable unless there was an express limitation on removal.[70]

After quoting all the relevant constitutional provisions, Taft spent a good deal of time discussing history, particularly the Decision of 1789. For the Court, Taft insisted that "there is not the slightest doubt after an examination of the record, that the vote is and was intended to be, a legislative declaration that the power to remove officers appointed by the President and the Senate was vested in the Senate alone."[71] Taft noted that the first Congress's constitutional conclusions were based on the Executive Power Clause and on the claim that because the President could appoint, he could remove as well.

Drawing upon the debates in the House in the first Congress, Taft made the pragmatic argument that the President must have the power to remove those who help exercise statutory authority granted to the President. But even when statutory authority is vested with the officer rather than the President, the President must be able to remove or else he cannot secure a "unitary and uniform executions of the laws" as required by the Faithful Execution Clause.[72] Reserving the question of whether the President has the power to overrule or revise quasi-judicial decisions made by purely executive officers, Taft concluded that the President could remove such officers based on their exercise of their

---

[68] William E. Leuchtenberg, *The Case of the Contentious Commissioner: Humphrey's Executor v. U.S.*, in *Freedom and Reform* 276, 292 (Harold M. Hyman & Leonard W. Levy, 1969).

[69] 2 Henry Pringle, *The Life and Times of William Howard Taft* 1024 (1939).

[70] Myers v. United States, 272 U.S. 52, 116 (1926).

[71] *Id.* at 114.

[72] *See* U.S. Const. art. II, § 3.

statutory authority. The President "can consider the decision after its rendition as a reason for removing the officer, on the ground that the discretion ... has not been only whole intelligently or wisely exercised. Otherwise, the President cannot discharge his faithful execution duty."[73] Taft thereby indicated that officers who had quasi-judicial functions were subject to presidential removal.

Taft went on to emphasize that posterity had come to regard the Decision of 1789 as a legislative declaration that the Constitution granted the President a power of removal. Subsequent statutes were written with the understanding that the President had a constitutional power to remove. And early Presidents removed hundreds of officers, presumably unilaterally. Taft concluded there had been acquiescence to the "legislative decision of 1789 for nearly three-quarters of a century by all branches of the Government" and that the Court had previously said as much.[74]

According to Taft, even those who might be counted as dissenters had come to recognize the force of the Decision of 1789. Hamilton, who had claimed that the President could remove only with the Senate's consent, changed his view.[75] John Marshall, who had claimed in *Marbury v. Madison* that the President could not remove justices of the peace,[76] subsequently claimed that the Decision of 1789 was considered "as a full expression of the sense of the legislature" on the question of removal, thereby suggesting his agreement with the Decision.[77]

Taft's opinion also added a gloss on *Marbury v. Madison*. *Marbury* famously distinguished discretionary political duties from mandatory statutory duties. The former were never examinable in court, while the latter could be made the subject of a suit.[78] When it came to removal of officers, however, the Court rubbished this distinction. "There is nothing in the Constitution which permits a distinction between the removal of a head of a department or bureau, when he discharges a political duty of the President or exercise his discretion, and the removal of executive officers engaged in the discharge of their other normal duties."[79] In other words, the President's removal power extended beyond those officers who exercised discretion in a manner contrary to presidential policies.

---

[73] *Myers*, 272 U.S. at 173–74.

[74] *Id.* at 146.

[75] *Id.*

[76] Marbury v. Madison, 5 U.S. 137, 162 (1803).

[77] *Myers*, 272 U.S. at 142.

[78] *Marbury*, 5 U.S. at 165–66.

[79] *Myers*, 272 U.S. at 132.

The President could remove officers for no other reason than that he disagreed with their execution of mandatory, statutory duties.

The Court ended its opinion by criticizing the many acts passed in the wake of the Civil War that sought to limit the President's power to remove. Those acts were the product of a power struggle between President Andrew Johnson and Radical Republicans and were not enough to overcome the unbroken practice that preceded them.

Although *Myers* is often seen as endorsing an unqualified and illimitable presidential removal power and as endorsing broad presidential power more generally, in reality, the Court reserved judgment on several crucial issues. For instance, it declined to comment on whether the President had a right to remove non-article III judges.[80] More importantly, the Myers' majority opinion did not say that the President had an absolute right to remove all executive officers. Instead the opinion said that Congress could not limit the President's power of removal when appointments were made by the President, with the Senate's consent.[81]

Indeed, the majority opinion expressly withheld comment on whether the Congress could regulate presidential removals when Congress permitted the President to appoint without Senate consent. At times, it intimated that perhaps Congress could not limit removal by the President in such situations.[82] But the Court never came out and said as much. Moreover, the Court's opinion could be read as suggesting that Congress could prevent or regulate presidential removals when it delegated the appointment of inferior officers to the department heads and courts. *Perkins v. United States*[83] had made clear that Congress could regulate the ability of department heads to remove those inferior officers whom they had unilaterally appointed. What was unclear after *Perkins* is whether Congress could regulate *presidential* removal of inferior officers appointed by the department heads and courts. The Court did nothing to answer this question. Hence, it left open the possibility that Congress might regulate removals by the President when Congress delegated the sole power to make appointments to inferior offices to the President, the department heads and the courts. In short, nothing in *Myers'* precluded congressional regulation of presidential removal of inferior officers, including postmasters, in the future.

Finally, the majority opinion left open the question of whether (and the extent to which) the President can direct officers in their exercise of

---

[80] *See id.* at 116.

[81] *See id.* at 164, 176.

[82] *See id.* at 162.

[83] *See* United States v. Perkins, 116 U.S. 483, 485 (1886).

statutory discretion. "There may be duties of a quasi-judicial character imposed on executive officers and members of executive tribunals whose decisions . . . the President can not in a particular case properly influence or control."[84] This statement could be read to suggest sympathy for the proposition that the President could not direct the quasi-judicial duties of executive officers. But it also could be read to suggest that the President could control the *executive* duties of such officers. For why else would the Court single out quasi-judicial duties, unless the Court wished to suggest a distinction between those duties and other duties imposed on executive officers? This debate about presidential directive authority has extended from the earliest days of the Republic,[85] to the opinions of attorneys general,[86] and to the pages of modern law reviews.[87]

Justices Oliver Wendell Holmes, James McReynolds, and Louis Brandeis each wrote dissenting opinions. Holmes was brief, saying that because Congress could create and abolish the office of first class postmaster, it could preclude presidential removals or condition removals on the Senate's concurrence. The claimed constitutional basis for a presidential removal power—the executive power, the take care clause, and the power to commission all officers—seemed to him "spider's webs inadequate to control the dominant" fact of congressional control over the office.[88]

In contrast to Holmes, McReynolds was verbose, having composed a rambling 18–part, sixty-two page dissent. McReynolds had served as Attorney General and one might have supposed that he would favor broad readings of executive power. In fact, he voiced the narrowest view

---

[84] *Myers*, 272 U.S. at 173–74.

[85] *See James Madison in The Congressional Register* (June 16, 1789), *reprinted in 11 Documentary History of the First Federal Congress, 1789–1791*, 868 (1992) ("I conceive that if any power whatsoever is in its nature executive it is the power of appointing, overseeing, and *controling* [sic] those who execute the laws.").

[86] *Compare* 1 Op. Att'y Gen. 624, 625 (1823) (President cannot exercise statutory authority committed to officers) *with* 7 Op. Att'y Gen. 453, 469–71 (1855) (officers cannot lawfully exercise discretion in defiance of presidential directives).

[87] For the proposition that the President can direct and exercise statutory authority, *see* Steven G. Calabresi & Saikrishna B. Prakash, *The President's Power to Execute the Laws*, 104 Yale L.J. 541, 549–50 (1994); Saikrishna B. Prakash, *The Essential Meaning of Executive Power*, 2003 U. Ill. L. Rev. 701. For the proposition that the President can only oversee discretion and not direct it or exercise it, *see* Cynthia R. Farina, *The Consent of the Governed: Against Simple Rules for a Complex World*, 72 Chi.-Kent L. Rev. 987, 987–89 (1997); Kevin M. Stack, *The President's Statutory Powers to Administer the Laws*, 106 Colum. L. Rev. 263, 267 (2006); Peter L. Strauss, *Overseer, or "The Decider"? The President in Administrative Law*, 75 Geo. Wash. L. Rev. 696 (2007).

[88] *Myers*, 272 U.S. at 76 (Holmes, J., dissenting).

of presidential power, reading the grant of executive power as vesting no more than the powers found elsewhere in Article II.

McReynolds began by emphasizing the broad nature of the claim that the President had an absolute constitutional power to remove all presidentially appointed officers. He admitted that the act of removing was an executive deed but insisted that prescribing "the conditions" for removal was legislative. He believed that the central issue of the case was whether any constitutional provision "definitively limited the otherwise plenary power of Congress over postmasters" when they are appointed by the President with the Senate's consent. His answer was no. The President must enforce the laws using whatever resources and powers Congress granted and if they did not give him a right to remove unilaterally, the President lacked such power.

As far as practice went, McReynolds asserted that for 47 years prior to the 1876 Act, the President "could neither appoint nor remove any postmaster" because Congress had vested the right of appointing postmasters with the Postmaster General. He admitted that the President was understood to have the power to remove many officers. But he equivocated as to the source of this power. Sometimes he intimated that the Constitution granted the President a removal power; more often he claimed that Congress had expressly or implicitly authorized such removals.

Indeed, much of McReynolds' opinion rejected the claim that the Executive Power Clause of Article II actually vested any power. The Clause merely indicated who would have the powers found in the remainder of Article II, claimed McReynolds. There was no shared understanding of executive power at the founding; varying conceptions from many nations had influenced the Framers. Moreover, he asserted that the states did not have the view that "executive power" meant something more than the particular grants found in state constitutions. Discussing the U.S. Constitution in particular, McReynolds said it "is beyond the ordinary imagination to picture forty or fifty capable men ... vainly discussing, in the heat of a Philadelphia summer, whether express authority to require opinions in writing should be delegated to a President" if they believed he had a generic executive power.[89]

Finally, McReynolds made much of *Marbury v. Madison*. Chief Justice Marshall had held that *Marbury* could not be removed because he had a five-year term. If the President had a constitutional power to remove, as the government argued, Marshall and his colleagues' assumption that Marbury could not be removed was a mistake. *Marbury*'s discussion about removal was not dictum, said McReynolds. It was a necessary part of the case because it was a means of avoiding the

---

[89] *Id.* at 205 (McReynolds, J., dissenting).

constitutional question about the Court's jurisdiction. Had William Marbury been removable from his office of the Justice of the Peace, there would have been no occasion to discuss the constitutional question. Hence McReynolds read *Marbury* as necessarily establishing that when Congress provides a term of office and does not mention the possibility of any premature removal, the officer was not removable by the President. And if Congress could preclude removals entirely, as McReynolds said it did in *Marbury*, it might condition removal on the Senate's consent.

Rather than reading his dissent, McReynolds delivered "an acrid extemporaneous speech."[90] McReynolds complained that the Court's decision was "revolutionary, and the sooner the thinking people of this country understand it the better. Yesterday, we supposed we had a government of definitely limited and specified powers. Today, no one knows what those powers are."[91]

Though Justice Brandeis wrote a much more narrow opinion, his opinion was also quite prolix, running some 56 pages. He emphasized that what was at stake was whether the Congress could grant the Senate a check on the removal of inferior officers. According to Brandeis, the President had no inherent power to remove such officers because he certainly had no power to appoint them. Congress had to grant such authority. The President had an essential power to suspend, because that was necessary to the effective functioning of government. He might suspend an officer and designate someone else to act in the officer's stead. But removal was different because it was not essential for efficient government. To imply a removal power would unjustifiably limit congressional power over inferior officers.

Brandeis went on to argue that Congress had long distinguished inferior offices from other officers. It had placed many restrictions on the President's power to remove such officers from Lincoln's Administration onwards. Moreover, presidents after Andrew Johnson had complied with statutes requiring the Senate's assent to removals. When an office was occupied, presidents would send a proposed candidate to the Senate and if the Senate approved, the appointment of the new officer would simultaneously displace the previous occupant. This practice of Senate concurrence for the removal of inferior officers had existed for more than half a century prior to the *Myers* case and had covered a great majority of offices. Citing *United States v. Midwest Oil Co.*,[92] Brandeis said that the long acquiescence of two branches "should be deemed tantamount to

---

[90] William E. Leuchtenberg, *The Case of the Contentious Commissioner: Humphrey's Executor v. U.S.*, in *Freedom and Reform* 276, 293 (Harold M. Hyman & Leonard W. Levy, 1969).

[91] *Id.*

[92] United States v. Midwest Oil Co., 236 U.S. 459, 469 (1915).

judicial construction, in the absence of any decision by any court to the contrary."[93]

At the end of his opinion, Brandeis emphasized that the President was responsible for executing the laws. But he could only execute the laws with the means that Congress provided. If Congress did not permit removal of inferior officers or limited it in some way, then the President would have to faithfully execute the law using other means at his disposal. The separation of powers, intoned Brandeis, did not make each branch autonomous. The "separation of powers was adopted by the Convention of 1787, not to promote efficiency but to preclude the exercise of arbitrary power." Moreover, the separation of powers was erected not to avoid friction but to use friction to "save the people from autocracy," claimed Brandeis.[94]

Brandeis's dissent is notable for its many footnotes. These footnotes make the opinion seem more like a piece of scholarship, for the magnitude of the footnotes approaches the size of the text of the opinion. In these footnotes, Brandeis cites all the statutes that limited the President's power to remove inferior officers and discusses various episodes in history that might support and detract from his claims. Brandeis' clerk, James Landis, later boasted that the dissent represented "as thorough a piece of historical research as you would find in the Supreme Court reports anywhere."[95] Brandeis, embarrassed by the length of his dissent, offered to pay for its printing.[96] Though Taft complained privately that Brandeis "can not avoid writing an opinion . . . as if he were writing an article for the Harvard Law Review,"[97] Taft told Brandeis that the congressional appropriation for printing would be sufficient to cover the cost.[98]

Contemporary Reactions

Taft regarded *Myers* as a "monument"[99] and claimed that he "never wrote an opinion that I felt to be so important in its effects."[100] Yet he

---

[93] *Myers*, 272 U.S. at 283.

[94] *Id.* at 293.

[95] William E. Leuchtenberg, *The Case of the Contentious Commissioner: Humphrey's Executor v. U.S.*, in *Freedom and Reform* 276, 293 (Harold M. Hyman & Leonard W. Levy, 1969).

[96] *Myers*, 272 U.S. at 293; Alpheus Thomas Mason, *William Howard Taft: The Chief Justice* 226 (1964).

[97] William E. Leuchtenberg, *The Case of the Contentious Commissioner: Humphrey's Executor v. U.S.*, in *Freedom and Reform* 276, 293 (Harold M. Hyman & Leonard W. Levy, 1969).

[98] Alpheus Thomas Mason, *William Howard Taft: The Chief Justice* 226 (1964).

[99] *Id.* at 225.

[100] 2 Henry Pringle, *The Life and Times of William Howard Taft* 1025 (1939).

was embittered by his failure to secure a unanimous opinion. He attacked Brandeis as someone who "loves the kicker, and is therefore in sympathy with the power of the Senate to prevent the Executive from removing obnoxious persons, because he always sympathizes with the obnoxious person."[101] He also said the attitude of "socialists" was to oppose effective administration until a "small number" of them "acquire absolute power" and then insist upon "unit administration with a vengeance."[102] Both McReynolds and Brandeis, Taft complained, "belong to a class of people that have no loyalty to the court and sacrifice everything to the gratification of their own publicity."[103]

As one might expect, *Myers* got much press and criticism. Solicitor General Beck claimed that the decision would be a "landmark in constitutional law for many years to come."[104] Princeton Professor Edward Corwin said the case "captured" the front pages of the newspapers for the first time since the 1899 Insular Cases.[105] Corwin criticized the opinion for failing to recognize that the power to remove "should vary with the *nature of the office involved*."[106] He also said that a "mere fraction of a fraction, a minority of a minority" of the members of the First Congress believed that the President had a constitutional power to remove.[107] Thomas Reed Powell, a Harvard Law Professor, called it lame, inconclusive, and the history "far from compelling."[108] Republican Senator Hiram Johnson of California claimed that the opinion satisfied those who thought the nation required a Mussolini.[109]

Of course, there were concerns about the decision's effect on the civil service and on the various independent commissions. Indeed, Bran-

---

[101] Alpheus Thomas Mason, *William Howard Taft: The Chief Justice* 226 (1964).

[102] *Id.*

[103] 2 Henry Pringle, *The Life and Times of William Howard Taft* 1025 (1939).

[104] *President's Ouster Power Without Senate Consent Upheld by Supreme Court*, N. Y. Times, Oct. 26, 1926, at 1.

[105] Edward S. Corwin, *The President's Removal Power under the Constitution* v (1927).

[106] *Id.* at vii (emphasis in original).

[107] Edward S. Corwin, *The President's Removal Power under the Constitution* 13 (1927). For a critique of Corwin's analysis of the Decision of 1789, *see* Saikrishna Prakash, *New Light on the Decision of 1789*, 91 Cornell L. Rev. 1021 (2006).

[108] William E. Leuchtenberg, *The Case of the Contentious Commissioner: Humphrey's Executor v. U.S.*, in *Freedom and Reform* 276, 294–95 (Harold M. Hyman & Leonard W. Levy, 1969).

[109] *Id.* at 295.

deis had discussed the spoils system that might result from the opinion,[110] while McReynolds had lamented that a whole host of officers of commissions and boards now hold their offices "subject to the President's pleasure or caprice."[111] Some scholars shared those concerns.[112] Senator Pepper later said that the decision was written too broadly because it went beyond the question of removal of inferior officers by discussing superior officers.[113]

Others read the case more narrowly. One of those was former Solicitor General Beck. Writing in 1930, Beck said that Myers clearly covered executive officers "who are not quasi-judicial."[114] Going further, Beck claimed that *Myers* may be "regarded as having left undecided some minor questions as to whether quasi-judicial bodies ... are within the scope of the decision."[115] Other scholars said that it was unlikely that the Court would conclude in a future case that the President could remove the heads of administrative tribunals.[116] And still others suggested that presidents were too smart to remove these commissioners willy-nilly because of the political fallout that would ensue.[117]

Subsequent Supreme Court Decisions

A little more than a decade later, a rather narrow reading of *Myers* triumphed. In 1935 the Supreme Court both heard and decided *Humphrey's Executor v. United States* in the span of one month.[118] President Franklin D. Roosevelt had sent a letter to William E. Humphrey removing him from the Federal Trade Commission (FTC) because Roosevelt did not "feel that [our minds] go along together on either the policies or the administering of the Federal Trade Commission."[119] The FTC was charged with enforcing anti-trust laws.

---

[110] *Myers*, 272 U.S. at 276–85.

[111] *Id.* at 181–82.

[112] *See* 13 Va. L. Rev. 122 (1926); Galloway, *"The Consequences of the Myers Decision,"* 61 Am. L. Rev. 481 (1927).

[113] George Wharton Pepper, *Philadelphia Lawyer* 362 (1944). Without a trace of glee, Pepper noted that the discussion of superior officers turned up as an embarrassment in the Humphrey's case. *See id.* at 362–33.

[114] James M. Beck, *The Appointing and Removal Power of the President of the United States by Charles E. Morganston*, 78 Penn. L. Rev. 444, 445 (1930) (book review).

[115] *Id.*

[116] *See* James Hart, *The Bearing of Myers v. United States upon the Independence of Federal Administrative Tribunals*, 23 Am. Pol. Sci. Rev. 657, 671–672 (1929).

[117] *See* Howard Lee McBain, *Consequences of the President's Unlimited Power of Removal*, 41 Pol. Sci. Q. 596, 600–03 (1926).

[118] Humphrey's Executor v. United States, 295 U.S. 602 (1935).

[119] William E. Leuchtenberg, *The Case of the Contentious Commissioner: Humphrey's Executor v. U.S.*, in *Freedom and Reform* 276, 287 (Harold M. Hyman & Leonard W. Levy, 1969).

Prior to sending the letter, the Roosevelt Administration was quite confident that it could remove Humphrey. It had sought the advice of James Landis, the clerk responsible for the Brandeis dissent. Landis said that Taft was "insistent" that the language claiming that that the President could remove executive officers with quasi-judicial duties remain in the opinion. If that language had not been there, said Landis, "I doubt whether some of the dissents would have been as bitter as they were."[120] Based on such advice, the Roosevelt Administration was so confident that it had a winning case that before it went before the Supreme Court, it identified the *Humphrey's* case as a sure winner.[121] How wrong that proved to be.

George Sutherland wrote a fourteen-page opinion for a unanimous court (which included three other members of the *Myers* majority and two of the *Myers* dissenters) holding that Congress could limit the President's ability to remove officers who exercised non-executive functions. The statute creating the office of Commissioner of the FTC provided that "any commissioner may be removed by the President for inefficiency, neglect of duty, or malfeasance in office." Distinguishing the *Shurtleff* case,[122] the Court concluded that the FTC statute was meant to limit removals for only the causes listed in the statute and hence the question was whether such constraints on presidential removal were constitutional.

The rationale of *Myers*, the *Humphrey's* Court claimed, was limited to "purely executive officers." To be sure, the *Myers* opinion had some statements that suggested a broader reading. But those discussions were mere dicta, not necessary to decide the case, said the *Humphrey's* Court. Applying its narrow reading of *Myers*, the Court concluded that Commissioners of the FTC were not purely executive officers, but were primarily quasi-legislative and quasi-judicial officers. In administering the details of the statute's unfair competition standard, the commission acted in part quasi-legislatively and in part quasi-judicially.[123] While the Commis-

---

[120] *Id.* at 296.

[121] *Id.* at 291.

[122] In *Shurtleff*, the Court had concluded that statutes that merely list reasons why the President could remove would not be read as precluding presidential removal for other reasons. Congress would have to clearly intend to constrain presidential removals in order for the courts to regard statutes as actually attempting to constrain such authority. *See* Shurtleff v. United States, 189 U.S. 311 (1903).

[123] The commission had no rulemaking authority, so the court presumably was referring to the judicial lawmaking said to be part of giving meaning to vague statutory standards. *See* Antonin Scalia, *Historical Anomalies in Administrative Law* (1985).

sion may have had some executive functions, those functions were merely necessary to discharge their non-executive functions.[124]

Humphrey's never claimed that the President had no power to remove officers with quasi-judicial duties. It merely said that the President had no absolute constitutional power to remove officers like the FTC Commissioner. It admitted that there would now be a "field of doubt" between *Myers* and *Humphrey's*, and said that future cases would have to resolve such doubts.[125]

Was *Myers'* discussion of the President's ability to remove executive officers with quasi-judicial functions *dicta* as *Humphrey's* suggested? Not at all. While one can imagine a *ratio decendi* that only covered executive officers or postmasters specifically, *Myers* never offered such a rationale. Instead *Myers*, notwithstanding its many caveats, held that the President had a constitutional power, arising out of the grant of executive power, the Faithful Execution Clause, and the appointment power, to remove *all* officers nominated by the President with the Senate's advice and consent. Moreover, it specifically noted that its rationale covered executive officers who had some quasi-judicial duties. The fact that one can imagine a more narrowly reasoned opinion does not make the broad reasoning actually found in an opinion mere *obiter dicta*.

Brandeis, who dissented in *Myers,* now found himself with the *Humphrey's* majority in ruling against an absolute presidential removal power and he was "greatly pleased."[126] In a confidential interview, Brandeis said "we would have in effect a dictatorship or totalitarian state" if the "men on the Federal Trade Commission and similar government agencies are not allowed to exercise their independent judgment."[127] Imagine what would happen if "Huey Long were President" and the *Myers* doctrine prevailed?[128] Whether McReynolds was similarly gratified to be with the majority in *Humphrey's* is unknown. He did, however, make clear that he continued to adhere to the views he expressed in *Myers*.[129]

---

[124] *But see Constitutional Law, Executive Officers, Congressional Limitation upon the President's Power of Removal*, 49 Harv. L. Rev. 330, 331 (1935) (claiming that FTC was primarily involved in law enforcement and its general purpose was "executive").

[125] Humphrey's Executor v. United States, 295 U.S. 602, 632 (1935).

[126] Alpheus Thomas Mason, *Brandeis: A Free Man's Life* 619 (1946).

[127] *Id.*

[128] *Id.*

[129] *Humphrey's*, 295 U.S. at 632.

Humphrey's came down on "Black Monday," the same day as two other cases, one of which was *Schechter Poultry*.[130] All three were 9–0 decisions against the President's agenda. Roosevelt was upset, but was particularly "outraged" by *Humphrey's*. According to William Leuchtenberg, the decision seemed "a deliberate assault" on the President's prerogatives.[131] Roosevelt also felt that the Court was "personally hostile to him."[132] Apparently, such grievances were the impetus behind Roosevelt's court-packing plan.[133]

Sutherland's claim that the FTC was not an executive institution was met with astonishment, even by those who favored his judgment.[134] Edward Corwin, who had been quite critical of *Myers*, said that Sutherland's opinion provoked "wonderment" by asserting that the FTC was not part of the executive branch. "If a Federal Trade Commissioner is not in the executive department, where is he?"[135]

Some two decades later, a unanimous Supreme Court extended the *Humphrey's* logic in *Wiener v. United States*.[136] The case concerned the removal of a member of the War Claims Commission. The Commission adjudicated compensation claims by those who allegedly had been injured in some way by the enemy. The decisions of the Commission were final, with no possibility of judicial review. Though the statute did not limit presidential power to remove, the Court concluded that Congress must have wanted the adjudications to be uninfluenced by political considerations. This was an extension of *Humphrey's Executor*, for prior cases had supposed that the President could remove at will in the absence of statutory constraints on removal. The Court rejected that reasoning, arguing that the President lacked a constitutional removal authority over officers with judicial authority and that Congress had not granted the President any statutory removal authority over War Claims

---

[130] A.L.A. Schechter Poultry Corp. v. United States, 295 U.S. 495 (1935), was a Supreme Court decision that invalidated regulations of the poultry industry promulgated under the authority of the National Industrial Recovery Act of 1933. The regulations were invalidated on the grounds that they were issued pursuant to a statute that unconstitutionally delegated legislative power.

[131] William Leuchtenberg, *Franklin D. Roosevelt's Court Packing Plan*, 1966 Sup. Ct. Rev. 347, 357.

[132] *Id.* at 382. *See also* Marian C. McKenna, *Franklin Roosevelt and the Great Constitutional War: The Court–Packing Crisis of 1937*, 98 (2002) (saying that Roosevelt regarded decision as a slap in the face).

[133] *Id.*

[134] William E. Leuchtenberg, *The Case of the Contentious Commissioner: Humphrey's Executor v. U.S.*, in *Freedom and Reform* 276, 300 (Harold M. Hyman & Leonard W. Levy, 1969).

[135] *Id.*

[136] 357 U.S. 349 (1958).

Commissioners. In sum, the Court rather clearly concluded that the President lacked any constitutionally grounded removal authority over members of adjudicatory bodies.

Finally, in 1988, the Supreme Court wholly eviscerated *Myers*. *Morrison v. Olson* sustained the independent counsel statute.[137] Under that law, the independent counsel could be removed "only for good cause, physical disability, mental incapacity, or any other condition that substantially impairs the performance of such independent counsel's duties." The independent counsel concededly exercised "purely" executive duties, so one might have thought the *Myers* rule applied. Or one might have supposed that given the Court's conclusion that the independent counsel was an inferior officer and given that the counsel was not appointed by the President with the Senate's advice and consent, the case finally presented the question that the Court had previously chosen not to address: Could Congress regulate the President's ability to remove inferior officers appointed outside the process of presidential nomination and Senate consent?

Instead, the Court approached *Myers* through the lens of *Humphrey's*, largely at the invitation of the government.

> [O]ur present considered view is that the determination of whether the Constitution allows Congress to impose a "good cause"-type restriction on the President's power to remove an official cannot be made to turn on whether or not that official is classified as "purely executive." The analysis contained in our removal cases is designed not to define rigid categories of those officials who may or may not be removed at will by the President, but to ensure that Congress does not interfere with the President's exercise of the "executive power" and his constitutionally appointed duty to "take care that the laws be faithfully executed" under Article II.[138]

The logic of the Court's conclusion suggested that while Congress could not give the Senate a check on removal of first class postmasters, Congress might have limited or precluded removal of postmasters so long as it could be said that "the removal restrictions are of such a nature that they [do not] impede the President's ability to perform his constitutional duty." In other words, if Congress could constrain the ability to remove a prosecutor, it could likewise constrain the President's ability to remove postmasters in charge of delivering mail because such constraints likely would not impede the President's ability to see the laws faithfully executed. After all, how crucial is a postmaster or a prosecutor

---

[137] 487 U.S. 654 (1988). For more on *Morrison v. Olson*, see Chapter 11 in this volume.

[138] *Morrison*, 487 U.S. at 689–90. The Court actually *realized* that *Myers* had not established the rule that Presidents could remove all executive officers. *See id.* at 690 n.27.

in the larger scheme of law execution? Will law execution wholly go to pieces if some negligent or bumbling executive officer remains in office? Of course not. By setting up this test, the Court made the President's removal power (and his control of the executive branch) susceptible to death by a thousand different cuts.

In any event, Congress already had limited the President's removal power over postmasters. In 1971, Congress established the United States Postal Service as "an independent executive establishment."[139] While the Postmaster General position has not been abolished, the President no longer appoints him or her. Rather, the President has the authority to appoint nine members of a Board of Governors who appoint a Postmaster General who serves as "chief executive officer" for the Postal Service.[140] Likewise, there are still postmasters—defined as those who manage a post office[141]—but the statutes preclude presidential removal, making postmasters subject to the civil service.[142] Hence what Solicitor General Beck warned would come to pass if the Court did not rule in favor of the President has come to pass notwithstanding the President's victory in that case. Indeed, *Myers* itself suggested the possibility that postmasters might be subject to civil service protections, thus foreshadowing what was to come.

The current fate of *Myers*, it would seem, is to be a polestar for those who imagine that it reflects the proper (or at least a superior) understanding of the President's power to remove and the President's executive power granted by Article II, section 1 of the Constitution. *Myers'* other fate is that it will remain in the constitutional and administrative law casebooks as an example of a case whose holding and rationale have been undermined by successive opinions that have been rather unkind to it.

Still as much as *Humphrey's*, *Morrison*, and other cases may have gutted *Myers*, it still remains the case that Congress cannot participate in the removal of officers of the United States.[143] Perhaps more impor-

---

[139] 39 U.S.C. § 201.

[140] 39 U.S.C. § 202–203.

[141] 39 U.S.C. § 1004.

[142] 39 U.S.C. § 1001(b).

[143] *See* Bowsher v. Synar, 478 U.S. 714, 726 (1986); Morrison v. Olson, 487 U.S. 654, 685–66 (1988). More precisely, the chambers of Congress may only remove via the impeachment process. *See Bowsher*, 478 U.S. at 726. Elsewhere I have argued that while Congress cannot limit the President's power to remove executive officers, the Constitution authorizes Congress to remove by statute all executive officers and all non-Article III judicial officers of the United States, *see* Saikrishna Prakash, *Removal and Tenure in Office*, 92 Va. L. Rev. 1799 (2006).

tantly, the Court has never restored an officer removed by a President.[144] Moreover, in *Morrison* itself, the Court left open the precise meaning of "good cause" and included a discussion that suggested that under the statutory standard, the President retained a fair amount of removal authority over the independent counsel.[145] For such reasons, some have argued that it is unlikely that the courts will ever second-guess a President who removes for cause, as long as he is somewhat savvy about giving reasons for the removal.[146] *

---

[144] William E. Leuchtenberg, *The Case of the Contentious Commissioner: Humphrey's Executor v. U.S.*, in *Freedom and Reform* 276, 302 (Harold M. Hyman & Leonard W. Levy, 1969).

[145] *Morrison*, 487 U.S. at 692–93.

[146] *Id.*

* Thanks to Curtis Bradley, Chris Schroeder, and Kevin Stack for insightful comments and criticisms. Thanks to Carolyn Kuduk for comments and research assistance.

6

H. Jefferson Powell

The Story of *Curtiss–Wright Export Corporation*

Many well-known Supreme Court decisions have in fact not just one story but several. There is nothing mysterious about this. Consider perhaps the earliest example. William Marbury petitioned the Supreme Court for a writ of mandamus because he and his fellow plaintiffs genuinely wanted official recognition of their appointment as justices of the peace in the District of Columbia. *Marbury v. Madison*[1] however, is far more than that mildly-interesting bit of legal history. The story of Marbury's action is a small part of the broader history of the development of American political institutions after the election of 1800 resulted in the first transfer of national political power from Marbury's defeated Federalists to James Madison's triumphant Republicans. And for modern American lawyers, the decision is the symbol and canonical statement of the practice of judicial review. This last story sits rather loosely to the others: *Marbury v. Madison*'s importance in that regard came (long) after the fact. But all three accounts are part of what the case means today.

United States v. Curtiss–Wright Export Corporation[2] shares this characteristic of standing for multiple stories, and does so to an extraordinary degree. The case was a bona fide federal criminal prosecution that ultimately resulted in the imposition of substantial fines on Curtiss–Wright Export Corporation and the other defendants. (I shall refer to the case as *Curtiss–Wright* and to the leading defendant as Curtiss–Wright Export.) The law under which the defendants were convicted was the product of an intersection between a tragic episode in the history of South America, the Gran Chaco War, and the attempt by President Franklin D. Roosevelt to implement his own approach to foreign policy

---

[1] 5 U.S. (1 Cranch) 137 (1803).

[2] 299 U.S. 304 (1936).

without jeopardizing his domestic programs or his political base in the teeth of principled and emphatic opposition. The Supreme Court's decision in the case is a part, although a somewhat enigmatic one, of the story of the Court's response to the New Deal in the mid-Nineteen Thirties. The opinion of the Court in *Curtiss–Wright* seems, at first reading anyway, almost willfully obtuse, a story of the justices being willing to permit the opinion's author, Justice George Sutherland, to ride a favorite hobby-horse at the expense of doctrinal clarity. In retrospect, however, the crucial story in *Curtiss–Wright* has turned out to be its role in the struggle between the president and Congress for dominance in the conduct of United States foreign policy.

These stories sometimes overlap only slightly: for example, the actual decision of the Court says almost nothing about the distribution of power over international relations. Furthermore, not all of the stories are, it appears, of equal interest. Almost no one in the early Twenty-first Century is concerned with the case because of its connection to the Chaco War (in the United States at any rate), or (with the exception of historians of FDR's administration) even what it says about the politics of foreign affairs in the Thirties. As a result, the issues lawyers and scholars now concern themselves with in discussing *Curtiss–Wright* seldom include either the horrors of the war or the interplay between Congress and the president in fashioning American policy toward the world beyond the Republic's borders. The stories of *Curtiss–Wright* are autonomous, and sometimes even antithetical, in ways that go beyond the norm represented by *Marbury v. Madison*. That suggests the possibility that there is yet another story to be found in *Curtiss–Wright*: the tale of how a Supreme Court decision can escape almost entirely all of its contemporary context, how lawyers and others can reinvent such a decision so that what it stands for has virtually nothing to do with the original case. *Marbury v. Madison* rested the power of the Court to determine constitutional meaning on the duty of the judicial branch to decide cases; *Curtiss–Wright* suggests that the Court's constitutional role may be, at times anyway, very different.

The Chaco War

The Gran Chaco (*chaqu* is Quechua for "hunting land") is a very large, mostly arid low-lying plain in what is now northern Argentina, southeastern Bolivia, and northern Paraguay, which changes to humid jungle-like conditions in its eastern reaches. Because of its inhospitable climates, it was sparsely populated in the early Twentieth Century and remains so today; the most numerous ethnic-linguistic group indigenous to the Chaco speaks Guaraní, which was (and is) spoken as well by virtually the entire population of Paraguay. For reasons based on the borders of the Spanish colonial administrative districts, Bolivia claimed sovereignty over most of the Chaco from independence through the 1920s, but until the close of the Nineteenth Century the government in La Paz periodically asserted its legal claims but otherwise paid little attention to the region. This policy of neglect began slowly to change after Chile defeated Bolivia and its Peruvian allies in the War of the Pacific in 1879–83: as part of the peace settlement, Bolivia was forced to recognize Chile's annexation of the former's one seacoast province, leaving it landlocked. The possibility of regaining direct access to the sea by establishing a port on the navigable Paraguay River, which runs through the Chaco and as to which there were international accords guaranteeing freedom of navigation, increasingly aroused the interest of Bolivian politicians and businesspeople.[3]

Paraguay had its own reasons for interest in the Chaco. During the disastrous War of the Triple Alliance that the nation fought against Brazil, Uruguay and Argentina between 1864 and 1870, Paraguay lost probably sixty percent of its total population as well as much of the territory it claimed, and only remained a marginally viable independent state because Brazil rejected Argentine suggestions that the two victors divide it between them. The physical and emotional effects of the war were devastating and prompted a search among leaders in Asunción for ways to rebuild the country. The cultural affinities between Paraguay and the population of the Chaco, however small, and the general passivity of the Bolivian government led by the early 1900s to a deliberate policy on the part of the Asunción government of encouraging settlement and agricultural expansion in the Chaco. (The lower lying areas in the area are well-suited to growing mate, a plant from which a kind of tea is made and in the early Twentieth Century the most important cash crop in Paraguay.)

The event that turned a long-running but low-level conflict of interest into a bloody war was the discovery of oil. The American petroleum giant Standard Oil organized a Bolivian subsidiary in 1921 and in 1928 oil was discovered in the foothills of the Andes to the west of the Chaco; the assumption was widespread—and shared in particular by politicians in both La Paz and Asunción—that the Chaco would turn out to be rich in petroleum. In Bolivia, oil fever and the older interest in a port on the Paraguay River merged: the port now appeared a necessity if Bolivia's oil profits were not to be absorbed by Argentine or Brazilian middlemen. Bolivian troops began building new outposts in what Paraguay had come to see as its own territory and Paraguay responded militarily. The first clash, the Paraguayan sack of a Brazilian fort, took place in December 1928, and prompted a series of futile attempts by the League of Nations and various individual governments to persuade the

---

[3] Bruce W. Farcau, *The Chaco War: Bolivia and Paraguay, 1932–1935*, at 8 (1996).

two countries to negotiate a settlement, interspersed by occasional fighting. In June 1932, however, the Bolivian army attacked a Paraguayan outpost in the north-central Chaco and general hostilities commenced.[4]

Despite almost continuous efforts by the League and leading European governments to bring an end to the fighting, the Chaco War lasted from 1932 until the two sides finally agreed to a ceasefire on June 12, 1935. Bolivia initially enjoyed a two and half to one advantage in population, a vastly superior arsenal of modern weapons, and access to essentially unlimited oil (Standard Oil of Bolivia was reported to be selling much of its production to the La Paz government at very low prices), but these advantages were canceled by incompetent generalship and a sharp divide between the Bolivian elite, which was enthusiastic about the War, and the large number of Bolivian army conscripts who were from the high Andes and both uninterested in the Chaco and ill-suited to endure its harsh, lowland conditions. A military coup in November 1934 undermined the legitimacy of Bolivian political authority but led to some improvement in the army's performance on the battle-field. By the time of the 1935 ceasefire, Paraguay held most of the disputed territory and had troops on indisputably Bolivian soil as well, but both sides were in fact exhausted.

The Chaco War was, in some dry military sense, a Paraguayan victory but it was an undeniable human catastrophe. The War is some-times thought of as a Western Hemisphere reprise of the First World War, and the analogy is an apt one. The War cost about 100,000 lives, about two-thirds of them Bolivian, and was enormously destructive of both countries' wealth and natural resources, comparable in these re-spects (proportionately) in the suffering it caused to the Great War's impact on the European powers. In the deployment of fast modern aircraft (chiefly by Bolivia until late in the War) and state of the art Nineteen Thirties armor (used rather ineffectively, again mostly by the Bolivians), the War also foreshadowed the Second World War. And the failure of the international community, and of the League of Nations in particular, to prevent the War, to end it quickly, or even to curtail the shipment of arms to the belligerents for much of its course, presaged the failures shortly to come over the Spanish Civil War, and Italian, Japanese and German militarism. For believers in international cooperation as the central tool for the maintenance of peace, the Chaco War was a warning that such cooperation can be difficult to attain and almost impossible to render effective.

Perhaps surprisingly, the June 1935 truce held, and on October 28 of that year, the peace conference being held in Buenos Aires adopted a

---

[4] David H. Zook, Jr., *The Conduct of the Chaco War* 69–72 (1960).

resolution affirming that the war was over. The boundary set by arbitrators drawn from other Latin American states under the Treaty of Buenos Aires of 1938 awarded almost all of the Chaco to Paraguay.

There was, it turned out, no oil in the Gran Chaco.[5]

Political Context

Franklin Delano Roosevelt began his political career on the national stage as a committed believer in a robust internationalism as the centerpiece of United States foreign policy. FDR was a warm admirer of the two preeminent American internationalists of the early Twentieth Century: his cousin Theodore Roosevelt and Woodrow Wilson, in whose administration FDR served as assistant secretary of the Navy, and the young FDR's views were a combination of their not-entirely compatible approaches. In his December 1904 message to Congress, the elder Roosevelt announced an "interpretation" of the venerable Monroe Doctrine (that the United States would not accept further European colonization or interference with the independent nations of the Western Hemisphere) that was startling in its implications:

> All that this country desires is to see the neighboring countries stable, orderly, and prosperous. Any country whose people conduct themselves well can count upon our hearty friendship. If a nation shows that it knows how to act with reasonable efficiency and decency in social and political matters, if it keeps order and pays its obligations, it need fear no interference from the United States. Chronic wrongdoing, or an impotence which results in a general loosening of the ties of civilized society, may in America, as elsewhere, ultimately require intervention by some civilized nation, and in the Western Hemisphere the adherence of the United States to the Monroe Doctrine may force the United States, however reluctantly, in flagrant cases of such wrongdoing or impotence, to the exercise of an international police power.[6]

This "Roosevelt Corollary" served as an express justification for repeated American intervention in the affairs of several Caribbean states over the next two decades, and the legitimacy of unilateral American action to maintain or restore order—or the order that American interests preferred—became axiomatic among many American internationalists. Although Wilson trumpeted disinterested United States support for national self-determination in his rhetoric, in practice Wilsonian idealism led to much the same foreign policy in inter-American relations as Roosevelt's more unabashed nationalism.

---

[5] David H. Zook, Jr., *The Conduct of the Chaco War* 192 (1960).

[6] Theodore Roosevelt, State of the Union Address (Dec. 6, 1904), *in* 3 *Theodore Roosevelt, Presidential Addresses and State Papers* 176–77 (1910).

At first FDR seems to have agreed with his cousin on all of this. He played a role in drafting the constitution the United States imposed on Haiti after President Wilson ordered the occupation of the island country in 1915, and as late as 1922 he defended the American protectorate over Haiti as an appropriate exercise of American power. By 1928, however, FDR had repudiated the Roosevelt/Wilson view of inter-American relations. "The time has come when we must accept . . . a newer and better standard in international relations. . . . Single-handed intervention by us in the affairs of other nations must end." His views on Wilson's great project, the League of Nations, underwent a similar evolution. As the Democratic vice presidential candidate in 1920, Roosevelt campaigned vigorously for American membership in the League, but as it became clear that American public opinion was irrevocably opposed to entry into the League, FDR gradually distanced himself from it, and after entering the race for the Democratic presidential nomination in January 1932, he publicly stated that he no longer favored American participation in what had become (contrary, he said, to Wilson's intentions) "a mere meeting place for the political discussion of strictly European national difficulties." Roosevelt remained committed to "the prevention of war and a settlement of international difficulties in accordance with fundamental American ideals," but said little about how he would pursue those goals during the presidential campaign.[7]

The Roosevelt administration's foreign policy during his first term in the White House was dominated by two themes. FDR announced the first, his famous Good Neighbor policy, in his inaugural address on March 4, 1933: "In the field of world policy I would dedicate this Nation to the policy of the good neighbor—the neighbor who resolutely respects himself and, because he does so, respects the rights of others—the neighbor who respects his obligations and respects the sanctity of his agreements in and with a world of neighbors."[8] The United States would take an active role in seeking international cooperation and resolving international differences, but on the terms of peaceful, multilateral action. While stated in general terms, the policy obviously applied with special force to the Latin American states. The second theme arose out of FDR's concern over the threat that militarism posed to world peace, a concern fueled in large part by his prescient reading of the likely intentions of Adolf Hitler, who came to power in Germany in January 1933. A commitment to peace did not, in FDR's view, require the United States to ignore the difference between aggressors and their victims, and the president ought to have the authority to take peaceful steps to

---

[7] Robert Dallek, *Franklin D. Roosevelt and American Foreign Policy, 1932–1945*, at 11–20 (1979).

[8] Franklin D. Roosevelt, First Inaugural Address (Mar. 4, 1933), *in* Davis Newton Lott, *The Inaugural Address of American Presidents* 233 (1961).

identify and punish aggression. Key to this strategy, in his view, was the discretion to impose an embargo on the sale of American arms and munitions when it would be effective and against whomever the president determined to be an aggressor. Shortly after taking office, FDR submitted draft legislation to Congress that would have given him such discretionary authority. The House of Representatives passed the bill in its administration form, but the Senate amended it to require the president to impose any embargo on all parties to an armed conflict. In the end, Roosevelt secured the amended bill's defeat.[9]

The fate of this 1933 legislative proposal set the pattern for interaction between the White House and Congress on the issue for the next several years. The administration consistently (if sometimes privately) sought a completely discretionary authority for the president so that the executive could employ an arms embargo as a selective tool of foreign policy, while a powerful group of senators and representatives consistently argued that any embargo should be even-handed and mandatory upon the outbreak of war. In their view neither the idea of being a good neighbor nor the goal of deterring aggression justified any deviation from a strict policy of American neutrality. As Congressman Hamilton Fish III, a bitter critic of the administration, explained their views, a law giving the president the power to determine which warring side was the aggressor and punish it alone would be "an act of war and not an act of peace."

> I should rather join the League of Nations than give the President the power to lay an embargo on the aggressor nation—a measure to provoke war and the right the declare war. You might as well take all the constitutional powers away from Congress and give them to the President.[10]

In February 1934, an administration proposal for discretionary arms-embargo power again passed the House but once again was amended in the Senate to deny the president any discretion. Roosevelt, preferring no authority at all to a totally non-discretionary power, decided to put aside for the time being his quest for general arms-embargo authority.[11]

The ongoing tragedy of the Chaco War produced a partial exception to the standoff between FDR and his opponents. The ever-increasing death toll, in a war fought in the Western Hemisphere, claimed significant public attention, as did a series of exposés of the role played by

---

[9] Robert Dallek, *Franklin D. Roosevelt and American Foreign Policy, 1932–1945*, at 47–48 (1979).

[10] 78 Cong. Rec. 9374 (1934).

[11] Robert Dallek, *Franklin D. Roosevelt and American Foreign Policy, 1932–1945*, at 71–72 (1979).

arms-makers in the human suffering in the Chaco and elsewhere. In early 1934, the great investigative journalist George Seldes published a book, *Iron, Blood and Profits*, that labeled the arms industry—including, emphatically, its American component—"the greatest and most profitable secret international of our time—the international of bloodshed and profits."[12] Secretary of State Cordell Hull stated the administration's official view in a May 22, 1934 public letter: the Chaco War "has involved the loss of thousands of lives and, if it is permitted to continue unchecked, the destruction of life is likely to assume appalling proportions." The large-scale participation of American arms manufacturers "for the sake of profits" in the provision of arms and munitions to enable the warring governments to carry on a "useless and sanguinary conflict" was a moral embarrassment. In addition, the secretary pointed out, American inaction made a mockery of the ambitions of the Good Neighbor policy: "War in any part of the world is a matter of concern to this government. But war between two American republics is of special and vital concern, which neither our humanitarian sentiment nor our feeling of American solidarity will permit us to ignore."[13] Concern over the sale of American arms and munitions to Bolivia and Paraguay, furthermore, was not limited to supporters of the president. In April, isolationist Senator Gerald Nye, a leading critic of the administration's quest for discretionary anti-aggressor legislation, launched an investigation of the arms trade,[14] and it was increasingly clear that a properly crafted bill to curtail arms sales to the Chaco belligerents could pass Congress. On May 18, administration supporters in Congress introduced a bill to that effect and within six days, it was awaiting the president's signature.

The haste with which FDR and his allies pushed legislation on the Chaco War excited some skepticism in the press. The papers reported speculation that the real issue was over American investment in Bolivia. Paraguayan advances in the spring of 1934 had put the oil fields and refinery of Standard Oil of Bolivia within their reach, and the company's deep involvement with the Bolivian government rendered a Paraguayan occupation a threat to the company even if its facilities were physically undamaged.[15] In fact, however, the administration's desire to end Ameri-

---

[12] Quoted in Robert A. Divine, *The Case of the Smuggled Bombers, in Quarrels That Have Shaped the Constitution* 214 (John A. Garraty ed., 1964); *see* George Seldes, *Iron, Blood and Profits: An Exposure of the World-wide Munitions Racket* (1934).

[13] Letter from Sec'y Cordell Hull to Rep. Samuel McReynolds (May 22, 1934), *in Chaco Arms Ban Pressed in House; Hull Spurs Action*, N.Y. Times, May 23, 1934, at 1, 15.

[14] Robert Dallek, *Franklin D. Roosevelt and American Foreign Policy, 1932–1945*, at 102 (1979).

[15] *Chaco Arms Ban Pressed in House; Hull Spurs Action*, N.Y. Times, May 23, 1934, at 1.

can involvement in supplying the War was sincere, if not altogether disinterested. The timing was a product of international relations: in early May the British began pressuring the United States for action and on May 20, a committee of the League of Nations formally called on the administration to match a proposed League embargo with an American parallel.[16] For FDR, always a careful student of public opinion, this seemed the chance to align his institutional interest in enhancing the president's foreign affairs discretion with a popular cause, and one that he fully shared on the merits. The issue of discriminating between evil aggressors and righteous victims, the ultimate point of disagreement with his critics in Congress, was not in play: in the administration's view both the La Paz and the Asunción governments were responsible for the War's continuation.[17] FDR was perfectly willing, as a result, to apply whatever ban Congress imposed to both countries, thus satisfying opponents of anti-aggressor legislation such as Fish.

In addition, a legal twist peculiar to the Chaco situation made it possible to draft what seemed to be effective legislation to address it that would not serve as a damaging precedent in future attempts to secure a discretionary and general arms-embargo power. The United States had long-standing treaties with both Bolivia and Paraguay forbidding the imposition of any embargo on U.S. trade with those countries that was not generally applicable. An actual embargo would abrogate those treaties, which the administration did not wish to do, in part because of its sensitivity to Latin American fears that abrogation would amount to a return (in the economic sphere) to the unilateral coercion characteristic of the Roosevelt Corollary. The solution the administration proposed was a prohibition on the sale *in the United States* of American arms and munitions to either Bolivia or Paraguay, in form and effect a purely domestic piece of criminal legislation that would leave for another day the question whether the president ought as a general matter to have the authority to use an arms embargo as a tool for punishing aggressors. The result was House Joint Resolution 347.

> The proposed joint resolution was brief:

> Resolved by the Senate and House of Representatives of the United States of America in Congress assembled, That if the President finds that the prohibition of the sale of arms and munitions of war in the United States to those countries now engaged in armed conflict in the Chaco may contribute to the reestablishment of peace between those countries, and if after consultation with the governments of other American Republics and with their cooperation, as well as that

---

[16] Letter from Sec'y Cordell Hull to Rep. Samuel McReynolds (May 22, 1934), *in Chaco Arms Ban Pressed in House; Hull Spurs Action*, N.Y. Times, May 23, 1934, at 15.

[17] *Id.*

of such other governments as he may deem necessary, he makes proclamation to that effect, it shall be unlawful to sell, except under such limitations and exceptions as the President prescribes, any arms or munitions of war in any place in the United States to the countries now engaged in that armed conflict, or to any person, company, or association acting in the interest of either country, until otherwise ordered by the President or by Congress.

Sec. 2. Whoever sells any arms or munitions of war in violation of section 1 shall, on conviction, be punished by a fine not exceeding $10,000 or by imprisonment not exceeding two years, or both.[18]

As the arguments in *Curtiss–Wright* were later to show, it is possible to discern an ambiguity in section one of the joint resolution. Would the president's authority depend on his determination of a fact (that the prohibition would "contribute to the reestablishment of peace"), as the verb "finds" suggests? Or was he being empowered to make a discretionary judgment, as the non-mandatory phrase "if . . . he makes proclamation to that effect" implies? It is somewhat curious that administration critics raised no objection to the president's apparent authority to choose whether to issue the proclamation: perhaps the point seemed completely theoretical since Roosevelt was committed to exercising his authority if Congress adopted the joint resolution. In any event, they did not, and the result was that the Joint Resolution Congress adopted went part of the way toward FDR's preference for discretion to use control over the sale of American arms as a tool for the prosecution of the executive's foreign policy goals. It also planted the seeds of a constitutional attack on its validity, as we shall see.

Neither house of Congress spent much time debating Joint Resolution 347. The bill came before the House of Representatives on May 23, 1934. After a brief introduction by the chairman of the Foreign Affairs Committee, Fish spent fifteen minutes on a fierce if irrelevant denunciation of the administration's quest for discretionary arms-embargo authority that concluded "I am ready at any time to vote to take the profits out of war." Other than a brief and equally irrelevant colloquy between Fish and several administration supporters over Fish's views about anti-aggressor legislation, that was the entirety of the House discussion, after which the joint resolution passed unanimously. The Senate "debate" on the following day, May 24, was even less consequential: the chairman of the Committee on Foreign Relations asked that the Senate consider the joint resolution immediately (contrary to the Senate's usual rules of procedure), the minority leader asked what emergency justified a waiver of the rules, and was told that "[t]he emergency is simply that two South

---

[18] Congress enacted the draft without change. *See* H.R.J. Res. 347, 73d Cong., ch. 365, 48 Stat. 811 (1934).

American countries are warring and have been for a long time." The Senate then approved the joint resolution unanimously.[19]

Four days later, on May 28, Roosevelt signed the joint resolution into law and issued the proclamation contemplated by the resolution: "I have found that the prohibition of the sale of arms and munitions of war in the United States to those countries now engaged in armed conflict in the Chaco may contribute to the reestablishment of peace between those countries, and ... I have consulted with the governments of other American Republics and have been assured of the cooperation of such governments as I have deemed necessary as contemplated by the said joint resolution...."[20] The language of the proclamation, whether intentionally or not, implied the narrower, fact-determination reading of the joint resolution: read with legal nicety, it could be argued, all FDR did was report two facts, one (implicitly statistical, but then that is the nature of many assertions of fact) about the probable impact of invoking his authority and the other about his consultation with other governments, and then invoke the authority Congress had conferred in the event those two facts could be asserted.

The May 28, 1934 proclamation remained in effect until the Buenos Aires peace conference announced on October 28, 1935 that the Chaco War was over. Two weeks later, President Roosevelt issued a new proclamation terminating the prohibition on arms sales to Bolivia and Paraguay.[21]

Joint Resolution 347 proved to be an aberration in the struggle between President Roosevelt and the Congress over authority to control the sale of arms that held for the rest of the decade. A year later, FDR's critics successfully forced on him the authority he had resisted, the mandatory power to impose an impartial arms embargo in the event of war between foreign states leaving him no discretion whatever. The president's supporters were able to place a time limit on this Neutrality Act of 1935, but another, similar bill was enacted and signed by a reluctant Roosevelt in 1936, and it was only after the fall of France in May and June of 1940 that the administration began to build momentum in Congress to support a form of neutrality that clearly distinguished fascist aggressors from democratic combatants.[22] In the immediate context, whatever minor advantage FDR got from securing the passage of

---

[19] 78 Cong. Rec. 9373–75, 9432–33 (1934).

[20] Proclamation No. 2087, 44 Stat. 1744 (1934).

[21] Proclamation No. 2147, 49 Stat. 3480 (1935).

[22] *See* Neutrality Act of 1935, ch. 837, 49 Stat. 1081, *amended by* Neutrality Act of 1937, ch. 146, 50 Stat. 121; Neutrality Act of 1936, ch. 106, 49 Stat. 1153; Neutrality Act of 1939, ch.2, 54 Stat. 4.

the Chaco joint resolution was swallowed up by his repeated defeats on
the Neutrality Acts. The great case of *Curtiss–Wright*, located in its
contemporaneous setting, concerned the validity of a ticket good for one
ride only.

Criminal Prosecution and the Delegation Doctrine

In July 1929, the Wright Aeronautical Corporation (the corporate
descendant of the company formed by Orville and Wilbur Wright after
their success in achieving heavier-than-air flight) and Curtiss Aeroplane
and Motor Company (founded by Glenn Curtiss, who beat out the
Wright brothers in a major international 1909 aviation meet), merged.
The resulting Curtiss–Wright Corporation operated through twelve subsidiaries and had extensive holdings in aircraft and engine manufacture
as well as airlines, but the stock market crash three months after its
formation threatened it with bankruptcy. The corporation's response to
its financial woes, in part, was to exploit its extensive research and
development contracts with the United States government by modifying
aircraft designs generated by its business with the American military
and selling the resulting planes to foreign governments; transactions
with those governments were handled by a subsidiary, Curtiss–Wright
Export Corporation, and its president Clarence K. Webster. Webster saw
the Chaco War as a splendid business opportunity, and by the spring of
1933 Curtiss–Wright Export had a practical monopoly on the sale of
warplanes to Bolivia, whose military increasingly relied on air power to
offset the Paraguayans' tactical superiority on the ground. The monopoly, maintained through a 5% kickback to the Bolivian comptroller
general, was so lucrative that Webster formed a separate corporation
(with himself as president) to handle its transactions and attempted,
secretly but unsuccessfully, to sell planes to Paraguay as well.[23]

The passage of House Joint Resolution 347 and President
Roosevelt's implementing proclamation posed a serious threat to Curtiss–Wright's financial recovery (sales to Bolivia had accounted for two-
thirds of the company's export profits in 1933), a threat pointedly
underlined when the federal government seized five Curtiss–Wright
fighters and four bombers in June 1934 on the ground that, although
Bolivia had ordered them in February, Curtiss–Wright still held title to
them. The Department of Justice ultimately concluded that the fighters,
which had been finished prior to FDR's proclamation, did not fall within
the prohibition and could be shipped, but that the bombers, unfinished
on May 28, could not. In response, Richard Hoyt, chairman of the board

---

[23] Unless otherwise noted, the factual details about the Curtiss Wright Export conspir-
acy and the subsequent prosecution are found in Robert A. Divine, *The Case of the
Smuggled Bombers, in Quarrels That Have Shaped the Constitution* 210–21 (John A.
Garraty ed., 1964).

of the parent corporation, Webster, and John Allard (Webster's successor as president of Curtiss–Wright Export), devised a plan for collecting on the bombers: mechanics removed the bomb racks and gun turrets and installed passenger seats, while Curtiss–Wright sold the revamped "airliners" to a shell corporation for ultimate delivery to Bolivia. Hoyt died shortly thereafter of complications following an operation for a liver disease, but Webster and Allard continued with the scheme. The bombers left the United States at the end of March 1935, shortly after Hoyt died, but the Department of State caught wind of the scam, and the government of Peru cooperated with the United States in preventing the bombers from completing the last stage of their journey to Bolivia.

The Justice Department correctly saw the Curtiss–Wright venture as a paradigm of what Joint Resolution 347 was about and the highly respected United States Attorney for the Eastern District of New York, Martin Conboy, resigned his position in order to undertake the investigation and prosecution of the scam. Despite a personal visit to Lima, Conboy was unable to develop an adequate case that the bombers were warplanes intended for Bolivia, but while in Lima Conboy found the evidence he needed to prosecute Curtiss–Wright Export, Webster and Allard. When the Justice Department authorized the shipment of the five fighters it had seized in June 1934, it specifically prohibited the inclusion of fifteen machine guns that it correctly inferred were to be mounted in the bombers. Webster, Allard, and a clerk had nonetheless crated the embargoed guns with the fighters and then filed false export declarations about the contents of the crates, which left the United States in September. After returning to the United States, Conboy secured indictments for conspiracy to sell the machine guns to Bolivia against Webster, Allard, Curtiss–Wright Export and a couple of subordinates at the end of January 1936.

As a factual matter, Conboy's case against the *Curtiss–Wright* defendants was solid, if it targeted only a small part of the actual scheme. But events entirely unconnected to his investigation, Curtiss–Wright Export, or the Chaco War had conspired to undercut the entire prosecution. In early 1936, the defendants demurred to the charge of conspiracy for which, they asserted, "there is no constitutional basis." On March 24, District Judge Mortimer Byers sustained the defendants' constitutional claim, a decision he reaffirmed on April 6 after allowing reargument on that point at the government's request.[24] (The demurrer asserted two other grounds for dismissing the indictment: the president's alleged failure to engage in the required consultations, and his second proclamation rescinding the prohibition on arms sales to Bolivia

---

[24] United States v. Curtiss–Wright Exp. Corp., 14 F.Supp. 230 (S.D.N.Y. 1936) (reporting both the court's original decision and its supplementary opinion after reargument).

and Paraguay, which according to the defendants eliminated the statutory basis for the prosecution. The district court ruled against them on both points and the Supreme Court affirmed it as to those issues.)[25]

The constitutional problem Judge Byers discerned in Conboy's case stemmed from a well-known but up to this point rather innocuous principle that judges had attributed to the Constitution since the time of John Marshall: Congress may not delegate its authority to make laws to either of the other two branches of the federal government. House Joint Resolution 347 was plainly a conferral of authority on the president: rather than imposing of its own force a prohibition on arms sales, the joint resolution did so in the event that the president issued the contemplated proclamation. The constitutional issue this raised was whether in doing so Congress had violated the delegation rule. As we have seen, the joint resolution was ambiguous, at least arguably, about the nature of the steps the president was required to take in order to issue the proclamation, but that had seemed of little moment in May 1934. Legislation authorizing the president to impose or remit limitations on trade with particular countries was no novelty, the earliest examples dating from the 1790s. In the 1813 case of *The Aurora*, the Supreme Court accepted the applicability of the delegation principle to such laws but concluded that the 1810 act under review merely authorized the president to determine whether a certain event had occurred.[26] Subsequent cases applied the delegation principle in a variety of contexts, but as of 1934 the Court had never invalidated an act of Congress on that ground.

Only six years before Congress passed the Chaco joint resolution, a unanimous Court decided *J.W. Hampton, Jr., Co. v. United States*, in which it sustained the validity of a trade provision empowering the president to change tariff rates if he found that existing ones did not equalize the differences in production costs between United States and foreign manufacturers. Such a determination was hardly the same as deciding whether a foreign government had rescinded specified edicts (the finding required in the act upheld in *The Aurora*); as the government pointed out in *Curtiss–Wright* a substantial body of opinion supported the conclusion that "costs are in the last analysis matters of opinion and are not susceptible of scientific determination."[27] In *J.W. Hampton*, the Supreme Court appeared to dismiss such considerations as

---

[25] The district court's discussion of these arguments is found at *id.* at 235–38, and the Supreme Court's at 299 U.S. 304, 330–33 (1936).

[26] Cargo of the Brig Aurora v. United States, 11 U.S. (7 Cranch) 382, 388 (1813).

[27] Brief for the United States at 14 n.5, *Curtiss–Wright*, 299 U.S. 304 (No. 98) (quoting *Report of Special Committee of the Senate on Investigation of the Munition Industry*, S. Rep. No. 944, pt. 2, at 6 (1935)).

constitutionally insignificant. The principle forbidding the delegation of Congress's powers, the Court asserted, put no obstacle in the way of Congress "seeking assistance from" the president in carrying out the policies that Congress chooses: "Congress has found it frequently necessary to use officers of the executive branch within defined limits, to secure the exact effect intended by its acts of legislation, by vesting discretion in such officers to make public regulations interpreting a statute and directing the details of its execution." The *J.W. Hampton* Court rejected the argument that there were precise rules cabining Congress's power to vest discretion in this manner. "[T]he extent and character of that assistance must be fixed according to common sense and the inherent necessities of the governmental co-ordination." "[S]uch legislative action is not a forbidden delegation of legislative power" as long as "Congress shall lay down by legislative act an intelligible principle" governing the executive's exercise of discretion.[28] Under this approach, House Joint Resolution 347 appeared safe from attack on delegation grounds.

Enter, stage left, the Roosevelt administration and the National Industrial Recovery Act of 1933 (NIRA).[29] NIRA was the centerpiece of the so-called "first New Deal," the administration's and Congress's initial attempt to combat the ravages of the Great Depression by creating a comprehensive federal industrial policy that would be enforced through a combination of mandatory management-labor cooperation and federal bureaucratic oversight. NIRA and similar legislation deliberately cast the executive's supervisory powers in broad and discretionary terms, often with the aim of enabling government regulators to obtain "voluntary" private sector compliance through the threat of mandatory regulation, and stated the statutory purposes at a very high level of abstraction and at times without relating specific grants of discretion to any particular purpose.

The drafting process in Congress that produced NIRA had included a variety of features intended to incorporate the willing participation of business in the statutory scheme, but within a year and a half corporate opposition to the statute and to its chief implementing agency, the National Recovery Administration (NRA) was turning to constitutional litigation as a tool for resisting a system that many sincerely viewed as statist and ineffective.[30] The reasons were various: the NRA's erratic leadership and NIRA's inherent ambiguities had produced "a crazy quilt

---

[28] 276 U.S. 394, 406, 409 (1928).

[29] *See* National Industrial Recovery Act, ch. 90, 48 Stat. 195 (1933), *invalidated by* A.L.A. Schechter Poultry Corp. v. United States, 295 U.S. 495 (1935).

[30] *See generally* George McJimsey, *The Presidency of Franklin Delano Roosevelt* 55–75 (2000).

of business arrangements, accompanied by continuing struggles for dominance of [particular industries' regulatory] authorities" while there
were few signs that NIRA was stimulating a significant economic up-
turn.[31] During the first half of 1935, the Supreme Court decided two
cases in which the validity of discretionary executive power under NIRA
was in question, and in both cases the Court ruled, almost unanimously,
that the statute had violation the rule against delegation of governmental power.

Panama Refining Co. v. Ryan, decided in January, invalidated
section 9(a) of NIRA, which authorized the president to forbid the
interstate or international transportation of oil produced or removed
from storage in violation of state law without furnishing any express
criterion whatever for when the president should do so. With Justice
Benjamin Cardozo the lone dissenter, the Court held that the provision
gave the president

> an unlimited authority to determine the policy and to lay down the
> prohibition, or not to lay it down, as he may see fit. And disobedi-
> ence to his order is made a crime punishable by fine and imprison-
> ment.
>
> . . . .
>
> . . . The Congress left the matter to the President without
> standard or rule, to be dealt with as he pleased.[32]

A.L.A. Schechter Poultry Corp. v. United States, which came down in
May, involved another provision of NIRA, section 3, under which the
president was empowered to approve "codes of fair competition" governing business practices in a given industry (drafted by business and labor
interests in that industry) that were then enforceable by criminal
penalties. Before doing so, section 3 required the president to assure
himself that the drafting process had been open, and to "find" that the
code was not designed to promote monopolies or to eliminate or oppress
small enterprises, and will not operate to discriminate against them; the
putative goal of "fair competition" was not otherwise defined. The Court
held that this requirement failed to satisfy the constitutional principle
that Congress must provide a "standard or rule" to guide the president's
exercise of discretion.

> But these restrictions leave virtually untouched the field of policy
> envisaged by [NIRA's general purposes of spurring economic recov-

---

[31] *Id.* at 73.

[32] Panama Ref. Co. v. Ryan, 293 U.S. 388, 415–18 (1935); *cf. id.* at 440 (Cardozo, J.,
dissenting) (concluding that section 9(a) should be read in light of NIRA's overall purposes
and that doing so provided "a sufficient definition of a standard to make the statute
valid").

ery and eliminating "unfair competitive practices"], and, in that wide field of legislative possibilities, the proponents of a code, refraining from monopolistic designs, may roam at will, and the President may approve or disapprove their proposals as he may see fit. That is the precise effect of the further finding that the President is to make—that the code "will tend to effectuate the policy of this title." While this is called a finding, it is really but a statement of an opinion as to the general effect upon the promotion of trade or industry of a scheme of laws. . . .

. . . .

. . . [T]he discretion of the President in approving or prescribing codes, and thus enacting laws for the government of trade and industry throughout the country, is virtually unfettered. We think that the code-making authority thus conferred is an unconstitutional delegation of legislative power.[33]

Even Justice Cardozo, a consistent defender of broad congressional power, thought section 3 went too far. "The delegated power of legislation which has found expression in this code is not canalized within banks that keep it from overflowing. It is unconfined and vagrant. . . . Here in effect is a roving commission to inquire into evils and upon discovery correct them."[34]

Taken together, the "hot oil" and "sick chicken" cases appeared substantially to rewrite the constitutional law of delegation and in doing so to set a very serious question mark against the validity of House Joint Resolution 347. Neither decision, to be sure, purported to overrule *J.W. Hampton* and the Court's opinion in *Panama Refining* distinguished the tariff acts of the early Republic as conferring on the president "an authority which was cognate to the conduct by [the president] of the foreign relations of the government"—although the Court also commented, more ominously, that "these early acts were not the subject of judicial decision."[35] The joint resolution, furthermore, was not truly subject to the feature of section 9(c), the complete absence of any indication of Congress's specific objective or other limitation on the authority vested in the president, that proved fatal in *Panama Refining*: Judge Byers agreed with the government that Congress's policy and goals were clear.[36]

---

[33] A.L.A. Schechter Poultry Corp. v. United States, 295 U.S. 495, 538, 542 (1935).

[34] *Id.* at 551 (Cardozo, J., concurring).

[35] *Panama Refining*, 293 U.S. at 422.

[36] United States v. Curtiss–Wright Exp. Corp., 14 F.Supp. 230, 239 (S.D.N.Y. 1936).

The Chaco law was, however, arguably indistinguishable from NIRA section 3: as with section 3, all the joint resolution required of the president was some process (in the Chaco case, consultation with other governments) and what the *Schechter Poultry* Court termed "a statement of an opinion as to the general effect" of exercising the president's discretion[37] ("if the President finds that the prohibition of the sale of arms and munitions of war in the United States to those countries now engaged in armed conflict in the Chaco may contribute to the reestablishment of peace between those countries"). That, at any rate, was Judge Byers's conclusion. Unlike earlier laws that the Supreme Court had upheld, Byers thought that the joint resolution did not require the president to make "a true finding" about "if or when a given state of facts" is so. Instead, what the joint resolution "called a finding . . . by its nature is an opinion or forecast" that "if certain transactions were forbidden, the interdiction would have ability (capacity) to contribute a desired future result," the restoration of peace in the Chaco. The joint resolution was, therefore, squarely within the rule of *Schechter Poultry*, and an invalid delegation of legislative power to the executive. On reargument, Conboy vigorously pressed the argument that a decision invalidating the law would play havoc with "the successful conduct of the foreign relations of this government," but Byers thought it beside the point that the joint resolution "deals primarily with matters of international relations." His reasoning on this issue was somewhat opaque but seems in part to have rested on his view that the conduct of foreign affairs is not "necessarily involved" in a criminal prosecution for conduct that took place within the United States. The joint resolution was, therefore, unconstitutional and as a consequence the president's proclamation invoking it was a legal nullity.[38]

Judge Byers's decision posed an obvious and immediate threat not just to the administration's Chaco policy but to FDR's longer-term objective of obtaining the authority to use arms embargos as a discretionary tool for the conduct of American foreign policy toward aggressor states. More broadly still, if Byers's interpretation of *Schechter Poultry* was correct, it would be difficult to defend FDR's vision of a government that acted on broad concepts such as "the public interest" or "national purpose" that allowed the details of public law to emerge through interaction between government and various interest groups.[39] The executive therefore took the case up to the Supreme Court under a 1907 statute allowing such direct appeals in criminal cases where a district

---

[37] *Schechter Poultry*, 295 U.S. at 538.

[38] *Curtiss–Wright*, 14 F.Supp. at 239.

[39] *See generally* George McJimsey, *The Presidency of Franklin Delano Roosevelt* 293–96 (2000).

court sustained a demurrer on the ground that the act of Congress supporting a criminal charge was unconstitutional. As we shall see in the next section, in December 1936, the Court reversed Byers on the delegation issue, which allowed *Curtiss–Wright* to return to the district court.

After the Supreme Court remanded the case, Conboy secured a new indictment of the original defendants as well as others (including two other Curtiss–Wright companies) in December 1937. The January 1939 trial ended in a mistrial after Judge Vincent L. Leibell discovered that a juror had engaged defendant John Allard in a sidewalk conversation outside the courthouse. A second trial ended in a hung jury on most of the counts. By this time, the Curtiss–Wright empire's financial worries were long past—the corporate group sold over 159 million dollars in warplanes and engines to American and foreign governments in 1938 alone, as the approach of World War Two made the demand for military aircraft rise precipitously—and its management had become interested in avoiding the negative publicity that a third and possibly lengthy trial might bring. The defendants therefore pled guilty, and on February 15, 1940, Judge John W. Clancy imposed a fine of $260,000 on the Curtiss–Wright corporate defendants and $11,000 each on Allard and Clarence Webster. The government did not seek a prison sentence for either man on the stated ground that they had acted on Chairman Hoyt's orders. Three other individual defendants, almost certainly far less central to the scheme than Allard and Webster, received sentences of a year and a day.[40]

The Supreme Court Decision

We return now to *Curtiss–Wright*'s sojourn in the high Court. The government's brief, apparently the product of collaboration between Conboy and the office of Solicitor General Stanley Reid, inadvertently testified to its authors' fear that Judge Byers had read *Schechter Poultry* correctly and that under that decision Congress could not validly confer discretionary authority on the president when the constraint on that discretion was a duty to arrive at an opinion or forecast of future events as opposed to a "true" finding of present fact. The first part of the brief's discussion on the merits argued that the validity of House Joint Resolution 347 was not actually open to challenge in light of the very longstanding practice "in the conduct of our foreign relations ... of

---

[40] In addition to the discussion in Robert A. Divine, *The Case of the Smuggled Bombers, in Quarrels That Have Shaped the Constitution* (John A. Garraty ed., 1964), see *$328,000 Assessed in Arms–Ban Case*, N.Y. Times, Feb. 16, 1940, at 2; *Indictments Charge Arms Sale to Chaco*, N.Y. Times, Dec. 22, 1937, at 4; *New Neutrality Trial On*, N.Y. Times, Jan. 17, 1939, at 6; *Plane Embargo Case Goes to Trial Here*, N. Y. Times, Jan. 10, 1939, at 21.

conferring upon the President power similar to that conferred" by House
Joint Resolution 347. In other words, it was simply too late in the day to
apply *Schechter Poultry*.[41]

Assuming nonetheless that the constitutional issue was not settled,
and further assuming that Byers was right to find in *Schechter Poultry* a
constitutional distinction between findings of act and forecasts of the
future, the brief went on, the president's obligation under the joint
resolution fell on the present-fact side of the line. "The President must
find a fact presently existing at the time of proclamation, to wit, will the
prohibition of arms *now* contribute to the reestablishment of peace in
the Chaco *now*." That the joint resolution addressed an issue involving
"the external relations of the United States" was highly relevant, but as
with the argument from practice only to support an argument ultimately
grounded elsewhere. The considerations necessary to determine "the
ultimate fact of the effect of the prohibition of sales of arms" were
"peculiarly available to the President" because they required an evaluation of "the constantly changing situation of the belligerents and the
complex and varying attitudes of other nations as revealed by continuous
diplomatic correspondence." The joint resolution thus satisfied *Schechter
Poultry* even on the district court's reading of that decision.

The administration's concern over the outcome in *Curtiss–Wright*
went far beyond its interest in the now-obsolete Chaco law, of course,
and its lawyers' ultimate goal was to minimize the impact of *Schechter
Poultry* on congressional flexibility and executive discretion. The brief
for the United States reflects this priority. The government's most basic
argument in the *Curtiss–Wright* brief was accordingly a flat rejection of
Judge Byers's fact/forecast dichotomy. The brief pointed to many cases—
carefully *not* citing *Schechter Poultry* at this point—in which the Court
had upheld statutes requiring decisions based in part on judgments
about the future effects of a given action: quoting one of the most
familiar expressions in New Deal legislation, the brief noted that
"[w]hether continuation of or change in the present situation is most apt
to be 'in the public interest' in the future has been held a proper basis
for the exercise of delegated authority." Under the Court's decisions
(now including *Schechter Poultry* in a string citation), "the proper test,
and the only test, of the validity of authority vested by Congress in the
executive is the absence of a free and arbitrary discretion." *Schechter
Poultry*, according to the government, was simply *J.W. Hampton*.

The extremely able lawyers for the main *Curtiss–Wright* defendants
defended the district court's fact/forecast distinction, hammered at the
weaknesses in the government's arguments, and brought up further

---

[41] Brief for the United States at 7–9, United States v. Curtiss–Wright Exp. Corp., 299
U.S. 304 (1936) (No. 98).

difficulties with its position. The argument from practice, they argued, amounted to a claim that in the area of foreign affairs, "the separation of powers under the Constitution may be disregarded," a proposition supported neither by principle nor by any decision of the Court.

> The prohibition against unwarranted delegations to the President can make no distinction between legislation generally on the one hand and legislation which may affect our foreign relations on the other, or among legislation which regulates interstate trade and commerce, legislation which regulates foreign commerce, legislation which imposes taxes, or legislation which declares a state of war to exist. All are equally subject to the same standards and the same limitations.

Under the government's logic, Congress could authorize the president to go to war if he found that doing so would contribute to the reestablishment of peace between warring nations, in which case "it [would be] the President and not Congress who decided whether this country should go to war."[42]

The defendants' lawyers forcefully pointed out the logical difficulty with the government's argument that the joint resolution was valid under *Schechter Poultry*. Even if the "finding" required by the law met that decision's requirements, which of course they did not concede, the joint resolution allowed and indeed required a further step: "Th[e] proclamation is a final essential. But the President is under no obligation to proclaim anything. Whether he shall do so or not is purely optional. He may ... decline for any ... reason, or indeed, for no reason at all...." Even if the president concluded that an arms prohibition would end the Chaco War immediately and had secured the cooperation of other governments, the joint resolution gave him "unfettered discretion" over whether to invoke his authority under the joint resolution. Even under the government's view of the rule governing delegation, this could not be constitutional. "If the option ... to decide whether the law shall take effect or not, is not a surrender of the legislative power to make or not to make a law, it is hard to conceive what would amount to such a surrender."[43]

---

[42] Brief for Appellees, John S. Allard, Clarence W. Webster and Samuel J. Abelow at 20, *Curtiss–Wright*, 299 U.S. 304 (No. 98); *see also* Brief for Appellees, Curtiss–Wright Export Corporation and Curtiss Aeroplane & Motor Company, Inc. at 16–26, *Curtiss–Wright*, 299 U.S. 304 (No. 98).

[43] Brief for Appellees, Curtiss–Wright Export Corporation and Curtiss Aeroplane & Motor Company, Inc. at 17–19, *Curtiss–Wright*, 299 U.S. 304 (No. 98); *see also* Brief for Appellees, John S. Allard, Clarence W. Webster and Samuel J. Abelow at 10–21, *Curtiss–Wright*, 299 U.S. 304 (No. 98).

The constitutional ban on delegations to the executive of unlimited discretion, furthermore, was no mere formalism but a necessary corollary to the Constitution's express provisions governing the enactment of federal laws. If Congress can leave the decision whether to bring legislation into effect entirely up to the president's will, it can give him what amounts to "a deferred veto—one that the Congress could never vote or override, and one not provided for in the Constitution," since he can sign it into law, or even veto it and have his veto overridden, and then "refuse to make the proclamation." If valid, the procedure authorized by the joint resolution "would invest the President with a power far more effective than the constitutional veto."[44]

In light of what ensued, the most striking feature of all the substantive briefs in *Curtiss–Wright* is the subordinate role played by ideas about the exercise of power over foreign affairs. There were lawyers in the Roosevelt administration at the time who were arguing internally for a more forceful assertion of the president's independent authority in the external domain. Assistant Secretary of State R. Walton Moore, for example, wrote a memorandum in August 1935 asserting that Congress ought to allow wide executive discretion in wielding the arms-embargo tool in part because it is "the President . . . who is primarily responsible for our international affairs." The idea that denying the president discretion to target aggressor states in imposing an embargo could prevent him from involving the United States in war without congressional approval was simply naive given the president's unilateral constitutional authority: "That power exists [already] because as Commander-in-Chief . . . he can attack and invade some other country and in conducting our foreign relations, he can place our country in such an attitude toward some other country as to make war inevitable."[45] But the lawyers drafting the administration's brief in *Curtiss–Wright* made no such claims. Their invocation of the president's "conduct . . . of the foreign relations of the Government" (the phrase itself was a quote from the Court's opinion in *Panama Refining*) was more limited, intended to define an area of legislation in which, whether because of settled practice, presidential access to facts, or the Court's own language, the delegation principle might cut less deeply.[46] And as we have seen, the

---

[44] Brief for Appellees, Curtiss–Wright Export Corporation and Curtiss Aeroplane & Motor Company, Inc. at 18–19, *Curtiss–Wright*, 299 U.S. 304 (No. 98); *see also* Brief for Appellees, John S. Allard, Clarence W. Webster and Samuel J. Abelow at 10–21, *Curtiss–Wright*, 299 U.S. 304 (No. 98).

[45] Moore, Memorandum on Neutrality (Aug. 27, 1935), *in* Justus D. Doenecke & Mark A. Stoler, *Debating Franklin D. Roosevelt's Foreign Policies 1933–1945*, at 97, 98–99 (2005).

[46] Brief for the United States at 8, *Curtiss–Wright*, 299 U.S. 304 (No. 98) (quoting Panama Ref. Co. v. Ryan, 293 U.S. 388, 422–25 (1935)).

defendants' lawyers, who stood to lose ground if the Court put any weight on the foreign-affairs aspect of the case, labored mightily to insist that the delegation principle necessarily applied in the same way to the Chaco law as it had to NIRA. Nothing in any of the briefs would have suggested to their first readers that *Curtiss–Wright* would become a central player in debates over who controls American foreign policy.

Curtiss–Wright was argued on November 19 and 20, 1936. Martin Conboy represented the government and George Z. Medalie, like Conboy a former United States Attorney, argued for the defendants. The justices were, for that era, unusually active, with Chief Justice Charles Evans Hughes (a former Secretary of State) and Associate Justices James C. McReynolds and George Sutherland (former members of the Senate Foreign Relations Committee) repeatedly questioning Conboy and Medalie about the foreign-affairs aspects of the case. Perhaps aware that Congress would be considering new arms control legislation early in the new year, the Court moved with considerable speed to decide the case, and the decision was announced on December 21, in an opinion written by Justice Sutherland. Six other justices joined in Sutherland's conclusion that *Schechter Poultry* was not controlling in *Curtiss–Wright* and that the joint resolution was constitutional: Judge Byers had erred and his judgment had to be reversed. Justice McReynolds dissented without opinion, noting only that he was "of opinion that the court below reached the right conclusion and its judgment ought to be affirmed."[47] Justice Stone, who was ill, did not participate.

* * *

George Sutherland was seventy-four in December 1936 and had been a member of the Court for fourteen years. Sutherland previously served in the Utah state legislature and in both the House (1901–03) and Senate (1905–17) of the U.S. Congress, and in 1916–17 he was the president of the American Bar Association.[48] While serving in the Senate, Sutherland showed both a strong interest in and strong views on issues of constitutional power. He was a critic of expansive interpretations of Congress's power to regulate interstate commerce. He argued against a 1909 proposal to use the power to ban interstate shipment of goods produced with convict labor, for example, on the ground that if it were legitimate the entire system of enumerated powers would be overthrown: "there would seem to be no phase of the business of domestic manufacture which it could not in the same way control." At the same time, Sutherland supported a Teddy Roosevelt robust approach to foreign policy and argued in the 1909 debates that the federal government's

---

[47] *Curtiss–Wright*, 299 U.S. at 333 (McReynolds, J., dissenting).

[48] For Sutherlands' biography, see generally Joel F. Paschal, *Mr. Justice Sutherland: A Man Against the State* (1951).

powers in that area rested on very different grounds than its domestic authority. "I deny that it is a Government of delegated powers when it comes to deal with a foreign nation. In our dealings with foreign nations, as I claim, the Government of the United States is a sovereign power dealing with foreign nations in its sovereign capacity." In that same year Sutherland issued a Senate document sketching out in more detail this distinction between the domestic and foreign affairs powers of the government, which he published in March 1910 as an essay entitled "Internal and External Powers of the National Government."[49]

Defeated for reelection as a senator in 1916, Utah's first popular election to the Senate, Sutherland went into private practice in Washington. By that time he had enjoyed a cordial relationship for several years with the president of Columbia University, Nicholas Murray Butler; Butler genuinely admired Sutherland's learning (Columbia awarded Sutherland an honorary degree in 1913, recognizing him as "profoundly versed in the law and polity of the Constitution"), and subsequent to Sutherland's electoral defeat Butler invited him to deliver the Blumenthal Lectures at Columbia in December 1918. The invitation was a signal honor: previous Blumenthal Lecturers included Presidents Wilson and Taft. Sutherland responded with energy and verve, using his 1910 essay as a starting point, and delivered *Constitutional Power and Foreign Affairs* in person and then (with remarkable swiftness) as a book that Columbia University Press published in February 1919.[50]

Sutherland's central aim in his lectures was to develop at some length the theory he had advocated since at least 1909 that the domestic and international powers of the national government are essentially different in source and scope. The Constitution is the source of the domestic powers of the government, which it enumerates and grants, for the most part to Congress, by carving out those powers from the authority originally possessed by the states. "In all matters of *internal* sovereignty ... the original reservoir of power was in the states; portions therefrom were delegated to the national government; the residue was retained by the states." In contrast, the source of the government's powers over foreign affairs lay in the powers of international sovereignty originally possessed by the Crown, powers which were plenary and defined not by local political arrangements but by the law of nations. "These powers passed directly to the Nation as the result of successful revolution.... When the Constitution was framed, therefore, the undi-

---

[49] 44 Cong. Rec. 2506 (1909); George Sutherland, *The Internal and External Powers of the National Government*, 191 N. Am. Rev. 373, 388 (1910).

[50] G. Edward White, *The Transformation of the Constitutional Regime of Foreign Relations*, 85 Va. L. Rev. 1, 56 (1999); *see also* Joel F. Paschal, *Mr. Justice Sutherland: A Man Against the State* 87, 96–99 (1951); *Columbia Turns Out Its Largest Class*, N.Y. Times, June 5, 1913, at 6.

vided powers of *external* sovereignty were in the Union, which antedated the Constitution and was made 'more perfect' by it." The Constitution therefore did not confer those powers on the federal government—they were already possessed by the federal government of the day, the Confederation Congress—although it did regulate and distribute them among the new instrumentalities of national authority.[51]

For Sutherland this was no mere theoretical point: it was, instead, the basis for the only sound approach to the interpretation of federal power. Any federal claim to domestic authority "must be justified by the express grants of the Constitution" and doubts are to resolved against its validity, while any federal claim to authority over external affairs is presumptively valid, "justified unless the powers are prohibited by the Constitution, or unless contrary to the fundamental principles upon which it was established." In either case, "[t]he sovereign will of the Nation is embodied in the Constitution and its exercise is measured thereby; but in the one case it is manifested by what that instrument affirms and in the other case by what it fails to negative." The distinction between domestic and foreign powers is therefore fundamental on a practical as well as a theoretical level: in the domain of external affairs, the federal government has the legitimate authority to do *anything* a sovereign may legally do under international law in the absence of an explicit constitutional prohibition.[52]

It is easy to exaggerate the radical character of Sutherland's argument in *Constitutional Power and World Affairs*. While it is true that Sutherland's historical assertions about the founders' views on the source of the federal foreign affairs powers are debatable, his nationalistic view of their scope was hardly novel, being essentially the same professed by Thomas Jefferson and many others in the early Republic.[53] Sutherland's description of the foreign affairs powers as "extra-constitutional"[54] was inconsistent with the language in some Supreme Court opinions but close to that found in others;[55] only a year after the book

---

[51] George Sutherland, *Constitutional Power and World Affairs* 43–44 (1919).

[52] *Id.* at 46–47.

[53] *See generally* David M. Golove, *Treaty-Making and the Nation: The Historical Foundations of the Nationalist Conception of the Treaty Power*, 98 Mich. L. Rev. 1075 (2000).

[54] George Sutherland, *Constitutional Power and World Affairs* 55 (1919).

[55] *Compare* Fong Yue Ting v. United States, 149 U.S. 698, 711 (1893) ("The United States are a sovereign and independent nation, and are vested by the constitution with the entire control of international relations, and with all the powers of government necessary to maintain that control, and to make it effective.") *with* Cunningham v. Neagle, 135 U.S. 1, 64 (1890) (president's powers include the power to enforce "the rights, duties, and

appeared the Supreme Court vindicated a specific example Sutherland gave when it upheld a federal migratory bird act as a valid execution of the treaty power while assuming that Congress could not have enacted the law under its enumerated powers.[56] Sutherland carefully disavowed any claim that the federal government could legitimately ignore a constitutional prohibition by invoking its external powers: the extra constitutional source of those powers does not license the violation of a negative limitation the Constitution places on the government.

Sutherland, finally, said surprisingly little about the constitutional powers of the president. He did affirm (in a rather low key manner) the president's exclusive role in negotiations with foreign powers, although he implied that the Senate's exclusion, at least where a treaty is being negotiated, is as much a matter of lacking the means as of lacking the legitimate authority to participate directly. In fact he put greater emphasis on the significance of the Senate's constitutional power to give the president advice on treaties which, he insisted, could not properly be reduced to that of an up or down vote on the final product of negotiations.[57] Finally, by the standards of early twenty-first century debates, Sutherland stated a distinctly pro-Congress view of the line between legislative and executive power with respect to involving the United States in armed conflict.[58] In tone, moreover, the lectures were far indeed from an encomium to unilateral presidential authority. "The office of President has grown in potency and influence to an extent never dreamed of by those who framed and adopted the Constitution"—no constitutional compliment coming from Sutherland. "Even in normal times, Congress has been subjected to such a degree of executive domination as to threaten the stability of the principle of departmental independence involved in the distribution of the several powers among the three branches of government." In times of international crisis, Sutherland continued, "the people . . . are coming to regard him as the sole repository of their power which, very decidedly, he is not."[59]

Whatever one makes of Sutherland's constitutional theory, *Constitutional Power and World Affairs* clearly showed him to be one of the justices best prepared to handle *Curtiss–Wright* with both learning and

---

obligations growing out of the constitution itself, our international relations, and all the protection implied by the nature of the government under the constitution").

[56] *See* Missouri v. Holland, 252 U.S. 416 (1920); *see also* George Sutherland, *Constitutional Power and World Affairs* 154–55 (1919).

[57] George Sutherland, *Constitutional Power and World Affairs* 122–28 (1919); *see especially id.* at 123 ("the power of the Senate . . . is to advise as well as consent, and its power is co-ordinate, throughout, with that of the President").

[58] *See id.* at 71–76, 110–11.

[59] *Id.* at 75–76.

celerity, and that may well be the main reason that Chief Justice Hughes assigned him to write the opinion of the Court. Hughes may also have thought that Sutherland would be likely to keep the Court from splintering badly since Sutherland's general adherence to the narrow-construction view of congressional (domestic) power might prevent other justices belonging in that camp from straying into dissent. If these assumptions are correct, Hughes achieved his immediate goals: a substantial opinion, written quickly, and with only one justice dissenting (and even he declined to write). The Chief Justice's decision about who should write the opinion was nonetheless momentous, as it turned out, for how Justice Sutherland carried out his assignment has proven, in the long run, more important than the actual ruling that his opinion announced.

After introducing the case and stating the defendants' main constitutional arguments, Sutherland announced that the Court was not going to decide what was for the administration and its lawyers the most fundamental issue lurking in the case: "[w]hether, if the Joint Resolution had related solely to internal affairs, it would be open to the challenge that it constituted an unlawful delegation of legislative power to the Executive." Thus almost from the outset, the government's lawyers knew that the Court was not going to loosen the grip its 1935 delegation cases had put on New Deal flexibility, while the defendants' lawyers understood that their lengthy arguments that the Court could not pick and choose in applying the delegation doctrine of *Panama Refining* and *Schechter Poultry* had gone for naught. The only question the Court would answer was whether, "assuming (but not deciding) that the challenged delegation, if it were confined to internal affairs, would be invalid, may it nevertheless be sustained on the ground that its exclusive aim is to afford a remedy for a hurtful condition within foreign territory?"[60]

With the question before the Court narrowed in this way, Sutherland launched into a direct reprise of the fundamental thesis of *Constitutional Power and World Affairs*. "[That there are] differences between the powers of the federal government in respect of foreign or external affairs and those in respect of domestic or internal affairs," he wrote, "and that these differences are fundamental, may not be doubted." The opinion's next three pages in the United States Reports are taken up with a brisk summary of chapters two and three of the 1919 book, at the conclusion of which Sutherland asserted that "we have shown [that] the federal power over external affairs [is] in origin and essential character different from that over internal affairs...."[61] At this point, however, Sutherland's 1936 opinion diverged sharply from his lectures in tone. He

---

[60] United States v. Curtiss–Wright Exp. Corp., 299 U.S. 304, 315 (1936).

[61] *Id.* at 315–19.

began by linking his distinction between internal and external powers to another idea almost entirely absent from *Constitutional Power and Foreign Affairs*: "participation in the exercise of the power [over external affairs] is significantly limited." What immediately follows this rhetorical linkage is the most famous passage in the opinion, also unparalleled in his earlier lectures.

> In this vast external realm, with its important, complicated, delicate and manifold problems, the President alone has the power to speak or listen as a representative of the nation. He makes treaties with the advice and consent of the Senate; but he alone negotiates. Into the field of negotiation the Senate cannot intrude; and Congress itself is powerless to invade it. As Marshall said in his great argument of March 7, 1800, in the House of Representatives, 'The President is the sole organ of the nation in its external relations, and its sole representative with foreign nations.'
>
>   . . . .
>
> It is important to bear in mind that we are here dealing not alone with an authority vested in the President by an exertion of legislative power, but with such an authority plus the very delicate, plenary and exclusive power of the President as the sole organ of the federal government in the field of international relations—a power which does not require as a basis for its exercise an act of Congress, but which, of course, like every other governmental power, must be exercised in subordination to the applicable provisions of the Constitution.[62]

Gone are the 1919 cautions about the constitutional "right and authority of the Senate to participate in the making of treaties at any stage of the process," gone the worry that in an international crisis "Congress will be driven from its traditional and constitutional place in public thought, as a co-ordinate branch of the government."[63] At the heart of Sutherland's opinion in *Curtiss–Wright* is an account of the constitutional order reoriented from his 1919 defense of the foreign-affairs authority of the national government (and Congress in particular) against federalism and narrow-construction attack to an assertion of the foreign-affairs authority of the president that stresses its independence of Congress.

It is impossible to absolve Sutherland of the accusation of leaving some ambiguity about just what all this has to do with the question of delegation that was actually before the Court, but if one reads his opinion charitably its logic is tolerably clear. Since they do not stem from the Constitution, the foreign-affairs powers are not defined by that

---

[62] *Id.* at 319–20 (citation omitted).

[63] George Sutherland, *Constitutional Power and World Affairs* 76, 123 (1919).

instrument and are plenary except as limited by "applicable provisions of the Constitution." In distributing these powers it does not create, the Constitution makes the president the "sole organ of the federal government in the field of international relations," and places few prohibitions on his conduct of those relations: it is therefore the president's power in this domain that is, for the most part, "delicate, plenary and exclusive." As the primary decisionmaker in foreign policy, the president determines the principles governing that policy, and it follows that a delegation rule crafted to preserve Congress's role in defining policy is simply, logically, inapplicable. Furthermore, and here Sutherland began to adopt part of the government's argument, when Congress legislates with respect to foreign-affairs objectives, it therefore properly takes account of the executive's control, in practice and principle, of the tools of intelligence, secrecy and negotiation that are essential to success in the area.

> [T]he legislator properly bears in mind the important consideration that the form of the President's action—or, indeed, whether he shall act at all—may well depend upon the nature of the confidential information which he has or may thereafter receive, or upon the effect which his action may have upon our foreign relations.[64]

By this point in hearing or reading the opinion, it had long been clear what the Court's holding was going to be, but Sutherland was not through with the delegation issue. He proceeded for several pages to review the history of legislation granting the president broad discretion over international trade and related issues, which he agreed with the government went "a long way in the direction of proving the presence of unassailable ground for the constitutionality of the practice." While he conceded that the Court was not bound by the course of legislative precedent, he once again agreed with the government that holding the Chaco joint resolution unconstitutional would implicitly invalidate a "uniform, long-continued and undisputed legislative practice.... [E]ven if the practice found far less support in principle than we think it does, we should not feel at liberty at this late date to disturb" it. Detailed consideration of the defendants' criticisms of the details of the joint resolution was unnecessary "both upon principle and in accordance with precedent, [which provide] sufficient warrant for the broad discretion vested in the President to determine whether the enforcement of the statute will have a beneficial effect upon the re-establishment of peace in the affected countries [and] whether he shall make proclamation to bring the resolution into operation...."[65] In short, neither Judge Byers's distinction between finding facts and making predictions, nor the defendants' demonstration that the joint resolution left the president una-

---

[64] *Curtiss–Wright*, 299 U.S. at 321–22.

[65] *Id.* at 327–29.

bridged discretion to determine whether to invoke his authority once he made the required finding, were constitutionally relevant. In the vast external realm of foreign affairs, Congress can empower the president to act on the basis of forecast and opinion, and the president can be left with the absolute discretion whether to act at all. The joint resolution was constitutional, in the end, because congressional authorization to make domestic arms sales to the Chaco combatants a criminal offense was only a modest legislative assist to the essentially presidential power of determining whether the United States ought to ban such sales as part of its—his—foreign policy.

* * *

The day before the Supreme Court announced its decision in *Curtiss–Wright*, an informed odds-maker might have thought it rational to bet either way on the outcome. The (near-)unanimity of the 1935 delegation cases indicated that all of the justices were prepared to treat the delegation principle seriously as a constraint on federal power, and four members of the Court, including Justice Sutherland, appeared to many people to be consistent opponents of attempts to expand the administrative power of government. On the other hand, *Panama Refining Co. v. Ryan* had suggested a reluctance to retreat from the Court's historic acquiescence in broad delegations of power in the area of international trade.[66] Furthermore, barely more than seven months before, in the most recent decision involving the scope of congressional power, *Carter v. Carter Coal Co.*, Justice Sutherland's opinion for a bare majority alluded to his theory about the radical distinction between the two sets of federal power. ("The question in respect of the inherent power of that government as to the external affairs of the Nation and in the field of international law is a wholly different matter which it is not necessary now to consider.")[67] The Court's decision in *Curtiss–Wright* was neither a shocking surprise nor obviously preordained.

There are, nevertheless, mysteries about the outcome in the case. The lawyers for Curtiss–Wright Export and the other defendants skillfully argued to the Court that House Joint Resolution 347 was, in the final analysis, even more constitutionally defective than Judge Byers had realized. The problem with the law was not just the arguably technical difference between finding a fact and making a prediction—the joint resolution allowed the president, after he did some preliminary work, to make arms sales to Bolivia and Paraguay a crime or not simply by choosing. No on the Court seems to have been troubled by this except perhaps the pugnacious Justice McReynolds, who only suggested that he disagreed on the technical difference on which Byers relied. The Court

---

[66] 293 U.S. 388, 421–22 (1935).

[67] 298 U.S. 238, 295 (1936).

was, to be sure, only four months away from *NLRB v. Jones & Laughlin Steel Corp.*, which turned out to be a decisive turn away from restrictive views of congressional power, but that decision too was not predictable and the Court made it over Sutherland's objections.[68]

It also remains a mystery why Sutherland himself reworked in the president's favor the theory that *Curtiss–Wright* gave him the chance to write into law. If the crudest of the legal-realist arguments then in vogue were correct, one would have expected Sutherland, a "conservative" Republican opposed in principle to much of the New Deal trajectory in federal government, to look for chances to embarrass FDR, a "liberal" Democrat and the very symbol of the New Deal. Crude legal realism, however, is obviously useless in this context, and Sutherland's most recent advocate, political theorist Hadley Arkes, argues that Sutherland had come to see that in principle and practice only the executive branch could carry out many of the functions that his theory ascribed to the national government.[69]

The Immediate and Longer-term Impact of Curtiss–Wright

The national press identified the Court's decision in *Curtiss–Wright* as a broad vindication of the "President's Vast Power in Foreign Field" and of the Roosevelt administration's persistent search for "authority for him to exercise wide discretion in limiting exports to combatants." Assistant Secretary of State Moore was reported by the New York Times to have predicted, no doubt with relish, that the decision was "likely to have marked effect on the future of neutrality legislation." The Times indicated some skepticism about Moore's comments, although the Post asserted that *Curtiss–Wright* "was generally believed to open the door for a more vigorous neutrality course, providing the approach is discretionary with the President, rather than mandatory."[70]

Moore, it turned out, was a poor forecaster. While the sort of anti-aggressor authority FDR had long sought would clearly be immune from constitutional attack under Sutherland's opinion, *Curtiss–Wright* played no apparent role in the struggle between the administration and its congressional opponents over whether to grant the president discretionary arms-embargo authority or impose on him a mandatory and impartial duty of neutrality in terminating American arms sales to warring states. FDR's foes continued to have the upper hand throughout the rest

---

[68] 301 U.S. 1 (1937). Sutherland joined Justice McReynolds's dissent. *Id.* at 76.

[69] *See* Hadley Arkes, *The Return of George Sutherland: Restoring a Jurisprudence of Natural Rights* 196–241 (1994).

[70] Robert C. Albright, *Highest Court Affirms Arms Embargo Act*, Wash. Post, Dec. 22, 1936, at 1; *High Court Backs Neutrality Power Held by President*, N.Y. Times, Dec. 22, 1936, at 1.

of the decade, and the Neutrality Acts of the period expressly denied the president discretion of the sort *Curtiss–Wright* allowed; the suggestion that the decision required Congress to afford the executive such discretion was ignored. More broadly, as the press recognized, Sutherland's opinion left *Panama Refining* and *Schechter Poultry* untouched, and it was the Supreme Court's famous recession from its narrow view of federal power beginning in March 1937, not *Curtiss–Wright*, that ultimately proved to have freed Congress and the executive from the constraints the 1935 delegation decisions appeared to have fashioned.

Curtiss–Wright played only a narrow role as precedent in the Court's decisions in the first few years after it was decided. Four and a half months after delivering the opinion in *Curtiss–Wright*, Justice Sutherland again spoke for the Court in a case involving foreign affairs. *United States v. Belmont* involved the legality of the agreement by which the Soviet Union assigned to the United States its interest in various assets within the latter's jurisdiction in return for formal recognition. Writing for a six-justice majority (Justices Stone, Brandeis and Cardozo concurred in the result), Sutherland relied on his favored distinction between internal and external powers in concluding that the national government had the power to enter into the agreement, and invoked the language, though not the name, of *Curtiss–Wright*, in further concluding that "in respect of what was done here, the Executive had authority to speak as the sole organ of th[e United States] government."[71] He expressly cited his earlier opinion only for the general proposition that state laws and policies cannot interfere with federal decisions in the realm of foreign affairs.[72] Sutherland retired from the Court on January 18, 1938, and his personal role in the saga of *Curtiss–Wright* came to an end. The Court applied *Belmont* in a 1942 decision called *United States v. Pink* in an opinion by Justice William O. Douglas that again invoked *Curtiss–Wright*,[73] but other than that, before *Johnson v. Eisentrager* in 1950 opinions of the Court cited *Curtiss–Wright* rarely and inconsequentially.[74]

Commentary in the law reviews was rather muted at first. A student comment in the Harvard Law Review described Justice Sutherland's account of the origin and character of the foreign affairs power as "novel

---

[71] United States v. Belmont, 301 U.S. 324, 330 (1937).

[72] *Id.* at 331, 332.

[73] 315 U.S. 203 (1942). Unlike Sutherland in *Belmont*, in *Pink* Douglas expressly quoted *Curtiss–Wright*'s description of the president as "sole organ." *See id.* at 229.

[74] 339 U.S. 763, 789 (1950) (citing *Curtiss–Wright* for the proposition that "the President is exclusively responsible" for "diplomatic and foreign affairs" in the context of denying that an enemy alien held by the United States abroad in the wake of World War Two could challenge his detention in an American court.)

and broad ... but how far the delegation [of power by Congress] may go remains for future clarification," while the Georgetown Law Review editors observed that "[o]n the face of it the case is a long step toward executive autonomy in the field of foreign relations." Other references to the decision tended to focus on its relationship to the "stricter attitude toward delegation manifested by the Supreme Court during the past two years." The first thorough academic discussion of Sutherland's opinion came out ten years after the decision, and was highly critical.[75]

Despite occasional assertions to the contrary, there is little reason to attribute great importance to the role of *Curtiss–Wright* in the first couple of decades after it was handed down. The period was one in which after 1940 executive discretion and independent authority in the international arena increased exponentially, but *Curtiss–Wright* was at most a bit player in this drama, a useful source of rhetoric about the president as "sole organ" and his "delicate, plenary and exclusive" powers for those arguing on quite other grounds for the legitimacy of unilateral presidential action. Attorney General Robert Jackson's famous opinion in the 1940 destroyers-for-bases arrangement with Britain is a good example. Jackson quoted the entire "plenary and exclusive" paragraph from *Curtiss–Wright* but made no analytical use of it—he immediately acknowledged that the president's "plenary" authority "is not unlimited," and spent the rest of his opinion parsing the discretion Congress had permitted the president under the relevant statutes.[76]

The Supreme Court's celebrated decision invalidating President's Truman's seizure of the steel industry in *Youngstown Sheet & Tube Co. v. Sawyer*, decided in 1952, marks an appropriate end-point for an examination of *Curtiss–Wright*'s immediate impact.[77] By 1952, the delegation issue had receded in importance, and *Curtiss–Wright*'s specific holding seemed unexceptionable ... and also unimportant. Cases such as *Belmont*, *Pink*, and *Johnson v. Eisentrager* showed that the Court continued to share Justice Sutherland's reluctance to be "in haste" to interfere with the president's conduct of foreign affairs, although in no instance had the Court employed Sutherland's opinion to narrow or limit Congress's powers in the interest of executive autonomy.

---

[75] Recent Decisions, 36 Colum. L. Rev. 1162, 1164 (1936); Recent Decisions, 25 Geo. L.J. 738, 740 (1937); Recent Cases, 50 Harv. L. Rev. 691, 692 (1937); *see* David M. Levitan, *The Foreign Relations Power: An Analysis of Mr. Justice Sutherland's Theory*, 55 Yale L.J. 467 (1946).

[76] Acquisition of Naval and Air Bases in Exchange for Over–Age Destroyers, 39 Op. Att'y Gen. 484, 486–88 (1940).

[77] 343 U.S. 579 (1952). Sutherland's "in haste" comment quoted later in the paragraph is from *Curtiss–Wright*, 299 U.S. at 322.

The Steel Seizure Case on its face left *Curtiss–Wright* without any real significance. Writing for the Court, Justice Hugo Black appeared to reject Sutherland's concept of extra constitutional federal power entirely (if implicitly). Like *Curtiss–Wright*, *Youngstown* involved executive action within the United States but directed toward an external goal (in *Youngstown*, the federal seizure of steel mills in order to ensure the continued supply of munitions to the United States armed forces fighting the Korean War). "The President's power, if any, to issue the [seizure] order must stem either from an act of Congress or from the Constitution itself," Black wrote, and he found in the Constitution no independent executive power to carry out the policy Truman's order sought to effect.[78] Justice Jackson's concurrence, later to become the best known and most influential of the *Youngstown* opinions, relegated *Curtiss–Wright* to a footnote that described Sutherland's opinion as largely dicta and in any event irrelevant to issues involving the separation of powers between Congress and the president other than delegation. "It was intimated that the President might act in external affairs without congressional authority, but not that he might act contrary to an Act of Congress."[79]

After *Youngstown*, one might well have expected *Curtiss–Wright* to drop out of sight altogether from constitutional debate, a period piece that later developments had left behind. That this did not occur was the result, I suspect, of the basically common-law mindset of American lawyers. *Curtiss–Wright*, after all, is a decision of the United States Supreme Court that has never been overruled and indeed, viewed narrowly as a decision, no one has ever seriously questioned. It is, in short, an "authority" apparently available for use. For lawyers (and others) interested in defending unilateral presidential action in the realm of foreign affairs or in resisting congressional efforts to limit the president's discretion there, Justice Sutherland's flamboyant language has proven irresistible—"this vast external realm, with its important, complicated, delicate and manifold problems ... the President alone has the power to speak or listen ... Congress itself is powerless to invade ... the very delicate, plenary and exclusive power of the President as the sole organ of the federal government in the field of international relations—a power which does not require as a basis for its exercise an act of Congress." And executive-branch lawyers and apologists have, understandably, not resisted. "Among government attorneys, Justice Sutherland's lavish description of the president's powers ... is so often cited that it has come to be known as the '*Curtiss–Wright*-so-I'm-right' cite—a

---

[78] 343 U.S. at 585.

[79] *Id.* at 635 n.2 (Jackson, J., concurring).

statement of deference to the president so sweeping as to be worthy of frequent citation in any government foreign-affairs brief."[80]

Pro-executive enthusiasm about *Curtiss–Wright* has in turn sparked a considerable backlash among scholars. Much of the criticism has echoed Justice Jackson's dismissal of Sutherland's language as dicta, although what is perhaps the most careful and elaborate examination of the opinion's legal and historical underpinnings, a 1973 article by historian Charles A. Lofgren, came to the conclusion that most of Sutherland's argument was relevant to the holding but "shockingly inaccurate" history. "If good history is requisite to good constitutional law, then *Curtiss–Wright* ought to be relegated to history."[81] In recent years, a small but growing number of scholars have sought to rehabilitate the *Curtiss–Wright* opinion, but I believe it is still fair to say that the scholarly mainstream still treats the opinion as "a muddled law review article wedged with considerable difficulty between the pages of the United States Reports."[82] To be sure, the critics' efforts to demolish Sutherland's opinion have not kept it out of briefs or judicial opinions: "for every scholar who hates Curtiss–Wright, there seems to exist a judge who loves it,"[83] although the high Court justices have made rather circumspect express use of the decision. (No post–*Youngstown* decision by the Supreme Court clearly rests on *Curtiss–Wright* as controlling precedent.) It is curiously difficult, as a result, to describe the current status of *Curtiss–Wright*. Is it a decisional antique containing a discredited and misleading account of the president's powers or "authoritative doctrine"[84] on which judges and executive decisionmakers can and should rely?

The Continuing Importance of Curtiss–Wright Today

What one is to make of *Curtiss–Wright* today depends on which of the stories that the case generates is in view. Take the delegation issue: it is easy enough to conclude that the Supreme Court's holding and (narrow) rationale—House Joint Resolution 347 was constitutional because the delegation principle is less constraining when Congress is addressing foreign affairs—are beyond question. But I wonder. Justice Sutherland did not actually address the defendants' argument that the

---

[80] Harold Hongju Koh, *The National Security Constitution: Sharing Power After the Iran–Contra Affair* 94 (1990).

[81] Charles A. Lofgren, United States v. Curtiss–Wright Export Corporation: *An Historical Reassessment*, 83 Yale L.J. 1, 32 (1973).

[82] Michael Glennon, *Two Views of Presidential Foreign Affairs Power:* Little v. Barreme *or* Curtiss–Wright?, 13 Yale J. Int'l L. 5, 13 (1988).

[83] Anthony Simones, *The Reality of* Curtiss–Wright, 16 N. Ill. U. L. Rev. 411, 415 (1995).

[84] Louis Henkin, *Foreign Affairs and the Constitution* 25–26 (1972).

joint resolution gave the president what amounts to a deferred veto, unconstrained and congressionally uncontrollable discretion to turn on or off the criminal-law authority of the United States. In 1998, the Court invalidated the Line Item Veto Act because it allowed the president to sign a bill into law and then "cancel" the effects of some of its provisions. If that is correct, why should it be constitutional for Congress to permit the president to decide, after approving a law, to conclude that it will remain a nullity even though he or she has determined that it will achieve Congress's goals?[85] Perhaps the formal difference between that act and *Curtiss–Wright*-style discretion is an adequate justification, but the issue seems at least open to discussion.

Curtiss–Wright did not address directly the boundary between federal and state authority, or the supremacy of national law, but Justice Sutherland's introduction into his opinion of his Blumenthal Lectures theory gives the decision a role in those issues. On that score, the judicial and academic critique of his historical account of the Crown-to-nation transmission of extra-constitutional powers has been withering ... but in practical terms Sutherland's approval of plenary national power has prevailed.

In the early Twenty–First Century, the real significance of *Curtiss–Wright* lies in what the decision may say about one of the most contestable issues of our day, the relationship between the powers of Congress and those of the president over foreign affairs. Critics of broad, independent executive authority view as radically incorrect Justice Sutherland's language about "the very delicate, plenary and exclusive power of the President as the sole organ of the federal government in the field of international relations." Sutherland's quotation of John Marshall on the "sole organ" point, they often argue, is a cheat—all Marshall meant was that foreign governments communicate with the United States through the president, not that the president decides what to say or do in response.[86] Executive apologists, in contrast, continue to play the

---

[85] *See* Clinton v. City of New York, 524 U.S. 417 (1998). The Court cited *Curtiss–Wright* for the general proposition that in the area of foreign affairs the president enjoys "a degree of discretion ... which would not be admissible were domestic affairs alone involved," but carefully avoided any reference to the fact that the discretion upheld in *Curtiss–Wright* was apparently completely unfettered. *See id.* at 445 (quoting *Curtiss–Wright*, 299 U.S. at 320).

[86] *See* Charles A. Lofgren, United States v. Curtiss–Wright Export Corporation: *An Historical Reassessment*, 83 Yale L.J. 1, 30–31 (1973); Michael Glennon, *Two Views of Presidential Foreign Affairs Power:* Little v. Barreme *or* Curtiss–Wright?, 13 Yale J. Int'l L. 5, 11–12 (1988); *cf.* H. Jefferson Powell, *The Founders and the President's Authority over Foreign Affairs*, 40 William & Mary L. Rev. 1471, 1521–28 (1999) (concluding that the critics are right about the meaning of the "sole organ" passage in Marshall's speech but that Marshall nevertheless thought the president enjoys independent policymaking authority over foreign affairs).

"*Curtiss–Wright*-so-I'm-right" card: "What don't you understand about plenary and exclusive?" is the point. On this view, Congress's role in foreign affairs is that of a quartermaster supplying the tools that the president needs.[87] Argument over what to make of Sutherland's opinion in this regard is endless, but (I suggest) instrumental: when the president's independent power is at stake, comments about the meaning of *Curtiss–Wright* tend to be ideological weapons rather than stages in a real effort to discern the best answer to a question of constitutional law.

There is no single, incontrovertible way to tell the story, the stories, of *Curtiss–Wright*. In many respects the decision is obsolete or unimportant. It is, furthermore, truly bizarre to think that profound questions about the foreign policy of the United States might turn on Sutherland's words: no one embraces Sutherland's cherished theory about the twofold nature of federal power and the opinion probably doesn't make sense without the theory. Nevertheless, Sutherland's opinion in *Curtiss–Wright* remains the single most obvious judicial source of language about the relative positions of the legislature and executive in making foreign policy. *Curtiss–Wright* invites us to address an issue that more recent decisions have not always squarely addressed: to what extent do the Constitution's arrangements of institutional responsibility place foreign relations in the president's sphere? In doing so, however, the decision raises a question that it does not resolve, unless we are to take adjectives for answers.*

---

[87] *See, e.g.*, The President's Constitutional Authority to Conduct Military Operations Against Terrorists and Nations Supporting Them, 2001 WL 34726560, at *6 (O.L.C. Sept. 25, 2001) (quoting *Curtiss–Wright* in describing the president's foreign affairs power as exclusive and plenary).

* I am grateful to Jasper Liou for his outstanding assistance and for the many opportunities to think the issues through with Sarah ans Sara Powell.

*

7

Patricia L. Bellia

The Story of the *Steel Seizure* Case

Youngstown Sheet & Tube & Co. v. Sawyer, in which the Supreme Court invalidated President Truman's seizure of the nation's steel industry, is perhaps the best known of the Court's presidential power cases. For modern students of constitutional law, the *Steel Seizure* case is typically the framing separation-of-powers case, offered both to illustrate the "formal" and "functional" threads in the Court's decisions and to introduce the Court's approach to questions about the relative powers of the President and Congress in foreign affairs. Some observers regard the *Steel Seizure* case not only as a significant case in the Supreme Court's separation-of-powers canon, but also as a turning point in the Court's handling of politically charged constitutional questions.[1]

When President Truman announced the seizure of the nation's steel industry on April 8, 1952, few could have predicted the steel controversy's legacy. President Truman's action was taken in the midst of the Korean conflict, at a time when high-level military advisers claimed that the United States and its allies were holding the line against the advance of Communism with ammunition rather than soldiers' lives. Past presidents had seized private property—even entire industries—when necessary to preserve wartime production. In this case, moreover, the President and many of his advisers saw no legitimate labor-management dispute, but instead believed that the steel companies were using the specter of a strike to strong-arm the government into raising steel prices. The seizure was a way to maintain steel production while bringing the industry back to the bargaining table, not an opportunity to litigate great and unanswered questions of presidential power.

---

[1] *See generally* Maeva Marcus, *Truman and the Steel Seizure Case: The Limits of Presidential Power* (1977). Marcus's work remains the definitive treatment of the *Steel Seizure* case. For a collection of more recent reflections on the impact of the *Steel Seizure* case, *see Youngstown at Fifty: A Symposium*, 19 Const. Comm. 1 (2002).

In the weeks that followed the seizure, however, a series of tactical blunders by the government brought those questions to the fore in district court. When the government defended the seizure by invoking an extremely broad theory of presidential power, the image of profit-hungry steel companies gave way to the image of a power-hungry President. The pillars of the government's theory were far from novel. Indeed, they had been propounded or otherwise supported by three of the sitting Justices of the Supreme Court, including two who had served as advisers to President Roosevelt when he faced threatened work stoppages before and during World War II[2] and one who, as President Truman's Attorney General, had supported a broad conception of "inherent" presidential powers to act in an emergency.[3] But the government's position before the district court was so extreme that even a prompt disavowal could not save the case.

The story of the *Steel Seizure* case provides important context for modern readers who might perceive a chasm between what the decision stands for and what it says. The decision has tremendous rhetorical and symbolic significance in justifying judicial policing of executive action in a range of contexts. Yet as a matter of doctrine, it is difficult to see why the case occupies this position. The decision leaves open a major question about executive power—whether the President can ever claim a nontextual constitutional power to act in an emergency absent, or even contrary to, congressional action. Even the most enduring opinion of the case, Justice Jackson's concurrence, can support both narrow and broad judicial constructions of presidential power.

In resolving the *Steel Seizure* case, the district court and the Supreme Court could have avoided deciding the underlying constitutional question at several turns. That fact is significant. After the executive branch's own actions provoked the district court to forcefully reject the government's claims, the government moderated its claims, thus inviting the Supreme Court to uphold the seizure on narrow factual grounds. The significance of the *Steel Seizure* case lies in part in the fact that the Court chose to forgo this path. Courts now invoke the *Steel Seizure*

---

[2] Justice Robert H. Jackson, of course, served as President Roosevelt's Attorney General. Chief Justice Fred M. Vinson had served, among other positions, as Director of the Office of Economic Stabilization, and in that capacity had filed an affidavit in connection with President Roosevelt's December 1944 seizure of the plants and facilities of Montgomery Ward & Co. *See* Affidavit No. 8, United States v. Montgomery Ward & Co., No. 44 C 1611; Box No. 899; Civil Action Files; U.S. District Court for the Northern District of Illinois (N.D.Ill.); Records of District Courts of the United States, Record Group 21 (RG21); National Archives and Records Administration—Great Lakes Region (Chicago) (NARA–Chicago).

[3] Justice Tom C. Clark served as President Truman's Attorney General before being appointed to the Court. For discussion of his advice to President Truman, *see* text accompanying notes 39, 218.

precedent in the most delicate of cases involving perceived government abuses of power.

In celebrating the *Steel Seizure* case's implications for the judiciary, however, we should not overlook its messages to the political branches, particularly the messages of Justice Jackson's concurrence. The concurrence is famous for the framework it supplies for courts to evaluate presidential power claims—a framework that turns out to be less robust in theory and more malleable in practice than those who celebrate it might prefer. The concurrence's most pointed messages about how to preserve the balance of power between Congress and the President, however, are directed to the political branches. The story of the *Steel Seizure* case holds lessons not only for those who decide separation of powers questions, but also for those who generate them.

Factual Background

The Labor and Price Dispute

The dispute that precipitated President Truman's seizure of the steel mills was not purely a dispute between labor and management. The United States' involvement in the Korean conflict had produced considerable inflationary pressure. Government price controls were a key component of the administration's plan to control those pressures. The Defense Production Act, passed in 1950 to give the President discretionary authority to establish price ceilings on individual goods and services, simultaneously required the President to stabilize wages in affected industries when he did so.[4] To implement the Act, the President established separate entities to deal with wage and price stabilization issues, the Wage Stabilization Board (WSB) and the Director of Price Stabilization respectively.[5] As of the time of the steel dispute, the President by Executive Order had given the WSB the power to make recommendations to the President when a labor dispute threatened the national defense.[6]

On November 1, 1951, the United Steelworkers of America, C.I.O., provided notice of its intent to seek a new contract for its members. The union believed that, despite government price controls, the steel industry was operating at a high level of profits. The union therefore sought a substantial package of wage and benefit changes as well as a union shop in the steel mills. Almost immediately, the steel companies indicated that they would not grant a wage increase without a price increase.[7] The

---

[4] Defense Production Act of 1950, ch. 932, § 402(b), 64 Stat. 798, 803.

[5] Exec. Ord. 10,161, 3 C.F.R. § 339 (1949–1953).

[6] Exec. Ord. 10,233, 3 C.F.R. § 743 (1949–1953).

[7] A.H. Raskin, *Steel Puts Pay Rise Up to Government*, N.Y. Times, Nov. 16, 1951, at 17.

United States, meanwhile, refused to provide the steel companies any assurances that they would receive a price increase. Under the administration's approach to such cases, the Director of Price Stabilization would grant a price increase only under its existing formula, which tied price increases to the industry's profit level over a period of years.[8]

From the start, then, the steel dispute's awkward trilateral posture hampered productive negotiations between the union and the companies. The steel companies refused to make an offer to the union.[9] As the December 31 contract expiration date approached and the threat of a strike loomed, President Truman referred the dispute to the WSB to recommend a settlement.[10] The WSB's recommendations would not be binding on the parties, but they would be submitted to the President for further action. While the WSB considered the wage issue, the Office of Price Stabilization considered whether the steel industry would be entitled to price relief. The union, meanwhile, postponed its threatened strike.

The WSB recommended a package of wage and benefit measures to the President on March 20, over the objection of the industry members of the Board. Over the next two weeks, government officials attempted to work out a package of wages and benefits that would satisfy the union as well as a price adjustment that would satisfy the steel companies. Just days before the threatened strike, however, the steel companies and the government remained far apart. The average price of steel stood at approximately $110 per ton.[11] The Office of Price Stabilization wished to grant the steel industry a price increase of about $3 per ton, while the steel companies claimed that only an increase of $12 a ton would offset the increased labor costs.[12]

Throughout the dispute, the union had agreed that it would provide a least 96 hours' notice of a strike, to enable the industry to bank its

---

[8] More specifically, under the "industry earnings standard," OPS would increase a price ceiling only when an industry could not absorb cost increases without reducing its earnings below 85 percent of the three best years of the 1946–1949 period. *See* Office of Price Stabilization, Price Operations Memorandum No. 25 (Feb. 15, 1952) (on file with author) (discussing industry earnings standard announced on April 21, 1951); *see also* James A. Durham, *The Present Status of Price Control Authority*, 52 Colum. L. Rev. 868, 873 (1952).

[9] Maeva Marcus, *Truman and the Steel Seizure Case: The Limits of Presidential Power* 59 (1977).

[10] Statement by the President on the Labor Dispute in the Steel Industry, 1951 Pub. Papers 651 (Dec. 22, 1951).

[11] *Wilson Declares Steel Plan Blow to Stabilization*, N.Y. Times, Mar. 25, 1952, at 1.

[12] Maeva Marcus, *Truman and the Steel Seizure Case: The Limits of Presidential Power* 73–74 (1977).

furnaces. On April 4, the union affirmed that a strike would begin at 12:01 a.m. on April 9, and the steel companies began the process of shutting down the mills.

The Seizure Decision

As the strike loomed, the White House considered its options for maintaining an uninterrupted supply of steel for U.S. military efforts in Korea. The problem of how to prevent a threatened work stoppage from interfering with defense efforts was not a new one. In 1917 alone, the year the United States entered World War I, more than one million workers engaged in more than 4,000 strikes.[13] The federal government intervened when strikes threatened output in major industries, mainly by creating sector-specific boards to mediate disputes. Because the boards could neither compel the parties to submit to their jurisdiction nor bind the parties to accept a particular resolution, they were often ineffective in resolving disputes short of a strike. Immediately before and during the war, Congress passed statutes granting the President seizure authority in limited circumstances.[14] President Wilson seized numerous businesses throughout the war, sometimes citing specific statutory authority and sometimes citing the Constitution and laws of the United States.[15]

On the eve of U.S. involvement in World War II, President Roosevelt sought to prevent strikes by extracting a no-strike/no-lockout pledge from industry and labor leaders and by creating agencies—in this case, national and regional rather than sector-specific—to resolve disputes.[16] As in World War I, when such efforts failed, the government resorted to seizure to prevent labor disputes from disrupting war production. The first seizure episode occurred six months before the attack on Pearl Harbor. The dispute concerned the North American Aviation plant in Inglewood, California. The plant produced one-fifth of the nation's

---

[13] Melvyn Dubofsky & Foster Rhea Dulles, *Labor in America: A History* 82–86 (7th ed. 2004) (1949).

[14] In one such statute, the Army Appropriations Act of 1916, Congress authorized the President to take control of any system of transportation necessary to move troops or equipment. Act of Aug. 29, 1916, ch. 418, 39 Stat. 619, 645. In December 1917, President Wilson relied on this statute to place major railroads—then beset by numerous strikes—under federal control. Pres. Procl. of Dec. 26, 1917, 40 Stat. 1733. Congress specifically ratified the President's action the following year. Act of Mar. 21, 1918, ch. 25, 40 Stat.451, 451.

[15] The seizures are catalogued in Appendix II to Justice Frankfurter's opinion in the *Steel Seizure* case. 343 U.S. 579, 620–21 (Frankfurter, J., concurring).

[16] *E.g.*, Exec. Ord. 8716, § (2), 6 Fed. Reg. 1532 (1941) (creating National Defense Mediation Board); Exec. Ord. 9017, 7 Fed. Reg. 237 (1942) (creating National War Labor Board).

military airplanes, and the U.S. and British militaries had placed $200 million worth of orders with the plant. After a strike closed the plant in early June of 1941, the government considered how to ensure that its orders would be filled. National union leaders claimed that the strike was called by local union leaders without their approval and that the strike reflected the maneuvering of the Communist Party.[17] At the time, no statute spoke directly to how the government could respond to threatened unrest in a vital defense industry. President Roosevelt issued an Executive Order directing the Secretary of War to take charge of the plant,[18] and the striking workers yielded to 2,500 federal troops.[19]

Following issuance of the Executive Order, Robert H. Jackson, then serving as President Roosevelt's Attorney General, opined as follows on the legality of the Order:

> The Presidential proclamation rests upon the aggregate of the Presidential powers derived from the Constitution itself and from statutes enacted by Congress.

> The Constitution lays upon the President the duty "to take care that the laws be faithfully executed." Among the laws which he is required to find means to execute are those which direct him to equip an enlarged Army, to provide for a strengthened Navy, to protect Government property, to protect those who are engaged in carrying out the business of the Government, and to carry out the provisions of the Lease–Lend Act. For the faithful execution of such laws the President has back of him not only each general law enforcement power conferred by the various acts of Congress but the aggregate of all such laws plus that wide discretion as to method vested in him by the Constitution for the purpose of executing the laws.

> The Constitution also places on the President the responsibility and vests in him the powers of Commander in Chief of the Army and of the Navy. These weapons for the protection of the continued existence of the nation are placed in his sole command and the implication is clear that he should not allow them to become paralyzed by failure to obtain supplies for which Congress has appropriated the money and which it has directed the President to obtain.

> The situation at the North American plant more nearly resembles an insurrection than a labor strike. The President's proclama-

---

[17] *Text of Frankensteen's Declaration on Aviation Strike*, N.Y. Times, June 8, 1941, at 37.

[18] Exec. Ord. 8773, 6 Fed. Reg. 2777 (1941).

[19] Foster Hailey, *Bayonets on Coast*, N.Y. Times, June 10, 1941, at 1.

tion recites the persistent defiance of Governmental efforts to mediate any legitimate labor differences. The distinction between loyal
labor leaders and those who are following the Communist Party line
is easy to observe. Loyal labor leaders fight for a settlement of labor
grievances. Disloyal men who have wormed their way into the labor
movement do not want settlements; they want strikes. That is the
Communist Party line which those who have defied both the Government and their own loyal leaders to prevent a settlement of the
strike have followed. There can be no doubt that the duty constitutionally and inherently rested upon the President to exert his civil
and military, as well as his moral, authority to keep the Defense
effort of the United States a going concern.[20]

The North American Aviation seizure, and in particular its reliance
on the President's constitutional authority, would become an important
precedent for subsequent seizures. Although the government did not
invoke any specific statutory authority in the North American Aviation
seizure in 1941, between 1940 and 1944 Congress passed several laws
authorizing seizures in a variety of circumstances. The most significant
of these was the War Labor Disputes Act, passed in June 1943 over
President Roosevelt's veto. The statute authorized the President to take
over plants in which labor disputes threatened to disrupt war production.[21] President Roosevelt invoked this authority to seize more than 40
businesses throughout World War II.[22]

President Roosevelt also seized plants when the application of the
War Labor Disputes Act was highly questionable, and arguments regarding the President's *constitutional* powers figured prominently in those
disputes. Among the more notable seizures was the seizure of the
Chicago offices of Montgomery Ward & Co. in April 1944 by U.S. Army
troops, four months into a nationwide strike by the company's 12,000
workers. Montgomery Ward had refused to comply with a War Labor
Board order to recognize the United Retail, Wholesale and Department
Store Union and institute the terms of a collective bargaining agree-

---

[20] Statement of Attorney General Robert H. Jackson, June 9, 1941. This statement was
excerpted in the major newspapers. *See, e.g.*, Louis Stark, *Roosevelt Explains Seizure;
Jackson Cites Insurrection*, N.Y. Times, June 10, 1941, at 1, 16. The full statement appears
in the district court record in the *Montgomery Ward* case, accompanied by a letter from the
Assistant Solicitor General indicating that the Department of Justice considered the
statement to constitute an opinion of the Attorney General. Letter of Jan. 12, 1945, from
Hugh B. Cox, Assistant Solicitor General, to Al Woll, United States Attorney, United States
v. Montgomery Ward & Co., No. 44 C 1611; Box No. 899; Civil Action Files; N.D.Ill.; RG21;
NARA—Chicago.

[21] *See* War Labor Disputes Act, § 3, Pub. L. No. 89, 57 Stat. 163, 164 (1943).

[22] The seizures are catalogued in Appendix II to Justice Frankfurter's opinion in the
Steel Seizure case. 343 U.S. 579, 622–26 (Frankfurter, J., concurring).

ment. The Executive Order directing the seizure did not cite statutory authority.[23] Eight months later, when Montgomery Ward continued to refuse to recognize the union, President Roosevelt issued an Executive Order seizing all of Montgomery Ward's property nationwide, citing the War Labor Disputes Act as well as his power under the Constitution as Commander in Chief.[24]

The seizure was legally questionable because, by its terms, the War Labor Disputes Act authorized seizure of "any plant, mine, or facility *equipped for the manufacture, production, or mining* of any articles or materials which may be required for the war effort or which may be useful in connection therewith."[25] Montgomery Ward was a retail and mail order business and therefore claimed that it was not "equipped" for "manufacture, production, or mining." The day after the President issued the Executive Order, the United States filed suit in federal district court seeking a declaratory judgment that the seizure was proper and moved for a preliminary injunction prohibiting the company from interfering with its possession. In addition to arguing that the term "production" in the War Labor Disputes Act should be broadly construed to encompass Montgomery Ward's business, the government argued that the President had inherent constitutional authority to seize the company's property.[26] Fred M. Vinson, who would serve as Chief Justice when the Court heard the *Steel Seizure* case, was then Director of Economic Stabilization and filed an affidavit in the case.[27]

The district court rejected the government's statutory and constitutional arguments and directed the return of the company's property.[28] On appeal, however, the U.S. Court of Appeals for the Seventh Circuit reversed the district court on the statutory interpretation question[29] and

---

[23] Exec. Ord. 9438, 9 Fed. Reg. 4459 (1944).

[24] Exec. Ord. 9508, 9 Fed. Reg. 15079 (1944).

[25] War Labor Disputes Act § 3, 57 Stat. at 164 (emphasis added).

[26] Brief for the United States in Support of its Motion for a Temporary Injunction at 48, United States v. Montgomery Ward & Co., No. 44 C 1611; Box No. 899; Civil Action Files; N.D. Ill.; RG 21; NARA–Chicago.

[27] Affidavit No. 8, United States v. Montgomery Ward & Co., No. 44 C 1611; Box No. 899; Civil Action Files; N.D. Ill.; RG21; NARA–Chicago.

[28] United States v. Montgomery Ward & Co., 58 F.Supp. 408 (N.D. Ill. 1945).

[29] United States v. Montgomery Ward & Co., 150 F.2d 369 (7th Cir. 1945). The court reasoned that the word "production," although undefined in the War Labor Disputes Act, should be construed in the same manner as the term "production" under the Fair Labor Standards Act. Under that statute, production is defined as "produced, manufactured, mined, handled, or in any other manner worked on in any State," and the court concluded that the definition was broad enough to encompass transportation of products. *Id.* at 377.

declined to address the constitutional question.[30] In 1945, President Truman ended the seizure and the Supreme Court dismissed a pending appeal as moot.[31]

The legal landscape changed significantly after the end of World War II. Fueled in part by public hostility to the wave of strikes that followed World War II, the congressional elections of 1946 brought an end to the stronghold of Roosevelt New Deal Democrats. In June 1947, Congress adopted the Labor Management Relations Act, also known as the Taft–Hartley Act, which reduced the power of unions. The seizure provisions of the War Labor Disputes Act were to expire of their own force on June 30, 1947, six months after President Truman proclaimed the cessation of hostilities of World War II.[32] The Taft–Hartley Act took a different approach to the problem of strikes that threatened defense industries. Rather than authorizing seizure, the statute permitted the President to appoint a board of inquiry when he believed that a threatened strike would "imperil the national health or safety."[33] Once the board issued its report, the Attorney General could petition a federal district court to enjoin a strike for a period of 80 days.[34] Congress supplemented those provisions in 1948 with an amendment to the Selective Service Act. The amendment permitted the President to take possession of facilities that failed to fill orders placed by the government for goods required for national defense purposes.[35] In addition, in 1951, Congress amended the Defense Production Act to authorize the President to institute condemnation proceedings to requisition property when needed for the national defense.[36]

The legal and political landscape facing President Truman and his advisers at the time of the steel crisis was thus complex. On the one hand, multiple Presidents had seized property for defense efforts, sometimes under specific statutory authority, sometimes with questionable interpretations of existing statutes, and on occasion with no claim of

---

[30] *Id.* at 382.

[31] Montgomery Ward & Co. v. United States, 326 U.S. 690 (1945).

[32] *See* War Labor Disputes Act, Pub. L. No. 89, § 10, 57 Stat. 163, 168 (1943); 3 C.F.R. § 77 (1946 Supp.) (proclaiming on December 31, 1946, the termination of hostilities of World War II).

[33] Labor Management Relations Act, ch. 120, § 206, 61 Stat. 136, 155 (1947).

[34] *Id.* §§ 208–210, 61 Stat. at 155–56.

[35] Selective Service Act of 1948, ch. 625, § 18(a), 62 Stat. 604, 626.

[36] *See* Defense Production Act of 1950, ch. 932, § 201(a), 64 Stat. 798, 799–800 (authorizing President to requisition property); Amendments to Defense Production Act of 1950, ch. 275, § 102, 65 Stat. 131, 132 (requiring President to institute condemnation proceedings to obtain real property).

statutory authority whatsoever. On the other hand, the legal framework had changed significantly over time. The World War I patchwork of sector-specific responses to labor unrest had given way to the more comprehensive regulation of labor-management relations. And although the post-World War II amendments to the labor laws tended to shift the balance of power back towards management, the severe anti-strike provisions of the War Labor Disputes Act had expired. The Taft–Hartley Act authorized injunctions to ward off strikes but omitted any mention of seizure authority. The injunction mechanism was supplemented only by the fairly narrow provisions of the Selective Service Act addressing government orders and the condemnation provisions of the Defense Production Act.

Against this backdrop, President Truman's options were limited.[37] He had already referred the dispute to the Wage Stabilization Board, and union members had continued to work since December 31 without a contract. By the time the WSB issued its report on March 20, the union had postponed its strike for 80 days—all that could have been achieved under the Taft–Hartley Act. Congress had passed the Taft–Hartley Act over President Truman's veto and he and was therefore hostile to invoking it; moreover, numerous advisers perceived invoking it in these circumstances to be grossly unfair to the union, since the government had already achieved the full relief to which it was entitled.[38]

In short, the President's advisers could not identify a statute clearly supporting the President's authority to intervene in operation of the steel mills so as to prevent a curtailment of steel production. On the question of what powers the President might have under the Constitution, President Truman's legal advisors apparently gave mixed advice. In 1949, then-Attorney General Tom C. Clark had written of a President's "inherent" powers to act in an emergency—powers that he characterized as "exceedingly great."[39] Advisers could cite instances involving presidential seizure of businesses, some under statutory authority and a handful involving questionable interpretations of statutes or no statutory authority at all. But no court had directly addressed the scope of the President's constitutional powers to seize and operate a private business—except perhaps the district court in *Montgomery Ward*, which had

---

[37] For discussion of the advice President Truman received, *see* Maeva Marcus, *Truman and the Steel Seizure Case: The Limits of Presidential Power* 74–80 (1977).

[38] *Id.* at 75–76.

[39] Hearings on S. 249 Before the S. Comm. on Labor and Public Welfare, 81st Cong., 1st Sess. 232 (1949); *see also* Maeva Marcus, *Truman and the Steel Seizure Case: The Limits of Presidential Power* 338 n. 51 (1977) (discussing Clark's support for President's inherent powers).

cast doubt upon the legality of such action and which the Court of Appeals had reversed on statutory rather than constitutional grounds.

President Truman announced his decision to the nation in a radio address at 10:30 pm on April 8, 1952. The President stated that he had ordered Secretary of Commerce Charles Sawyer to operate the steel mills on behalf of the government of the United States. The Executive Order itself claimed that "steel is an indispensable component of substantially all" of the weapons and other materials needed by U.S. and other armed forces, that steel is "likewise indispensable to the carrying out of programs of the Atomic Energy Commission of vital importance to our defense efforts," and that a "continuing and uninterrupted supply of steel is also indispensable to the maintenance of the economy of the United States, upon which our military strength depends."[40]

The President's speech, however, went considerably beyond the terms of the order. The President rebuked the steel companies for demanding a significant price increase. He argued that stabilization formulas had been applied to the dispute and accepted by the union, but that the steel companies were using the threatened work stoppage to extort a substantial profit, at the expense of economic stability. The President described the companies' position as "about the most outrageous thing I ever heard of. They not only want to raise their prices to cover any wage increase; they want to double their money on the deal."[41]

Within an hour of the President's address, lawyers for two of the major steel companies, Youngstown Sheet & Tube and Republic Steel Corporation, arrived at the home of Judge Bastian of the U.S. District Court for the District of Columbia to request a temporary restraining order barring Secretary Sawyer from carrying out the President's Executive Order. Judge Bastian declined to grant the order without notice to the government and directed the lawyers to provide such notice at 9:00 am the following day and appear in court for a hearing at 11:30 am.[42]

As the legal proceedings began the following day, President Truman sent the first of two messages to Congress concerning the steel seizure. After explaining the reasons for his action, he concluded:

> On the basis of the facts that are known to me at this time, I do not believe that immediate Congressional action is essential; but I

---

[40] Exec. Ord. 10,340, 17 Fed. Reg. 3139 (1952).

[41] Press Release of April 8, 1952, at 4, *reprinted in The Constitutional Crisis over President Truman's Seizure of the Steel Industry in 1952*, 30 Documentary History of the Truman Presidency 109, 112 (Dennis Merrill, ed.) (2001).

[42] Maeva Marcus, *Truman and the Steel Seizure Case: The Limits of Presidential Power* 102 (1977).

would, of course, be glad to cooperate in developing any legislative proposals which the Congress may wish to consider.

If the Congress does not deem it necessary to act at this time, I shall continue to do all that is within my power to keep the steel industry operating and at the same time make every effort to bring about a settlement of the dispute so the mills can be returned to their private owners as soon as possible.[43]

Twelve days later, the President reiterated his position in a letter to the President of the Senate: "The Congress can, if it wishes, reject the course of action I have followed in this matter."[44]

The District Court Proceedings

Lawyers for Youngstown Sheet & Tube and Republic Steel, along with lawyers for five other major steel companies, appeared at 11:30 am on April 9 before Judge Alexander Holtzoff, who was assigned to hear motions that day.[45] Because the steel companies sought temporary restraining orders, they had to demonstrate not only that they would likely succeed on the merits, but also that the government's actions would lead to immediate and irreparable injury and that the steel companies would not have any adequate remedy at law. Proving immediate and irreparable injury was going to be difficult. The Executive Order stated that, despite the plants being under the direction of the Secretary of Commerce, "the managements of the plants, facilities, and other properties ... shall continue their functions."[46] The Secretary of Commerce had sent telegrams designating the President of each steel company covered by the order an "Operating Manager" for the United States. The telegrams directed each President "to continue operations for the United States" and required all officers and employees "to perform their usual functions and duties in connection with plant and office operation, and sale and distribution of products."[47] In other words, business would proceed as usual, except that the companies would fly the flag of the United States and post a notice of the United States' possession.[48]

---

[43] H.R. Doc. No. 82–422 (1952), *reprinted in* 1952 U.S.C.C.A.N. 883.

[44] Cong. Rec., Apr. 21, 1952, p. 4192.

[45] Transcript of Hearing of April 9, 1952, before Judge Holtzoff, *in* Transcript of Record, *Youngstown Sheet & Tube Co. v. Sawyer*, Nos. 744 & 745, at 217, *available in* U.S. Supreme Court Records and Briefs, 1832–1978 (Thomson Gale Doc. No. DW3901733850).

[46] Exec. Ord. 10,340, par. 3, 17 Fed. Reg. 3139 (1952).

[47] Telegram from Charles Sawyer, Attachment to Defendant's Opposition to Plaintiff's Motion for a Preliminary Injunction, *in* Transcript of Record, *Youngstown Sheet & Tube Co. v. Sawyer*, Nos. 744 & 745, at 21, *available in* U.S. Supreme Court Records and Briefs, 1832–1978 (Thomson Gale Doc. No. DW3901733850).

[48] *Id.*

If the seizure meant only that the steel companies' plants and facilities would fly the flag of the United States, then it was difficult to see how the companies would suffer irreparable injury. In the hearing before Judge Holtzoff, the companies argued principally that the government would alter the terms of employment and then require the steel companies to accept the new terms as a condition of the return of the companies' property. The companies' argument thus rested on a provision of the Executive Order, not yet invoked, empowering the Secretary of Commerce to "determine and prescribe terms and conditions of employment under which the plants, facilities, and other properties possession of which is taken pursuant to this order shall be operated."[49] The companies pointed out that the government had taken precisely this course in connection with its seizures of the coal industry in 1943 and 1945. Judge Holtzoff, however, viewed the mere possibility that the government would displace management or supersede its control over labor relations as insufficient to demonstrate immediate and irreparable injury. His brief opinion denied temporary relief but noted that the steel companies could renew their applications if circumstances changed.[50]

The occasion for the plaintiffs to renew their applications for preliminary relief arrived within ten days. On April 18, Secretary Sawyer announced that he would examine the terms of employment in the steel industry[51]—an announcement amplified two days later by his public statement that there would "certainly" be "some" wage increases.[52] Since April 10, Youngstown and Republic Steel had supplemented their complaints with motions for preliminary injunctions, and the other steel companies, including Bethlehem Steel, United States Steel, Armco Steel, and E.J. Lavino & Co., had also filed complaints. The task of considering the preliminary injunction motions fell to Judge David A. Pine, who set a hearing for April 24, 1952. Before the steel companies filed memoranda supporting their motions for preliminary injunctions, the Justice Department filed a memorandum of law in opposition. The steel companies filed responsive memoranda supporting the motion on the morning of the district court hearing.

When the hearing arrived, the steel companies apparently perceived that they would be fighting an uphill battle, and that Judge Pine was unlikely to focus on the merits of the seizure itself, let alone to enjoin it.

---

[49] Exec. Ord. 10,340, par. 3, 17 Fed. Reg. 3139 (1952).

[50] Transcript of Hearing of April 9, 1952, before Judge Holtzoff, *in* Transcript of Record, *Youngstown Sheet & Tube Co. v. Sawyer*, Nos. 744 & 745, at 265, *available in* U.S. Supreme Court Records and Briefs, 1832–1978 (Thomson Gale Doc. No. DW3901733850).

[51] *Sawyer Says He Will Order Steel Pay Boosts Next Week Unless Accord Is Reached*, Wall St. J., Apr. 19, 1952, at 2.

[52] *Steel Union To Get Raise, Sawyer Says*, Wash. Post, Apr. 21, 1952, at 1.

The companies' strategy was to steer Judge Pine toward a moderate course of action: that of enjoining changes to the terms and conditions of employment and thus protecting the companies' interests without ruling against the government on the ultimate question of the seizure's legality. The six attorneys who planned to argue on behalf of the large steel companies[53] at the April 24 hearing had divided the issues, with some focusing on the propriety of granting equitable relief and others focusing on the purported legal basis for the seizure. The steel companies opened with an argument by Theodore Kiendl, representing the United States Steel Company. Rather than addressing the purported legal basis for the seizure, Kiendl moved directly to whether the steel companies would have an adequate remedy at law in the absence of injunctive relief and whether the injury claimed by the steel companies was in fact immediate and irreparable.[54] The claim as to the immediacy of the injury again rested on the possibility—now more concrete in view of Secretary Sawyer's public statements—that the government would change the terms and conditions of employment. In light of this claimed injury, Kiendl stated that his client sought a preliminary injunction against the Secretary of Commerce's *threatened change in the terms of employment* rather than a preliminary injunction against the government's *possession of the steel mills*.[55] The strategy here seems clear, and it is difficult to believe that it had not been embraced by all of the steel companies: The companies sought to offer Judge Pine a middle course—a way to protect the companies' interests without ruling against the government on the underlying constitutional issue.

Judge Pine was surprised by the limited nature of the requested relief. He could not fathom why the steel companies would seek a preliminary ruling on the legality of the seizure but request an injunction that would perpetuate the claimed illegality—that is, Sawyer's continuing possession and control of the property.[56] As the steel compa-

---

[53] The six large steel companies included United States Steel, Bethlehem Steel, Republic Steel, Armco, Jones & Laughlin, and Youngstown. These companies claimed to account for approximately 70 percent of the steel industry. Transcript of Proceedings, Motion for Preliminary Injunction, Youngstown Sheet & Tube v. Sawyer, Civ. Action No. 1550–52, *in* Transcript of Record, *Youngstown Sheet & Tube Co. v. Sawyer*, Nos. 744 & 745, at 291, *available in* U.S. Supreme Court Records and Briefs, 1832–1978 (Thomson Gale Doc. No. DW3901733850). E.J. Lavino & Co. was also a party to the case and argued in the district court. In addition to the general arguments about the legality of the government's actions, E.J. Lavino & Co. also argued that it was not engaged in manufacturing steel and should not have been subject to the Executive Order or the implementing order issued by the Secretary of Commerce. *Id.* at 421.

[54] *Id.* at 285.

[55] *Id.* at 311.

[56] *Id.*

nies' lawyers began to recognize the significance of the judge's skepticism about Kiendl's position, they quickly broke ranks with Keindl and shifted strategy. When Judge Pine began polling the other parties concerning the relief they sought, Bruce Bromley, the lawyer for Bethlehem Steel, was the first to respond. Bethlehem Steel, he said, wanted "the whole hog"[57]—a preliminary injunction against the government's continued possession of its mills. When Judge Pine asked Youngstown's counsel, "If you should convince me of [the illegality of the seizure], you wouldn't want me to perpetuate the illegality, would you?," counsel responded, "I never look a gift horse in the face, Your Honor."[58] Ultimately, Kiendl was alone in arguing that the court need not consider whether to enjoin the government's continued possession of the mills.

Judge Pine's focus on the underlying legality of the seizure exposed a significant misstep on the government's part. Recall that the government filed its brief opposing the preliminary injunction motion first, despite the fact that the government was the non-moving party. As the non-moving party, the government should have tried to emphasize the equities surrounding the grant of preliminary relief rather than on the legality of the seizure. The government's brief, however, devoted over forty-five pages to the question of the President's constitutional authority to order the seizure of the mills—more than twice what it devoted to all of the equity issues combined.[59]

The government's ability to marshal a full argument on the question of presidential power in the short period of time between the filing of the plaintiffs' complaint and the filing of its memorandum of law was likely attributable to the litigation in the *Montgomery Ward* case. The government was the plaintiff and the moving party in *Montgomery Ward*, and it had fully briefed the question of the President's constitutional authority to seize private property in wartime at the district court,[60] in a petition for a writ of certiorari prior to judgment in the court of appeals,[61] and in

---

[57] *Id.* at 313.

[58] *Id.* at 315.

[59] *Compare* Memorandum of Points and Authorities in Opposition to Plaintiffs' Motion for Preliminary Injunction at 25–69, Youngstown Sheet & Tube v. Sawyer, No. 1550–52, Box No. 1160; Civil Action Files; U.S. District Court for the District of Columbia (D.D.C.); Records of the District Courts of the United States, Record Group 21 (RG21); National Archives Building, Washington D.C. (NAB), *with id.* at 7–24.

[60] *See* Brief for the United States in Support of its Motion for a Temporary Injunction, United States v. Montgomery Ward & Co., No. 44 C 1611; Box No. 899; Civil Action Files; N.D. Ill.; RG21; NARA–Chicago.

[61] Petition for Writ of Certiorari at 21–27, United States v. Montgomery Ward, 324 U.S. 858 (1945), No. 949.

the court of appeals.[62] Although the *Montgomery Ward* case involved a statutory issue not present in the *Steel Seizure* case—whether Montgomery Ward was engaged in "production" for purposes of the War Labor Disputes Act—the government had defended the seizure on constitutional grounds as well. The government's brief in the *Steel Seizure* case simply replicated these constitutional arguments, with some organizational changes.[63]

The government's posture as plaintiff in *Montgomery Ward* and defendant in the *Steel Seizure* case, however, made that strategy highly questionable. As plaintiff in *Montgomery Ward* seeking a declaratory judgment that its seizure action was proper, and as the movant for preliminary injunctive relief rather than the party opposing it, the government in *Montgomery Ward* necessarily would have sought to direct the court's attention to its central contentions about the legality of the Executive Order rather than the other equitable factors involved. As the non-moving party in the *Steel Seizure* case, however, the government should have sought to direct the court's attention to the inappropriateness of preliminary injunctive relief on the facts of that particular case.[64] The government's tactical error both allowed the steel companies to use their own memoranda of law to engage the government on the merits more fully than otherwise would have been possible and drew Judge Pine's attention squarely to that issue.

When the government finally took to the podium late in the afternoon of April 24, the task of arguing on behalf of the Secretary of

---

[62] The available files on the *Montgomery Ward* case do not contain the government's brief before the court of appeals, but the fact that the government focused heavily on that issue is apparent both from the court of appeals decision, United States v. Montgomery Ward, 150 F.2d 369, 381 (1945) (noting that the government advanced its constitutional arguments "even more elaborately than the point on which we rest our decision"), and from Montgomery Ward's petition for a writ of certiorari after the court of appeals decision, Petition for a Writ of Certiorari at 21–23, Montgomery Ward v. United States, 326 U.S. 690 (1945), No. 408.

[63] Stanley Temko, who was among U.S. Steel's attorneys during the *Steel Seizure* case, has suggested that the government largely copied its *Montgomery Ward* court of appeals brief into its district court brief in the *Steel Seizure* case. *See President Truman and the Steel Seizure Case: A 50–Year Retrospective*, 42 Duq. L. Rev. 685, 699 (2003); *see also* Maeva Marcus, *Truman and the Steel Seizure Case: The Limits of Presidential Power* 302–03 n.51 (1977). The absence of the court of appeals brief from the available *Montgomery Ward* files makes it difficult to confirm the extent of this claim. Archival research does, however, confirm the government's heavy reliance on the *Montgomery Ward* materials. *Compare* Memorandum of Points and Authorities in Opposition to Plaintiffs' Motion for Preliminary Injunction at 25–57, Youngstown Sheet & Tube v. Sawyer, No. 1550–52, *with* Brief for the United States in Support of its Motion for a Temporary Injunction at 48–58, 63–66, United States v. Montgomery Ward & Co., No. 44 C 1611.

[64] Marcus reaches a similar conclusion. *See* Maeva Marcus, *Truman and the Steel Seizure Case: The Limits of Presidential Power* 111 (1977).

Commerce fell to Holmes Baldridge, Assistant Attorney General for the Claims Division (now known as the Civil Division) of the Department of Justice. The government tried unsuccessfully to shift the court's focus back to questions surrounding the propriety of granting injunctive relief, arguing both that the steel companies had an adequate remedy at law and that the balance of equities favored the government. Judge Pine, however, quickly brought Baldridge back to the merits. Baldridge initially described the government's position as follows:

> Mr. Baldridge: We say that when an emergency situation in this country arises that is of such importance to the entire welfare of the country that something has to be done about it and has to be done now, and there is no statutory provision for handling the matter, that it is the duty of the Executive to step in and protect the national security and the national interests. We say that Article II of the Constitution, [which] provides that the Executive power of the Government shall reside in the President, that he shall faithfully execute the laws of the office and he shall be Commander-in-Chief of the Army and of the Navy and that he shall take care that the laws be faithfully executed, are sufficient to permit him to meet any national emergency that might arise, be it peace time, technical war time, or actual war time.[65]

Although this starting point was not far from the government's past arguments in relation to specific seizure episodes such as the North American Aviation incident or the Montgomery Ward incident, Judge Pine's highly critical questioning led Baldridge into statements from which the government would never recover, either in court or in the press:

> The Court: So you contend the Executive has unlimited power in time of an emergency?
>
> Mr. Baldridge: He has the power to take such action as is necessary to meet the emergency.
>
> The Court: If the emergency is great, it is unlimited, is it?
>
> Mr. Baldridge: I suppose if you carry it to its logical conclusion, that is true. But I do want to point out that there are two limitations on the Executive power. One is the ballot box and the other is impeachment.
>
> The Court: Then, as I understand it, you claim that in time of emergency the Executive has this great power.

---

[65] Transcript of Proceedings, Motion for Preliminary Injunction, Youngstown Sheet & Tube v. Sawyer, Civ. Action No. 1550–52, *in* Transcript of Record, *Youngstown Sheet & Tube Co. v. Sawyer*, Nos. 744 & 745, at 371, *available in* U.S. Supreme Court Records and Briefs, 1832–1978 (Thomson Gale Doc. No. DW3901733850).

Mr. Baldridge: That is correct.

The Court: And that the Executive determines the emergencies and the Courts cannot even review whether it is an emergency.

Mr. Baldridge: That is correct.[66]

Asked for "any case that sustains such a position as that,"[67] Baldridge sought to rest on past instances of executive seizures in the absence of statutory authorization. Judge Pine rejected the relevance of executive practice in the absence of judicial interference, arguing that "[t]he fact that a man reaches in your pocket and steals your wallet is not a precedent for making that a valid act."[68] The court recessed for the day and asked the government to be prepared to provide such authority the following morning.

The following morning, the district court's pointed questioning of the government's position continued unabated:

The Court: . . . Supposing the President should declare that the public interest required the seizure of your home and directed an agent to seize it and to dispossess you: Do you think or do you contend that the court could not restrain that act because the President had declared an emergency and because he had directed an agent to carry out his will?

Mr. Baldridge: I would rather, Your Honor, not answer a case in that extremity. We are dealing here with a situation involving a grave national emergency. . . . I do not believe any President would exercise such unusual power unless, in his opinion, there was a grave and an extreme national emergency existing. . . .[69]

In response to further questioning, Baldridge asserted that the Constitution distinguishes between the legislative and executive branches by enumerating only specific powers that Congress can exercise but vesting all executive power in the President. Judge Pine was astounded by the breadth of the government's argument: "So, when the sovereign people adopted the Constitution, it enumerated the powers set up in the Constitution [and] limited the powers of the Congress and limited the powers of the judiciary, but it did not limit the powers of the Executive. Is that what you say?" When Baldridge confirmed that "[t]hat is the way we read Article II of the Constitution," Judge Pine observed that "I have

---

[66] *Id.* at 371–72.

[67] *Id.* at 372.

[68] *Id.* at 372–73.

[69] *Id.* at 376

never heard that view expressed in any authoritative opinion of any court."[70]

The public reaction to the government's claims was swift and negative. President Truman disavowed the claims almost immediately,[71] and the government submitted a supplemental memorandum "clarifying" its position in light of "misunderstandings which may have arisen during the course of oral argument": "[T]he President possesses the constitutional power and duty to take action in a grave national emergency such as existed here. Beyond this, of course, we do not go."[72]

The memorandum, filed on April 29, 1952, could not undo the damage. The district court issued its opinion in the case the same day. The court focused first on whether the seizure was authorized by law. Unsurprisingly, the court's opinion on this point was a scathing indictment of the government's theory of presidential power. The court concluded that the Constitution did not grant the President the authority "to take such action as he may deem to be necessary ... whenever in his opinion an emergency exists requiring him to do so in the public interest."[73] After canvassing the cases cited by the government and concluding that all involved the President's exercise of authority under specific statutes, the court responded to the argument that past executive practice supported the legality of the President's action:

> [I]t is difficult to follow [the] argument that several prior acts apparently unauthorized by law, but never questioned in the courts, by repetition clothe a later unauthorized act with the cloak of legality. Apparently, according to [this] theory, several repetitive, unchallenged, illegal acts sanctify those committed thereafter. I disagree.[74]

The court concluded its discussion of executive power by noting the "utter and complete lack of authoritative support for defendant's position."[75] The court then analyzed the equities and held that they weighed

---

[70] *Id.* at 376–78.

[71] *See* Letter of April 27, 1952, from President Truman to C.S. Jones at 3, *reprinted in The Constitutional Crisis over President Truman's Seizure of the Steel Industry in 1952*, 30 Documentary History of the Truman Presidency 190, 192 (Dennis Merrill, ed.) (2001) ("The powers of the President are derived from the Constitution, and they are limited, of course, by the provisions of the Constitution...."); Joseph A. Loftus, *Truman Quoted as Resting Powers Issue With Courts*, N.Y. Times, Apr. 29, 1952, at 1.

[72] Supplemental Memorandum of Defendant at 1, Youngstown Sheet & Tube v. Sawyer, No. 1550–52, Box. No. 1160; Civil Action Files; D.D.C.; RG21; NAB.

[73] Youngstown Sheet & Tube Co. v. Sawyer, 103 F. Supp. 569, 573 (D.D.C. 1952).

[74] *Id.* at 575.

[75] *Id.* at 576.

in favor of granting the injunction. The court observed that it was unwilling to issue the more limited injunction proposed by United States Steel because of its "stultifying implications": "I could not consistently issue such an injunction which would contemplate a possible basis for the validity of defendant's acts."[76] The court thus invited United States Steel to withdraw its request for limited relief and request the same injunction issued as to the other plaintiffs. On the morning of Wednesday, April 30, the court signed the injunction, as to all plaintiffs, and denied the government's request for a stay pending appeal.

The Supreme Court Proceedings

The government proceeded immediately to the U.S. Court of Appeals for the D.C. Circuit and secured a stay enabling it to seek a writ of certiorari in the Supreme Court prior to judgment in the court of appeals. The following day, the steel companies asked the D.C. Circuit to condition the stay on the government not altering the prevailing terms of employment. After hearing oral argument en banc, the court denied the steel companies' application; four judges who had opposed the stay dissented. In releasing its opinion on May 2, the D.C. Circuit indicated that it had "at least a serious question as to the correctness of the view of the District Court."[77]

Because the statute governing petitions for writs of certiorari permits any party to a case, not merely the losing party, to seek a writ of certiorari,[78] both the government and the steel companies filed petitions, with the steel companies filing their petition first. The Supreme Court took up the petitions at its conference on Saturday, May 3.[79] Six of the Justices favored granting the writ. Justice Jackson abstained from voting,[80] while Justice Frankfurter and Justice Burton both opposed bypassing the court of appeals. Despite a written plea from Justice Reed that "if you could bring yourself to go with the [Court] on cert it would be most helpful,"[81] Justice Burton filed a dissenting opinion that he had prepared before the conference, which Justice Frankfurter joined. Because the D.C. Circuit had set its stay to expire upon the Court's

---

[76] *Id.* at 577.

[77] Youngstown Sheet & Tube v. Sawyer, 197 F.2d 582 (D.C. Cir. 1952).

[78] 28 U.S.C. § 1254(1).

[79] Justice Burton's papers contain the only detailed account of the conference. Notes on 744–745, Container 211, Harold H. Burton Papers, Manuscript Division, Library of Congress, Washington, D.C.

[80] *Id.*

[81] Note from SR, Container 211, Harold H. Burton Papers, Manuscript Division, Library of Congress, Washington, D.C.

granting of a writ of certiorari, the Court then had to consider whether to grant a stay of the district court's injunction. As in the D.C. Circuit, the steel companies' response to the government's petition requested that the Court condition any stay on the government not altering the terms of employment. The Justices voted in favor of a stay and conditioned it on the government not changing the terms and conditions of employment; Justice Jackson apparently abstained again.[82]

The Court's decision to condition the stay on the government maintaining the status quo had a devastating effect on ongoing negotiations. Shortly after the D.C. Circuit had granted the government a stay, the President asked union leaders to meet with the presidents of six steel companies at the White House on Saturday, May 3. The threat that the government would increase wages while the appeal was pending brought the steel companies back to the bargaining table. In the midst of those negotiations, however, the participants received word that the Supreme Court had conditioned the stay on the government maintaining the status quo.[83] That news removed the steel companies' incentive to settle, and the negotiations—which by some accounts had proceeded to the point where the parties were actually drafting an agreement—collapsed.[84]

All parties filed their briefs on May 10, and the Supreme Court heard oral argument on May 12 and 13. The briefs and oral arguments focused on three broad themes.[85] First, the parties considered the significance of the *statutory landscape* as it related to the present dispute—that is, whether Congress had spoken to the issue through specific statutes or otherwise had indicated their intent. Second, the parties looked to past and present *legislative approaches* to seizures during national emergencies as a barometer of Congress's views about the scope of the President's constitutional powers. Finally, the parties considered whether past *executive practice* should have any bearing on a Court's interpretation of the President's constitutional powers.

---

[82] Justice Burton's notes regarding Justice Jackson's position on the stay are illegible, but his conference sheet records Justice Jackson as having passed. Conference Sheet on 744–745, Container 208, Papers of Harold H. Burton, Manuscript Division, Library of Congress, Washington, D.C.

[83] Maeva Marcus, *Truman and the Steel Seizure Case: The Limits of Presidential Power* 143–48 (1977).

[84] *Id.* at 147–48; David A. Feller, *Thoughts About the Steel Seizure Case*, 41 Duq. L. Rev. 735, 740 (2003) (noting that Arthur Goldberg, counsel for the union, had instructed his associates to draft settlement documents before the Supreme Court conditioned the stay).

[85] The briefs and transcript of argument are reprinted in volume 48 of Landmark Briefs and Arguments of the Supreme Court of the United States: Constitutional Law (1975).

The Statutory Landscape

On the question of whether Congress had spoken to the present dispute, the government essentially conceded that no statute specifically authorized the President's action. Former Solicitor General John W. Davis, however, arguing the case on behalf of the steel companies,[86] observed that the Taft–Hartley Act did more than simply not authorize the President's action. The Taft–Hartley Act, Davis argued, specifically precluded the President from seizing property to avoid a strike, because it provided an alternative remedy for the precise type of emergency that a potential steel strike would have created: an 80–day injunction against a strike. In other words, if the President wished to prevent a strike that would threaten the national interest, he could do so by following the Taft–Hartley procedures.[87] The steel companies also noted that the House had rejected a proposed amendment to the Taft–Hartley Act that would have provided for governmental seizure in the event of emergency.[88]

Arguing on behalf of the United States, Philip Perlman, the Solicitor General and the Acting Attorney General, advanced a much different view of the relevance of Taft–Hartley. He claimed that although the President might have followed the Taft–Hartley procedures in December of 1951 in response to the union's initial threat to strike, those procedures were not mandatory. Having chosen instead to refer the dispute to the Wage Stabilization Board, the President could not now invoke Taft–Hartley's injunctive remedy. As of the time of the seizure on April 8, the union had already delayed its strike by 99 days—longer than the Taft–Hartley Act contemplated. Following the procedures of Taft–Hartley thus would have accomplished nothing that the course chosen by the President did not achieve. As Perlman put it, the President had already complied with the spirit of the Taft–Hartley Act.[89]

In addition to disputing the availability of the Taft–Hartley procedures on April 8, the parties took different views of Congress's failure to act in response to the President's Executive Order. A day after the President issued the order, he reported his action in a message to

---

[86] At the time, the Supreme Court's rules provided that when cross-petitions were filed, the plaintiff in the court below had the right to open and close oral argument. Because the steel companies had filed their own petition, over the objection of the government the Court permitted the steel companies to argue first.

[87] Transcript of Oral Argument, *reprinted in* 48 Landmark Briefs and Arguments of the Supreme Court of the United States: Constitutional Law 887–88 (1975).

[88] Brief for Plaintiff Companies at 22, *reprinted in* 48 Landmark Briefs and Arguments of the Supreme Court of the United States: Constitutional Law 441 (1975).

[89] Transcript of Oral Argument, *reprinted in* 48 Landmark Briefs and Arguments of the Supreme Court of the United States: Constitutional Law 937–38 (1975).

Congress and indicated that if Congress favored a different course he would abide by its wishes. Congress, however, had not acted. The parties vigorously debated what to make of this legislative inaction. The steel companies noted that members of Congress had taken to the floor to denounce the President's actions and that the Senate had proposed an amendment to an appropriations bill providing that no funds could be expended to carry out the seizure.[90] The government seized upon the fact that this bill never became law, and that Congress had not passed a statute directing the President to relinquish the mills or to take any other steps, as evidence that Congress did not disagree with the President's action.[91] At oral argument, at least some of the Justices expressed skepticism that anything could be made out of Congress's failure to respond to the President's message: Justice Burton, echoed by Justice Jackson, suggested that Congress simply might be waiting for the courts to resolve the pending lawsuits.[92]

Legislative Practice as Evidence of the President's Constitutional Powers

Both parties also relied on congressional action (and inaction) as a barometer of Congress's views of the scope of the President's constitutional powers. For the steel companies, the fact that Congress had passed specific statutes authorizing presidential seizures indicated that Congress understood the power to seize as one given by Congress rather than inhering in the presidency. Moreover, the steel companies argued that Congress intended that such power should be granted, if at all, only sparingly, for specific reasons, for limited purposes, and with appropriate safeguards.[93] The government presented past statutes authorizing seizure in a different light: rather than demonstrating that Congress understood the power to be exclusively legislative, the statutes merely confirmed, simplified, or supplemented a power that Congress understood to inhere in the President. The government focused in particular on Congress's responses to President Roosevelt's pre-war and wartime seizures.[94]

Executive Practice as Evidence of Executive Power

Finally, the parties disagreed with each other over whether past executive practice could shed any light on the President's constitutional

---

[90] Brief for Plaintiff Companies at 48, *reprinted in* 48 Landmark Briefs and Arguments of the Supreme Court of the United States: Constitutional Law 441 (1975).

[91] Transcript of Oral Argument, *reprinted in* 48 Landmark Briefs and Arguments of the Supreme Court of the United States: Constitutional Law 905–06 (1975).

[92] *Id.* at 906, 936.

[93] *Id.* at 887.

[94] *Id.* at 927–28.

power. The government, of course, had repudiated Baldridge's broad
assertions in district court that the President possessed all of the powers
of which he was capable, subject only to the checks of impeachment or
the ballot box. The government's claim, however, remained a nontextual
one: the government sought to rely on the aggregate of the President's
enumerated powers to support its action and buttressed its position with
arguments about past executive practice. Judge Pine had found such
practice to be irrelevant if a court had not passed upon its legality.
Although the Court seemed more willing to consider the relevance of
executive practice than Judge Pine had been, the Justices closely questioned Perlman on whether all of the examples were as relevant as he
suggested. Particularly sensitive for Justice Jackson was the government's reliance on the North American Aviation strike, which he had
supported as Attorney General under Roosevelt.[95] From the bench,
Justice Jackson catalogued the factual differences between the North
American Aviation seizure and the steel seizure, and in particular the
fact that the NAA plant had contracts with the government and that the
owners of the plant acquiesced in the seizure. "I looked it up because I
wondered how much of this was laid at my door."[96] When the Solicitor
General emphasized that Jackson's legal opinion did not turn on these
facts, Jackson replied that "I claimed everything, of course, like every
other Attorney General does. It was a custom that did not leave the
Department of Justice when I did."[97]

The Court's Decision

On May 16, the Court met in conference for nearly four hours to
discuss the case.[98] The Justices spoke in order of seniority. As it hap-

---

[95] See text accompanying notes 17–20.

[96] Transcript of Oral Argument, reprinted in 48 Landmark Briefs and Arguments of
the Supreme Court of the United States: Constitutional Law 920 (1975).

[97] Id.

[98] Justice Burton noted the length of the conference in his diary. Diary Entry for May
16, 1952, Container 2, Papers of Harold H. Burton, Manuscript Division, Library of
Congress, Washington, D.C.

There are four sets of conference notes available: those of Justice Burton, Container
211, Papers of Harold H. Burton, Manuscript Division, Library of Congress, Washington,
D.C. (hereinafter Burton Conference Notes); those of Justice Douglas, Container 221,
Papers of William O. Douglas, Manuscript Division, Library of Congress, Washington, D.C.
(hereinafter Douglas Conference Notes); those of Justice Frankfurter, Reel 60, The Felix
Frankfurter Papers, Part I: Supreme Court of the United States Case Files of Opinions and
Memoranda, October Terms, 1938–1952, Manuscript Division, Library of Congress, Wash-
ington, D.C. (hereinafter Frankfurter Conference Notes); and those of Justice Jackson,
Container 176, Papers of Robert H. Jackson, Manuscript Division, Library of Congress,
Washington, D.C. (hereinafter Jackson Conference Notes).

pened, however, the first two to speak—Chief Justice Vinson and Justice Black—staked out the opposing poles, with the remaining Justices positioning themselves in the vast middle ground between them.

The Chief Justice began with a lengthy defense of the President's conduct. While acknowledging that the President's powers are not unlimited, the Chief Justice argued that the President acted in good faith and with humility in the face of a real emergency. President Truman, he claimed, would have been thought "derelict" in his duty had he not seized the mills.[99] Also of particular importance for the Chief Justice was the fact that the President had informed Congress almost immediately of his action and had invited congressional correction, and "Congress [had] done nothing."[100] As for the broader legislative landscape, the Chief Justice urged the Court to consider not only the Taft–Hartley Act, but also the wide range of congressional authorizations and appropriations for augmenting the armed forces. Congress had placed new responsibilities on the President and the President was doing no more than carrying out his obligations to execute the laws. Indeed, the Chief Justice argued, the United States' military commitments were heavier and more definite than those during World War II,[101] when President Roosevelt had seized property on a number of occasions.

Justice Black immediately dismissed most of the Chief Justice's discussion as "irrelevant."[102] A decision to seize constituted an exercise of the lawmaking function, and the lawmaking function is committed to Congress. For Justice Black, past seizures had no bearing on the constitutional question: If President Roosevelt had seized property without statutory authority, Justice Black claimed, he would have held that President Roosevelt acted without authority. Although most of Justice Black's discussion focused on the legal authority question, according to Justice Douglas's notes his comments also betrayed some doubt as to whether the emergency President Truman faced was real: "This is not a

---

Existing accounts of the conference tend to rely exclusively on the notes of Justice Douglas. *See, e.g.*, Howard Ball & Phillip J. Cooper, *Of Power and Right: Hugo Black, William O. Douglas, and America's Constitutional Revolution* 132–33 & 342 nn. 152–154 (1992); Howard Ball, *Hugo L. Black: Cold Steel Warrior* 179–81 & 279–80 nn. 56–59 (1996). Because of discrepancies among the notes, unless otherwise indicated I use quotation marks only for those phrases that appear in more than one set of notes.

[99] Burton Conference Notes; Douglas Conference Notes; Jackson Conference Notes.

[100] Burton Conference Notes; Douglas Conference Notes; Frankfurter Conference Notes; Jackson Conference Notes.

[101] Burton Conference Notes; Douglas Conference Notes.

[102] Burton Conference Notes; Douglas Conference Notes; Jackson Conference Notes.

case of the President tearing down a house in order to stop the fire—
conditions are not that serious."[103]

Only Justice Reed, speaking third, and Justice Minton, speaking
last, sided with the Chief Justice in defending the seizure. Justice Reed
suggested that the practice of Presidents and the assent of the people
shape constitutional law;[104] the President was not limited to seizing
property only when statutory authorization existed. Justice Minton
argued that the President has implied power to act in an emergency to
defend the United States. Both emphasized that the emergency President Truman faced was real.[105] Justice Minton—pounding the table,
according to Justice Douglas—argued that the nation was in its "extremity"[106] and that the President had no choice but to defend the nation in a
"day of peril."[107]

The remaining Justices voted to affirm the district court's judgment,
but some offered different rationales than Justice Black had. Justice
Douglas's brief comments placed him closest to Justice Black in the view
that the power to seize is a legislative function.[108] Like Justice Black,
Justice Frankfurter seemed to have doubts about the extent of the
"emergency of steel" President Truman faced: According to Justice
Douglas's notes, Justice Frankfurter suggested that the steel might be
released for "civilian use."[109] On the legal question, however, Justice
Frankfurter, unlike Justice Black, said that he would not conclude that
in every case the President lacks the power to seize private property in
an emergency. If no statutes concerning seizure existed, he claimed, the
President might have been able to seize the steel mills temporarily so as
to permit Congress to legislate. Justice Frankfurter also offered a fuller
account of the legislative landscape and past executive practice than had
other Justices. First, he emphasized that past congressional action
demonstrated that when Congress passed statutes containing seizure
authority, it perceived itself to be granting power rather than recognizing a preexisting power. Echoing Davis's comments at oral argument, he
observed that between 1862 and 1916 there were no statutes dealing
with seizure. Seizure statutes since 1916 were detailed in the findings
they required, the conditions they imposed, and the compensation they

---

[103] Douglas Conference Notes; *see also* Jackson Conference Notes.

[104] Douglas Conference Notes; Jackson Conference Notes.

[105] On Justice Reed, *see* Burton Conference Notes; Douglas Conference Notes.

[106] Burton Conference Notes; Douglas Conference Notes.

[107] Douglas Conference Notes.

[108] Burton Conference Notes; Jackson Conference Notes.

[109] Douglas Conference Notes. For further discussion of the adequacy of the steel
supply and the release of steel for civilian use, *see* Maeva Marcus, *Truman and the Steel
Seizure Case: The Limits of Presidential Power* 225–26 (1977).

required. Second, in reviewing past executive conduct—particularly seizures undertaken during the Roosevelt administration—Justice Frankfurter noted that most relied on statutory authorities. As for those that
did not, Justice Frankfurter found them unimportant: general conditions, he argued, not exceptions, were most significant.[110]

Justice Jackson, by his own account, thought that the Court should
affirm while "doing [as] little damage as possible."[111] He emphasized
that the Court should not pass on the factual question of whether an
emergency existed. Rather, the Court should accept the fact of the
emergency and ask what the President could do in this emergency. On
that question, he found the President's position "untenable."[112] According to Justice Douglas's account, Justice Jackson despaired that "the
Department of Justice has been demoralized. The crowd that wants to
claim everything has taken over."[113]

Justice Burton's was the decisive fifth vote to affirm. Like Justices
Black and Douglas, he observed that the power to seize rests with
Congress, but he also believed that the Taft–Hartley Act itself foreclosed
the President's conduct.[114] The President was not compelled to invoke
the Taft–Hartley procedures, but the decision to use the Wage Stabilization Board could not put the President in a better position than use of
Taft–Hartley would have.[115] Justice Clark's views echoed Justice Jackson's. He emphasized that the Court should not pass on whether an
emergency existed and should limit its decision to this particular case.[116]

As the most senior Justice in the majority, Justice Black assigned
the opinion to himself. It is often the case that Justices' views evolve
after the Court's conference; the task of drafting, circulating, and
revising opinions is the task of building an institutional consensus
regarding the rationale for a decision. In the *Steel Seizure* case, however,
no such institutional consensus appears to have been possible. At the
conference, Justice Frankfurter apparently observed that he hoped all
nine Justices would write in the case.[117] The Court also recognized that it
had to release its decision quickly. Others were at work on their own

---

[110] Burton Conference Notes; Douglas Conference Notes.

[111] Jackson Conference Notes.

[112] Burton Conference Notes; Douglas Conference Notes.

[113] Douglas Conference Notes.

[114] Douglas Conference Notes; Jackson Conference Notes.

[115] Douglas Conference Notes.

[116] Douglas Conference Notes; *see also* Burton Conference Notes, Jackson Conference
Notes.

[117] Burton Conference Notes; Douglas Conference Notes.

writings before the conference vote, and after Justice Black circulated his opinion on May 28, a flurry of concurring opinions followed. All of the opinions had been circulated by May 30.

On June 2, 1952, less than three weeks after hearing oral argument, the Court announced its decision. What is striking about the opinions is how closely those in the majority hewed to their comments at conference. Justice Black wrote for himself and four others—Justice Frankfurter, Justice Douglas, Justice Jackson, and Justice Burton. Justice Clark provided the sixth vote to affirm the district court's judgment but did not join Justice Black's opinion.

Justice Black's opinion devoted a mere three-and-a-half pages to resolving the constitutional question.[118] He reasoned that "[t]he President's power, if any, to issue the order must stem either from an act of Congress or from the Constitution itself."[119] Because he found no statute that authorized the President to take possession of the steel mills nor any express constitutional language granting the power, Justice Black turned to the claim that "presidential power should be implied from the aggregate of . . . powers under the Constitution."[120] Justice Black declined to sustain the Executive Order under this theory. He viewed the power to dictate the terms under which the government could take possession of private property as a "lawmaking" power—resting within Congress's "exclusive constitutional authority to make laws necessary and proper to carry out the powers vested by the Constitution" in the federal government.[121] Because the seizure of property was "a job for the Nation's lawmakers, not for its military authorities," the designation of the President as Commander in Chief could not justify the action.[122] And the provisions granting the President the executive power and requiring that he take care that the laws be faithfully executed "refute[] the idea that he is to be a lawmaker."[123] While Justice Black acknowledged the government's argument that "other Presidents without congressional authority have taken possession of private business enterprises in order to settle labor disputes," he stated that even if this were true, "Congress has not thereby lost its exclusive constitutional authority" to make laws.[124]

---

[118] Youngstown Sheet & Tube Co. v. Sawyer, 343 U.S. 579, 585–89 (1952).

[119] Id. at 585.

[120] Id. at 587.

[121] Id. at 588–89.

[122] Id. at 587.

[123] Id.

[124] Id. at 588.

Justice Black's opinion for the Court thus reads much like a toned-down version of Judge Pine's opinion at the district court level. Predictably, however, the four Justices who joined Justice Black's majority opinion wrote separately, and all but Justice Douglas highlighted significant disagreement with Justice Black's rationale.[125] Indeed, in an unusual separate statement appended to the Court's opinion, Justice Frankfurter noted the importance of "[i]ndividual expression of views in reaching a common result," because "differences in attitude toward [the] principle [of separation of powers] . . . can hardly be reflected by a single opinion for the Court."[126] When the Justices announced and read their opinions from the bench, Justice Jackson described Justice Black's approach as the "least common denominator" with which those joining the opinion could agree.[127]

Only Justice Douglas explicitly embraced Justice Black's characterization of the President's action as "legislative" in nature.[128] For the other three Justices who joined Black's opinion—Justices Frankfurter, Jackson, and Burton—and for Justice Clark, who concurred only in the judgment,[129] the case turned not on the characterization of the seizure as a "lawmaking" act nor on a narrow construction of enumerated executive powers, but instead on the perception that the President's action in seizing the steel mills conflicted with the authorities Congress had provided the President to deal with potential industrial disruptions. In a now famous passage of his opinion, Justice Jackson suggested that presidential powers "are not fixed but fluctuate, depending upon their disjunction or conjunction with those of Congress."[130] He offered the following grouping of presidential actions and their legal consequences:

> 1. When the President acts pursuant to an express or implied authorization of Congress, his authority is at its maximum, for it includes all that he possesses in his own right plus all that Congress can delegate. . . .

---

[125] *See id.* at 593 (Frankfurter, J., concurring); *id.* at 629 (Douglas, J., concurring); *id.* at 634 (Jackson, J., concurring); *id.* at 655 (Burton, J., concurring).

[126] *Id.* at 589 (separate statement of Frankfurter, J.).

[127] John P. Frank, *The United States Supreme Court: 1951–52*, 20 U. Chi. L. Rev. 1, 12 (1952). Contemporaneous newspaper accounts do not report this statement, but the "least common denominator" phrase is penciled in on the copy of the concurrence that appears in Justice Jackson's files. At least one source attributes this comment to Justice Frankfurter, in erroneous reliance on the Frank article cited above. *See* Roger K. Newman, *Hugo Black: A Biography* 417, 687 n.5 (1997).

[128] *Youngstown*, 343 U.S. at 630 (Douglas, J., concurring).

[129] *Id.* at 660 (Clark, J., concurring in judgment).

[130] *Id.* at 635 (Jackson, J., concurring).

2.   When the President acts in absence of either a congressional grant or denial of authority, he can only rely upon his own independent powers, but there is a zone of twilight in which he and Congress may have concurrent authority, or in which its distribution is uncertain. Therefore, congressional inertia, indifference or quiescence may sometimes, at least as a practical matter, enable, if not invite, measures on independent presidential responsibility. In this area, any actual test of power is likely to depend on the imperatives of events and contemporary imponderables rather than on abstract theories of law.

3.   When the President takes measures incompatible with the expressed or implied will of Congress, his power is at its lowest ebb, for then he can rely only upon his own constitutional powers minus any constitutional powers of Congress over the matter. Courts can sustain exclusive presidential control in such a case only by disabling the Congress from acting upon the subject.[131]

Justice Jackson viewed President Truman's action as falling within the third category, as a measure "incompatible with the expressed or implied will of Congress."[132] Justices Frankfurter and Burton agreed, as did Justice Clark. More specifically, the President's seizure was inconsistent with the three mechanisms that Congress had provided the President for responding to threatened industrial disruptions—the Taft–Hartley Act, which provided for injunctive relief rather than presidential seizure;[133] the Selective Service Act's provisions permitting seizure to ensure that government orders would be fulfilled;[134] and the Defense Production Act's condemnation procedures.[135]

---

[131] *Id.* at 635–38 (footnotes omitted).

[132] *Id.* at 637.

[133] *Id.* at 599–600 (Frankfurter, J., concurring) ("Authorization for seizure as an available remedy for potential dangers was unequivocally put aside."); *id.* at 639 (Jackson, J., concurring) (noting that the President did not invoke the Taft–Hartley Act); *id.* at 656, 658 (Burton, J., concurring) ("The accuracy with which Congress [in the Taft–Hartley Act] describes the present emergency demonstrates [the Act's] applicability.... The President, however, chose not to use the Taft–Hartley procedure."); *id.* at 663 (Clark, J., concurring in judgment) (noting that the President did not invoke the Taft–Hartley Act).

[134] *Id.* at 608 n.16 (Frankfurter, J., concurring) (noting that President had not used his authority to seize plants under the Selective Service Act); *id.* at 665–66 (Clark, J., concurring in judgment) ("[T]he Government made no effort to comply with the procedures established by the Selective Service Act of 1948....").

[135] *Id.* at 658 & nn.5, 6 (Burton, J., concurring) (noting that the President had referred the controversy to the Wage Stabilization Board under the Defense Production Act, but had not invoked the separate provisions of the Defense Production Act allowing condemnation); *id.* at 663 (Clark, J., concurring in judgment) ("The Defense Production Act ...

Having established that the President's action was inconsistent with the mechanisms Congress provided, each of the Justices went on to discuss whether the President's action could nevertheless be sustained as an incident of the President's constitutional authority. Here again, the concurring opinions were in tension with Justice Black's majority opinion. None of the concurring Justices articulated a conception of presidential power as narrow and rigid as that found in Justice Black's opinion for the majority.

First, Justice Frankfurter rejected Justice Black's suggestion that past executive practice is irrelevant to an assessment of the President's constitutional authority:

> The Constitution is a framework for government. Therefore the way the framework has consistently operated fairly establishes that it has operated according to its true nature.... In short, a systematic, unbroken, executive practice, long pursued to the knowledge of the Congress and never before questioned, engaged in by Presidents who have also sworn to uphold the Constitution, making as it were such exercise of power part of the structure of our government, may be treated as a gloss on "executive Power" vested in the President by § 1 of Art. II.[136]

Justice Frankfurter concluded, however, that the past seizures the government identified did not amount "in number, scope, duration or contemporaneous legal justification" to the kind of unquestioned executive practice that could be viewed as a gloss on executive power.[137] Similarly, Justice Jackson argued that it was important to "give to the enumerated powers the scope and elasticity afforded by what seem to be reasonable, practical implications instead of the rigidity dictated by a doctrinaire textualism."[138] But he too rejected the notion that the historical precedents the government cited provided "color of legality" for President Truman's actions.[139]

Second, on the broader question of what power the President might have to act without congressional authorization in responding to a national emergency—a power that Justice Black's opinion seemed to reject—the concurring opinions broke with the majority and either implicitly or explicitly suggested that such a power may exist in some

---

grants the President no power to seize real property except through ordinary condemnation proceedings, which were not used here....").

[136] *Id.* at 610–11 (Frankfurter, J., concurring).

[137] *Id.* at 613.

[138] *Id.* at 640 (Jackson, J., concurring).

[139] *Id.* at 648.

cases. Justice Frankfurter thought it unnecessary to pass on the scope of the President's powers:

> The issue before us can be met, and therefore should be, without attempting to define the President's powers comprehensively.... We must ... put to one side consideration of what powers the President would have had if there had been no legislation whatever bearing on the authority asserted by the seizure....[140]

Justice Burton likewise distinguished President Truman's action from steps taken when "Congress takes no action and outlines no governmental policy."[141] Justice Burton acknowledged the possibility that nontextual powers to act in an emergency exist, but found them unavailable to the President in the situation he faced, which was "not comparable to that of an imminent invasion or threatened attack."[142] Justice Clark explicitly embraced the concept of such powers: "In my view ... the Constitution does grant to the President extensive authority in times of grave and imperative national emergency. In fact, to my thinking, such a grant may well be necessary to the very existence of the Constitution itself."[143]

Justice Jackson's position on the subject was perhaps the most ambiguous, but even his opinion can be read as accepting that the President possesses at least some powers to act in response to a national emergency. He rejected the notion that the Court could declare the existence of inherent presidential powers as broad as necessary to meet *any* emergency or that the executive would have unreviewable discretion to determine that an emergency existed. On the other hand, Justice Jackson's recognition of a "zone of twilight" in which the President and Congress "may have concurrent authority, or in which its distribution is uncertain," presupposes that the President can act in the absence of specific authority—and, in Justice Jackson's view, the evaluation of such action will likely depend "on the imperatives of events" rather than "abstract theories of law."[144] In addition, Justice Jackson declared himself unwilling "to circumscribe, much less to contract, the lawful role of the President as Commander in Chief,"[145] suggesting that the President should have latitude to respond to foreign threats to the nation's security.

---

[140] *Id.* at 597 (Frankfurter, J., concurring).

[141] *Id.* at 659 (Burton, J., concurring).

[142] *Id.*

[143] *Id.* at 662 (Clark, J., concurring in judgment).

[144] *Id.* at 637.

[145] *Id.* at 645.

In sum, although Justices Frankfurter, Jackson, and Burton joined Justice Black's opinion for the Court purporting to reject the existence of a presidential power to respond to a national emergency in the absence of congressional action, their concurrences do not reject the existence of such a power. And, of course, the three dissenting Justices were prepared to recognize such a power as well.[146] The district court, with its narrow construction of presidential powers and its explicit rejection of executive practice as an indicator of the scope of constitutional power, had resisted the notion that such a power existed. But only Justice Black and Justice Douglas agreed. The remaining Justices did not rule out the possibility that courts should construe the President's enumerated powers more broadly than Justice Black had construed them or that the President could claim powers based on the structure that the words of the Constitution ordain rather than the words themselves. For the concurring Justices, the case was not about the scope of the President's constitutional power in the face of congressional silence, but about whether the President could take certain action when Congress had foreclosed it.

The Impact of the Steel Seizure Case

The public reacted positively to the Supreme Court's decision in the *Steel Seizure* case.[147] For legal commentators, however, the case was more complicated. As one commentator put it, "[w]e can hardly expect that the lasting outgrowth of the steel controversy will be the *Youngstown* case."[148] For Professor Edward S. Corwin, the decision was "a judicial brick without straw"—the opinion of the Court resting on a "purely arbitrary construct,"[149] Justice Jackson's "rather desultory" concurring opinion containing "little that is of direct pertinence to the constitutional issue,"[150] and the other concurring opinions contributing nothing "to the decision's claim to be regarded seriously as a doctrine of

---

[146] The dissenting Justices argued that the relevant statutes did not prohibit the seizure. *Id.* at 704–07 (Vinson, C.J., dissenting). But they also emphasized that the President should be able to take action in an emergency to preserve Congress's legislative prerogatives. *See id.* at 701.

[147] Maeva Marcus, *Truman and the Steel Seizure Case: The Limits of Presidential Power* 212 (1977).

[148] Jerre Williams, *The Steel Seizure: A Legal Analysis of a Political Controversy*, 2 J. Pub. L. 29, 34 (1953).

[149] Edward S. Corwin, *The Steel Seizure Case: A Judicial Brick Without Straw*, 53 Colum. L. Rev. 53, 64 (1953).

[150] *Id.* at 63.

constitutional law."[151] Political scientist Glendon Schubert pronounced the decision "destined to be ignored."[152]

Those predictions may seem naïve in light of the prominence of the *Steel Seizure* case in the constitutional law canon. In evaluating the impact of the *Steel Seizure* case, however, it is important to distinguish the case's symbolic or rhetorical significance from its doctrinal significance. The former may not have been apparent to contemporary commentators, while the tension between Justice Black's majority opinion and the accompanying concurrences detracted from the latter.

For courts and commentators, Justice Jackson's opinion has now emerged as the most authoritative among the various *Steel Seizure* opinions. Although that opinion is often thought to provide concrete guidance on how to resolve presidential power claims, particularly with respect to foreign affairs, it leaves many questions unanswered. As I will argue, however, the strength of the Jackson opinion lies less in its doctrinal categories than in its critique, explicit and implicit, of the decision-making in the political branches that gave rise to the *Steel Seizure* case.

The Steel Seizure *Case in the Courts*

Measuring the influence of any separation-of-powers case is difficult. Separation-of-powers controversies arrive infrequently in court and the facts of the disputes tend to be highly individual. Indeed, if one were to assess the influence of the *Steel Seizure* case based on citation frequency alone, one would reach the ironic conclusion that the case is most influential in supplying courts with an avenue to *avoid* finding a violation of separation-of-powers principles.[153] Courts most often cite the case for the same unremarkable reason that it is typically placed first in a Constitutional Law casebook's separation-of-powers chapter: that Justice Frankfurter's opinion and Justice Jackson's opinion, in contradistinction to Justice Black's, illustrate the "functional" approach to resolving separation-of-powers questions.[154]

Less frequently but more significantly, courts also use the *Steel Seizure* case to affirm their powers to invalidate the acts of a coordinate branch of government. Historian Maeva Marcus's seminal book on the *Steel Seizure* case, written on the heels of the Nixon presidency, views the case as launching a trend of judicial intervention in politically charged cases. She sees the imprint of the *Steel Seizure* case in the

---

[151] *Id.* at 65.

[152] Glendon A. Schubert, Jr., *The Steel Case: Presidential Responsibility and Judicial Irresponsibility*, 6 W. Pol. Q. 61, 65 (1953).

[153] *See* Patricia L. Bellia, *Executive Power in* Youngstown's *Shadows*, 19 Const. Comm. 87, 108–09 (2002).

[154] *Id.* at 109.

school desegregation cases[155] as well as in the Court's involvement in reapportionment disputes.[156] Although at least one scholar suggests that Marcus overstates the *Steel Seizure* case's influence in those contexts,[157] the influence of the *Steel Seizure* case on Nixon-era separation-of-powers disputes is unmistakable. The *Steel Seizure* case provided the courts with an important precedent for rejecting former President Nixon's claims that certain actions of the executive branch were not subject to review by the judiciary.[158] In *United States v. Nixon*,[159] for example, the Court cited the *Steel Seizure* case as one instance of the judiciary invalidating another branch's exercise of power,[160] and the precedent allowed the Court to resist Nixon's claim of absolute privilege in certain presidential communications, subject to no judicial review.[161] The lower courts made similar use of the case in rejecting Nixon's assertions of privilege as well as his claim that the courts would lack authority to enforce any adverse ruling on the privilege issue.[162]

A more recent Clinton-era decision illustrates a similar use of the *Steel Seizure* case to establish a court's authority to act in the face of perceived abuses of power. In *Clinton v. Jones*,[163] the Court rejected President Clinton's claim that separation-of-powers principles required a district court to postpone, until the end of his presidency, civil proceedings in a dispute arising out of conduct that occurred prior to his time in office. The President argued that permitting the proceedings to go forward would cause undue judicial interference with the "effective performance of his office."[164] The Court rejected this argument, concluding that the fact that a court's exercise of jurisdiction may burden the

---

[155] *See* Maeva Marcus, *Truman and the Steel Seizure Case: The Limits of Presidential Power* 229 (1977) (calling the desegregation cases "the most spectacular example of the Court's new willingness to face basic constitutional questions").

[156] *Id.* at 229–30 (arguing that the *Steel Seizure* case helped the Court to explain in *Baker v. Carr*, 369 U.S. 186 (1962), why the Court could intervene in reapportionment disputes).

[157] William H. Harbaugh, *The Steel Seizure Case Reconsidered*, 87 Yale L.J. 1272, 1281–83 (1978).

[158] *See* Maeva Marcus, *Truman and the Steel Seizure Case: The Limits of Presidential Power* 240–48 (1977).

[159] 418 U.S. 683 (1974). For more on the *Nixon* case, see Chapter 9 in this volume.

[160] *Nixon*, 418 U.S. at 703.

[161] *Id.* at 707.

[162] *See* Maeva Marcus, *Truman and the Steel Seizure Case: The Limits of Presidential Power* 240–45 (1977).

[163] 520 U.S. 681 (1997).

[164] *Id.* at 702.

time and attention of the President "is not sufficient to establish a violation of the Constitution."[165] The Court cited the *Steel Seizure* case as "the most dramatic" example of a case in which the judiciary had, in effect, imposed a burden on the President by virtue of its authority to determine "whether [the President] has acted within the law."[166] The Court's use of the *Steel Seizure* case there, and elsewhere in the opinion,[167] is surprising because the two cases are so different. Any burden that the President's involvement in the *Steel Seizure* case created arose out of his official duties, and it is therefore difficult to view a requirement that he respond to legal process as an interference in any way analogous to that which President Clinton had claimed.[168] In invoking the case throughout its opinion, and in emphasizing the case as a precedent for courts' authority to determine whether the President has acted within the law, the Court seemed to rely on the decision more as an illustration that the President is not above the law than for the case's doctrinal relevance to the dispute at hand.

These cases suggest, as Marcus has put it, that much of the significance of the *Steel Seizure* case "lies in the fact that it was made."[169] When the courts police the domain of a coordinate branch of government or seek to combat perceived abuses of power, even on questions unrelated to those the Court considered in connection with President Truman's seizure of the steel mills, it is the *Steel Seizure* case that lends the legal if not moral weight.[170]

Also beginning with the Nixon era, however, the *Steel Seizure* case began to have important ramifications in disputes with facts more closely related to those in the *Steel Seizure* case—when the President

---

[165] *Id.* at 703.

[166] *Id.* ("Perhaps the most dramatic example of such a case is our holding that President Truman exceeded his constitutional authority when he issued an order directing the Secretary of Commerce to take possession of and operate most of the Nation's steel mills in order to avert a national catastrophe.").

[167] *See id.* at 696 (quoting Justice Jackson's observation that historical and scholarly materials concerning the Framers' intent with respect to separation of powers point in different directions); *id.* at 699 (quoting Justice Jackson's description of the power in the Presidency); *id.* at 701 & n.35 (relying on the *Steel Seizure* case, among other cases, for the proposition that "the lines between the powers of the three branches are not always neatly defined").

[168] *Cf. id.* at 718 (Breyer, J., concurring in judgment) (stating that the *Steel Seizure* precedent "does not seem relevant in this case").

[169] Maeva Marcus, *Truman and the Steel Seizure Case: The Limits of Presidential Power* 228 (1977).

[170] *See* Patricia L. Bellia, *Executive Power in* Youngstown*'s Shadows*, 19 Const. Comm. 87, 110–13 (2002).

claimed the power, in times of crisis, to take certain actions. Two cases decided in the early 1970s are illustrative. The *Steel Seizure* case was decisive in neither, but it arguably framed the issues in both. First, in the *Pentagon Papers* case,[171] the government requested an injunction against the continued publication of a classified Defense Department history of the United States' political and military involvement in the Vietnam War. The government claimed that the executive branch had unreviewable discretion to determine whether national security required suppressing the study. Just as the concurring Justices in the *Steel Seizure* case rested their decision on the fact that the legislative landscape was inconsistent with President Truman's conduct, three concurring Justices in the *Pentagon Papers* case rested their rejection of the government's request on the ground that Congress, in enacting statutes to protect national security information, had declined to authorize the President to seek injunctive relief.[172] Second, in the *Keith* case,[173] the Court considered whether the Executive could intercept communications without judicial authorization when facing an alleged domestic threat to national security. The Court's decision rested on Fourth Amendment grounds: The Court concluded that the Fourth Amendment required the government to seek judicial authorization for the surveillance.[174] But the case was similar to the *Steel Seizure* case in that the executive branch essentially claimed that it had the power to protect national security in the absence of an authorizing statute, and indeed in the face of a federal statute that did not specifically authorize the executive branch to carry out the surveillance.[175] The Court did not directly confront the presidential power issue, assuming that the President had constitutional authority to protect the United States "against those who would subvert or overthrow it by unlawful means."[176] The court below had specifically

---

[171] New York Times Co. v. United States, 403 U.S. 713 (1971).

[172] *Id.* at 740 (White, J., joined by Stewart, J., concurring) ("Congress has addressed itself to the problems of protecting the security of the country and the national defense from unauthorized disclosure of potentially damaging information. It has not, however, authorized the injunctive remedy against threatened publication.") (internal citations omitted); *id.* at 743 (Marshall, J., concurring) ("Congress has on several occasions given extensive consideration to the problem of protecting the military and strategic secrets of the United States.").

[173] United States v. U.S. District Court for the Eastern District of Michigan (*Keith*), 407 U.S. 297 (1972). For more on the *Keith* case, see Chapter 8 in this volume.

[174] *Keith*, 407 U.S. at 317.

[175] *See id.* at 299–308 (concluding that federal wiretap statute neither authorized Executive to conduct surveillance in domestic security matters without prior judicial approval nor recognized an existing constitutional authority to conduct such surveillance).

[176] *Id.* at 310.

considered the presidential power issue,[177] and the influence of their treatment of the issue is apparent both in the Supreme Court's discussion of past executive practice of engaging in surveillance in domestic security cases[178] and in the Court's premise that Congress could adopt procedures for domestic security surveillance that did not precisely track those that the Fourth Amendment was thought to require for surveillance in criminal investigations.[179] The *Steel Seizure* case was not decisive in *Keith*, but it surely influenced the premises from which the Court operated.

The Jackson Concurrence in the Courts

A third case involving presidential power in times of crisis marked a decisive shift in courts' reliance on the *Steel Seizure* case. In *Dames & Moore v. Regan*,[180] the Supreme Court confronted whether the President could suspend the claims of U.S. citizens against Iran and its nationals. The case involved an Executive Order implementing the executive agreement by which the United States secured the release of the U.S. hostages from Iran. The opinion for the Court by then-Justice Rehnquist—one of Justice Jackson's law clerks when the Court heard the *Steel Seizure* case—characterized Justice Jackson's opinion as bringing together "as much combination of analysis and common sense as there is in this area."[181] The Court analyzed the Executive Order through the lens of Justice Jackson's three categories, concluding that Congress had implicitly approved the President's conduct.[182]

Justice Jackson's concurrence continues to predominate in presidential power cases touching on foreign affairs. Even when the Court itself does not explicitly apply Justice Jackson's categories, those categories can frame the parties' arguments. In *Hamdi v. Rumsfeld*,[183] for example, the Court considered whether the President could order the detention of citizens whom the government believed to be "enemy combatants." The government claimed both that the President had constitutional power to detain enemy combatants and that Congress had, in the Authorization for the Use of Military Force (AUMF) adopted shortly after the September 11 attacks, authorized such detention.[184] A plurality of the Court

---

[177] United States v. United States District Court, 444 F.2d 651, 660–61 (6th Cir. 1971).

[178] *Keith*, 407 U.S. at 310–11.

[179] *Id.* at 322–23.

[180] 453 U.S. 654 (1981). For more on *Dames & Moore*, see Chapter 10 in this volume.

[181] *Dames & Moore*, 453 U.S. at 661.

[182] *Id.* at 680.

[183] 542 U.S. 507 (2004).

[184] Brief for Respondent at 21, Hamdi v. Rumsfeld, 542 U.S. 507 (2004), No. 03–6696 (filed Mar. 29, 2004).

adopted the latter argument,[185] with Justice Thomas providing a fifth vote on this point.[186] Two years later, in *Hamdan v. Rumsfeld*,[187] the Court examined whether the President could establish military commissions to try enemy combatants. Again Justice Jackson's framework structured the arguments and some of the opinions, with the government arguing both that the AUMF authorized the President to establish military commissions and that the President had inherent authority to do so.[188] The Court rejected these claims and concluded that the Uniform Code of Military Justice limited the circumstances in which the President could authorize military commissions. Although Justice Stevens mentioned the *Steel Seizure* case only in passing,[189] Justice Kennedy's concurrence invoked and applied Justice Jackson's framework in reaching the conclusion that the UCMJ limits the President's use of military commissions.[190] Most recently, in *Medellín v. Texas*,[191] Justice Jackson's concurrence framed the Court's consideration, and ultimately its rejection, of the claim that the President could direct state courts to provide reviews of criminal convictions in accordance with the terms of an International Court of Justice decision and without regard for state procedural default rules.[192]

At least since *Dames & Moore*, then, courts have viewed Justice Jackson's opinion as providing the "accepted framework"[193] for evaluating presidential power claims. But some scholars argue that Justice Jackson's framework does more work than that: that the framework embodies a *normative* commitment to congressional "primacy" in foreign affairs. Congressional primacy scholars read the Constitution to lodge most foreign affairs powers with Congress, and take Justice Jackson's concurrence to instruct courts to resolve most foreign affairs disputes in favor of Congress.[194]

The claim that Justice Jackson's concurrence embodies a normative commitment to congressional primacy in foreign affairs proves proble-

---

[185] *Hamdi*, 542 U.S. at 517 (plurality opinion).

[186] *Id.* at 587 (Thomas, J., dissenting).

[187] 548 U.S. 557 (2006). For more on *Hamdan*, see Chapter 12 in this volume.

[188] Brief for Respondent at 16, 20, Hamdan v. Rumsfeld, 548 U.S. 557 (2006).

[189] *Hamdan*, 548 U.S. at 593 n. 23.

[190] *Id.* at 638–43 (Kennedy, J., concurring in part and concurring in the judgment).

[191] 128 S.Ct. 1346 (2008).

[192] *Id.* at 1368–71.

[193] *Id.* at 1368.

[194] For a discussion of the strands of congressional primacy claims, *see* Patricia L. Bellia, *Executive Power in* Youngstown's *Shadows*, 19 Const. Comm. 87, 117–21 (2002).

matic, however, both in theory and in practice. To be sure, Justice Jackson's central premise is that how, if at all, Congress has acted should influence how presidential conduct is evaluated. In at least some "category three" cases, as in the *Steel Seizure* case, how Congress has acted will be decisive, by foreclosing presidential conduct inconsistent with Congress's action. To suggest that presidential power is at its "lowest ebb" when it conflicts with congressional policy, however, is not to suggest that presidential conduct in conflict with congressional power is always unconstitutional.[195]

Moreover, the congressional primacy view depends not only on the conclusion that the President's choice of policy must yield to Congress's, but also on two further claims: first, that courts must narrowly construe statutes by which Congress authorizes presidential conduct;[196] and second, that courts must narrowly construe the foreign affairs powers that the Constitution does expressly grant to the Executive (such as the power to serve as Commander in Chief and the power to receive ambassadors). But Justice Jackson's concurrence gives relatively little guidance to courts on how to determine when congressional authorization exists and how to assess the scope of executive power in its absence. As to congressional authorization, Justice Jackson's opinion refers to the "express *or implied*" authorization of Congress. The opinion thus presupposes that it is possible to infer congressional approval of a particular executive practice even in the absence of a specific statute. In the *Steel Seizure* case itself, of course, several Justices inferred congressional *disapproval* of executive action. Their conclusions that the President's action was inconsistent with the course prescribed by Congress were based not on a specific statute barring seizure but on the fact that the House had rejected a seizure option in its consideration of the Taft–Hartley Act and that Congress had effectively already occupied the field. If such inferences from the legislative landscape are fair game in an assessment of Congress's implied *opposition* to executive conduct, it is

---

[195] *Cf.* David A. Barron & Martin S. Lederman, *The Commander in Chief at the Lowest Ebb—A Constitutional History*, 121 Harv. L. Rev. 941, 1099 (2008) (discussing mistaken view that constitutional history establishes a Commander in Chief power that is preclusive of congressional control, but acknowledging that this alone does not explain what should happen at the "lowest ebb").

[196] *See, e.g.*, David Gray Adler, *Court, Constitution, and Foreign Affairs* in David Gray Adler and Larry N. George, eds., *The Constitution and the Conduct of American Foreign Policy* 19, 32–35 (1996) (criticizing the Supreme Court's treatment of congressional delegation to Secretary of State of power to issue passports); Harold Hongju Koh, *The National Security Constitution* 146 (1990) ("[T]he Supreme Court's reading of these statutes has enhanced presidential power by encouraging lawyers throughout the executive branch to construe their agency's authorizing statutes to permit executive initiatives extending far beyond the intended scope of those statutes.").

unclear why such inferences would not also be in an assessment of Congress's implied *approval* of presidential conduct.

Quite apart from how to construe legislative will in the absence of a specific statute, Justice Jackson's concurrence provides limited guidance on how courts should construe specific statutes. In a case raising such an issue, a substantive question is intertwined with an institutional one. The substantive question is whether the statute authorizes the challenged conduct, and the institutional question relates to who is in the best position—courts or the Executive—to interpret the statute, or, put another way, whether the courts owe the Executive's interpretation of the statute any deference. Here, of course, foreign affairs law intersects with a well developed body of administrative law dealing with deference to the Executive in its interpretation of ambiguous statutes.[197] Congressional primacy scholars imply that courts should construe congressional delegations in the foreign affairs context more narrowly than other congressional delegations. That approach necessarily depends on the premise that only a narrow construction of a delegation will preserve congressional prerogatives in foreign affairs. Whether or not that view is correct, Justice Jackson concurrence simply does not speak to it.

Perhaps even more problematic is the congressional primacy view that Justice Jackson's opinion should be read to instruct courts to narrowly construe the President's *constitutional* powers. Justice Jackson's opinion states that "because the President does not enjoy unmentioned powers does not mean that the mentioned ones should be narrowed by a niggardly construction."[198] Justice Jackson also notes that in any event courts are likely to have a limited role in policing presidential conduct when Congress is silent: "In this area, any actual test of power is likely to depend on the imperatives of events and contemporary imponderables rather than on abstract theories of law."[199] The point seems predictive rather than normative, but it supplies the basis for two normative arguments for why a court should avoid construing the President's constitutional powers when Congress is silent—first, that the political branches are more likely to arrive at a narrow resolution that will preserve government flexibility in later, unforeseen circumstances, and that a court should therefore stay its hand;[200] and second, that

---

[197] *See, e.g.*, Curtis A. Bradley, *Chevron Deference and Foreign Affairs*, 86 Va. L. Rev. 649, 663 (2000); Patricia L. Bellia, *Executive Power in* Youngstown's *Shadows*, 19 Const. Comm. 87, 126–39 (2002).

[198] 343 U.S. at 640 (Jackson, J., concurring).

[199] *Id.* at 637.

[200] This view seemed to animate Justice Powell's concurrence in the Supreme Court's decision to deny review in *Goldwater v. Carter*, 444 U.S. 996 (1979), a dispute over President Carter's termination of the United States' mutual defense treaty with Taiwan.

because the Constitution confers authority over foreign affairs and national security to the political branches, there is a "risk that judicial intervention will itself be a serious violation of separation of powers."[201]

These conceptual problems with overreading Justice Jackson's concurrence manifest themselves in cases in which courts attempt to apply Justice Jackson's framework. Critics of the Supreme Court's decision in *Dames & Moore*, for example, suggest that the Court failed to adhere in that case to the boundaries between Justice Jackson's three categories— that the Court has too-broadly construed particular legislative action to constitute "authorization," thus transforming congressional silence or congressional opposition into congressional approval.[202] Justice Jackson's concurrence, however, seems to leave that avenue open. The *Medellín* case arguably illustrates the opposite phenomenon, with the Court concluding that the Senate's ratification of a treaty lacking provisions that "clearly" accorded the treaty domestic effect constituted an implicit *prohibition* on the President's implementation of the treaty.[203]

Justice Powell argued that judicial intervention was inappropriate because Congress and the President had not yet reached a "constitutional impasse." *Id.* at 997 (Powell, J., concurring in judgment). The Senate had considered a resolution declaring that Senate approval is necessary for termination of a treaty but had taken no final action. *Id.* at 998. Justice Powell suggested that "[i]t cannot be said that either the Senate or the House has rejected the President's claim. If the Congress chooses not to confront the President, it is not our task to do so." *Id.*

[201] H. Jefferson Powell, *The President's Authority over Foreign Affairs: An Executive Branch Perspective*, 67 Geo. Wash. L. Rev. 527, 537 (1999). Under this theory, judicial intervention would be inappropriate where Congress is silent, and may not even be appropriate when there is a conflict between congressional and presidential will. Four of the Justices who concurred in the decision not to grant review in *Goldwater* took this view. Because the Justices found no constitutional provision expressly governing the termination of treaties, the dispute presented a political question. 444 U.S. at 1003 (Rehnquist, J., concurring in judgment). The concurring Justices observed that a court's resolution of a political question can create "disruption among the three coequal branches of Government." *Id.* at 1005–06.

[202] *See, e.g.*, Harold Hongju Koh, *The National Security Constitution* 142 (1990) (discussing cases, including Dames & Moore v. Regan, 453 U.S. 654 (1981), and INS v. Chadha, 462 U.S. 919 (1983), that "dramatically alter the application of Justice Jackson's tripartite *Youngstown* analysis in cases on foreign affairs"); Gordon Silverstein, *Imbalance of Powers* 11–12 (1997) (arguing that courts "began to soften the barriers" between Justice Jackson's categories in the decades following the *Steel Seizure* decision, thus lending "legitimacy to the emerging executive claim to prerogative powers in foreign policy").

[203] The *Medellín* case is particularly interesting for its re-envisioning of *Dames & Moore*. In *Medellín*, the Court rejected the argument that congressional acquiescence in a course of presidential conduct could be taken as a sign of congressional *authorization* in category one; the Court deemed congressional acquiescence to be relevant only to the question of the President's *constitutional* power in category two. *Medellín*, 128 S.Ct. at 1370. Although the *Medellín* Court's approach appears to be more faithful to Justice Jackson's approach in the *Steel Seizure* case than *Dames & Moore* was, it seems to narrow

In addition to raising questions about how to measure Congress's "express" or "implied" will, these cases demonstrate a reluctance to explore the President's *constitutional* powers in any detail. I have discussed elsewhere the costs to our constitutional system of courts' reluctance to explore the scope of the President's constitutional foreign affairs powers.[204] The seeds of the political question doctrine—arguably planted in Justice Jackson's concurrence—tend to sprout into executive power. In addition, courts' reluctance to explore questions about the constitutional powers of the President deprives the executive branch of authoritative guidance, developed in the crucible of contested cases and controversies, about its own conduct, thus compromising one of the most effective restraints on executive branch conduct—the executive branch itself.

The Jackson Concurrence in the Political Branches

The discussion above suggests that, in the courts, Justice Jackson's opinion does far less to restrain presidential conduct than congressional primacy scholars think it should. That observation, however, should not detract from the opinion, for the opinion is directed as much if not more toward the political branches than it is to the courts.

To Congress, Justice Jackson's message was that congressional inertia would expand presidential power and that courts could do little to stop it. In describing his second grouping of presidential action—action in the absence of a congressional grant or denial of authority—Justice Jackson noted that "congressional inertia, indifference or quiescence may sometimes, at least as a practical matter, enable, if not invite, measures on independent presidential responsibility."[205] Justice Jackson later observed that he had "no illusion that any decision by this Court can keep power in the hands of Congress if it is not wise and timely in meeting its problems. A crisis that challenges the President equally, or perhaps primarily, challenges Congress.... We may say that power to legislate for emergencies belongs in the hands of Congress, but only Congress itself can prevent power from slipping through its fingers."[206]

To the executive branch, Justice Jackson spoke as legal-adviser-turned-judge. The message was clear: that the advice that President Truman had legal authority to seize the mills never would have been

---

Dames & Moore while purporting to apply it. Interestingly, Chief Justice Roberts, who wrote the opinion in *Medellín*, served as a law clerk to then-Justice Rehnquist when *Dames & Moore* was decided.

[204] Patricia L. Bellia, *Executive Power in* Youngstown's *Shadows*, 19 Const. Comm. 87, 145–54 (2002).

[205] 343 U.S. at 637 (Jackson, J., concurring).

[206] *Id.* at 654.

given or followed in President Roosevelt's time. Although Justice Jackson's three-part framework is the most famous part of his opinion, the opinion also contains several direct comments on executive decision-making both before and during the *Steel Seizure* litigation. The opinion condemns the government's district court claims, stating that "I did not suppose, and I am not persuaded, that history leaves it open to question, at least in the courts, that the executive branch, like the Federal Government as a whole, possesses only delegated powers."[207] Similarly, the Solicitor General's argument before the Court concerning the Commander in Chief Clause provoked Justice Jackson to comment that presidential advisers "would not waive or narrow [the clause] by nonassertion yet cannot say where it begins or ends."[208] He continued that although advisers often make broad claims under the rubric of this clause, "advice to the President in specific matters usually has carried overtones that powers, even under this head," are much narrower; and "[e]ven then, heed has been taken of any efforts of Congress to negative [the President's] authority."[209] Echoing a comment he made at conference to the effect that "[w]isdom in [the Executive's] use of the power in the past has been in keeping it out of the courts,"[210] Justice Jackson suggested that "prudence has counseled that actual reliance on such nebulous claims stop short of provoking a judicial test."[211] In the accompanying footnote, Justice Jackson went so far as to draw a parallel to the Tudors' use of the power of legislation by proclamation, quoting Holdsworth as saying that the legal question regarding the extent of their use " 'was never finally settled ... because the Tudors made so tactful a use of their powers that no demand for the settlement of this question was raised.' "[212]

This pointed critique of executive branch decision-making may be lost on modern constitutional law students, for casebooks, while including Justice Jackson's rebuttal of the Solicitor General's understanding of executive power, omit much of the language quoted above.[213] Even a reader of the full opinion might miss the extent to which Justice Jackson's critique is truly an *intra*-executive branch critique rather than a judicial critique, pitting the claims of current advisors to President

---

[207] *Id.* at 640.

[208] *Id.* at 641.

[209] *Id.* at 645.

[210] Douglas Conference Notes.

[211] *Youngstown*, 343 U.S. 647 (Jackson, J., concurring).

[212] *Id.* at 648 n.16.

[213] *See, e.g.*, Kathleen M. Sullivan & Gerald Gunther, *Constitutional Law* 348–49 (15th ed. 2004) (omitting all but the fourth of the five quotations above).

Truman against the narrower claims of advisors past. Justice Jackson's involvement in the North American Aviation seizure made a discussion of that episode necessary, and in that discussion Justice Jackson twice distinguished between his role as adviser and his role as judge.[214] Elsewhere in the opinion, however, Justice Jackson relied squarely but silently on his own advice to President Roosevelt to show the error of the government's position. In claiming that, in the past, "heed has been taken of any efforts of Congress to negative" the President's authority as Commander in Chief, Justice Jackson cited legal advice to President Roosevelt concerning a proposed transfer of vessels to Great Britain. The Justice Department had advised President Roosevelt that he could not transfer certain so-called "mosquito boats" because doing so would violate a statute.[215] The advice was Justice Jackson's,[216] as was the advice in a second opinion cited on the same point.[217] Justice Jackson also quietly defended Justice Clark, whose claim that the President's "inherent power to deal with emergencies" was "exceedingly great" had been taken to support the seizure of the steel mills.[218] Justice Jackson contended that the citations following the Attorney General's reference to "inherent power" identified instances of congressional authorization, and that the "specific advice" given by the Attorney General had ample basis in the President's duty to see that the laws are faithfully executed.[219]

In the final opinion, then, Justice Jackson's critique of executive branch decision-making seems to be offered at arms' length, deemphasizing his own role in shaping executive branch precedents. The availability of earlier drafts of the opinion, however, shows that the opinion began as an *insider*'s critique of the government's position and that Justice Jackson gradually—but never completely—de-personalized the opinion. Justice Jackson's papers include notes and multiple draft opinions from

---

[214] *Youngstown*, 343 U.S. at 647 (Jackson, J., concurring) ("[A] judge cannot accept self-serving press statements of the attorney for one of the interested parties as authority in answering a constitutional question, even if the advocate was himself."); *id.* at 649 n.17 ("I do not regard [the North American seizure] as a precedent for this, but, even if I did, I should not bind present judicial judgment by earlier partisan advocacy.").

[215] *See* Acquisition of Naval and Air Bases in Exchange for Over-age Destroyers, 39 Op. Atty. Gen. 484.

[216] *Id.*

[217] *See* Training of British Flying Students in the United States, 40 Op. Atty. Gen. 58.

[218] Justice Clark had made these comments while he was Attorney General. Hearings on S. 249 Before the S. Comm. on Labor and Public Welfare, 81st Cong., 1st Sess. 232 (1949); *see also* Maeva Marcus, *Truman and the Steel Seizure Case: The Limits of Presidential Power* 338 n. 51 (1977) (discussing Clark's support for President's inherent powers).

[219] *Youngstown*, 343 U.S. at 649–50 n. 17.

the case.[220] As early as May 7, three days before the Court received the briefs in the case and five days before it heard oral argument, Justice Jackson had begun drafting segments of material that he would eventually incorporate into his concurrence.[221]

The segments dealing head-on with Justice Jackson's personal involvement as an advisor to President Roosevelt provide a useful starting point. The initial May 7 segment on Justice Jackson's advice to President Roosevelt on presidential power questions is essentially a justification of his decision to participate in the *Steel Seizure* case at all. Justice Jackson wrote that "[c]andor requires me to state that I have considered whether I should sit in this case."[222] He concluded that "my experience is too remote to carry any insurmountable predilections [that] warrant withdrawal" and that "practical experience with the problems of this case may contribute" something to the presidential powers debate.[223] A revised version of this segment placed more emphasis on the unique vantage point that Jackson's position as Attorney General provided and less on the possibility of recusal: "Few experiences could make one more aware of the magnitude, advantages and dangers of the forces controlled by a dynamic Executive through the combination of law and leadership than to have served as legal advisor to a resourceful President in time of crisis. As Attorney General, it was my duty to advise President Roosevelt in urgent matters which raised sharp issues of presidential power that are cited as precedents here."[224] These highly personal comments on Justice Jackson's "duty" in advising President Roosevelt as to matters cited as precedent for the steel seizure were largely de-personalized in later drafts. In his final opinion, Justice Jackson opened by alluding to his experience: "That comprehensive and undefined presidential powers hold both practical advantages and grave dangers for the country will

---

[220] Container 176, Papers of Robert H. Jackson, Manuscript Division, Library of Congress, Washington, D.C.

[221] The May 7 segments cover a range of topics and reflect extensive edits in Justice Jackson's hand; there are also cleaner versions dated May 8. The small opinion segments are separately paginated, making it difficult to provide unique citations. Below I cite the May 7 and May 8 opinion segments with descriptive titles that do not appear on the opinions themselves. (All drafts are located in Container 176 of Justice Jackson's papers.) By May 22, the small opinion segments had been merged into a complete opinion, also reflecting extensive edits in Justice Jackson's hand. The concurring opinion had taken substantially final shape by May 29, within four days of the Court's June 2 announcement of its decision.

For another account of the evolution of Justice Jackson's opinion, *see* Adam J. White, *Justice Jackson's Draft Opinions in the Steel Seizure Cases*, 69 Alb. L. Rev. 1107 (2006).

[222] Roosevelt Involvement Segment, May 7, at 1.

[223] *Id.*

[224] Roosevelt Involvement Segment, May 8, at 1.

impress anyone who has served as legal adviser to a President in time of transition and public anxiety."[225] In doing so, however, he eliminated any specific reference to President Roosevelt and to the government's reliance on his own legal advice as precedent.

Justice Jackson's efforts to grapple with and distinguish the Roosevelt-era precedents in which he played a role reflect a similar evolution. Indeed, one might go so far as to say that Justice Jackson's famous three-part framework initially developed not as an abstract tool for resolving presidential power disputes, but as a tool for contextualizing Justice Jackson's own advice to President Roosevelt and distinguishing it from the advice upon which President Truman acted. Of particular interest is *how* one can determine whether presidential action falls into Justice Jackson's first category—that involving congressional authorization. The first opinion segment setting up the three-part framework, likely prepared on May 7, contemplated that executive action could be classified as "in accordance with congressional authority," "contrary to the enacted policy of Congress," and where there is "no rule or policy of Congress."[226] These formulations left open the question of how one should discern what is "in accordance with congressional authority." The next draft referred to an "express Act or *general policy* of Congress,"[227] wording that survived in later versions before eventually giving way in a May 22 draft to the "express or *implied* authorization" wording that appears in the final opinion.[228]

The recognition that one could discern congressional approval from a general policy or by implication was important for purposes of classifying the most obvious Roosevelt-era precedent—that involving the seizure, on then-Attorney General Jackson's advice, of the North American Aviation plant.[229] Justice Jackson's first draft of a discussion of the

---

[225] *Youngstown*, 343 U.S. 579 (Jackson, J., concurring).

[226] This segment, although dated May 8, appears to be the first segment discussing the framework for evaluating executive action. Justice Jackson's undated handwritten notes on the case contain an early outline of the three categories of executive action Justice Jackson presents in his final opinion. Undated Handwritten Notes, Container 176, Papers of Robert H. Jackson, Manuscript Division, Library of Congress, Washington, D.C. Although undated, it is almost certain that these notes pre-dated the earliest typed opinion segments, which expand upon the central points in the notes. The segment described in the text most closely matches Justice Jackson's handwritten notes. Other versions dated May 7 and May 8 expand upon it. Adam White reaches a similar conclusion about the mis-dating of this segment in his analysis of the draft opinions. *See* Adam J. White, *Justice Jackson's Draft Opinions in the Steel Seizure Cases*, 69 Alb. L. Rev. 1107, 1114 n. 37 (2006).

[227] Classification Segment, May 7, at 1.

[228] May 22 Draft at 2; *Youngstown*, 343 U.S. at 635.

[229] Justice Jackson's undated handwritten notes, like the early opinion segments, tend to support the view that the three-part framework developed in part to distinguish and

North American Aviation seizure characterized that seizure as "rest[ing] upon the provisions of two statutes."[230] A memo from Justice Jackson's law clerk noted that the stated justification for the NAA neither invoked nor was consistent with the "only relevant statute," the Selective Service Act of 1940.[231] In the next version, after recounting differences between the North American Aviation seizure and the steel seizure, Justice Jackson categorized the North American Aviation seizure, without elaboration, as being "in accordance with the policy of Congress."[232]

Although the May 7 segments on the Roosevelt-era precedents discussed only the North American Aviation seizure, Justice Jackson soon supplemented that example with other specific instances of his advice to President Roosevelt. As with the North American Aviation example, Justice Jackson dealt head-on with the fact that he was President Roosevelt's advisor on such matters. For example, a May 8 segment cited an instance during Justice Jackson's time as Attorney General in which the President sought congressional authorization to seize foreign merchant vessels lying immobilized in United States waters. Justice Jackson pointed out that the seizure could have been justified as within the power of the Commander in Chief "far better than the seizure now before us," and yet President Roosevelt had sought statutory authority for his action.[233] Justice Jackson defended another of his opinions as Attorney General—one that he said had "been frequently criticized as pushing powers of the President to the extreme limit."[234] That opinion—relating to the transfer of overage destroyers—relied upon the specific authorization of Congress to dispose of the destroyers in question. As noted earlier, however, the same opinion also advised

---

justify President Roosevelt's conduct. Undated Handwritten Notes, Container 176, Papers of Robert H. Jackson, Manuscript Division, Library of Congress, Washington, D.C. The outline of the framework and notes on its application to the steel seizure are immediately followed by a catalog of the differences between President Roosevelt's seizure of the North American Aviation plant and President Truman's seizure of the steel mills. See Undated Handwritten Notes, Container 176, Papers of Robert H. Jackson, Manuscript Division, Library of Congress, Washington, D.C.

[230] Roosevelt Precedent Segment, May 7, at 2.

[231] See Memorandum from CGN, Presidential Seizure Power, May 8, 1952, at 2, Container 176, Papers of Robert H. Jackson, Manuscript Division, Library of Congress, Washington, D.C. (noting that reliance on the Selective Service Act seems not to have been contemplated at the time, and that "the press reports say nothing of it, except to indicate through reports of suggested amendatory legislation that the 1940 Act played no part in the seizure").

[232] Roosevelt Precedent Segment, May 8, at 1.

[233] Id. at 2.

[234] Id.

that certain so-called "mosquito boats" could not be transferred because doing so would violate a statute.[235]

In short, early segments of Justice Jackson's opinions reflect not only the development of the three-part framework included in his final opinion, but also an effort to situate his own advice to President Roosevelt within that framework. As with his more general comments on his involvement in the Roosevelt administration, however, Justice Jackson sought to de-personalize these segments. The Roosevelt-era examples developed in the May 7 and May 8 segments were demoted to footnotes, stripped of any reference to the fact that they involved advice given by Jackson himself, and placed alongside practices of other Presidents.[236] Only in connection with the North American Aviation seizure did Justice Jackson allude to the extent to which his own past legal advice contributed to the breadth of the government's current claims about presidential power.[237]

Two other aspects of the opinion's de-personalization are notable as well. The first involved Justice Jackson's account of a disagreement he had with President Roosevelt over a presidential power issue—specifically, his advice to the President that the Lend–Lease Act did not encroach upon executive power merely because the act provided for its termination upon a joint resolution of Congress. Despite Jackson's advice, President Roosevelt maintained that the Act thereby unconstitutionally deprived the President of the power to exercise a veto on Congress's decision. Justice Jackson introduced this disagreement in a May 22 draft but removed it from a later version.[238] Finally, Justice Jackson's May 22 draft spoke rather forcefully to the role of a legal-advisor-turned-judge in a parallel to the English experience:

> [I]t is the duty of the Court not to be the first but to be the last to give up our constitutional system of power only under law. We

---

[235] *See* Acquisition of Naval and Air Bases in Exchange for Over-age Destroyers, 39 Op. Atty. Gen. 484.

[236] As noted earlier, the final opinion still contains an account of Jackson's advice to President Roosevelt concerning the transfer of the overage destroyers, but without an indication that the advice was Jackson's, as well as a citation to another of Justice Jackson's opinions concerning U.S. training of British flying students. *Id.* at 645 (citing Training of British Flying Students in the United States, 40 Op. Atty. Gen. 58). The final version also includes a footnote that discusses President Roosevelt's request for congressional authorization to seize immobilized vessels in American harbors, placing that episode alongside those involving other Presidents. *Id.* at 647–48 n.16.

[237] *See* Kathleen M. Sullivan & Gerald Gunther, *Constitutional Law* 348–49 (15th ed. 2004).

[238] A year later, Justice Jackson revealed President Roosevelt's memorandum in an article in the Harvard Law Review. Robert H. Jackson, *A Presidential Legal Opinion*, 66 Harv. L. Rev. 1353 (1953).

follow a judicial tradition instituted by one who had been a subservient, partisan Attorney General but who lives in history as an exemplary judge. On a memorable Sunday in 1612, King James took great offense at his defense of judicial independence and, in rage, declared: "Then I am to be *under* the law—which it is treason to affirm." ... Chief Justice [Coke] replied to the King who had appointed him: "Thus wrote Bracton, 'The King ought not to be under any man, but he is under God and the Law.' "[239]

In handwritten edits to the May 22 draft, Justice Jackson excised the implicit parallel between his own role and that of Chief Justice Coke.[240] He then relegated the example to a footnote in the near-final copy edited version.[241]

The de-personalization of Justice Jackson's opinion, of course, was never complete. Justice Jackson still consciously spoke as legal-advisor-turned-judge. But if Justice Jackson's three-part framework emerged from, and as a way to justify the decisions he made in, his role as Attorney General, it is perhaps better understood as a guide for the executive branch to avoid separation-of-power disputes than as a prescription for courts to resolve them.

How, then, does Justice Jackson's opinion fare in the executive branch, if its message is one of prudence and stewardship in the exercise of power? In the final footnote of her book, Maeva Marcus quotes a deputy assistant attorney general in the Justice Department's Office of Legal Counsel (OLC)—the branch of the Justice Department charged with rendering advice on constitutional matters—as saying in a 1974 interview that "[a]ttorneys in the office do not often cite the [*Steel Seizure*] case, but it is always in the back of their minds."[242] The statement is ambiguous, for it could mean either that the *Steel Seizure* case indirectly but firmly shapes OLC's advice or that attorneys can simply set it aside. In a more recent reflection, almost thirty years after the interview, Marcus cast the observation in the more pessimistic light:

---

[239] Draft Opinion of May 22, at 30, Container 176, Papers of Robert H. Jackson, Manuscript Division, Library of Congress, Washington, D.C.

[240] *Id.*

[241] Undated Draft Opinion at 22, Container 176, Papers of Robert H. Jackson, Manuscript Division, Library of Congress, Washington, D.C.; *see Youngstown*, 353 U.S. at 655 n.27 ("We follow the judicial tradition instituted on a memorable Sunday in 1612, when King James took offense at the independence of his judges and, in rage, declared: 'Then I am to be *under* the law—which it is treason to affirm.' Chief Justice Coke replied to his King: 'Thus wrote Bracton, "The King ought not to be under any man, but he is under God and the Law." ' ").

[242] Maeva Marcus, *Truman and the Steel Seizure Case: The Limits of Presidential Power* 358 n. 31 (1977) (quoting Leon Ulman).

"*Youngstown* rarely affects the advice the office gives the president on the legality of contemplated actions. They know the decision exists, but it is not dispositive."[243]

But the heightened prominence of Justice Jackson's opinion over the last quarter-century may well have changed the stakes of executive advice-giving. To be sure, citations to the *Steel Seizure* case in published OLC opinions are balanced by citations to an opinion whose broad view of executive power Justice Jackson sought to rebut—*United States v. Curtiss–Wright Export Corp.*[244] One could argue, however, that the shadow the *Steel Seizure* case casts on executive decision-making in foreign affairs cases is so long that the executive branch can only avoid the case's implications by refusing to acknowledge it at all.[245] And although Justice Jackson's framework can be as fluid in the hands of the executive branch as it may seem in the hands of courts,[246] the *Steel Seizure* case

---

[243] Maeva Marcus, *Will* Youngstown *Survive?*, 41 Duq. L. Rev. 725, 732 (2003).

[244] 299 U.S. 304 (1936). For more on *United States v. Curtiss–Wright*, see Chapter 6 in this volume.

[245] Many critics of the rescinded Torture Memo have noted that OLC's analysis of the federal anti-torture statute omitted any citation to the *Steel Seizure* case. *See, e.g.*, Neil Kinkopf, *The Statutory Commander in Chief*, 81 Ind. L.J. 1169, 1171 (2006) ("[OLC] failed even to cite to Justice Jackson's seminal opinion from *Youngstown*."); Cornelia Pillard, *Unitariness and Myopia: The Executive Branch, Legal Process, and Torture*, 81 Ind. L.J. 1297, 1304–05 (2006) ("[T]he Torture Memo's sweeping commander-in-chief analysis ... glaringly omitted even mere mention of the paradigmatic *Steel Seizure* case."); Lawyers' Statement on Bush Administration's Torture Memo, Aug. 7, 2004, at 2, *available at* http://www.hrw.org/pub/2004/lawyers-statement.pdf ("One of the surprising features of these legal memoranda is their failure to acknowledge the numerous sources of law that contradict their own positions, such as the Steel Seizure Case."). The portion of the Torture Memo addressing the President's Commander in Chief power suggests that Congress is powerless to limit the executive's interrogation of enemy combatants. Memorandum from Jay S. Bybee, Assistant Attorney General, Office of Legal Counsel, to Alberto R. Gonzales, Counsel to the President, Aug. 1, 2002, at 31. Professor Neil Kinkopf argues that the failure to cite Justice Jackson's opinion "is no mere violation of citation etiquette, for it led OLC to fail to acknowledge that Congress has any relevant authority whatsoever." Neil Kinkopf, *The Statutory Commander in Chief*, 81 Ind. L.J. 1169, 1171 (2006).

[246] The Justice Department's "White Paper" on the National Security Agency's terrorist surveillance program provides a case in point. Legal Authorities Supporting the Activities of the National Security Agency Described by the President, Jan. 19, 2006. The opinion acknowledged the centrality of the *Steel Seizure* framework. But it characterized the NSA program as a "category one" event—as being supported by an express or implied congressional authorization. More specifically, the opinion concluded that the Authorization for the Use of Military Force (AUMF), which permits the President to use "all necessary and appropriate force against those nations, organizations, or persons he determines planned, authorized, committed, or aided the terrorist attacks" of September 11, 2001, placed the President's authority to conduct surveillance at its zenith. *Id.* at 2, 11. Surveillance to gather foreign intelligence information is extensively regulated by the Foreign Intelligence Surveillance Act, 50 U.S.C. at § 1801 *et seq.*, and that statute deems

teaches that imprudent executive branch advice risks prompting judicial intervention to re-set the balance between the President and Congress.[247] The case thus counsels wise stewardship of executive power but serves a democracy-forcing function—requiring the cooperation of the political branches—when that fails.[248]

Conclusion

We can confidently say that the Supreme Court's decision in the *Steel Seizure* case was never "destined to be ignored."[249] What is surprising about the story of the case is how, at so many turns, the Court's final resolution of the dispute might have been avoided. Once the dispute reached the district court, most observers perceived the chances to be in the President's favor—to the point where the steel companies' attorneys thought their best strategy was to steer the district court toward a middle course of protecting the companies' interests without ruling against the government on the ultimate question of the seizure's legality. The Justice Department, meanwhile, not only opened the door for the district court's resolution of this ultimate question but also staked its defense of the seizure on an unreasonably broad theory of presidential power. Once the district court ruled, the Supreme Court unwittingly played into the steel companies' hands by staying the terms and conditions of employment and thereby dooming the ongoing negotiations.

Before the Supreme Court, the government moderated its claims. In siding with the steel companies, the Court rejected any sort of middle course by which it might have upheld the government's conduct on the

---

its procedures the "exclusive means" by which electronic surveillance to gather foreign intelligence information can occur. 18 U.S.C. § 2511(2)(f). The exclusivity provision suggests that the NSA surveillance would constitute a "category three" event. The White Paper sidestepped the difficulties created by the exclusivity provision in part by suggesting that interpreting FISA to preclude the surveillance would create a conflict between FISA and the President's power as Commander in Chief, and that the constitutional avoidance canon therefore counseled in favor of interpreting it otherwise. *See* Legal Authorities Supporting the Activities of the National Security Agency Described by the President, Jan. 19, 2006, at 28.

[247] The Court's decision in *Hamdan v. Rumsfeld*, 548 U.S. 557 (2006), interpreting the AUMF in the context of the President's claim of authority to set up military tribunals to try enemy combatants, essentially forecloses the White Paper's construction of the AUMF.

[248] *See Hamdan*, 548 U.S. at 636 (Breyer, J., concurring) ("Where, as here, no emergency prevents consultation with Congress, judicial insistence upon that consultation does not weaken our Nation's ability to deal with danger. To the contrary, that insistence strengthens the Nation's ability to determine-through democratic means-how best to do so. The Constitution places its faith in those democratic means. Our Court today simply does the same.").

[249] *See* Glendon A. Schubert, Jr., *The Steel Case: Presidential Responsibility and Judicial Irresponsibility*, 6 W. Pol. Q. 61, 65 (1953).

facts presented without broadly considering the scope of any inherent or residual power the President might have to act in an emergency. The importance of the *Steel Seizure* case thus stems in part from the weight it lends to claims that it is a court's duty to combat abuses of power by a coordinate branch of government. It also stems in part from Justice Jackson's concurrence, which courts and commentators treat as the most authoritative opinion in the case. As a matter of judicial doctrine, the concurrence does less to constrain presidential power claims that we might expect, for it both recognizes the importance of limiting presidential conduct and provides courts with ready avenues for upholding questionable presidential conduct. The opinion, however, is as much a primer on how to avoid courts' intervention in presidential power disputes as it is a guide for courts to resolve those disputes.*

* I thank research librarian Patti Ogden for expert assistance, the reference librarians at the Manuscript Division of the Library of Congress and the National Archives and Records Administration–Great Lakes Region for guidance with archival materials, and Jeffery Houin for excellent research assistance. Amy Barrett, A.J. Bellia, Peg Brinig, Nicole Garnett, Rick Garnett, Bill Kelley, Mary Ellen O'Connell, John Nagle, participants at a faculty workshop at Notre Dame, and other *Presidential Powers Stories* authors, especially Hal Bruff, provided helpful comments on prior drafts. I also thank participants in the D.C. Circuit Historical Society's program on *The Steel Seizure Case in Historical Perspective: Presidential Power in Wartime*, particularly Maeva Marcus and John Q. Barrett, for insightful discussions.

*

8

Trevor W. Morrison

The Story of *United States v. United States District Court (Keith)*: The Surveillance Power

May the President, acting in the interests of national security, authorize the electronic surveillance of persons within the United States without first obtaining a judicial warrant? The Supreme Court's first and still most important answer to that question came in *United States v. United States District Court for the Eastern District of Michigan, Southern Division*, better known as the *Keith* case.[1] In what the *New York Times* called "a stunning legal setback" for the government,[2] the Court concluded that "Fourth Amendment freedoms cannot properly be guaranteed if domestic security surveillance may be conducted solely within the discretion of the Executive Branch."[3] Thus, the Court held, a judicial warrant must issue before the government may engage in wiretapping or other electronic surveillance of domestic threats to national security. But the Court also limited its holding to cases involving "the domestic aspects of national security," and "express[ed] no opinion as to [the surveillance of the] activities of foreign powers or their agents."[4] Both in what it said and what it did not say, *Keith* has exerted great influence upon the judicial, legislative, and executive approaches to these issues in the years since.

---

[1] 407 U.S. 297 (1972). As recounted below, "Keith" refers to Damon J. Keith, the federal district judge in the case.

[2] Fred P. Graham, *High Court Curbs U.S. Wiretapping Aimed at Radicals*, N.Y. Times, June 20, 1972, at A1.

[3] *Keith*, 407 U.S. at 316–17.

[4] *Id.* at 321–22.

Keith is also a great story. Arising in a period of great social and political unrest in this country, its cast of characters features "White Panther" radicals, famed civil liberties lawyers, Watergate accomplices, a federal judge as a named party, and a junior Justice whose opinion for the Court no one would have predicted. Before meeting those characters, however, we need some background both on the law and practice of national security surveillance in general and on the circumstances giving rise to the *Keith* case in particular.

National Security Surveillance

When the *Keith* case arose in the early 1970s, warrantless wiretapping—that is, the electronic interception of telephone and other private communications—for purposes of national security was not a new phenomenon. Indeed, "[s]uccessive Presidents for more than one-quarter of a century ha[d] authorized such surveillance in varying degrees."[5] The first President to do so was Franklin Roosevelt. In 1940, he signed a memorandum empowering Attorney General Robert Jackson to direct government agents "to secure information by listening devices direct[ed] to the conversation or other communications of persons suspected of subversive activities against the Government of the United States, including suspected spies."[6]

Although it is unclear whether Roosevelt's authorization covered surveillance of wholly domestic entities,[7] in 1946 President Truman made that authority explicit by approving the use of wiretapping and other "special investigative measures ... in cases vitally affecting the domestic security, or where human life is in jeopardy."[8] As the Supreme Court later explained, "[t]he [warrantless] use of such surveillance in internal security cases [was] sanctioned more or less continuously by various Presidents and Attorneys General" from the time of Truman's authorization until the Court decided *Keith*.[9]

---

[5] *Id.* at 299.

[6] Memorandum from President Franklin D. Roosevelt to Robert Jackson, Att'y Gen. (May 21, 1940), *reprinted in Hearings Before the Senate Committee on the Judiciary on the Nominations of William H. Rehnquist, of Arizona, and Lewis F. Powell, Jr., of Virginia, to be Associate Justices of the Supreme Court of the United States*, 92d Cong. 254 (1971) [hereinafter "Powell Hearings"], *available at* http://www.gpoaccess.gov/congress/senate/judiciary/sh92–69–267/browse.html.

[7] *See Keith*, 407 U.S. at 310–11 n.10 (noting this uncertainty).

[8] Letter from Tom C. Clark, Att'y Gen., to President Harry S. Truman (Jul. 17, 1946), *reprinted in* Powell Hearings at 255. Truman's handwritten approval, appended to the bottom of Clark's letter, is dated July 17, *1947*. That seems to have been an error. *Cf. Keith*, 407 U.S. at 310 (treating 1946 as the date of Truman's authorization).

[9] *Keith*, 407 U.S. at 310. The only apparent exception came during the latter part of the Johnson administration, when Attorney General Ramsey Clark "sharp[ly] curtail[ed]" the warrantless use of electronic surveillance. *Id.* at 310–11 n.10.

When these surveillance policies were first put in place, there was no particular reason to think they implicated the Fourth Amendment's warrant requirement.[10] Under *Olmstead v. United States*,[11] the Fourth Amendment was understood to restrict only physical trespasses. Electronic surveillance not accompanied by some physical intrusion was simply not a Fourth Amendment event.[12]

In 1967, the Supreme Court overruled *Olmstead* in *Katz v. United States*.[13] *Katz* extended the Fourth Amendment's coverage to nontrespassory surveillance, rendering most warrantless electronic interceptions of private communications constitutionally unreasonable.[14] But the Court also confined its holding to the use of surveillance for ordinary law enforcement purposes; it expressed no opinion on "[w]hether safeguards other than prior authorization by a magistrate [that is, the issuance of a warrant] would satisfy the Fourth Amendment in a situation involving the national security."[15]

Legislative efforts by Congress in the late 1960s also avoided national security-based surveillance. In 1968, responding both to *Katz* and to the growing awareness that wiretapping and other forms of electronic surveillance were both vital law enforcement tools and substantial potential threats to individual privacy, Congress enacted Title III of the Omnibus Crime Control and Safe Streets Act.[16] As a general matter, the act prohibited wiretapping and electronic surveillance by anyone other than a duly authorized law enforcement officer, the Federal Communications Commission, or communications common carriers engaged in certain monitoring as part of their normal business practices. As for law enforcement, the act authorized the use of electronic surveillance, pursuant to a prior court order, in a limited set of criminal cases.[17] It laid out

---

[10] The Fourth Amendment provides: "The right of the people to be secure in their persons, houses, papers, and effects, against unreasonable searches and seizures, shall not be violated, and no Warrants shall issue, but upon probable cause, supported by Oath or affirmation, and particularly describing the place to be searched, and the persons or things to be searched." U.S. Const. amend. IV.

[11] 277 U.S. 438 (1928).

[12] Some instances of electronic surveillance might be accompanied by a physical invasion into the target's home in order, for example, to install certain electronic, video, or audio equipment. Even under *Olmstead*, cases of that sort would have triggered the Fourth Amendment.

[13] 389 U.S. 347 (1967).

[14] *Id.* at 353, 356–57.

[15] *Id.* at 358 n.23.

[16] 18 U.S.C. §§ 2510–20.

[17] *Id.* § 2516.

the kind of detailed and particularized showing required to obtain a court order, and it imposed certain conditions on the use of the authority conferred by the order.[18] In short, as the *Keith* Court later put it, the act was "a comprehensive attempt by Congress to promote more effective control of crime while protecting the privacy of individual thought and expression."[19]

Like the Supreme Court in *Katz*, however, Congress conspicuously avoided any pronouncement on national security-based surveillance. Instead, it included a provision that amounted to a national security disclaimer:

> Nothing contained in this chapter ... shall limit the constitutional power of the President to take such measures as he deems necessary to protect the Nation against actual or potential attack or other hostile acts of a foreign power, [or] to obtain foreign intelligence information deemed essential to the security of the United States.... Nor shall anything contained in this chapter be deemed to limit the constitutional power of the President to take such measures as he deemed necessary to protect the United States against the overthrow of the Government by force or other unlawful means, or against any other clear and present danger to the structure or existence of the Government.[20]

Yet just as this provision made clear Congress's intention not to limit the President's authority to act in the interests of national security, nothing in the act *enhanced* his authority to do so. Congress, in other words, simply took no position on whether the President had that power, nor on whether or when such power might be subject to Fourth Amendment or other constitutional limits.

In sum, by the time *Keith* came to the Court, it was clear that electronic surveillance for ordinary law enforcement purposes triggered the Fourth Amendment's warrant requirement. Title III also imposed various statutory restrictions on such surveillance. It was equally clear, though, that Title III did not apply to national security-based surveillance. What was not clear—and what became the central question in the case—was whether national security surveillance qualified for an exception to the Fourth Amendment's warrant requirement.

The case did not set up that way when it began, however. The next section addresses those beginnings.

---

[18] *Id.* § 2518.

[19] *Keith*, 407 U.S. 297, 302 (1972).

[20] 18 U.S.C. § 2511(3) (1976), *repealed by* Foreign Intelligence Surveillance Act, Pub. L. No. 95–511, 92 Stat. 1783 (1978) (codified as amended at 50 U.S.C. §§ 1801 *et seq.*).

Lawrence "Pun" Plamondon

The *Keith* case started as a criminal prosecution of Lawrence "Pun" Plamondon, John Sinclair, and John Waterhouse Forrest in connection with the bombing of a CIA office in Ann Arbor, Michigan.[21] Events relating to Plamondon in particular became the focal point of the surveillance component of the case. His story is part of the *Keith* story.

Life did not start easily for Plamondon. Born in 1945 to an alcoholic father and a syphilitic mother while both were institutionalized in a Michigan state mental hospital,[22] he was raised by adopted parents and eventually left home in his teens.[23] He was in frequent legal trouble: Between 1962 and 1966 he was arrested fourteen times in four different states and Canada for offenses ranging from underage drinking to assault and battery.[24] At age 21 he found himself in Detroit.[25] It was 1967, the year of Detroit's 12th Street Riot and a time of great unrest. Plamondon soon fell in with a group of "counterculture" artists, activists, and writers including John Sinclair, the founder of the Detroit Artists Workshop.[26] He "made sandals for money," and "[a]t night he dropped acid, smoked pot and ate hallucinogenic mushrooms while listening to the MC5, The Doors, and Iggy and the Stooges."[27]

Plamondon, Sinclair, and others moved to Ann Arbor in 1968.[28] They lived there in a kind of commune. At around that time, Plamondon read a newspaper interview with Huey P. Newton, a leader of the Black Panther Party, who told the reporter that if white people wanted to support the Black Panthers, "[t]hey can form a White Panther Party."[29] Plamondon and Sinclair soon did just that, with Sinclair serving as

---

[21] *See* Samuel C. Damren, *The* Keith *Case*, 11 *The Court Legacy* (Historical Society for the U.S. Dist. Ct. for the E.D. Mich.) at 1 (2003).

[22] *See* Pun Plamondon, *Lost from the Ottawa: The Story of the Journey Back* 16 (2004).

[23] *Id.* at 35–37; *see also* Marsha Low, *60s Radical Takes Long Trip Back to His Roots: White Panthers' Plamondon Surfaces with Memoir*, Detroit Free Press, Oct. 27, 2004, at B1.

[24] *See* Pun Plamondon, *Lost from the Ottawa: The Story of the Journey Back* 52–53 (2004).

[25] *See* Marsha Low, *60s Radical Takes Long Trip Back to His Roots: White Panthers' Plamondon Surfaces with Memoir*, Detroit Free Press, Oct. 27, 2004, at B1.

[26] *See* Samuel C. Damren, *The* Keith *Case*, 11 *The Court Legacy* (Historical Society for the U.S. Dist. Ct. for the E.D. Mich.) at 8 (2003).

[27] Marsha Low, *60s Radical Takes Long Trip Back to His Roots: White Panthers' Plamondon Surfaces with Memoir*, Detroit Free Press, Oct. 27, 2004, at B1.

[28] *Id.*

[29] Pun Plamondon, *Lost from the Ottawa: The Story of the Journey Back* 114–15 (2004).

Chairman and Minister of Information and Plamondon as Minister of Defense.[30] The "White Panther Manifesto," which Sinclair wrote in 1968, declared the group's mission:

> Our program is Cultural Revolution through a total assault on the culture, which makes us use every tool, every energy and any media we can get our collective hands on.... Our culture, our art, the music, newspapers, books, posters, our clothing, our homes, the way we walk and talk, the way our hair grows, the way we smoke dope and fuck and eat and sleep—it is all one message, and the message is FREEDOM! ... We demand total freedom for everybody! And we will not be stopped until we get it.... ROCK AND ROLL music is the spearhead of our attack because it is so effective and so much fun.... With our music and our economic genius we plunder the unsuspecting straight world for money and the means to carry out our program, and revolutionize its children at the same time.[31]

On September 29, 1968, a bomb exploded in front of a CIA recruitment office in Ann Arbor.[32] Shortly after the bombing, Plamondon went underground. He traveled across the country and the world for nearly a year, "bouncing from San Francisco to Seattle to New York to Toronto, Germany, Italy, and Algeria."[33] In Algeria he spent time with members of the Black Panthers living in self-imposed exile.[34] By the middle of 1969, Plamondon was on the Federal Bureau of Investigation's "Ten Most Wanted" list.[35]

In the fall of 1969, a federal grand jury returned indictments against Plamondon, Sinclair, and Forrest.[36] It charged them with conspiring to destroy government property, and additionally charged Plamondon with

---

[30] See Samuel C. Damren, The Keith Case, 11 The Court Legacy (Historical Society for the U.S. Dist. Ct. for the E.D. Mich.) at 1, 8 (2003).

[31] Reprinted in id. at 3.

[32] Id. at 1.

[33] Marsha Low, 60s Radical Takes Long Trip Back to His Roots: White Panthers' Plamondon Surfaces with Memoir, Detroit Free Press, Oct. 27, 2004, at B1.

[34] See Pun Plamondon, Lost from the Ottawa: The Story of the Journey Back 195–205 (2004).

[35] See Marsha Low, 60s Radical Takes Long Trip Back to His Roots: White Panthers' Plamondon Surfaces with Memoir, Detroit Free Press, Oct. 27, 2004, at B1.

[36] See United States v. United States District Court, 444 F.2d 651, 653 (6th Cir. 1971). Quoting the government's statement of facts in its petition, the Sixth Circuit's opinion identifies the date of the indictment as December 7, 1969. Id. Damren, however, sets the date as October 7, 1969. See Samuel C. Damren, The Keith Case, 11 The Court Legacy (Historical Society for the U.S. Dist. Ct. for the E.D. Mich.) at 1 (2003). Nothing material turns on this discrepancy.

destroying government property in connection with the CIA office bombing.[37] Plamondon was still on the lam at that point, but he soon grew tired of life abroad and returned to Michigan.[38] He evaded the authorities' notice for a while. But when a state trooper observed empty beer cans being thrown out of a Volkswagen van as it traveled down the highway, he pulled it over to find Plamondon and two other White Panthers inside.[39] The trooper soon saw through Plamondon's false identification, realized who he was, and arrested him.[40]

Later recalling the beer cans, Plamondon told the *Detroit Free Press* that his arrest was due to a "lack of revolutionary discipline."[41]

The Case in the Lower Courts

The case against Plamondon, Sinclair, and Forrest was filed in the U.S. District Court for the Eastern District of Michigan, in Detroit. It was randomly assigned to Judge Damon J. Keith.[42] Appointed to the bench in 1967, Judge Keith would go on to serve as Chief Judge of his district from 1975 to 1977. He was elevated to the U.S. Court of Appeals for the Sixth Circuit in 1977 and remains on that court today, having taken senior status in 1995.

The United States Attorney in charge of the case was Ralph Guy, whom President Nixon had appointed to the position in 1970.[43] He went on to join Judge Keith as a judge on the U.S. District Court for the Eastern District of Michigan and, like Keith, was later elevated to the Sixth Circuit.[44]

On the defense side, Sinclair and Plamondon were represented by famed civil liberties lawyers William Kuntsler and Leonard Weinglass.[45] Forrest was represented by a young lawyer from the National Lawyers

---

[37] *United States District Court*, 444 F.2d at 653.

[38] "I was a fish out of water," Plamondon explained to a reporter in 2004. "There were no hippie girls, no hippie guys, no rock 'n roll, no beer. I was lonely and homsesick. I came home unannounced." Marsha Low, *60s Radical Takes Long Trip Back to His Roots: White Panthers' Plamondon Surfaces with Memoir*, Detroit Free Press, Oct. 27, 2004, at B1.

[39] *Id.*

[40] *Id.*

[41] *Id.*

[42] *See* United States v. Sinclair, 321 F.Supp. 1074 (E.D. Mich. 1971).

[43] *See* Samuel C. Damren, *The* Keith *Case*, 11 *The Court Legacy* (Historical Society for the U.S. Dist. Ct. for the E.D. Mich.) at 1, 7 (2003).

[44] *Id.* at 7.

[45] *Id.* at 1.

Guild named Hugh Davis.[46] Kuntsler and Weinglass had already gained substantial notoriety for their defense of the Chicago Seven, a group of political radicals charged with conspiring to incite a riot at the 1968 Democratic National Convention in Chicago.[47] As in the Chicago case, the defense team saw the prosecution as a "politically motivated" attack, this time against the White Panther Party.[48]

The government's principal witness in the case was one David Valler, who had earlier pleaded guilty to a separate bombing and was currently in prison for that and other offenses.[49] Linked by the media to a number of other Detroit-area bombings during that period, Valler told authorities that he had supplied the explosives used in the Ann Arbor bombing.[50] He was evidently prepared to implicate some or all of the defendants in a conspiracy to carry out the attack. But there were substantial reasons to doubt his credibility. Defense counsel claimed that Valler himself had made numerous statements in which he questioned his own sanity. They filed a motion challenging Valler's competency and requesting a psychiatric evaluation. But Judge Keith denied the motion, reasoning that the defense's arguments went to Valler's credibility and not his basic competency.[51] The jury could consider those issues when deciding how much weight to give to his testimony.

In October 1970, still before trial, the defense filed a motion seeking "all [government] logs, records, and memoranda of electronic surveillance directed at any of the defendants or co-conspirators not indicted."[52] A supporting affidavit by attorney Kuntsler stated that although he had no direct knowledge of electronic surveillance in this particular case, he knew of other instances in which the government had conducted illegal surveillance of supposed counterculture radicals.[53] In addition to disclosure of any such surveillance in this case, the defense also requested a hearing "to determine whether any of the evidence upon which the

---

[46] *Id.*

[47] *See Judge Keith, the Constitution, and National Security from* Haddad *to* Sinclair, 5 J. L. Soc'y 359, 386 (2004) (remarks of Judge Keith) [hereinafter "Keith Remarks"].

[48] *Judge Keith, the Constitution, and National Security from* Haddad *to* Sinclair, 5 J. L. Soc'y 359, 370 (2004) (remarks of Hugh M. Davis, defense counsel for Forrest in the *Keith* case) [hereinafter "Davis Remarks"].

[49] *See* Samuel C. Damren, *The* Keith *Case,* 11 *The Court Legacy* (Historical Society for the U.S. Dist. Ct. for the E.D. Mich.) at 3 (2003).

[50] *Id.*

[51] *Id.*

[52] United States v. Sinclair, 321 F.Supp. 1074, 1076 (E.D. Mich. 1971).

[53] *See* Samuel C. Damren, *The* Keith *Case,* 11 *The Court Legacy* (Historical Society for the U.S. Dist. Ct. for the E.D. Mich.) at 4 (2003).

indictment is based or which the Government intends to introduce at trial is tainted by such surveillance."[54] The motion was based in part on the Supreme Court's decision in *Alderman v. United States*,[55] which held that the government must disclose to the defense evidence of any conversations the defendant participated in or that occurred on his premises which the government monitored or overheard during illegal surveillance. Disclosure, in other words, is required when the surveillance in question was done illegally. And the point of the disclosure is to determine whether any illegally obtained information has tainted the evidence upon which the government is relying in the case at bar.

In response to the disclosure motion, U.S. Attorney Guy and his prosecution team entered into a stipulation with the defense.[56] The prosecutors stated that they had no knowledge of any electronic surveillance of any of the defendants, but that they had asked the Justice Department to check with the FBI in Washington to see if it had any record of any such surveillance.[57] If those requests produced anything, the prosecutors stipulated that they would turn the information over to Judge Keith for his inspection.[58]

The complexion of the case began to change on December 14, 1970, when the government filed an affidavit signed by United States Attorney General John Mitchell. In it, Mitchell acknowledged that "[t]he defendant Plamondon has participated in conversations which were overheard by Government agents who were monitoring wiretaps which were being employed to gather intelligence information deemed necessary to protect the nation from attempts of domestic organizations to attack and subvert the existing structure of the Government."[59] The wiretaps had been authorized by the Attorney General but not by any court. In compliance with the earlier stipulation, the government submitted the logs of the surveillance to Judge Keith for his *in camera* inspection. But it refused to disclose them to the defense on the ground that doing so would "prejudice the national interest."[60]

As discussed below, the government held fast to that refusal even after losing the case at the Supreme Court. Thus, it is difficult to know

---

[54] *Id.*

[55] 394 U.S. 165 (1969).

[56] *See* Samuel C. Damren, *The* Keith *Case*, 11 *The Court Legacy* (Historical Society for the U.S. Dist. Ct. for the E.D. Mich.) at 5 (2003).

[57] *Id.*

[58] *Id.*

[59] *Keith*, 407 U.S. 297, 300 n.2 (1972) (reprinting the affidavit).

[60] *Id.*

for certain what the "overheard" conversations in question were all about. The government repeatedly stressed that "Plamondon was not the object of the surveillance," and that the Attorney General's authorization of the wiretaps was not designed to collect information about Plamondon.[61] It is reasonable to infer, then, that Plamondon was overheard having conversations with some other person or persons who were the object of the surveillance, or who were present at a location targeted by the surveillance. Decades after the trial, Hugh Davis (who had represented Forrest in the trial) offered one possibility along those lines:

> I believe [the surveillance] was a National Security Agency intercept from when Pun Plamondon was in Algeria with [Black Panther leader] Eldridge Cleaver, who was also on the run. They were calling Huey Newton at the Black Panther headquarters in Oakland. And ... if we'd have had a taint hearing, I think we would have lost [because the conversations had nothing to do with the Ann Arbor bombing].[62]

The government, however, did not try to win the battle at a taint hearing. Instead, it simply refused to disclose the logs, arguing that the surveillance was perfectly legal and thus that it was under no obligation of disclosure. Specifically, the government contended that the combination of the Attorney General's affidavit and the sealed logs established that although the surveillance was conducted without prior judicial approval, it was "a reasonable exercise of the President's power (exercised through the Attorney General) to protect the national security."[63] In other words, the government answered the question left open in *Katz* by arguing that national security was indeed an exception to the general Fourth Amendment requirement that the government obtain advance judicial approval before engaging in electronic surveillance.

Judge Keith disagreed. Stressing that "[w]e are a country of laws and not of men"[64] and that "the Constitution is the Supreme Law of the Land,"[65] he saw no basis for exempting presidentially authorized electronic surveillance from the requirements of the Fourth Amendment. The Fourth Amendment's warrant requirement ensures that assertions of government power are checked by the objective review of an independent magistrate, and Judge Keith was "loath to tolerate" replacing that check with an arrangement in which "law enforcement officials would be

---

[61] United States v. United States District Court, 444 F.2d 651, 653 n.1 (6th Cir. 1971).

[62] Davis Remarks at 370.

[63] *Id.* at 301.

[64] United States v. Sinclair, 321 F.Supp. 1074, 1077 (E.D. Mich. 1971).

[65] *Id.* at 1078.

permitted to make their own evaluation as to the reasonableness [of the] . . . search" in question.[66]

Although he did not develop the point at length, Judge Keith also drew a distinction between surveillance targeting purely domestic entities and surveillance targeting foreign powers:

> An idea which seems to permeate much of the Government's argument is that a dissident domestic organization is akin to an unfriendly foreign power and must be dealt with in the same fashion. There is great danger in an argument of this nature for it strikes at the very constitutional privileges and immunities that are inherent in United States citizenship. It is to be remembered that in our democracy all men are to receive equal justice regardless of their political beliefs or persuasions. The executive branch of our government cannot be given the power or the opportunity to investigate and prosecute criminal violations under two different standards simply because certain accused persons espouse views which are inconsistent with our present form of government.[67]

Judge Keith's distinction between domestic and foreign intelligence-gathering can be read in at least two different ways. One way is to stress the passage referring to the constitutional rights that come with being a citizen of the United States. Yet citizenship itself generally does not mark the boundary of the Fourth Amendment's protections; non-citizens prosecuted in U.S. courts enjoy the Amendment's protections just as citizens do. Another (perhaps more descriptively accurate and normatively attractive) reading would treat the distinction as having to do with whether the government's actions have any proximate connection to the domestic criminal justice system, without regard to the citizenship of those involved. On this reading, the point is that the Fourth Amendment must apply fully to "dissident domestic organization[s]" precisely because such organizations are subject to the domestic criminal justice system. "[F]oreign power[s]," on the other hand, are not likely to face prosecution in the U.S. courts. More generally, the domestic sovereign's relationship to them is qualitatively different than it is to domestic individuals and organizations. Thus, it makes sense from this perspective to distinguish between domestic and foreign targets of the government's surveillance efforts.

The rule embraced by Judge Keith did precisely that: "[I]n wholly domestic situations, there is no national security exemption from the warrant requirement of the Fourth Amendment."[68] Phrased this way,

---

[66] *Id.* at 1078–79.

[67] *Id.* at 1079.

[68] 321 F. Supp. at 1080 (quoting United States v. Smith, 321 F.Supp. 424, 429 (C.D. Cal. 1971)). *Smith* was a district court case that involved the same issues as the case before

the rule carried no necessary implications for national security surveillance in situations involving foreign powers or that were otherwise not
purely domestic. But because the Attorney General's affidavit described
this case in "wholly domestic" terms, and because the surveillance in
this case took place without a judicially issued warrant, it violated the
Fourth Amendment. Accordingly, under *Alderman* Judge Keith ordered
the government to disclose to Plamondon his overheard conversations.

The government acted quickly to challenge Judge Keith's order
before the U.S. Court of Appeals for the Sixth Circuit. Because it was a
pretrial interlocutory order, the judge's order was not immediately
subject to a conventional appeal.[69] In addition, it fell outside the limited
set of interlocutory orders that Congress had singled out as immediately
appealable.[70] So the ordinary appellate avenues were unavailable. There
were other avenues, however, and the government took one of them.
Relying on the jurisdiction conferred by the All Writs Act,[71] the government pursued its appeal in the form of a petition for a writ of mandamus. This move made the district court below (and Judge Keith himself)
the respondent in the case before the appellate courts, which is how
Keith got its name.

A divided three-judge panel of the Sixth Circuit denied the government's petition, thus upholding Judge Keith's order.[72] The court did
agree to review the case via mandamus, stressing that "this is in all
respects an extraordinary case," that "[g]reat issues are at stake for all
parties concerned," and that the government claimed that affirming the
disclosure order will have the effect of forcing the government to dismiss
the case against Plamondon.[73] On this last point, the government was
thus saying that it would never publicly disclose the surveillance logs. If
the disclosure order stood, the government would simply abandon its
case against Plamondon.[74] Thus, although the government contended—

Judge Keith, complete with an identical Attorney General affidavit. The author of the
Smith opinion was Judge Warren Ferguson. In several places in his opinion, Judge Keith
stressed his agreement with and admiration for Judge Ferguson's reasoning. *See, e.g., id.*
at 1077 (calling the *Smith* opinion "[p]articularly noteworthy" and "exceptionally well-
reasoned and thorough").

[69] *See* 28 U.S.C. § 1291; *see also* 18 U.S.C. § 3731 (addressing criminal appeals in
particular).

[70] *See id.* § 1292.

[71] 28 U.S.C. § 1651.

[72] United States v. United States District Court, 444 F.2d 651 (6th Cir. 1971).

[73] *Id.* at 655.

[74] The government confirmed this point in its petition for certiorari to the Supreme
Court. *See* Petition for a Writ of Certiorari at 5, United States v. United States District

and no one meaningfully disputed—that the surveillance in question was never targeted at Plamondon and was not conducted with the purpose of developing evidence for any criminal case against him, the legality of the surveillance became the decisive factor in whether his case would proceed at all.

On the merits, the Sixth Circuit reached the same conclusion as Judge Keith. It summarized the basic inadequacy of the government's position as follows:

> The government has not pointed to, and we do not find, one written phrase in the Constitution, in the statutory law, or in the case law of the United States, which exempts the President, the Attorney General, or federal law enforcement from the restrictions of the Fourth Amendment in the case at hand.[75]

Accordingly, the court embraced a rule quite similar to the one articulated by Judge Keith: "[I]n dealing with the threat of domestic subversion, the Executive Branch of our government ... is subject to the limitations of the Fourth Amendment ... when undertaking searches and seizures for oral communications by wire."[76] Like Judge Keith's rule, this rule was limited to domestic cases. Situations involving "forces or agents of a foreign power" were a different matter, and the court expressed no view on them.[77]

The Sixth Circuit issued its decision on April 8, 1971. The government quickly sought certiorari from the Supreme Court, and certiorari was granted on June 21 of that year.

Justice Powell and Wiretapping

The Supreme Court that decided *Keith* was a Court in flux. Hugo Black and John Marshall Harlan, two longstanding members of the Court, had recently departed. Their replacements, Lewis Powell and William Rehnquist, arrived after certiorari had already been granted in *Keith*. That point was not lost on the Senate as it considered the nominations, especially Powell's. Indeed, the case was referenced on numerous occasions during Powell's confirmation hearings, and he faced extensive questioning about his views on wiretapping and related surveillance matters.

Powell had a paper trail on wiretapping in particular as well as criminal justice more generally. He came to national prominence in 1964

Court (Keith), 407 U.S. 297 (1972) (No. 07–153), *reprinted in* 72 *Landmark Briefs and Arguments of the Supreme Court of the United States: Constitutional Law* 554 (Philip B. Kurland & Gerhard Casper eds., 1975) (No. 1687) [hereinafter "Landmark Briefs"].

[75] *United States District Court*, 444 F.2d at 665.

[76] *Id.* at 667.

[77] *Id.*

upon becoming president of the American Bar Association.[78] And "[a]l-
though Powell had never prosecuted or acted as defense counsel in a
criminal case, as ABA president, '[m]ostly, he talked about crime.' "[79] In
doing so, Powell often staked out strong law-and-order positions and
expressed criticism of some of the Warren Court's rulings on issues of
constitutional criminal procedure.[80] In 1965, President Johnson appointed Powell to a newly established Commission on Law Enforcement and
the Administration of Justice.[81] In 1967, the Commission issued a report
entitled *The Challenge of Crime in a Free Society*.[82] One of the Commission's recommendations was for Congress to pass legislation regulating
the use of wiretaps in criminal cases, which helped pave the way for Title
III of the Omnibus Crime Control and Safe Streets Act of 1968, discussed above.[83] The Commission was careful to note, however, that
"matters affecting the national security not involving criminal prosecution" fell outside its mandate, and that its wiretapping-related recommendations were not meant to apply in that context.[84]

Powell also served on a Criminal Justice Committee of the American
Bar Association that, shortly before his nomination to the Court, issued
a set of recommended standards for the regulation of wiretapping and
related surveillance activities.[85] The Committee Report expressly ap-

---

[78] *See* John C. Jeffries, Jr., *Justice Lewis F. Powell* 194 (1994) ("Becoming president of
the ABA put Powell on the national map.").

[79] Tracey Maclin, *The Bush Administration's Terrorist Surveillance Program and the
Fourth Amendment's Warrant Requirement: Lessons from Justice Powell and the* Keith
Case, 41 U.C. Davis L. Rev. 1259, 1269 (2008) (quoting *id.* at 210).

[80] *Id.*

[81] *See* Powell Hearings at 206–07 (describing the Commission's work).

[82] President's Comm'n on Law Enforcement & Admin. of Justice, *The Challenge of
Crime in a Free Society* (1967).

[83] *Id.* at 473. This recommendation was made by a majority of the Commission,
including Powell, but was not unanimous. Dissenting members agreed that the current
state of the law of electronic surveillance was a disorganized mess, but harbored "serious
doubts about the desirability" of federal wiretap legislation. *Id.* For further discussion of
the Commission's recommendations on this point, see Tracey Maclin, *The Bush Administration's Terrorist Surveillance Program and the Fourth Amendment's Warrant Requirement: Lessons from Justice Powell and the* Keith *Case*, 41 U.C. Davis L. Rev. 1259, 1270–71
(2008).

[84] President's Comm'n on Law Enforcement & Admin. of Justice, *The Challenge of
Crime in a Free Society* 473 (1967); *see* Tracey Maclin, *The Bush Administration's Terrorist
Surveillance Program and the Fourth Amendment's Warrant Requirement: Lessons from
Justice Powell and the* Keith *Case*, 41 U.C. Davis L. Rev. 1259, 1271 (2008).

[85] *See* ABA Project on Minimum Standards for Criminal Justice, Standards Relating to
Electronic Surveillance § 3.1 (Approved Draft 1971).

proved electronic surveillance without prior judicial approval in cases involving a "foreign power":

> The use of electronic surveillance techniques by appropriate federal officers for the overhearing or recording of wire or oral communications to protect the nation from attack by or other hostile acts of a foreign power or to protect military or other national security information against foreign intelligence activities should be permitted subject to appropriate Presidential and Congressional standards and supervision.[86]

The Report took no formal stance on the President's authority to order warrantless surveillance in purely *domestic* cases. Yet the Committee was not entirely silent on that issue. The commentary to the Report stated that the Committee "rejected any reading of the fourth amendment that would invariably require compliance with a court order system before surveillance in interest[s] [of] national security could be termed constitutionally reasonable."[87] Even without adopting any firm affirmative position, that rejection placed the Committee—and, thus, Powell—at odds with the decisions of the lower courts in *Keith*. As noted below, however, Powell would later claim during his confirmation hearings that the Committee simply "did not address the far more troublesome area of internal security surveillance."[88]

Powell's most significant statements on the surveillance issue were made in his personal capacity, not as part of any commission or committee. In an April 15, 1971 speech to the Richmond Bar Association,[89] Powell reiterated the view that the President had the power to order warrantless surveillance in national security cases involving foreign threats, but noted that "the President's authority with respect to internal security is less clear."[90] Powell went on, however, to question the stability of the foreign/domestic distinction as "far less meaningful now that radical [domestic] organizations openly advocate violence."[91]

Powell reiterated that point in even sharper terms in an August 1, 1971 op-ed in the *Richmond Times–Dispatch*, entitled "Civil Liberties

---

[86] *Id.* § 3.1.

[87] *Id.* § 3.1 cmt. at 12. For more on the Committee's position, see Tracey Maclin, *The Bush Administration's Terrorist Surveillance Program and the Fourth Amendment's Warrant Requirement: Lessons from Justice Powell and the* Keith *Case*, 41 U.C. Davis L. Rev. 1259, 1273 & n.62 (2008).

[88] Powell Hearings at 207.

[89] The speech is reprinted in Powell Hearings at 244–48.

[90] *Id.* at 247.

[91] *Id.*

Repression: Fact of Fiction?"[92] The piece was in many respects a refutation of the growing concern among civil libertarians over the government's use of wiretapping. Powell's description of the controversy, including his reference to the *Keith* case itself, is worth quoting at length:

> Civil libertarians oppose the use of wiretapping in all cases, including its use against organized crime and foreign espionage. Since [enactment of Title III of] the 1968 Act, however, the attack has focused on its use in internal security cases and some courts have distinguished these from foreign threats. The issue will be before the Supreme Court at the next term.
>
> There can be legitimate concern whether a president should have this power with respect to internal 'enemies.' There is, at least in theory, the potential for abuse. This possibility must be balanced against the general public interest in preventing violence (e.g. bombing the Capitol) and organized attempts to overthrow the government.
>
>   . . . .
>
> There may have been a time when a valid distinction existed between external and internal threats. But such a distinction is now largely meaningless. The radical left, strongly led and with a growing base of support, is plotting violence and revolution. Its leaders visit and collaborate with foreign Communist enemies. Freedom can be lost as irrevocably from revolution as from foreign attack.
>
> The question is often asked why, if prior court authorization to wiretap is required in ordinary criminal cases, it should not also be required in national security cases. In simplest terms the answer given by the government is the need for secrecy.
>
> Foreign powers, notably the Communist ones, conduct massive espionage and subversive operations against America. They are now aided by leftist radical organizations and their sympathizers in this country. Court-authorized wiretapping requires a prior showing of probable cause and the ultimate disclosure of sources. Public disclosure of this sensitive information would seriously handicap our counter-espionage and counter-subversive operations.
>
>   . . . .
>
> The outcry against wiretapping is a tempest in a teapot. There are 210 million Americans. There are only a few hundred wiretaps annually, and these are directed against people who prey on their

---

[92] Lewis F. Powell, Jr., *Civil Liberties Repression: Fact or Fiction?—"Law–Abiding Citizens Have Nothing to Fear*," Richmond Times–Dispatch, Aug. 1, 1971, *reprinted in* Powell Hearings at 213–17.

fellow citizens or who seek to subvert our democratic form of government. Law-abiding citizens have nothing to fear.[93]

A number of things stand out in this passage. First, and most obviously, Powell combined great trust in the government's actions with a dismissiveness of civil libertarians' concerns as nothing but "a tempest in a teapot."[94] Second, he came very close to explicitly endorsing the government's secrecy argument—that imposing a warrant requirement would necessarily compromise the secrecy of the government's "counter-espionage and counter-subversive operations," which in turn would undermine the efficacy of those operations.[95]

Third, Powell became more pointed in his criticism of the foreign/domestic distinction. Noting that "some courts have distinguished [domestic threats] from foreign threats" and that "[t]he issue will be before the Supreme Court at the next term," Powell then proceeded to dismiss the distinction as "largely meaningless."[96] This was a direct reference to, and rejection of the reasoning of, the lower court decisions in *Keith*. The rejection was both descriptive and prescriptive. On the descriptive side, Powell observed that the most serious domestic threats to national security are in fact allied with and connected to hostile foreign entities, including "foreign Communist regimes."[97] Thus, a hard distinction between foreign and domestic threats simply did not fit reality. On the prescriptive side, by stressing that internal entities can be just as dangerous as external ones, he implied that aggressive government measures are just as appropriate against the former as against the latter. The "radical left" within the United States was "plotting violence and revolution," he maintained, and "[f]reedom can be lost as irrevocably from revolution as from foreign attack."[98] It was the government's responsibility to guard against all such threats.[99]

When Powell came before the Senate Judiciary Committee for his confirmation hearings, members of the Committee pressed him on his views in this area. Senator Birch Bayh of Indiana led the questioning. Powell, however, revealed very little:

---

[93] *Id.* at 214–15.

[94] *Id.* at 215.

[95] *Id.*

[96] *Id.* at 214.

[97] *Id.* at 215.

[98] *Id.*

[99] For more on Powell's op-ed, see Tracey Maclin, *The Bush Administration's Terrorist Surveillance Program and the Fourth Amendment's Warrant Requirement: Lessons from Justice Powell and the* Keith *Case*, 41 U.C. Davis L. Rev. 1259, 1274–77 (2008).

SEN. BAYH: . . . . Could you give us your thoughts relative to whether . . . it would not be a fair test to subject all wiretapping, to have the one who is going to use the wiretap to get a court order?

MR. POWELL: . . . . The ABA standards did incorporate provisions with respect to national security cases but did not require a prior court order. This involves action by a foreign power in espionage or comparable situations. The ABA standards did not address the far more troublesome area of internal security surveillance.

I have never studied that. I alluded to it in two of the talks which I sent to you. I understand that at least one case is either on the docket or on its way to the Court, and I doubt whether I should go beyond what I have said on that topic.

. . . .

SEN. BAYH: Do you anticipate that the Court will have difficulty in trying to distinguish between domestic insurgents or domestic agents and international agents?

MR. POWELL: Senator, I wish you wouldn't ask me that question. I don't think I ought to speculate as to just what the Supreme Court might do, whether or not I am on it.

. . . .

SEN. BAYH: . . . . But is it conceivable that you have already expressed such strong views in this area that you might be compelled to excuse yourself in a case that came before you on the subject matter?

MR. POWELL: I would reserve final judgment until I were confronted with the problem, but I would say without any hesitation as I think my Richmond Bar talk demonstrated, I have no fixed view on the delicate area that you have been discussing. . . .

SEN. BAYH: . . . [reads aloud the passage of Powell's article where he calls the foreign/domestic distinction "now largely meaningless" and refers to the "radical left . . . plotting violence and revolution"] Now, that may or may not be true. If they are, we have to deal with it. But first of all perhaps I should ask does . . . this article reflect your present views and aren't those views rather strong in this area? Aren't you rather specific in an area where you said you had not made up your mind already?

MR. POWELL: . . . I think the language you read . . . was addressed primarily to this hazy area where internal security and national security, where internal dissidents are cooperating or working affirmatively with, or are very sympathetic to countries, other powers, that may be enemies of the United States. This is a very difficult area. Drawing that line, as I have said, is very perplexing.

But to come back to your question, I do not consider it was a fixed view considering the circumstances under which it was expressed, the brevity of expression—I was not writing a law review article. And yet I would add one other point, Senator, just to be absolutely clear: If I should go on the Court, and this Sixth Circuit case comes up after I come on the Court, I will be very conscious of the fact that I have written a few things, very few, really, in this area; and it may well be that I will disqualify myself. At the moment I would rather not say positively that I will or I won't.[100]

The Judiciary Committee ultimately gave the Powell nomination its unanimous support, and the full Senate confirmed it with a vote of 89 to 1.[101]

As the parties prepared to argue *Keith* before the Court, Powell's confirmation had to come as good news to the government and bad news to the defense. Although Powell insisted during the hearings that he did not have a "fixed view" when it came to the legality of warrantless wiretapping in the interests of internal security (or for that matter whether it was possible to distinguish between internal and external security in that context),[102] he must have looked like a good bet for the government. Indeed, when Powell arrived at the Court, the defendants could reasonably have believed that their best hope with him was recusal.

Counsel and Arguments Before the Court

Oral argument took place on February 24, 1972, before an eight-member Court. Justice Powell did not recuse; Justice Rehnquist did.[103]

Arthur Kinoy, a professor at Rutgers University School of Law and co-founder of the Center for Constitutional Rights, argued on behalf of

---

[100] Powell Hearings at 207–13.

[101] Senator Bayh was among the "yeas." The lone "nay" was Senator Fred Harris of Oklahoma. *See* 117 Cong. Rec. 44,857 (1971); Henry J. Abraham, *Justices, Presidents, and Senators: A History of the U.S. Supreme Court Appointments from Washington to Clinton* 15 (4th ed. 1999).

[102] Powell Hearings at 211.

[103] Justice Rehnquist offered no public reason for his recusal at the time. But in a later opinion explaining his decision not to recuse in a different case, he noted that while serving in the Justice Department's Office of Legal Counsel before joining the Court, he had "assisted in drafting" one of the government's briefs in the *Keith* litigation, and he cited that as the reason for his recusal. Laird v. Tatum, 409 U.S. 824, 828–29 (1972) (Rehnquist, J., on motion to recuse).

the defense.[104] Kuntsler, Weinglass, and Davis remained on the brief.[105] As the named target of the mandamus petition, Judge Keith had his own counsel before the Court. William T. Gossett, formerly the President of the American Bar Association, argued on his behalf. With him on the brief was Abraham Sofaer, then a professor at Columbia Law School and later himself a federal district judge.

Ordinarily, the government's argument would have been presented by someone in the Solicitor General's Office.[106] The Solicitor General at the time was Erwin Griswold, former Dean of the Harvard Law School and a familiar and powerful presence before the Court.[107] Yet while his name was on the government's brief,[108] neither he nor any other member of his office argued the case. This did not go unnoticed. The *New York Times* attributed Griswold's absence to his own disagreement with the government's use of warrantless surveillance,[109] and there is reason to think the *Times* was right. Decades later, Judge Keith recalled a conversation with Griswold during Thurgood Marshall's 80th birthday party, in which Griswold told Keith: "Judge, the reason I didn't want to argue that case was that I didn't believe that the government had this type of authority. . . . I thought you were absolutely right."[110]

Instead, Robert C. Mardian, Assistant Attorney General in charge of the Justice Department's Internal Security Division, argued on behalf of the government.[111] Mardian was a controversial figure. As head of the Internal Security Division—an office originally established during the McCarthy era but largely inactive for many years until the Nixon

---

[104] *See* 72 Landmark Briefs at 1035; Fred P. Graham, *High Court Curbs U.S. Wiretapping Aimed at Radicals*, N.Y. Times, June 20, 1972, at 23.

[105] *See* 72 Landmark Briefs at 723.

[106] There were and continue to be exceptions to that practice, but it was and remains the general rule.

[107] President Johnson first appointed Griswold Solicitor General in 1967. He retained the office under President Nixon, serving until 1973. By then he had occupied the office longer than anyone since John Davis, who served from 1913 to 1918.

[108] *See* 72 Landmark Briefs at 569.

[109] *See* Fred P. Graham, *High Court Curbs U.S. Wiretapping Aimed at Radicals*, N.Y. Times, June 20, 1972, at 23 (stating that the wiretapping program overseen by Attorney General Mitchell was "so controversial among career attorneys that when the case reached the Supreme Court no member of the Solicitor General's office argued the government's case").

[110] Keith Remarks at 385 (quoting Griswold); *see also* Davis Remarks at 372 (stating that "Erwin Griswold . . . found the government's position to be so unpalatable, that he declined to argue the case for the United States").

[111] *See* 72 Landmark Briefs at 1035; Fred P. Graham, *High Court Curbs U.S. Wiretapping Aimed at Radicals*, N.Y. Times, June 20, 1972, at 23.

administration revived it—he presided over hundreds of investigations and grand jury proceedings (but few actual convictions) targeting elements of the "New Left."[112]

A close political ally of President Nixon and former Attorney General Mitchell (who by then had left the Justice Department to manage Nixon's re-election campaign), Mardian, along with Mitchell and White House Chief of Staff H.R. Haldeman, would later be convicted of conspiracy to hinder the investigation into the break-in at the Washington, DC headquarters of the Democratic National Committee—that is, the Watergate break-in.[113] That break-in turned out to have been the work of people associated with the Committee to Re-elect the President, which Mitchell ran. Indeed, Mitchell was among the principal players in the attempted cover-up of the break-in, which, as is well known, ultimately led to President Nixon's resignation. Moreover, investigations conducted by Senate and House Committees revealed that the Watergate break-in was just one of many illegal activities authorized and carried out by Nixon's staff. Others included campaign fraud, other illegal break-ins, and warrantless wiretapping on a massive scale, including of the press and regular citizens.[114] Seen with the benefit of hindsight, the fact that the government's position in *Keith* turned on the assertions contained in an affidavit by Mitchell is more than a little ironic. Along with Haldeman, Mitchell himself had "ordered warrantless wiretaps to be placed on the telephones of newsmen and certain employees of the executive branch."[115] A clearer case of the fox guarding the henhouse is hard to imagine.

Things were not so clear when *Keith* was argued, however. To be sure, civil libertarians already suspected that the administration was

---

[112] *See* Judith Berkan, *The Federal Grand Jury: An Introduction to the Institution, Its Historical Role, Its Current Use and the Problems Faced by the Target Witness*, 17 Rev. Juridica U. Inter. P.R. 103, 109 (1983) ("In the three-year period from 1970 to 1973, the [Internal Security Division] conducted over 100 investigations, principally directed at 'New Left' groups in the United States. Between 1000 and 2000 witnesses were called before Grand Juries, and 200 indictments resulted. Of those cases in which indictments were issued, only 10% resulted in convictions, a very low rate when compared to the average 65.2% conviction rate in ordinary cases.").

[113] The D.C. Circuit subsequently reversed Mardian's conviction on procedural grounds, and the special prosecutor declined to re-try him. *See* United States v. Mardian, 546 F.2d 973 (D.C. Cir. 1976); *see also* United States v. Haldeman, 559 F.2d 31, 51–59 (D.C. Cir. 1976) (per curiam).

[114] *See Final Report of the Senate Select Comm. To Study Governmental Operations with Respect to Intelligence Activities and the Rights of Americans*, S. Rep. No. 94–755, pt. 2, at 169 (1976).

[115] Peter E. Quint, *The Separation of Powers Under Nixon: Reflections on Constitutional Liberties and the Rule of Law*, 1981 Duke L.J. 1, 20–21.

engaged in widespread surveillance of its political enemies. During
Kinoy's presentation to the Court, for example, he asserted that Mitchell
had authorized warrantless wiretapping of "leaders of the anti-war
movement, black movements, Catholic activist pacifists, advocates of
youth culture."[116] But the Watergate scandal was months away[117] and the
various congressional investigations still years off, so claims of this sort
did not yet have the credibility they would gain later on.[118] Thus, to
understand the story of *Keith* as it actually unfolded, it is important to
bear in mind that although many of the key players in the case were also
central figures in the Watergate scandal, the two did not coincide in
time.

Even without the taint of Watergate, however, Mardian faced a
skeptical Court. Much of his opening argument was spent addressing
questions from Justice White[119] about the application of Title III of the
1968 Act, and about whether the Attorney General's affidavit complied
with the statutory limitations established by the Act. Other members of
the Court seemed impatient with the statutory issue, however. Another
Justice finally complained that Mardian "ke[pt] ducking the Fourth
Amendment," and urged him to turn to it.[120]

Mardian obliged. He did so against the backdrop of briefing by the
government that had advanced a more modest position on the Fourth
Amendment issue than the one it had pressed in the lower courts. As the
Sixth Circuit put it, the government at that stage had argued that "the

---

[116] 72 Landmark Briefs at 1063.

[117] The break-in took place on June 17, 1972, four months after *Keith* was argued and,
coincidentally, just two days before the Court announced its decision. But it was not until
much later that the involvement of the White House and others in the Nixon administration came to light. For more on the Watergate break-in and the indictments that ensued,
see chapter 9 in this volume.

[118] Moreover, Kinoy himself did not seem to carry much weight with the Court. Justice
Blackmun was certainly not impressed with his argument. Although he went in to the
argument tentatively inclined to affirm the Sixth Circuit, Justice Blackmun wrote in his
notes that Kinoy "alm[ost] los[t] t[he] case for me." Harry Blackmun Papers, Library of
Congress, box 141, folder 10. He described Kinoy as "very dramatic," "preaching," "loud,"
and "a tense guy." *Id.* The Court as a whole asked Kinoy literally no questions during his
argument, a likely sign that the Justices saw little to be gained from dialog with him. *See
generally* 72 Landmark Briefs at 1061–70.

[119] The oral argument transcripts produced at the time do not identify which Justice is
speaking, but it seems fair to infer that Justice White led the questioning on this point.
First, at one point in his discussion of the statute, Mardian referred to Justice White by
name in a way that suggests he had been the questioner. *See* 72 Landmark Briefs at 1042.
Second, as noted below, the statutory issue ultimately formed the basis for Justice White's
separate concurrence in the case. *Keith*, 407 U.S. 297, 335 (1972) (White, J., concurring in
the judgment).

[120] 72 Landmark Briefs at 1051.

President of the United States, in his capacity as Chief Executive, has unique powers of the 'sovereign' which serve to exempt him and his agents from the judicial review restrictions of the Fourth Amendment."[121] The President's inherent power to act in the interests of national security, in other words, rendered the Fourth Amendment simply inapplicable. Before the Supreme Court, the government's briefs were more restrained. Rather than seeking a categorical exemption from the Fourth Amendment, the government argued that the Fourth Amendment's only requirement was that searches not be "unreasonable," and that a decision by the President (or the Attorney General on his behalf) to authorize electronic surveillance in the interests of national security "is not unreasonable solely because it is conducted without prior judicial approval."[122] The government thus conceded that the reasonableness constraint applied to presidentially ordered surveillance. It requested only that warrantless surveillance of this sort not be deemed categorically unreasonable for lack of a warrant.[123]

Mardian tried to maintain that position during oral argument, but it unraveled. On one hand, he continued to stress that the government was "not asking for an exemption from the Fourth Amendment."[124] Yet on the other, his account of what the government *was* seeking sounded very much like an exemption: "We simply suggest that in the area in which he has limited but exclusive authority, the President of the United States may authorize electronic surveillance; *and, in those cases, it is legal.*"[125] This was precisely what the government's brief had disclaimed: an argument that the President's (or Attorney General's) authorization itself rendered the surveillance lawful. Recognizing this point, a member of the Court asked Mardian whether, under the theory he was articulating, it was "possible [for] ... the President [to] make an unreasonable intrusion into the private life of a citizen of this country."[126] Once "the President decides it's necessary to bug John Doe's phone," was there truly "nothing under the sun John Doe can do about it?"[127] Mardian seemed to say that John Doe indeed had no judicial recourse, and

---

[121] United States v. United States District Court, 444 F.2d 651, 657 (6th Cir. 1971).

[122] Brief for the United States at 6, *Keith*, 407 U.S. 297 (No. 70–153), *reprinted in* 72 Landmark Briefs at 583 (No. 1687).

[123] *Id.* at 10, *reprinted in* 72 Landmark Briefs at 587 ("The government makes no claim that ... authorization by the Attorney General itself establishes compliance with the Fourth Amendment standard of reasonableness; it urges the Court only to hold that the absence of prior judicial approval does not invalidate the search under that standard.").

[124] 72 Landmark Briefs at 1051.

[125] *Id.* (emphasis added).

[126] *Id.*

[127] *Id.*

suggested that relying at that point on the President's own duty of fidelity to the Constitution "is an attribute of our Government which exists and has always existed."[128] Thus did Mardian's opening argument undermine the modesty of the government's briefs.

Things did not get much better for the government when Mardian rose for rebuttal. A member of the Court pressed him on the point that, in contrast to the system of judicial warrants envisioned by the Fourth Amendment, the government's position provided for no adversarial testing of the asserted basis for a wiretap.[129] Mardian responded by saying that Gossett, as Judge Keith's attorney in the proceedings before the Sixth Circuit and the Supreme Court, was entitled to review the logs and other material that the government had originally submitted to Judge Keith for his *in camera* review.[130] He did not explain how such ex post review in the context of a mandamus proceeding could be an adequate substitute for the ex ante review entailed in the Fourth Amendment's warrant procedure. But in any event, Gossett himself evidently did not understand that he had the right of review Mardian claimed he had, and under questioning Mardian acknowledged that no one in the government had ever told Gossett that he could see the materials.[131] Mardian insisted, however, that "had Mr. Gossett requested the opportunity to see the *in camera* exhibit, Mr. Gossett's reputation is such that there would be no question that the Government would have acquiesced in that demand."[132] What, then, of Plamondon, the person actually facing criminal charges? "Can his lawyer see it?" the Court asked. Mardian said no.[133] He was not pressed further on the point. But according to defense counsel Davis, "Thurgood Marshall, who ... had argued [*Brown v. Board of Education*] with Kinoy in the Supreme Court, turned his chair around and never again looked at the government's lawyer during the entire argument. It was a stunning and telling moment."[134]

That moment came quite near the end of the argument, and by the time it was over Mardian would have had relatively little reason for optimism.

---

[128] *Id.* Mardian's answer brings to mind President Nixon's now-infamous statement some years later that "[w]hen the President does it, that means that it is not illegal." *Nixon: A President May Violate the Law*, U.S. News & World Rep., May 30, 1977 at 65 (reporting on a May 19, 1977 interview with David Frost).

[129] *See* 72 Landmark Briefs at 1071.

[130] *Id.* at 1071–72.

[131] *See id.* at 1072.

[132] *Id.* at 1076.

[133] *Id.* at 1072.

[134] Davis Remarks at 372.

Deliberations

In their post-argument conference, all eight Justice voted to affirm—that is, to uphold Judge Keith's disclosure order.[135] But there was substantial disagreement on the grounds. Five members of the Court—Douglas, Brennan, Stewart, Marshall, and Powell—voted to affirm "on the Constitution,"[136] which meant agreeing with Judge Keith and the Sixth Circuit that the surveillance in question violated the Fourth Amendment. The other three—Burger, White, and Blackmun—voted to affirm "on the statute,"[137] which meant concluding that the Attorney General's affidavit did not establish that the wiretapping at issue fell within the bounds of the "national security disclosure" in Title III of the 1968 Act.[138] A holding of that sort would have the virtue of avoiding a direct constitutional confrontation with the executive branch.[139] But it would also leave entirely unresolved an issue of increasing national significance, namely the extent of the President's authority to order warrantless surveillance in the interests of national security. A statutory holding would simply tell future Attorneys General that their affidavits must more closely track the language in Title III's disclaimer provision. It would amount to little more than a lesson in affidavit drafting.

Burger initially assigned the opinion to White, who was firmly in favor of affirming on the statute. Douglas objected, pointing out that the statutory ground had only three votes while the constitutional ground had five.[140] He proposed that the Chief give Powell the assignment instead.[141] Alternatively, Douglas said he could make the assignment

---

[135] *See* Letter from Justice Douglas to Chief Justice Burger (Mar. 6, 1972), in Harry Blackmun Papers, Library of Congress, box 136, folder 2 [hereinafter "Douglas Letter"] (describing the initial vote as unanimous to affirm, though on different grounds).

[136] *Id.*

[137] Douglas's letter to Burger does not mention Blackmun by name, but instead says that Justice White "and two others including yourself voted to affirm on the statute." *Id.* Because Douglas expressly lists himself, Brennan, Stewart, Marshall, and Powell as affirming on the Constitution, the other vote for the statutory basis has to have been Blackmun.

[138] *See* 18 U.S.C. § 2511(3).

[139] *See generally* Ashwander v. TVA, 297 U.S. 288, 345–46 (1936) (Brandeis, J., concurring) (discussing virtues of avoiding constitutional issues where possible, and cataloging methods of such avoidance).

[140] *See* Douglas Letter.

[141] *Id.* ("With all respect, I think Powell represents the consensus. I have not canvassed everybody, but I am sure that Byron, who goes on the statute, will not get a court. To save time, may I suggest you have a huddle and see to it that Powell gets the opinion to write?").

himself.[142] This was a canny move by Douglas, the senior liberal on the Court. Undoubtedly pleased and perhaps even surprised (given his past statements on the issue) that Powell appeared willing to affirm on constitutional grounds, Douglas may have suggested assigning the opinion to Powell in order to help "lock in" his vote. It would also ensure that this new Nixon appointee took a strong stand against the President that had appointed him, something Douglas surely would have enjoyed. At the same time, the veiled threat that Douglas himself might take over the assignment prerogative raised the possibility that he might keep it for himself or give it to someone like Brennan, thus raising the possibility of an extremely aggressive constitutional opinion that might still command a majority. As between that and allowing Powell to write, the typically conservative, more government-friendly Burger should have preferred the latter.

Burger went part way there. In a letter responding to Douglas, he said that both Powell and White should go ahead and write their opinions.[143] He suggested that he thought White might have "substantial" support for his statutory holding, and that he was not sure Powell and White were truly that far apart in their approaches.[144] Thus, he said, it made sense for both to proceed with their opinions and see what resulted.[145]

Burger did not explain why he thought Powell's and White's positions might actually be similar, and in fact they were not. When White circulated his draft on March 14, it relied exclusively on the Mitchell affidavit's failure to track the language of Title III's national security exception.[146] A memorandum to Justice Blackmun from one of his law

---

[142] *Id.* ("Or if you want me to suggest an assignment, that would be fine.").

[143] Letter from Chief Justice Burger to Justice Douglas (Mar. 6, 1972), in Harry Blackmun Papers, Library of Congress, box 136, folder 2 [hereinafter "Burger Letter"].

[144] *Id.* ("[T]here may be much likelihood of Byron's securing substantial support and I am not sure Byron's and Lewis' views are not rather close.").

[145] The account in the text is based upon copies of the actual correspondence among the Justices, found in the Blackmun Papers. It differs from the account offered by Bob Woodward and Scott Armstrong in their 1979 book, *The Brethren*. According to Woodward and Armstrong, "White rejected the assignment [of the majority opinion], noting that he and the Chief were alone in their view. Douglas immediately reassigned the case to Powell. . . ." Bob Woodward & Scott Armstrong, *The Brethren: Inside the Supreme Court* 264 (1979). In fact, however, the correspondence in the Blackmun Papers shows that there was no formal reassignment, only a suggestion of such by Douglas and an agreement by Burger that both White and Powell ought to press forward with their respective drafts.

[146] *See* Memorandum from GTF to Justice Blackmun (Mar. 14, 1972), in Harry Blackmun Papers, Library of Congress, box 136, folder 2 [hereinafter "GTF Memo I"] (describing White's draft). "GTF" are the initials of Justice Blackmun's law clerk working on the case. They stand for George T. Frampton, Jr., who later served as a Watergate

clerks also suggested that the draft may have been written and circulated "in a hurry to stake out Justice White's position," and that it had "the feeling of an off-the-cuff, unedited opinion: sparsely documented, and pregnant with potentially suggestive language when it touches the merits."[147] Although Justice Blackmun originally voted to affirm on the statutory ground, his clerk urged him not to join White's opinion.[148] Blackmun waited, as did everyone else: White's opinion attracted no votes.

Powell circulated his opinion in early May. Douglas, Marshall, and Stewart joined the opinion immediately, apparently without requesting any changes.[149] Blackmun waited several weeks before finally joining on June 12.[150] By then, Powell's opinion commanded a clear majority. When the decision was issued the following week, everyone but Burger and White had joined the Powell opinion. Douglas also wrote a separate concurrence excoriating the government for its abusive intrusions on personal privacy and characterizing its appeals to national security as the symptoms of "another national seizure of paranoia, resembling the hysteria which surrounded the Alien and Sedition Acts, the Palmer Raids, and the McCarthy era."[151] White concurred only in the judgment, adhering to his position that the case should be resolved on statutory grounds.[152] And Burger, inexplicably, concurred in the result without writing or joining any opinion at all.[153]

The Court's Opinion

Powell's opinion for the Court stressed that while the question before the Court was an important one, it was also narrow. That

---

special prosecutor and, much later, as Deputy Secretary of the Interior under President Clinton.

[147] *Id.*

[148] *See* GTF Memo I.

[149] *See* join letters collected in Harry Blackmun Papers, Library of Congress, box 136, folder 2. Douglas did say that he "may possibly file a separate opinion, not in derogation of what [Powell had] written, but in further support of it." *Id.* He ultimately did so, although he also joined the Powell opinion in full. *See Keith*, 407 U.S. 297, 324 (1972) (Douglas, J., concurring). The Blackmun Papers do not contain anything indicating the date or terms of Brennan's join. But there is no evidence that he pressed for any changes in Powell's draft, and it seems reasonable to infer that he joined the opinion at around the same time as Stewart, Marshall, and Douglas.

[150] *See* join letter (June 12, 1972), in Harry Blackmun Papers, Library of Congress, box 136, folder 2.

[151] *Keith*, 407 U.S. at 324, 329 (Douglas, J., concurring).

[152] *Id.* at 335 (White, J., concurring in the judgment).

[153] *Id.* at 324.

question, the Court explained, was the one left open in *Katz*: "Whether safeguards other than prior authorization by a magistrate would satisfy the Fourth Amendment in a situation involving the national security."[154] To address the question, the Court began by acknowledging that the President may sometimes "find it necessary to employ electronic surveillance to obtain intelligence information on the plans of those who plot unlawful acts against the Government."[155] Indeed, the use of such surveillance could well be a critical means of "safeguard[ing] [the government's] capacity to function and to preserve the security of its people."[156] In this respect, the Court conceded that the President—and, implicitly, his designee the Attorney General—had the basic constitutional authority to order electronic surveillance in the interests of national security.

But to acknowledge a constitutional authority is not to say it is without limit. The Court stressed in particular that the interests of national security do not eliminate the constitutional concerns surrounding warrantless surveillance. To the contrary, national security cases "often reflect a convergence of First and Fourth Amendment values not present in cases of 'ordinary' crime."[157] This connection between the First and Fourth Amendment is an important theme in the opinion. As the Court put it:

> History abundantly documents the tendency of Government—however benevolent and benign its motives—to view with suspicion those who most fervently dispute its policies. Fourth Amendment protections become the more necessary when the targets of official surveillance may be those suspected of unorthodoxy in their political beliefs. The danger to political dissent is acute where the Government attempts to act under so vague a concept as the power to protect "domestic security."[158]

To those who remembered Powell's op-ed in the *Richmond Times–Dispatch* the previous summer, this passage must have been striking. Where earlier he had painted the domestic targets of electronic surveillance as leaders of a "radical left . . . plotting violence and revolution,"[159]

---

[154] *Id.* at 309 (quoting Katz v. United States, 389 U.S. 347, 358 n.23 (1967)).

[155] *Id.* at 310.

[156] *Id.* at 312.

[157] *Id.* at 313.

[158] *Id.* at 314.

[159] Lewis F. Powell, Jr., *Civil Liberties Repression: Fact or Fiction?—"Law–Abiding Citizens Have Nothing to Fear*," Richmond Times–Dispatch, Aug. 1, 1971, *reprinted in* Powell Hearings at 215.

now he saw them as dissident voices vulnerable to government repression on account of their "unorthodo[x] ... political beliefs."[160]

The link between the First and Fourth Amendment values helped support the next key move in the opinion: the conclusion that constitutional values "cannot properly be guaranteed if domestic security surveillances may be conducted solely within the discretion of the Executive Branch."[161] Such an arrangement, the Court said, is at odds with the institutional roles contemplated by the Fourth Amendment. The job of the executive is "to enforce the laws, to investigate, and to prosecute," while the duty of the judiciary is to constrain the executive in its quest for enhanced power.[162] Whether or not the executive might in fact be capable of checking itself in some cases, that it not a risk that the Fourth Amendment tolerates.[163] Thus, although the Court "recognize[d] ... the constitutional basis of the President's domestic security role," it held that the role "must be exercised in a manner compatible with the Fourth Amendment."[164] Here, that meant complying with "an appropriate prior warrant procedure."[165]

Having announced its core holding, the Court then addressed and rejected a number of the government's arguments. Here again, Powell seemed to turn 180 degrees from his position in the *Times-Dispatch* article. Whereas earlier he expressed sympathy with the government's worry that a judicial warrant procedure would destroy the secrecy of its national security efforts,[166] on behalf of the Court he rejected that very concern: "The investigation of criminal activity has long involved imparting sensitive information to judicial officers who have respected the confidentialities involved. Judges may be counted upon to be especially conscious of security requirements in national security cases."[167] The Court likewise rejected the government's related argument that "internal security matters are too subtle and complex for judicial evalua-

---

[160] *Keith*, 407 U.S. at 314. Of course, neither description purported to apply to all possible cases, but the shift is significant nonetheless.

[161] *Id.* at 316–17.

[162] *Id.* at 317.

[163] *Id.* ("The Fourth Amendment contemplates a prior judicial judgment, not the risk that executive discretion may be reasonably exercised." (footnote omitted)).

[164] *Id.* at 320.

[165] *Id.*

[166] *See* Lewis F. Powell, Jr., *Civil Liberties Repression: Fact or Fiction?—"Law–Abiding Citizens Have Nothing to Fear,"* Richmond Times–Dispatch, Aug. 1, 1971, *reprinted in* Powell Hearings at 215.

[167] *Keith*, 407 U.S. at 320–21.

tion."[168] In a passage ringing with professional pride, the Court insisted that judges "regularly deal with the most difficult issues of our society. There is no reason to believe that federal judges will be insensitive to or uncomprehending of the issues involved in domestic security cases."[169] And besides, the Court said with near indignation, if the Attorney General and other senior law enforcement officers are incapable of communicating the significance of a particular threat to a court, perhaps the threat is not so significant after all.[170]

The Court concluded by reemphasizing the narrowness of its holding. There are two key points here. First, the Court left open the possibility that Congress could establish legislative standards for the use of electronic surveillance in national security cases that departed from the standards applicable in criminal cases under Title III of the 1968 Act.[171] In that sense, the Court stressed that the precise contours of the warrant requirement it was upholding were subject to legislative specification.[172] The Court even identified a number of procedures Congress might want to adopt—including, for example, designating a special court in Washington, D.C. as responsible for evaluating warrant applications in national security cases.[173]

Second, adopting the same basic distinction observed by Judge Keith and the Sixth Circuit, the Court stressed that the instant case "involves only the domestic aspects of national security. We have not addressed, and express no opinion as to, the issues which may be involved with respect to activities of foreign powers or their agents."[174] The Court dropped a footnote at that point, citing two lower court cases, as well as the ABA Committee whose standards Powell had earlier worked on, as examples of authorities embracing "the view that warrantless surveillance, though impermissible in domestic security cases, may be constitutional where foreign powers are involved."[175] An earlier draft of the

---

[168] *Id.* at 320.

[169] *Id.*

[170] *Id.* ("If the threat is too subtle or complex for our senior law enforcement officers to convey its significance to a court, one may question whether there is probable cause for surveillance.").

[171] *Id.* at 322–24.

[172] *Id.* at 324 (explaining that although the Court held that "prior judicial approval is required for the type of domestic surveillance involved in this case," it also allowed that "such approval may be made in accordance with such reasonable standards as the Congress may prescribe").

[173] *Id.* at 323.

[174] *Id.* at 321–22.

[175] *Id.* at 322 n.20 (citations omitted).

opinion contained a more detailed list of authorities on that point, suggesting more strongly that foreign surveillance cases would come out the other way.[176] The modification of the footnote suggests that at least some on the Court truly did not want to suggest anything one way or the other about cases involving foreign targets.

The Court's embrace of the domestic/foreign distinction arguably marks another important difference between it and Powell's earlier statements. The precise distinction that Powell had once derided as "largely meaningless" emerged by the end of *Keith* as potentially decisive for Fourth Amendment purposes. How should we read this shift? One possibility is simply that Powell changed his mind. After immersing himself in the *Keith* materials, he may have become convinced that a distinction he earlier deemed empty could sometimes make sense.

Another possibility, however, is that Powell embraced the distinction *precisely because* he thought it meaningless in most cases. The Mitchell affidavit in *Keith* was striking in its exclusive focus on domestic threats.[177] At the time it was drafted, the government had no particular incentive to characterize the threats any other way, since the domestic/foreign distinction did not yet have the legal salience that *Keith* would give it. But if Powell was right in his *Times-Dispatch* op-ed that domestic and foreign threats are so frequently interconnected that the domestic/foreign distinction is essentially irrelevant in many cases, then embracing that very distinction was a way to minimize the impact of the *Keith* decision. If a significant portion of serious domestic threats can readily be described as involving foreign entities as well, then the constitutional holding in *Keith* is vanishingly small. Indeed, one might even say that the Court's holding, like Justice White's statutory concurrence, amounts to little more than a lesson in affidavit drafting: to bypass *Keith*, the government need only highlight the connections between the domestic and foreign elements of the target.

However one reads *Keith*'s treatment of the domestic/foreign distinction, that and other aspects of the Court's opinion had enormous impact on the law of national security surveillance in the years that followed. The next section addresses that impact.

Keith's Impact

The effect of the *Keith* decision might be best appreciated by distinguishing among at least three different effects: the reactions it

---

[176] *See* Memorandum from GTF to Justice Blackmun (May 18, 1972), in Harry Blackmun Papers, Library of Congress, box 136, folder 2 (describing the earlier version of footnote 20 as "strongly suggest[ing] that the foreign intelligence or espionage situation would go the other way").

[177] *See Keith*, 407 U.S. at 300 n.2 (referring to "attempts of domestic organizations to attack and subvert the existing structure of the Government").

provoked in the press; its direct doctrinal effect on warrantless surveillance cases in the years immediately following; and its connection to
executive and legislative efforts to regulate intelligence-related surveillance, especially the enactment in 1978 of the Foreign Intelligence
Surveillance Act. This section considers each effect in turn.

The Press Reaction

The *Keith* decision created headlines as soon as it was issued.[178]
Echoing the sentiments of many in the press, a *New York Times* editorial
hailed it as "a sharp rebuke to those ideologues of the executive branch
who consider the President's 'inherent powers' superior to the Constitution."[179] Depicted in these terms, the decision hardly seemed narrow or
confined. It was, rather, a sweeping reaffirmation of "the historic lesson
that a blank check of official powers is the prelude to their abuse."[180] The
Court was lauded for having "ignor[ed] the usual division between
'liberal' and 'conservative'" to "remin[d] the Government that it is just
because its powers are so awesome that their exercise cannot be left to
the discretion of men without precise restraint of law, under the Constitution."[181] *Keith*, then, was received as nothing less than a triumph of
the rule of law itself.

Direct Doctrinal Impact

Keith's direct doctrinal impact was less sweeping. This was due in
large part to the Court's embrace of the domestic/foreign distinction and
its insistence that its holding applied only to purely domestic cases.
Warrantless surveillance of foreign targets thus remained an open question after *Keith*. Lower courts soon took it up. The year after *Keith* was
decided, the Fifth Circuit upheld the legality of surveillance in which an
American citizen was incidentally overheard on a warrantless wiretap
that had been set up for foreign intelligence purposes.[182] Addressing the
precise question reserved in *Keith*, the court held that "the President's
constitutional duty to act for the United States in the field of foreign
affairs, and his inherent power to protect national security in the

---

[178] *See, e.g.*, Fred P. Graham, *High Court Curbs U.S. Wiretapping Aimed at Radicals*,
N.Y. Times, June 20, 1972, at A1; Glen Elsasser, *Court Rules Wiretaps Need OK*, Chi. Trib.,
June 20, 1972, at 1A; John P. MacKenzie, *Court Curbs Wiretapping of Radicals*, Wash.
Post, June 20, 1972, at A1.

[179] Editorial, *The Restraint of Law*, N.Y. Times, June 20, 1972, at 38.

[180] *Id.*

[181] *Id.*

[182] *See* United States v. Brown, 484 F.2d 418 (5th Cir. 1973), *cert. denied*, 415 U.S. 960
(1974).

conduct of foreign affairs" empower him to "authorize warrantless wiretaps for the purpose of gathering foreign intelligence."[183] The Third Circuit reached a similar result the following year after determining that the primary purpose of the warrantless surveillance in question was to obtain foreign intelligence.[184] And in 1977, the Ninth Circuit stated confidently that "[f]oreign security wiretaps are a recognized exception to the general warrant requirement."[185]

The lower courts were not unanimous on this point. In a case involving surveillance of a purely domestic organization, the D.C. Circuit questioned in dicta whether any national security exception to the warrant requirement could pass constitutional muster, foreign target or not.[186] But that was a minority position. After *Keith*, most lower courts were prepared to conclude that "in foreign-related matters of national security the Government is indeed excused from its normal obligation to obtain a warrant."[187]

This tendency to recognize a "foreign surveillance exception" put pressure on the domestic/foreign distinction itself, the very distinction Powell had once derided as "largely meaningless."[188] The problem was definitional. What, precisely, are the boundaries of foreign security surveillance? As a 1974 Note in the *Harvard Law Review* put it, "[a]lmost any problem of governmental concern could be said to relate, at least remotely, to the national security, and to bear, at least potentially, on the country's relations with foreign powers. If loosely drawn, a foreign security exception to the warrant requirement could thus be very broad."[189] And of course, *Keith* itself said nothing about how loosely or tightly any such exception should be drawn.

---

[183] *Id.* at 426.

[184] *See* United States v. Butenko, 494 F.2d 593 (3d Cir.) (en banc), *cert. denied sub nom.* Ivanov v. United States, 419 U.S. 881 (1974).

[185] United States v. Buck, 548 F.2d 871 (9th Cir.), *cert. denied*, 434 U.S. 890 (1977).

[186] *See* Zweibon v. Mitchell, 516 F.2d 594, 613–14 (D.C. Cir. 1975), *cert. denied*, 425 U.S. 944 (1976) ("[A]n analysis of the policies implicated by foreign security surveillance indicates that, absent exigent circumstances, all warrantless electronic surveillance is unreasonable and therefore unconstitutional...." (footnote omitted)).

[187] Note, *Foreign Security Surveillance and the Fourth Amendment*, 87 Harv. L. Rev. 976, 977 (1974); *see also id.* at 977 n.8 (collecting cases).

[188] Lewis F. Powell, Jr., *Civil Liberties Repression: Fact or Fiction?—"Law–Abiding Citizens Have Nothing to Fear*," Richmond Times–Dispatch, Aug. 1, 1971, *reprinted in* Powell Hearings at 214.

[189] Note, *Foreign Security Surveillance and the Fourth Amendment*, 87 Harv. L. Rev. 976, 977 (1974).

Longer Term Executive and Legislative Responses

Foreign security surveillance did not remain entirely unregulated, however. Not long after the *Keith* decision, the executive branch developed its own standards governing foreign intelligence surveillance. Under those standards, warrantless electronic surveillance was to be employed only in cases where the targets were foreign powers or their agents, and where the purpose of the surveillance was to obtain foreign intelligence information. The executive's standards also limited the uses to which the fruits of such surveillance could be put.[190]

Such executive self-policing did not satisfy Congress. Spurred by the Watergate scandal, congressional investigations in the mid–1970s uncovered evidence of a broad range of abuses of government authority, especially in the area of purported national security intelligence gathering. The 1976 conclusions of the Church Committee are representative:

> Virtually every element of our society has been subjected to excessive government-ordered intelligence inquiries. Opposition to government policy or the expression of controversial views was frequently considered sufficient for collecting data on Americans. The committee finds that this extreme breadth of intelligence activity is inconsistent with the principles of our Constitution which protect the rights of speech, political activity, and privacy against unjustified governmental intrusion.[191]

More specifically, the Church Committee found that warrantless surveillance had been used against numerous U.S. citizens having no discernible connection to any foreign power and posing no credible threat to national security.[192] It traced those abuses in part to the lack of clear standards governing foreign intelligence surveillance.[193]

In 1978, Congress responded by passing the Foreign Intelligence Surveillance Act (FISA).[194] As the Senate Judiciary Committee explained in a statement outlining the need for the legislation, "This legislation is in large measure a response to the revelations that warrantless electron-

---

[190] *See Electronic Surveillance Within the United States for Foreign Intelligence Purpose: Hearings on S. 3197 Before the Subcomm. on Intelligence and the Rights of Americans of the S. Select Comm. on Intelligence*, 94th Cong. 77 (1976) (statement of Attorney General Levi).

[191] *Final Report of the Senate Select Comm. To Study Governmental Operations with Respect to Intelligence Activities and the Rights of Americans*, S. Rep. No. 94–755, pt. 2, at 169 (1976).

[192] *Id.* at 5.

[193] *Id.* at 186–87.

[194] Pub. L. No. 95–511, 92 Stat. 1783 (1978) (codified as amended at 50 U.S.C. §§ 1801 *et seq.*).

ic surveillance in the name of national security has been seriously abused."[195] Congress sought to " 'curb the practice by which the Executive Branch may conduct warrantless electronic surveillance on its own unilateral determination that national security justifies it,' while [still] permitting the legitimate use of electronic surveillance to obtain foreign intelligence information."[196]

FISA is sometimes viewed as a response to the Supreme Court's suggestion in *Keith* that Congress adopt special standards for surveillance in national security cases.[197] Yet, while *Keith* and FISA are certainly connected in important respects,[198] FISA does not take up the precise invitation issued in *Keith*. That invitation applied to the category of surveillance addressed in the case—so-called "domestic security" surveillance for intelligence purposes.[199] FISA does not cover such surveillance. In fact, "[n]o congressional action has ever been taken regarding the use of electronic surveillance in the domestic security area."[200] For cases falling in that area, therefore, *Keith*'s direct application of the Fourth Amendment continues to govern.

FISA, in contrast, regulates at least part of the category of surveillance left untouched by *Keith*—surveillance targeting foreign powers or their agents.[201] Specifically, it establishes a framework for the use within the United States of "electronic surveillance"[202] to acquire "foreign

---

[195] S. Rep. No. 95–604(I) at 8 (1977), 1978 U.S.C.C.A.N. 3904, 3909.

[196] Elizabeth B. Bezan & Jennifer K. Elsea, Memorandum, Cong. Research Serv., *Presidential Authority to Conduct Warrantless Electronic Surveillance to Gather Foreign Intelligence Information* 13 (Jan. 5, 2006), *available at* http://www.fas.org/sgp/crs/intel/m 010506.pdf (quoting *id.*).

[197] *See, e.g.*, Robert Bloom & William J. Dunn, *The Constitutional Infirmity of Warrantless NSA Surveillance: The Abuse of Presidential Power and the Injury to the Fourth Amendment*, 15 Wm. & Mary Bill Rts. J. 147, 159 (2006) ("Congress would accept [*Keith*'s] invitation to provide a separate but integrated protective scheme for electronic surveillance driven by national security interests with the passage of FISA.").

[198] *See generally* Tracey Maclin, *The Bush Administration's Terrorist Surveillance Program and the Fourth Amendment's Warrant Requirement: Lessons from Justice Powell and the* Keith *Case*, 41 U.C. Davis L. Rev. 1259, 1296–98 (2008) (describing the connection and claiming that "there is a direct line connecting *Katz*, Title III, *Keith*, and FISA").

[199] *See Keith*, 407 U.S. 297, 322–24 (1972).

[200] Americo R. Cinquegrana, *The Walls (and Wires) Have Ears: The Background and First Ten Years of the Foreign Intelligence Surveillance Act of 1978*, 137 U. Pa. L. Rev. 793, 803 (1989).

[201] In so doing, FISA replaced Title III's "national security exception." *See* 18 U.S.C. § 2511(3) (1976), *repealed by* Foreign Intelligence Surveillance Act, Pub. L. No. 95–511, 92 Stat. 1783 (1978) (codified as amended at 50 U.S.C. §§ 1801 *et seq.*).

[202] FISA defines "electronic surveillance" to cover, *inter alia*:

intelligence information."[203] It generally requires the government to obtain a judicial warrant before engaging in such surveillance[204] and creates a special court (the FISA court, or FISC) for the issuance of such warrants.[205] The FISC consists of a small number of federal judges appointed by the Chief Justice. It "meet[s] secretly in a sealed, secure room in Washington, DC" and employs streamlined procedures enabling expedited consideration of the government's applications.[206] Most significantly, it applies a substantive standard that is considerably more lenient than the Title III standard for electronic surveillance in the criminal justice context.[207] To obtain a FISA warrant, the government

---

(1) the acquisition . . . of the contents of any wire or radio communication sent by or intended to be received by a particular, known United States person who is in the United States, if the contents are acquired by intentionally targeting that United States person, under circumstances in which a person has a reasonable expectation of privacy and a warrant would be required for law enforcement purposes; [or]

(2) the acquisition . . . of the contents of any wire communication to or from a person in the United States, without the consent of any party thereto, if such acquisition occurs in the United States. . . .

50 U.S.C. § 1801(f).

[203] FISA defines "foreign intelligence information" as follows:

(1) information that relates to, and if concerning a United States person is necessary to, the ability of the United States to protect against—

(A) actual or potential attack or other grave hostile acts of a foreign power or an agent of a foreign power;

(B) sabotage or international terrorism by a foreign power or an agent of a foreign power; or

(C) clandestine intelligence activities by an intelligence service or network of a foreign power or by an agent of a foreign power; or

(2) information with respect to a foreign power or foreign territory that relates to, and if concerning a United States person is necessary to—

(A) the national defense or the security of the United States; or

(B) the conduct of the foreign affairs of the United States.

Id. § 1801(e).

[204] FISA does recognize two narrow exceptions to the warrant requirement. First, where the government does not have enough time to obtain a judicial warrant in advance, the Attorney General may approve the surveillance provided he then seeks a judicial warrant from the FISA court within seventy-two hours of the initiation of the surveillance. Id. § 1805(f)(2). Second, FISA permits the Attorney General to authorize warrantless electronic surveillance during the first fifteen days after a declaration of war. Id. § 1811.

[205] See id. § 1805.

[206] Stephen J. Schulhofer, The New World of Foreign Intelligence Surveillance, 17 Stan. L. & Pol'y Rev. 531, 534 (2006).

[207] See Tracey Maclin, The Bush Administration's Terrorist Surveillance Program and the Fourth Amendment's Warrant Requirement: Lessons from Justice Powell and the Keith Case, 41 U.C. Davis L. Rev. 1259, 1299 (2008).

must show probable cause to believe that the surveillance target is the "agent of a foreign power."[208] As long as the target is not a U.S. citizen or permanent resident alien, however, no showing of likely criminal activity is required.[209] In addition, FISA originally required the government to certify that "the purpose[] of the surveillance is to obtain foreign intelligence information."[210] However, the USA PATRIOT Act,[211] passed in the wake of the attacks of September 11, 2001, amended FISA to require only that obtaining foreign intelligence information be "a significant purpose of the surveillance."[212]

Key aspects of the FISA regime—its use of a specialized, secret court with streamlined procedures and its articulation of a more lenient substantive standard than the conventional probable cause requirement—mirror quite closely the standards and procedures that *Keith* had proposed for domestic security surveillance. In that sense, FISA's regulation of foreign surveillance was at least indirectly inspired by *Keith*'s treatment of domestic surveillance.

Keith and FISA also share a more overarching and significant similarity: an unwillingness to grant the executive branch exclusive, unchecked power to engage in electronic surveillance in the name of national security. Just as *Keith* concluded that "Fourth Amendment

---

[208] 50 U.S.C. § 1805(a)(3). The statute defines "foreign power" to include not only any foreign government or faction, but also any "foreign-based political organization, not substantially composed of United States persons" and, perhaps most significantly, any "group engaged in international terrorism or activities in preparation therefor." *Id.* § 1801(a). In addition, Congress in 2004 expanded the definition of "agent of a foreign power" to include not only persons affiliated with foreign powers as just described, but also non-U.S. citizens or permanent residents who "engage[] in international terrorism or activities in preparation therefor," even if they are acting alone. *Id.* § 1801(b)(1)(C). This is FISA's so-called "lone wolf" provision. *See generally* Tricia L. Bellia, *The "Lone Wolf" Amendment and the Future of Foreign Intelligence Surveillance*, 50 Vill. L. Rev. 425 (2005).

[209] If the target *is* a U.S. citizen or permanent resident alien, the government must show probable cause to believe the target it committing a crime related to clandestine intelligence gathering or comparable offenses. *Id.* § 1801(b)(2).

[210] Pub. L. No. 95–511, § 104(a)(7)(B), 92 Stat. 1789 (1978).

[211] Uniting and Strengthening America by Providing Appropriate Tools Required to Intercept and Obstruct Terrorism (USA PATRIOT) Act of 2001, Pub. L. No. 107–56, 115 Stat. 272.

[212] 50 U.S.C. § 1804(a)(7)(B), *amended by* USA PATRIOT Act § 218 (2001). One district court has found FISA's requirement of "significant purpose" unconstitutional under the Fourth Amendment. Mayfield v. United States, 504 F. Supp. 2d 1023, 1039 (D. Or. 2007) ("FISA now permits the Executive Branch to conduct surveillance and searches of American citizens without satisfying the probable cause requirement of the Fourth Amendment."). *But see* United States v. Mubayyid, 521 F. Supp. 2d 125, 135–36 (D. Mass. 2007) (citing several other courts that have "ruled that FISA does not violate the Fourth Amendment").

freedoms cannot properly be guaranteed if domestic security surveillance may be conducted solely within the discretion of the Executive Branch,"[213] FISA represents Congress's determination to protect constitutional values by subjecting even foreign intelligence surveillance to the constraints of a judicial warrant procedure.[214] In that respect, a key component of FISA is its replacement of Title III's "national security exception"[215] with a provision stating that that FISA and Title III together "shall be the exclusive means by which electronic surveillance . . . may be conducted."[216] In other words, the foreign intelligence surveillance covered by FISA is lawful only insofar as it complies with FISA itself. In regulating such surveillance in this manner, Congress did not deny that the Constitution empowers the President to order electronic surveillance for national security purposes.[217] Rather, just as *Keith* held that the President's constitutional authority to order domestic security surveillance was subject to the constraints of the Fourth Amendment, Congress in FISA exercised its authority to "regulate the conduct of [electronic] surveillance [for foreign intelligence purposes] by legislating a reasonable procedure" and making it "the exclusive means by which such surveillance may be conducted."[218]

Events relating to the "war on terror" have put pressure on the FISA regime. In late 2005, news broke that the President had authorized the National Security Agency to engage in warrantless electronic surveillance of communications involving suspected terrorists, even when U.S. citizens within the United States are party to the communications.[219] On its face, this surveillance program—known by the government as the Terrorist Surveillance Program, or TSP—would seem to run afoul of FISA. The government resisted that conclusion on two grounds. First, it

---

[213] *Keith*, 407 U.S. 297, 316–17 (1972).

[214] *See* Tracey Maclin, *The Bush Administration's Terrorist Surveillance Program and the Fourth Amendment's Warrant Requirement: Lessons from Justice Powell and the* Keith *Case*, 41 U.C. Davis L. Rev. 1259, 1296 (2008) (treating FISA as an extension of *Keith*).

[215] *See* 18 U.S.C. § 2511(3) (1976), *repealed by* Foreign Intelligence Surveillance Act, Pub. L. No. 95–511, 92 Stat. 1783 (1978) (codified as amended at 50 U.S.C. §§ 1801 *et seq.*).

[216] 18 U.S.C. § 2511(2)(f).

[217] *See* Letter from Curtis A. Bradley, David Cole, Walter Dellinger, Ronald Dworkin, Richard Epstein, Philip B. Heymann, Harold Hongju Koh, Martin Lederman, Beth Nolan, William S. Sessions, Geoffrey Stone, Kathleen Sullivan, Laurence H. Tribe & William Van Alstyne to Sen. Bill Frist, Majority Leader, et al. (Jan. 9, 2006), *reprinted in On NSA Spying: A Letter to Congress*, 53 N.Y. Rev. Books (Feb. 9, 2006) [hereinafter "Letter from Curtis A. Bradley, *et al.*"].

[218] H.R. Rep. No. 95–1283, pt. I, at 24 (1978).

[219] *See* James Risen & Eric Lichtblau, *Bush Lets U.S. Spy on Callers Without Courts*, N.Y. Times, Dec. 16, 2005, at A1.

argued that legislative developments after the attacks of September 11, 2001 (in particular the Authorization for Use of Military Force, passed by Congress on September 18, 2001) had effectively amended FISA to permit warrantless surveillance of this sort. Second, and alternatively, the government contended that to the extent FISA prohibits the President from ordering this surveillance in his capacity as Commander-in-Chief, it unconstitutionally infringes his inherent powers under Article II of the Constitution.[220] Those arguments have faced substantial opposition and critique,[221] and their status remains uncertain.

Meanwhile, Congress has contemplated permanently amending FISA to better accommodate the government's asserted need for greater surveillance authority in connection with the war on terror. As of this writing it remains to be seen what will become of the regulatory regime established by FISA and inspired, albeit indirectly, by *Keith*.

Conclusion

In addition to delivering "a stunning legal setback" to the government's assertions of executive authority,[222] *Keith* won Pun Plamondon and his co-defendants their freedom. Rather than comply with the Court's order to disclose the surveillance records involving Plamondon—records that very likely would have confirmed the lack of any connection between the surveillance and the criminal charges against him—the government simply abandoned the prosecution.[223] The case ended there.

Yet *Keith*'s impact endures. Although the future of the major statutory regime it inspired is now uncertain, *Keith*'s underlying constitutional holding remains in place. And although that holding is formally confined to instances of purely domestic security surveillance, it is still the Supreme Court's most important statement on the general topic of warrantless electronic surveillance. The Court, at least, has stuck with that statement. Indeed, as of this writing, "the Supreme Court has never upheld warrantless wiretapping within the United States, *for any purpose*."[224]

---

[220] *See* U.S. Dep't of Justice, *Legal Authorities Supporting the Activities of the National Security Agency Described by the President* (Jan. 19, 2006), *available at* http://news.lp.findlaw.com/hdocs/nsa/dojnsa11906wp.pdf. For further discussion of the government's statutory argument, see Trevor W. Morrison, *Constitutional Avoidance in the Executive Branch*, 106 Colum. L. Rev. 1189, 1250–58 (2006).

[221] *See, e.g.*, Letter from Curtis A. Bradley, *et al.*

[222] Fred P. Graham, *High Court Curbs U.S. Wiretapping Aimed at Radicals*, N.Y. Times, June 20, 1972, at A1.

[223] *See* Samuel C. Damren, *The* Keith *Case*, 11 *The Court Legacy* (Historical Society for the U.S. Dist. Ct. for the E.D. Mich.) at 8 (2003).

[224] David Cole, *Reviving the Nixon Doctrine: NSA Spying, the Commander-in-Chief, and Executive power in the War on Terror*, 13 Wash. & Lee J.C.R. & Soc. Just. 17, 34 (2006) (emphasis added).

*

9

Christopher H. Schroeder

The Story of *United States v. Nixon*: The President and the Tapes

In July and August of 1948, the House Committee on Un–American Activities (HUAC) was holding hearings critical to its survival, as President Truman had let it be known that he would seek to abolish the Committee should he beat Dewey in the fall.[1] Seeking to unearth an active communist cell within the State Department, the Committee called Whittaker Chambers, an admitted former Communist, to testify about communists in the executive branch. Chambers named Alger Hiss, claiming to have known him in the 1930s, when Hiss had been a low level State Department employee. Subsequently, Hiss had risen in the ranks to senior positions, including membership in the delegation to the three-power talks at Yalta. By 1948, he was well connected in Democratic circles (soon-to-become Secretary of State Dean Acheson helped prepare Hiss's opening statement[2]) and was President of the Carnegie Endowment for International Peace. Hiss demanded an opportunity to defend himself. Two days later, he delivered a bravado defense before the Committee.[3] HUAC then sought to obtain government personnel files in order to bolster their case against Hiss and others. According to acting HUAC Chairman Mundt, "if the White House refus[ed] to cooperate in turning over the personnel files, we will crucify the administration. If they [did cooperate], we are going to be able to dig out more stuff to plague them in the fall campaign."[4] President Truman chose non-

---

[1] Stephen E. Ambrose, *Nixon* 166–67 (1987).

[2] *Id.* at 170. Hiss also had friends across the aisle. John Foster Dulles, the odds-on favorite to be Secretary of State had Dewey defeated Truman, was chairman of the Carnegie Endowment Board, and also one of Hiss's benefactors. *Id.* at 178.

[3] *Id.* at 170–71.

[4] *Quoted in* Irwin F. Gellman, *The Contender: Richard Nixon, the Congress Years* 199 (1999).

cooperation, and issued an executive order instructing federal agencies to release no information on federal employees to committees of Congress.[5] Freshman Congressman and HUAC member Richard Nixon then took to the House floor to denounce the President's refusal to turn over information. Nixon argued that the President was wrong "from a constitutional standpoint and on the merits," because he was preventing Congress from exercising its proper investigative authority.[6]

Nixon's fellow Republicans on HUAC, thinking the hearings were going badly, wanted to get rid of Hiss and Chambers by turning the issue of who was lying over to the Justice Department. Nixon, though, did not trust the Truman administration to investigate someone Secretary of State Acheson had defended and whose investigation Truman had agreed was a "red herring." Nixon was determined to "prevent a cover up" by the Executive Branch,[7] and he pressed forward aggressively. His investigations unearthed inconsistencies in Hiss's story that were exposed during a dramatic second set of hearings several weeks later.[8] When Hiss was later called before a grand jury investigating espionage, he perjured himself and ended up being sentenced to five years in prison. Years afterwards, when the Nixon White House was being investigated for a cover-up of its own, President Nixon would tell his aides that Hiss could have weathered the HUAC hearings if only he had told the truth from the beginning.

* * *

This chapter tells the story of *United States v. Nixon*.[9] The case shows conclusively that President Nixon came to endorse a very different interpretation of presidential authority than Congressman Nixon had. It also suggests that at a crucial moment in his Presidency, he seems to have forgotten his own take-away lesson from the Hiss/Chambers incident.

The issue in *Nixon* centered on a clash between the judicial branch's claims for information and the President's claim of confidentiality. Its larger story reveals a President asserting a broad theory of strong presidential authority—much stronger than simply the claim that he alone was to decide when his confidential conversations were to be revealed. As has been true throughout our history, the President's main

---

[5] Stephen E. Ambrose, *Nixon* 173 (1987).

[6] Stanley I. Kutler, *The Wars of Watergate* 347 (1990).

[7] Stephen E. Ambrose, *Nixon* 173 (1987).

[8] Geoffrey Stone, *Perilous Times* 329–31, 370–72 (2004); Stephen E. Ambrose, *Nixon* 180–86 (1987).

[9] 418 U.S. 684 (1974).

protagonist in the struggle over presidential power was the Congress, with the political arena—and ultimately the Congress' rarely invoked impeachment process—the main battlegrounds. The judiciary found itself injected into the political struggle because subordinates of the President were charged with the common crimes of breaking and entering and obstruction of justice. When a federal district court issued a criminal subpoena for tapes of conversations in the Oval Office and the President refused to turn them over to the special prosecutor, the prerequisites were in place for litigation in the Supreme Court. The decision in *United States v. Nixon* proved to be the factor that turned the President's remaining base of political support against him. President Nixon resigned when it became apparent to all that he could not prevail against the impeachment proceedings that had been running in parallel with the subpoena litigation.

Before turning to the litigation itself, the next section sets the larger political context, describing President Nixon's understanding of the powers of the presidency. The following section focuses on the Watergate break-in and the escalating investigations into the break-in that were the immediate precursors to the subpoena that was challenged in *United States v. Nixon*. The concluding sections discuss the Court's unanimous decision, situate that decision into the larger political context that was swirling around it, and describe the decision's continuing influence.

The Political Context

Somewhere between the House of Representatives and the White House, Richard Nixon had become convinced of the superiority of the presidency in policy making, national leadership, and Constitutional stature. By the time he ran for the presidency, he had little positive to say about the other branches. Nixon's first director of the White House office of congressional relations, Bryce Harlow, described Richard Nixon "as the type of individual who wanted to be President with the least possible interference from other actors in the political system."[10]

The makings of a tense relationship between the President and the Congress were cemented in place while Nixon was a presidential candidate. During the 1968 campaign, Nixon showed disdain for Congress, frequently making statements that ignored the role of Congress entirely, and running on the argument that national leadership had to be exercised by "the President and the people together." Throughout the campaign, he "offered no recognition of shared power whatsoever."[11]

---

[10] Kenneth E. Collier, *Between the Branches* 119–20 (1997).

[11] Stanley I. Kutler, *The Wars of Watergate* 131 (1990).

Once in office, Nixon and his advisers viewed Congress with thinly veiled contempt. In Nixon's view, the President was the only public figure who could legitimately speak for the people of the United States, and to give voice to the Silent Majority. This attitude was reflected even in the esteem within the White House in which those assigned to deal with congressional relations were held. They were never within the first circle of power in the Nixon White House. "To the White House inner circle, Congress was enemy territory."[12] The other branch of government was simply an obstacle to be worked around, undermined and avoided.[13]

Unfortunately for someone with his attitude toward Congress, when Nixon took the oath of office in January, 1969, he became the first newly elected President since Zachary Taylor in 1848 to face a Congress in which both houses were controlled by the opposing party. His first term thus inaugurated the contemporary period of contentious divided government.[14] This presented enormous problems for the President, because Nixon had inherited a brutal domestic and foreign policy agenda that would necessitate collaboration with Congress more often than Nixon would have preferred. The war in Southeast Asia, which had been the prime reason that Lyndon Johnson had not run for a second term, remained for Nixon the greatest concern. Besides Vietnam, however, Nixon was beset with a clutch of domestic problems daunting in and of themselves. The economic problems and budget deficits generated by Johnson's guns and butter strategy, the demands of the civil rights movement, urban and civil unrest, including some of the worst riots American cities have ever experienced, record numbers of bombings by self-described revolutionary groups and other dissidents, campus violence—all of these elements contributed to a growing anxiety that the country was fissuring in ways that might not be reparable. The challenges of this national agenda would have placed strains on any President facing an opposition Congress. In Nixon's case, policy disagreements were exacerbated by the manner in which the President asserted presidential authority to act free from any interference by the Congress.

The Unitary Executive and Presidential Imperialism:
Two Facets of Presidential Power

Nixon's approach to executive power can be broken into two compartments. The first addressed how much control the president should

---

[12] Matthew Crenson & Benjamin Ginsberg, *Presidential Power: Unchecked and UnBalanced* 192 (2007).

[13] Matthew Crenson & Benjamin Ginsberg, *Presidential Power: Unchecked and UnBalanced* 192 (2007).

[14] In the forty year period between 1968 and 2008, at least one house of Congress has been in the hands of the opposing party for thirty of those years.

be able to assert over the actions of his subordinates. Here, Nixon was an exponent of a strong theory of the unitary executive (although scholars had not yet designated it by that name). That theory rests in turn on a strong reading of Article II, Section 1 of the Constitution, which vests the "executive power ... in a President." How completely the executive power is "vested" in a single individual raises questions of the president's *control* over his subordinates. These questions are distinct from questions of the scope or extent of presidential power. What can the President do without congressional authorization? What can he do even if Congress has enacted prohibitory statutes? Here, Nixon believed that the Constitution vested the President with substantial powers with which the other branches of government simply could not interfere. When Arthur Schlesinger described the Nixon Presidency as the apogee of the "imperial presidency," he referred primarily to Nixon's views on the *scope* of presidential authority. Textually, Nixon's imperialism rested on a strong reading of the provision of Art. II making him commander-in-chief, as well on the interpretation of presidential authority found in the *Curtiss–Wright* decision declaring the president to be the "sole organ" of the country in foreign relations.[15] Many of Nixon's famous face-offs with the Congress—and later the courts—concerned this second issue, the scope of presidential authority.

To Schlesinger, the imperialistic assertion of presidential authority typified by the Nixon Presidency constituted a shift in the balance of constitutional powers, amounting to nothing less than "the appropriation by the Presidency ... of powers reserved by the Constitution and by long historical practice to Congress.... The essence of [Nixon's New American Revolution] was not, as [Nixon] said [in his 1971 Inaugural Address] power to the people. The essence was power to the presidency."[16] Presidential imperialism now sometimes travels under the label "presidentialism."[17] In either case, advocates of this view contend that the Constitution bestows on the President substantial substantive authorities that cannot be limited or controlled by the Congress or reviewed by the courts. Nixon's assertion of absolute authority to impound funds that Congress had appropriated, of absolute control over what information Congress would receive from the executive branch and of absolute discretion to decide what actions best protected the national

---

[15] On *Curtiss–Wright*, see Chapter 6 in this volume.

[16] Arthur M. Schlesinger, Jr., *Foreword to the 1973 Edition*, in *The Imperial Presidency* xxvi (2004), and *id.* at 252.

[17] For works that use the term "presidentialism," see Matthew Crenson & Benjamin Ginsberg, *Presidential Power: Unchecked and UnBalanced* (2007); Peter Shane, *Madison's Nightmare* (forthcoming 2008).

security were all emanations of the imperialism or presidentialism that characterized his presidency.

In discussions of presidential authority, the issues of the control and scope are sometimes elided. For example, during the confirmation hearings of Samuel Alito in 2006, Senators questioned the nominee about his role in developing and advocating unitary executive principles during his time in President Reagan's Department of Justice. The Senators often seemed, however, more interested in asking about the scope of presidential authority vis-à-vis Congress' authority, rather than about the President's ability to direct the bureaucracy. Senator Leahy, for instance, asked Judge Alito whether "[u]nder a unitary theory of government, one could argue that [the President] has an absolute right to ignore a law that the Congress has written?"[18] The Senator's immediate concern was to question the contents of a statement President G. W. Bush had issued as he was signing into law a restriction on American personnel committing torture, in which President Bush had suggested that his authority as commander-in-chief would enable him to disregard the law if necessary.[19] Judge Alito, however, treated the question as one asking about the President's power to control his subordinates. He replied that "the question of the unitary executive, as I was explaining yesterday, does not concern the scope of executive powers, it concerns who controls whatever power the executive has. You could have an executive with very narrow powers and still have a unitary executive. So those are entirely different questions."[20]

One cannot tell from the hearing transcript whether Senator Leahy was satisfied with that answer, but Judge Alito correctly noted that a robust theory of the unitary executive can co-exist with a modest interpretation of the scope of presidential authority, and vice versa. In Richard Nixon's case, the nation experienced a President with a quite robust position on both. Each was on full display during the two years of the Watergate story, culminating with the Supreme Court's decision in *United States v. Nixon*, the House Judiciary Committee's affirmative vote on three articles of impeachment, and President Nixon's resignation on August 8, 1974. Even prior to Watergate, though, each of these two strands of Nixon's theory of the presidency had generated considerable controversy and animosity between the President and Congress. These prior controversies served to drain the reservoirs of congressional support that Nixon might otherwise have had to draw upon during the impeachment controversy.

---

[18] Confirmation hearings of Samuel A. Alito, Jan. 11, 2006, 2006 WL 53273 (F.D.C.H.) (Westlaw).

[19] *Id.*

[20] *Id.*

Control of the Bureaucracy

Congress was not the only institution in Washington that seemed eager to thwart Nixon's presidential ambitions. Especially as regards his unitary executive views, the bureaucracy was often a formidable opponent, and Nixon's efforts to circumvent the bureaucracy contributed to the circumstances that led to Watergate, the *United States v. Nixon* decision, and his eventual demise.

Over the years, arguments about the unitary executive have been waged over three discrete issues, each involving a mechanism that the President might use to gain control over his subordinates: the President's power of removal; the President's power to direct other officials' exercises of discretionary executive power; and the President's power to nullify or veto other officials' exercises of discretionary executive power.[21] Nixon believed strongly that he ought to possess full authority in all three areas, and he worked hard to put his theory of presidential control of the executive into practice. In both foreign policy and domestic affairs, he sought to concentrate decision making in the White House, rather than in the various departments of government. The White House wanted "direct and operational control of policy-making ... Kissinger's expansion of his role as National Security Adviser is the most obvious case, although by 1973 John Ehrlichman's Domestic Council had developed the same tendency."[22] To gain further control over the executive branch agencies, Nixon expanded the supervisory functions available through White House review of the budget. He instituted a quality of life review for agency rules that was the precursor of even more vigorous oversight of agency rulemaking through the Office of Information and Regulatory Analysis within the Office of Management and Budget (OMB), as an additional means of concentrating authority in the Executive Office of the President.[23]

These efforts to concentrate power and decision-making within the orbit of his immediate advisers instead of within the agencies reflected Nixon's deep distrust of the bureaucracy. In conversation with his key aides, Bob Haldeman and John Ehrlichman, Nixon frequently inveighed against the departments, lamenting the White House's inability to successfully implement greater operational control. He told Ehrlichman that "we have no discipline in this bureaucracy. We never fire anybody.

---

[21] *See, e.g.*, Steven G. Calabresi and Christopher S. Yoo, *The Unitary Executive During the First Half–Century*, 47 Case W. Res. L. Rev. 1451, 1458 (1997).

[22] Stanley I. Kutler, *The Wars of Watergate* 96 (1990).

[23] Robert C. Percival, *Checks Without Balance: Executive Office Oversight of the Environmental Protection Agency*, 54 Law & Contemp. Probs. 127, 132–134 (1991) ("While publicly emphasizing the importance of EPA's independence, OMB was acting to assert greater control over EPA's regulatory activities.").

We never reprimand anybody. We never demote anybody. We always promote the sons-of-bitches that kick us in the ass."[24] Some of the invective was directed at bureaucratic foot-dragging in implementing presidential programmatic priorities. It was also fueled, however, by frustration with not getting rapid responses to Nixon's more partisan political agendas, like performing tax audits of people on his enemies list.[25]

The White House imperative for control contributed directly to the showdown over the Watergate tapes and to Nixon's resignation. After Daniel Ellsberg had stolen and leaked the Pentagon Papers first to the New York Times and subsequently to the Washington Post, Nixon demanded that such leaks of confidential information be plugged. Nixon did not trust the FBI's reliability and responsiveness, so he tasked the job of plugging the leaks to the newly-created Special Investigations Unit—quickly dubbed the Plumbers—under the direct control of White House aides. "At this point, the White House moved across the line from . . . prodding other agencies into direct operations more appropriate to a secret-police force."[26] While FBI agents might well have resisted when asked to turn their talents to breaking and entering the Democratic National Committee's office in the Watergate complex, the Plumbers unit would later voice no opposition. Their botched break-in on the night of June 16, 1972—presumably to rearrange electronic surveillance gear planted earlier—initiated the chain of events that would lead to the Supreme Court showdown in *United States v. Nixon*.

Friction With Congress

Needless to say, Nixon's unitary executive views were not well received on Capitol Hill, where members of Congress tend to guard its own mechanisms of control over the bureaucracy rather jealously. The legislation through which Congress lays down its basic policies and instructions amounts to only the beginning of an on-going relationship between Congress and the bureaucracy. Subsequently, through oversight, appropriations, reauthorization and constituent casework activities, members of Congress continue to make their preferences known to the agencies. The result too often can be an "iron triangle" in which key congressional committees, civil service bureaucrats and lobbyists exercise great control over agency behavior, whatever the desires of the President might be.[27] Regardless of whether the agencies were part of an iron

---

[24] Box 14, Ehrlichman Papers, Hoover Institution Archives, Stanford, California, *as quoted in* Stanley I. Kutler, *The Wars of Watergate* 94 (1990).

[25] Stanley I. Kutler, *The Wars of Watergate* 640 n.34 (1990).

[26] J. Anthony Lukas, *Nightmare: The Underside of the Nixon Years* 94 (1988).

[27] Stanley I. Kutler, *The Wars of Watergate* 139 (1990).

triangle, when President Nixon took office the bureaucracies had operated under Democratic Presidents for twenty-eight of the previous thirty-six years, and were thought to be staffed with individuals largely sympathetic to programs that Republican President Nixon intended to change. Congress, which remained in Democratic hands, was predictably resistant both to the changes and to the President's efforts to exert his own control over the bureaucracy. So when President Nixon promised to go after the "bureaucratic elites in Washington," whose "fragmented fiefdoms" were having a "hobbling effect ... on elected leadership and, therefore, on the basic principles of democratic government,"[28] he threw down a challenge that the Congress did not ignore.

Nixon and Congress clashed numerous times in disputes over control of the executive branch. One dispute arose when Nixon undertook to augment the power of the Office of Management and Budget over the federal bureaucracy. To protect its own influence, Congress proposed to abolish the offices of director and deputy director of OMB and then reestablish them as positions requiring Senate confirmation.[29] Nixon opposed that measure as a backdoor effort to remove his incumbent appointees (and then to replace them with individuals more acceptable to the Senate and subsequently more subject to congressional oversight), thereby usurping a removal power that the President claimed belonged to him. Nixon was eventually successful in defending his removal power. At the same time, Congress gained an increased measure of control, because, while it backed away from trying to oust the incumbents, it did change the offices to ones requiring Senate confirmation in the future.[30]

---

[28] Richard Nixon, *Special Message to the Congress on Executive Branch Reorganization, Mar. 25, 1971*, The American Presidency Project (John T. Woolley and Gerhard Peters, eds.), http://www.presidency.ucsb.edu/ws/?pid=2951.

[29] Christopher S. Yoo, Steven G. Calabresi & Anthony J. Colangelo, *The Unitary Executive in the Modern Era, 1945–2004*, 90 Iowa L. Rev. 601, 657 (2005).

[30] When they are called upon to resolve separation of powers questions, courts look to incidents such as these to determine the views of the other two branches of government concerning how constitutional power has been allocated. Unfortunately, the lessons of this particular dispute are decidedly ambiguous, as is so often the case. Did the members of Congress acquiesce because they recognized the force of a constitutional objection to its backdoor removal effort; because enough of them recognized the force of the practical arguments made by the President and his defenders about the undesirable consequences of Congress' removing key presidential subordinates in this way; because enough Democratic members feared the consequences of establishing a precedent that might come back to bite Presidents that they supported; because the President cajoled or arm-twisted enough votes to get his way through more bare knuckles means ... or some combination of these? Frequently it is simply impossible to tell what lesson is to be drawn from altercations such as these.

See chapter 5 in this volume on *Myers v. United States* and chapter 11 on *Morrison v. Olson* for discussion of two cases in which the Supreme Court has addressed the removal power.

Nixon and the Congress also engaged in an ongoing dispute over the President's authority to impound funds. Presidential impoundment of congressionally appropriated monies has a pedigree extending back to 1803, when President Jefferson reported to Congress that he had decided not to expend $50,000 that Congress had appropriated for gunboats on the Mississippi River because "the favorable and peaceful turn of affairs . . . rendered an immediate execution of the law unnecessary."[31] Thus began a history of the occasional exercise of such presidential authority. In more recent times, President Franklin Roosevelt ordered the "deferment of construction funds not essential to the war effort," in order to establish fiscal reserves. Several years later, President Truman withheld funds to build a 58–wing Air Force because he thought a 48–wing Air Force was sufficient. President Johnson also impounded funds for a number of domestic programs. President Nixon built on this history, but also went "further than his predecessors."[32] In a January 31, 1973 press conference he transformed the occasional exercise of withholding funds under circumstances in which congressional approval might plausibly be anticipated into a matter of Constitutional right regardless of congressional priorities, declaring that it was "the Constitutional right for the President of the United States to impound funds . . . when the spending of money would mean . . . increasing prices or increasing taxes for all the people." "The right," he said, "is absolutely clear."[33]

In the name of fiscal restraint and his claimed presidential authority, Nixon proceeded to impound more funds than any President in history. By 1971, a Senate report calculated that the total had reached $12.76 billion.[34] The impoundment dispute between Congress and the President came to a head over the Federal Water Pollution Control Act of 1972, which included a public works program to assist states and localities in building modern water treatment facilities. Nixon vetoed the legislation, citing as the major reason these public works expenditures, which he viewed as unnecessary pork barrel spending. Congress promptly overrode the veto and appropriated funds for the state and local assistance program. Nixon instructed his administrator of the Environmental Protection Agency, William Ruckelshaus, not to spend the appropriated funds. As Nixon's deputy attorney general, Ruckelshaus

---

[31] 1 *Messages and Papers of the Presidents: 1789–1897* 330 (James Richardson ed., 1896).

[32] *The Issue of Impounding*, Time, Feb. 12, 1973, *available at* http://www.time.com/time/magazine/article/0,9171,903811,00.html.

[33] 9 *Weekly Compilation of Presidential Documents* 110 (1973).

[34] *Hearings on Executive Impoundment of Appropriated Funds before the Subcommittee on Separation of Powers of the Senate Committee on the Judiciary*, 92d Cong., 1st Sess. 165 (1971).

would later refuse to follow the President's direction to fire Archibald Cox, the first special prosecutor appointed to investigate Watergate. When it came to impoundment, however, EPA Administrator Ruckelshaus complied.

To many, Nixon's approach to the water pollution control bill seemed to stand on its head the President's constitutional obligation to take care that the laws of the United States are "faithfully executed." Here, Congress had passed a bill authorizing the expenditure of funds to assist state and localities in meeting the requirements of the law. After the President vetoed the bill, Congress overrode the veto, invoking its Constitutional authority to enact policy over the President's objections, provided it could muster the supermajorities necessary. Subsequently it appropriated the funds to implement its program. Nixon's impoundment effectively left the Congress with no capacity to assert its will further. Under these circumstances, the Second Circuit ruled, "the challenged impoundment policy ... is a violation of the spirit, intent and letter of the Act and a flagrant abuse of executive discretion."[35] In a unanimous decision, the Supreme Court agreed.[36] Congress responded further in the Congressional Budget and Impoundment Control Act of 1974 by placing statutory restrictions on presidential impoundment. Nixon's assertions of absolute presidential authority to impound appropriated monies had generated enough resentment in Congress that these actions would later be considered by the House Judiciary Committee as the possible basis of a separate article of impeachment. The Committee's staff report acknowledged, however, that the historical precedents provided some justification for at least some of Nixon's decisions, and it recommended against this being considered a "high crime or misdemeanor" by the Committee, which ended up not approving an impeachment article based on these actions.

The controversy over the OMB director and deputy director raised unitary executive questions, questions of controlling the bureaucracy. The impoundment dispute was over the scope of executive authority vis-à-vis the Congress. The question of executive privilege, the subject upon which *United States v. Nixon* would eventually turn, combined elements of both control and scope, as President Nixon claimed both the authority to resist disclosure of presidential communications and also the authority to control whether his subordinates complied with congressional requests for information. As with impoundment, earlier Presidents had invoked the right to maintain the confidentiality of presidential communications, as illustrated by President Truman's refusing to provide congressional access to documents or to make aides available to testify

---

[35] City of New York v. Train, 494 F.2d 1033, 105 (D.C. Cir. 1974).

[36] Train v. City of New York, 420 U.S. 35 (1975).

during HUAC's investigation of Alger Hiss and others.[37] Once again, however, Nixon would push past the historical precedents. By 1973, Nixon had deployed the doctrine as a means to restrict disclosing information to Congress more frequently than any previous President.[38]

Nixon clashed with the courts as well as with the Congress over his claimed authority to control the flow of information out of the executive branch. When it attempted to enjoin the publication of the Pentagon Papers, the administration claimed broad powers to suppress speech in the interests of national security.[39] It also claimed a large authority to gather up information in the first place: when it engaged in warrantless surveillance of the White Panthers, it defended its actions on the basis of a broad presidential national security authority.[40]

Extension of Historical Precedent

In these areas and others, although Nixon's assertions of presidential authority were seldom completely discontinuous with historical precedent, he systematically pressed for more authority than his predecessors had. His conception of the presidency diverged sharply from some of his predecessors. When President Harding, for instance, had ambitious ideas for changes in the tariff and tax laws, federal promotion of aviation, highways and the like, he nonetheless viewed it as Congress' responsibility to shape and then enact the specific policies that would bring these ideas to fruition after he suggested them. Once Harding had called Congress into session to address his ambitious agenda, "the president sat back and waited for Congress to work out the details of his program and enact it. He did not think it proper for the executive to meddle in the business of the legislative branch."[41] In such a context of deference to Congress's primacy as policy formulator, party leaders in

---

[37] Strictly speaking, neither Truman nor any prior President invoked "executive privilege." The Eisenhower administration was to first to make use of that term. Mark. J. Rozell, *Executive Privilege: Presidential Power, Secrecy, and Accountability* 39 (2nd Ed., rev. 2002). Beginning with George Washington, however, Presidents have asserted a right to withhold some information from Congress and the public. Rozell's book recounts the history. *See also* Archibald Cox, *Executive Privilege*, 122 U. Pa. L. Rev. 1383 (1974).

[38] Raoul Berger, *How the Privilege for Governmental Information Met Its Watergate*, 25 Case W. Res. L. Rev. 747, 775 (1975). By Nixon's third year in office, "Congress was in fact being denied a vast amount of information that it sought from the executive branch." Philip Kurland, *Watergate and the Constitution* 42 (1975).

[39] The Court declined to recognize that authority in the Pentagon Papers case, *New York Times v. United States*, 403 U.S. 713 (1971).

[40] Again, the Court disagreed. *See* United States v. U.S. Dist. Court (*Keith*), 407 U.S. 297 (1972). For more on *Keith*, see Chapter 8 in this volume.

[41] Matthew Crenson & Benjamin Ginsberg, *Presidential Power: Unchecked and Unbalanced* 143 (2007).

the Congress were ascendant forces and overt clashes between the two branches were modest.

In contrast, the model of the presidency that Richard Nixon employed was dramatically different. It can trace its roots to the tenure of Franklin Delano Roosevelt. In his early days, FDR frequently consulted with congressional leaders, on both sides of the isle, and listened to their advice.[42] After the 1934 mid-term elections, however, he became bolder as his program proposals became more liberal in their orientation—still, however, in keeping with the general tenor of Congress, which had also moved more heavily democratic and liberal in 1934. By 1936, however, FDR had begun to establish the modern-day electoral democratic coalition, with first-time voters flooding into the presidential election in record numbers to support him.[43] Riding this tide of heretofore unaffiliated voters, Roosevelt started creating an "executive democracy" whose dependence on the state party mechanisms in which members of Congress were often so influential was sharply attenuated.[44] While President Nixon won office on the votes of a quite different constituency than FDR, Nixon's belief that the President spoke directly for the people of the country and that governance was essentially his right and responsibility had its beginnings in the executive democracy of FDR.

Early in 1937, FDR sought to solidify his control of the executive branch by submitting an extensive executive organization plan. The plan would have expanded White House staff, strengthened presidential control over the budget and integrated independent agencies and commissions into cabinet departments. The next month he then sought to expand the scope of that authority further by announcing his court-packing plan, with the intention of adding Justices to the Court who would be more sympathetic to his New Deal program's legal initiatives, complete with their typically broad delegations of authority to executive branch agencies. In each of these attempts, he was partially successful. Although his court-packing plan was rejected, the switch-in-time of Justice Roberts gave him a 5–4 majority for a greatly expanded federal power over the economy, and he later solidified that power with eight appointments of Justices sympathetic to the New Deal. Congress gave him less than what he wanted in reorganizing the executive branch, but the modest reorganization package it did approve began the evolution toward greater centralization of executive decision making.

The efforts during FDR's second term to accrete power to the executive branch set a tone of presidential ambitions that continued into

---

[42] *Id.* at 159.

[43] *Id.* at 165.

[44] *Id.*

the post-Roosevelt era. Whether or not FDR's second term marks the beginning of the "modern presidency,"[45] all Presidents since FDR have shared his conviction that the President is the leader of the country, distinct from Congress and political party. As elections began to become less party focused and more candidate focused, Presidents developed a sense of primacy with respect to national policymaking that both was stimulated by that shift and contributed to it. Presidential candidates now needed to present themselves as individuals worth electing, and the key attribute that recommends a presidential candidate to the electorate is leadership. Incumbents express leadership by exercising the powers of the office to address the nation's problems. "[T]he same drive that animates candidate-centered campaigns also motivates Presidents and their staff assistants to expand the formal powers and administrative resources of the presidency. In the process, they bring into being an institution with a structural interest in defending and expanding executive authority."[46] Or, as Nixon's OMB deputy director put it before the 1972 campaign, "the President's unique asset in the forthcoming campaign [is] his control of the executive branch," through which he could demonstrate leadership, as well as reward his friends and punish his enemies.[47] Hence a considerable degree of activism and oftentimes more than a considerable amount of impatience toward Congress have become standard presidential attributes.

So Richard Nixon's view of the presidency and what it took to be an effective President was nurtured in the post-World War II environment and reflected the move toward executive democracy that had begun to develop under FDR. Nixon's desire to control the bureaucracy continued an inclination that his post-World War II predecessors had shared, propelled by an urge to implement a set of presidential priorities and a presidential program. That required mastery of the tools at the President's disposal, including the constituent parts of the executive branch. Post–World War II Presidents may appreciate that they share control of the bureaucracy with Congress as a matter of practical reality, but it is a reality that they are motivated to resist for political, policy and personal reasons. When faced with resistance on the part of Congress, and sometimes even without such resistance but simply out of a desire to act

---

[45] There is much debate about whether the hallmarks of the "modern" Presidency hearken back to FDR or can be seen even earlier, perhaps in the McKinley presidency. *See* Lewis I. Gould, *The Modern American Presidency* 7–15 (2003) (advocating for McKinley). By focusing here on FDR, I do not mean to choose sides in that debate, but only to use FDR as a leading example of a contrasting presidential attitude from Presidents like Harding.

[46] Matthew Crenson & Benjamin Ginsberg, *Presidential Power: Unchecked and UnBalanced* 177 (2007).

[47] J. Anthony Lukas, *Nightmare: The Underside of the Nixon Years* 19–21 (1988).

swiftly, Presidents increasingly want to go their own way. With Nixon, these urges reached an apex, with respect to both his ambitions to exert absolute control over the executive branch and his assertions of absolute authority.

When Nixon assumed the office, a considerable sentiment, especially among liberals, lay behind the idea that a strong and activist President was necessary to deal with the nation's problems. Liberals thought the country was afflicted by a "deadlock of democracy."[48] Both houses of Congress were effectively in the control of a Republican–Southern Democratic coalition that was considerably more conservative than the liberal wing of the Democratic party. That coalition had long been intransigent on civil rights, the great moral and political domestic issue of the day. As a consequence, liberals viewed Congress as a roadblock and obstacle. Decrying the politics of deadlock, and attracted to the idea of a single elected President (who until Nixon in the post WW II era had been a Democrat, with the exception of Eisenhower) leading the country, liberal intellectuals promoted the advantages of a strong presidential role.

When Nixon entered office in 1968, his conception of a strong presidency was thus, as a theoretical matter, more in tension with the conventional views of his own party than it was with the views of his liberal opposition. This is what Alexander Bickel had in mind when he wrote, "I don't know when Richard Nixon caught the liberals bathing, but he did walk off with their clothes."[49] Bickel's specific indictment against liberals was for their too-ready endorsement of a dangerous view of the presidency. But the indictment went to a deeper point as well: Bickel meant to criticize the collapse of legal and especially constitutional barriers in the name of supposedly higher imperatives, a charge which he most famously leveled against the Warren Court's seeming disregard of constitutional constraints in its efforts to achieve results that the Court thought were fair or just in particular cases. As a comment on the Nixon excesses, Bickel's implication was that by being insufficiently attentive to maintaining the proper limitations of presidential power within our system of separated powers, liberals had helped create the conditions that produced those excesses.

Eventually, the Congress did respond to the Nixonian excesses. Although the modern Congress has often been accused of being complicit in the shift toward presidential imperialism,[50] this was not the case in

---

[48] *See* James MacGregor Burns, *Deadlock of Democracy* (1963). Burns develops the theme that the United States system of separated powers gives the presidency insufficient power and flexibility to address modern problems.

[49] Alexander Bickel, *Watergate and the Legal Order*, 57 Commentary 19, 26 (1974).

[50] *E.g.*, Andrew Rudalevige, *The New Imperial Presidency* 15 (2007) ("Congress itself has not been run over so much as it has lain supine [in the post-Wategate era]").

the closing years of Nixon's presidency and for a while afterward. Congress enacted budget legislation to regularize Congress' role and bring the President's impoundment authority under statutory control; federal election reform legislation to reduce some of the corrupt campaign financing practices brought to light by the Ervin Committee in 1973; foreign intelligence surveillance legislation to institute judicial approval of wiretaps done for foreign intelligence gathering purpose; and war powers legislation seeking to control the President's ability to commit troops to combat. These actions were all taken in response to the efforts by the Nixon presidency to acquire more and more power for that office.

In responding in these ways, the post-Watergate Congress was signaling that the Nixon presidency indeed was excessive in its broad assertions of unilateral presidential authority, even after giving due regard for the historical precedents set by earlier Presidents, for the contemporary displeasure with the politics of gridlock, and for the frustrations that any President would feel when dealing with an opposition Congress on divisive issues. Nixon's conception of executive power may not have been wholly unique, but his presidency manifested "extraordinary attempts to concentrate power in the executive branch at the expense of other organs of government."[51]

Notwithstanding these excesses, it is likely that Nixon would have completed his second term in office had he not made the crucial mistake of coming to equate defending the powers of the institutional presidency with defending his own political success. He showed little compunction in turning the full powers he claimed for the presidency to the service of his own re-election ambitions. Consequently, when polls in the early summer of 1972 were showing a close contest between Nixon and his Democratic opponent, George McGovern,[52] the Special Investigations Unit of the White House—set up initially to stop leaks of national security information—was sent to break into the Democratic National Committee headquarters in the Watergate complex in order to again partisan political intelligence.

---

[51] Peter Quint, *The Separation of Powers Under Nixon: Reflections on Constitutional Liberties and the Rule of Law*, 1981 Duke L.J. 1, 2 (1981). *See also* Alexander Bickel, *Watergate and the Legal Order*, 57 Commentary 19, 25 (1974) ("The accumulation of power in the Presidency did not begin with Richard M. Nixon, of course, but it reached heights made possible by the populism of the day. There was a time there, soon after the election of 1972, when Mr. Nixon gave the impression that he thought the American political process had taken place, so to speak, that it was over for a while, and that he could just rule.").

[52] A May 1972 Harris poll of likely voters, for instance, showed Nixon with a slim five point lead in a three-way contest. *Survey by Louis Harris & Associates* (May 9–May 10, 1972) *in* the iPOLL Databank, The Roper Center for Public Opinion Research, University of Connecticut, http://www.ropercenter.uconn.edu/ipoll.html (last visited Jan. 15, 2008).

It took two years for the ripple effects of the break-in to result in the Supreme Court decision in *United States v. Nixon*. That two-year national drama, known now simply as "Watergate," was in President Nixon's own words an "epic battle," in which he threw "down a gauntlet to Congress, the bureaucracy, the media, and the Washington establishment."[53] Although one can say that our constitutional system stood stronger at the end of the ordeal, Watergate shook the belief of many Americans in that system to their very foundations, because at the heart of it was a President who massively abused the power of his office and then lied about it and obstructed justice in an attempt to remain in office. The lesson that Nixon had drawn from the Hiss/Chambers hearings had been lost on Nixon himself.

Factual Background and the Proceedings Below[54]

On the night of June 16, 1972, Bernard Barker, Virgilio Gonzalez, Eugenio Martinez, James W. McCord and Frank Sturgis were caught breaking into the Democratic National Committee offices in the Watergate complex in Washington, D.C. McCord was security director of the Committee to Re-elect the President (CRP) and the others were part of the Special Investigations Unit in the White House—the Plumbers. In September, these five, along with E. Howard Hunt and G. Gordon Liddy would be indicted for burglary.

The target of the break-in, coupled with the connection between the burglars, the CRP and the White House, led immediately to speculation of political motivations for the burglary. In the succeeding days, the White House and the President's supporters cavalierly dismissed the charges. With no evidence yet indicating that higher-ups in the campaign or the White House were involved, Press Secretary Larry Ziegler was free to describe the incident as "third-rate burglary," while RNC Chairman Robert Dole urged the Democrats to "stop trying to make a political issue" out of the break-in.[55] The press seemed to agree, because press coverage of the burglary was slight. The press was concentrating on the campaign itself and failed to see any important connection between the break-in and the national election contest between Nixon and McGovern. The public did not think the President is implicated in the event, either. In an October 1972 Harris Poll only 13% of respondents believed the

---

[53] Richard Nixon, 2 *RN: The Memoirs of Richard Nixon* 386 (1979).

[54] This account relies primarily on Stanley I. Kutler, *The Wars of Watergate* (1990). It and numerous other book length accounts describe the events of Watergate in much greater detail than can be done in this chapter, beginning with Carl Bernstein and Bob Woodward, *All the President's Men* (1973) and Richard Nixon's own Memoirs, *RN: The Memoirs of Richard Nixon* (1978).

[55] Bob Woodward and Carl Bernstein, *Jury Bares New Details Of Break In*, Wash. Post, Sept. 16, 1971, at A1.

President was involved, while 62% responded that the break-in was "just politics," the kind of shenanigans that both parties practiced.[56]

Unknown to the public or the press at the time, key White House officials and the President were much more anxious about the break-in than they were admitting. Just a week after the break-in, Nixon held three meetings with John Haldeman, his chief of staff, to discuss the potential that either the White House or the campaign committee could be implicated. They examined ways to deflect the criminal investigation being conducted by the FBI so that neither connection would be made. Haldeman and Nixon explicitly discussed how to enlist CIA Director Richard Helms to block the FBI's investigation of the break-in.[57] Nixon's own audio taping system caught him saying that Helms should be instructed to warn the FBI that further inquiry would "open the whole Bay of Pigs thing ... [The CIA] should call the FBI in and say that '...for the country, don't go any further into this case, period.' "[58] Two years later, when the President finally complied with a criminal subpoena to produce the White House tapes, this statement would become the "smoking gun" confirming Nixon's early role in orchestrating an obstruction of justice. Nixon may not have known of the plans for the break-in before hand, but whether he did or not would prove immaterial to his downfall. That descent began on June 23, 1972 with his undeniable involvement in covering up CRP and White House involvement. The cover-up, and not the break-in itself, formed the basis for one of the articles of impeachment approved by the House Judiciary Committee.

By the summer of 1973, numerous revelations from others would erode the public's opinion of Nixon, and his continuing efforts to hide his complicity would be greeted with great skepticism by the American people. In the immediate aftermath of the break-in, however, the cover-up proved successful. John Dean, the White House Counsel, assumed major responsibility for managing the efforts to keep the story from unraveling, including arranging for hush money to go to Howard Hunt and others. On September 15, 1972, he assured the President that matters would stay under wraps through the November election, and therefore would have no impact on the election. Dean's later testimony about this conversation before the Senate Select Committee Presidential

---

[56] UNC Odum Institute for Research in the Social Sciences, Harris Survey No. 2235 (Oct. 19, 1972).

[57] "During the course of at least three meetings covering more than two hours on June 23, Nixon and Haldeman took steps to impose a blanket on the investigation and to cover up any links between the burglars, CREEP, and the White House." Stanley I. Kutler, *The Wars of Watergate* 218 (1990).

[58] *White House Transcripts of 3 Nixon–Haldeman Conversations on June 23, 1972*, N.Y. Times, Aug. 6, 1974, at A14.

Campaign Activities became one of the key events in the Watergate story. Anxious that he not be shown to have known anything about the cover-up prior to the elections, Nixon would deny Dean's description of the September conversation, insisting that he knew nothing about the cover-up until March of 1973.[59]

In the short term, however, Dean was good to his word, and Nixon cruised to victory in November, besting McGovern by 23% of the popular vote and carrying 49 states (all but Massachusetts). For several months after the election, the break-in continued to attract very little attention of the press or the public. Even the continuing forward movement of the criminal justice process failed to stimulate renewed interest. In January 1973, the seven individuals charged in connection with the break-in went on trial in Judge John Sirica's courtroom in the Federal District Court for the District of Columbia. In opening the trial, Judge Sirica expressed the hope that testimony will bring to light the full range of those implicated in the break-in,[60] but this was not to be. Five of the seven pled guilty and the other two, Gordon Liddy and James McCord, were convicted after a short trial. No witness testified to any broader conspiracy. At the conclusion of the trial, Judge Sirica remarked, "I am still not satisfied that all the pertinent facts that might be available—I say might be available—have been produced before an American jury."[61]

Just as the trial was winding down, the Congress began to organize its own proceedings. In the same month as the trial, the Senate voted unanimously to authorize a special inquiry into alleged irregularities in the 1972 presidential campaign, including the Watergate break-in. Chaired by Senator Sam Ervin of North Carolina and with Howard Baker of Tennessee as its ranking member, the Senate Select Committee on Presidential Campaign Activities—widely known as either the Ervin Committee or the Watergate Committee—began to gather staff and to prepare for public hearings to be held in the summer of 1973.

Now the tempo of damaging revelations began to accelerate. In March, James McCord delivered a letter to Judge Sirica in advance of sentencing in which he alleged that perjury had been committed during the trial. McCord denied that Watergate was a CIA operation, which many people suspected, but claimed that it did involve high ranking government officials. When the day of the sentencing hearing arrived, Judge Sirica postponed sentencing, and urged the defendants to cooper-

---

[59] *Statement of Richard M. Nixon, President of the United States, Apr. 29, 1974,* reproduced in *Earlier Nixon Statements on Watergate,* N.Y. Times, Aug. 9, 1974, at A15.

[60] Bob Woodward and Carl Bernstein, *Watergate Trial Judge Wants "Exploration",* Wash. Post, Jan. 11, 1973, at A15.

[61] Bob Woodward and Carl Bernstein, *Still Secret: Who Hired Spies and Why,* Wash. Post, Jan. 31, 1973, at A1.

ate with the Senate investigation, telling them that their candor would have a bearing on the severity of the sentences. The import of this extraordinary move by Judge Sirica was lost on no one, including the defendants: it was intended to put pressure on them to reveal the further dimensions of the break-in that the trial had been unable to expose.

Soon thereafter, the Ervin Committee indicated that it intended to ask key White House aides to testify. President Nixon strongly resisted testimony by his aides, claiming a broad testimonial immunity. In a prepared statement for the press, the President declared:

> "Under the doctrine of separation of powers, the manner in which the President personally exercises his assigned executive powers is not subject to questioning by another branch of Government. If the President is not subject to such questioning, it is equally appropriate that members of his staff not be so questioned, for their roles are in effect an extension of the Presidency."[62]

In this same March 13, 1973 statement the President also issued an extended defense of the confidentiality of presidential communications, invoking precedents back to Washington. He asserted that the President must be sole arbiter of executive privilege and pledged that he would not invoke it to block disclosures of criminal wrongdoing or "embarrassing information," but only to prevent disclosures "harmful to the public interest."[63]

Nixon's March 13 statement embraced both a unitary executive position and imperialism. In keeping with the vision of a single President exercising all of the executive power, officials in the executive branch were to be considered simply extensions of the President. The decision whether they should be permitted to talk on any subject hence was the President's to make. In keeping within a strong brand of imperialism, that decision was absolute, not subject to review by anyone else. These two essential prongs of the President's position—that the decision was his and was unreviewable—would be developed and refined as the controversies over the White House tape recordings proceeded, eventually becoming the organizing principles for Nixon's defense in the Supreme Court, but the core claims were clearly laid out early on in the March 13 statement. A month later, Attorney General Kleindienst amplified both points. In testimony before a Senate subcommittee, Kleindienst stated that under the Constitution the President could order *any* member of the executive branch to refuse information to the Congress. This prompted Senator Muskie to ask, rather incredulously, if he had heard

---

[62] Pub. Papers 160 (Mar. 13, 1973).

[63] *Id.*

the Attorney General correctly. "This Congress, in your view," Muskie asked, "has no power to command the production of testimony or information by anyone in the executive branch under any circumstances?" None, Kleindienst replied, "[y]our power to get what the President knows is in the President's hands."[64]

These two statements from Kleindienst and Nixon left no doubt as to how much President Nixon's view of executive privilege been had been transformed from the view of Congressman Nixon. Then, Nixon had strenuously protested Truman's decision to deny HUAC access to government personnel files. "I say that [the] proposition [that the President has a right to withhold information from the Congress] cannot stand from a constitutional point of view," Nixon had said. "That would mean that the President could have arbitrarily issued an Executive order in ... any ... case denying the Congress of the United States information it needed to conduct an investigation of the executive department and the Congress would have no right to question his decision."[65] Now, President Nixon embraced the position he had criticized Truman for holding.

Some members of the Ervin Committee were eager to challenge President Nixon's stance on testimonial immunity,[66] despite the President's considerable support on his side of the aisle, reflecting the fact that Nixon had just won an electoral landslide and remained the undisputed leader of his party. At the same time, though, there was no love lost in the relationship between members of Congress (on both sides of the aisle) and Nixon's aides, who were widely viewed as arrogant and condescending. Commenting on the prospects of Nixon's aides facing subpoenas and possibly contempt citations, one Republican Senator observed that "it couldn't happen to a better bunch of guys."[67]

April of 1973 proved to be a very bad month for the President and the cover-up efforts. News leaked out that James McCord was cooperating the Ervin Committee investigators, providing particulars as to the roles of former Attorney General John Mitchell as well as of important Nixon aides, including John Dean, Jeb Magruder, and Charles Colson.[68] Just as importantly, the Senate Judiciary Committee held hearings in

---

[64] *Executive Privilege, Secrecy in Government, Freedom of Information: Hearings before the S. Subcomm. on Intergovernmental Relations*, 93d Cong., 1st Sess., vol. I, 20, 45, 51 (Apr. 10, 1973) (statement of Richard Kleindienst, Att'y Gen. of the United States).

[65] 84 Cong. Rec. H4783 (1948).

[66] Stanley I. Kutler, *The Wars of Watergate* 290 (1990).

[67] *Defying Nixon's Quest for Power*, Time, Apr. 16, 1973, *available at* http://www.time.com/time/magazine/article/0,9171,878518–4,00.html.

[68] Stanley I. Kutler, *The Wars of Watergate* 290 (1990).

late March and April on the confirmation of Patrick Gray to be the new FBI director. Gray had been acting director since J. Edgar Hoover's death the year before. In his testimony Gray revealed that he had been in close contact with the White House throughout the Watergate investigation, providing Dean with regular updates on the progress of the investigation that (we now know) Dean and others in the White House were trying to obstruct. Senators on the Judiciary Committee warned the President that unless White House aides testified to explain their roles, Gray's nomination was doomed. This apparently suited Nixon, who had lost faith in Gray's ability to be a total team player and was no longer interested in having him become FBI director. As Ehrlichman famously described it, the White House would let Gray "twist slowly in the wind."

Gray ended up withdrawing his nomination on April 5, but the damage had been done. His testimony placed enormous pressure on President to permit his aides to testify in some forum about the Watergate affair. Meanwhile, Gray's testimony, McCord's cooperation and other leads were pointing Henry Peterson, who was the Assistant Attorney General of the Department of Justice's criminal division and in charge of the investigation, toward former Attorney General Mitchell (who headed Nixon's Committee to Re-elect) and then onto Dean, Haldeman and Ehrlichman. The White House aides attempted to make Mitchell the fall guy, hoping both to stop the unraveling of the conspiracy short of them and also to encourage Peterson to urge Ervin not to press for their testimony, lest it interfere with the criminal investigation. Soon, though, the President came to realize that the taint surrounding Watergate would continue to blanket the White House as long as the implicated aides remained there. In separate meetings, he told each of them that they must resign, and on April 27, Dean, Haldeman, and Ehrlichman did so. Attorney General Kleindienst resigned on the same day, having independently become convinced that the investigation's turn toward his old friend and boss Mitchell was bringing the investigation too close to him for him to remain effective.

These developments helped make April 1973 a turning point in the road leading to *United States v. Nixon* and the President's resignation. Key evidence suggesting Oval Office obstruction of justice had surfaced. The President had taken drastic measures to try to prevent the scandal from reaching him, firing two of his closest and most important aides and attempting to deflect all the responsibility onto his old friend and former law partner, John Mitchell. The pressures of the April developments finally forced Nixon's hand in two additionally important ways. First, he agreed to the appointment of a special prosecutor, which he had been resisting. Second, he permitted his aides, former and current, to testify before the Ervin Committee. Even these desperate moves did not come in time to save Nixon from slipping badly in the polls. Early April Gallup polls showed a 59% approval rating, but by early May this was down to 44%. What is more, these concessions served only to accelerate the investigations into White House activities.[69]

The President nominated Elliot Richardson to replace Kleindienst as attorney general. During his confirmation hearings, Richardson pledged to appoint a special prosecutor and to ensure the prosecutor's independence, including his ability to contest assertions of executive privilege should they be raised. Richardson appointed as special prosecutor Harvard Law Professor Archibald Cox, Richardson's former teacher. The selection of a special prosecutor was a set back for Henry Peterson and the career professionals in the Justice Department's criminal division, who had been pursuing the case conscientiously and in fact had amassed, collated and organized a wealth of information that would prove invaluable to the special prosecutor's new team. The appointment also did not sit well with Nixon, who although publicly greeting the selection with warm approval, was wary because Cox was closely identified with Nixon's old nemesis, the Kennedy family, particularly Senator Ted Kennedy.[70]

While Richardson's confirmation hearings were going on, the Ervin Committee began it hearings into irregularities in the 1972 presidential election. On the opening day, Baker asked his famous question, "What did the president know and when did he know it?" At the time, Baker intended the question as a defense of the President, using it to highlight the fact that no one had yet testified in any proceeding as to any personal involvement by the President in any of the events prior to the break-in or afterwards.

In June, 1973, Dean took the stand to answer Senator Baker's question, becoming the star witness of the proceedings. Over the span of a week, Dean testified in great detail about activities within the White House, exposing the existence of the "enemies list," discussing ways in which the White House used the IRS and the FBI to harass political opponents or members of the press, detailing efforts that he and others made to cover up the break-in, and reporting about his conversations with the President. He testified in particular about the September 15,

---

[69] The unraveling of the Nixon presidency proceeded along more fronts than can be discussed in this chapter. Significant collateral investigations were going on into the Justice Department's settlement of the ITT anti trust case, into allegations that Nixon backdated a deed in order to gain tax deductions, into the plea bargains and trials of second-or third-tier White House or campaign personnel as well as into other matters. Again, there are numerous more detailed accounts of these additional matters. *E.g.*, Stanley I. Kutler, *The Wars of Watergate* 349 (1990) (six committees of Congress investigating these various accusations).

[70] Stanley I. Kutler, *The Wars of Watergate* 330 (1990).

1972 briefing he gave the President on cover-up efforts, which the President subsequently denied. Dean's week of testimony was devastating, but it remained a case of he-said-he-said. On July 9, 1973, *Time* magazine published with a cover saying, "Can Nixon Survive Dean?" Formulating this as a question comported with the views of many that the answer remained open, as many Nixon's supporters continued to think that a wounded Nixon could nonetheless survive.

Litigation Over the Tapes

Time's question might have been more to the point if it had asked, "Can Nixon Survive Butterfield?" On July 16, Alexander Butterfield dropped the biggest bombshell of the Ervin Committee proceedings when he disclosed the existence of a taping system in the Oval Office. Now all attention focused on the tapes. The country immediately grasped their import, as reflected in a New York Times editorial on July 18: "Suddenly and unexpectedly, instead of being forced into an unsatisfactory judgment of one man's word against another's, the American public has learned of specific evidence which could establish what Mr. Nixon knew and when he knew it."[71] That same day, an op-ed put the President's predicament succinctly:

> "[T]he President finds himself in an impossible situation. The tapes must be in some way incriminating. Otherwise, it is hard to believe that the White House would not have made them available immediately after Mr. Dean's testimony and thereby delivered a crushing unanswerable rebuttal."[72]

The same op-ed then uncannily anticipated the eventual end game when it speculated about what might happen it the President refuses to deliver the tapes:

> But would the Supreme Court uphold a claim of absolute privilege when the documents in question may be evidence of a crime? It is absurd to contend that litigation over this question must be tied up in the courts for years. When the issue is of overriding importance the Supreme Court can act promptly.[73]

Special Prosecutor Cox followed up quickly on Butterfield's revelations. He secured a grand jury subpoena on July 23, seeking specific conversations that Dean had referred to in his testimony, after negotiations with Nixon's lawyer, Charles Alan Wright, failed to produce them voluntarily. The Ervin Committee also issued its own subpoenas.

---

[71] *The Nixon Tapes*, N.Y. Times, July 18, 1973, at A36.

[72] William H. Shannon, *The Dangling Man*, N. Y. Times, July 18, 1973, at A37.

[73] *Id.*

The President attempted to quash the Cox subpoena. In a letter to Cox, Charles Alan Wright stated the President's position:

> It is for the President and only for the President to weigh whether the incremental advantage that these tapes would give you in criminal proceedings justifies the serious and lasting hurt that disclosure of them would do to the confidentiality that is imperative to the effective functioning of the Presidency. In this instance the President has concluded that it would not serve the public interest to make the tapes available.[74]

As with the President's earlier defense of testimonial immunity for his aides, Wright's position contained both a unitary executive and an imperialist inflection. The unitary executive claim was directed at Cox, and anticipated the position that would be developed more fully as the legal contest over the tapes developed: that the question of whether or not the public interest is best served by disclosure, *insofar as it is a disagreement between Cox and Nixon*, is a dispute between two executive branch officials and is internal to the executive branch. Such an intra-branch dispute, the President argued, could only be won by one person. The subpoena should be quashed because the President had determined it not to be in the public interest, and that must be the end of the matter. The imperialist element was then directed at the court's power— or, better, its powerlessness—to question the President's choice once it has been made. If accepted, these paired arguments provided a basis to quash the subpoena.

While awaiting a ruling from Judge Sirica, President Nixon held a press conference, at which he stated that he would comply with "a definitive order of the Supreme Court" regarding the tapes.[75] He declined to clarify what characteristics an order would have to possess to be "definitive," despite questioning then and at several subsequent press conferences. Subsequently, Judge Sirica issued an order enforcing the grand jury subpoena for nine specific tapes. The President appealed and the Court of Appeals for the District of Columbia Circuit expedited review. On October 12, in a 5–2 decision, two judges having recused themselves, the court upheld the subpoena.[76]

As a final attempt to resolve the matter in a manner satisfactory to him, Nixon offered to satisfy the subpoena by producing a written transcript whose accuracy would be verified by Senator John Stennis of

---

[74] Water Special Prosecution Task Force, Report 91 (1975).

[75] Richard Nixon, *The President's News Conference of August 22nd, 1973*, The American Presidency Project (John T. Woolley and Gerhard Peters, eds.), http://www.presidency.ucsb.edu/ws/?pid=3937.

[76] Nixon v. Sirica, 487 F.2d 700 (D.C.Cir. 1973).

Mississippi, an old friend of Nixon's. In the course of announcing this proposal, Nixon continued to be defiant regarding his right to protect presidential communications. "I am confident that the dissenting opinions ... would have been sustained upon review by the Supreme Court," he said. "I have concluded, however, that it is not in the national interest to leave this matter unresolved for the period that might be required for a review by the highest court."[77] This remark would later only add to the speculation over the President's willingness to comply with a "definitive" order. If the Supreme Court issued a similarly divided judgment, would the President comply, or would the division in the Court permit the President to say, "I agree with the dissenters?"

Cox and his team did not think much of the Stennis proposal. Over the course of the summer, Nixon had voluntarily released some tapes after making transcripts available, and Cox's team was well aware how inaccurate the transcripts were. (Many of the tapes were of quite poor quality, and Senator Stennis had some hearing loss.) Still, the President had announced the Stennis proposal as his final offer. Exercising his views of unitary executive authority, Nixon directed Richardson to instruct Cox to accept this compromise. When Cox rejected it, Nixon ordered Cox fired. Richardson resigned rather than follow these instructions, feeling himself bound by commitments he had made to the Senate Judiciary Committee during his confirmation hearings. Nixon's order then was directed to Ruckelshaus, but Ruckelshaus reached the same conclusions as had Richardson, and submitted his resignation rather than carry out the President's order. Finally, Solicitor General Robert Bork, the third ranking official in the Department, and now acting Attorney General, carried out the instruction to fire the special prosecutor. This chain of events of Saturday, October 20, immediately became known as the Saturday Night Massacre.

The country, in the words of Al Haig, the new White House chief of staff, reacted in a "firestorm" of protest,[78] forcing the White House to alter course. On October 23, Charles Alan Wright informed Judge Sirica that President would comply fully with the grand jury subpoena. As for the special prosecutor, even "top Republican leaders, who had stood beside the President during the long Watergate crisis, urged him ... to restore public confidence in the investigation by naming a [new] special prosecutor."[79] The President acceded to the demands for a replacement, and by November 1, Leon Jaworski, a partner in a leading Houston law

---

[77] Richard Nixon, *Nixon: Reasonable Proposal for Compromise*, Wash. Post, Oct. 20, 1973, at A8.

[78] Stanley I. Kutler, *The Wars of Watergate* 429 (1990).

[79] Anthony Ripley, *Senate Republican Leaders Ask Nixon to Name New Prosecutor; Impeachment is Widened*, N.Y. Times, Oct. 25, 1973, at A1.

firm, had been selected to replace Cox. Later that month, the subpoenaed tapes were indeed turned over, although not without further
developments embarrassing to the President. The White House had to
inform Judge Sirica that one of the tapes contained a mysterious
eighteen and a half minute gap, which later forensic study concluded was
the product of six distinct erasures. The cause of the erasure was never
found. Nixon's long time secretary, Rose Mary Woods, took responsibility, claiming the erasure was accidental.

The impeachment inquiry that had been proceeding informally in
the House Judiciary Committee quickened its pace after the Saturday
Day Night Massacre. The House formally authorized the House Judiciary Committee in February of 1974 to investigate impeachment charges
against the President, with many believing that the outcome of the
impeachment inquiry hinged on whether the White House tapes were
made public. "The case for or against the president in the arena of
public opinion hinged on what the tapes could show he did or did not
say."[80] Even before the Saturday Night Massacre, 59% of the public
believed that the President knew about the cover-up and 71% thought he
was withholding vital information.[81] Afterwards, 43% thought the President should resign.[82] And yet, the public remained ambivalent about
impeaching a sitting President. As William Greider explained in a
Washington Post op-ed, "the public opinion polls have presented a
persistent paradox. A growing majority has disapproved of Mr. Nixon's
performance considering him guilty of one thing or another, and would
like him out of office. Yet only a fraction has favored impeachment ...
talk about removing him or putting him on trial summons up deep,
unspoken feelings."[83]

Before Jaworski agreed to take the job as special prosecutor, he and
congressional leaders insisted on even greater assurances of independence in the investigation than Cox had been given. In an effort to give
them, Acting Attorney General Robert Bork issued several pronouncements, which were placed in the Federal Register. These gave the special
prosecutor "full authority for investigating and prosecuting offenses
against the United States arising out of the unauthorized entry into the
Democratic National committee Headquarters at the Watergate,"[84] and

---

[80] Stanley I. Kutler, *The Wars of Watergate* 441 (1990).

[81] UNC Odum Institute for Research in the Social Sciences, Harris Survey No. 2344
(Aug. 1973).

[82] UNC Odum Institute for Research in the Social Sciences, Harris Survey No. 7483
(Mar. 1974).

[83] William Greider, *Nixon's Fate and Ours: The Fear of Following the Leader*, Wash.
Post, Mar. 3, 1974, at B1.

[84] 38 Fed. Reg. 30738–9 (Nov. 2, 1973).

further provided that the special prosecutor "will not be removed from his duties except for extraordinary improprieties on his part and not without the President's first consulting the majority and minority leaders and the chairmen and ranking minority members of the Judiciary Committees of the Senate and the House of Representatives and ascertaining that their consensus is in accord with his proposed action."[85]

As Jaworski and the grand jury continued with the criminal investigation, Nixon assured the public that he was cooperating fully. For some time after the events of October 20, the criminal investigation front in the President's "epic battle" remained comparatively quiet. That quiet ended on March 1, 1974, when the grand jury indicted Colson, Ehrlichman, Haldeman, Mardian, Parkinson and Strachan, all former key aides, as well as former Attorney General Mitchell, charging them with conspiracy to obstruct justice and other offenses. Unknown to the public at the time, the grand jury had named Nixon as an unindicted coconspirator. By now, twice as many people believed John Dean's Senate testimony than the President's protestations of cooperation and innocence.[86]

The indictments turned impeachment into a real possibility. "Up to now," Joseph Kraft wrote, "most of the Congress has tended to regard Watergate as a media event. But criminal indictments, as Dr. Johnson once said about the prospect of hanging, tend to concentrate the mind. As never before, Republicans now see that association with the administration is politically disastrous, while Democrats sense an enormous opportunity in taking on the President. Thus the odds on impeachment have shifted dramatically."[87]

On April 16, 1974, Jaworski issued a trial subpoena pursuant to Fed. R. Crim. Proc. 17(c) for the tapes of sixty-four additional conversations. Jaworski's subpoena *duces tecum* included an appendix individually detailing the trial relevance of each conversation, contending that there was prima facie evidence that they would reveal aspects of a conspiracy to obstruct justice. Among the subpoenaed conversations were the "smoking gun" conversations between the President and Haldeman on June 23, 1972. Jaworski's subpoena came one week after the House Judiciary Committee issued its own subpoena for its own set of conversations, including many sought by Jaworski. The near-contemporaneous issuance of parallel subpoenas made vivid the closely intertwined relationship between the judicial and the House proceedings, and called attention to the fact that, as important and visible as the clash between

---

[85] 38 Fed. Reg. 30739 (Nov. 19, 1973).

[86] UNC Odum Institute for Research in the Social Sciences, Harris Survey No. 5483 (Mar. 1974).

[87] Joseph Kraft, *Impeachment Prospects*, Wash. Post, Mar. 3, 1974, at A21.

the President and the special prosecutor was and would remain, the real danger the President faced came from the Congress.

On April 29, 1974, Nixon responded to the House subpoena by announcing that he would release an edited transcript of some 1300 pages that "include all the relevant portions of all of the subpoenaed conversations that were recorded, that is, all portions that relate to the question of what I knew about Watergate or the cover-up and what I did about it."[88] The transcript release did the President little good. Now a majority of 59% supported impeachment and removal if Congress determined he was involved in the cover-up, and for the first time a plurality (47% to 45%) thought the President should resign.[89]

In May, Judge Sirica held hearings on the subpoena over a several day period. These were closed to the public so that sealed court records could be debated (including whether as a constitutional matter Nixon could be named as an unindicted co-conspirator). In public statements Nixon's new attorney, James St. Clair, refused to answer categorically whether the President would comply with a court order. Newspapers wrote that delay was to the President's advantage, because it would string along the impeachment proceedings, allowing time for some other significant event to take the public's attention away from Watergate.[90]

In the briefs before Judge Sirica, St. Clair vigorously advocated the President's two arguments against compelled disclosure, shaping them into the form they would eventually take before the Supreme Court. The unitary executive claim—that the matter involved an intra-branch dispute between two executive branch officials that the President must win because the Constitution vests him with the executive power—was now framed as an objection to justiciability: there is no judicially cognizable case or controversy when a subordinate officer and the President disagree about where the public interest lies. The imperialist claim was that, even if a court does not accept the first argument, the President must still prevail because his control over confidential presidential communications is absolute.

On May 20, 1974, Judge Sirica issued an opinion and order enforcing the trial subpoena, which the President immediately appealed. Jaworski then sought certiorari in the Supreme Court prior to a court of appeals judgment, a step available under the Supreme Court rules, but

---

[88] Richard Nixon, *The President's News Conference of August 22nd, 1973*, The American Presidency Project (John T. Woolley and Gerhard Peters, eds.), http://www.presidency.ucsb.edu/ws/?pid=3937.

[89] UNC Odum Institute for Research in the Social Sciences, Harris Survey No. 2421 (May 1974).

[90] *E.g.*, Lesley Oelsner, *Time Viewed as Nixon's Biggest Gain in Subpoena Fight*, N.Y. Times, May 9, 1974, at A34.

something that had been successfully done only five times in the nation's history. Signaling their own understanding of the magnitude of the "epic battle," the Justices granted Jaworski's petition.

To help their position in every way possible, the Special Prosecutor's office went to lengths to depict the case as a garden-variety appeal challenging a criminal subpoena by an ordinary federal prosecutor. This included the office's unilateral decision to file their briefs using the distinctive gray cover page reserved for briefs of the United States filed by the Solicitor General, forcing the President's lawyers to take different colors.[91] The extraordinary nature and the broader ramifications of the case were not lost on the Court, however. Even though the parallel impeachment proceedings were never mentioned by the Court in its opinion, without their pendency and a sense of urgency to resolve them there would be nothing about a truly garden-variety challenge to a criminal subpoena that would justify accepting a certiorari petition prior to a judgment in the court of appeals.

Preparing for the Supreme Court show down, Jaworski's team was cautiously optimistic that they could obtain a 5–3 decision in their favor. Due to the President's evasiveness as to what he would consider a "definitive" order, they also worried that this might not be a sufficient victory.[92] Throughout the arguments below as well as in private negotiations, St. Clair had pointedly not taken non-compliance off the table as a possibility.[93]

The stage was now set. With the country fretting over the eventual impeachment actions that might be taken by the House and the Senate, equally fretful over the question of whether the President would comply with an adverse outcome or throw the country into still more uncharted constitutional waters, and anxious generally about the cohesiveness of the social fabric still frayed over Vietnam, domestic violence, civil rights and economic woes, it waited for the Supreme Court to act. Many people thought that the well-being of the country depended on a speedy resolution to the Watergate scandal and the questions surrounding the President's involvement in covering up evidence of criminal behavior relating to attempts to influence the presidential election. In his 1974 State the Union address, Nixon had proclaimed that it was time to move on, that "one year of Watergate is enough." As the country marked the second

---

[91] Phillip Lacovara interview, Nov. 21, 1987, Hofstra University, *quoted in* Howard Ball, *We Have a Duty* 75 (1990).

[92] *Id.*

[93] This hedging carried over to oral argument in the Supreme Court, where St. Clair sparred with Thurgood Marshall over the conditions under which the issue was being submitted to the Court for its resolution. St. Clair declined to state categorically that the President would abide by the Court's decision.

anniversary of the break-in, however, it was deeper into Watergate than ever.

The Supreme Court Decision[94]

The Decision

After granting Jaworski's request for certiorari in advance of judgment, the Supreme Court set a briefing schedule and heard arguments on July 8, 1974. Sixteen days later it handed down a unanimous decision, 8–0, upholding the trial subpoenas.[95] It was clearly a defeat for the President, although not necessarily for the presidency, as we shall see.

The Court first addressed the unitary executive question, now framed as an issue of justiciability. After acknowledging Nixon's claim that this was purely an intra-branch dispute, the Court stated that "[o]ur starting point is the nature of the proceeding for which the evidence is sought."[96] This formulation of a starting point distinctly favored Jaworski, because it depicted the question in terms of the court's competence to decide the validity of a trial subpoena in a criminal case. That was a question federal courts had decided routinely in the course of many federal criminal prosecutions. Jaworski's efforts to frame the case in just that matter-of-fact manner thus had been successful,[97] and the Court found in his favor on this threshold question.

On the question of confidentiality of presidential communications, the Court initially declared that protection for such communications was grounded in the Constitution. In contrast to the justiciability analysis, the advantage now went to the President, for Jaworski had argued that any privilege that the Court might find rested on a common law basis. Throughout the Watergate controversy, however, the President had been asserting constitutional status for a privilege protecting confidential conversations, arguing that this was an imperative in order for the President to receive the full, candid advice that was necessary to discharge his constitutional responsibilities. The Supreme Court agreed. "Human experience teaches," the Court wrote, "that those who expect

---

[94] Note on citations and references in this section: The briefs of the parties and excerpts of the transcript of the oral argument have been reproduced in Leon Friedman, *United States v. Nixon* (1975). When referring to these materials, citations are to the Friedman book.

[95] Associate Justice William Rehnquist recused himself because he had worked closely with several of the defendants in the underlying criminal case while he was in Department of Justice.

[96] United States v. Nixon, 418 U.S. 683, 694–95 (1974).

[97] This is made even clearer in the very next sentence: "It is a judicial proceeding in a federal court alleging violations of the federal laws and it is brought in the name of the United States as sovereign." *Id.* at 695.

public dissemination of their remarks may well temper candor with a concern for appearances and for their own interests to the detriment of the decision making process."[98] "[T]he privilege," it continued, "can be said to derive from the supremacy of each branch within its own assigned areas of constitutional duties. Certain powers and privileges flow from the nature of enumerated powers; the protection of the confidentiality of Presidential communications has similar constitutional underpinnings."[99]

Having recognized the privilege's constitutional grounding, however, the Court's answer to the next critical question—how the privilege is to be defined—was not at all to the President's liking. The Court declined to give the privilege an imperialist interpretation. The President's interest in confidentiality deserved recognition, but in this case there was a countervailing interest in disclosure, namely the integrity of a criminal proceeding and the public's claim to "every man's evidence."[100] One interest must be balanced against the other and, crucially, it was the proper role of the federal courts to perform that balance. Under the facts presented, the Court concluded that disclosure of presidential confidences on the infrequent occasions when such communications are directly relevant to a criminal proceeding, satisfying the subpoena requirements of Rule 17(c), would not cause advisors so to temper their candor as to tip the balance in the President's favor. Hence, the President's "generalized interest in confidentiality . . . cannot prevail over the fundamental demands of due process of law in the fair administration of criminal justice."[101] The Court then added that the outcome would be different had the circumstances included "a claim of need to protect military, diplomatic, or sensitive national security secrets,"[102] despite the fact that no one had claimed that the particular assertion of privilege in *Nixon* itself rested on any such claim of need.

Assessing the Court's Work

When momentous decisions such as *United States v. Nixon* reach the Supreme Court, the Court itself often must seek to reconcile two different dimensions of its function. On the one hand, it faced significant and difficult legal issues, the resolution of which will affect how future disagreements of like type will be resolved. In this instance, conflicts between the President and the other branches of government over

---

[98] *Id.* at 705.

[99] *Id.* at 705–06.

[100] *Id.* at 409, *quoting* Branzburg v. Hayes, 408 U.S. 665, 688 (1972).

[101] *Id.* at 713.

[102] *Id.* at 706.

disclosure of information were certain to recur. As a court of law, then, the Court needed to make hard legal judgments and to declare "what the law is."[103] On the other hand, cases such as *Nixon* also implicate questions of governance. The entire country was anxious about the Watergate situation and how it would be resolved, and for good reason. The Court's action was certain to play a pivotal role in a course of events having potentially much greater consequences for the country than simply resolving the legal issues presented by the case. The House impeachment proceedings would be greatly affected by how the Court dealt with the criminal subpoena, and consequently the fate of the Presidency and to some extent the well-being of the country were in the balance, too. The Justices were quite aware of the spotlight shining on them, and they were just as aware of the facts that had been revealed so far about the cover-up and the President's involvement in it. They felt and accepted what can only be described as a governance responsibility, a responsibility to help stabilize and lead the country through a difficult period in its history.

There was no way to ignore either of these two dimensions, even if the Justices had been so inclined. In responding to each of them, the Court perforce had to fold its responses into a single instrument, namely the decision that it rendered. In the case of *United States v. Nixon*, there were a number of junctures at which the legal decisions the Court made were evidently influenced by their sense of governance responsibility.

The first evidence of this influence came in the Court's decision to accept the expedited petition for certiorari. As already suggested, were the proceedings below an ordinary trial for obstruction of justice or even much more serious charges, there would have been no justification for doing this. Much of the conversation in the initial conference focused on the importance to the country of taking the case. Justice Brennan's notes report that although only he and Marshall initially favored expedited action, the others eventually saw that "after two years of Watergate, it was time the nation had access to the evidence that would reveal the truth about Watergate."[104] The "truth" about Watergate could only have been a reference to the truth about the President's involvement. That truth was not directly relevant to Judge Sirica's trial, because Nixon had not been indicted. It was clearly relevant, however, to the House impeachment inquiry, which was considering an obstruction of justice article of impeachment. The Court's sense of urgency thus had less to do with the judicial proceedings below, and a great deal to do with the House impeachment proceedings.

---

[103] Marbury v. Madison, 5 U.S. (1 Cranch) 137 (1803).

[104] Letter from William Brennan to Howard Ball, *quoted in* Howard Ball, *We Have a Duty* 88 (1990).

The Justices were fully aware of those House proceedings. Even if they had not been, St. Clair had made a point of bringing them front and center in oral argument, using them as the basis for asserting both that the Court was entering into a political thicket by adjudicating the privilege claim with impeachment looming, as well as asserting that the Congressional venue was the constitutionally preferable forum to resolve these issues. This latter point prompted an exchange with Justice Marshall:

> Justice Marshall: How are you going to impeach him if you don't know about it? [i.e., If Congress is also barred by executive privilege from securing the necessary evidence.]

> Mr. St. Clair: Well, if you know about it, then you can state the case. If you don't know about it, you don't have it.

> Justice Marshall: So there you are. You're on the prongs of a dilemma, huh?

> Mr. St. Clair: No, I don't think so.

> Justice Marshall: If you know the President is doing something wrong, you can impeach him, but the only way you can find out is this way; you can't impeach him, so you don't impeach him. You lose me some place along there.

> [Laughter][105]

The Justices thus were keenly aware that how they decided this dispute between Jaworski and Nixon, in the context of a subpoena *duces tecum*, would have a profound impact on the House proceedings, and eventually the Senate trial, if it came to that. It could not have benefited Nixon's prospects in the Supreme Court that the Justices had by this time read the sealed portions of the grand jury record upon which Jaworski's Rule 17(c) had been based, which were very damning for the President. They all must have either believed the President to have had early involvement in the cover-up conspiracy or believed that there was an excellent chance that this was so. If this were so, furthermore, it would mean that the President had lied on a number of occasions in addresses to the American people and in statements to the press. To be sure, it might have been difficult under any circumstances to persuade the Supreme Court of the President's strong theories of presidential authority, but with the mindset the Justices must have had about the underlying behavior of the President, it proved to be impossible.

The impeachment proceedings and the political context of which they were a part may have also exerted subtler effects on how the

---

[105] Transcript of Oral Argument in *United States v. Nixon, reprinted in* Leon Friedman, *United States v. Nixon* 579–80 (1975).

decision in *United States v. Nixon* was written. The Justices had concerns about how their decision would be received by elected officials in Washington, as well as by the President himself. Although Nixon's public opinion ratings were dismal, the plurality of people unqualifiedly favoring impeachment was still narrow, and Nixon retained some staunch support among Republican members of the House and Senate on the ultimate question of his being removed from office. His defenders continued to protest that the impeachment proceedings were being driven by partisan politics. In that environment, a decision in which the Court overtly referred to the impeachment proceedings, or one that recited damaging facts about the President's apparent culpability in order to justify its outcome might itself have been vulnerable to the charge that it was politically motivated.[106] That in turn could have formed part of the basis for the President declining to comply with the court order, an option that still seemed very much a live possibility at the time.

The Supreme Court's opinion seemed designed to skirt these pitfalls. The sole mention of the Congress appears in a footnote in which the Supreme Court says its decision focuses exclusively on balancing the competing claims of the presidency and judiciary.[107] No explicit mention at all is made of how the Court's analysis might translate to the congressional-executive arena, where the vast majority of such disclosure disputes arise. No mention, either, is made of Watergate or the long saga of attempts to determine what the President knew and when he knew it. The crimes of which the defendants are accused are described in the most generic ways possible. Someone reading the opinion without independent knowledge of the political controversy swirling around the tapes would have no idea that this was a case about a President thought by many to himself be guilty of obstruction of justice and other abuses of power, facing a Congress poised to impeach him.

The urge to write such an antiseptic opinion may well have influenced more than the rhetoric of the decision. It might have influenced the decision's substance as well, especially the nature of the test announced by the Court for when a "presumptively valid" assertion of privilege might be overcome by opposing public interest claims. Jaworski's brief had offered the court a narrow exception to executive privilege. The special prosecutor had argued that when there was a "prima facie showing that the officials participating in the deliberations did so as

---

[106] *See, e.g.*, Paul J. Mishkin, *Great Cases and Soft Law: A Comment on* United States v. Nixon, 22 UCLA L. Rev. 76 (1974) (exploring this possibility and its consequences for the way the opinion was written).

[107] *Nixon*, 418 U.S. at 712 n.19 (1974) ("[W]e are not here concerned with the balance between the President's generalized interest in confidentiality ... and congressional demands for information.").

part of a continuing criminal plan ... the President is foreclosed from invoking a privilege that exists only to protect and promote the legitimate conduct of the Nation's affairs."[108] Jaworski was suggesting that conversations that were themselves a part of an ongoing conspiracy could not be protected by executive privilege, just as they are not protected under other privileges, such as attorney-client. President Nixon himself had earlier acknowledged that he would only assert executive privilege to protect communications with respect to the official duties of the President and not to conceal evidence of wrongdoing. Thus deciding the case on the narrow grounds offered by Jaworski ought ordinarily to have had some considerable appeal, and in any other context, one might have anticipated that the Court would accept the invitation to create a narrow exception to a constitutional privilege, one just sufficient to decide the case before it. Reciting facts in the opinion to show that a prima facie case of relevance had been established would, however, have required stating the evidence that tended to show the President engaging in a criminal conspiracy. This could be interpreted by the President's supporters as a partisan jab. Instead, the vague balancing test that the Court announced required no such specificity, but it also set a much lower bar for overcoming a claim of privilege than the resolution of this particular dispute required.

The Court's justiciability holding may also been influenced by the Justices' sense of the significance of their role in responding to the needs of the country, which required them to reach the merits. The Court concluded that President was bound by the Department of Justice regulations that acting Attorney General Bork had issued, ensuring the independence of Jaworski, which remained in effect. Because Jaworski had not been fired in accordance with the procedures set forth in the Federal Register, he remained competent to represent the interests of the United States. For this reason, he was a proper party before the Court, and the contest between the special prosecutor and the President was justiciable.

This formulation of the justiciability question, however, failed to confront the most persuasive version of the President's argument. Regardless of whether the Special Prosecutor remained a federal employee and had not been discharged, President Nixon was raising a claim about who precisely within the executive branch had the final say in a dispute between two executive branch officials as to what the executive interests of the United States were. As William Van Alstyne ably expressed the point shortly after the decision,[109] once it was accepted that the interest

---

[108] Brief of the United States in *United States v. Nixon, reprinted in* Leon Friedman, *United States v. Nixon* 224 (1975).

[109] William Van Alstyne, *A Political and Constitutional Review of* United States v. Nixon, 22 UCLA L. Rev. 116, 121–22 (1974).

being represented by Jaworski was an executive interest, "the court should have deferred to the superior executive authority of the President of the United States: The President had made it plain that he did not believe any executive interest would be advanced by issuance of the subpoena, and there simply was no other interest whatever to serve as a basis for issuing that subpoena.... The issue is not at all whether the President ... might delegate some portion of the executive power.... [T]he existence of an outstanding and unrevoked agency is in no sense inconsistent with the executive superiority of the President when a district court is confronted with conflicting assertions of what constitutes *the* executive interest in a given case."[110]

The Continuing Significance of the Decision

The immediate impact of *United States v. Nixon* could hardly have been more dramatic and significant. In the days after the decision, President Nixon sequestered himself in the White House, contemplating his options while the country held its breath to see whether the President would comply with the Supreme Court's mandate to release the tapes. Meanwhile, during the evening of the day the decision was handed down, the House Judiciary Committee convened to continue its impeachment inquiry, which had moved to considering specific articles of impeachment.[111] Three days later it voted, 27–11, to approve an article based on obstruction of justice.[112] On July 30, it approved a second article predicated on abuse of power, 28–10,[113] followed the next day by a third for failure to turn over to the Committee materials subpoenaed as part of its impeachment inquiry, this time by a nearly party-line vote of 21–17.[114] Public and congressional Republican support had nearly entirely slipped away from the President by this time, and on August 5, the President ended the national suspense by releasing the tapes. Transcripts of the crucial conversations were printed verbatim in papers throughout the country, including the conversations with Haldeman on June 23, 1972. They confirmed people's worst beliefs about the President's involvement in the obstruction of justice. Three days later Richard Nixon became the first and only President of the United States to resign from office. Had the Supreme Court ruled in favor of the Presi-

---

[110] Alexander Bickel had made a similar argument in an op-ed after Judge Sirica had dismissed the justiciability concerns. *See* Alexander Bickel, *Mr. Jaworski's Quarrel with Mr. Nixon*, N.Y. Times, May 23, 1974, at A41.

[111] *See* Stanley I. Kutler, *The Wars of Watergate* 516–26 (1990).

[112] *Id.* at 526.

[113] *Id.* at 529.

[114] *Id.* at 529.

dent, or even if there had been a significant dissent, the path of this history would have been quite different.

Beyond its immediate consequences for the public career of Richard Nixon, the decision has also had important implications for both the institution of the Special Prosecutor and the Presidency. For the Special Prosecutor, when the Court ratified Jaworski's authority to stand before the Court to represent the prosecutorial position in the case, it helped pave the way for the Ethics in Government Act of 1978,[115] which institutionalized an office of special prosecutor. *Nixon* did not resolve the constitutional doubts surrounding such a position—these would later be faced by the Supreme Court in *Morrison v. Olson*[116]—but a contrary ruling on the justiciability of the intra-branch dispute between Jaworski and the President would have called a statutory special prosecutor's office into considerable doubt at the outset.[117]

The implications of the case for the institution of the Presidency were more complex. *Nixon* ratified the authority of the special prosecutor to assert a position in court directly contrary to the instructions of the President. That ruling might have been expected to have implications for the issue raised by the theory of the unitary executive, namely the extent of the President's authority under the Constitution to control the acts of subordinates in the executive branch. To the contrary, the ruling failed to resolve any significant questions about that authority, which continues to be a source of disagreement between the President and Congress. For instance, when Congress enacted measures that purport to grant subordinate executive branch officials the right to convey information directly to Congress without the approval of their superiors, President George W. Bush objected on presidential power grounds. After the Congressional Research Service (CRS) concluded that executive branch superiors "do not have the right to prevent or prohibit their officers or employees ... from presenting information to the United States Congress ... concerning relevant policy issues,"[118] President Bush's Office of Legal Counsel (OLC) offered the administration's perspective. OLC contended that "Congress may not bypass the procedures the President establishes to authorize the disclosure to Congress of classified and other privileged information by vesting lower-level employ-

---

[115] Ethics in Government Act, Pub. L. No. 95–521, tit. VI, 92 Stat. 1324, 1867–73 (1978).

[116] 487 U.S. 654 (1987).

[117] For more on *Morrison v. Olson*, see Chapter 11 in this volume.

[118] Memorandum for Honorable Charles Rangel, House Committee on Ways and Means, from Jack Maskell, Legislative Attorney, American Law Division, Congressional Research Service, Re: Agency Prohibiting a Federal Officer from Providing Accurate Cost Information to the United States Congress 1–2 (Apr. 26, 2004).

ees with a right to disclose such information to Congress without authorization."[119]

In this dispute, *Nixon's* holding that Jaworski could prosecute the case against the President was not cited by either CRS or OLC. *Nixon* has not had any influence in this and similar disputes because the Court relied upon the existence of executive branch regulations restricting the conditions under which the special prosecutor could be removed from office, and did not directly confront the question of who should prevail when the President and a subordinate in the executive branch disagree over where the interests of the executive branch lie in the absence of such a delegation within the executive branch. President Nixon would have been in a better position to press the unitary executive issue if he had directed the Attorney General to rescind the regulations, but without that having been done, the Court was able to treat the matter as one of the executive branch being required to follow its own procedures until they were changed.

Even though *Nixon* was not cited at all by CRS or OLC, another holding in the decision was quite relevant to their disagreement, and very much influenced the content of their exchange. *Nixon's* holding that executive privilege enjoys a constitutional status forms the foundation for executive branch arguments that the privilege can trump statutory law. Thus, in resisting the right to disclose provision that Congress had enacted, OLC grounded its objection on the claim that "statutes may not override the constitutional doctrine of executive privilege, [therefore] they may not act to prohibit the supervision of the disclosure of any privileged information, be it classified, deliberative process or other privileged material."[120] *Nixon* is, of course, the seminal judicial decision upon which this position is based.

Presidents beginning with George Washington have claimed the right to preserve the confidentiality of some communications and information.[121] Prior to the Supreme Court's decision in *Nixon*, however, the legal status—as well as the appropriate boundaries—of that right had remained in doubt throughout the country's entire history. If the privilege were ultimately grounded solely in the common law, Congress would

---

[119] Letter Opinion for the General Counsel Department of Health and Human Services, from Jack L. Goldsmith III, Assistant Attorney General, Office of Legal Counsel, Re: Authority of Agency Officials to Prohibit Employees from Providing Information to Congress (May 21, 2004), *available at* http://www.usdoj.gov/olc/crsmemoresponsese.htm.

[120] *Id.*

[121] *See, e.g.*, Archibald Cox, *Executive Privilege*, 122 U. Pa. L. Rev. 1383, 1395–1405 (1979). For a general history of executive privilege, but focusing on the Nixon presidency forward, see Mark J. Rozell, *Executive Privilege: Presidential Powers, Secrecy, and Accountability* (2d ed. rev. 2002).

be able to enact legislation revising it or even eliminating it, just as it could with respect to any other common law right. Even in the absence of such legislation, were the privilege grounded only in the common law, Congress could claim that its own constitutionally recognized powers of investigation permit it to decide on a case-by-case basis whether to accept a claim of privilege.[122] If, on the other hand, the privilege is grounded in the Constitution, there are limits to the powers that Congress can claim to have, either legislatively or by virtue of its own case-by-case determinations, to overcome an assertion of privilege.[123] The constitutional status of the privilege also lends weight to unitary executive claims such as those raised during the right to disclose debate, because the President can claim at least a certain degree of vertical control within the executive branch is necessary to make the right to withhold information effective.

In providing this constitutional foundation for executive privilege, *Nixon* has profoundly shaped the struggles over executive privilege between congress and the executive. This continues to be the decision's most significant feature. The balancing approach the Court used to determine the scope of the privilege has also had an important corollary role in framing those struggles. That the privilege is constitutional has meant that Congress is not able to overcome it by asserting its investigative authority or legislating the privilege away. That assessing any particular claim of privilege requires a balancing of the competing interests of the two branches has meant that the executive branch has been unable simply to stiff-arm congressional inquiries and requests for information. The result has been a situation that is untidy from a strictly legal point of view. Because it limited itself so carefully to considering the balance between judicial interests and those of the executive, *Nixon* has next to nothing to say about how conflicts between Congress and the President ought to be resolved. In the years since the

---

[122] *See, e.g.*, CRS Congressional Oversight Manual, CRS Order Code RL30240 (Updated Jan. 3, 2007) at 46 ("Although there has never been a definitive Supreme Court ruling on the question, the strong constitutional underpinnings of the legislative investigative power, long-standing congressional practice, and recent appellate court rulings casting doubt on the viability of common-law privilege claims by executive officials in the face of grand jury investigations, support the position that committees may determine, on a case-by-case basis, whether to accept claims of privilege.").

[123] It may be that neither Congress nor the Executive should accept the Court's interpretation of executive privilege as authoritative for purposes of their own inter-branch disagreements. The idea that as co-equal branches of government these two branches have their own authority to develop constitutional meaning within their own spheres has been much debated in recent years. For a review of that debate, see Dawn E. Johnsen, *Functional Departmentalism and Nonjudicial Interpretation: Who Determines Constitutional Meaning?*, 67 Law & Contemp. Probs. 105 (2004). As a practical matter, both Congress and the Executive appear to accept the constitutional status of the privilege as it was announced in *United States v. Nixon*.

decision, the Court has not re-entered the congressional-executive privilege field.[124]

While legally untidy, the decision fares better when appreciated as an exercise in the management of our political system. *United States v. Nixon* has had the effect of committing questions of executive privilege to the other two branches, which are more accustomed and institutionally qualified to address each other's shifting claims, to accept admittedly compromise resolutions and to weigh questions of urgency and priority that are so difficult to make sensibly amenable to judicial resolution. Thus, a decision that was heavily influenced by the Justices' sense of their role as one of the three governing institutions of our federal system, resulting in an opinion that can be questioned as a matter of legal craft, continues to wear well over time as an exercise in the sound stewardship of our system of separation of powers.*

---

[124] Since *United States v. Nixon*, four lower court decisions have directly involved litigation over a request for information by Congress. Three arose out of the same incident, in which the House Committee on Interstate and Foreign Commerce subpoenaed records of AT&T. The Committee was seeking information about a warrantless surveillance program conducted for national security purposes where the FBI had enlisted the cooperation of the telephone company. The United States sued AT&T to prevent its compliance with a committee subpoena. After the district court agreed with the Ford Administration and quashed the subpoena, the court of appeals reversed, upholding the injunction against AT&T compliance, but concluding that separation of powers required the Congress and the executive to accommodate each other's legitimate interests. The court asked the two branches to negotiate to that end, prior to any judicial intervention. Eventually, the Committee became satisfied it had received sufficient information, and the litigation ended without any ruling on the appropriate balance between congressional and executive interests. *See* United States v. AT&T, 419 F. Supp. 454 (D.D.C. 1976); United States v. AT&T, 551 F.2d 384 (D.C. Cir. 1976) and United States v. AT&T, 567 F.2d 121 (D.C. Cir. 1977). In the fourth case, the Department of Justice filed suit against the House of Representatives to have a claim of executive privilege made by EPA Administrator Anne Gorsuch Burford declared valid, and hence to forestall efforts by the House to enforce a subpoena about to be issued against her. United States v. House of Representatives, 556 F.Supp. 150 (D.D.C. 1983). The court refused to reach the merits and, following the *AT&T* precedent, urged the two branches to negotiate their disagreement, with each side accommodating the other's legitimate interests. The subpoena dispute was then resolved without further judicial proceedings.

* My thanks to Ryan Purcell, Duke Law class of 2009, for terrific research assistance, and to the faculty of George Washington University Law School for their comments and suggestions on a preliminary version of this chapter.

*

10

Harold H. Bruff

The Story of *Dames & Moore*: Resolution of an International Crisis by Executive Agreement

All of the images of the Iranian Hostage Crisis were vivid. On November 4, 1979, American television sets carried pictures of blindfolded American Embassy personnel in Tehran, stumbling in the grasp of swarming young Iranians. Before long, ABC's Nightline program featured Ted Koppel with a graphic behind him that counted the days of "America Held Hostage": 100, 200, 300, 400. In April, 1980, news photos showed the charred remains of American airplanes and airmen in a remote Iranian desert, after a failed military attempt to rescue the hostages. Finally, on a cold Inauguration Day in 1981, Ronald Reagan, with his actor's acute sense of timing, announced that the airplane carrying 52 freed Americans was wheels up at Tehran Airport, and the crowd cheered as some shed tears of relief.

Both the genesis and settlement of the Iranian Hostage Crisis had roots in the long and conflicted history of the relationship between two nations embodying the fundamentally different cultures of their peoples. The solution, when it came, was the product of both patient negotiation by diplomats and skilled counseling by lawyers who used every tool available to the Executive Branch of the United States Government. And even when the new President announced the results of a deal with Iran that was the work of his predecessor Jimmy Carter, resolution was not final. The deal was embodied in an "executive agreement," which is a non-treaty agreement between the United States and another nation. These agreements between the Executive Branch and other countries have long existed, but since they exclude the Senate from the partic-

ipation that it would enjoy in approving a treaty, they have always raised
constitutional issues.[1]

Whether such a device could validly settle the outstanding differences between the United States and Iran quickly became the subject of
a litigation that reached the Supreme Court of the United States within
months of the release of the hostages. The case, *Dames & Moore v.
Regan,*[2] upheld the settlement of the crisis by executive agreement. In so
doing, the Supreme Court created an important precedent in American
constitutional and foreign relations law. The decision is also important
for its approach to statutory interpretation. The modern Court had been
working out its approach to the intersection between constitutional and
statutory authority. In *Dames & Moore,* the Court sparked controversy
because it avoided a constitutional ground for decision by upholding
executive action on the basis of a tenuous link to statutory authority. To
understand *Dames & Moore* and its legacy, it is necessary to revisit the
Iranian Hostage Crisis and the legal initiatives that finally resolved it.

Background: Crisis, Negotiation, Resolution

The 1970s witnessed a profound change in the government of Iran,
and in its relationship with the United States.[3] Iran had a long history of
autocratic government under its kings, the shahs, who claimed to embody the ancient traditions of Persia. Constant pressure from Islamic
clerics, who sought political power and wished no separation between
church and state, was constrained by force. The last shah, Mohammed
Reza Pahlavi, was educated in Europe. He ruled uneasily from 1941
until 1979 by building his army and his internal security service (the
infamous SAVAK[4]), and by playing off factions in the nation and in the
parliament, the Majlis. A charismatic and xenophobic Majlis leader,
Mohammed Mossadeq, temporarily overthrew the shah in 1951. But
prompt intervention by the Central Intelligence Agency ousted Mossadeq
and restored the shah. This action bonded the shah to the United
States.[5] Many Iranians would never forgive the United States.

---

[1] *See generally* Louis Henkin, *Foreign Affairs and the United States Constitution* 215–
30 (2d ed. 1996); Lawrence Margolis, *Executive Agreements and Presidential Power in
Foreign Policy* (1986).

[2] 453 U.S. 654 (1981).

[3] For the historical background to the 1979 crisis, see James A. Bill, *The Eagle and the
Lion: The Tragedy of American–Iranian Relations* (1988); Michael Ledeen & William
Lewis, *Debacle: The American Failure in Iran* (1981).

[4] *Sazeman-e Ettela'at va Amniyat-e Keshvar* (National Intelligence and Security Organization).

[5] As President Kennedy would later put it: "He's not much of a shah, but he's our
shah." Michael Ledeen & William Lewis, *Debacle: The American Failure in Iran* 122
(1981).

By the 1970s, the shah faced opposition both from the impoverished masses, who responded to the Islamic fundamentalists, and from an alienated middle class. New revenues from price increases in oil did not find their way to the people. Rather they flowed into massive purchases of arms and other goods from the United States, as the shah sought to overawe his people and to spur the economic development of the nation. Yet the shah lacked the ruthlessness that marked so many twentieth-century rulers. He neither crushed his opposition nor appeased it. The stage was set for revolution.

In 1977, the incoming administration of President Jimmy Carter rejected Nixon–Kissinger realpolitick in favor of a more moralistic foreign policy. President Carter pursued human rights values, as did his Secretary of State, Cyrus Vance, and Vance's deputy, Warren Christopher. The more hawkish National Security Adviser, Zbigniew Brzezinski, was happy to use the new emphasis on human rights to flay the Soviet Union. Before long, the Carter team began pressing Iran to improve its human rights record. The administration was unprepared, however, for the startling events that soon unfolded.

Unrest grew in Iran in 1977–78. Ominously, religious and secular opponents of the regime drew together in an alliance of convenience. The shah, who was dying of cancer, wavered between force and appeasement. From his exile in Paris, Ayatollah Ruhollah Khomeini skillfully managed the opposition. He nurtured a vision, largely unknown to American observers, of a theocratic Iran freed from the unbelievers. Western influences, so visible in Iran, must go, along with the shah's alliance with the United States.

The American government, ambivalent about the shah, watched bemused in early 1979 as the shah fled and Khomeini toppled him. The clerics then began consolidating their power, aided by their revolutionary guards. Khomeini proclaimed an Islamic republic and set out to purify the nation. The United States decided to accommodate itself to the new regime, which was still poorly understood, and to abandon the shah—but not entirely. In late October, he received a visa to enter the United States for medical care.[6] Outrage erupted in Iran, where many feared that the United States planned to repeat the restoration of the shah in the 1950s, destroying the Iranian revolution.

In the predawn hours of November 4, 1979, the Iranian Hostage Crisis began with telephone calls to the State Department from the American Embassy in Tehran, announcing that a large mob of young Iranians, composed of local university students, had stormed the com-

---

[6] Months later, the shah left the United States. After some sad travels, he died in Egypt in July, 1980.

pound and were breaking into the buildings.[7] The Embassy staff soon decided to surrender rather than to resist, in hopes of a rescue by Iranian authorities that never occurred.

It is unclear whether Khomeini knew of the students' intentions in advance. Nevertheless, he speedily blessed the takeover, making the captors official instruments of the Revolution. The students called themselves the "Muslim Student Followers of the Imam's Line at the Den of Espionage." While this moniker may lack the ring of, say, "the Minutemen," it accurately described the two characteristics of the group that would greatly retard solutions to the hostage crisis. First, the students would take direction only from Khomeini and not from any other entity within the Iranian government. Second, in their revolutionary naïveté, they were deeply convinced that the Embassy was a nest of spies who were bent on undoing the Iranian Revolution and who deserved no sympathy.

Although the hostages were adequately fed during their long captivity and were neither tortured nor placed on trial, their treatment was inhumane. They were sometimes bound and blindfolded, constantly subjected to political hectoring about the crimes of the United States in supporting the shah, sometimes beaten (especially for defying or insulting their captors), often placed in solitary confinement in close quarters, and once subjected to a mock execution. Moreover, for fourteen months they lived with constant uncertainty about their ultimate fate. Their courage and endurance were remarkable.

The fate of the hostages soon became a political football in Iran's turbulent politics. The adroit and ruthless Khomeini used the students and the hostages to keep revolutionary ardor high. This enabled him to draw power away from the westernized "moderates" who inhabited the provisional government at the time of the seizure. Within days, that government had resigned, leading to an extended period of reconstituting the Majlis in appropriate post-revolutionary form. Astute observers correctly warned Americans that the United States would not retrieve its hostages as long as their presence served Khomeini's internal purposes, no matter what sanctions we imposed. Iranians addressed America in religious terms, as "the Great Satan." Americans addressed the Iranians in legal terms, calling them international outlaws. A wide gulf required bridging. The U.S. intelligence community could be of little help in that effort. Having relied on the shah for information, it was blinded by the Revolution. The government was also hampered throughout the crisis by

---

[7] For a vivid account of the Iranian Hostage Crisis from the viewpoint of the hostages, see Mark Bowden, *Guests of the Ayatollah: The First Battle in America's War with Militant Islam* (2006). The view from within the United States Government is in Gary Sick's excellent analytic memoir, *All Fall Down: America's Tragic Encounter with Iran* (1986).

the essential difficulty of dealing with any nation that is in the throes of revolutionary turmoil.

The crisis that followed the hostage-taking stretched for an endless 444 days until their release occurred at the sunset of the Carter administration. This period was long enough for the American response to develop several aspects: legal, diplomatic, financial, and military.[8] The President himself closely supervised management of the crisis, never letting it go until his own time to go. Each aspect of the response took prominence at some phase of the crisis.

Within days of the hostage-taking, the Executive Branch realized that Iranian authorities had no intention of intervening to release the captives. The United States imposed economic sanctions on Iran by freezing about $12 billion in Iranian assets held by U.S. banks. Having seized this bargaining chip, the Government also initiated appeals to the International Court of Justice and the United Nations Security Council. The Court issued a judgment that the hostage-taking violated international law, as surely it did, and the Council adopted resolutions calling for the hostages' release.

Protracted and frustrating negotiations ensued via intermediaries who were thought to have some influence in Iran. As shifts of power constantly occurred within an Iran that was still completing its revolution, American negotiators could never be sure who could speak for the Iranian government or who had decisive control of the hostages themselves. Repeatedly, a settlement appeared close at hand. Repeatedly, a statement by Khomeini dashed expectations and sent the negotiators back to try again. Throughout, the United States took the unbending position that it would not address Iranian grievances until the hostages had been freed. By March, 1980, the negotiations had stalled. Another round of economic and diplomatic sanctions ensued.

Throughout the crisis, military options remained on the table. Early on, President Carter had warned Iran that any harm to the hostages or any attempt to put them on trial would trigger a military response. After collapse of the negotiations, the frustrated President authorized an ill-fated military effort to rescue the hostages. This complicated and obviously high-risk airborne and land-based operation turned back before reaching Tehran. It aborted in the Iranian desert after some helicopters became disabled by mechanical malfunctions caused by a dust storm. On departure, an aircraft accident killed eight American servicemen. No Iranians were harmed.

---

[8] For a valuable analysis of the crisis by many of the major participants, see Warren Christopher, Harold H. Saunders, Gary Sick, Robert Carswell, Richard J. Davis, John E. Hoffman, Jr., & Roberts B. Owen, *American Hostages in Iran: The Conduct of a Crisis* (1985).

In the fall of 1980, after the outbreak of its war with Iraq, Iran showed signs of favoring a settlement. In an intense final period of negotiations led by Warren Christopher, the U.S. working groups began preparing the legal and financial elements of a proposed deal that had to meet several main objectives. First, Iran could not be left better off than at the outset of the crisis, lest cries of ransom be heard. Second, the $12 billion in frozen assets had to be movable when and where the settlement demanded. And third, Americans having claims against Iran and its assets had to obtain some means for seeking relief. For this last item, international claims settlement procedures provided a well-trodden path to follow. They were quickly incorporated into American proposals, which called for directing a portion of the frozen assets into an escrow account to satisfy claims.

To gain cooperation from the banks holding Iranian money, the banks were allowed to satisfy loans that Iran owed them out of funds on deposit before transferring the remaining balance. This was a sensitive decision because it placed the banks in a preferred position among creditors. On the other hand, the bank claims were for liquidated amounts, and many other creditors were claiming damages in undetermined amounts. Finally, and perhaps the bitterest pill to swallow, Iran insisted that the United States waive any claims against it by the hostages themselves. Knowing that it was unlikely that freed hostages could bring successful litigation against Iran, the American team included this item, hoping that Congress would attend to the needs of the hostages.

A looming deadline pressed the Iranians to a final decision. The Carter administration notified Iran that on Inauguration Day, its proposals would expire. Then the Iranians could deal with incoming President Reagan, who had been referring to them as "barbarians." An appropriately religious Majlis was finally in place, and Khomeini made a speech outlining the terms of a deal. A final flurry of international communications followed, ending on the morning of Inauguration Day.

The Executive Agreement that ended the crisis was embodied in two declarations by the Government of Algeria (usually called the Algiers Accords), embodying agreements with each contending nation.[9] Algeria served as a very helpful intermediary, because Iran would not deal directly with the United States. Iran released the hostages and the United States returned most of the frozen Iranian funds, but held back $1 billion to form a pool of money to be used by an international arbitral panel to satisfy the outstanding legal claims against Iran. Several hours

---

[9] Declaration of the Government of the Democratic and Popular Republic of Algeria (Algiers Accords), Jan. 19, 1981, Iran–U.S., 20 I.L.M. 224. Implemented in Exec. Orders Nos. 12,276–12,285, 3 C.F.R. 104–18 (1982), *reprinted in* 50 U.S.C. § 1701 at 150–55 (1982). President Reagan ratified the Jan. 19 executive orders on Feb. 24, 1981. Exec. Order No. 12,294, 3 C.F.R. 139–40 (1982), *reprinted in* 50 U.S.C. § 1701 at 155 (1982).

before the inauguration, the last steps occurred: glitches in the financial arrangements were removed and the money flowed into an escrow account at the Bank of England. Half an hour after Reagan took the oath of office, an airplane lifted off at Tehran with the 52 freed Americans aboard. The American negotiators, many of them no longer employed by the Government, went home to sleep for the first time in days.

Legal Advice for the President

From the beginning of the crisis, lawyers assumed a prominent role, for the simple reason that the President needed to know what legal options he possessed. The President's primary legal adviser is the Attorney General of the United States, who since 1789 has been charged with providing legal advice to the President and the heads of cabinet departments.[10] Within the Department of Justice, this function is mostly delegated to the Office of Legal Counsel (OLC), an elite group of about twenty lawyers that includes both expert career lawyers and recent law school graduates gathering experience before commencing other careers.[11] During the Iranian Hostage Crisis, OLC constantly assessed the legality of possible executive initiatives for the Attorney General, the White House, the State Department, and the numerous special groups working on the crisis within the Executive Branch. The advice consisted of formal memoranda responding to requests for the Office's opinion, together with a stream of informal advice provided in letters, meetings, and telephone conversations.[12] President Carter also received advice from the White House Counsel, from the Legal Adviser's office in the State Department, and from the general counsels of other agencies.

Each President assumes a duty to assure the legality of actions he or she proposes to take. As prescribed by the Constitution, the oath of office requires a pledge to "preserve, protect, and defend the Constitution...."[13] Each of the President's lawyers, upon entering the federal

---

[10] 28 U.S.C. §§ 511–12.

[11] During the period of the Iranian Hostage Crisis, I was a Senior Attorney–Adviser in OLC. John Harmon was the Assistant Attorney General in charge of the Office, and his deputies were Larry Hammond, Larry Simms, and Leon Ulman. They were all superb public servants. For analyses of OLC, see Douglas W. Kmiec, *OLC's Opinion Writing Function: The Legal Adhesive for a Unitary Executive*, 15 Cardozo L. Rev. 337 (1993); John O. McGinnis, *Models of the Opinion Function of the Attorney General: A Normative, Descriptive, and Historical Prolegomenon*, 15 Cardozo L. Rev. 375 (1993); Cornelia T.L. Pillard, *The Unfulfilled Promise of the Constitution in Executive Hands*, 103 Mich. L. Rev. 676 (2005).

[12] For a collection of 25 opinions generated by OLC regarding the hostage crisis, see 4A Op. O.L.C. 69–333 (1980). OLC's website is www.usdoj.gov/olc. There are also several other volumes of published OLC opinions in hardcopy.

[13] U.S. Const. art. II, § 1, cl. 8. The full oath is: "I do solemnly swear (or affirm) that I will faithfully execute the Office of President of the United States, and will to the best of my Ability, preserve, protect and defend the Constitution of the United States." *Id.*

service, also pledges to defend the Constitution.[14] Moreover, in representing any client, every lawyer is expected to "exercise independent professional judgment and render candid advice."[15] The President's lawyers must balance these obligations against the incentives they encounter to support the legality of actions that may be intensely desired by the administration.[16] Their detachment is bolstered by the knowledge that the President's claim to receive deference from Congress and the courts for actions taken in the heat of crisis depends on the fact that careful legal analysis has preceded them.

In the Iranian Hostage Crisis, there certainly was a steady flow of legal advice to President Carter. The Executive Branch relied on existing constitutional and statutory authority, and sought no special legislation to authorize its initiatives. Although the administration made careful efforts to keep Congress informed, it feared that seeking new legislation might lead to an uncontrollable reaction within Congress that could hamper the delicate negotiating process. Secretary of State Cyrus Vance later estimated that he and his deputy Warren Christopher spent two hours daily briefing Members of Congress until the crisis was resolved.[17]

Within the Justice Department, OLC found itself responding to constant requests to assess the legality of various options the President had under consideration. These included many options that were eventually rejected, such as rounding up Iranian diplomats to exchange for the hostages or expelling the thousands of Iranian students in the United States to punish Iran. By pointing out the serious legal difficulties attending such steps, OLC successfully deterred their selection. Without specifically addressing the dubious wisdom of these options, OLC reviewed the adverse consequences that would flow from them. Hence, the guidance that the President's lawyers provided steered the policymakers away from options that presented the greatest legal hazards and toward safer choices.

---

[14] 5 U.S.C. § 3331. This statute implements the command of Article VI, Clause 3 of the Constitution that "all executive ... Officers ... of the United States ... shall be bound by Oath or Affirmation, to support this Constitution...."

[15] American Bar Ass'n, Model Rules of Professional Conduct 2.1 (2003). Government attorneys are governed by the ethics rules of their state bars. The states usually codify the Model Rules.

[16] The "central dilemma" for OLC is to provide clients advice "they find generally congenial while at the same time upholding the reputation of the office as an elite institution whose legal advice is independent of the policy and political pressures associated with a particular question." John O. McGinnis, *Models of the Opinion Function of the Attorney General: A Normative, Descriptive, and Historical Prolegomenon*, 15 Cardozo L. Rev. 375, 422 (1993).

[17] *See* Cyrus Vance, *Hard Choices: Critical Years in America's Foreign Policy* 14 (1983).

In general, OLC first sought statutory sources of executive authority before moving to constitutional ground. The main exception to this cautious practice concerned the President's power to use military force against Iran, which the Justice Department supported as a constitutional matter, most prominently in approving the doomed raid to rescue the hostages.

The legal steps that eventuated in the *Dames & Moore* litigation invoked both statutory and constitutional powers. The first major step taken by President Carter, the freezing of Iranian assets, had a long statutory pedigree. During World War I, Congress enacted the Trading with the Enemy Act (TWEA),[18] to allow the President to seize assets of an enemy nation and its citizens, and then to take title to the assets and use them for purposes that included satisfying claims of Americans against the enemy. Over the years, TWEA was repeatedly used to freeze and dispose of enemy assets. The statute was also used in some surprising ways, most prominently by President Franklin Roosevelt to close the nation's banks on his first inauguration day.

TWEA was one among many emergency statutory powers that Congress conferred on the President over the years. After World War II, concern grew within Congress that the emergency powers needed comprehensive revision. Even more important was the need to repair the breakdown in relations between Congress and the Executive Branch that accompanied the Vietnam War and the Watergate scandal. Congress, intent on asserting its own constitutional role in matters involving foreign affairs and war, enacted several statutes to provide a framework for congressional-executive relations.[19] The National Emergencies Act (NEA) terminated some declared national emergencies that had existed for decades and required Presidents to make explicit findings when announcing new national emergencies and to renew them periodically after reexamining the need for them.[20] Congress also bifurcated TWEA, confining its authority to take foreign property to wartime. At the same time, Congress retained TWEA's grant of broad power to control assets of foreign nations in times of declared emergency, shifting it to the new International Emergency Economic Powers Act (IEEPA).[21]

---

[18] 40 Stat. 411 (1917) (codified as amended at 50 U.S.C. App. § 5(b)).

[19] In addition to the statutes discussed in text, the War Powers Resolution of 1973, Pub. L. No. 93–148, 87 Stat. 555, was especially prominent.

[20] Pub. L. No. 94–412, 90 Stat. 1255 (1976) (codified at 50 U.S.C. § 1621 *et seq.*).

[21] Pub. L. No. 95–223, 91 Stat. 1625 (1977) (codified at 50 U.S.C. §§ 1701–1706). Under § 1701(a), the President's authority "may be exercised to deal with any unusual and extraordinary threat, which has its source in whole or substantial part outside the United States, to the national security, foreign policy, or economy of the United States, if the President declares a national emergency with respect to such threat."

Ten days after the hostage-taking, President Carter declared a national emergency pursuant to the NEA and IEEPA. Simultaneously he blocked the removal or transfer of "all property and interests in property of the Government of Iran, its instrumentalities and controlled entities and the Central Bank of Iran which are or become subject to the jurisdiction of the United States...."[22] Carter delegated authority to implement the order to the Treasury Department.[23] The next day the Treasury's Office of Foreign Assets Control promulgated regulations carrying out the blocking order.[24] Treasury had decades of experience with implementing freeze orders during international crises. The President then authorized a general license allowing judicial proceedings against Iran, but not allowing the "entry of any judgment or of any decree or order of similar or analogous effect...."[25] By consenting to the initiation of these lawsuits, the administration began an inventory of outstanding claims against Iran and reduced incentives for claimants to bring immediate judicial challenges to the President's orders.

Along with the statutes granting specific foreign policy powers, such as IEEPA, the administration sought legal authority wherever it could find it. A curious statute was soon unearthed, which the administration happily named the Hostage Act of 1868.[26] Although it had never been

---

[22] Exec. Order No. 12,170, 44 Fed. Reg. 65,729 (Nov. 14, 1979). The order invoked § 203 of IEEPA, 50 U.S.C. § 1702(a)(1) (1980), to authorize these actions. Its core provision authorizes the President to:

> (B) investigate, regulate, direct and compel, nullify, void, prevent or prohibit, any acquisition, holding, withholding, use, transfer, withdrawal, transportation, importation or exportation of, or dealing in, or exercising any right, power, or privilege with respect to, or transactions involving, any property in which any foreign country or a national thereof has any interest by any person, or with respect to any property, subject to the jurisdiction of the United States.

[23] *Id.*

[24] The initial regulation provided that "[u]nless licensed or authorized ... any attachment, judgment, decree, lien, execution, garnishment, or other judicial process is null and void with respect to any property in which on or since [November 14, 1979,] there existed an interest of Iran." 31 C.F.R. § 535.203(e) (1980). The regulations also stated that any licenses granted could be "amended, modified, or revoked at any time." § 535.805.

[25] Dames & Moore v. Regan, 453 U.S. 654, 663 (1981) (quoting 31 C.F.R. § 535.504(a) (1980)). On December 19, 1979, a clarifying regulation stated that "the general authorization for judicial proceedings ... includes pre-judgment attachment." § 535.418.

[26] An Act concerning the Rights of American Citizens in foreign States, ch. 249, § 3, 15 Stat. 223, 224 (1868) (codified as amended at 22 U.S.C. § 1732). The Act provides:

> Whenever it is made known to the President that any citizen of the United States has been unjustly deprived of his liberty by or under the authority of any foreign government, ... if it appears to be wrongful and in violation of the rights of American citizenship, the President shall forthwith demand the release of such citizen, and if the release so demanded is unreasonably delayed or refused, the President shall use such

invoked, its text allowed the President to "use such means, not amounting to acts of war" as he chose to obtain the release of Americans held hostage by foreign nations.[27] Although the administration was never sure how much authority it could squeeze out of this statutory relic, it cited the Act as a source of support throughout the crisis.

The Constitution became prominent once negotiations began to include the prospect of claims settlement by executive agreement. Here, some background is necessary. It is initially surprising that the executive would have any power to enter international agreements other than by treaty, since the Constitution provides a specific process only for treaties. In addition, treaties are the only form of international agreement that the Supremacy Clause of the Constitution makes the supreme law of the land.[28]

Nevertheless, a simple, practical reason explains why other kinds of agreements have arisen. It would make no sense to require the full dignity and cumbersomeness of the treaty process every time the State Department wants to create a utility easement in an overseas embassy or wants to alter the number of accredited personnel in a foreign embassy here. Instead, these matters are handled by various forms of correspondence between the nations involved—executive agreements. In some situations, Congress participates by authorizing or ratifying an executive agreement ("Congressional-executive agreements"). In others, the President proceeds on his own by entering "sole" executive agreements. Can the simple and flexible tool of the sole agreement be used to settle claims of foreign nations and nationals against the United States and its nationals, and vice versa? Ever since the technique was first used for that purpose in 1799, the answer has been yes, but there is an obvious—and still unresolved—problem of limits.[29]

To the President's legal advisers, two Supreme Court decisions from the 1930s appeared to confirm a plenary power to settle claims by sole executive agreement, free of any need for congressional authorization or of any obligation to obey any contrary state law. Both decisions arose after President Roosevelt had decided, at long last, to recognize the Soviet Union. The Russian Revolution and its expropriation of private

---

means, not amounting to acts of war, as he may think necessary and proper to obtain or effectuate the release. . . .

Id.

[27] *Id.*

[28] The other types of agreements made supreme are the Constitution itself and statutes. U.S. Const. art. VI, cl. 2.

[29] For a recounting of the historical practice regarding claims settlement by sole executive agreement, see Ingrid Brunk Wuerth, *The Dangers of Deference: International Claim Settlement by the President*, 44 Harv. Int'l L.J. 1, 19–41 (2003).

property had created a blizzard of claims that hampered the normalization of relations between the two nations. As he formally recognized the Soviet government, FDR exchanged letters with their Foreign Minister, Maxim Litvinov, agreeing to marshal the various claims that citizens of each nation had against the other and to send them to a settlement process.

The Supreme Court twice upheld aspects of this "Litvinov Assignment." In *United States v. Belmont*,[30] it affirmed the President's power to recognize the Soviet Union and to settle outstanding claims by executive agreement. And in *United States v. Pink*,[31] it held that the Government's power to control the assets overrode an attempt by New York courts to distribute them to foreign claimants. Both Justice Sutherland in *Belmont* and Justice Douglas in *Pink* wrote in their typically broad strokes, emphasizing the need for the President to have an effective claims settlement power to implement American foreign policy.[32] Both opinions relied in part on the Court's sweeping rhetoric endorsing broad executive power in foreign affairs in the recent *Curtiss–Wright* case.[33] Accordingly, OLC relied on these two cases in advising President Carter that he could use an executive agreement to engineer a settlement with Iran.[34]

The Algiers Accords stated that "[i]t is the purpose of [the United States and Iran] . . . to terminate all litigation as between the Government of each party and the nationals of the other, and to bring about the settlement and termination of all such claims through binding arbitration."[35] The Accords provided for the establishment of an Iran–United States Claims Tribunal to provide binding arbitration.[36] The United States was obligated

> to terminate all legal proceedings in United States courts involving claims of United States persons and institutions against Iran and its state enterprises, to nullify all attachments and judgments obtained

---

[30] 301 U.S. 324 (1937).

[31] 315 U.S. 203 (1942).

[32] *See Belmont*, 301 U.S. at 760 ("That the negotiations, acceptance of the assignment and agreements and understandings in respect thereof were within the competence of the President may not be doubted."); *id.* at 223.

[33] United States v. Curtiss–Wright Exp. Corp., 299 U.S. 304 (1936). For more on *Curtiss–Wright* see chapter 6 in this volume.

[34] *Presidential Authority to Settle the Iranian Crisis*, 4A Op. O.L.C. 248, 249 (Sept. 16, 1980).

[35] Declaration of the Government of the Democratic and Popular Republic of Algeria (Algiers Accords), Jan. 19, 1981, Iran–U.S., 20 I.L.M. 224, 224.

[36] *Id.* at 230.

therein, to prohibit all further litigation based on such claims, and to bring about the termination of such claims through binding arbitration.[37]

In addition, the United States had to bring about the transfer by July 19, 1981, of all Iranian assets held in this country by American banks.[38] An escrow account in the Bank of England would hold $1 billion of the funds, to satisfy awards against Iran by the Claims Tribunal.[39]

On January 19, 1981, President Carter issued a series of Executive Orders implementing the Accords.[40] The orders revoked all licenses affecting the Iranian funds and required the banks to transfer them to the Federal Reserve Bank of New York, to be sent onward as agreed. A month later, President Reagan ratified Carter's orders.[41] He also suspended "[a]ll claims which may be presented to the ... Tribunal" and asserted that the claims "shall have no legal effect in any action now pending in any court of the United States...."[42] The suspension of a claim would terminate if the Claims Tribunal found that it lacked jurisdiction over it,[43] and claims would be discharged for all purposes when the Claims Tribunal either awarded some recovery (and the award was paid), or determined that no recovery was due.[44]

Claimants Pursue Iran and Challenge the Settlement

In December, 1979, Dames & Moore, a multinational engineering and construction company, filed suit in a United States District Court in California against the Government of Iran, the Atomic Energy Organization of Iran, and various Iranian banks.[45] Through one of its subsidiaries, Dames & Moore had contracted with the Atomic Energy Organization to conduct site studies for a proposed nuclear power plant in Iran.[46] The project was part of the Shah's efforts to modernize Iran and transform it

---

[37] *Id.* at 224.

[38] *Id.* at 225.

[39] *Id.* at 229.

[40] Exec. Orders Nos. 12,276–12,285, 46 Fed. Reg. 7913–7932 (Jan. 19, 1981), *reprinted in* 50 U.S.C. § 1701 at 150–55 (1982).

[41] Exec. Order No. 12,294, 46 Fed. Reg. 14111 (Feb. 24, 1981).

[42] *Id.* § 1.

[43] *Id.* § 3.

[44] *Id.* § 4.

[45] Complaint, Dames & Moore v. Atomic Energy Org. of Iran, No. CV 79–04918 LEW (Px) (C.D. Cal. filed Dec. 19, 1979). *See* Dames & Moore v. Regan, 453 U.S. 654, 663–64 & n.4 (1981).

[46] *Dames & Moore*, 453 U.S. at 664.

into a leading industrial nation. When Khomeini took power, he renounced all contracts with American companies, including Dames & Moore. The company claimed that it was owed about $3.5 million for services performed before the contract termination.[47] Dames & Moore's lawsuit against Iran was typical of the commercial claims. By the time the crisis ended, over 400 similar suits were pending in the federal courts.

Dames & Moore persuaded the district court to issue attachment orders against the defendants.[48] During the long pendency of the crisis, the company obtained summary judgment in the district court, notwithstanding the Treasury regulation forbidding the entry of any form of final judgment against Iran.[49] The court did, though, stay any attempt at execution.[50] Dames & Moore subsequently filed an action "for declaratory and injunctive relief against the United States and the Secretary of the Treasury, seeking to prevent enforcement of the executive orders and the Treasury Department regulations implementing the [Algiers Accords]" on both constitutional and statutory grounds.[51]

Dames & Moore had two basic arguments, which it would soon pursue before the Supreme Court. First, the company argued that when IEEPA restricted the President's power to take foreign assets to wartime, it allowed him only to freeze assets temporarily and not to take any action that would dispose of them permanently, such as sending them back to Iran.[52] Second, the company argued that Congress had fundamentally altered the President's claims settlement authority by enacting the Foreign Sovereign Immunities Act of 1976 (FSIA),[53] which created federal jurisdiction over suits brought by claimants against the commercial (but not governmental) activities of foreign states, eliminating their sovereign immunity to that extent.[54] Therefore, now that Americans could pursue foreign governments in federal court for the kind of ordinary breach of contract claim that Dames & Moore possessed, the President was no longer free to take these private claims for use in settling international crises. And if he did so anyway, the company

---

[47] Id.

[48] Id.

[49] Id. at 666.

[50] Id.

[51] Id. at 666–67.

[52] Brief for Petitioner at 7, Dames & Moore, 453 U.S. 654 (No. 80–2078), 1981 WL 390300.

[53] Pub. L. No. 94–583, 90 Stat. 2891 (codified at 28 U.S.C. §§ 1330, 1602 et seq.).

[54] Brief for Petitioner at 6–7, Dames & Moore, 453 U.S. 654 (No. 80–2078).

argued, that was a taking of private property for which the Fifth Amendment required compensation.[55]

The district court denied a preliminary injunction and dismissed the complaint for failure to state a claim upon which relief could be granted.[56] Appeal to the Ninth Circuit followed, and while it was pending, the district court reacted to new Treasury regulations requiring transfer of the Iranian funds by granting an injunction "prohibiting the United States from requiring the transfer of Iranian property that [was] subject to 'any writ of attachment, garnishment, judgment, levy, or other judicial lien' issued by any court in favor of [Dames & Moore]."[57] The company then sought an extraordinary remedy—a writ of certiorari before judgment in the court of appeals.[58]

The Supreme Court granted the writ, probably for three reasons. First, although the district court's opinions were unreported, leaving the Supreme Court without lower court guidance in this case, two courts of appeals had already upheld the President's program with full opinions.[59] Second, the cases in the lower courts were in disarray. Some had been stayed in compliance with the Government's requests; others were proceeding. Third and most important, the July 19, 1981 deadline loomed. Under the Algiers Accords, the United States was obligated to return funds remaining in American banks to Iran by that date.[60] The nation urgently needed a conclusive determination of the legality of the settlement, and only the Supreme Court could provide that. The Court granted the writ on June 11th, adopted an expedited briefing schedule, and set the case for oral argument on June 24th.[61] The Court's decision appeared eight days after oral argument. Thus it was not only the

---

[55] *Id.* at 7.

[56] *Dames & Moore*, 453 U.S. at 667.

[57] *Id.* at 667 (quoting App. to Pet. for Cert. 151–52, *id.* (No. 80–2078)) ("On June 4, the Treasury Department amended its regulations to mandate 'the transfer of bank deposits and certain other financial assets of Iran in the United States to the Federal Reserve Bank of New York by noon, June 19.' ").

[58] *Id.* at 667–68; *see* 28 U.S.C. § 2101(e); S.Ct. Rule 18.

[59] *Id.* at 667; *see Charles T. Main Int'l, Inc. v. Khuzestan Water & Power Authority*, 651 F.2d 800 (1st Cir. 1981); *American Int'l Group, Inc. v. Islamic Republic of Iran*, 657 F.2d 430 (D.C. Cir. 1981).

[60] *See* Declaration of the Government of the Democratic and Popular Republic of Algeria (Algiers Accords), Jan. 19, 1981, Iran–U.S., 20 I.L.M. 224, 226 ("[T]he United States will act to bring about the transfer to the Central Bank, within six months from [date of the agreement], of all Iranian deposits and securities in U.S. banking institutions in the United States. . . .").

[61] Dames & Moore v. Regan, 452 U.S. 932 (1981) (granting certiorari and establishing expedited schedule).

Executive Branch's negotiators who operated under extreme time pressure in the hostage crisis. Lawyers for both the executive and the private companies and even the Justices themselves faced tight deadlines. When the Court's opinion emerged, it visibly reflected the pressured circumstances of its generation.

The Supreme Court Decision

Justice William H. Rehnquist's opinion for the Court began with a bow in the direction of Justice Robert Jackson, whose concurrence in the steel seizure case, *Youngstown Sheet & Tube Co. v. Sawyer,*[62] is the greatest modern opinion on the separation of powers between Congress and the President. As a young man, Rehnquist had served as a law clerk to Jackson when *Youngstown* was before the Court. Three decades later, he vividly remembered the executive's arguments for essentially unlimited power in that case, and the adverse reaction they sparked in the nation and within the Court.[63] As it turned out, there was a third generation of Supreme Court Justices involved in *Dames & Moore.* One of Justice Rehnquist's law clerks that Term was John G. Roberts, Jr., who would succeed him as Chief Justice in 2005. It is said that Roberts "played a leading role in drafting Rehnquist's opinion" in the case.[64]

Having endorsed Jackson's approach, Justice Rehnquist emphasized the danger of excessive reliance on Justice Sutherland's broad dicta in *Curtiss–Wright.*[65] After quoting Sutherland's famous reference to the "very delicate, plenary and exclusive power of the President" in foreign relations,[66] Rehnquist quoted Jackson's response to the claims of unbounded executive power that had been advanced in *Youngstown*:

> The example of such unlimited executive power that must have most impressed the forefathers was the prerogative exercised by George III, and the description of its evils in the Declaration of Independence leads me to doubt that they were creating their new Executive in his image.[67]

---

[62] Youngstown Sheet & Tube Co. v. Sawyer, 343 U.S. 579, 634 (1952) (Jackson, J., concurring). For more on *Youngstown* see chapter 7 in this volume. *See generally* Harold H. Bruff, *Balance of Forces: Separation of Powers Law in the Administrative State* 106–13 (2006).

[63] William H. Rehnquist, *The Supreme Court: How It Was, How It Is*, chs. 1–3 (1987).

[64] Charlie Savage, *Takeover: The Return of the Imperial Presidency and the Subversion of American Democracy* 255 (2007).

[65] United States v. Curtiss–Wright Exp. Corp., 299 U.S. 304 (1936). For more on *Curtiss–Wright* see chapter 6 in this volume.

[66] Dames & Moore v. Regan, 453 U.S. 654, 661 (1981) (quoting *id.* at 319–320).

[67] *Id.* at 662 (quoting *Youngstown*, 343 U.S. at 641 (Jackson, J., concurring)).

Rehnquist demonstrated the lesson he took from the steel crisis in his approach to the resolution of the hostage crisis. He said he would confine his opinion to questions necessary to decision, avoiding broad analytic strokes that might create an unfortunate precedent ripe for future exploitation by the executive.[68] He echoed Jackson's lament about the difficulty of applying any simple analytic formula to the messy facts and law of a real controversy.[69] Moreover, like *Youngstown*, the hostage case had been litigated under great time pressure: caution could avoid mistakes.

The Iranian hostage litigation gave Rehnquist an opportunity both to reaffirm the insights of his mentor and to revise and extend them in application to a new context. Jackson had identified three categories of congressional support for presidential action: first, the presence of express or implied statutory authority, which would elevate presidential power to its maximum; second, a "zone of twilight," where Congress had neither granted nor denied authority; third, express or implied denial of authority, where presidential power would be at its "lowest ebb," reliant on some overriding constitutional grant alone.[70] In *Dames & Moore*, Rehnquist emphasized Jackson's concession that these categories were somewhat oversimplified, and suggested that it might be more accurate not to conceive of executive action as falling cleanly into one of the categories, but as existing "along a spectrum running from explicit congressional authorization to explicit congressional prohibition."[71] He thought that this slight reformulation would be especially apt when considering presidential "responses to international crises the nature of which Congress can hardly have been expected to anticipate in any detail."[72] In this uncertain realm, then, there would be more twilight and less sunshine.

After reciting the complex factual background of the case, Rehnquist turned to the first main issue, the validity of nullifying the attachments and ordering the transfer of the frozen assets. The Government argued that the plain language of IEEPA authorized both actions.[73] Dames & Moore responded that the President could only freeze assets temporarily, and could not dispose of them.[74] The Court disagreed. It relied on the

---

[68] *Id.*

[69] *Id.* at 669.

[70] *Youngstown*, 343 U.S. at 635–38 (Jackson, J., concurring).

[71] *Dames & Moore*, 453 U.S. at 669.

[72] *Id.*

[73] *Id.* at 670.

[74] *Id.* at 671–72.

text of IEEPA and TWEA, which "authorize[d] the President to 'direct and compel' the 'transfer, withdrawal, transportation, ... or exportation of ... any property in which any foreign country ... has any interest....' "[75] Here, the United States was not taking title to the assets, for which it would need TWEA authority; instead, it was sending them to Iran and to the banks. The Court also noted that Dames & Moore's attachments were subsequent to both the blocking order and the Treasury regulations, which made all attachments subject to revocable licenses.[76] Hence, the company knew that its interests in these assets were contingent. More importantly, the purpose of freezing assets was to allow the President to use them as a "bargaining chip" to assert leverage against a hostile nation.[77] The Court thought that it would be odd to read the statute "to allow individual claimants throughout the country to minimize or wholly eliminate this 'bargaining chip' through attachments...."[78]

From the text and purposes of IEEPA, the Court drew the conclusion that the orders nullifying the attachments and ordering transfer of the assets were specifically authorized by Congress, and therefore fell in Justice Jackson's first category.[79] "A contrary ruling would mean that the Federal Government as a whole lacked the power exercised by the President, and that we are not prepared to say."[80]

Having disposed of the issue that it considered easy, the Supreme Court turned to the cloudier issues surrounding the claims settlement agreement. Here, IEEPA could be of no use. The Court noted correctly that litigation claims of Americans against Iran could not be understood as Iranian property—indeed, the point of the lawsuits was to separate Iran from some of its property.[81]

Nor would the Court read the curious Hostage Act to authorize the settlement, although its text would support an argument for any action short of war.[82] Justice Rehnquist emphasized that the Act responded to a

---

[75] *Id.* at 672 n.5 (quoting 50 U.S.C. § 1702). Also, the Court cited *Orvis v. Brownell*, 345 U.S. 183 (1953).

[76] *Id.* at 673.

[77] *Id.*

[78] *Id.*

[79] *Id.* at 674.

[80] *Id.* (citing Youngstown Sheet & Tube Co. v. Sawyer, 343 U.S. 579, 636–37 (1952) (Jackson, J., concurring)).

[81] *Id.* at 675.

[82] Although the Court did not say so, it may have been influenced in its reluctance to put weight on this statute by Judge Mikva's separate statement in one of the cases that

century-old crisis that was almost the opposite of the Iranian one.[83] As its text suggests, the Act condemned the forced repatriation of naturalized American citizens by other nations, not the holding of U.S. citizens for ransom.[84] Moreover, the Act contemplated reprisals against other nations and their citizens, not the resolution of claims held by Americans.[85]

Having declined to stand on either of these two statutes, however, the Court would not dismiss them entirely. Justice Rehnquist thought that both statutes were "highly relevant in the looser sense of indicating congressional acceptance of a broad scope for executive action in circumstances such as those presented in this case."[86] He stressed that Congress could not be expected to foresee the nature of future international crises.[87] Therefore, the lack of explicit authority did not "imply 'congressional disapproval'" of executive action.[88] Instead, grants of broad discretion in the vicinity of a particular situation could be considered, in Jackson's formula, to "invite" presidential initiative, at least where no statute exuded contrary implications.[89] This qualification was critically important, for Rehnquist's approach at this point otherwise paralleled the *dissent* in *Youngstown*, which had relied on the presence of statutes authorizing conduct of the Korean War to support the validity of President Truman's seizure of the steel mills.[90]

Needing to distance himself from the *Youngstown* dissent, Rehnquist argued that for claims settlement there was "a history of congressional acquiescence in conduct of the sort engaged in by the President."[91]

---

had upheld the settlement, *American International Group, Inc. v. Islamic Republic of Iran*, 657 F.2d 430, 452 (D.C. Cir. 1981), in which he argued that the name Hostage Act was "a sobriquet newly coined for the purposes of the Iranian crisis," and counseled against relying on it.

[83] *Dames & Moore*, 453 U.S. at 676–77.

[84] *Id.* at 676.

[85] *Id.* at 677.

[86] *Id.*

[87] *Id.* at 678.

[88] *Id.* (quoting Haig v. Agee, 453 U.S. 280, 291 (1981)).

[89] *Id.*; *see* Youngstown Sheet & Tube Co. v. Sawyer, 343 U.S. 579, 637 (1952) (Jackson, J., concurring).

[90] *See Youngstown*, 343 U.S. at 667, 671–72 (Vinson, C.J., dissenting).

[91] *Dames & Moore*, 453 U.S. at 678–79. Justice Frankfurter's concurrence in *Youngstown* had engaged in an elaborate analysis of congressional acquiescence in wartime industrial seizures, and had found it to have been withdrawn in the case at hand. *See Youngstown*, 343 U.S. at 593 (Frankfurter, J., concurring).

The Court began its review of the history by noting the long pedigree of international claims settlements as a means for nations to eliminate "sources of friction" between them.[92] From the Federalist Era onward, Presidents had settled claims by sole executive agreement "in return for lump-sum payments or the establishment of arbitration mechanisms."[93] In doing so, the executive had pursued the interests of the nation, whether or not they coincided with the interests of the claimants.[94] Here the Court, as it so often does, was using longstanding historical practice to support a gloss on the text of the Constitution.[95]

"Congress ha[d] implicitly approved the practice of claims settlement by executive agreement" by creating the Foreign Claims Settlement Commission and giving it jurisdiction to decide claims of Americans against settlement funds.[96] Subsequently, Congress had frequently amended this legislation to address problems surrounding particular agreements, without withdrawing the underlying authority to enter them.[97] Finally, there was the odd history of the Case Amendment. After World War II, some Members of Congress sought to constrain presidential use of executive agreements. After various attempts to legislate a limitation, in 1972 Congress finally settled for the symbolic requirement that the text of significant executive agreements be transmitted to it.[98]

---

[92] *Dames & Moore*, 453 U.S. at 679 (quoting United States v. Pink, 315 U.S. 203, 225 (1942)). The Court also cited Louis Henkin, *Foreign Affairs and the Constitution* 262–63 (1972).

[93] *Dames & Moore*, 453 U.S. at 679.

[94] *Id.* at 680.

[95] *See* Harold H. Bruff, *Balance of Forces: Separation of Powers Law in the Administrative State* 65–66 (2006).

[96] *Dames & Moore*, 453 U.S. at 680; *see* International Claims Settlement Act of 1949, 64 Stat. 13 (codified as amended at 22 U.S.C. § 1621 (1976 ed. & Supp. IV)).

[97] *Id.* at 681. The Court also thought that "the legislative history of IEEPA further reveals that Congress has accepted the authority of the Executive to enter into settlement agreements." *Id.* It quoted a disclaimer: " '[n]othing in this act is intended . . . to interfere with the authority of the President to [block assets], or to impede the settlement of claims of U.S. citizens against foreign countries.' " *Id.* at 681–82 (alteration in original) (quoting S. Rep. No. 95–466, at 6 (1977); 50 U.S.C. § 1706(a)(1) (1976 ed., Supp. III)).

[98] *Id.* at 682 n.10; *see* Pub. L. No. 92–403, § 1, 86 Stat. 619 (1972) (codified as amended at 1 U.S.C. § 112b). The Court said that "the legislative history . . . further reveals that Congress has accepted the President's authority to settle claims." Senator Case, the sponsor of the Act, conceded:

"I think it is a most interesting [area] in which we have accepted the right of the President, one individual, acting through his diplomatic force, to adjudicate and settle claims of American nationals against foreign countries. But that is a fact."

Id. at 682 n.10 (alteration in original) (quoting *Transmittal of Executive Agreements to Congress: Hearings on S. 596 before the S. Comm. on Foreign Relations*, 92d Cong. 74 (1971)).

In addition to this pattern of congressional acquiescence in the President's power to settle claims, there was Supreme Court precedent upholding it. The *Dames & Moore* Court cited *Pink*, describing it as resting on a judgment that settling "claims was integrally connected with normalizing United States' relations with a foreign state."[99] Thus the Court was able to combine the acquiescence doctrine with deference to the President's independent constitutional powers in foreign affairs in order to justify an executive action—but without having to specify any precise content for either the statutory or constitutional powers.[100]

One obstacle remained. Dames & Moore had argued that Congress ended claims settlement authority by enacting the FSIA in 1976, with its grant of federal jurisdiction over commercial suits against other nations.[101] This was a serious contention, since it is conventional to assume that sole executive agreements, unlike treaties, do not displace prior and inconsistent statutes.[102] The Court disagreed. It understood the FSIA to be directed to a separate problem, the practice within the executive of making ad hoc judgments about the recognition of another nation's sovereign immunity when a particular claimant asked for relief.[103]

The Court concluded "the President was authorized to suspend pending claims pursuant to Executive Order No. 12294."[104] By using the passive voice, the Court left the ultimate basis of the President's authority unclear. Its discussion had touched on both constitutional and statutory powers; apparently their sum sufficed. In closing, the Court again quoted its prior opinions establishing the acquiescence doctrine. It expressed pleasure that the creation of the Claims Tribunal would give claimants a means of redress. And it noted that Congress, well aware of the Iranian settlement, had expressed no displeasure. Still, the Court wished to "re-emphasize the narrowness of our decision. We do not decide that the President possesses plenary power to settle claims, even as against foreign governmental entities."[105] Unable to anticipate the future, the Court would not make statements about it.

---

[99] *Id.* at 683; *see* United States v. Pink, 315 U.S. 203 (1942).

[100] This has been a frequent strategy for the Court to follow. *See, e.g.*, Regan v. Wald, 468 U.S. 222 (1984); Haig v. Agee, 453 U.S. 280 (1981).

[101] *Dames & Moore*, 453 U.S. at 684; *see* 28 U.S.C. §§ 1330, 1602 *et seq.*

[102] *E.g.*, United States v. Guy W. Capps, Inc., 204 F.2d 655, 659–60 (4th Cir. 1953) ("We think that whatever the power of the executive with respect to making executive trade agreements regulating foreign commerce in the absence of action by Congress, it is clear that the executive may not through entering into such an agreement avoid complying with a regulation prescribed by Congress.").

[103] *See Dames & Moore*, 453 U.S. at 685 (discussing "the principle purpose of the FSIA").

[104] *Id.* at 686.

[105] *Id.* at 688.

The majority declined to decide whether the suspension of claims might be a taking of property in violation of the Fifth Amendment. That question was not ripe for decision, but the Court did decide that the Court of Claims would have jurisdiction to consider the issue.[106] Justice Powell dissented in part, arguing that the nullification of attachments might "effect a taking of property interests giving rise to claims for just compensation."[107] He would have left the issue to the Court of Claims.[108] Signaling his own views, he said that "[t]he Government must pay just compensation when it furthers the Nation's foreign policy goals by using as 'bargaining chips' claims lawfully held by a relatively few persons and subject to the jurisdiction of our courts."[109]

The Immediate Impact of Dames & Moore

The most important immediate consequence of *Dames & Moore* lay in what the Court did *not* do: it did not declare that some or all of the arrangements ending the Iranian crisis were illegal, either for transgressing statutory limits or for evading the Constitution's requisites for

---

[106] *See id.* at 688–89 (noting jurisdiction would lie under the Tucker Act, 28 U.S.C. § 1491 (1976 ed., Supp. III)). Justice Stevens wrote a short concurrence to say that the prospect of a " 'taking' is so remote that I would not address the jurisdictional question...." *Id.* at 690 (Stevens, J., concurring in part).

[107] *Id.* at 690 (Powell, J., concurring and dissenting in part).

[108] *Id.* In a footnote Justice Powell explained:

Even though the Executive Orders purported to make attachments conditional, there is a substantial question whether the Orders themselves may have effected a taking by making conditional the attachments that claimants against Iran otherwise could have obtained without condition. Moreover, because it is settled that an attachment entitling a creditor to resort to specific property for the satisfaction of a claim is a property right compensable under the Fifth Amendment, there is a question whether the revocation of the license under which petitioner obtained its attachments suffices to render revocable the attachments themselves.

Id. at 690 n.1 (citation omitted).

In a footnote of its own, the majority responded to Justice Powell's concern:

Our construction of petitioner's attachments as being "revocable," "contingent," and "in every sense subordinate to the President's power under the IEEPA," in effect answers petitioner's claim that even if the President had the authority to nullify the attachments and transfer the assets, the exercise of such would constitute an unconstitutional taking of property in violation of the Fifth Amendment absent just compensation. We conclude that because of the President's authority to prevent or condition attachments, and because of the orders he issued to this effect, petitioner did not acquire any "property" interest in its attachments of the sort that would support a constitutional claim for compensation.

Id. at 674 n.6 (majority opinion).

[109] *Id.* at 691 (Powell, J., concurring and dissenting in part).

making treaties. Such an outcome would have created a truly impressive legal mess. Hence, the holding of the case was not surprising. In addition, *Dames & Moore* was not a departure from the Court's own precedents. In crafting the Algiers Accords, the Executive Branch had relied explicitly on the Court's decisions in *Belmont* and *Pink*, upholding the normalization of relations with the Soviet Union through similar claims settlement measures. Moreover, the severe pressures of time and evolving events late in the hostage negotiations were well suited to executive initiative, not to the stately dance of senatorial ratification. Perhaps for these reasons, observers have not displayed much surprise or outrage at the outcome of the case.[110]

In the event, the settlement did produce recovery for many American claimants. The Claims Tribunal, consisting of three American, three Iranian, and three neutral judges, was responsible for resolving 4,700 American claims.[111] The Tribunal had a rocky start, as the Iranian judges disrupted its organizing efforts. Eventually, the Tribunal awarded over $2.1 billion to American claimants. Over 85% of the claims were private claims by individuals or companies against the government of the other country—overwhelmingly suits by American parties against Iran.[112]

Dames & Moore itself was less fortunate, however. In 1983, the Claims Tribunal dismissed its main contract claim of $3.5 million for lack of jurisdiction.[113] The declaration creating the Tribunal had excluded from its purview claims under any contract that called for litigation of disputes in the courts of Iran, and that is what the company's contract provided. After the dismissal, theoretically the company could have revived the claim in an Iranian court, although it is difficult to imagine a forum more hostile. The Tribunal did give Dames & Moore some relief, though. It awarded $208,000 plus interest at 10% for two other claims (under another contract and for Iran's expropriation of some company

---

[110] For a good overview of the issues, see Symposium, *Dames & Moore v. Regan*, 29 UCLA L. Rev. 977 (1982).

[111] *See generally* Stewart & Sherman, *Developments at the Iran–United States Claims Tribunal: 1981–1983*, 24 Va. J. Int'l L. 1 (1983).

[112] These figures are as of April, 2007. *See* Iran–United States Claims Tribunal, *at* http://www.iusct.org (last visited June 2, 2008). Other claims involved disputes between the two governments or between banks of the two countries. Ironically, the time taken by the tribunal to begin processing the claims had at least one beneficial effect; the $1 billion security fund initially created for the settlement of claims grew substantially because interest on the fund exceeded the amount of the awards paid out.

[113] Dames & Moore v. The Islamic Republic of Iran, 4 Iran–U.S.C.T.R. 212 (1983), *reconsideration denied*, 8 Iran–U.S.C.T.R 107 (1985). *See generally* Stein, *Jurisprudence and Jurists' Prudence: The Iranian–Forum Clause Decisions of the Iran–U.S. Claims Tribunal*, 78 Am. J. Int'l L. 1 (1984).

property).[114] The unfavorable outcome of this long process of litigation for Dames & Moore shows why the company was so determined to preserve its access to American courts by attaching Iranian assets here, and so willing to incur the expense of litigation in the Supreme Court.

Nevertheless, the overall fate of the claimants demonstrates that many of them were better off than if no claims settlement had occurred, because there was an accessible and ample pool of funds to satisfy them. In *United States v. Sperry Corporation*,[115] the Court later held that a statute requiring successful litigants in the Claims Tribunal to pay a portion of any award to the United States did not create any obligation of just compensation. Explaining why Sperry suffered no compensable loss, the Court said: "Had the President not agreed to the ... Tribunal ..., Sperry would have had no assurance that it could have pursued its action against Iran to judgment or that a judgment would have been readily collectible."[116]

The Continuing Importance of Dames & Moore

Two aspects of *Dames & Moore* have created continuing controversy: the Court's treatment of property rights and the separation of powers implications of its method of decision. Dean Harold Koh, in an excellent and influential book,[117] has criticized *Dames & Moore* sharply on both counts. Let us consider them in turn. Koh deplored the Court's unwillingness to demand a "clear statement" from Congress that it was authorizing the President to suspend claims.[118] This is a venerable way for courts to avoid endorsing executive decisions touching on individual rights until Congress has considered and explicitly authorized them.[119] Hence, the clear statement approach is an interpretive device that both

---

[114] *Id.*

[115] 493 U.S. 52 (1989). Lower courts also rejected claims that the executive orders had caused takings of property. *See E–Systems Inc. v. United States*, 2 Cl. Ct. 271 (1983); *American Int'l Group v. Islamic Republic of Iran*, 657 F.2d 430 (D.C. Cir. 1981); *see also Itek Corp. v. First Nat'l Bank of Boston*, 730 F.2d 19 (1st Cir. 1984); Phillip R. Trimble, *Foreign Policy Frustrated*—Dames & Moore, *Claims Court Jurisdiction and a New Raid on the Treasury*, 84 Colum. L. Rev. 317 (1984).

[116] 493 U.S. at 63; *see also Belk v. United States*, 858 F.2d 706 (Fed. Cir. 1988) (executive agreement securing release of the hostages and forbidding U.S. hostages to sue Iran held not a compensable taking). The hostages later tried to obtain relief against Iran in U.S. courts, but were unsuccessful. *See Roeder v. Islamic Republic of Iran,* 333 F.3d 228 (D.C. Cir. 2003).

[117] *The National Security Constitution: Sharing Power After the Iran–Contra Affair* 139–43 (1990).

[118] *Id.*

[119] Curtis A. Bradley & Jack L. Goldsmith, *Congressional Authorization and the War on Terrorism*, 118 Harv. L. Rev. 2047, 2102–06 (2005).

minimizes direct adjudication of constitutional rights and maximizes the participation of all three branches in sensitive decisions. The Court has invoked it rather unpredictably. Perhaps the paradigmatic case for requiring a clear statement is *Hamdan v. Rumsfeld*, the military commissions case, in which the Justices displayed marked uncertainty about the extent of both the executive's constitutional powers and the detainees' constitutional rights.[120]

Whether the clear statement principle should be deployed ought to depend, then, on the comparative strength of the claims of individual rights and executive power in any particular context. The *Dames & Moore* Court, finding claims of individual right relatively weak and claims of executive necessity relatively strong, was prepared to uphold the President's action, although not without some cautionary utterances.

Since the rights asserted were a form of property—claims for money damages against the Iranian government—the fair expectations of the claimants mattered. In turn, these expectations depended on the law of foreign sovereign immunity, which had evolved over the years in ways that gave each of the three branches of government dominance over whether claims could be satisfied.[121] Before the late 1930s, the courts treated the immunity as a common law doctrine that they would define, with episodic deference to the views of the executive. In general, there was an absolute bar to recovery against foreign governments, at least unless the executive took up a particular claim and successfully urged a court to ignore the immunity. The *Pink* decision exuded the attitude that those dealing with foreign governments took their chances with this legal regime.

After *Pink* there ensued a period of increasing deference to Executive Branch lawmaking about the immunity. Under the "Tate Letter" regime (from 1952–1976), litigants could sue directly in court for commercial claims and would not be barred unless the government affirmatively objected to the claim. Congress then intervened by enacting the FSIA, asserting its own control over the susceptibility of a foreign nation to suit in U.S. courts.

The FSIA removed immunities for actions based on a foreign state's commercial activities in the United States. But Congress did not consider the fact that it was creating two coexisting legal regimes. Under the first regime—routine claims against a foreign nation—the executive preferred to avoid any further involvement. By avoiding a decision on whether to

---

[120] 548 U.S. 557 (2006). For more on *Hamdan* see Chapter 12 in this volume. *See generally* Cass R. Sunstein, *Clear Statement Principles and National Security:* Hamdan *and Beyond*, 2006 Sup. Ct. Rev. 1.

[121] *See* Curtis A. Bradley, Chevron *Deference and Foreign Affairs*, 86 Va. L. Rev. 649, 709–14 (2000).

"espouse" them and thereby urging a court to deny sovereign immunity, there would be no foreign policy interest of the United States in view. Hence, before the FSIA, most of these claims were merely irritants to the executive. The other regime, however—settling whole categories of claims against a foreign nation to ease relations or to end a crisis—did involve critical foreign policy interests of the United States. Since the Justice and State Departments helped draft the FSIA, it is not likely that they meant to give away the executive's longstanding claims settlement authority. And as the Supreme Court noted in *Dames & Moore*, the legislative history of the FSIA is bare of any suggestion that preexisting understandings about claims settlement power were being altered as well.

If we combine the presence of presidential claims settlement authority with the presence of the FSIA, a complex and somewhat muddled set of claimants' expectations emerges. They know that in an increasingly globalized economy, they can conduct routine relationships with foreign governments, including the power to pursue claims for damages. They are subject to the uncertainties, however, of determining which activities of another nation are commercial, and not immune, from those that are governmental, and still immune.[122] In addition, claimants must know that they are dealing with foreign governments, not private organizations, and that large forces may arise to defeat their hopes, including the possibility that the President will make a claims settlement that affects them. In any international crisis, many business plans evaporate. The Iranian revolution defeated the expectations of Dames & Moore and others who had dealt with the Government of Iran. The company's contract to litigate in Iran suddenly became a very bad bargain indeed, but the claims settlement left them to pursue it. Other claimants were left better off than they had been.

Presidents need a constitutional authority to settle claims against foreign nations, subject to controls enacted by Congress, but not subject to clear statement rules that require prior statutory authority. Consider the painful and convoluted story of the Iranian Hostage Crisis and its eventual resolution. This was a real emergency, not a false one fabricated for public posturing or to bulwark argument in litigation. The traditional power of claims settlement was central to President Carter's capacity to end the crisis. The Executive Branch possessed no bargaining chip other than the frozen Iranian assets. It could not negotiate effectively unless it could control those assets. Hence, the executive could not let them be diverted to the pockets of private claimants, many of whom had no special relation to the assets.

---

[122] For an analysis of the difficulty of this distinction by the future Justice Breyer, see *Charles T. Main Int'l, Inc. v. Khuzestan Water & Power Auth.*, 651 F.2d 800, 816–17 (1st Cir. 1981) (concurring opinion).

If Presidents lacked adequate claims settlement authority, they would tend to be drawn toward military responses to crises. That would not be a beneficial development. Justice Powell's suggestion in *Dames & Moore* that Presidents could use private claims as bargaining chips, but on condition of paying for taking them, could deter settlements that would be in the interests of the nation. Presidents might fear protracted litigation over un-liquidated claims, leading to large liabilities. Hence, the facts of the Iranian Hostage Crisis do not support any special sympathy to individual rights that should constrict traditional claims settlement authority.

Criticisms of the Court's decision in *Dames & Moore* from the standpoint of separation of powers have taken two opposite tacks. First, some have seen it as an unjustified retreat from *Belmont* and *Pink*.[123] The value of these precedents to the executive during the Iranian crisis lay in their broad and apparently unqualified assurance that executive agreements could be employed to accomplish the tasks needed to free the hostages. They provided a firm platform on which to stand. The repeated notes of caution in *Dames & Moore*, on the other hand, together with the Court's emphasis on close, context-specific analysis, reduce the usefulness of the older precedents in other, perhaps somewhat dissimilar situations, as Justice Rehnquist no doubt intended. Caution has its virtues, and its price.

In contrast, other critics see *Dames & Moore* as too willing to uphold unilateral executive adventures in the foreign policy realm.[124] Harold Koh has argued that Justice Rehnquist placed too much emphasis on the broad text of IEEPA and ignored its legislative history, which demonstrated a desire to cabin prior instances of unrestrained executive power. Therefore, he disagreed with the Court's reliance on the acquiescence doctrine to turn legislative silence into consent, thereby elevating an executive action based on dubious authority to Justice Jackson's almost unassailable category of actions blessed by statutes. Koh argued that the President should have asked "Congress for a swift joint resolution of approval."[125] The risk created by *Dames & Moore*, then, was that it "championed unguided executive activism and congressional acquiescence in foreign affairs over the constitutional principle of balanced institutional participation."[126] Under the *Dames & Moore* formula, Koh

---

[123] *See, e.g.,* Philip R. Trimble, *Foreign Policy Frustrated*—Dames & Moore, *Claims Court Jurisdiction and a New Raid on the Treasury*, 84 Colum. L. Rev. 317 (1984).

[124] For a textualist argument against *Dames & Moore* as an evasion of the treaty power, see Michael D. Ramsey, *The Constitution's Text in Foreign Affairs* 214–16 (2007).

[125] Dean Harold Koh, *The National Security Constitution: Sharing Power After the Iran–Contra Affair* 140 (1990).

[126] *Id.* He noted that in a decision issued a week before *Dames & Moore*, the Court also relied on the acquiescence doctrine in upholding the State Department's power to revoke passports. *Id.* (citing Haig v. Agee, 453 U.S. 280 (1981)).

argued, Presidents could expect to prevail in foreign policy whenever they did not visibly contravene statutes.[127] He also noted that the broadly phrased Hostage Act has a history of misuse, most notoriously by Oliver North, who would later argue that it authorized him "to do whatever [was] necessary" during the Iran–Contra affair.[128]

Similarly, Professor Kevin Stack found that the "most startling aspect of *Dames & Moore* is that the Court aggregated delegations of statutory authority to find a power that it could not trace to any individual authorization, or even to any interlocking set of authorizations."[129] He argued that deciding what qualifies as congressional authorization is critical to the rule of law in foreign relations.[130] Given the power of the President's veto, the traditional acceptability of broad statutory delegations in foreign policy, and the executive's natural institutional advantages in that realm, a judicial finding that statutory authority exists for an action is extremely difficult for Congress to overturn or modify. In sum, both scholars found that *Dames & Moore* is far less modest in effect than in iteration.[131]

The *Dames & Moore* Court was trying to tread a narrow path between shackling executive power and endorsing executive adventuring. In addressing this kind of separation of powers issue, the Court's decision whether to invoke clear statement principles can have long-term implications for the distribution of powers between the two political branches. A remand to Congress for statutory authority concentrates the power of initiative in the legislature; an endorsement of executive discretion to act without statutory support concentrates that power in the President. In the claims settlement context, the course of the Iranian hostage crisis shows why a general requirement for advance statutory

---

[127] *Id.* at 142; *see also* William N. Eskridge, Jr., *Interpreting Legislative Inaction*, 87 Mich. L. Rev. 67, 74 (1988) (concluding that in foreign affairs, "the Court will routinely infer legislative approval of executive practices, where 'Congress has consistently failed to object to [them] . . . even when it has had an opportunity to do so.' " (quoting Dames & Moore v. Regan, 453 U.S. 654, 682 n.10 (1981))).

[128] Dean Harold Koh, *The National Security Constitution: Sharing Power After the Iran–Contra Affair* 197 (1990).

[129] Kevin M. Stack, *The Statutory President*, 90 Iowa L. Rev. 539, 567 (2005).

[130] *Id.*; *see also* Samuel Issacharoff & Richard H. Pildes, *Emergency Contexts Without Emergency Powers: The United States' Constitutional Approach to Rights During Wartime*, 2 Int'l J. Const. L. 296 (2004).

[131] *See also* Louis Henkin, *Foreign Affairs and the United States Constitution* 227 (2d ed. 1996) ("*Dames & Moore* . . . is less sweeping than *Belmont* in its rhetoric but no less broad in what it holds."); Peter J. Spiro, *Treaties, Executive Agreements, and Constitutional Method*, 79 Tex. L. Rev. 961 (2001); Lee R. Marks & John C. Grabow, *The President's Foreign Economic Powers After* Dames & Moore v. Regan: *Legislation by Acquiescence*, 68 Cornell L. Rev. 68 (1982).

authority might prove unwise. Just as the Carter administration was reluctant to seek a statute supporting its efforts to settle the crisis, out of fear that it would provide insufficient discretion, Congress could reasonably have been reluctant to provide one, fearing that it would license more discretion than actually would be needed. In the event, the administration proceeded with a caution that was influenced by uncertainty about the limits to its power.

Before *Dames & Moore* was decided, the conventional understanding of claims settlement law as articulated in *Belmont* and *Pink* was that the President possessed a plenary constitutional power to settle claims, subject to unknown powers of control by Congress. Justice Rehnquist's opinion studiously avoided saying anything that could be understood to limit congressional power to enact limits to claims settlements, either in general or relating to particular settlements. Compared to the opinion that the Court *could* have written—*Belmont/Pink II*—the opinion that it *did* write looks more modest.

The statutory context of *Dames & Moore* was an appropriate one for invocation of the acquiescence doctrine. Congressional concern about presidential emergency powers had recently led to the inter-branch settlement that was incorporated in the NEA and IEEPA. Congress, knowing that it is difficult to legislate substantive standards for foreign policy in advance, relied on two process controls that were designed to assure the political accountability of presidential action and to preserve a full opportunity for subsequent congressional control through legislation. These were requirements that the President take personal responsibility for his determinations of necessity by making particular findings, and that Congress be kept fully informed by reporting and consultation. Not long after *Dames & Moore* was decided, the Iran/Contra scandal would demonstrate that when these process controls are ignored, the risks of substantively illegal executive action become severe.[132] When they are abided, however, Congress can appropriately confide broad substantive discretion to the executive. In the Iranian Hostage Crisis, President Carter obeyed the process controls—and the spirit—of the statutes, and Congress was willing to acquiesce in his actions.

Consider the incentives for executive advisers before and after *Dames & Moore* was decided. In place of the relative certainties of *Belmont* and *Pink,* which might encourage executive adventuring, the Court has commanded a counseling process that reads the Constitution cautiously and takes statutes seriously. The importance of this reminder should never be discounted. For there is another view of executive power that competes for acceptance, and it lacks the careful qualifications that suffuse *Dames & Moore.* That is the view of executive hegemony in

---

[132] *See generally* Theodore Draper, *A Very Thin Line: The Iran–Contra Affairs* (1991).

foreign affairs that is drawn from the expansive dicta in *Curtiss–Wright* that Justice Rehnquist disapproved, a view that has little respect for statutory efforts to control executive action. It is refuted by the Court's approach in *Dames & Moore*.

The *Dames & Moore* decision has also had consequences for American federalism. Recall that one of its precedents, *Pink*, had forbidden New York courts to control the distribution of assets under a claims settlement agreement. In *American Insurance Ass'n v. Garamendi*, the Court reiterated that "valid executive agreements are fit to preempt state law...."[133] It held that an executive agreement entered by President Clinton in the very sensitive context of Holocaust insurance claims overrode a California statute that addressed the subject.[134] Citing *Dames & Moore*, the Court restated its reliance on tradition and congressional acquiescence as supports for presidential claims settlement authority.[135] In addition, the majority "accorded preemptive effect" to the agreement even though no such intention was explicitly stated in it.[136] *Garamendi* is quite protective of the executive's capacity to set controlling foreign policy, at least when a formal executive agreement is entered.[137]

A recent Supreme Court decision, however, suggests that in the absence of either statutory authority or a valid executive agreement, the executive will be unable to bind the states. In *Medellin v. Texas*, a Mexican national who had been convicted of murder and sentenced to death by a Texas state court appealed on the ground that he had been denied notification of his right to seek assistance from his consulate as required by a treaty ratified by the United States.[138] President Bush directed the state courts to honor a decision of the International Court of Justice that called for reconsideration of convictions and sentences to remedy this violation of international law in Medellin's case and others.[139] In the Supreme Court, the United States argued as *amicus curiae* that the President's directive should have preemptive effect on any state

---

[133] 539 U.S. 396, 416 (2003).

[134] *Id.* at 420–21.

[135] *Id.* at 415.

[136] *Id.* at 436 (Ginsburg, J., dissenting).

[137] The *Garamendi* Court characterized its earlier decision in *Barclays Bank PLC v. Franchise Tax Bd. of Cal.*, 512 U.S. 298 (1994), as involving only informal policy statements by executive officers, which were overborne by a congressional policy that the Court detected. The *Barclays Bank* Court had distinguished these statements from executive agreements and other actions having the force of law.

[138] 128 S.Ct. 1346 (2008).

[139] *Id.* at 1355.

law to the contrary.[140] Texas countered that the directive was not pursuant to an executive agreement with Mexico, but rather was an interpretation of preexisting treaty rights that was due no deference by Texas state courts.[141]

Chief Justice Roberts wrote an opinion for the Court that gave Texas a victory by ruling that President Bush's directive exceeded his powers.[142] The Court stressed that the treaties involved were not self-executing, but rather required statutory implementation to have the force of law in the U.S.[143] Applying Justice Jackson's tripartite analysis of powers from *Youngstown,* the Court held that when the Senate ratifies a treaty on the understanding that it is not self-executing, a presidential effort to execute it lies in Jackson's third category of actions inconsistent with congressional will.[144] The *Medellin* Court thought that this situation was "of a different nature" from the claims settlements that it had upheld in *Dames & Moore* and other cases.[145] In the claims settlement context, congressional acquiescence had been sufficient to imply executive authority; treaties that were not self-executing could not support an acquiescence argument.[146] The Court's refusal to approve free-wheeling presidential execution of such treaties implies that in the future, even formal executive agreements may need closer ties to statutory authority than has been the case since *Dames & Moore.*

Conclusion

Dames & Moore is best viewed as a decision that attempts to balance both of the large tradeoffs involved: those between executive power and individual rights; and those between executive and legislative power. Its animating concern can be traced directly back to *Youngstown* and to Justice Rehnquist's memory of the claims of unbounded executive power that were made and rejected there. The important feature of Justice Jackson's famous three categories of power is that they treat the existence of congressional restrictions on executive action as a real possibility to be examined in the case at hand. Jackson was explicitly cautious about recognizing claims to exclusive executive power, and

---

[140] *Id.* at 1367 (quoting Brief for the United States as Amicus Curiae at 5).

[141] *Id.* at 1356 (quoting *Ex parte* Medellin, 223 S.W.3d 315, 352 (Tex. Crim. App. 2006)).

[142] Justice Stevens concurred in the judgment; Justice Breyer dissented, joined by Justices Ginsburg and Souter.

[143] *Medellin,* 128 S.Ct. at 1357.

[144] *Id.* at 1369.

[145] *Id.* at 1371.

[146] *Id.* at 1372.

Rehnquist's opinion shares this caution. The point of view that is shared between these two Justices, both reacting to the same great moment in the Court's history, is essential to maintaining the separation of powers in the United States constitutional system.

The competing model of executive hegemony in foreign affairs, the one drawn from dicta in *Curtiss–Wright* but never adopted as the actual basis of a decision by the Court, is profoundly destabilizing. The great virtue of the *Dames & Moore* opinion is that it avoids that reef. The note of caution that it injects into executive decision-making is the correct one, and one with which all executive advisers should be prepared to live. It simply calls for an examination of whether a pattern of acquiescence in executive discretion has been broken by some statute relevant to the problem at hand. If so, the assumption is that the will of Congress prevails, unless truly extraordinary considerations support a claim to preclusive executive power.

11

Kevin M. Stack

The Story of *Morrison v. Olson*: The Independent Counsel and Independent Agencies in Watergate's Wake

Watergate motivated a wide variety of institutional reforms. One of the most significant was Congress's enactment of the independent counsel statute in 1978.[1] With it, Congress sought to strengthen the institutions responsible for investigating criminal conduct at the highest reaches of the executive branch. The independent counsel statute created a new form of prosecutor to be appointed by a specially designated federal court and to be removable by the Attorney General only for good cause.

In *Morrison v. Olson*,[2] the Supreme Court upheld the constitutionality of this exercise in institutional design. The *Morrison* decision has acquired two conventional readings. First, the decision is regarded as one

---

[1] The first independent counsel provisions were enacted as part of the Ethics in Government Act of 1978, Pub. L. No. 95–521, 92 Stat. 1824, 1867 (1978). This Act referred to the prosecutor it created as a "special prosecutor," and specified that the prosecutor could be removed, other than by impeachment, only by the Attorney General "only for extraordinary impropriety, physical disability, mental incapacity, or any other condition that substantially impairs ... performance...." *Id.* § 596(a)(1). The 1983 reenactment and amendments to these provisions changed the name of the prosecutor to "independent counsel," and changed "extraordinary improprieties" to "good cause." Pub. L. No. 97–409, §§ 2, 6(d), 96 Stat. 2039, 2042 (1983). The provisions were reenacted with amendments in 1987, Pub. L. No. 100–191, 101 Stat. 1293 (1987), and in 1994, Pub. L. No. 103–270, 108 Stat. 732 (1994). I refer to the statute that created this prosecutor in 1978 and afterwards as the "independent counsel statute," and the prosecutor it created as the "independent counsel." For a compact summary of the legislative amendments to the independent counsel statute, see Charles A. Johnson & Danette Brickman, *Independent Counsel: The Law and the Investigations* 253–313 (2001).

[2] 487 U.S. 654, 697 (1988).

of the most significant defeats for a strongly unitary conception of the executive because it upheld the statute's good-cause restriction on the President's power to remove the independent counsel. Second, with continued experience under the independent counsel statute following *Morrison*, many have come to believe that the *Morrison* Court fundamentally misjudged the risks the statute posed.

The story of *Morrison* complicates both of these conventional views of the decision. The stage for understanding *Morrison*'s contribution to the unitary executive debate is President Reagan's Department of Justice and its separation-of-powers litigation. During the Reagan administration, the Department of Justice sought to implement a strongly unitary conception of the executive, including challenging the constitutionality of independent agencies. The independent counsel shared the same objectionable feature as independent agencies—insulation from plenary presidential removal. This link between the two framed the way in which the independent counsel statute came to be presented to the Supreme Court, the character of arguments before the Court, and the Court's opinion.

Morrison's ultimate intervention on this turf was enigmatic. Although the *Morrison* Court validated, at least in form, Congress's authority to restrict the President's removal power, it did so in a curious manner, highlighting the similarities between the independent counsel and the Watergate special prosecutors, who enjoyed no statutory removal protections. The independent counsel, the Court's analysis suggested, was merely a variant of the removable special prosecutor. Rather than marking a strong affirmation of restrictions on the president's removal power, the decision (re)ignited the question of how much actual protection from presidential influence good cause restrictions provide.

The *Morrison* Court's analogy between the independent counsel and the Watergate special prosecutor also calls into question the conventional charge that the Supreme Court failed to see the risks posed by the independent counsel statute, and thus upheld a cure that was worse than the disease. From this critical perspective, the perceived excesses of the Independent Counsel Kenneth Starr's investigation of President Clinton served to vindicate Justice Scalia, who had warned in his *Morrison* dissent that the statute allowed a retaliatory prosecution, enabled by "judges hostile to the administration, the independent counsel an old foe of the President, the staff refugees from the recently defeated administration," and leaving "no one accountable to the public to whom the blame could be assigned."[3] As one participant put it, during the Starr investigation, "the parade of horribles envisioned by Justice

---

[3] *Morrison*, 487 U.S. at 731 (Scalia, J., dissenting).

Scalia" was "marching right down Pennsylvania Avenue."[4] On this reading, Congress's decision not to reauthorize the statute in 1999 operated as a confirmation of *Morrison*'s errors.

A closer look at *Morrison* reveals a more complex picture of the Court's decision. The Court rejected a facial attack on the constitutionality of the independent counsel statute. But it did so in part by construing the independent counsel's protection from presidential removal as only incrementally stronger than the protections afforded to the Watergate special prosecutors. Once the independent counsel was normalized within the familiar frame of the Watergate special prosecutor, the risks of abuse that so animated Justice Scalia appeared less pressing when compared to the evident benefits the country had gained through the Watergate investigations conducted by Archibald Cox and Leon Jaworski. Whatever failings the Watergate special prosecutor model had, it could not be said to have left no one accountable for the public to blame. What is more, once the independent counsel and the Watergate special prosecutor are construed as fundamentally similar, it is less clear that the manner in which later Presidents (and independent counsels) chose to act under the statute may be put at the feet of the *Morrison* Court.

This chapter traces these two strains—*Morrison* and the investigation of executive misconduct, and *Morrison* and debate over agency independence—separately in the political and legal context preceding the decision, and illustrates their connections in the Supreme Court's opinion. The chapter begins by briefly describing the Watergate controversy out of which the independent counsel statute arose, highlighting contrast between the special prosecutor model of Watergate (and today) and the independent counsel model for investigating executive misconduct. It then turns to how the independent counsel statute became entwined in the larger effort of President Reagan's Department of Justice to challenge the constitutionality of independent agencies. In that context, the chapter surveys the political dispute between the Department of Justice, the Environmental Protection Agency, and the House of Representatives that ultimately led to the independent counsel investigation of Theodore Olson, a top Department of Justice lawyer during Reagan's first term. In describing the litigation leading up the *Morrison* decision, the chapter shows how the Department of Justice's efforts to avoid constitutional review of the independent counsel statute ended up suggesting a fundamental similarity between the independent counsel and the special prosecutor, and as a result, strengthening the grounds for upholding the statute. Finally, it examines how that similarity featured in the *Morrison* opinion and shapes its legacy.

---

[4] Linda Greenhouse, *Blank Check; Ethics in Government: The Price of Good Intentions*, N.Y. Times, Feb. 1, 1998, § 4, at 1 (quoting Walter Dellinger).

From Special Prosecutor to Independent Counsel

The independent counsel statute traces its origins to Saturday, October 20, 1973, the day President Nixon succeeded in dismissing the first Watergate Special Prosecutor, Archibald Cox, in the midst of his investigation.[5] In response to Cox's plan to compel President Nixon's compliance with court orders requiring disclosure of tapes and documents of White House conversations, President Nixon ordered his Attorney General, Elliot Richardson, to fire Cox.[6] Richardson refused, and resigned. The next in the chain of command at the Department of Justice, William Ruckelshaus, also refused to dismiss Cox, and resigned.[7] In the end, Solicitor General Robert Bork, third at the Department of Justice, fired Cox.[8]

At the time the Watergate scandal arose, the country had a relatively long history of appointing *ad hoc* special prosecutors, from President Grant's 1875 appointment of a special prosecutor to investigate corruption in the reporting of whiskey production, to President Truman's appointment, through his Attorney General, of a special prosecutor to investigate misconduct in the revenue service.[9] That history also included notable firings. President Grant directly ordered his Attorney General to fire the special prosecutor that President Grant had himself appointed and to find a suitable replacement.[10] A replacement special prosecutor

---

[5] For a detailed account, see, for example, *Watergate: Chronology of A Crisis* 353–67 (Wayne Kelley ed., 1975); Ken Gormley, *Archibald Cox: Conscience of a Nation* 338–77 (1997). For more on *United States v. Nixon* see chapter 9 in this volume.

[6] Letter from Elliot Richardson, U.S. Att'y Gen., to President Richard Nixon (Oct. 20, 1973), *reprinted in Watergate: Chronology of a Crisis* 371–72 (Wayne Kelley ed., 1975).

[7] Letter from William D. Ruckelshaus, Deputy Att'y Gen., to President Richard Nixon (Oct. 20, 1973), *reprinted in Watergate: Chronology of a Crisis* 372 (Wayne Kelley ed., 1975).

[8] Letter from Robert H. Bork, Solicitor Gen., to Archibald Cox, Special Prosecutor (Oct. 20, 1973), *reprinted in Watergate: Chronology of a Crisis* 372 (Wayne Kelley ed., 1975).

[9] Charles A. Johnson & Danette Brickman, *Independent Counsel: The Law and the Investigations* 8–11 (2001); Katy J. Harriger, *Independent Justice: The Federal Special Prosecutor in American Politics* 15–16 (1992); David A. Logan, *Historical Uses of a Special Prosecutor: The Administrations of Presidents Grant, Coolidge, and Truman* (Congressional Research Service Nov. 23, 1973); Terry Eastland, *Ethics, Politics and the Independent Counsel: Executive Power, Executive Vice 1789–1989* 7–16 (1989); *Historical Encyclopedia of U.S. Independent Counsel Investigations* 231–33 (Gerald S. Greenberg ed., 2000).

[10] Terry Eastland, *Ethics, Politics and the Independent Counsel: Executive Power, Executive Vice 1789–1989* 14 (1989); Charles A. Johnson & Danette Brickman, *Independent Counsel: The Law and the Investigations* 9 (2001); David A. Logan, *Historical Uses of a Special Prosecutor: The Administrations of Presidents Grant, Coolidge, and Truman* 12 (Congressional Research Service Nov. 23, 1973) ("You will advise General Henderson of his discharge from further service," President Grant wrote on December 10, 1875.).

was installed the next day.[11] President Truman's Attorney General fired a special prosecutor, apparently misjudging Truman's wishes and prompting the Attorney General's own firing.[12]

Thus Archibald Cox was not the first special prosecutor appointed to investigate allegations of criminal misconduct at the highest reaches of the executive branch, nor the first to be fired by the President or an Attorney General, nor the first whose firing resulted in the appointment of a replacement. But none of the prior firings registered in the national imagination the way President Nixon's firing of Cox did. In Watergate, the wrong-doing included the President himself. Something else, however, bolstered the sense of shock and betrayal that came with the Cox firing, and ultimately undergirded the long-term legislative momentum toward reform of the institutional arrangements under which Cox (and his successor) operated.

President Nixon had made a public commitment to a full inquiry into the Watergate matter.[13] Just as important, during his confirmation hearings, Attorney General Richardson extensively and publicly committed himself to the independence of the special prosecutor.[14]

The special prosecutor model as Richardson defended it had four basic features. First, the special prosecutor was an *ad hoc* appointment of the Attorney General, and therefore the Attorney General had the power to terminate the special prosecutor at will. At the time of the Watergate scandal, as today, the Attorney General had statutory authority to delegate any function of the Attorney General to any officer of the Department of Justice, and specifically to appoint attorneys to conduct any legal proceeding on behalf of the United States.[15] It was this grant of

---

[11] David A. Logan, *Historical Uses of a Special Prosecutor: The Administrations of Presidents Grant, Coolidge, and Truman* 13 (Congressional Research Service Nov. 23, 1973).

[12] Charles A. Johnson & Danette Brickman, *Independent Counsel: The Law and the Investigations* 10 (2001); Katy J. Harriger, *Independent Justice: The Federal Special Prosecutor in American Politics* 16 (1992).

[13] President Nixon's Television Address to Nation, April 30, 1973, *reprinted in Watergate: A Chronology of a Crisis* 35 (1975) ("I know that as Attorney General, Elliot Richardson will be both fair and fearless in pursuing this case wherever it leads. I am confident that with him in charge, justice will be done.").

[14] *Nomination of Elliot Richardson to be Attorney General, Hearings Before the S. Comm. on the Judiciary*, 93rd Cong. (1973) (hereinafter "Richardson Hearings").

[15] 28 U.S.C. §§ 510, 515. Richardson also pointed to the statutory requirement that "the conduct of litigation in which the United States . . . is a party . . . is reserved to officers of the Department of Justice, under the direction of the Attorney General," 28 U.S.C. § 516, and a more general duty that "the Attorney General shall supervise all litigation to which the United States . . . is a party," 28 U.S.C. § 519. Richardson Hearings at 69. When pressed by the Senate, Richardson clearly stated that he did not see how a

statutory authority that Richardson said he would, and did, invoke to appoint a special Watergate prosecutor.[16] As such, Richardson consistently explained throughout his confirmation hearings that the Attorney General must maintain "ultimate responsibility" for the investigation.[17]

Second, Richardson committed to granting the special prosecutor "complete authority" with respect to the investigation of matters arising out of the Watergate break-in.[18] Third, he pledged to protect the independence of the special prosecutor "with the greatest degree of independence that is consistent with the Attorney General's statutory accountability for all matters falling within the jurisdiction of the Department of Justice."[19] He backed that up by articulating an extremely high standard for removal: "The Special Prosecutor will not be removed from his duties except for extraordinary improprieties on his part."[20] And finally, Richardson committed to selecting a special prosecutor of high integrity; he found that Cox, a former Solicitor General and Harvard Law School professor fit that bill.

Richardson's testimony revealed his confidence in this arrangement as adequate to the task of ensuring the independence of the investigation. Asked by Senator Hart to explain whether the President could dismiss the special prosecutor by firing Richardson as Attorney General, Richardson testified:

> No. No.... He could dismiss me, but the special prosecutor would be my appointee.... And if I were directed to fire him and I refused, and I would refuse in the absence of some overwhelming evidence of cause, the President's only recourse would be to replace me.[21]

In the same breath, Richardson miscalculated the prospect of such an event occurring. His testimony continued:

---

special prosecutor could constitutionally be created outside the ultimate responsibility of the Attorney General and thus the President, because the prosecutor would be "part of the executive branch, ... in any event [would] be responsible to the President, in whom ultimate Executive authority is vested." Richardson Hearings at 141.

[16] Richardson Hearings at 72 ("Well, of course, this is the section that I would use in vesting authority in the special prosecutor.").

[17] *See, e.g., id.* at 6, 67, 72 ("I have tried in these hearings to make clear that if I have appointed somebody and given him full authority, I would retain ultimate responsibility not simply regarding the manner in which he exercised his delegated power, but in standing back of what he did." Richardson Hearings at 72.).

[18] *See, e.g., id.* at 144.

[19] *Id.* at 145 (reproducing "Duties and Responsibilities of the Special Prosecutor").

[20] *Id.*

[21] *Id.* at 72–73.

Now, again, these are things that in the present circumstances are so remotely possible as to be practically inconceivable....

Now ... given the kinds of public interest at stake, for the President to intervene in the matter of the appointment or the way the special prosecutor does his job and so on, would be totally at variance with the whole approach he set forth. It just will not happen.[22]

Prior to Cox's firing each of the elements of Richardson's proposed "three-layered insurance policy"[23] were satisfied. Richardson had committed to Cox's independence and powers, and carried through on his promises, resigning as opposed to executing President Nixon's order to fire Cox. Thus, when President Nixon fired Cox, his action appeared to shatter not only the Watergate investigation itself, but also the special prosecutor model in which it operated. The weakness appeared to rest with the structure of the special prosecutor as an *ad hoc* appointee of the Attorney General.

Within weeks of Cox's firing, several proposals emerged for creating a new special prosecutor based on statutory independence from the President. Two of the most controversial features of the independent counsel statute that was eventually enacted surfaced in this first round of bills: appointment of the special prosecutor by a court, and protection of the special prosecutor from removal by the Attorney General or President.[24] In the midst of the Watergate story, the overwhelming political pressure to replace Cox, and the confidence generated by his nearly immediate replacement, Leon Jaworski, blunted immediate legislative interest in these broad institutional reforms. Through Jaworski's efforts, culminating in successful litigation to the Supreme Court to

---

[22] *Id.*

[23] *Id.* at 141.

[24] Senate Bill No. 2611 had the most initial legislative interest, acquiring the backing of 55 Senators (47 Democrats and eight Republicans), with eight members of the Senate select committee among its sponsors. *See Watergate: Chronology of a Crisis* 378 (Wayne Kelly ed., 1975). It vested the appointment of the special prosecutor in the chief judge of the United States District Court for the District of Columbia, as Cox himself had recommended following his dismissal, *see Special Prosecutor, Hearings Before the S. Comm. on the Judiciary*, 93d Cong. Part 1, 19 (Oct. 29, 1973) ("appointment by the district court would be the wisest, wisest by a good deal, I think.") with the special prosecutor to be removable only by the appointing court upon a showing he "willfully violated" the act or "committed extraordinary improprieties," *see* S. 2611, 93rd Cong. § 10 (1973). The bill expressly prohibited the President or Attorney General to direct, otherwise interfere with, or remove the special prosecutor. *See id.* § 11. Another bill proposed the creation of an office of the special prosecutor to be selected by the chief judge of the federal district court in the District of Columbia, and removable only by impeachment. *See* S. 260, 93rd Cong. § 5 (1973). Senator Ervin proposed a bill to make the Department of Justice itself an independent agency, with the Attorney General removable only for cause. *See* S. 2803, 93rd Cong. § 2(a) (1973).

require President Nixon to disclose the White House tapes, the nation came to know that President Nixon had become part of the effort to cover-up the Watergate affair, and on August 9, 1974, President Nixon resigned.

With the underlying facts of Watergate revealed and with Nixon's resignation, one is tempted to say that the special prosecutor model defended by Richardson ended up working rather well.[25] The shortcomings in its institutional arrangements, on the one hand, became apparent in President Nixon's firing of Cox. At the same time, the responsiveness of Congress and the executive branch more generally led to the rapid appointment of a replacement, who by most accounts, straightforwardly fulfilled his mission. While the Watergate special prosecutor model allowed politics to trump legal process in the short term, it was not without political accountability for President Nixon.

Congress did not, however, have such a charitable view of the overall performance of the process, and legislative interest in a newly devised arrangement for a special prosecutor persisted following Nixon's resignation. After several years of legislative impasse, in 1978, President Carter signed into law the Ethics in Government Act. The Act's Title VI ostensibly completed the transformation from Richardson's special prosecutor model to the independent counsel vision.

The Act required the Attorney General to conduct a "preliminary investigation" upon "receiving specific information" that individuals covered by the statute had committed a violation of federal criminal law.[26] The Attorney General then had 90 days to determine whether the matter is "so unsubstantiated as not to warrant further investigation."[27] If the Attorney General either found that further investigation was warranted or failed to make a determination within 90 days, the Attorney General was required to apply to a special division of the United States Court of Appeals for the District of Columbia for the appointment of an independent counsel.[28]

---

[25] See, e.g., Harold H. Bruff, *Balance of Forces: Separation of Powers Law in the Administrative State* 440–41 (2006) (noting the promise of the Watergate model); see also The American Enterprise Institute and The Brookings Institution, Robert Dole & George J. Mitchell, Co–Chairs, *Project on the Independent Counsel Statute, Report and Recommendations* 9 (1999) (recommending emulation of key aspects of the Watergate special prosecutor experience); Christopher H. Schroeder, *Putting Law and Politics in the Right Places—Reforming the Independent Counsel Statute*, 62 Law & Contemp. Probs. 163, 180–81 (1999) (arguing that placing decision to prosecute in hands of President or Attorney General would be more sound course).

[26] Ethics in Government Act of 1978, Pub. L. No. 95–521, §§ 591(a), 592(a), 92 Stat. 1824, 1867 (1978).

[27] *Id.* § 592(c)(1).

[28] *Id.* § 592(c).

Under the Act, the power to appoint the independent counsel was vested in that special division, along with the power to define the prosecutor's jurisdiction.[29] The Act provided the independent counsel with "full power and independent authority to exercise all investigative and prosecutorial functions and powers of the Department of Justice."[30] As to removal, the statute provided that the independent counsel could be removed, other than by impeachment and conviction, only by the Attorney General "for extraordinary impropriety, physical disability, mental incapacity, or any other condition that substantially impairs the performance of such special prosecutor's duties."[31] The "extraordinary impropriety" language traced Attorney General Richardson's standard for removal of Cox. The Act bolstered this high standard for removal with a provision for judicial review, by the special division, including a possible remedy of reinstatement.[32] The Act also included a sunset provision for five years from the date of enactment.[33]

The Senate Report summarized the core ambition of the Act as placing criminal investigation of high-ranking government officials in the hands of a prosecutor who is "independent, both in reality and appearance, from the President and the Attorney General."[34] With that ambition, and choice of mechanism to achieve it, the independent counsel provisions of the Ethics in Government Act of 1978 set in motion a constitutional clash about the scope of executive power.

Theodore Olson, the Reagan Department of Justice, and Executive Power

The early years of the independent counsel statute coincided with President Reagan's first term in office. President Reagan campaigned for and sought to implement a broadly deregulatory agenda.[35] Implementing that agenda required asserting control over administrative agencies. It fell to the administration's top lawyers to develop a legal strategy that would enable the administration to gain the necessary influence over the vast administrative state. Those lawyers developed a conception of the President's constitutional power that allowed for greater presidential

---

[29] *Id.* §§ 593(b)-(c).

[30] *Id.* § 594(a).

[31] *Id.* § 596(a)(1).

[32] *Id.* § 596(a)(3).

[33] *Id.* § 598.

[34] S. Rep. No. 95–170, at 65–66 (1978).

[35] *See, e.g.,* David A. Stockman, *The Triumph of Politics: How the Reagan Revolution Failed* 103 (1986) ("Sweeping deregulation was another pillar of the supply-side platform.").

control of administrative action; that conception left no constitutional space for independent agencies—agencies protected from removal under a good cause standard—much less the independent counsel statute.

Administration lawyers argued that Article II's vesting of "executive power" in the President[36] combined with the President's authority to "take Care that the Laws be faithfully executed"[37] requires that the President have power to supervise and control the implementation of all federal law, and bars Congress from imposing restrictions on his power to fire executive officers at will. And for those with constitutional or political objections to independent agencies, the independent counsel statute was, as one participant put it, an "outrage."[38] The statute imposed removal restrictions on an officer whose functions seem to be the paradigm of exercises of executive power—criminal investigation and prosecution.

Shortly after taking office, President Reagan took an important step in implementing greater control over federal agencies. He issued his widely-discussed executive order providing for centralized review of major agency actions.[39] The executive order required executive agencies to conduct cost-benefit analysis of their significant regulations and to submit the regulations and their analysis for review by the Office of Management and Budget. The executive order gave the White House a right to review an agency's proposed regulation, and grounds to require the agency to alter its regulations to conform to White House priorities.

While the Office of Legal Counsel (OLC) within the Department of Justice had advised the White House that it could constitutionally apply the proposed executive order to independent agencies,[40] the White House declined to do so. The conventional view is that the White House's decision not to extend the order to independent agencies was a political one: "the political costs of arousing congressional opposition, perhaps to the order as a whole, would be too great."[41]

---

[36] U.S. Const. art. II, § 1, cl. 1.

[37] *Id.* art. II, § 3, cl. 4.

[38] Charles Fried, *Order and Law: Arguing the Reagan Revolution—A Firsthand Account* 137 (1991).

[39] Exec. Order No. 12,291, 46 Fed. Reg. 13,193 (Feb. 17, 1981).

[40] Memorandum for Honorable David Stockman, Director, Office of Management and Budget, Re: Proposed Executive Order on Federal Regulation, *reprinted in* Peter M. Shane & Harold H. Bruff, *The Law of Separation of Powers* 521–23 (2d ed. 2005).

[41] Peter L. Strauss, *The Place of Agencies in Government: Separation of Powers and the Fourth Branch*, 84 Colum. L. Rev. 573, 593 (1984); *see* Jerry L. Mashaw, Richard A. Merrill & Peter M. Shane, *Administrative Law: The American Public Law System, Cases and Materials* 275 (5th ed. 2003) (White House viewed it as prudent to avoid a "turf battle"

In this light, the Reagan administration viewed independent agencies as a problem. Their "independence of presidential authority was considered the extreme example, a kind of emblem, of one of the biggest obstacles to the administration's program."[42] To bring these agencies within direct presidential supervision, lawyers at the Department of Justice hoped to establish grounds for a Supreme Court decision that "would hold that agency commissions served at the pleasure of the President, and that statutory limitations on their removal were unconstitutional."[43]

Theodore Olson held one of the key positions at the Department of Justice as Assistant Attorney General in charge of OLC, and helped to lay the groundwork for such an assault. He issued several legal opinions at OLC on relatively low-stake issues that suggested the possible foundation for a challenge to independent agencies.

In March of 1982, Olson took the view that the primary functions of the Advisory Council on Historic Preservation were "executive in nature, and thus not such as would permit Congress constitutionally to insulate its members from the President's removal power,"[44] despite the Council's statutory designation as "independent."[45] In March 1983, Olson concluded that allowing the EEOC to take a litigation position contrary to that of the Attorney General would not only exceed the agency's statutory authority, but also be "inconsistent with the constitutional principle of the unitary executive,"[46] because the "whole of the Executive power . . . is vested exclusively in the President."[47] In November 1983, Olson concluded that a statute requiring the FAA to report concurrently

---

over independent agencies with Congress.); *cf.* Remarks of C. Boyden Gray, Counsel to Vice President Bush and the Presidential Task Force on Regulatory Relief, Hall of Flags Regulatory Reform Briefing Before the United States Chamber of Commerce, Apr. 10, 1980, *reprinted in Role of the Office of Management and Budget in Regulation: Hearings Before the Subcomm. On Oversight and Investigations of the H. Comm. on Energy and Commerce*, 97th Cong. 94 (1981) ("We chose not to do it really because of policy reasons that we had our plate more than full with the Executive Branch Agencies which impose by far the greatest percentage of capital costs.").

[42] Charles Fried, *Order and Law: Arguing the Reagan Revolution—A Firsthand Account* 154–55 (1991).

[43] *Id.* at 157.

[44] Removal of Members of the Advisory Council on Historic Preservation, 6 Op. Off. Legal Counsel 180, 180 (Mar. 11, 1982).

[45] *Id.* at 181 (noting 16 U.S.C. § 470i designation).

[46] Litigation Authority of the Equal Employment Opportunity Commission in Title VII Suits Against State and Local Government Entities, 7 Op. Off. Legal Counsel 57, 57 (Mar. 13, 1983).

[47] *Id.* at 64.

to Congress and the President would violate separation of powers principles. Separation of powers, Olson wrote, "requires that the President have ultimate control over subordinate officials who perform purely executive functions, which includes the right to supervise and review the work of such officials."[48]

Based on these positions, it followed that the removal restrictions on the independent counsel, who exercises purely executive functions, would also be unconstitutional. Olson's opinions, however, stopped short of concluding that removal restrictions on independent agencies were themselves invalid.

The Department of Justice's own victory in *INS v. Chadha*[49] in 1983 bolstered the logic for taking that further step. As indicated by Olson's opinion on the Advisory Council on Historical Preservation, longstanding Supreme Court doctrine recognized that the President had the power to remove "purely executive" officers at will. That position was culled from the Supreme Court's two most important decisions on the removal power, *Humphrey's Executor v. United States*[50] and *Myers v. United States*.[51] In *Myers*, the Supreme Court invalidated a statute that required Senate advice and consent prior to removal of a postmaster, with Chief Justice Taft's majority opinion embracing a broad view that congressional restrictions on removal where the appointment was made by the President were nearly always impermissible.[52] In *Humphrey's Executor*, the Court cut back on the broader implications of *Myers*, and validated a good cause restriction on removal for Federal Trade Commissioners. *Humphrey's Executor* distinguished *Myers* on the ground that the character of the office at issue in *Myers* was purely executive, while the FTC Commissioners performed "quasi legislative" and "quasi judicial functions."[53]

Chadha added an important dimension to the *Myers–Humphrey's Executor* analysis. In *Chadha*, the Supreme Court invalidated the one-House legislative veto, in a manner which emphasized the formal separation of powers among the branches. The Constitution, the Court wrote, "divide[d] the delegated powers of the new Federal Government into three defined categories, legislative, executive, and judicial, to assure, as

---

[48] Constitutionality of Statute Requiring Executive Agency to Report Directly to Congress, 6 Op. Off. Legal Counsel 632, 632 (Nov. 5, 1982).

[49] 462 U.S. 919 (1983).

[50] 295 U.S. 602 (1935).

[51] 272 U.S. 52 (1926).

[52] *Id.* For more on *Myers v. United States* see chapter 5 in this volume.

[53] 295 U.S. at 628–29.

nearly as possible, that each Branch of government would confine itself to its assigned responsibility."[54] The Court concluded that "legislative power" may be exercised only through bicameralism and presentment to the President. Thus, once the Court concluded that the one-House veto was an exercise of legislative power, it followed as a matter of course that the one-House veto was unconstitutional.[55]

One implication of the more formal mode of separation of powers analysis embraced in *Chadha* is that all independent agencies would have to be classified within one of these three silos of power, not in an uncertain constitutional spot as "quasi-legislative" or "quasi-judicial." And among the three silos, logic would place them clearly within the executive branch. Indeed, Chief Justice Burger's opinion in *Chadha* suggested that when "quasi-legislative" functions, like rulemaking, are undertaken by agencies, they are executive in nature.[56]

Thus, *Chadha* could be read to suggest that it was no longer possible for an office to be something other than "purely executive" or "purely legislative" or "purely judicial." On that view, all agencies would fall within the executive branch. But once that is true, per *Meyers*, all executive officers would be within the President's power to remove at will. In short, the logic of *Chadha* plus *Myers* provided grounds to mount a challenge to the constitutionality of independent agencies.[57] As Attorney General Meese had argued in a widely-cited set of remarks in 1985, in the post-*Chadha* era, "federal agencies performing executive functions are themselves properly agents of the executive. They are not 'quasi' this, or 'independent' that."[58]

But the theory had not yet been tested in a challenge to a removal restriction. As it happened, the initial test of the theory came in *Bowsher v. Synar*,[59] the Supreme Court's decision striking down the Gramm–Rudman–Hollings Act.[60] The Supreme Court's decision in *Bowsher* foreshadowed its resistance to the broad *Chadha*-plus-*Myers* logic that any

---

[54] 462 U.S. at 951.

[55] *Id.* at 952, 958–59.

[56] *Id.* at 954 n.16; *see* Peter L. Strauss, *The Place of Agencies in Government: Separation of Powers and the Fourth Branch*, 84 Colum. L. Rev. 573, 635 (1984) (noting *Chadha*'s characterization of "quasi-adjudication" and "quasi-legislation" within the executive branch).

[57] I thank Professor John Harrison for suggesting this discussion.

[58] Edwin Meese, III, *Towards Increased Government Accountability*, 32 Fed. B. News & J. 406, 408 (1985).

[59] 478 U.S. 714 (1986).

[60] The formal name of the act is the Balanced Budget and Emergency Deficit Control Act of 1985, Pub. L. 99–177, 99 Stat. 1038 (1982).

executive official must serve at the President's pleasure ultimately put directly before the Court in *Morrison*.

The Gramm–Rudman–Hollings Act, aimed at reducing the federal deficit, granted the Comptroller General power the Court understood to be executive in nature.[61] The Comptroller General, however, is removable only by impeachment or by a joint resolution of Congress on the grounds of good cause.[62] Because these removal restrictions both included a good cause restriction and vested removal authority in Congress, they were open to two different grounds for challenge. The more narrow challenge, relying on *Myers* alone, was that the Congress cannot grant itself any role in the removal of federal officials. The broader logic, invoking the *Chadha*-plus-*Myers* view, was that the President must have authority to remove the Comptroller General at will because the Comptroller exercises executive power. The United States challenged the Act on both theories.[63]

Whether the Court adopted the broad or narrow argument, of course, would make all the difference for the constitutional status of independent agencies, and the independent counsel. Justice O'Connor's exchange with Solicitor General Fried at oral argument nicely conveys the Court's clear understanding of these stakes. Fried began his argument suggesting that the government's position did not throw overboard the constitutional foundation for independent agencies, and the suggestions by the opposing counsel to the contrary were merely meant to "scare."[64] To that, Justice O'Connor interjected, "Well, Mr. Fried, you certainly scared me."[65]

Fried's position did not, it later became clear, scare Chief Justice Burger. Chief Justice Burger's first draft of the opinion in *Bowsher* came very close to adopting the broader logic. In its Part III, the Chief Justice wrote that because the "power of removal over Executive Branch officers resides in the President" Congress may not "retain the sole power of removal of an officer charged with the execution of the laws."[66] In

---

[61] *See Bowsher*, 478 U.S. at 726.

[62] *Id.* at 720, 728.

[63] *See* Brief for the United States at 31–32, 48, *Bowsher*, 478 U.S. 714 (Nos. 85–1377, 85–1378 & 85–1379).

[64] Transcript of Oral Argument at 47, *Bowsher*, 478 U.S. 714 (Nos. 85–1377, 85–1378 & 85–1379).

[65] *Id.*; *see also* Charles Fried, *Order and Law: Arguing the Reagan Revolution—A Firsthand Account* 159–60 (1991) (recounting the exchange).

[66] Bernard Schwartz, *An Administrative Law "Might Have Been"—Chief Justice Burger's* Bowsher v. Synar *Draft*, 42 Admin. L. Rev. 221, 243 (1990) (reproducing withdrawn *Bowsher v. Synar* first draft).

response to the draft, Justice O'Connor wrote to Chief Justice Burger "with the possible exception of Bill Rehnquist, those who voted to affirm hope to make sure that the opinion not cast doubt on the constitutionality of independent agencies.... I fear that the opinion as now written, especially Part III, does just that."[67] All of the other members of the conference majority except for Justice Rehnquist objected to Chief Justice Burger's draft.[68]

The ultimate opinion in *Bowsher* rested on the narrower ground that "Congress cannot reserve for itself" the power of removal of an officer charged with the execution of the laws.[69] Justice White's dissent highlighted this distinction: "I wish to emphasize what it is that the Court quite pointedly and correctly does *not* hold: namely, that 'executive' powers of the sort granted to the Comptroller by the Act may only be exercised by officers removable at will by the President."[70]

Bowsher, then, although a technical victory for the Reagan Justice Department, was a partial defeat for its strongly unitary conception of presidential control. The Court had the chance to embrace that vision, but the fact that the statute granted removal power to Congress allowed the Court to side-step the issue, and resolve the case on a more narrow ground. Following *Bowsher*, the question remained whether the Court would embrace a strongly unitary conception of the executive in the context of a statute in which Congress granted to itself no role in removal.

That question was posed squarely by removal restrictions on independent agencies and by the independent counsel statute. While the Justices' deliberations in *Bowsher* clearly suggested the Court would not go so far as to strike down all removal restrictions, their deliberations in response to Chief Justice Burger's first draft were not public. The Reagan lawyers had only the signal that the Court had declined to embrace their broader challenge in *Bowsher*. Raising the issue in the context of a challenge to the independent counsel statute, however, posed a strategic problem for the Justice Department: the independent counsel had a Watergate-reform appeal unmatched by independent agencies. For the Reagan administration, the litigation challenging the independent counsel statute, including Olson's own, became an undesired stalking horse for the constitutionality of independent agencies.

---

[67] Letter from Justice Sandra Day O'Connor to Chief Justice Warren Burger (June 2, 1986), quoted in *id.* at 227.

[68] *Id.* at 227–29.

[69] *Bowsher*, 478 U.S. at 726.

[70] *Id.* at 760 (White, J., dissenting).

Factual and Litigation Background

At the same time as a possible legal challenge to independent agencies was developing in the Reagan Department of Justice and unfolding in the courts, it was Theodore Olson's advice on another aspect of executive power that ended up leading to the appointment of an independent counsel to investigate him. Olson had advised President Reagan and the EPA to assert executive privilege in response to subpoenas from the House. That advice, and statements about it before the House, lead to a call from the House for an independent counsel investigation of him and others, and a fierce political clash between the House and the Reagan Administration.

In the fall of 1982, while the House was under Democratic leadership, two House Subcommittees began concurrent investigations into EPA's implementation of the Superfund hazardous cleanup legislation, seeking a broad range of documents regarding EPA's activities under the legislation as well as information about specific Superfund sites. The Subcommittees had obtained information from current and former EPA employees suggesting that partisan political considerations had influenced the EPA's handling of Superfund enforcement actions.[71] For instance, EPA staff members alleged that political appointees within EPA purposefully delayed a proposed agreement on cost sharing between the federal government and California concerning the clean-up of the Stringfellow Site until after the November elections.[72] At the time, then-Governor Jerry Brown was seeking election to the U.S. Senate for California against Pete Wilson. The implication was that if the settlement had been reached prior to the election, Governor Brown could have taken credit for the cooperative agreement in his re-election bid.[73] There were allegations that similar political considerations had influenced EPA action with regard to sites in Indiana,[74] Michigan, and Oklahoma.[75]

The EPA sought advice from the OLC on the scope of its obligations to disclose information to Congress in response to these requests. After negotiations with the House Subcommittees collapsed, the OLC recom-

---

[71] *Report of the Independent Counsel Concerning Theodore B. Olson and Robert M. Perry* at 33–34, D.C. Cir., Div. for Purpose of Appointing Independent Counsels, Div. No. 86–1 (Dec. 27, 1988) (hereinafter "Morrison Report").

[72] *Investigation of the Role of the Department of Justice in the Withholding of Environmental Protection Agency Documents From Congress in 1982–83*, H.R. Rep. No. 99–435, at 38–40, 32–33 (1985) (hereinafter "House Report"). The site was the Stringfellow Acid Pits in Riverside County, California. *See id.* at 32.

[73] *See id.* at 38–40, 32–33.

[74] *Id.* at 33–34.

[75] Morrison Report at 33–34.

mended to President Reagan that the EPA assert executive privilege and withhold documents found in "open investigative files" reflecting "law enforcement strategy."[76] President Reagan then directed the Administrator of the EPA at the time, Anne Gorsuch, to assert executive privilege in response to the House subpoenas.[77] Administrator Gorsuch followed President Reagan's directive, and the full House of Representatives ended up voting to hold her in contempt for failure to comply with the subpoena.[78] It was a historic first contempt citation for a Cabinet-level official, and Olson's advice to assert executive privilege had played an important role in it.

If only to highlight the level of acrimony between the Executive and Legislative branches, on the same day as the contempt citation, the Department of Justice and Administrator Gorsuch filed a civil lawsuit against *the House of Representatives*, several of its subcommittees, the Speaker and the subcommittee chairs. The suit's caption succinctly conveyed the charged political atmosphere: on the one side it named the United States of America, along with Administrator Gorsuch, as the plaintiffs, and the other side of the "v." (and the aisle) it named the House of Representatives as the lead defendant, resulting in *United States v. House of Representatives*.[79] The plaintiffs sought a declaration of the validity of Administrator Gorsuch's assertion of executive privilege and corresponding injunctive relief. Olson reviewed the complaint after it was filed, and prepared a memorandum that suggested filing an amended complaint.[80] With the filing of the civil action, the clash between the Executive and the Legislature had escalated beyond a battle; "the War of the Branches," declared a New York Times headline on December 18, 1982.[81]

---

[76] Memorandum from Theodore B. Olson, Office of Legal Counsel, to President Ronald Reagan (Oct. 25, 1982), *reprinted in* House Report at 1018–22.

[77] Memorandum from President Reagan For the Administrator, Environmental Protection Agency (Nov. 30, 1982), *reprinted in* House Report at 1166–67. During the course of these events, Administrator Gorsuch was married, and became Anne Burford. I refer to her as Anne Gorsuch throughout. *See* House Report at 4 n.2.

[78] H.R. Res. 632, 128 Cong. Rec. H10040 (daily ed. Dec. 16, 1982); *see* 2 U.S.C. § 192 (providing that a person subpoenaed who refuses to produce papers upon any matter under inquiry of the House or any of its committees shall be guilty of a misdemeanor) and § 194 (providing that following contempt the Speaker of the House is to certify the contempt citation to the U.S. Attorney, who is required to bring the matter to the grand jury).

[79] *See* Michael Herz, United States v. United States: *When Can the Federal Government Sue Itself?*, 32 Wm. & Mary L. Rev. 893, 991 (1991).

[80] Morrison Report at 84; House Report at 381.

[81] Editorial, *The War of the Branches*, N.Y. Times, Dec. 18, 1982, § 1 at 26.

The district court dismissed the civil suit on jurisdictional grounds,[82] and shortly thereafter, individuals in the Department of Justice, including Olson, learned that documents regarding possible political manipulation of EPA Superfund sites had been withheld from the House subcommittees. That revelation resulted in the firing and eventual prosecution of a top EPA official, Rita Lavelle.[83] And in rapid succession, the Department of Justice and EPA dropped their claims of executive privilege, and disclosed the remaining documents with evidence of political manipulation, including those involving the Stringfellow site in California, to the House.[84] With their revelation, Administrator Gorsuch resigned, and the House voted to withdraw its contempt citation.

In view of all these questions of disclosure, the House Judiciary Committee commenced an investigation into the way EPA and the Department of Justice handled the EPA documents.[85] On March 10, 1983 Olson had appeared before the House Judiciary Subcommittee on Monopolies and Commercial Law for hearings on oversight and authorization of the Office of the Legal Counsel. The House Judiciary Committee's investigation of Olson focused on this March 1983 appearance. Though the appearance was not under oath, questions were raised about the truthfulness of several aspects of Olson's responses, and transcript corrections of his responses.

After two years of investigation, the House Judiciary Committee issued a multi-volume report in December 1985 concluding that Olson's statements in his March 1983 appearance had been false and misleading.[86] The Report also concluded that Carol Dinkins, Lands Division Assistant Attorney General, and Deputy Attorney General Edward Schmults had wrongfully withheld documents from the Committee. The Committee adopted the report on partisan lines, with all the Republicans except one voting against accepting the report. The Report then led to a request to the Attorney General on behalf of the full House Judiciary Committee to seek appointment of an independent counsel to investigate possible criminal conduct, triggering the Attorney General's review under the independent counsel statute. In the spring of 1986, Attorney

---

[82] With the court dismissal, Olson's position that a U.S. Attorney is not required to refer a contempt finding to the grand jury in circumstances where the basis for contempt is the assertion of executive privilege was relegated to an OLC opinion, appearing about a year later. *See* Theodore B. Olson, Prosecution for Contempt of Congress of an Executive Branch Official Who Has Asserted a Claim of Executive Privilege, 8 Op. Off. Legal Counsel 101 (1984).

[83] Morrison Report at 92.

[84] *Id.* at 100.

[85] *Id.* at 101.

[86] House Report at 9.

General Meese referred Olson, but not Schmults nor Dinkins, to the special division of the D.C. Circuit Court of Appeals for appointment of an independent counsel, leading commentators to question whether Olson was a political scapegoat.[87] Olson recalled reacting to Attorney General Meese's decision, "It was a confluence of unreality, I thought, this is unjustified, unfair. It didn't make any sense."[88]

Finally, in April 1986, more than three years after Olson's March 1983 statements, the Special Division appointed an independent counsel to investigate Olson. When its first appointment, James C. McKay, resigned on the grounds of an appearance of a conflict of interest with another case handled by his firm, the Special Division appointed Alexia Morrison, McKay's deputy.

The Independent Counsel Statute Goes to Court

By the time the Olson investigation had reached this point—several years from the underlying events—the high-drama of the confrontation between the EPA and the House had faded, and the Iran–Contra independent counsel investigation filled the front pages. Lt. Col. Oliver North, a principal in the scheme to trade arms with Iran to fund the Nicaraguan contras, challenged the independent counsel statute. Although the *North* litigation did not turn out to be the vehicle for constitutional review of the independent counsel statute before the Supreme Court, it ended up strengthening Independent Counsel Morrison's hand in defending the statute in unanticipated ways.

In October and November of 1986, news broke of a possible secret government operation in which weapons were sold to Iran, and the proceeds of the sale were directed to fund Nicaraguan contras fighting to overthrow Nicaragua's Sandinista government.[89] Internal Justice Department investigations culminated in Attorney General Meese's application to the Special Division to appoint an independent counsel to investigate Lt. Col. North's involvement in this scheme; the special division appointed former Judge Lawrence E. Walsh as independent counsel.[90]

North took an aggressive litigation posture. One month after Walsh had empanelled a grand jury, North brought a civil suit challenging the

---

[87] *See* Alison Frankel, *Ted Olson's Five Years in Purgatory*, Am. Law., Dec. 1988, at 68, 74 ("Was Olson a scapegoat thrown to a hungry throng of Democrats by a pressured and controversial attorney general?").

[88] *See id.* at 74 (quoting Olson).

[89] *See* Charles A. Johnson & Danette Brickman, *Independent Counsel: The Law and the Investigations* 163 (2001) (describing the beginning of the Iran–Contra scandal).

[90] *In re* Sealed Case, 829 F.2d 50, 51–52 (D.C. Cir. 1987).

constitutionality of the independent counsel statute.[91] At this point, given the pace of the North investigation and vigor of North's litigation, it seemed plausible that this would be the case that took a constitutional challenge to the independent counsel statute to the Supreme Court.

From the perspective of Reagan's Department of Justice, North's litigation created a dilemma. Despite the Department's view that the independent counsel statute was unconstitutional, it also wanted to avoid Supreme Court review of the statute for fear that it had "too strong an appeal to the public's common sense,"[92] and thus would survive challenge notwithstanding the substantial groundwork the Department had laid for a challenge to independent agencies. Moreover, even among independent counsel cases, the *North* litigation was the worst vehicle to mount a challenge. The Iran–Contra investigation had captured public attention and would be a "terrible case[] in which to challenge a law that the public was told guaranteed impartial justice."[93]

The Department of Justice devised a clever strategy to bar judicial review of the independent counsel statute, while allowing the investigation of North to continue.[94] The Attorney General offered the independent counsel a "parallel" appointment within the Department of Justice as a special prosecutor, under the same statutory authority that had been used to create the Watergate special prosecutor's office. The regulations establishing the parallel appointment granted the counsel identical authority, jurisdiction, and removal protection as provided by the independent counsel statute,[95] but were issued under the Attorney General's statutory authority to appoint *ad hoc* special prosecutors.

With regard to North, the gambit worked. Walsh accepted the parallel appointment the day it was offered.[96] North now had to show that his constitutional objections to the independent counsel statute

---

[91] *Id.* at 52.

[92] Charles Fried, *Order and Law: Arguing the Reagan Revolution—A Firsthand Account* 160 (1991).

[93] *Id.* at 137.

[94] Office of Independent Counsel, General Powers and the Establishment of Independent Counsel—Iran/Contra, 52 Fed. Reg. 7270, 7270 (March 10, 1987) (codified at 28 C.F.R. §§ 600 & 601 (1987)) (Attorney General Meese introduced the parallel appointment regulations with a summary saying, "I have found it advisable to assure the courts, Congress and the American people that this investigation will proceed in a clearly authorized and constitutionally valid form regardless of the eventual outcome of the North litigation [challenging the independent counsel statute].").

[95] *See id.* at 7270–302. On the provisions for removal protection, compare 28 U.S.C. § 596 with the parallel provisions of 28 C.F.R. § 600.7(c)–(d); *see also In re* Sealed Case, 829 F.2d at 52–53 (noting the parallel in removal protection).

[96] *In re* Sealed Case, 829 F.2d at 52–53.

were ripe for review despite the fact that Walsh had been granted nearly identical authority in a constitutionally uncontroversial way. The D.C. Circuit held that North's constitutional challenges to the independent counsel statute were not reviewable in view of the parallel appointment, over a partial dissent by Judge Williams.[97] At the center of the court's reasoning were its conclusions that there was no difference in the actions Walsh would take if he were acting solely on the basis of the authority vested in him by the Attorney General and those he would take with the addition of the protections of the independent counsel statute, and therefore no point in review.[98]

Although the Department of Justice had sought this outcome, it held important consequences when the Supreme Court eventually did reach the merits of a constitutional challenge to the independent counsel statute in the Olson litigation. If the D.C. Circuit's conclusion was sound, it raised a foundational question about how much additional independence the independent counsel provisions furnished the independent counsel beyond that of the Watergate special prosecutors. Indeed, it ends up suggesting an essential similarity between the two forms of prosecutors.

Judge Williams' partial dissent in the *North* appeal pounced on the point. In view of the apparently huge gulf between tenure provided by the Attorney General's parallel appointment—which, as an *ad hoc* regulation issued by the Attorney General, the Attorney General could set aside at will—and the steel-plated tenure provided by the independent counsel statute, Judge Williams argued that it was self-evident that these different protections would make a difference in the conduct of Walsh's investigation.[99] Indeed, that difference was a principal motivation for the enactment of the independent counsel provisions. Judge Williams did not have to wait long for an opportunity to reach the merits of the challenge to the independent counsel statute. At the time of the D.C. Circuit's decision in the *North* appeal, it was little more than three weeks away from the oral arguments in Olson's challenge to the statute in the D.C. Circuit, with Judge Williams on the panel.

Unlike North's litigation, Olson's challenge to the independent counsel statute arose in a way that eluded the efforts of the Department of Justice to avoid a Supreme Court review of the constitutionality of the statute. The Department of Justice offered parallel appointments to all active independent counsels,[100] but Independent Counsel Morrison

---

[97] *Id.* at 62.

[98] *Id.* at 59–62.

[99] *Id.* at 65 (Williams, J., concurring in part and dissenting in part).

[100] Earl C. Dudley, Jr., Morrison v. Olson: *A Modest Assessment*, 38 Am. U. L. Rev. 255, 258 (1989). This piece provides an excellent first-hand account of *Morrison* litigation.

declined the appointment. One of Morrison's chief deputies, Earl C. Dudley, Jr., explained this decision as grounded in several considerations. The investigation of Olson had nowhere near the public interest in a timely resolution that was presented by the Iran–Contra investigation and so the prospect of delay in the constitutional litigation of the independent counsel statute did not weigh as heavily in favor of accepting the appointment as it did for Walsh.[101] Moreover, the Justice Department had been an adversary of Independent Counsel Morrison in litigation over her jurisdiction, and Morrison's investigation concerned allegations of wrong-doing at the Department of Justice itself. These entanglements with the Department of Justice posed the risk that the parallel appointment would make the appearance of independence under the parallel appointment illusory (as Judge Williams' dissent in the *North* litigation had concluded).[102]

As a subject of an independent counsel inquiry, Olson clearly sought to prompt review of the statute, the legal strategy of his former employer, Department of Justice, notwithstanding. He did so by moving, along with Carol Dinkins and Edward Schmults, to quash grand jury subpoenas Morrison had issued to each of them on the grounds of the statute's unconstitutionality and then declining to comply with district court orders enforcing Morrison's subpoena. Days before the D.C. Circuit's decision on North's challenge to the statute, the district court held all three in contempt. It was Olson's and his co-parties' appeal of that contempt citation, presenting a facial challenge to the independent counsel statute, that reached the Supreme Court.

Although the Department of Justice and Olson, along with his co-parties, had opposing interests in obtaining review, they still stood on the same side of the statute's constitutionality. In Olson's appeal of the contempt citation to the D.C. Circuit, the Department of Justice took the unusual step of filing an amicus brief in support of Olson's challenge;[103] eventually the Solicitor General did the same before the Supreme Court. Senate and leadership of the House filed briefs defending the statute in both the D.C. Circuit and Supreme Court.[104]

Between the D.C. Circuit's hearing of arguments and its decision, Olson's challenge gained another prominent friend. On December 15, 1987, President Reagan signed the bill reauthorizing the independent counsel statute, with some amendments. He issued a signing statement

---

[101] *See id.* at 258.

[102] *Id.* at 259.

[103] *See In re* Sealed Case, 838 F.2d 476, 477 (D.C. Cir. 1988) (noting Department of Justice as amicus urging reversal).

[104] *See id.* (noting House and Senate briefs).

expressing his doubts about the constitutionality of the legislation.[105] "An officer of the United States exercising executive authority in a core area of law enforcement," President Reagan wrote, "necessarily, under our constitutional scheme, must be subject to executive branch appointment, review, and removal."[106] President Reagan noted he was "gratified" that the constitutional questions presented by the statute were "squarely" presented to the D.C. Circuit, and that his administration would "continue to express our constitutional objections" in that litigation as it "moves through the courts."[107]

President Reagan's wish that the reauthorized Ethics Act would be struck down by the D.C. Circuit came true. In January 1988, the D.C. Circuit, in a decision authored by Judge Silberman and joined by Judge Williams, with then-Judge Ruth Bader Ginsburg dissenting, invalidated the independent counsel statute in a 30-page decision that was an across-the-board victory for Olson.[108] The D.C. Circuit's decision acknowledged more clearly than the Supreme Court would that the independent counsel statute was premised on a post-Watergate view of the "inability of the Department of Justice and the Attorney General to function impartially with full public confidence in investigating criminal wrongdoing of high-ranking government officials of the same political party."[109] The D.C. Circuit could see no limitation to the logic underlying the independent counsel statute under which the President and the Department of Justice are viewed as politically conflicted from criminal investigation of executive branch officials.[110] For the D.C. Circuit, that conflict-of-interest logic would lead to removing the Justice Department entirely from presidential influence, "which we think must be a constitutional *reductio ad absurdum*."[111]

The D.C. Circuit's decision resolved each of the constitutional questions raised by the statute, one after another, in the opposite direction from the way the Supreme Court would. The D.C. Circuit first concluded that the independent counsel was a principal, not an inferior officer, and therefore under the Appointments Clause, the independent counsel had

---

[105] President Reagan, Statement on Signing the Independent Counsel Reauthorization Act of 1987, Independent Counsel Reauthorization Act of 1987, 2 Pub. Papers 1524 (Dec. 15, 1987).

[106] *Id.*

[107] *Id.*

[108] *In re* Sealed Case, 838 F.2d 476.

[109] *Id.* at 504.

[110] *Id.* at 505.

[111] *Id.* at 505 (noting the existence of Senator Ervin's post-Saturday Night Massacre bill proposing to make the Department of Justice an independent agency).

to be appointed by the President, not a court.[112] The D.C. Circuit rejected the suggestion that the Attorney General was superior to the independent counsel—especially in view of Morrison's decision to decline the parallel appointment under which she would have been a subordinate of the Attorney General—and as well as the idea that the independent counsel's authority is temporary.[113] "The independent counsel's authority over the investigation is not temporary," the court wrote, "it is coterminous with the investigation itself."[114]

Expressly anticipating the prospect of Supreme Court review, the D.C. Circuit addressed Olson's other challenges to the statute. The court concluded that the appointment of the independent counsel by a court and the restrictions on the power of removal violated the President's Article II authority to take care that the laws are faithfully executed, and Article II's creation of a "unitary executive to ensure that the branch wielding the power to enforce the law would be accountable to the people."[115] On the critical question of the removal authority, the court concluded that the independent counsel's functions were the paradigm of executive functions, and so under *Humphrey's Executor* and *Myers*, the Constitution prohibited Congress from imposing any restrictions on the President's power to remove. In addition, the court emphasized that the removal restrictions in the independent counsel statute were more intrusive than the normal "good cause" restriction because the statute also afforded a removed independent counsel judicial review of the dismissal.[116]

Despite the D.C. Circuit's emphasis on this exceptional nature of the removal restrictions in the independent counsel statute, under the court's analysis, there was no escaping the question of the constitutional foundations of independent agencies. After demonstrating how *Humphrey's Executor* did not displace, but rather implicitly affirmed the core principle of *Myers*, the court went out of its way to take a shot at the core of *Humphrey's Executor*. "Supreme Court Justices have expressed dissatisfaction with the distinctions drawn in *Humphrey's Executor*," the court ventured, commenting that these Justices contended, "not without force," that the decision's "reliance on the [FTC] Commissioners' quasi-judicial and quasi-legislative functions is inadequate to explain the case—and to limit its future applicability."[117]

---

[112] *Id.* at 486–87.

[113] *Id.*

[114] *Id.*

[115] *Id.* at 488.

[116] *Id.* at 501–02.

[117] *Id.* at 499.

Arguments in the Supreme Court

So the gauntlet was thrown down before the Court. The very question of the constitutional foundations of removal restrictions that the Department of Justice had sought to avoid posing to the Supreme Court in the context of the independent counsel statute was front and center.

Independent Counsel Morrison's brief seized on the potentially sweeping implications of striking down the statute's removal provisions. "Longstanding governmental arrangements—*unless they are all unconstitutional*," Morrison argued, support Congress's authority to insulate aspects of law implementation from the President's removal authority, including "establish[ing] agencies independent of the President's control," private causes of action to supplement government enforcement, and qui tam actions.[118] These examples, Morrison urged the Court, refute the conception of a "unitary executive" embraced by the D.C. Circuit and Olson under which "all 'executive' business, or all law enforcement duties, must be performed by agents under the direct control of the President or those who serve at his pleasure and act at his direction."[119]

Olson's brief emphasized that each of the powers of the federal government is "inherently distinct."[120] As to the exercise of authority that is indisputably executive in nature, Olson advocated that "the President alone must discharge that power and, under Article II, § 3, he must 'take Care' that the laws are faithfully executed."[121] Accordingly, the independent counsel statute "disables the President from performing the function which, above all others, in placed in his care by Article II."[122]

The amicus brief of the United States filed by Solicitor General Fried labored to craft a principle that would invalidate the independent counsel statute, but sweep no further. "[O]ur argument in this case," the United States explained, "does not require that the President's power of 'superintendence' entail, in every case, the power of appointment to office *and* plenary power of direction while in office *and* plenary power of removal from office, especially in the case of officers whose functions are not purely executive."[123] And in case the point was lost on

---

[118] Brief for Appellant at 50, Morrison v. Olson, 487 U.S. 654 (1988) (No. 87–1279) (emphasis added) (hereinafter "Morrison Brief").

[119] *Id.* at 51 (emphasis added).

[120] Brief for Appellee at 18, *Morrison*, 487 U.S. 654 (No. 87–1279) (hereinafter "Olson Brief").

[121] Olson Brief at 19.

[122] *Id.*

[123] Brief for the United States as Amicus Curiae Supporting Appellees at 9, *Morrison*, 487 U.S. 654 (No. 87–1279) (hereinafter "United State Brief"); *see also id.* at 32.

the reader, "That issue is not in this case."[124] And so too, the brief later returned to "emphasize that the removability of members of 'independent agencies' presents quite a different question."[125] Another amicus intervened in the briefing solely to defend the constitutionality of "good cause" restrictions generally.[126]

On the day of oral argument before the Supreme Court, April 26, 1988, the Supreme Court's courtroom was packed to capacity, with four lawyers to argue, Appellant Alexia Morrison, defending the constitutionality of the statute, Michael Davidson, Counsel to the Senate on behalf of appellant, Thomas Martin on behalf of Olson and the other appellees, and Solicitor General Charles Fried, supporting the appellees, for an exceptional 90–minute argument.

Morrison argued first. Her argument, while touching on the full range of issues before the Court, emphasized the practical operation of the statute as well as the multiple points of connection between the independent counsel and the Attorney General. Attorneys General have complete discretion to decline to trigger an independent counsel, Morrison argued, noting that on repeated occasions the Attorneys General had declined to request appointment. Morrison emphasized that she viewed herself as bound by statute to follow the Department of Justice's prosecution manuals, and noted her own office's communication with career officers at the Department on policy and procedure. Morrison highlighted the power that the good cause removal standard still gives the Attorney. It gives the Attorney General the obligation "if he finds that an independent counsel is proceeding less than faithfully in executing the independent counsel provisions, to step in and cause that independent counsel's removal."[127] And of course, as Morrison reminded the Court, the President retains the power to pardon.

Michael Davidson's argument centered on a defense of the statute as consistent with Article III and the Appointments Clause.[128] At the end of his argument, he emphasized that the statute's removal provision had been extensively amended twice, in 1982 and 1987, in response to concerns of the executive branch.

---

[124] United States Brief at 9.

[125] *Id.* at 32.

[126] Brief of the American Federation of Labor and Congress of Industrial Organizations As Amicus Curiae in Support of Neither Party at 4–5, *Morrison*, 487 U.S. 654 (No. 87–1279).

[127] Transcript of Oral Argument at 17, *Morrison*, 487 U.S. 654 (No. 87–1279).

[128] The Article III challenge is that the independent counsel statute conferred on the special division powers beyond the scope of the judicial power under Article III. *See Morrison*, 487 U.S. at 678–79.

The heat of the argument and pace of questioning by the Court picked up immediately with Thomas Martin's argument. "The independent counsel is an anomaly in our system," Martin began, "She performs an Executive function but she is not under the President."[129] Justice White responded, "[a]nd the fact that he or she is not subject to the usual control of the President doesn't necessarily make it unconstitutional."[130] And Martin replied, "I think it does, Mr. Justice White," to which the next question immediately interrupted, "You mean Congress may never create an office in the Executive Branch that is not subject to unlimited power by the President?,"[131] echoing the point of emphasis in his dissenting opinion in *Bowsher v. Synar*. Martin then retreated from the breadth of the suggestion, noting that the case is "narrowly focused" on prosecutorial power.

The rapid pace of the Court's questioning came to an abrupt halt when Solicitor General Fried took the podium. Fried first expressly invited revisiting the conventional wisdom that the special prosecutor model had failed:

> [T]he Watergate episode ... is thought to teach the necessity for this provision. With respect we submit that that episode teaches the exact opposite lesson. True, the dismissal of Special Prosecutor Cox was regrettable, but it was not a constitutional catastrophe. Had Special Prosecutor Jaworski been dismissed, had the Watergate task force been disbanded, had those prosecutions been abandoned, that would have been another matter. But everyone knows that those prosecutions proceeded to their denouement without missing a beat.

As to the points of constitutional doctrine, Fried focused on the appointments clause challenges, which offered the narrowest route for the Court to strike down the statute. Fried argued uninterrupted for most of his time. A solitary substantive question from the Court about an early appointments clause decision finally interrupted Fried's argument. After that one question, the Court did not stir again until Fried sat down, with a customary "Thank you, General Fried," from the Chief Justice. Solicitor General Fried read the Court's silence during his argument as spelling defeat.[132]

---

[129] Transcript of Oral Argument at 37, *Morrison*, 487 U.S. 654 (No. 87–1279).

[130] *Id.*; *see* Bowsher v. Synar, 478 U.S. 714, 760 (1986) (White, J., dissenting) ("I wish to emphasize what it is that the Court quite pointedly and correctly does *not* hold: namely, that 'executive' powers of the sort granted the Comptroller by the Act may only be exercised by officers removable at will by the President.").

[131] Transcript of Oral Argument at 37–38, *Morrison*, 487 U.S. 654 (No. 87–1279).

[132] Interview with Charles Fried, Professor, Harvard Law School, in Boston, Mass. (Oct. 11, 2007).

Justice Blackmun's notes from the Supreme Court's conference on the case on April 29, 1988 reflected the seven-one split (with Justice Kennedy recused) of the ultimate decision.[133] Justice Blackmun's notes suggest that Chief Justice Rehnquist set out his position in some detail. He "disagree[d]" with the D.C. Circuit on the Appointments Clause; he did not think the independent counsel was "a superior officer," and he disagreed with Olson's "subordinacy" argument.[134] The special court appointment power was "not unusual," nor did the special court have "supervisory" power. Rather the "AG has termination author[ity]. Construe and uphold."[135] As to the removal issue, Chief Justice Rehnquist affirmed "[r]emoval is in the Pres[ident]/AG. *Myers* is excellent law,"[136] suggesting some sympathy with construing the removal provision as allowing adequate influence from the President.

Justice Brennan indicated his "anal[ysis] [was] close to CJ's." Likewise Justice White suggested "no great differ[ence] in this inter'g case," and so too with Justice Blackmun, and Justice O'Connor.[137] Justice Stevens noted that "Cox himself shows n[ot] a wild departure,"[138] likely referring to the amicus brief on which Cox was of counsel that emphasized the historical record of prosecutions conducted outside of executive control.[139] Justice Scalia, to dissent, noted that he admired Ed Levi, and he "knew t[he] practicalities." Attorney General Levi along with two other former Attorneys General, Griffin Bell and William French Smith, had filed an amicus brief challenging the constitutionality of the statute largely pointing to the prospect for abuse it invited, including as an appendix Justice Jackson's famous remarks on the Federal Prosecutor, quoted at length in Justice Scalia's dissent. Justice Scalia noted that the statute keeps the Executive Branch "in a cloud," which he prophesied "would make a dif[ference] in t[he] future."[140] As to the basis of Scalia's dissent, Justice Blackmun records his colleague as

---

[133] Harry A. Blackmun, Supreme Court Conference Notes, Morrison v. Olson, 87–1279, Apr. 29, 1988, Library of Congress, Manuscript Division, The Harry A. Blackmun Papers, Box 507.

[134] *Id.*

[135] *Id.*

[136] *Id.*

[137] *Id.*

[138] *Id.*

[139] Brief of Common Cause as Amicus Curiae in Support of the Constitutionality of the Independent Counsel Law at 11–17, Morrison v. Olson, 487 U.S. 654 (1988) (No. 87–1279).

[140] *Id.*

stating that if the officer is inferior, he must be subject "to control of President."[141]

Chief Justice Rehnquist circulated his first draft of the opinion for the Court on June 1, 1988. With a few stylistic changes, it is virtually identical to the published decision. By June 8th, Justices Brennan, White, Marshall, Blackmun, Stevens, and O'Connor all indicated that they would join the Chief Justice's opinion. Justice Scalia circulated his dissenting opinion on June 25th. On June 29th, the final day of opinions for the 1987–88 Term, the Court announced its decision along with eight other decisions. In a rare event for the Court at the time, Justice Scalia summarized his dissent aloud from the bench in a nine-minute statement to the packed courtroom.

The *Morrison* decision was, as the The New York Times reported in leading front page stories, "a stunning rebuff to the Reagan Administration,"[142] and a "stinging political and philosophical blow to the Administration's vision,"[143] handed out by President Reagan's own selection as Chief Justice. Morrison's own brief was clearly a strong guide-post for the Court, adding further sting to Olson and the Department of Justice. And because the Court addressed point-for-point each of the challenges Olson made, the decision includes an unusually high number of constitutional holdings, including under the Appointments Clause, Article III, and separation-of-powers more generally.

The Decision

The *Morrison* opinion's analysis begins with whether the independent counsel is a principal or inferior officer. The manner in which the Court addressed this first question reveals that it viewed the independent counsel existing on a par with, if not falling within, the special prosecutor model, as opposed to representing a stark departure from it. Making that analogy between the independent counsel and the special prosecutor fundamentally shaped the decision.

The Court eschewed embracing a clear doctrinal test to distinguish "inferior" and "principal" officers within the Appointments Clause, concluding instead that four factors supported its conclusion that the independent counsel was an inferior officer.[144] Because the Attorney General possessed the power to remove the independent counsel, the

---

[141] *Id.*

[142] Stuart Taylor, Jr., *Supreme Court Vote Upholds Law on Special Prosecutors; 7–1 Ruling is Rebuff to Reagan; Scalia in Dissent*, N.Y. Times, June 30, 1988, at A1.

[143] Linda Greenhouse, *Fetters on the Executive; By Finding No Threat in Prosecutor Law, The Court Rejects a Constitutional Vision*, N.Y. Times, June 30, 1988, at A1.

[144] *Morrison*, 487 U.S. at 671–673.

Court reasoned, the counsel is "to some degree 'inferior' in rank and authority," even if not "subordinate" in her exercise of powers.[145]

Having put aside the suggestion that "subordinacy" was a litmus test for whether the officer is inferior or principal, the Court went on to focus on a functional consideration of the duties and scope of power of the independent counsel. The Court concluded that the independent counsel's duties and jurisdiction were "certain" and "limited" as prescribed by the statute and referral from the Attorney General.[146] Finally, the Court noted that the independent counsel's tenure is " 'temporary' in the sense an independent counsel is appointed essentially to accomplish a single task."[147]

This conclusion, the Court stated, was consistent with its reference in *United States v. Nixon* to the Watergate Special Prosecutor "whose authority was similar to that of appellant," as a "subordinate officer."[148] The Court thus declined to equate the greater "independence" with being a "principal" officer. By seeing the good cause removal standard as not only a wedge that separates the independent counsel from the Attorney General (and President), but also a factor suggesting the counsel is inferior "in rank," the Court inclined further toward viewing the independent counsel in the shoes of the Watergate special prosecutor.

The Department of Justice's parallel appointments may have bolstered that logic. As Morrison argued in her brief, the Attorney General as "head of a department" may appoint only "inferior" officers.[149] But the powers and duties given to the independent counsels under the parallel appointments, as the D.C. Circuit had confirmed in the *North* litigation, were the same as those granted by the independent counsel statute.[150] If one acting under a parallel appointment were an inferior officer, then why would a prosecutor with identical powers but operating only under the independent counsel statute be a principal officer?

One answer is that the independent counsel, as distinct from the special prosecutor acting under a parallel appointment, has very different tenure protection. The independent counsel's tenure protection would suggest that she was not subordinate to the Attorney General in the sense of being subject to his day-to-day supervision.

---

[145] *Id.* at 671.

[146] *Id.*

[147] *Id.* at 672.

[148] *Id.* at 673 (quoting United States v. Nixon, 418 U.S. 683, 694 n.8 (1974)).

[149] Morrison Brief at 34–35 & n.44.

[150] *In re* Sealed Case, 829 F.2d 50, 52–53 (D.C. Cir. 1987).

The Court, however, had distinguished principal and inferior officers on the basis of the character of their duties and scope of authority, not on the basis of day-to-day subordinancy. As a result, because both appointments granted identical powers and jurisdiction, the independent counsel appointments and parallel appointments would have to stand as inferior officers, or fall as principal officers together.[151] With both the parallel appointments and the Watergate special prosecutors squarely viewed as inferior officers, so too must the independent counsel.

The Department of Justice's strategic ploy to avoid Supreme Court review of the independent counsel statute by granting parallel appointments thus undercut its substantive argument that the independent counsel was a principal officer under the Appointments Clause. The parallel appointments (and the D.C. Circuit's conclusion in the *North* litigation that the parallel appointment prevented constitutional review of the Act) domesticated the very aspect of the independent counsel— statutory independence via removal protection—likely to distinguish the counsel from the constitutionally uncontroversial special prosecutor.

Olson had an alternative Appointments Clause challenge. He argued that even if the independent counsel were an inferior officer, the fact that the statute provided for the counsel's appointment by a court of law, as opposed to by a member of the executive branch, was an unconstitutional "interbranch appointment." This argument appeared to be Olson's weakest, and the Court swiftly rejected it. The language of the Appointments Clause, the Court pointed out, offered no aid to Olson; its "Exceptions Clause" permits Congress to vest the appointment of inferior officers, "in the President alone, in the courts of Law, or in the Heads of Departments."[152] Nor, the Court concluded, is there any inherent incongruity in having a court appoint prosecutorial officers. As Morrison's brief had emphasized, the Court had previously recognized that courts may appoint private attorneys to act as prosecutors for judicial contempt proceedings, and lower courts had upheld their own powers to appoint interim U.S. Attorneys, a power that had been granted by statute.[153] In view of the statute's prohibition on the judges of the Special Division from participating in matters relating to an independent counsel they had appointed, the Court did not see the statute as creating a constitutionally prohibited incongruous interbranch appointment.[154]

---

[151] Morrison's brief put the point as follows: "[I]t is inconceivable that the identical office is an 'inferior' one when its occupant is appointed by a 'Head of Department' and a 'principal' one when its occupant is appointed by a 'Court of Law.' " Morrison Brief at 34 n.44.

[152] U.S. Const. Art. II, § 2, cl. 2.

[153] *Morrison*, 487 U.S. at 676.

[154] *Id.* at 677.

The Court also rejected Olson's argument that the powers granted to the Special Division violated Article III. The Court found the Special Division's authority to terminate the independent counsel the most troublesome statutory power because it was the least traditionally judicial task. But the Court concluded that this provision could be construed narrowly to grant the Special Division to terminate only after the duties of the counsel were completed or substantially completed such that no further action from the independent counsel is necessary.[155] So construed, the Court concluded that the statute did not "pose a sufficient threat of judicial intrusion into matters that are more properly within the executive's authority" to invalidate the Act.[156] As the Chief Justice had suggested in conference: "Construe and uphold."

The Court's most momentous doctrinal announcements appeared in its assessment of the twin separation-of-power challenges—whether the good cause removal provision itself unconstitutionally interferes with the President's constitutional functions and whether the act as a whole impermissibly interferes with the President's powers.

On the particularly potent removal issue, Olson and the United States had a strong doctrinal argument, embraced by the Court of Appeals below, that under the Supreme Court's decisions in *Myers*[157] and *Humphrey's Executor*,[158] Congress was prohibited from imposing any removal restrictions on "purely executive" officers. As the *Morrison* Court recounted, in *Humphrey's Executor*, the Court upheld the good cause removal restriction for FTC Commissioners.[159] *Humphrey's Executor* distinguished *Myers* on the ground that the office at issue in *Myers* was "purely executive," and as a result *Myers'* prohibition on the congressional restrictions on the President's removal power reached only "purely executive officers," not officers performing "quasi legislative or quasi judicial powers."[160] But based on that distinction, Olson argued that *Myers* should govern here,[161] and suggested a simple syllogism, the basis for which appeared years before in his own OLC memos: no restriction on removal of "purely executive officers" is permissible; the independent counsel is a purely executive officer; and therefore the statute's removal restrictions are unconstitutional.

---

[155] *Id.* at 682.

[156] *Id.* at 683.

[157] 272 U.S. 52 (1926).

[158] 295 U.S. 602 (1935).

[159] 487 U.S. at 687.

[160] *Humphrey's Ex'r*, 295 U.S. at 628.

[161] Olson Brief at 29 & n.91.

The Court had a two-pronged rejection of this argument. First, it distinguished *Myers* and its recent decision in *Bowsher v. Synar*[162] on the ground that the statutes at issue in both cases involved "an attempt by Congress itself to gain a role in the removal of executive officials other than its established powers of impeachment and conviction."[163] In those statutes, the Court concluded that Congress had attempted to aggrandize its power. In contrast, the independent counsel statute did not reserve to Congress any role in removal. Rather, the statute put removal "squarely in the hands of the Executive Branch."[164] As a result, it had to address head-on the argument stemming from *Humphrey's Executor* and *Myers* that Congress can impose no restriction on the President's removal power over purely executive officers that the Court had evaded in *Bowsher*.

The Court's most widely criticized portion of its opinion is its abrupt casting aside of this argument:

> We undoubtedly did rely on the terms "quasi-legislative" and "quasi-judicial" to distinguish the officials involved in *Humphrey's Executor* and *Wiener* from those in *Myers*, but our present considered view is that the determination of whether the Constitution allows Congress to impose a "good cause"-type restriction on the President's power to remove an official cannot be made to turn on whether or not that official is classified as "purely executive."[165]

For law students, for lawyers, and typically for courts, a "present considered view" does not distinguish a prior decision. Faced with doctrine from *Humphrey's Executor* and *Myers* that would have invalidated the independent counsel statute, the Court jettisoned the doctrine, while preserving the results in those decisions.

The Court's footnote to this passage is telling. The Court claims: "this Court has never held that the Constitution prevents Congress from imposing limitations on the President's power to remove *all* executive officials simply because they wield 'executive' power."[166] At one level, this statement is just an elaboration of its rejection of the idea that purely executive offices are immune from removal restrictions. But it also puts that rejection more directly than the text of the Court's opinion. In that regard, it seems to take a jab at the broader logic that

---

[162] 478 U.S. 714 (1986).

[163] *Morrison*, 487 U.S. at 686. Professor Peter Strauss had advanced this distinction in *The Place of Agencies in Government: Separation of Powers and the Fourth Branch*, 84 Colum. L. Rev. 573, 614–15 (1984).

[164] *Morrison*, 487 U.S. at 686.

[165] *Id.* at 689.

[166] *Id.* at 690 n.27.

would sweep aside independent agencies and the Solicitor General's emphasis that the independent counsel statute's removal provision could be distinguished from the provisions creating independent agencies. In the absence of stable ground between the removal restriction in the independent counsel statute and those more generally, the Court balked and cast aside the basic premise supporting the Department's logic. The skepticism in Justice White's emphatic opening question to Mr. Martin in oral argument held the day.

In the place of the distinction between the functions of the office-holder—whether "purely executive," or "quasi-legislative" or "quasi-judicial" of *Humphrey's Executor*—the Court adopted a new test to judge the constitutional validity of removal restrictions on the President, focused not on the functions of the officer, but rather on whether "the removal restrictions are of such a nature that they impede the President's ability to perform his constitutional duty."[167] And under that new test, the Court concluded that the President's need to control the exercise of the independent counsel's discretion was not "so central to the functioning of the Executive Branch as to require as a matter of constitutional law that the counsel be terminable at will by the President."[168]

In support of this new test, the Court cited no authority, lending the appearance that the doctrine emerged from the Court's own cogitations. This test, rather, appears to derive from the Court's decision in *Nixon v. Administrator of General Services*,[169] cited later in the *Morrison* opinion.[170] *Nixon v. Administrator of General Services* upheld the constitutionality of the Presidential Recordings and Materials Preservation Act. In an opinion delivered by Justice Brennan, the Court rejected the suggestion that the Constitution creates a complete division of authority between the branches. Instead, invoking Justice Jackson's celebrated concurrence in *Youngstown Sheet & Tube Co. v. Sawyer*,[171] the Court stated that in determining whether the legislation disrupts the separation of powers, the "proper inquiry focuses on the extent to which it *prevents the Executive Branch from accomplishing its constitutionally assigned functions*."[172] Only when such a potential for disruption is present does the court inquire as to whether that disruption is justified by "an overriding need to promote objectives within the constitutional

---

[167] *Id.* at 691.

[168] *Id.* at 691–92.

[169] 433 U.S. 442 (1977).

[170] *See Morrison*, 487 U.S. at 694.

[171] 343 U.S. 579 (1952).

[172] Nixon v. Adm'r of Gen. Servs., 433 U.S. 425, 443 (1977) (emphasis added).

authority of Congress."[173] Then–Justice Rehnquist dissented in *Nixon v. Administrator of General Services*. But by the time of *Morrison*, Chief Justice Rehnquist latched onto the inquiry of *Nixon v. Administrator of General Services* into the extent to which the statute interferes with the Executive's capacity to perform his constitutionally assigned functions. In that regard, Chief Justice Rehnquist followed Morrison's brief, which took *Nixon v. Administrator of General Services* as the framing doctrine for separation-of-powers analysis.[174]

The extent to which the *Morrison* Court accommodated the independent counsel statute within the general mold of the Watergate special prosecutor comes out all the more strikingly in the Court's comment on the scope of authority the Attorney General retains to terminate the independent counsel. Even under the Act's "good cause" limitation on removal, the Court ventured that the Attorney General retains "ample authority to assure that the counsel is competently performing his or her statutory responsibilities in a manner that comports with the provisions of the Act,"[175] though it declined to specify what more is encompassed within the statute's "good cause" standard. Not only was the independent counsel statute's removal provision insufficient to make the counsel a principal officer, but that removal provision itself affords the Attorney General adequate authority to ensure the counsel's compliance with the statute. The difference between the Attorney General's authority over a special prosecutor and the independent counsel becomes a matter of degree. And, so understood, it would be difficult to conclude that those differences in degree would, under the new functional test, prevent the President from performing his constitutional duty to ensure the faithful execution of the law.

Finally, the Court's rejection of the argument that the statute as a whole violates separation of powers helped to solidify anti-aggrandizement as a grounding separation-of-powers principle. Because the statute did not reserve a role to Congress in removal, the Act did not constitute a usurpation of executive functions by Congress. Nor did the Act constitute a "judicial usurpation" of executive functions. Under the Act, the court retained no power to supervise or control the independent counsel's conduct. More generally, the Court emphasized that under its reading of the removal provision in the Act, the President retained

---

[173] *Id.*

[174] *See* Morrison Brief at 49 (quoting *Nixon v. Administrator of General Services'* two-part test and stating that "we follow that approach here"); *cf.* Peter L. Strauss, *The Place of Agencies in Government: Separation of Powers and the Fourth Branch*, 84 Colum. L. Rev. 573, 636 (1984) (suggesting that the approach of *Nixon v. Administrator of General Services* is appropriate for the analysis of the constitutional place of agencies).

[175] *Morrison*, 487 U.S. at 692.

"substantial ability" and "sufficient control" to ensure that the laws were "faithfully executed."[176]

In one of his most well-known opinions, Justice Scalia dissented. He bristled with outrage both at the Court's conclusion, and at every aspect in the Court's analysis. He offered his own point-for-point dissection of the Court's constitutional analysis, but also turned repeatedly to suggest the practical possibilities that the Court's validation of the independent counsel statute allows.

As to constitutional considerations, Justice Scalia viewed the case as a very straightforward one. For Justice Scalia, as for Olson, the major premise of the argument is that all purely executive powers must fall within the full control of the President. The question is not, *how much* of the "purely executive powers of government must be within the full control of the President. The Constitution prescribes that they *all* are."[177] No party contested the minor premise, that the independent counsel exercises purely executive functions. From these two premises, Justice Scalia argued, it follows the counsel must be within the full control of the President. Even with the Court's generous reading of the "good cause" removal restriction as affording adequate control to the Attorney General, it deprives the Attorney General (and thus the President) of full control. That is the point of the removal restriction.[178]

Justice Scalia also would have concluded that the independent counsel was a principal officer under the Appointments Clause, but would have reached that conclusion on the ground that to be an "inferior" officer the officer must be "subordinate."[179] Because the independent counsel is not subordinate, in the sense of subject to the supervision of a superior officer, to the Attorney General or the President, the counsel cannot be an inferior officer.[180]

As to practical considerations, Justice Scalia's description of the prospects for abuse of the independent counsel statute came to be viewed by many as prophetic. Building on the brief filed by the Edward Levi and the two other former Attorney Generals, Justice Scalia warned, as noted above, that the act provides no remedy, not even a political one if the judges of the special division are "politically partisan, as judges have been known to be, and select a prosecutor antagonistic to the adminis-

---

[176] *Id.* at 696.

[177] *Id.* at 709. *See also id.* at 710 ("We should say here that the President's constitutionally assigned duties include *complete* control over investigation and prosecution of violations of the law . . . .").

[178] *Id.* at 706–07.

[179] *Id.* at 719–22.

[180] *Id.*

tration."[181] Moreover, Justice Scalia suggested, quoting the Levi brief at length, the isolation of the independent counsel "is designed to heighten, not to check, all of the occupational hazards of the dedicated prosecutor; the danger of too narrow a focus, of the loss of perspective, of preoccupation with the pursuit of one alleged suspect to the exclusion of other interests."[182]

Morrison's Immediate Impact—the Independent Counsels

For the Reagan administration, the decision was unwelcome on several fronts. Not only was the decision perceived as a rebuke to the administration, but it also removed any residual doubt about the constitutionality of proceedings in the three other independent counsel investigations of Reagan administration officials pending at the time of the decision. Independent Counsel Whitney North Seymor obtained a conviction of Michael Deaver, President Reagan's former deputy chief of staff and assistant, on one count of perjury before a congressional subcommittee, and two counts of false declaration before a grand jury on October 19, 1987. Deaver was awaiting sentencing pending the Supreme Court's resolution of *Morrison*. The other two active investigations, the Iran–Contra investigation, and that of Franklyn C. Nofziger, a former White House official ultimately convicted of lobbying violations, operated under the grants of parallel appointments by the Attorney General, though surely the opposite result in *Morrison* would likely have provoked renewed litigation.

The Supreme Court's decision had an immediate effect for Olson, who faced continued investigation. He did not, however, have to endure an independent counsel investigation for long. On August 17, 1988, Olson agreed to be interviewed by Independent Counsel Morrison. Less than two weeks later, on August 26, 1988, Independent Counsel Morrison announced her decision not to seek an indictment. On December 27, 1988, Morrison issued a comprehensive report exonerating Olson of wrongdoing.[183] The Morrison Report provided a detailed account of the origins of the controversy in the House of Representative's dispute with EPA and the Department of Justice, and an analysis of the central aspects of Olson's testimony on March 10, 1983 that the House Judiciary Committee's report had called into question.

Morrison concluded that Olson's answers on level of intra executive branch agreement on the executive privilege claims were technically

---

[181] *Id.* at 730.

[182] *Id.* at 731–32 (quoting Brief for Edward H. Levi, Griffin B. Bell, and William French Smith as Amici Curiae in Support of Appellees at 11, *Morrison*, 487 U.S. 654 (No. 87–1279)).

[183] *See* Morrison Report.

acceptable; she found his testimony on the scope of document disclosure more troubling, but still not enough to proceed with the investigation.[184]

With the exoneration provided by Morrison's report, the remaining issue for Olson was over $1 million in fees he had expended in defending the investigation, and litigating his challenge to the independent counsel's constitutionality.[185] The whole affair did not unwind Olson's own

---

[184] Morrison Report at 155–97. As to the executive privilege claim, the House had asked Olson if he knew whether EPA "did indicate its willingness to turn over the documents," and Olson responded that he did not recall. Morrison Report at 106; *see also Oversight Hearings Before the H. Comm. on the Judiciary, Subcommittee on Monopolies and Commercial Law*, 99th Cong. 158 (1983) (hereinafter "Oversight Hearings"). Independent Counsel Morrison concluded that while some individuals at EPA could have been described as "willing" to produce documents, and there was evidence that Olson had some knowledge of these views, *see* Morrison Report at 163, Olson's answer could be literally true under a narrow reading of the question he had been asked. *See* Morrison Report at 166. Olson also stated that people at EPA, from those at the enforcement level through the Administrator, as well as people involved at the Department of Justice "agreed that this was a proper occasion for the invocation of the executive privilege." Morrison Report at 106–107; Oversight Hearings at 153–54. Morrison concluded that it was reasonable for Olson to interpret the question he had been asked to refer to the time period immediately preceding the EPA Administrator's assertion of executive privilege before the House Subcommittees in December 1982, and as to that time period the testimony was not false. *See* Morrison Report at 174. As to the scope of production, Olson was asked whether the Committee could assume that "all of the relevant documents have been provided, and the Department [of Justice] is not withholding any documents from the Committee." *Id.* at 107. Olson responded judiciously, noting that some of his own handwritten notes were not produced, and that "[w]e've included everything that we think is relevant to the questions that you've asked and to the advice that we've given." *Id.*; Oversight Hearings at 144. In Olson's correction of the transcript, he amended it to read "[w]e have included everything that we think is relevant to the questions you have asked and to the formal advice that we've given." Morrison Report at 114. Morrison concluded that this was the "by far the most troubling" aspect of his testimony, *see* Morrison Report at 182, in part because Olson's October 25, 1982 memorandum to the President recommending the assertion of executive privilege was not produced, and clearly included "formal" "advice" that was given. *See* Morrison Report at 185. Moreover, that memorandum had been incorrect in its assertion that none of the underlying documents reflected any misconduct of any sort by the administration, though it was unclear that Olson had knowledge of that. *See* Morrison Report at 186–87. Finally, Olson stated that he was "not sure" whether any of his advice regarding the civil suit brought against the House of Representatives was in writing, and corrected the transcript to read "I'm not sure, I believe that some of it was." Morrison Report at 108, 114; Oversight Hearings at 158. Olson had signed several memoranda on the lawsuit. Morrison Report, at 190. Morrison concluded that revision in the transcript was literally true. *Id.* at 191.

[185] The 1982 amendments and reauthorization to the independent counsel statute authorized the Special Division to award reasonable attorneys' fees if no indictment is brought against the individual. *See* Pub. L. No. 97–409, § 5, 96 Stat. 2039 (1983); *see also* Pub. L. No. 100–191, § 2, 101 Stat. 1293 (1987) (amending the independent counsel statute and keeping the provision for attorneys' fees). Olson sought $1,259,072.69 in attorneys' fees, and the court granted him $861,589.28, excluding costs Olson had incurred in the Attorney General's initial investigation. *In re* Theodore B. Olson, 884 F.2d 1415, 1418 (D.C.

career. He argued *Bush v. Gore*[186] on behalf of President George W. Bush, and served as his Solicitor General between 2001 and 2004.

The decision, of course, also kept the independent counsel statute on the books, but did not quell criticism that the act was used as an instrument of political partisanship. In particular, it was objected that the Iran–Contra investigation, resulting in the indictment of Defense Secretary Caspar Weinberger, had been politically motivated.[187] President George Bush's Justice Department also objected that independent counsels have "virtually unchecked" powers, without the constraints and centralizing influence of the Department of Justice. With the threat of a filibuster by 28 Republican senators, combined with the reluctance of the Democrats to challenge the filibuster, the statute lapsed in 1992.

Political winds changed rapidly with President Clinton's election in 1992. President Clinton's inauguration cleared away Justice Department objections to the statute. In November 1993, the news of potential financial improprieties involving President Clinton and Hillary Clinton in a land development scheme called Whitewater emerged. The delay between the disclosure of that news and Attorney General Reno's decision to appoint a special prosecutor in January 1994, added legislative momentum to the reenactment of the independent counsel statute.[188] President Clinton, now a possible witness or subject of an independent counsel investigation, signed the reauthorization of the independent counsel provisions in 1994. The law, President Clinton wrote, "ensures that no matter what party controls the Congress or the executive branch, an independent, nonpartisan process will be in place to guarantee the integrity of public officials and ensure that no one is above the law."[189]

Eleven independent counsel investigations were initiated subsequent to *Morrison v. Olson*, and seven of those initiated after the statute's reauthorization in 1994.[190] Only one of these investigations resulted in

---

Cir. 1989). The court excluded some fees in relation to the Attorney General's own investigation prior to the appointment of the independent counsel and reduced the fees and costs, leaving Olson just under $400,000 of unreimbursed fees. *See id.* at 1419–20; 1423–30.

[186] 531 U.S. 98 (2000).

[187] Helen Dewar, *GOP Filibuster Threat Kills Independent Counsel Bill*, Wash. Post, Sept. 30, 1992, at A11.

[188] The Senate approved reauthorization of the legislation by a voice vote on May 25, and the House by a vote of 317–105 on June 21.

[189] Statement on Signing the Independent Counsel Reauthorization Act of 1994, 1 Pub. Papers 1168–69 (June 30, 1994).

[190] *See* Charles A. Johnson & Danette Brickman, *Independent Counsel: The Law and the Investigations* 143–44 (2001).

prison terms.[191] In terms of occupying the national attention, Independent Counsel Kenneth Starr's investigation of the Whitewater/Lewinsky matter won the prize, beginning with the newly reauthorized special division of the D.C. Circuit's decision to replace Robert Fiske with Kenneth Starr, and culminating in Starr's submission to the House of a report with "specific and credible information that may constitute grounds for the impeachment" of President Clinton in September 9, 1998, the House vote to impeach President Clinton, and the Senate vote to acquit him of the changes. Starr resigned in October 1999, and with the appointment of one of Starr's deputies as a replacement, the investigation concluded days before the end of President Clinton's second term.

Independent Counsel Starr's investigation turned the political tables on the independent counsel statute. As it wound along, the investigation validated for a new constituency Justice Scalia's warning of the prospects for abuse under the law. At the conclusion of the Starr's investigation, the limits on the independent counsel that the Court relied upon to conclude he was an "inferior" officer—jurisdiction, limited tenure and duties—looked less convincing, and the "ample authority" of the Attorney General over the independent counsel more formal than practical.

In anticipation of Congress's decision not to reauthorize the statute in 1999, Attorney General Janet Reno circulated draft regulations governing the *ad hoc* appointment of the now-called "Special Counsel." The Attorney General issued the regulations in July 1999, invoking the same statutory authority relied upon by Attorney General Richardson to appoint Special Prosecutor Cox.[192]

The regulations restored the special prosecutor model of prosecution of high-level executive officers that Attorney General Richardson had so forcefully defended in his confirmation hearings—a promise of independence from day-to-day supervision, the grant of full investigative authority, specifying both that both the power to appoint and to remove the special counsel resides with the Attorney General.[193] But the Starr investigation also had an impact on these regulations. The regulations, like Richardson's, promised independence from "day-to-day supervision

---

[191] James McDougal was sentenced to three years in prison on conspiracy and fraud charges, and Susan McDougal served nearly 18 months in prison for contempt. President George H.W. Bush pardoned seven of the Iran-contra investigation's defendants in 1992. *See id.* at 216.

[192] Office of Special Counsel, A.G. Order No. 2232–99, 64 Fed. Reg. 37038–1 (July 9, 1999) (codified at 28 C.F.R. pt. 0 and 600 (invoking 28 U.S.C. §§ 509, 510, 515–19 and 5 U.S.C. § 301)).

[193] *See* 28 C.F.R. §§ 600.1–600.10 (2007) (describing the duties, limitations, responsibilities, and jurisdiction of the Special Counsel).

from the Justice Department."[194] But the new regulations also explicitly granted the Attorney General a veto over the Special Counsel's actions if the Attorney General "conclude[s] that the action is so inappropriate or unwarranted under established department procedures."[195]

These special counsel regulations, and the special prosecutor model they embody, still govern today.[196] With them, the institutional framework for investigating allegations of criminal conduct at the highest reaches of government has overcome a major piece of the reaction to Watergate.

Morrison's Constitutional Legacy—Agency Independence

Morrison's own constitutional wake extends beyond the statute that the opinion sustained, and it does so in complex ways.

The most stable achievement of the *Morrison* opinion is its reaffirmation of a principle of anti-aggrandizement as a core precept of separation-of-powers law. As applied to the specific question of removal, *Morrison* extends a clear line of precedent from *Myers* to *Bowsher* for the proposition that any attempt by Congress to retain for itself a role in the removal of executive officials is doomed. At most, Congress can impose a restraint, through a good cause standard, on the President's power to fire agency or other officials.

The decision also leaves no doubt as to Congress's power to impose such removal restrictions on the President's or Attorney General's power to remove. It casts aside the more formal conception of separation-of-powers under which Congress could not restrain removal authority whatsoever because the officer wields executive power. In that respect, *Morrison* creates a safe harbor for independent agencies. It also marks a turn from the more formal mode of analysis of its immediate separation-of-powers predecessors, *Chadha* and *Bowsher*. The doctrinal framework *Morrison* applies to determining whether such a restriction on removal authority is constitutional—whether it impedes the President's ability to perform his constitutional duty—returns to the functional mode of analysis reflected in *Nixon v. Administrator of General Services*.

The doctrine that *Morrison* applies to validate the removal provision, however, opens up a field of questions. How is the Court or

---

[194] *Id.*

[195] 28 C.F.R. § 600.7 (2007).

[196] Interestingly, in Acting Attorney General Comey's appointment of Special Counsel Patrick Fitzgerald to investigate Scooter Libby, Comey made Fitzgerald an *ad hoc* special counsel appointment, but did not limit Fitzgerald's position and authority to those "defined and limited by 28 C.F.R. part 600." *See* Letter from James B. Comey, Acting Attorney General, to Patrick J. Fitzgerald, Special Counsel (Feb. 6, 2004).

Congress to judge the kinds of functions that bear centrally on the functioning of the Executive Branch? What level of impairment is necessary to amount to an unconstitutional impediment? And why is the question of impairment of the President's constitutional functions the one that best explains the power of Congress to structure the executive branch in a way that imposes constraints on the President's removal power? *Morrison*'s more functionalist standard for judging removal restrictions displaces the formalism of *Humphrey's Executor* as the constitutional foundation for independent agencies, but postpones to a future day how the balancing shall be performed, and the underlying theory that justifies agency independence.

Executive branch interpreters have read *Morrison*'s contribution to this issue as relatively narrow. For instance, in a well-known 1996 memorandum on separation of powers by the Office of Legal Counsel, OLC highlighted the narrow range of officers to whom the *Morrison* decision applies. The *Morrison* Court's own analysis construed the removal restrictions in reference to an inferior officer with a narrow range of duties. Thus the decision, OLC pointed out, "had no occasion to consider the validity of removal restrictions affecting principal officers, officers with broad statutory responsibilities, or officers involved in executive branch policy formulation."[197] Those definitive questions, and even the constitutional doctrines in which that debate will proceed, still loom.

Morrison's comprehension of the independent counsel within the overall framework of the special prosecutor model provokes further and more fundamental questions. On the one hand, this understanding of the independent counsel statute helps blunt the critique that became more prominent after Independent Counsel Starr's investigation and Congress's decision to allow the statute to lapse. The reflective critique of *Morrison* is one of a complete failure to appreciate the dangers for abuse posed by the statute. The Court, however, saw the statute as one that could be construed to allow substantial control by the President over the investigation, but it was up to a President to so construe it.

The fact that Olson brought a facial challenge to the statute furthers this point. To prevail on a facial challenge, Olson would have to have shown—as Chief Justice Rehnquist had articulated in prior Term—that "no set of circumstances exists under which the Act would be valid."[198] The Court's analogy to the Watergate special prosecutor suggests that the Court could imagine a set of circumstances in which the removal restrictions would not impede the President's ability to exercise his

---

[197] The Constitutional Separation of Powers Between the President and Congress, 20 Op. Off. Legal Counsel 124, *28 (May 7, 1996).

[198] United States v. Salerno, 481 U.S. 739, 745 (1987).

constitutional duties. At the extreme, President Nixon's firing of the first Watergate special prosecutor did not impede his constitutional ability to take care that the law is faithfully executed. By upholding the statute under a facial challenge, the Court was not concluding that it could not be abused, only that it could be construed so as not to unconstitutionally impede the President.

By viewing the good cause restriction as allowing the President adequate authority to supervise the independent counsel, the Court also opened up the question of how much protection its validation of removal protections really provide to the independent counsel—or to independent agencies. If, as the Court suggested, a "good cause" removal provision gives "ample authority" to the Attorney General, would disobedience of a Presidential directive also constitute good cause for removal? Professor John Manning, for instance, has proposed that it should, at least in the context of the independent counsel statute.[199]

If so, then the proponents of a strongly unitary executive would have achieved all the presidential control they urge, but through statutory interpretation, as opposed to through wholesale declarations of the unconstitutionality of independent agencies. On this view, in *Morrison*, a Watergate reform became the vehicle for upholding the formal requirements for agency independence, but did so in a way that questions the extent of independence that form provides.

Executive branch interpreters, moreover, have taken steps in the direction of construing removal restrictions to allow significant presidential influence, while stopping short of fully disobeying a presidential directive as good cause. For instance, the Office of Legal Counsel's 1996 separation-of-powers memorandum also opines that *Morrison* and *Bowsher* together suggest that a "generous reading" of the President's power to remove an inferior officer "may be essential to the constitutionality" of the removal restrictions even when the officer's functions are narrow.[200]

On less momentous matters, *Morrison* still states the law on the topic of interbranch appointments. *Morrison* observed the very broad language of the "Excepting Clause"—providing that Congress may "by Law vest Appointment of such inferior Officers, as they think proper, in

---

[199] *See* John F. Manning, *The Independent Counsel Statute: Reading "Good Cause" in Light of Article II*, 83 Minn. L. Rev. 1285 (1999); *see also* Lawrence Lessig & Cass R. Sunstein, *The President and the Administration*, 94 Colum. L. Rev. 1, 110–111 (1994) (suggesting possibility of interpreting good cause provision this way). Professor Geoffrey Miller had taken this position prior to *Morrison*. *See* Geoffrey P. Miller, *Independent Agencies*, 1986 Sup. Ct. Rev. 41, 86–87.

[200] The Constitutional Separation of Powers Between the President and Congress, 20 Op. Off. Legal Counsel 124, at *28 n.117 (May 7, 1996).

the President alone, in the courts of Law, or in the Heads of Departments"—but acknowledged that vesting such an appointment power in a
court would be improper if there was "some 'incongruity' between the
functions normally performed by the courts and the performance of their
duty to appoint." There has been little occasion for revisiting that
question, and it is difficult to imagine that there would likely be any
such "incongruity" in any appointment vested in the President.[201] In
Mistretta v. United States,[202] the Court upheld the constitutionality of the
United States Sentencing Commission, relying on *Morrison* at multiple
points in its analysis. As to the assignment of nonadjudicatory tasks to
the federal courts, *Morrison* exerted a calming influence.[203]

The Supreme Court has been less favorable to *Morrison*'s multi-
factor analysis for determining whether an officer is inferior or principal
under the Appointments Clause. That doctrine has been largely super-
seded *sub silentio* by the Supreme Court's 1997 decision in *Edmond v.
United States*.[204] In *Edmond*, with Justice Scalia now writing for the
majority, the Court upheld the Secretary of Transportation's statutory
power to appoint civilian members of the Coast Guard Court of Criminal
Appeals and the constitutionality of the Secretary doing so because the
military judges on the court are inferior, not principal officers within the
meaning of the Appointments Clause. The Court in *Edmond* acknowledged that two of the *Morrison* factors suggested that the military judges
were principal officers—they, unlike the independent counsel are neither
limited in tenure, nor limited in jurisdiction—but deemphasized the
import of that conclusion. "*Morrison*," the Court emphasized, "did not
purport to set forth a definitive test for whether an office is 'inferior'
under the Appointments Clause."[205] The *Edmond* Court then proceeded
to do so: "Whether one is an 'inferior' officer depends on whether he has
a superior," in other words, an officer "whose work is directed and
supervised at some level by others who were appointed by Presidential
nomination with the advice and consent of the Senate."[206] Further
distancing its analysis from *Morrison*'s, the Court then rejected the idea
that lesser rank or less magnitude of responsibility matters. Instead,

---

[201] *Id.* at *17.

[202] 488 U.S. 361 (1989).

[203] *See id.* at 389 n.16, 396.

[204] 520 U.S. 651 (1997). For a thoughtful treatment, see Nick Bravin, Note, *Is* Morrison
v. Olson *Still Good Law? The Court's New Appointments Clause Jurisprudence*, 98 Colum.
L. Rev. 1103 (1998).

[205] *Edmond*, 520 U.S. at 661.

[206] *Id.* at 662–63.

what makes an officer "inferior," the Court explained, is that their work is "directed and supervised at some level" by a principal officer.[207]

The *Edmond* Court concluded that the Judge Advocate General's exercise of administrative oversight over the judges, and his power to remove them, combined with the review of their decisions by the Court of Criminal Appeals for the Armed Forces, renders the Coast Guard Court judges subordinate, and thus "inferior" officers. Justice Souter noticed the shift in analysis. While having a superior is necessary to being an inferior officer, Justice Souter pointed out, it is not sufficient, and was not sufficient in *Morrison*, where the Court then went on to evaluate the duties, tenure, and jurisdiction of the office.[208] Indeed, under the *Edmond* analysis, it is not clear that the independent counsel would be an inferior officer.

Conclusion

The story of *Morrison v. Olson* is the story of the shifting fate of an idea—that through institutional design, a prosecutor could be placed beyond the influence of politics—and its fallout for the unitary executive debate. In response to Watergate and in particular the Saturday Night Massacre, Congress enacted a statute that contained the critical elements that the Watergate special prosecutor model did not have: a statutory protection from removal for the independent counsel, and appointment by a court. With President Reagan's inauguration in 1980, the statute's limitation on the President's control was caught in a larger constitutional battle over the central ground of the unitary executive debate: Congress's authority to limit the President's power to remove executive officers at will. Despite the Reagan Justice Department's accumulation of precedent to challenge the constitutional foundation of independent agencies, the independent counsel statute's origins as a Watergate reform provided a vehicle for the Supreme Court to validate, at least in form, Congress's authority to restrict the President's removal power and thus independent agencies. The Court, however, premised its decision on the independent counsel's similarity to the Watergate special prosecutor. That analogy has an important wrinkle for the Court's validation of the removal restrictions; it calls into question how much protection those restrictions provide, either to the independent counsel, or to independent agencies. That analogy also complicates the view that Independent Counsel Starr's investigation of President Clinton confirms the misjudgments of the *Morrison* Court. The *Morrison* Court construed and upheld the independent counsel statute from a facial challenge. As a result, it is less clear the *Morrison* decision is answerable to the manner

---

[207] *Id.*

[208] *Id.* at 667–68 (Souter, J., concurring in part and concurring in the judgment).

in which later Presidents and independent counsels acted under the statute, or failed to challenge the statute as applied.

With Congress's decision not to reauthorize the independent counsel statute in 1999, a Watergate reform has fallen on itself, leaving a clear memory for more than one presidential administration and a puzzling mark on the constitutional foundations for agency independence from the President.*

---

* I am grateful to Lisa Schultz Bressman, Rebecca Brown, Harold Bruff, David Franklin, John Harrison, Trevor Morrison, Christopher Schroeder, Daniel Sharfstein, and Michael Vandenbergh, as well as to participants in a workshop at Duke University Law School for comments and suggestions. I am also grateful to John Haubenreich for research assistance.

12

Dawn E. Johnsen

The Story of *Hamdan v. Rumsfeld*: Trying Enemy Combatants by Military Commission

When may the federal government take away an individual's liberty? No question better illustrates the separation of powers fundamental to the United States' system of government than the role each of the three branches typically must play before an individual may be imprisoned. Ordinarily, Congress must first enact a constitutionally compliant statute that details the circumstances that warrant the deprivation of liberty. The executive must then seek to enforce that law against an individual. Finally, the courts must adjudicate the executive's claims according to constitutionally and statutorily decreed standards and procedures, and stand ready to hear any habeas corpus claim by an individual who alleges wrongful imprisonment. This system ordinarily safeguards liberty by denying the President the power of some dictators to imprison enemies without charge or trial.

Notwithstanding these constitutional norms, President George W. Bush claimed the unilateral, unchecked authority to detain individuals indefinitely and try them outside existing legal tribunals. His claims were highly controversial but not implausible, because they were made in the context in which presidential power typically is at its zenith: as Commander in Chief leading the nation in war and in the protection of national security. In the wake of the September 11, 2001 terrorist attacks, while the United States waged war in Afghanistan against those responsible, Bush began designating as "enemy combatants" some who had engaged in that conflict or, much more broadly, who had connections to suspected terrorists. He imprisoned them without access to courts or lawyers or any other opportunity for review even within the executive branch. Bush also sought to subject certain non-citizen enemy combatants to trial—not before existing federal courts or courts-martial, with their constitutional and statutory protections, but before specially created, far less protective military commissions designed by his administration. Under Bush's military commission procedures, for example, a detainee could be tried and convicted based on evidence he was not permitted to see or hear and on statements obtained through coercion.

President Bush's claims of authority provoked intense debate. The Bush administration cited the precedent of prior wartime Presidents who detained and militarily tried those engaged in armed combat against the United States. Further, it cited the need to protect the nation from the grave threat of future terrorist attacks. Critics responded that Bush's assertions of authority extended well beyond the contemporaneous military tribunals historically used for soldiers seized on a battlefield in a conventional war. Bush's enemy combatants included a broad range of people beyond those suspected of committing terrorist acts, and reached those suspected of connections to organizations the government believed were facilitating an indefinite "war on terror." They included a handful of individuals seized or held on U.S. soil for years without trial, as well as hundreds of people held for years in Guantanamo Bay, Cuba. The Bush administration held other enemy combatants it considered "high value" at secret locations abroad, known as black sites, where the Central Intelligence Agency interrogated them using methods long considered torture. The administration subjected still other detainees to extraordinary renditions, which included turning over some to countries known to torture prisoners. The Bush administration responded that the ways in which the war on terror differed from previous wars, far from undermining its claims, supported extraordinary presidential powers—including the authority to violate statutes that constrained the President's ability to fight terrorism in the ways he believed best.

The Supreme Court considered key aspects of the Bush administration's policies toward the detention and trial of individuals suspected of involvement with terrorism in 2004 in *Hamdi v. Rumsfeld*[1] and *Rasul v. Bush*,[2] and, the focus of this chapter, in June 2006 in *Hamdan v. Rumsfeld*.[3] In each case, the fundamental clash of values these policies raise did not result in unqualified victory for either side. The Bush administration, however, suffered substantial setbacks, both with regard to the particular policy under review and in its broader effort to expand presidential power. After *Hamdi* and *Rasul*, President Bush retained the ability to detain enemy combatants, but not with the full flexibility and

---

[1] 542 U.S. 507 (2004).

[2] 542 U.S. 466 (2004).

[3] 548 U.S. 557 (2006).

independence from the Courts and Congress that he had sought. The *Hamdan* Court held that President Bush's military commissions were illegal, for they failed to satisfy applicable statutory requirements, which among other things incorporated obligations under international law including Common Article 3 of the Geneva Conventions. The Court, however, limited its review to statutory issues, did not deny the President's authority to convene properly constituted military commissions, and avoided resolving the ultimate constitutional authorities of Congress and the President to structure military commissions.

In June 2008, the Court ruled in yet another challenge to President Bush's detainee policies. In *Boumediene v. Bush*, a sharply divided Court for the fourth time in four years held against the President, this time declaring unconstitutional a federal statutory provision enacted in the wake of *Hamdan* to deprive the federal courts of jurisdiction over habeas corpus claims brought by detainees held at Guantanamo.[4] As the Bush administration entered its final months and the American people prepared to elect a new President, all three branches of government continued to wrestle with the appropriate standards to govern the detention, interrogation and trial of suspected terrorists and those more loosely associated with organizations suspected of supporting terrorism. Looking ahead, the Supreme Court remains closely divided on key aspects of presidential power, and the balance may shift with the next appointment to the Court.

Political Context

September 11, 2001

On September 11, 2001, nineteen terrorists hijacked commercial jet airplanes and used them to kill almost three thousand people in suicide attacks on the World Trade Center, the Pentagon, and a thwarted attack reportedly aimed at the U.S. Capitol. Words cannot easily convey just how these attacks shocked the world. Many descriptions, including that of the official 9/11 Commission report, have contrasted the disorienting incongruity of the attacks with the flawless beauty of the morning.[5] In addition to the horrific loss of life, Americans suffered a deep—and in important respects unprecedented—blow to their sense of national and physical security.

The Manhattan skyline remains jarringly altered. The 9/11 attacks also dramatically transformed the political landscape. An overriding question was whether concerns about new security threats would lead to a strengthened presidency and diminished protections for individual

---

[4] 128 S.Ct. 2229 (2008).

[5] National Commission on Terrorist Attacks upon the United States, *The 9/11 Commission Report* 18 (2004).

liberty—not only temporarily as during past wars, but for the duration of an indefinite, potentially never-ending war on terror.

In the short term, change was certain. President Bush assumed office in January 2001 following one of the closest, most disputed presidential races in U.S. history. His rival Al Gore actually won the popular vote, and Bush won a majority of the electoral votes only after a controversial Supreme Court decision ended a recount underway in Florida due to voting irregularities.[6] Bush thus assumed office without a clear political mandate.

As the nation came together eight months later in the face of an external enemy, Bush's public approval rating skyrocketed to ninety percent, an all-time high in the history of recorded public opinion polls.[7] His likelihood of reelection increased. Congress enacted the Authorization for Use of Military Force (AUMF) just one week after 9/11 with only a single nay vote, which conferred on the President sweeping authority "to use all necessary and appropriate force against those nations, organizations, or persons he determines planned, authorized, committed, or aided the terrorist attacks that occurred on September 11, 2001, or harbored such organizations or persons...."[8] On the international scene, sympathy and support for the United States swelled to new heights.

Notwithstanding his strength at home and abroad—or perhaps emboldened by that support—President Bush repeatedly asserted expansive presidential power to implement his policies without first obtaining authorization from Congress, even when his policies seemed to conflict with existing statutes and when he almost certainly could have obtained congressional authorization. Vice President Dick Cheney was influential in formulating administration policy, which took advantage of favorable political conditions to advance views long held by him and his counsel (and later chief of staff) David Addington.[9] Cheney and Addington had

---

[6] Bush v. Gore, 531 U.S. 98 (2000).

[7] *A Snapshot Gives Bush 90% Approval*, N.Y. Times, Sept. 24, 2001, at B6.

[8] Authorization for Use of Military Force, Pub. L. No. 107–40, 115 Stat. 224 (2001). The Bush administration intentionally drafted the AUMF in this broad manner with an eye toward future assertions of extraordinary presidential war powers that Bush's advisors believed would be desirable, but which were not debated. In fact, the administration initially sought even broader language, but quickly abandoned that effort when it failed to attract adequate support. David Abramowitz, *The President, the Congress, and Use of Force: Legal and Political Considerations in Authorizing Use of Force against International Terrorism*, 43 Harv. Int'l L.J. 71 (2002).

[9] In addition to outstanding coverage in *The New York Times*, *The Washington Post* and *The New Yorker*, the best accounts of the inner workings of the Bush administration regarding the war on terror and presidential power include Jack Goldsmith, *The Terror*

worked together on the Iran–Contra investigation, Cheney as a member
and Addington as committee counsel. Cheney and other minority members of the Iran–Contra committee had issued a minority report on the
Iran–Contra investigation that defended the Reagan administration
against charges of unlawful action. The minority report endorsed expansive presidential authority and dissented from the majority report's
"aggrandizing theory of Congress' foreign policy powers that is itself
part of the problem."[10] Thus, Cheney assumed the vice presidency
believing that Congress had unduly encroached upon executive authority
in response to the Watergate scandal, and he openly declared his goal of
using his time in the White House to restore a strong presidency.[11]

Secretary of Defense Donald Rumsfeld and his lead counsel William
J. Haynes generally shared Cheney's objectives. They all found a critical
ally in John Yoo, a mid-level political appointee at the Department of
Justice's Office of Legal Counsel (OLC), which is the office entrusted
with advising the President and the executive branch on legal matters.
Yoo joined Addington, Haynes, and then-Counsel to the President Alberto Gonzales to form the group that regularly developed the legal rationales that supported the Bush administration's desired policies. Their
views on executive authority countenanced measures that not only
limited individual liberty, but also that realigned—in their view, recti-
fied—the balance of powers among the three branches, principally by
shifting power from Congress to the President. The Bush administration
sought to keep these controversial policies and legal determinations
secret, from the public and sometimes even from officials inside the
executive branch who might oppose them. Attorney General John Ashcroft at times was excluded even as his subordinate John Yoo directly
advised White House lawyers on the legality of proposed polices.

This expansive conception of executive authority played itself out in
the course of many of the decisions that needed to be made in the

---

Presidency: Law and Judgment Inside the Bush Administration (2007), and Charlie
Savage, *Takeover: The Return of the Imperial Presidency and the Subversion of American
Democracy* (2007).

[10] Select Comm. to Investigate Covert Arms Transactions with Iran, Report of the
Congressional Committees Investigating the Iran–Contra Affair with Supplemental, Minority, and Additional Views, S. Rep. No. 100–216 and H.R. Rep. No. 100–433, at 437 (1987);
see also Sean Wilentz, Op–Ed., *Mr. Cheney's Minority Report*, N.Y. Times, July 9, 2007, at
A17.

[11] *See, e.g.*, Charlie Savage, *Takeover: The Return of the Imperial Presidency and the
Subversion of American Democracy* 9 (2007) (quoting a 1996 speech by Cheney: "I clearly
do believe, and have spoken directly about the importance of a strong presidency. I think
there have been times in the past, oftentimes in response to events such as Watergate or
the war in Vietnam, where Congress has begun to encroach upon the powers and
responsibilities of the President; that it was important to go back and try to restore that
balance.").

aftermath of the 9/11 attacks, decisions that would shape the United States' prosecution of the war on terror. On the fundamental decisions to invade Afghanistan and later Iraq, President Bush did first obtain congressional authorization, although throughout he maintained that authorization was unnecessary because he possessed the constitutional authority to go to war without Congress.[12] On many other war on terror policies, presidential lawyers, acting on direction to be "forward-leaning" and push the legal envelope, gave the green light to controversial policies that the administration did not present to Congress.[13] Some prominent policies involved governmental action that seemed to conflict with federal statutory and treaty obligations, such as the National Security Agency's program of domestic electronic surveillance without compliance with the court order requirements of the Foreign Intelligence Surveillance Act.[14] A considerable portion of the Bush administration's counterterrorism policies focused on the detention, interrogation, or trial of persons the government suspected were actively participating in or aiding the terrorist threat. Prior to *Hamdan*, the Court had considered several cases that involved such issues.

Detention of Detainees: Hamdi and Rasul

Among the powers Bush asserted was the authority to declare individuals "enemy combatants"—a term without an established or clear definition—and to hold such persons until the end of the relevant war, without access to any legal process or any outside individual, including legal counsel or family. Bush based this authority on historical precedent in which the U.S. military captured enemy soldiers on the battlefield and held them for the duration of the war to prevent them from returning to fight.

---

[12] Memorandum from John C. Yoo, Deputy Assistant Att'y Gen., Office of Legal Counsel, U.S. Dep't of Justice to the Deputy Counsel to the President, The President's Constitutional Authority to Conduct Military Operations Against Terrorists and Nations Supporting Them 1 (Sept. 25, 2001) ("[T]he Constitution vests the President with the plenary authority, as Commander in Chief and the sole organ of the Nation in its foreign relations, to use military force abroad...."); *id.* at 19 (Congress may not "place any limits on the President's determinations as to any terrorist threat, the amount of military force to be used in response, or the method, timing, and nature of the response. These decisions, under our Constitution, are for the President alone to make.").

[13] Tim Golden, *After Terror, A Secret Rewriting of Military Law*, N.Y. Times, Oct. 24, 2004, at A1 (quoting former associate White House counsel Bradford Berenson); *see also* Jack Goldsmith, *The Terror Presidency: Law and Judgment Inside the Bush Administration* (2007); Charlie Savage, *Takeover: The Return of the Imperial Presidency and the Subversion of American Democracy* (2007).

[14] U.S. Dep't of Justice, *Legal Authorities Supporting the Activities of the National Security Agency Described by the President*, Jan. 19, 2006, *reprinted in* 81 Ind. L.J. 1374 (2006); James Risen & Eric Lichtblau, *Bush Lets U.S. Spy on Callers Without Courts*, N.Y. Times, Dec. 16, 2005, at A1.

Bush's theory, however, went beyond this historical precedent. In the context of a conflict that Bush himself declared to be "unlike any other we have ever seen" and that would "not end until every terrorist group of global reach has been found, stopped and defeated,"[15] the theory permitted quasi-permanent detention, at the President's sole discretion. Further, the Bush administration desired to hold enemy combatants, not only to prevent their return to the "battlefield" of terrorism, but also to question them, using extremely harsh methods and at times even methods of torture. Finally, the Bush administration took the position—controversial even within its own ranks, and ultimately rejected by the *Hamdan* Court—that detainees in the war on terror were not entitled to the protections of the Geneva Conventions.

Yasser Esam Hamdi's detention presented some additional twists. Hamdi was an American citizen captured in Afghanistan in November 2001 while fighting against the United States. Because he was a citizen, the military brought him to the United States, rather than Guantanamo Bay, and held him in South Carolina as an enemy combatant without charge, legal process, or access to anyone. In response to Hamdi's petition for a writ of habeas corpus, the Bush administration asserted that the President had the inherent authority as Commander in Chief to hold Hamdi without any congressional authorization. It argued in the alternative that the AUMF passed by Congress in the days after 9/11 had in fact authorized the detention. The administration added that the Court should not afford Hamdi any individual process out of "[r]espect for separation of powers and the limited institutional capabilities of courts in matters of military decision-making in connection with an ongoing conflict. . . ."[16]

Six Justices wrote opinions in *Hamdi*, with no one majority opinion. Only Justice Thomas embraced an expansive view of the President's constitutional authority similar to that of the Bush administration. A majority of the Justices did not reach this claim because five Justices agreed with the administration's alternative argument that the AUMF had authorized the detention of those seized on a traditional battlefield, even U.S. citizens, to prevent them from returning to fight. A different majority of six Justices, however, held that President Bush had overstepped that authority and denied Hamdi his constitutional right not to be deprived of liberty without due process of law by refusing to give him any process for challenging his designation as an enemy combatant.

---

[15] President's Address Before a Joint Session of the Congress on the United States Response to the Terrorist Attacks of September 11, 2 Pub. Papers 1140, 1141, 1142 (Sept. 20, 2001).

[16] Hamdi v. Rumsfeld, 542 U.S. 507, 527 (2004) (quoting Brief for the Respondents at 26 (No. 03–6696)).

Eight Justices emphasized constitutional protections against the ability of one branch acting alone to deprive an individual of liberty. The plurality opinion stated that the Constitution "envisions a role for all three branches when individual liberties are at stake" and contained the case's most quoted line: "a state of war is not a blank check for the President...."[17]

Thus, the Court held that the government had to afford Hamdi notice of the factual basis for the enemy combatant designation and a fair opportunity to challenge his detention before an impartial decision-maker. The Court left the government with some discretion in how it structured the necessary process, and did not require the full protections afforded a criminal defendant in federal court. The Bush administration, rather than provide Hamdi this required review after almost three years of detention, released him to Saudi Arabia on conditions that included that he renounce his citizenship and any claims he might have against the United States.

The plaintiffs in *Rasul v. Bush* and its companion case *Al Odah v. United States* also had been designated enemy combatants.[18] Because they were not U.S. citizens, however, the United States brought them, like hundreds of detainees, to the naval base at Guantanamo Bay, which, while not on U.S. soil, was under the control of the U.S. government. The government contended that because a treaty states that Cuba retains sovereign control over the area, the federal habeas corpus statute that affords access to federal courts did not apply to prisoners held there, and therefore the government could hold them indefinitely without access to any tribunal to challenge the legality of their detention. The Court rejected the government's argument and held that, because the United States exercised plenary and exclusive jurisdiction over Guantanamo Bay, the jurisdiction of the habeas statute extended to the plaintiffs, who thus were entitled to review in the federal courts. The Court also implicitly rejected the government's argument that for the Court to so hold would interfere with the President's constitutional authority, including by "directly interfer[ing] with the Executive's conduct of the military campaign against al Qaeda and its supporters."[19] Taken together, *Hamdi* and *Rasul* allowed President Bush to continue to designate and hold enemy combatants, but rejected key elements of his claimed authority and led to a system of Combatant Status Review Tribunals (CSRTs) within the Department of Defense to allow Guantanamo detainees to contest enemy combatant designations.

---

[17] *Id.* at 536.

[18] 542 U.S. 466 (2004).

[19] Brief for the Respondents at 42, *Rasul v. Bush*, 542 U.S. 466 (Nos. 03–334, 03–343).

Interrogation of Detainees: Padilla

Beyond this attempt at the unilateral, indefinite, incommunicado detention of enemy combatants, the Bush administration's most controversial counterterrorism policies and practices involved the interrogation of detainees during their lengthy detentions. Again, the administration rested its claims on the President's Commander-in-Chief authority. It sought to avoid congressional action on standards for detainee interrogations and to maximize its ability to use harsh techniques through Department of Justice legal opinions that would protect governmental actors from legal liability. It also sought to avoid liability by keeping noncitizen detainees outside the United States, relying instead on Guantanamo Bay, secret overseas black sites, and extraordinary renditions to other countries. And it also kept secret the details of its policies, practices, and legal analyses.

The *Hamdi* Court found that the President had the authority to hold enemy combatants seized on a traditional battlefield in order to keep combatants from returning to war. But the Bush administration wanted to hold enemy combatants in part for a very different purpose: to interrogate them in an attempt to gather intelligence. The facts of another Supreme Court case, *Rumsfeld v. Padilla*,[20] illustrate this goal. The government seized Jose Padilla not on a foreign battlefield but in Chicago, on the suspicion that he was involved in a terrorist plot to explode a dirty bomb. As the government made clear in the ensuing litigation, intelligence-gathering was an important motivation for holding Padilla as an enemy combatant, outside the protections of the existing justice system: to allow him access to a lawyer or a judge, the government contended, would give rise to hope and optimism, which would undermine the government's efforts to break him during his many months of interrogation and solitary confinement.[21] The government ultimately held Padilla for more than three years before transferring him to the criminal justice system, on different charges than the initial suspected terrorism plot, thereby mooting his enemy combatant case and

---

[20] 542 U.S. 426 (2004). The Court did not reach the merits of the challenge, because it found Padilla had filed the case in the wrong court.

[21] The government submitted to the Court, in support of Padilla's detention, a sworn declaration of Vice Admiral Lowell E. Jacoby, Director of the Defense Intelligence Agency, that stated:

> Only after such time as Padilla has perceived that help is not on the way can the United States reasonably expect to obtain all possible intelligence information from Padilla.... Providing him access to counsel now ... would break—probably irreparably—the sense of dependency and trust that the interrogators are attempting to create.

Brief of Respondent at 3 n.3, *Padilla*, 542 U.S. 426 (No. 03–1027) (quoting Jacoby declaration); *see also* Brief for the Petitioner at 10, 29, *Padilla*, 542 U.S. 426 (No. 03–1027) (relying upon Jacoby declaration).

preventing the Supreme Court from reaching his claim of unlawful detention.[22]

Soon after 9/11, the Bush administration sought legal advice on just how harsh those interrogations lawfully could be. A particular concern was legal constraints and liability for the Central Intelligence Agency (CIA) when interrogating suspected "high value" terrorists at black sites outside of the United States. President Bush determined, backed by OLC advice, that the protections of the Geneva Conventions (certain violations of which were punishable under federal law) did not apply to al Qaeda detainees. Among the grounds for his decision, ultimately before the Court in *Hamdan*: the Geneva Conventions govern only conflicts involving "High Contracting Parties" which must be states and therefore does not include al Qaeda, and Common Article 3 applies only to "armed conflict not of an international character" and therefore does not reach the conflict with al Qaeda which was international in scope. Gonzales also controversially opined that the nature of the war on terror "renders obsolete Geneva's strict limitations on questioning of enemy prisoners and renders quaint some of its provisions. . . . "[23] The President announced that "[a]s a matter of policy, the United States Armed Forces shall continue to treat detainees humanely and, to the extent appropriate and consistent with military necessity, in a manner consistent with the principles of Geneva."[24] Even the vague constraints of this directive, however, applied only to the military and not the CIA.

That left as a possible obstacle to CIA interrogators the federal statute that imposed criminal penalties for torture. Gonzales and Addington turned to OLC for an analysis of the anti-torture statute when, on March 28, 2002, the CIA captured and prepared to interrogate Abu Zubaida, believed to be a top al Qaeda operative. OLC gave a green light and later produced its now-infamous Torture Memo, authored primarily by John Yoo. The Torture Memo, dated August 1, 2002, was withheld from Congress and the public until leaked to the *Washington Post* in June 2004.[25] It began by interpreting the scope of the criminal prohibition exceedingly narrowly, limiting it, for example, to suffering "equivalent in intensity to the pain accompanying . . . organ failure, impairment

---

[22] Padilla ultimately was convicted of conspiracy charges related to terrorism and sentenced to seventeen years. *See* Kirk Semple, *Padilla Gets 17 Years in Conspiracy Case*, N.Y. Times, Jan. 23, 2008, at A14.

[23] Memorandum from Alberto R. Gonzales, Counsel to the President, to President George W. Bush (Jan. 25, 2002).

[24] Memorandum from President George W. Bush to Vice President Dick Cheney *et al.*, Humane Treatment of al Qaeda and Taliban Detainees (Feb. 7, 2002).

[25] Dana Priest & R. Jeffrey Smith, *Memo Offered Justification for Use of Torture*, Wash. Post, June 8, 2004, at A1.

of bodily function, or even death."[26] It then methodically explored all conceivable arguments whereby persons who engage in extreme interrogations, and even torture, could escape conviction. For example, it devised creative theories of necessity and self-defense, extended to self-defense of the nation.

Most significantly, the Torture Memo posited an extraordinarily broad theory of the President's authority as Commander in Chief to disregard statutory constraints. OLC concluded that Congress lacked the authority to prohibit the executive branch from using methods of torture when the President, as Commander in Chief, chooses to authorize it. OLC wrote, "Congress may no more regulate the President's ability to detain and interrogate enemy combatants than it may regulate his ability to direct troop movements on the battlefield."[27] The Memo neglected to cite the considerable war powers the Constitution expressly affords Congress[28] or relevant Supreme Court precedent, including the prevailing three-part analytical scheme that Justice Robert Jackson articulated in the Steel Seizure case.[29] Other secret OLC memoranda addressed additional interrogation issues: for example, approving specific extreme techniques such as waterboarding, a method long considered torture in which the detainee is subjected to drowning; advising the administration that it could turn detainees over to foreign governments known to use torture; and concluding that the military could ignore statutory limits on interrogations, including those contained in the Uniform Code of Military Justice.[30]

When the Torture Memo was leaked, it attracted strong criticism. Many commentators, including many former OLC attorneys, noted that

---

[26] Memorandum from Jay S. Bybee, Assistant Att'y Gen., Office of Legal Counsel, U.S. Dep't of Justice to Alberto R. Gonzales, Counsel to the President, Standards of Conduct for Interrogation Under 18 U.S.C. §§ 2340–2340A, at 1 (Aug. 1, 2002) [also known as the Torture Memo].

[27] *Id.* at 35.

[28] The Torture Memo failed to acknowledge Congress's authority to make rules for the government and regulation of the land and naval forces, U.S. Const. art. I, § 8, cl. 14; to declare war, grant letters of marque and reprisal, and make rules concerning captures on land and water, *id.* at cl. 11; and to define and punish piracies and felonies committed on the high seas and offenses against the law of nations, *id.* at cl. 10.

[29] Youngstown Sheet & Tube Co. v. Sawyer, 343 U.S. 579, 634 (1952) (Jackson, J., concurring). For more on *Youngstown* see Chapter 7 in this volume.

[30] As this book went to press, the Bush administration continued to keep secret some of these memoranda, but various sources have described them. In March 2008, the administration made public one additional memorandum, issued by OLC five years earlier. *See* Memorandum from John C. Yoo, Deputy Assistant Att'y Gen., Office of Legal Counsel, U.S. Dep't of Justice to William J. Haynes II, General Counsel, U.S. Dep't of Defense, Re Military Interrogation of Alien Unlawful Combatants Held Outside the United States (Mar. 14, 2003).

its results-oriented analysis was inappropriate for OLC, the office entrusted with providing the legal advice necessary to ensure lawful governmental action.[31] Such an approach serves the President poorly, including in his responsibility to uphold the Constitution and take care that the laws be faithfully executed.[32] The Bush administration ultimately disavowed the Torture Memo, but only after it was leaked to the public and a new Assistant Attorney General for OLC, Jack Goldsmith, insisted on its withdrawal. Goldsmith then resigned, after only nine months in office. Goldsmith later described his concern upon learning that the Torture Memo and some other OLC opinions "were deeply flawed: sloppily reasoned, overbroad, and incautious in asserting extraordinary constitutional authorities on behalf of the President. I was astonished, and immensely worried, to discover that some of our most important counterterrorism policies rested on severely damaged legal foundations."[33] Goldsmith's successor at OLC, Daniel Levin, issued a more reasonable-sounding replacement memorandum that opened by declaring torture "abhorrent."[34] The replacement torture memo simply dropped (but did not disavow) the earlier analysis of the President's Commander-in-Chief authority to disregard statutes.[35]

The Abu Ghraib scandal was of even greater political consequence than the leak of the OLC Torture Memo. On April 28, 2004, the very day of the *Padilla* argument, during which the government argued that the Court should trust and not second-guess the President regarding his enemy combatant policies,[36] CBS News and *The New Yorker* published photographs of U.S. soldiers abusing Iraqi prisoners at the Abu Ghraib military prison.[37] The images were circulated widely and quickly were

---

[31] *See* Dawn E. Johnsen, *Faithfully Executing the Laws: Internal Legal Constraints on Executive Power*, 54 UCLA L. Rev. 1559 (2007) (discussing ten "Principles to Guide the Office of Legal Counsel," which were developed by nineteen former OLC attorneys in reaction to the Torture Memo).

[32] U.S. Const. art. II, § 3.

[33] Jack Goldsmith, *The Terror Presidency: Law and Judgment Inside the Bush Administration* 10 (2007).

[34] Memorandum from Daniel Levin, Acting Assistant Att'y Gen., Office of Legal Counsel, to James B. Comey, Deputy Att'y Gen., Legal Standards Applicable Under 18 U.S.C. §§ 2340–2340A, at 1 (Dec. 30, 2004).

[35] The press reported that Levin also resigned over the torture issue while working on a never-issued memo that would have imposed tighter controls on interrogation techniques. Jan Crawford Greenburg & Ariane de Vogue, *Bush Administration Blocked Waterboarding Critic*, ABC News, Nov. 2, 2007, http://abcnews.go.com/ WN/DOJ/story?id=3814076.

[36] *See* Transcript of Oral Argument at 23, Rumsfeld v. Padilla, 542 U.S. 426 (2004) (No. 03–1027) ("[W]here there is a war . . . you have to trust the executive to make the kind of quintessential military judgments that are involved in things like that.").

[37] *See Slideshow: The Abu Ghraib Pictures*, The New Yorker, May 3, 2004, http://www.newyorker.com/archive/2004/05/03/slideshow_040503; Seymour M. Hersh, *Torture at Abu Ghraib*, The New Yorker, May 10, 2004, at 42.

etched in the world's collective memory: a hooded Iraqi forced to stand on a box with arms and legs outstretched and attached to wires, naked Iraqis forced into human pyramids while U.S. soldiers posed and grinned for the camera. These and hundreds of other photographs documented horrific cruelty and led to worldwide outrage.

President Bush immediately and repeatedly proclaimed that the United States does not engage in torture, though he continued to refuse to confirm which techniques were authorized, arguing that to divulge its methods would enable terrorists to prepare to withstand them. He sought to distance the government from what he described as the rogue actions of a few American troops. This contention was made difficult by the revelation of the OLC Torture Memo and other evidence that the government had authorized extreme treatment of detainees. It was disclosed, for example, that in December 2002 U.S. Secretary of Defense Donald Rumsfeld had approved harsh and controversial techniques for use at Guantanamo prison, including forced nudity and the use of attack dogs to induce panic. Even more disturbing reports came in 2005, of secret black sites overseas where the CIA's interrogation methods included waterboarding detainees and also repeatedly dousing them with extremely cold water while holding them in very cold cells.[38] As *Hamdan* worked its way to the Court, the press also covered the United States' use of extraordinary renditions to transfer custody of detainees to foreign countries known to use torture. The most publicized example involved Maher Arar, a Canadian whom the United States labeled a suspected terrorist and rendered to Syria in September 2002, where he was detained and tortured for almost a year. Ultimately, the Canadian government issued a formal apology, paid Arar ten million Canadian dollars, and filed a formal protest with the United States.[39]

As with some other counterterrorism policies, the administration's interrogation policies and practices encountered strong opposition from within the executive branch, most notably from within the military. Many lawyers throughout the government objected that the administration was acting pursuant to incorrect understandings of applicable legal constraints, but they failed to persuade policymakers who instructed them that OLC's legal advice was authoritative. The press reported on

---

[38] Brian Ross & Richard Esposito, *CIA's Harsh Interrogation Techniques Described*, ABC News, Nov. 18, 2005, http://abcnews.go.com/WNT/Investigation/story?id=1322866; Michael A. Fletcher, *Bush Defends CIA's Clandestine Prisons*, Wash. Post, Nov. 8, 2005, at A15.

[39] *See* Commission of Inquiry into the Actions of Canadian Officials in Relations to Maher Arar, *Report of the Events Relating to Maher Arar* (2006); David Cole & Jules Lobel, *Less Safe, Less Free: Why America is Losing the War on Terror* 23–28 (2007) (describing cases of Arar and Khaled El–Masri); Jane Mayer, *Outsourcing Torture: The Secret History of America's "Extraordinary Rendition" Program*, The New Yorker, Feb. 14, 2005, at 106.

this internal opposition. One particularly widely read and cited *New Yorker* article from February 2006 profiled the courage of Alberto J. Mora, general counsel of the U.S. Navy with the rank the equivalent of a four-star general, in raising "unequivocal, wide-ranging, and persistent" objections to what he viewed "as a disastrous and unlawful policy of authorizing cruelty toward terror suspects."[40]

Congress and the War on Terror

During the years following 9/11 and prior to the Court's June 2006 *Hamdan* opinion, President Bush enjoyed a highly supportive and deferential Congress. Republicans controlled both Houses of Congress from the time Bush took office in January 2001 until January 2007, except for a period from June 2001 to January 2003 when Democrats had an effective one-vote Senate majority. On the few occasions when Bush sought congressional action on war and terrorism issues, Congress was very responsive. Only one member of Congress voted against the Authorization to Use Military Force, passed one week after 9/11. Congress enacted the Patriot Act quickly and overwhelmingly, with remarkably little debate and consideration of its particulars. The October 2002 Authorization for the Use of Military Force Against Iraq passed with majorities of more than two-thirds in each house of Congress.

Although Congress generally was supportive, individual members criticized what they described as presidential overreaching—or even lawlessness. Democratic Senator Russ Feingold, among the most vociferous critics, introduced a resolution in March 2006 to censure President Bush for violating FISA with his warrantless domestic surveillance program, though this effort did not garner serious support even among Democrats. Patrick Leahy voiced strong concerns even in the months following 9/11, when he served as Chair of the Senate Judiciary Committee, about indefinite detentions and the President's announced plan to use military commissions. Senator Arlen Specter was the most consistent, though not the only, Republican critic of the administration. On the whole, however, prior to *Hamdan* Congress provided little oversight or new constraints on counterterrorism policies.

Congress's relative passivity is striking given that many of Bush's aggressive claims of authority involved controversial, often secret interpretations of federal statutes. President Bush raised constitutional concerns not only to existing statutes but also to record numbers of legislative provisions even as he signed them into law, frequently on the

---

[40] Jane Mayer, *The Memo: How an Internal Effort to Ban the Abuse and Torture of Detainees Was Thwarted*, The New Yorker, Feb. 27, 2006, at 32; *see also* Tim Golden & Eric Schmitt, *Detainee Policy Sharply Divides Bush Officials*, N.Y. Times, Nov. 2, 2005, at A1; Josh White, *Military Lawyers Fought Policy on Interrogations*, Wash. Post, July 15, 2005, at A1.

grounds they could be read to interfere with his expansive view of the powers of his office. Although prior Presidents also used signing statements to register constitutional objections, Bush's use (or, depending on one's perspective, abuse) of signing statements was widely criticized in the months before the Court decided *Hamdan*.

Some commentators have criticized Congress for failing to stand up for its institutional prerogatives: with regard to the Republicans, for allowing partisanship and support for their President to trump the safeguarding of the proper role and authorities of Congress; with regard to Democrats, for giving in to fear of being portrayed as soft on terrorism and war. On the other hand, when a President claims the authority to disregard many statutory provisions, sometimes secretly, Congress cannot easily constrain him. Simply enacting a law will not guarantee that the President actually will enforce it. In fact, when Congress reenacted a post-Nixon reform that required the government simply to notify Congress if it determined it would not enforce a statute on grounds of unconstitutionality, President Bush issued a signing statement suggesting he might not comply with that reporting requirement in some circumstances.[41] To check such presidential excesses, Congress is left with the possibilities of aggressive oversight, withholding funding or its consent to appointments, or the ultimate threat of impeachment—all steps that a Congress led by the President's own party will be loathe to take.

One issue on which Congress did take steps to constrain the President prior to *Hamdan* was the interrogation of detainees. In the wake of the Abu Ghraib scandal, the OLC Torture Memo, and reports of harsh interrogation techniques at Guantanamo Bay and secret black sites, Congress enacted the Detainee Treatment Act (DTA) in December 2005, by a vote of ninety to nine in the Senate and 308 to 122 in the House of Representatives.[42] The law provides that "[n]o individual in the custody or under the physical control of the United States government, regardless of nationality or physical location, shall be subject to cruel, inhuman, or degrading treatment or punishment."[43] The law's chief sponsor, Republican Senator John McCain, had special credibility on the issue, as a Vietnam veteran who had been tortured while held as a prisoner of war for more than five years.

---

[41] George W. Bush, President, Statement on Signing the 21st Century Department of Justice Appropriations Authorization Act (Nov. 2, 2002), *in* 38 Weekly Comp. Pres. Doc. 1971–73.

[42] Pub. L. No. 109–148, tit. X, 119 Stat. 2739 (2005) (to be codified in scattered sections of 10, 28 & 42 U.S.C.).

[43] 42 U.S.C. § 2000dd (West 2008).

The Bush administration initially worked hard to stop the bill, indicating that Bush would veto it because it would jeopardize the CIA's interrogation of detainees at secret black sites abroad. Ultimately, though, the overwhelming, veto-proof, bipartisan support for the bill made Bush's continued opposition untenable. The administration then turned its attention to seeking amendments to the bill, to minimize what it viewed as its harms, and it ultimately achieved significant changes. The precise meaning of one of the most controversial changes became a central issue of contention in *Hamdan*. That provision deprived the federal courts of jurisdiction over claims brought by Guantanamo detainees seeking to challenge the legality of their detention or treatment. At issue in *Hamdan* was whether the denial of jurisdiction applied to claims already pending in the courts at the time of the DTA's enactment. The DTA also defined cruel, inhuman, and degrading treatment narrowly and deemed some evidence obtained through coercion admissible in a CSRT's consideration of whether a detention was proper.

Notwithstanding what were, from his perspective, great improvements in the DTA's final form, President Bush issued a signing statement in December 2005 in which he appeared to claim the right not to comply with the new law if it hampered his decisions as Commander in Chief. His signing statement announced he would construe the DTA "in a manner consistent with the constitutional authority of the President . . . as Commander-in-Chief and consistent with the constitutional limitations on the judicial power. . . ."[44] In the months before the Court issued its decision in *Hamdan*, the press closely covered this controversy surrounding the DTA's enactment as well as Bush's use of signing statements to object to the constitutionality of hundreds of other statutory provisions.[45]

The year before the *Hamdan* decision also saw the appointment of two Supreme Court Justices, one as Chief Justice and the other to replace Sandra Day O'Connor who sat at the center of a Court that was closely divided on many issues. Separation of powers and civil liberties in wartime were central issues in the Senate Judiciary Committee's questioning of both John Roberts and Samuel Alito. Now–Chief Justice Roberts faced questions about his role in the *Hamdan* case itself: in July 2005, Roberts had ruled with the majority of the D.C. Court of Appeals'

---

[44] George W. Bush, President, Statement on Signing the Department of Defense, Emergency Supplemental Appropriations to Address Hurricanes in the Gulf of Mexico, and Pandemic Influenza Act, 2006 (Dec. 30, 2005), *in* 41 Weekly Comp. Pres. Doc. 1918, 1919.

[45] *See, e.g.*, Editorial, *Unchecked Abuse*, Wash. Post, Jan. 11, 2006, at A20 ("Without aggressive monitoring—and possibly further action—by Congress, illegal abuse of foreign prisoners in the custody of the United States is likely to continue."); Charlie Savage, *Bush Challenges Hundreds of Laws*, Boston Globe, Apr. 30, 2006, at A1.

three-judge panel in favor of the Bush administration and against Hamdan's claims.

The dominant issue on the political scene in the months while the Court deliberated *Hamdan* undoubtedly was the Iraq War. The length of that war and inaccuracies in assessments of Iraq's threat and possession of weapons of mass destruction ultimately contributed to the plummeting of President Bush's public approval rating, from the post 9/11 high of ninety percent to thirty-one percent in May 2006, the month before the Court issued its decision in *Hamdan*.[46] Growing opposition to the war helped Democrats take majorities in both Houses in the November 2006 elections.

Thus, as it deliberated in *Hamdan*, the Supreme Court was aware that President Bush—primarily through delegated authority to Vice President Cheney and a handful of executive branch lawyers—had vigorously promoted a new separation of powers paradigm that would afford the President greatly enhanced authority on issues of war, national security, and terrorism, with diminished protections for individual liberty. Presidential unilateralism was a hallmark of that paradigm, with congressional and judicial involvement opposed as undesirable and in many instances unconstitutional. Bush's most controversial claims involved expansive powers he viewed as both inherent, in the sense of stemming from constitutional authorities that required no additional statutory basis, and exclusive, in that Congress lacked the authority to constrain them. The President claimed authority, often in secret, to act in these spheres even in ways that Congress had expressly prohibited. The Court also knew of the lack of meaningful checks on presidential overreaching, from either Congress or from within the executive branch. At least on some important counterterrorism issues, OLC had abandoned its traditional core mission of preventing unlawful executive action and instead had provided advice outside the mainstream of legal thought that seemed designed to legitimate the administration's desired policies.

Legal and Factual Background

The Bush Administration's Military Commissions

On November 13, 2001, two months after the 9/11 attacks, President Bush issued a military order that authorized the creation of military commissions to try certain terrorism suspects. Entitled the "Detention, Treatment, and Trial of Certain Non–Citizens in the War Against Terrorism," the order authorized military commissions for any non-citizen the President determined "there is reason to believe:"

---

[46] Adam Nagourney & Megan Thee, *Bush's Public Approval at New Low Point*, N.Y. Times, May 9, 2006, at A1.

(i) is or was a member of al Qaida, (ii) has engaged in, aided or abetted, or conspired to commit, acts of international terrorism, or acts in preparation therefor, that have caused, threaten to cause, or have as their aim to cause, injury to or adverse effects on the United States, its citizens, national security, foreign policy, or economy; or (iii) has knowingly harbored one or more [such] individuals....[47]

The order did not provide many specifics about the new tribunals, but instead directed the Secretary of Defense to issue orders and regulations to fill in necessary details. The order did make clear, however, that it authorized the new tribunals to try suspected terrorists for war crimes under conditions less protective of the rights of the accused and more favorable to the prosecution than provided by federal courts or courts-martial. Conviction, for example, was possible on a two-thirds rather than unanimous vote, upon a lesser standard of proof than beyond a reasonable doubt, on evidence inadmissible in established tribunals and presented in secret proceedings, and with no right of appeal. A fundamental characteristic of the commissions was the concentration in the executive branch—in particular, in the military—of the authority to try, convict, and sentence individuals. Among the central justifications offered was the need for swift justice, sometimes in secret and based on evidence not admissible in existing tribunals.

President Bush did not ask Congress to authorize the creation of this military commission system. In a memo that the Bush administration continues to keep secret but the existence of which the *New York Times* reported, OLC assessed the legality of the military commissions. OLC concluded that, as Commander in Chief, the President possessed the inherent authority to proceed without congressional authorization and that he could use the commissions to try suspected terrorists for violating the law of war without providing the protections of the law of war that he found inapplicable, such as those of the Geneva Conventions.[48] Here, in addition to its controversial broad view of presidential power, the administration could rely on the historical use of military commissions during wartime, dating back to the Revolutionary War and particularly during the Civil War and World War II. The United States typically had used military commissions in theaters of ongoing military conflicts or where martial law was in effect; President Bush's order and subsequent proposed use were not so limited.

---

[47] Military Order of November 13, 2001: Detention, Treatment, and Trial of Certain Non–Citizens in the War Against Terrorism, 66 Fed. Reg. 57,833, *reprinted in* 10 U.S.C. § 801 (2006).

[48] Tim Golden, *After Terror, A Secret Rewriting of Military Law*, N.Y. Times, Oct. 24, 2004, at A1.

Twice before, atypical uses had led to Supreme Court review, with results difficult to reconcile. President Bush's lawyers sought to model their commissions on a World War II precedent, *Ex parte Quirin*, in which the Court upheld the convictions of eight Nazi saboteurs who were caught and tried before a military commission in the United States.[49] In an earlier case, *Ex parte Milligan*, the Court found unlawful the use of a Civil War military commission to try an Indiana citizen suspected of aiding the South, where the courts duly constituted in Indiana were open and available to hear the charges.[50] The *Quirin* Court distinguished *Milligan* on the grounds that the *Quirin* defendants were "unlawful combatants" while Milligan was "a non-belligerent, not subject to the law of war save as ... martial law might be constitutionally established."[51] The applicability of this precedent to President Bush's military commissions, and specifically the continued vitality of *Milligan* in light of *Quirin*, became one of many contested issues in *Hamdan*.[52]

Vice President Cheney championed the use of military commissions and personally obtained Bush's approval. Some other administration officials expressed concerns about whether the commissions were lawful and wise policy. Some key officials were excluded from the final development of the President's order. In October 2004, during the months *Hamdan* was working its way to the Supreme Court, the *New York Times* detailed the extraordinary process that had led to the order.[53] Among those intentionally excluded were the President's national security adviser Condoleezza Rice, Secretary of State Colin Powell, and career military lawyers and members of an interagency working group then meeting to evaluate options for prosecuting suspected terrorists. Rice and Powell learned of the President's order only when he announced it publicly. Some administration officials described the unusual internal process for developing the order as reflecting the administration's desire to strengthen executive power and "the determination of some influential officials to halt what they viewed as the United States' reflexive

---

[49] 317 U.S. 1 (1942).

[50] 71 U.S. (4 Wall.) 2 (1866). For more on *Ex parte Milligan* see Chapter 3 in this volume.

[51] *Ex parte Quirin*, 317 U.S. at 31, 45.

[52] *See, e.g.*, Curtis A. Bradley & Jack L. Goldsmith, *Congressional Authorization and the War on Terrorism*, 118 Harv. L. Rev. 2047 (2005); Neal K. Katyal & Laurence H. Tribe, *Waging War, Deciding Guilt: Trying the Military Tribunals*, 111 Yale L.J. 1259 (2002); Christopher Schroeder, *Military Commissions and the War on Terrorism*, 29 Litig. 28 (2002).

[53] Tim Golden, *After Terror, A Secret Rewriting of Military Law*, N.Y. Times, Oct. 24, 2004, at A1.

submission to international law."[54] Other officials stressed the urgency of the situation and the desire "to use existing legal models to assist in the process of saving lives, to get information. And the war on terror is all about information."[55] One clear impetus for the military commissions was the desire to use coercive methods of interrogation on the detainees that would render evidence gathered inadmissible in the otherwise-available courts.

In response to objections expressed within and without the administration to the initial order, the Department of Defense afforded detainees greater protections through implementing regulations. These protections included a "beyond a reasonable doubt" standard of proof, a requirement of unanimity among the members of the commission before imposition of the death penalty, and the provision of military lawyers and the right to retain civilian lawyers at detainees' own expense.[56] The regulations, however, still denied detainees some standard protections, including with regard to the admissibility of evidence and the possibility of appeal. The gap that remained between the military commissions and the structure and procedures required by the Uniform Code of Military Justice for courts-martial ultimately would lie at the heart of Salim Ahmed Hamdan's legal challenge.

Salim Ahmed Hamdan

The essential facts behind *Hamdan v. Rumsfeld* are not in dispute.[57] The very month the President issued the military commissions order, Hamdan was captured in Afghanistan. Hamdan was born in Yemen around 1970 (even he is unsure of the year). He was orphaned at a young age and grew up very poor, attaining only a fourth grade education. At the time of his capture, Hamdan worked as a personal driver for Osama bin Laden, the leader of al Qaeda responsible for the 9/11 attacks on the United States. He had worked for bin Laden since 1996, during which time al Qaeda also attacked two U.S. embassies in Africa (1998) and bombed the U.S.S. Cole (2000). After the United States' post–9/11 invasion of Afghanistan, Hamdan's wife and child (she was in her ninth month of pregnancy with their second child) fled to Pakistan, and eventually to Yemen. Hamdan claimed that he was captured (turned over to the United States by bounty hunters) while attempting to follow

---

[54] *Id.*

[55] *Id.*

[56] *See* Neil A. Lewis, *A Nation Challenged: The Military Tribunals; Rules on Tribunal Require Unanimity on Death Penalty*, N.Y. Times, Dec. 28, 2001, at A1.

[57] For comprehensive accounts of the facts behind the case, see Jonathan Mahler, *The Bush Administration v. Salim Hamdan*, N.Y. Times, Jan. 8, 2006, at 44; Marie Brenner, *Taking on Guantanamo*, Vanity Fair, Mar. 2007, at 328.

his family, but according to the government, when captured he was driving a vehicle containing two surface-to-air missiles in proximity to combat operations and therefore while supporting hostilities against the United States.[58] The United States first held Hamdan in prison camps in Bagram and Kandahar, Afghanistan, then in June 2002 moved him to the recently established detention center at Guantanamo Bay, Cuba.

Hamdan clearly was not the kind of high level al Qaeda operative for whom the administration originally designed the military commissions. He was not suspected of playing any direct role in the planning or execution of any terrorist attack. As the Supreme Court explained, "[t]here is no allegation that Hamdan had any command responsibilities, played a leadership role, or participated in the planning of any activity."[59] U.S. interrogators subjected Hamdan to far less extreme methods than the "enhanced" interrogation techniques, such as waterboarding, that were authorized for a small group of detainees believed to be part of the al Qaeda leadership and held until 2006 at secret black sited outside the United States.[60] Hamdan's lawyers and some news reports described him as a mere employee motivated more by the salary that came with the job than by religious or ideological belief.[61] Regardless of any mitigating facts, with five years of work as one of bin Laden's personal drivers, at stake for Hamdan was not whether but how (and perhaps for how long) the United States would detain him, for the government had concluded it would hold him as an enemy combatant even without a conviction from a military commission.

---

[58] A post-*Hamdan* military commission order relied on this to find Hamdan was an unlawful enemy combatant subject to the jurisdiction of the military commission. United States v. Hamdan, Order of Keith J. Allred, Captain, JAGC, U.S. Navy, On Reconsideration, Ruling on Motion to Dismiss for Lack of Jurisdiction 6 (Dec. 29, 2007). The order noted that the "missiles were in their carrying tubes, and did not have the launchers or firing mechanisms with them." *Id.* at 4.

[59] Hamdan v. Rumsfeld, 548 U.S. 557, 569 (2006).

[60] Hamdan's lawyers did claim, however, that he was "mistreated in several ways that may have violated the Geneva Conventions, including having his life threatened, being beaten and being kept in prolonged isolation." Neil A. Lewis, *Guantánamo Inmate Complains Of Threats and Long Isolation*, N.Y. Times, Aug. 7, 2004, at A9. In September 2006, President Bush announced that he had transferred fourteen "high value" detainees from black sites to Guantanamo. Dan Eggen & Dafna Linzer, *Secret World of Detainees Grows More Public*, Wash. Post, Sept. 7, 2006, at A18. In February 2008, the Bush administration for the first time admitted it had subjected three of the detainees to waterboarding. Dan Eggen, *Justice Dept. "Cannot" Probe Waterboarding, Mukasey Says*, Wash. Post Feb. 8, 2008, at A4.

[61] *See, e.g.*, Jonathan Mahler, *The Bush Administration v. Salim Hamdan*, N.Y. Times, Jan. 8, 2006, at 44; John Mintz, *Yemeni Likely to Face Early Trial*, Wash. Post, Feb. 11, 2004, at A9.

Hamdan of course was only one of close to eight hundred detainees held at some time at Guantanamo Bay, all of whom the government had determined could be held as enemy combatants. In the initial days, Secretary of Defense Rumsfeld described the detainees at Guantanamo as "the worst of the worst"[62] and had high hopes for their potential as sources of intelligence.[63] Those hopes were short-lived and soon turned to frustration at the quality of the intelligence the Guantanamo detainees provided. A leaked August 2002 top-secret C.I.A. report "described many of the detainees as having no meaningful ties to Al Qaeda."[64] This and other reports led some top officials, including National Security Advisor Condoleezza Rice, Secretary of State Colin Powell and Attorney General John Ashcroft, to express concerns within the administration and to urge improved review processes and release where appropriate. Change came slowly, however, due to extreme aversion to risking the mistaken release of someone who might turn out to be dangerous to the United States. Part of the problem, officials acknowledged privately, was that the conditions of detention exacerbated anti-American sentiment among the detainees, making release more problematic. Moreover, those suspected of the worst crimes—the "high value" detainees—were not brought to Guantanamo at all, but to secret black sites where they were subjected to the harshest interrogations, including torture such as waterboarding.

The *New York Times* reported shortly before the Court's *Hamdan* decision that the identities of the detainees "make[s] clear the long reach of the American campaign against terror."[65] Many were captured in Afghanistan, but many were not. A member of the original military prosecution team said of those captured in Afghanistan, "in many cases, we had simply gotten the slowest guys on the battlefield. We literally found guys who had been shot in the butt."[66] The detainees ranged in age at capture from as young as thirteen and dozens under eighteen to a man so old he was nicknamed "Al Qaeda Claus."[67] Generally, the lack of

---

[62] Dahlia Lithwick, *The Imperial Presidency*, Wash. Post, Jan. 14, 2007, at B2.

[63] Tim Golden, *Administration Officials Split Over Stalled Military Tribunals*, N.Y. Times, Oct. 25, 2004, at A1.

[64] *Id.*

[65] Tim Golden, *Voices Baffled, Brash and Irate in Guantanamo*, N.Y. Times, Mar. 6, 2006, at A1.

[66] Tim Golden, *Administration Officials Split Over Stalled Military Tribunals*, N.Y. Times, Oct. 25, 2004, at A1 (quoting Lt. Col. Thomas S. Berg).

[67] *Id.* The Bush administration released some of the youngest detainees and the man nicknamed "al Qaeda Clause" in the first years. As of 2008, the youngest detainee still at Guantanamo Bay was captured at age fifteen. William Glaberson, *A Legal Debate in Guantanamo on Boy Fighters*, N.Y. Times, June 3, 2007, at A1.

solid information about most of the detainees stymied the administration's original plans for the military commissions.

Prior Proceedings

On July 3, 2003, twenty months after issuing his military commissions order, President Bush issued his first order for their use, directing that Hamdan and five other Guantanamo Bay detainees were eligible for trial before a military commission. Of this group, the administration sought first to prosecute two British citizens, but abandoned that plan in the face of the British government's strong objections to how the military commissions had been structured—especially their failure to provide adequate review by civilian courts.

In December of 2003, the military appointed Charles Swift, a lawyer in the Navy's Judge Advocate General's (JAG) Corps, to represent Hamdan before the military commission. Swift and others—including the *New York Times*—have reported that his appointment initially was for the sole purpose of persuading Hamdan to enter a guilty plea, but the government denies this.[68] In any event, Swift instead challenged the legality of the system of military commissions on Hamdan's behalf. At the time of his appointment, Swift already had been working for six months with Georgetown Law professor Neal Katyal and other military lawyers on the question of the legality of the military commissions. Katyal, who ultimately argued *Hamdan* to the Court, brought with him expertise in constitutional and national security law, as well as access to exceptional law students and faculty at Georgetown and Yale who assisted in the case.

Katyal and Swift filed a demand for charges and a speedy trial under the Uniform Code of Military Justice (UCMJ). When that was denied, in April 2004 they filed a petition for a writ of habeas corpus in federal court, arguing that Hamdan's detention and prospective trial before a military commission violated statutory, constitutional and international law. Only then, in July 2004, did the government charge Hamdan with any offense. The charge was a single count of conspiracy, that he "willfully and knowingly joined an enterprise of persons who shared a common criminal purpose and conspired and agreed with [named members of al Qaeda] to commit the following offenses triable by military commission: attacking civilians; attacking civilian objects; murder by an unprivileged belligerent; and terrorism."[69] The charging document alleged that Hamdan committed the following "four 'overt acts:' " (1) he

---

[68] Editorial, *The Cost of Doing Your Duty*, N.Y. Times, Oct. 11, 2006, at A26. That same editorial condemned the Navy's refusal, just two weeks after the Court issued its decision in *Hamdan*, to promote Swift, thereby forcing him to retire.

[69] Hamdan v. Rumsfeld, 548 U.S. 557, 569 (2006).

served as Osama bin Laden's bodyguard and personal driver while knowing bin Laden and his associates were involved in terrorism, including the 9/11 attacks; (2) he transported weapons used by al Qaeda and arranged for their transport; (3) he drove or accompanied bin Laden to al Qaeda-sponsored events; and (4) he attended al Qaeda-sponsored camps where he received weapons training.[70]

As the military commission process progressed, on October 3, 2004 a Combatant Status Review Tribunal (CSRT) separately determined that Hamdan was an enemy combatant who warranted continued detention. The government provided this CSRT, like those for all Guantanamo detainees, as a consequence of the Supreme Court's decisions in *Hamdi* and *Rasul*.[71] Detainees challenged the adequacy of the CSRTs on many grounds, among them that the administration adopted a far broader definition of enemy combatant than it had presented to the Supreme Court: anyone "part of or supporting Taliban or al Qaeda forces or associated forces that are engaged in hostilities against the United States or its coalition partners" whether or not those forces had any connection to the 9/11 attacks or hostilities in Afghanistan.[72] The CSRT's determination meant that Hamdan could be held regardless of the outcome of the military commission.

In response to Hamdan's habeas petition, the government defended the legality of the Bush administration's military commissions on the merits, but also argued that the courts should abstain from reaching the merits until the completion of the proceedings before the military commission and the issuance of a final verdict. Both lower courts rejected the government's plea for abstention, but the courts split concerning the merits. On November 8, 2004 the United States District Court for the District of Columbia granted Hamdan's habeas petition.[73] The district court held that a competent tribunal had not determined that Hamdan's status was such that he could be tried before a military commission. The court further held that the planned military commission violated the UCMJ and Common Article 3 of the Geneva Conventions because, among other reasons, it allowed conviction based on evidence the accused would never see or hear. The Court of Appeals for

---

[70] *Id.*

[71] Hamdi v. Rumsfeld, 542 U.S. 507 (2004); Rasul v. Bush, 542 U.S. 466 (2004).

[72] Memorandum from Paul Wolfowitz, Deputy Sec'y of Defense, to the Sec'y of the Navy (July 7, 2004). At the conclusion of the first round of CSRT hearings, the Defense Department announced that of the 558 CSRT hearings held, 38 detainees were found to no longer meet the definition of enemy combatant. Gordon England, Sec'y of the Navy, Defense Department Special Briefing on Combatant Status Review Tribunals (Mar. 29, 2005).

[73] Hamdan v. Rumsfeld, 344 F. Supp. 2d 152 (D.D.C. 2004).

the District of Columbia reversed.[74] The Court held that the Geneva Conventions were not judicially enforceable and in any event did not apply to Hamdan. The Court also held that the military commissions did not violate the UCMJ or regulations intended to implement the Geneva Conventions.

Shortly after the Supreme Court announced it would review the Court of Appeals' decision, Congress enacted the Detainee Treatment Act, which provided the government with yet another argument: that Congress had deprived the Court of jurisdiction to hear the case. The government filed a motion to dismiss the case. The Supreme Court postponed ruling on this motion until after it heard argument on the merits.

The Supreme Court Decision

On June 29, 2006, the Supreme Court, by a vote of five to three, held that President Bush lacked the authority to establish his system of military commissions. Congress, the Court held, had conditioned whatever authority the President possessed to establish military commissions on compliance with the UCMJ, which among other things required compliance with "the rules and precepts of the law of nations."[75] The Court interpreted provisions in both the UCMJ itself and, by incorporation through the UCMJ, Common Article 3 of the Geneva Conventions to require military commissions to meet the standards Congress had established for courts-martial, absent an adequate showing of impracticability. President Bush's military commissions failed to meet those standards in several important respects, including structural differences that created less independence from the President and far less stringent evidentiary rules that, for example, allowed for conviction based on evidence obtained through coercion.[76]

The Justices' opinions in *Hamdan* are lengthy, complex, and highly technical. Six of eight participating Justices wrote opinions. Justice John Paul Stevens wrote an opinion that was in part for the majority of five, and in part for a plurality of four. Justices Anthony Kennedy and Stephen Breyer wrote concurrences, and Justices Antonin Scalia, Clar-

---

[74] Hamdan v. Rumsfeld, 415 F.3d 33 (D.C. Cir. 2005).

[75] *Hamdan*, 548 U.S. at 641 (quoting *Ex parte* Quirin, 317 U.S. 1, 28 (1942)).

[76] The Court assessed the procedures set forth in the Bush administration's then-most recent amendments to the commissions, dated August 31, 2005—which the Court noted was after Hamdan's prosecution already had begun. 548 U.S. at 612. Those rules allowed the admission of any evidence that, in the presiding officer's opinion, "would have probative value to a reasonable person." *Id.* (quoting amended order establishing the commission procedures). Moreover, a determination that evidence failed that standard could be overridden by a majority of the other commission members. 548 U.S. at 614.

ence Thomas and Samuel Alito each wrote dissents. The ninth Justice, Chief Justice John Roberts, recused himself from the case because just days before President Bush nominated him to the Court, he had ruled against Hamdan in the Court of Appeals, joining the opinion that the Supreme Court ultimately reversed. The Court thus effectively stood a closely divided five to four on the legality of Bush's military commissions, which revealed Justice Kennedy in his common position in the middle of the court.

Given the complexity of the Justices' analyses, an initial overview of the import of the Court's ruling might facilitate understanding of the many difficult issues raised by the parties. Not at all murky was the fact that the Bush administration had suffered a loss. How consequential a loss was a question that divided commentators. Many agreed with preeminent Supreme Court reporter Linda Greenhouse, who called the decision "a historic event."[77] Writing for the *New York Times*, Greenhouse ranked the opinion with the Court's most significant rulings regarding the separation of powers, up there with *United States v. Nixon*,[78] which ordered President Richard Nixon to turn over the Watergate tapes, and *Youngstown Sheet and Tube Co. v. Sawyer*,[79] which rejected President Harry Truman's seizure of the nation's steel mills. Leading Supreme Court advocate and former acting Solicitor General Walter Dellinger declared even more emphatically, "*Hamdan* is simply the most important decision on presidential power and the rule of law ever. Ever."[80]

Many other commentators, however, found the decision less momentous. Some critics of the Bush administration who celebrated the result tempered that praise with discussion of how the Court might have strengthened the opinion. Fordham Law School Professor Martin Flaherty, for example extolled the opinion, but also described its "shortcomings" and how the Court "pulled several punches" in not recognizing grounds for greater protection for the detainees—protection that, he emphasized, remained available to the Court in future cases.[81] The

---

[77] Linda Greenhouse, *Justices, 5–3, Broadly Reject Bush Plan to Try Detainees*, N.Y. Times, June 30, 2006, at A1.

[78] 418 U.S. 683 (1974).

[79] 343 U.S. 579 (1952).

[80] Walter Dellinger, *A Supreme Court Conversation: The Most Important Decision on Presidential Power. Ever.*, Slate, June 29, 2006, http://www.slate.com/id/2144476/entry/2144825/; *see also* Walter Dellinger, *A Supreme Court Conversation: Still "the Most Important Decision on Presidential Power Ever"*, Slate, June 30, 2006, http://www.slate.com/id/2144476/entry/2144911/.

[81] Martin S. Flaherty, *More Real than Apparent: Separation of Powers, the Rule of Law, and Comparative Executive "Creativity" in* Hamdan v. Rumsfeld, 2006 Cato Sup. Ct. Rev. 51, 51, 52.

reaction of the Bush administration and its supporters also tended to be mixed but from the opposite direction. They attacked what they saw as the Court's dangerous and self-aggrandizing failure to defer appropriately to President Bush and warned of dire consequences, but also emphasized how quickly and easily Congress could fix the problem.[82] The crux of most criticism from the Government's direction was the Court's lack of deference to the President as Commander in Chief.[83]

A common observation from analysts on all sides was that the Justices had wrestled with difficult and technical questions of statutory and treaty interpretation, but had not reached the related constitutional issues of ultimate presidential and congressional authority. Moreover, the Court rejected calls from both parties to interpret the statute in light of these related constitutional questions. The Court said that a straightforward interpretation of the relevant statutory provisions sufficed to resolve both the Court's jurisdiction and the merits of the case, so the Court need not (at least not expressly) resort to rules of construction that required constitutional analysis. Most important, as the Court stressed, its statutory focus meant that if President Bush was unhappy with the Court's reading of the relevant statutes, he had only to go to Congress to seek legislative action to change them.

Dellinger offered a convincing ground on which to reconcile the variations in assessments about *Hamdan*'s importance, arguing that they reflected "different levels of generality" from which the decision was viewed:

> [T]he farther back you stand, the more significant it appears. Up close, it's a case about Mr. Hamdan, or maybe about Hamdan and a dozen others. Whether it makes much difference to them is hard to say. If you look at it as a case about the validity of shortcut military commissions, it looks a bit more significant. . . .
>
> But that is not what *Hamdan* is really about. As Marty Lederman of Georgetown Law Center said . . . future historians are about as likely to think of *Hamdan* as a "military commissions case" as they are to think of [*Youngstown Sheet & Tube v. Sawyer*] as a

---

[82] *See, e.g., Concerning the Supreme Court's Decision in* Hamdan v. Rumsfeld: *Hearing Before the H. Comm. on Armed Servs.*, 109th Cong. (2006) (statement of Steven G. Bradbury, Acting Assistant Att'y Gen. for the Office of Legal Counsel), *available at* http:// armedservices.house.gov/comdocs/schedules/9–7–06BradburyStatement.pdf.

[83] *See, e.g.,* Julian Ku & John Yoo, Hamdan v. Rumsfeld: *The Functional Case for Foreign Affairs Deference to the Executive Branch*, 23 Const. Comment. 179 (2006); John Yoo, *An Imperial Judiciary at War:* Hamdan v. Rumsfeld, 2006 Cato Sup. Ct. Rev. 83. For competing views on the deference due the President on such matters of foreign relations, see Derek Jinks & Neal Kumar Katyal, *Disregarding Foreign Relations Law*, 116 Yale L. J. 1230 (2007); Eric A. Posner & Cass R. Sunstein, *Chevronizing Foreign Relations Law*, 116 Yale L. J. 1170 (2007).

decision about "steel mill law." *Hamdan* is about the OLC torture memo; and it's about whether the president can refuse to comply with the McCain Amendment. It's about all those laws the president says, as he signs them, that he will not commit to obey, if in his view foreign relations or deliberative processes of the executive or other matters may be affected. And, by the way, he won't even commit to tell Congress he is not obeying the law. That is what it's about.[84]

The Court, and the nation, understood well the broader context: almost five years of controversial counterterrorism measures through which the Bush administration strove when possible to act unilaterally, without seeking congressional authorization, in order to strengthen presidential power relative to the other branches of government. In reporting on the decision, Greenhouse acknowledged this context, remarking that "[t]he ruling marked the most significant setback yet for the administration's broad expansions of presidential power."[85]

Viewed from the big-picture perspective, five Justices in *Hamdan* soundly rejected Bush's unilateralism with respect to military commissions and recognized Congress's authority to establish and regulate them and the Court's own authority to evaluate their legality. Contrary to the government's request, the Court did not abstain from deciding the case or strongly defer to the Bush administration's legal judgments on the merits. The Court instead compelled the President to adhere to requirements it found Congress had imposed on military commissions and to return to Congress for any desired changes—a suggestion President Bush would promptly and successfully pursue.

A closer look at the issues and holdings in *Hamdan* reveals complexities. The government's brief and oral argument focused heavily on trying to persuade the Court that it should not even reach the merits of Hamdan's challenge because the Court lacked jurisdiction or, in the alternative, because it should decline to exercise any power it might possess to decide the case.[86] Among other things, the 2005 Detainee Treatment Act (DTA) removed the jurisdiction of the federal courts over habeas corpus actions brought by Guantanamo detainees and allowed only limited appeals to the Court of Appeals for the District of Columbia Circuit.[87] The government argued that this provision operated retroac-

---

[84] Walter Dellinger, *A Supreme Court Conversation: Still "the Most Important Decision on Presidential Power Ever"*, Slate, June 30, 2006, http://www.slate.com/id/2144476/entry/2144911/.

[85] Linda Greenhouse, *Justices, 5–3, Broadly Reject Bush Plan to Try Detainees*, N.Y. Times, June 30, 2006, at A1.

[86] Brief for Respondents, Hamdan v. Rumsfeld, 548 U.S. 557 (2006) (No. 05–184).

[87] Pub. L. No. 109–148, Title X, § 1005, 119 Stat. 2680, 2742 (2005) (to be codified as amended by the Military Commissions Act of 2006 at 28 U.S.C. § 2241(e)).

tively and that it required the Court to dismiss Hamdan's challenge. Hamdan replied that to interpret the DTA in this manner would raise grave constitutional questions about Congress's authority to limit the Supreme Court's appellate jurisdiction. The Court ruled that it need not consider that potential constitutional issue because its application of ordinary principles of statutory construction, which relied upon a close parsing of the statute's wording, established that the DTA's deprivation of jurisdiction did not apply retroactively. With a telling description of what was at stake, the Court also rejected the government's request that it voluntarily abstain from deciding the case until after the final outcome of the military commission proceeding:

> Hamdan and the Government both have a compelling interest in knowing in advance whether Hamdan may be tried by a military commission that arguably is without any basis in law and operates free from many of the procedural rules prescribed by Congress for courts-martial-rules intended to safeguard the accused and ensure the reliability of any conviction.[88]

Regarding the merits of the legality of the military commissions, the government argued that the President possessed the constitutional authority to establish military commissions in the absence of congressional authorization and, in the alternative, that Congress had authorized the commissions through the UCMJ, the post 9/11 Authorization to Use Military Force (AUMF), and the DTA. Hamdan contested each of these four claimed sources of authority and contended that even if some form of military commission was authorized, President Bush's commissions violated the UCMJ and international law. Hamdan's brief expressly acknowledged that he was not challenging Congress's authority to authorize military commissions, subject to constitutional requirements, but was arguing that Congress had not exercised that authority.[89]

The Court did not reach the President's claim of authority to act in the absence of congressional authorization. It said it would assume that Section 821 of the UCMJ authorized the President to convene military commissions under some circumstances. Section 821 states that the UCMJ's conferral of "jurisdiction upon courts-martial do[es] not deprive military commissions ... of concurrent jurisdiction with respect to offenders or offenses that by statute or by the law of war may be tried by military commissions...."[90] The Court cited *Ex parte Quirin's* holding that Congress, through a substantially identical predecessor to Section

---

[88] *Hamdan*, 548 U.S. at 588.

[89] Brief for Petitioner Salim Ahmed Hamdan at 13–17, Hamdan v. Rumsfeld, 548 U.S. 557 (No. 05–184).

[90] *Hamdan*, 548 U.S. at 641 (quoting Uniform Code of Military Justice (UCMJ), 10 U.S.C. § 821).

821, had authorized the military commission at issue there, which convicted eight Nazi saboteurs.[91] The Court described this holding as "controversial," but found no occasion to revisit it because the Court interpreted the UCMJ as imposing new requirements on military commissions—requirements, the Court went on to hold, that President Bush had failed to meet.[92] The Court further held that neither the post–9/11 AUMF nor the DTA authorized military commissions that failed to comply with the UCMJ. "Together, the UCMJ, the AUMF, and the DTA at most acknowledge a general Presidential authority to convene military commissions in circumstances where justified under the 'Constitution and laws,' including the law of war."[93]

Citing *Youngstown Sheet and Tube*, the Court noted that even if the President, as he claimed, had independent authority to establish military commissions in the absence of congressional authorization, he still would have to comply with limitations Congress placed on those commissions, as long as Congress had acted within its own powers. Although the Court noted that the "Government does not argue otherwise,"[94] it was well aware that in many other instances the Bush administration had argued precisely that the President possessed the constitutional authority to disregard statutes he viewed as inconsistent with his extremely broad view of his own constitutional authority. In *Hamdan* itself the government argued that "[t]he President's authority in this realm not only provides an independent basis for rejecting petitioner's challenge, but strongly counsels against reading the UCMJ to restrict the Commander in Chief's ability in wartime to hold enemy fighters accountable for violating the law of war."[95]

The Court did not adopt the deferential stance the government requested, but found, to the contrary, that compliance with the law of war was a condition upon which Section 821 granted the President the authority to convene military commissions. The Court emphasized that the President's authority to detain Hamdan for the duration of active hostilities, to prevent his return to the Afghan battleground, was not at issue; the Court had upheld some presidential authority to detain enemy

---

[91] 317 U.S. 1 (1942).

[92] *Hamdan*, 548 U.S. at 592. Four of the Justices in the majority, in a section Justice Kennedy did not join, emphasized further that *Quirin* marked the outer limits of the relevant executive authority: "[N]o more robust model of executive power exists; *Quirin* represents the high-water mark of military power to try enemy combatants for war crimes." 548 U.S. at 597.

[93] 548 U.S. at 593.

[94] 548 U.S. at 593 n.23.

[95] Brief for Respondents at 8–9, *Hamdan*, 548 U.S. 557 (No. 05–184).

combatants in *Hamdi*.[96] "But in undertaking to try Hamdan and subject him to criminal punishment, the Executive is bound to comply with the Rule of Law that prevails in this jurisdiction."[97]

The government urged acceptance of President Bush's determination that the relevant protections of the Geneva Conventions did not apply to members of Al Qaeda, such as Hamdan, and argued that in any event the Geneva Conventions did not themselves create judicially enforceable rights. The Court's interpretation of Section 821 to require military commissions to comply with the law of war avoided this difficult question of independent judicial enforceability in the absence of congressional authorization. On the merits, the Court rejected the Bush administration's determination that, because the struggle with al Qaeda did not fall within the scope of a "conflict not of an international character," the conflict was not covered by Common Article 3 of the Geneva Conventions. The Court reasoned instead that "not of an international character" meant not between two nation-states. The Court held that the conflict with al Qaeda therefore was covered and the protections of Common Article 3 extended to the United States' treatment of al Qaeda members.

The Court then considered whether Bush's military commissions satisfied the requirements of Common Article 3 and found applicable its prohibition on "the passing of sentences and the carrying out of executions without previous judgment pronounced by a regularly constituted court affording all the judicial guarantees which are recognized as indispensable by civilized peoples."[98] The Court interpreted this provision to require that a military commission, in order to constitute a "regularly constituted court," must adhere to the standards established by statute for courts-martial, absent a showing of some practical need for a deviation.

The Court similarly, and controversially, interpreted another provision of the UCMJ to reach essentially the same end. Section 836(b), a provision not emphasized by Hamdan's counsel, required that "[a]ll rules and regulations made under this article shall be uniform insofar as practicable."[99] The Court interpreted this language as requiring that "the rules applied to military commissions must be the same as those applied to courts-martial unless such uniformity proves impracticable."[100] Again, the Court declined the government's request for heavy deference

---

[96] 542 U.S. 507 (2004).

[97] *Hamdan*, 548 U.S. at 634.

[98] *Id.* at 628 (quoting 6 U.S.T. 3316, 3318).

[99] *Id.* at 639 (quoting 10 U.S.C. § 836 (2000 ed.)).

[100] *Id.* at 619.

to the President and held that the President had made no showing of impracticability adequate to support the many significant ways in which the military commissions deviated from courts-martial.

A plurality of four Justices (Justice Kennedy did not join these portions of the opinion) would have held for Hamdan on additional grounds. They wrote that the military commissions violated Common Article 3's requirement that tribunals afford "all the judicial guarantees which are recognized as indispensable by civilized peoples,"[101] because they allowed conviction on information kept secret from the defendant. That same plurality of four Justices also agreed with Hamdan's claim that the offense with which the government charged Hamdan, conspiracy, was neither an offense that Congress had made a war crime nor an offense against the law of war—and therefore Hamdan's conspiracy charge was not triable before a military commission. The plurality cited the need for caution when neither statute nor treaty defines the elements of the offense or the punishment, and it warned that to proceed otherwise would "risk concentrating in military hands a degree of adjudicative and punitive power in excess of that contemplated either by statute or by the Constitution." Citing *The Federalist Papers* and the Court's own precedent, the plurality noted the role played by the constitutional separation of powers among the three branches in safeguarding liberty.[102]

Although Justice Kennedy did not join this part of the opinion, he separately concurred and emphasized the same separation of powers concerns about the preservation of liberty, which he stressed supported the use of "regularly constituted" tribunals that check the executive using standards deliberated upon in advance of a crisis:

> Trial by military commission raises separation-of-powers concerns of the highest order. Located within a single branch, these courts carry the risk that offenses will be defined, prosecuted, and adjudicated by executive officials without independent review. Concentration of power puts personal liberty in peril of arbitrary action by officials, an incursion the Constitution's three-part system is designed to avoid. It is imperative, then, that when military tribunals are established, full and proper authority exists for the Presidential directive.[103]

Kennedy emphasized that in deviating from courts-martial, Bush's commissions failed to provide the degree of independence essential to a

---

[101] *Id.* at 628 (plurality opinion) (quoting 6 U.S.T. 3316, 3318). "[A]t least absent express statutory provision to the contrary, information used to convict a person of a crime must be disclosed to him." *Id.* at 634.

[102] "The accumulation of all powers legislative, executive and judiciary in the same hands ... may justly be pronounced the very definition of tyranny." *Id.* at 602 (plurality opinion) (quoting *The Federalist No. 47*, at 324 (James Madison) (J. Cooke ed., 1961)).

[103] *Id.* at 637 (Kennedy, J., concurring) (citation omitted).

"regularly constituted court." He extolled the great value of "standards deliberated upon and chosen in advance of a crisis, under a system where the single power of the Executive is checked by other constitutional mechanisms."[104]

All five of the Justices in the majority, in their various opinions, emphasized that the President could return to Congress and request any authority he believed necessary, and also that no emergency prevented such consultation with Congress. The plurality, for example, described the lack of military necessity as follows:

> Hamdan's tribunal was appointed not by a military commander in the field of battle, but by a retired major general stationed away from any active hostilities. Hamdan is [not] charged ... with an overt act for which he was caught redhanded in a theater of war and which military efficiency demands be tried expeditiously.... Any urgent need for imposition or execution of judgment is utterly belied by the record....[105]

As the government reminded the Court, it could continue to imprison Hamdan and others it determined to be enemy combatants, regardless of the Court's resolution of the case, just as it had for more than four years.

Justices Scalia, Thomas and Alito all wrote separate dissents, and joined many parts of each other's opinions. Scalia addressed the jurisdictional questions and Thomas and Alito the merits. The dissenting Justices framed their opinions largely as simple disagreements over the plain meaning of the relevant statutes. But it clearly is no coincidence that the Court split along familiar ideological lines. More than disagreements over statutory interpretation, the vote reflects competing visions of the separation of powers, and to a lesser extent, of the role international law should play in constraining governmental action.[106]

---

[104] *Id.*

[105] *Id.* at 611 (plurality opinion) (citation omitted). Justice Breyer's two paragraph separate concurrence in particular emphasized these points:

> Nothing prevents the President from returning to Congress to seek the authority he believes necessary.

> Where, as here, no emergency prevents consultation with Congress, judicial insistence upon that consultation does not weaken our Nation's ability to deal with danger. To the contrary, that insistence strengthens the Nation's ability to determine—through democratic means—how best to do so.

Id. at 635 (Breyer, J., concurring); *see also id.* at 634 (majority opinion) ("It bears emphasizing that Hamdan does not challenge, and we do not today address, the Government's power to detain him for the duration of active hostilities in order to prevent ... harm.").

[106] For an excellent discussion of the international law implications of *Hamdan*, see Oona A. Hathaway, Hamdan v. Rumsfeld: *Domestic Enforcement of International Law*, chapter in *International Law Stories* (2007).

Justice Thomas's opinion is the most revealing on this score. While the Justices in the majority emphasized the importance of interbranch checks on governmental power in order to safeguard liberty, Thomas chastised the Court for acting beyond its competence and authority in second-guessing the President's judgment on military and foreign affairs matters, thereby "openly flout[ing] our well-established duty" in ways "antithetical to our constitutional structure."[107] Thomas, joined by Scalia and usually also by Alito, stressed the Court's obligation to defer to the President: to his decision to try Hamdan before a military commission, to frame the charges as he did, to structure the commissions as he believed appropriate including in their deviations from courts-martial, and to interpret Common Article 3 of the Geneva Conventions as not applicable to the conflict with al Qaeda. In a portion of the opinion joined by all three dissenting Justices, Thomas decried "the illegitimacy of today's judicial intrusion onto core executive prerogatives in the waging of war where executive competence is at its zenith and judicial competence at its nadir."[108] He argued that Congress, far from setting forth the limits the majority described, fully authorized the President to establish his military commissions, primarily through the post–9/11 AUMF. Beyond his interpretation of the statutory framework, he extolled the presidency's structural advantages over Congress, which he concluded led the Framers to confer upon the President primary responsibility and the necessary power on matters of national security and foreign affairs.

Hamdan's Impact

As this book goes to press, at the close of the Bush administration and just two years after the Supreme Court's decision, assessments of *Hamdan*'s impact must be cautious. As discussed above, when the Court announced its ruling commentary varied widely, and Walter Dellinger insightfully noted that much of the disparity could be attributed to differences in the perspective—and especially the level of generality— from which the case was being evaluated.[109] Two years later, *Hamdan*'s significance remains dependent, for example, on whether viewed broadly, for what it reveals about judicial and congressional limits on presidential power during wartime, or narrowly, for its direct impact on the lives of Salim Ahmed Hamdan and other potential defendants before military commissions.

---

[107] *Hamdan*, 548 U.S. at 678 (Thomas, J., dissenting).

[108] *Id.* at 690.

[109] *See* Walter Dellinger, *A Supreme Court Conversation: The Most Important Decision on Presidential Power. Ever.*, Slate, June 29, 2006, http://www.slate.com/id/2144476/entry/2144825/.

Prior to the Supreme Court's ruling, Hamdan's principal lawyers extolled the historic nature of the case and what its very existence revealed about the U.S. system and its safeguards against presidential abuses of power. Neal Katyal, who argued the case before the Court, "recalled thinking 'how astonishing it was that "a little guy from Yemen" could be heard against "the biggest guys in America—the president and the secretary of defense." ' "[110] The day before the Court heard argument, Navy Lieutenant Commander Charles Swift, put it this way: "The question tomorrow is not: Did Mr. Hamdan do it? It is: Who are we? What kind of people are we? ... [O]nly in this country can a military officer take a disagreement with presidential power to court as a way of settling. Everywhere else they call that a coup."[111]

From this broad perspective, not only did Hamdan have his day in Court, he achieved a resounding victory. The Court ruled for the little guy and against the President. In interpreting the existing statutory framework and international law obligations, which were far from entirely clear on their face, the Court declined to defer to the President's interpretations and judgments, notwithstanding the military context. *Hamdan* had transformative implications for Bush administration counterterrorism policies beyond military commissions. The Court's determination that the protections of Common Article 3 of the Geneva Conventions applied to the detainees led the Court to declare the administration's military commissions unlawful, but at least as momentous was what it meant for the administration's interrogation policies.

It is now known that prior to *Hamdan*, the administration had used methods of torture such as waterboarding on some of the detainees it considered "high value." In a series of secret, later-discredited opinions, OLC had given the legal green light, including by contorting the law to read the criminal prohibition on torture incredibly narrowly. The protections of Common Article 3, however, prohibited not only torture, but also "cruel treatment" and "outrages upon personal dignity, in particular humiliating and degrading treatment."[112] In reaction to *Hamdan*, President Bush finally made public his CIA program of "enhanced" interrogations at secret black sites overseas, a program Bush complained the Court put at risk with its finding that Common Article 3's "vague and undefined" prohibitions applied. Bush announced at least a temporary halt to the CIA program and the transfer of fourteen detainees from the black sites to Guantanamo Bay, while he sought federal legislation to

---

[110] Marie Brenner, *Taking on Guantanamo*, Vanity Fair, Mar. 2007, at 328.

[111] *Id.*

[112] Geneva Convention Relative to the Treatment of Prisoners of War art. 3, Aug. 12, 1949, 6 U.S.T. 3316.

mitigate what he saw as the harm of *Hamdan*.[113] *Hamdan*'s precise
effects on interrogation practices remain unclear due to the Bush administration's continued secrecy. Even after *Hamdan* and into its final
months in office, however, the Bush administration—including its new
Attorney General Michael Mukasey—continued to refuse to acknowledge
that extreme interrogation methods such as waterboarding were unlawful and continued to oppose new legislation to clarify their illegality.[114]

Viewed narrowly from the personal perspective of Hamdan and
other detainees who faced possible trials before military commissions,
the Court's ruling changed little. In June 2006, Neal Katyal brought
Hamdan news of his victory in the Court and explained that for many
decades law students would be reading the case that bears his name;
Hamdan responded that perhaps he would change his name and that all
he wanted was to go home.[115] Hamdan's victory, of course, did not result
in his—or any detainee's—release. The United States continued to hold
him as an unlawful enemy combatant while developing its response.[116]

Within a few short months, at the Bush administration's urging,
Congress responded to the Court's ruling with the Military Commissions
Act of 2006,[117] which authorized much of what the Court found unlawful.
The *Hamdan* Court made clear that illegalities with the Bush military
commissions flowed from inconsistencies with the then-existing statutory framework, established by Congress and within Congress's authority
to change. The Bush administration helped draft the MCA such that the
new statutory framework governing military commissions, as well as
interrogation practices and treaty construction, would allow the administration to proceed largely along the lines it initially had sought to impose
unilaterally. The MCA also sought in effect to reverse *Hamdan*'s ruling
on jurisdiction by depriving the federal courts of jurisdiction over habeas
corpus claims brought by Guantanamo enemy combatants, and making
clear that deprivation applied retroactively to pending claims. Under the

---

[113] George W. Bush, President, Transcript, *President Discusses Creation of Military
Commissions to Try Suspected Terrorists*, Sept. 6, 2006.

[114] Dan Eggen, *Justice Official Defends Rough CIA Interrogations*, Wash. Post, Feb. 17,
2008, at A3; Dan Eggen, *Mukasey Hints at Wider CIA Probe*, Wash. Post, Jan. 31, 2008, at
A2. On March 8, 2008, President Bush vetoed a bill that would have even more explicitly
prohibited waterboarding and other extreme methods. Steven Lee Myers, *Veto of Bill on
C.I.A. Tactics Affirms Bush's Legacy*, N.Y. Times, Mar. 9, 2008, at A1.

[115] T.R. Goldman, *Katyal's Crusade*, Legal Times, July 31, 2006.

[116] Josh White, *Guantanamo Detainee Rejects Court Procedure*, Wash. Post, Apr. 30,
2008, at A4; *see* Josh White, *Justice System for Detainees Is Moving At a Crawl*, Wash.
Post, May 6, 2008, at A1.

[117] Pub. L. No. 109–366, 120 Stat. 2600 (2006) (to be codified in scattered sections of
10, 18, 28, and 42 U.S.C.).

headline "Detainee Bill Shifts Power to President," the *New York Times* reported that with the MCA President Bush "achieved a signal victory, shoring up with legislation his determined conduct of the campaign against terrorism in the face of challenges from critics and the courts."[118]

In June 2008, the Supreme Court, split five-four, for the fourth time ruled against the Bush administration's detainee policies, in *Boumediene v. Bush*.[119] The Court held unconstitutional the provision of the MCA that purported to deprive the federal courts of jurisdiction over Guantanamo detainees' habeas corpus claims. This ruling went to the very heart of the Bush administration's selection of Guantanamo for the detention of enemy combatants in order to avoid the ordinary jurisdiction of the federal courts. The Court held that Congress could deprive the detainees of the writ only through compliance with the Suspension Clause, which allows its suspension only "when in Cases of Rebellion or Invasion the public Safety may require it."[120] The Court further held that a process created in the Detainee Treatment Act to allow a detainee a limited appeal of a Combatant Status Review Tribunal (CSRT) determination of enemy combatant status did not constitute an adequate substitute. Four dissenting Justices each joined two dissents, of which Justices Scalia's was truly extraordinary for its graphic and extreme terms. He described "the disastrous consequences" of the Court's decision to second-guess the political branches' judgment on this matter of national security.[121] He warned that the "Nation will live to regret what the Court has done today" and that "[i]t will almost certainly cause more Americans to be killed."[122] The presidential candidates' reactions underscored what was at stake for the Court in the November 2008 election: Democrat Barack Obama praised *Boumediene* as "an important step toward re-establishing our credibility as a nation committed to the rule of law," while Republican John McCain described it as "one of the worst decisions in the history of this country."[123]

Notwithstanding its limited effect on the lives of Salim Hamdan and other Guantanamo detainees, *Hamdan* was a remarkable decision issued at a critical time. Together with *Hamdi*, *Rasul*, and *Boumediene*, it almost certainly will stand as a leading separation of powers precedent,

---

[118] Scott Shane & Adam Liptak, *Detainee Bill Shifts Power to President*, N.Y. Times, Sept. 30, 2006, at A1.

[119] 128 S.Ct. 2229 (2008).

[120] U.S. Const. art. I, § 9, cl. 2.

[121] *Boumediene*, 128 S.Ct. at 2294 (Scalia, J., dissenting).

[122] *Id*. at 2307 (Scalia, J., dissenting).

[123] Linda Greenhouse, *Justices Come Under Election–Year Spotlight*, N.Y. Times, June 14, 2008, at A10.

because of the Court's willingness to constrain the President during wartime regarding threats to national security. The *Hamdan* Court refused President Bush's plea to defer to his military judgments and rejected his interpretation of an important statute and treaty that vitally affected his exercise of his war powers. The profound importance of this refusal is especially apparent in light of one overriding objective behind the Bush administration's counterterrorism and war policies: to act unilaterally when possible, even if congressional authorization likely was obtainable, in order to establish expansive presidential power and pass on a strengthened presidency. The Court's repeated rejection of such unilateralism should counsel Presidents that overreaching of this sort can backfire and result in diminished power. And in *Boumediene*, the court took the additional step of declaring a federal statute violative of detainees' constitutional rights. The need for the Court to step in repeatedly should remind all of the critical importance of a vital judiciary.

Hamdan's most significant effect certainly was not to provide the Guantanamo detainees with substantive protections; the import there has been negligible. *Hamdan*'s greatest effect to date has been to force the President to work with Congress, within constitutional boundaries, to implement desired policies. That Congress ultimately chose to give the President substantial authority does not diminish the lasting significance of the Court's insistence on presidential adherence to the law. And that the plaintiff who prompted this reaffirmation of the rule of law was Salim Ahmed Hamdan, a personal driver to Osama bin Laden and a citizen of Yemen, is a powerful and extraordinary testament to the strength and principle of the American system of government.

Two years after the *Hamdan* ruling, as this book went to press in August 2008, the government finally implemented a new system of military commissions. Nearly seven years after President Bush first sought to authorize military commissions—citing the need for swifter and surer justice than Bush deemed otherwise possible—Hamdan himself became the first detainee tried before a military commission. This was also nearly seven years from the date of Hamdan's capture.

This time around, the charges against Hamdan were ten counts of "conspiracy" and "material support for terrorism," both of which are highly controversial "war crimes" charges and will certainly be challenged by future military commission defendants. For Hamdan, all of the counts stemmed from two basic allegations: (1) that Hamdan had provided transportation and bodyguard services to al Qaeda from 1996 to November 2001, with the knowledge and intent that such services would facilitate terrorist activity; and (2) that on November 24, 2001, Hamdan attempted to deliver one or two surface-to-air missiles to al Qaeda and/or Taliban forces in Afghanistan, to be used in the war against U.S. and coalition forces. Hamdan's lawyers again challenged the legality of the proceedings, on numerous grounds, but this time around a federal district court refused to stop the trial.

On August 6, 2008, the panel of six senior military officers that comprised Hamdan's military commission acquitted him of each of the conspiracy charges and of all of the charges related to the delivery of missiles. The commission convicted Hamdan, however, on five counts of providing "material support" to terrorism, principally on the basis of his having been a driver for Osama bin Laden while knowing his services would facilitate terrorism. The government urged the panel to sentence Hamdan to life imprisonment and a minimum of thirty years. Hamdan's lawyers sought a sentence of less than the time he already had been imprisoned.

The sentence imposed was very close to what Hamdan sought: a surprisingly short five and a half years (sixty-six months), with credit given for sixty-one months already served. Thus, Hamdan will have completed his sentence before the end of George Bush's time in office. As of the time this book went to press, however, the Bush administration had not yet determined whether it would release Hamdan upon completion of his sentence or continue to detain him as an enemy combatant. Hamdan has separately challenged his detention as an enemy combatant in a habeas proceeding before a U.S. District Court. Hamdan also plans to appeal his convictions on several constitutional grounds. Most important, Hamdan contends that the conduct for which he was convicted was not recognized as a war crime during the applicable period—a possible ex post facto violation—and that Congress violated the equal protection clause when, for the first time in U.S. history, it established specialized criminal tribunals and proceedings reserved only for aliens.*

---

* I am very grateful to Curtis Bradley and Christopher Schroeder for including me in this project and for their exceptionally helpful suggestions and guidance; to David Barron, Martin Flaherty and Martin Lederman for their excellent comments on drafts; and to Jeffrey Macey and Aaron Stucky for their outstanding research assistance.

*

Contributors to
Presidential Power Stories

Patricia L. Bellia is Professor of Law and Notre Dame Presidential Fellow at the Notre Dame Law School, where she teaches and researches in the areas of constitutional law, administrative law, cyberlaw, electronic surveillance law, and copyright law. She earned her A.B. summa cum laude from Harvard University and her J.D. from Yale Law School, where she served as editor-in-chief of the Yale Law Journal, executive editor of the Yale Journal of International Law, and student director of the Immigration Legal Services clinic. After graduating from law school, she clerked for Judge José A. Cabranes of the United States Court of Appeals for the Second Circuit and Associate Justice Sandra Day O'Connor of the Supreme Court of the United States. Before joining the Notre Dame faculty in 2000, Professor Bellia worked for three years as an attorney-advisor in the Office of Legal Counsel of the United States Department of Justice.

Curtis A. Bradley is the Richard and Marcy Horvitz Professor of Law and Professor of Public Policy Studies at Duke University. He has written extensively on issues relating to international law, U.S. foreign relations law, and presidential power. His publications include *The Military Commissions Act, Habeas Corpus, and the Geneva Conventions*, 101 Am. J. Int'l L. 322 (2007); *The International Legal Order and the Federal Judicial Power*, 2006 Sup. Ct. Rev. 59; *Presidential Signing Statements and Executive Power*, 23 Const. Comm. 307 (2007) (with Eric Posner); *Congressional Authorization and the War on Terrorism*, 118 Harv. L. Rev. 2047 (2005) (with Jack Goldsmith); and *Chevron Deference and Foreign Affairs*, 86 Va. L. Rev. 649 (2000). Professor Bradley graduated from Harvard Law School magna cum laude in 1988. He then clerked for Judge David Ebel of the U.S. Court of Appeals for the Tenth Circuit and Justice Byron White of the U.S. Supreme Court. After his clerkships, Professor Bradley practiced law for several years at Covington & Burling in Washington, D.C. He began teaching in 1995 at the University of Colorado School of Law, and he received tenure there in 1999. In 2000, he joined the faculty at the University of Virginia School of Law as a full professor. In 2004, he served as Counselor on International Law in the Legal Adviser's Office of the U.S. State Department. He is now a member of the Secretary of State's Advisory Committee on International Law, and he is also on the Board of Editors of the American Journal of International Law.

Harold Bruff is the Thomson Professor of Law at the University of Colorado School of Law, where he was dean from 1996–2003. He received his B.A. in American history and literature from Williams College, where he was elected to Phi Beta Kappa. He received his J.D. magna cum laude from Harvard Law School. He has been on the law faculties of Arizona State University, the University of Texas (as the John S. Redditt Professor of Law), and the George Washington University School of Law (as the Donald Rothschild Research Professor of Law). From 1979 to 1981, he served in the Office of Legal Counsel in the U.S. Department of Justice. He has testified before Congress on numerous occasions. Professor Bruff has authored two casebooks on the administrative process and separation of powers, a monograph on the latter, and numerous articles. He resides in Boulder with his wife Sherry and daughter Annie.

Martin S. Flaherty is Leitner Family Professor of Law and Co–Director of the Leitner Center for International Law and Justice. He is also a Visiting Professor at the Woodrow Wilson School of Public and International Affairs, where he was Fellow in the Program in Law and Public Affairs. He has also taught at China University of Political Science and Law in Beijing, Sungkyunkwan University in Seoul, and Queen's University Belfast. Previously Professor Flaherty served as a law clerk for Justice Byron R. White of the U.S. Supreme Court and Chief Judge John Gibbons of the Court of Appeals for the 3rd Circuit. He holds a B.A. from Princeton, his M.A. and M.Phil. from Yale (in history) and J.D. from the Columbia Law School. Formerly chair of the New York City Bar Association's International Human Rights Committee, he has led or participated in human rights missions to Northern Ireland, Turkey, Hong Kong, Mexico, Malaysia, Kenya, and Romania. Professor Flaherty is also a member of the Council on Foreign Relations. His publications focus upon constitutional law and history, foreign affairs, and international human rights. Selected publications include: *Executive Power Essentialism and Foreign Affairs* [with Curtis Bradley], Michigan Law Review; *The Most Dangerous Branch*, Yale Law Journal; and *History Right?: Historical Scholarship, Original Understanding, and Treaties as "Supreme Law of the Land,"* Columbia Law Review.

John Harrison is the D. Lurton Massee, Jr., and Herbert L. and Grace Doherty Charitable Foundation Professor of Law at the University of Virginia. A graduate of the University of Virginia (B.A., 1977) and the Yale Law School (J.D., 1980), he was a law clerk for Judge Robert Bork of the United States Court of Appeals for the District of Columbia Circuit (1982–1983) and then served for ten years in the United States

Department of Justice in a number of posts, including Special Assistant to the Attorney General and Deputy Assistant Attorney General in the Office of Legal Counsel. He teaches a variety of courses, including Administrative Law, Civil Procedure, Constitutional History, Corporations, Federal Courts, Foreign Relations Law, Remedies, and Torts. His scholarship focuses on structural constitutional law and constitutional history.

Dawn E. Johnsen is a Professor of Law at the Indiana University School of Law—Bloomington, where she teaches and writes about issues of constitutional law. Her recent publications on issues of presidential power include *Faithfully Executing the Laws: Internal Legal Constraints on Executive Power*, 54 UCLA L. Rev. 1559 (2007) and *What's a President to Do? Interpreting the Constitution in the Wake of the Bush Administration's Abuses*, 88 Boston U. L. Rev. 395 (2008). She served in the Office of Legal Counsel, U.S. Department of Justice, as the acting assistant attorney general heading that office (1997–98) and as a deputy assistant attorney general (1993–96). In that capacity, she provided constitutional and other legal advice to the attorney general, the President, and the general counsels of the various executive branch agencies. From 1988–93, she was the legal director of the National Abortion and Reproductive Rights Action League (NARAL). She clerked for the Honorable Richard D. Cudahy, U.S. Court of Appeals for the Seventh Circuit. She received a B.A from Yale University in 1983 and a J.D. from Yale Law School in 1986.

Thomas H. Lee is Professor of Law and Director of International Studies at Fordham University School of Law in New York, where he teaches in the areas of constitutional law, federal courts, and international law. He is the author of many articles, including publications in the Columbia Law Review and Northwestern University Law Review, and of a forthcoming book on the international laws of war and the American Civil War. He received his A.B. summa cum laude, an A.M., and a J.D. cum laude from Harvard University. Prior to teaching, he served as a U.S. naval intelligence officer from 1991 to 1995, and as a law clerk for Judge Michael Boudin of the United States Court of Appeals for the First Circuit and for Associate Justice David Souter of the United States Supreme Court. He has taught as a visiting professor at Columbia Law School, the University of Virginia School of Law, and at Sungkyunkwan University in Seoul, Korea.

Trevor W. Morrison is Professor of Law at Columbia Law School. He teaches and writes about constitutional law, the federal courts, and statutory interpretation, and has a particular interest in executive branch statutory and constitutional interpretation. Professor Morrison's recent scholarship includes *Suspension and the Extrajudicial Constitution*, 107 Colum. L. Rev. 1533 (2007); *Constitutional Avoidance in the*

Executive Branch, *106 Colum. L. Rev. 1189 (2006); Hamdi's* Habeas Puzzle: Suspension as Authorization? *91 Cornell L. Rev. 411 (2006); Private Attorneys General and the First Amendment, 103 Mich. L. Rev. 589 (2005); and, with Seth P. Waxman,* What Kind of Immunity? Federal Officers, State Criminal Law, and the Supremacy Clause, *112 Yale L.J. 2195 (2003). With Michael C. Dorf, he is the co-author of the forthcoming Constitutional Law: Principles & Theory (under contract with Oxford University Press). Professor Morrison received a B.A. from the University of British Columbia and a J.D. from Columbia Law School, and he was a Richard Hofstadter Fellow in History at Columbia University. He clerked for Judge Betty B. Fletcher of the United States Court of Appeals for the Ninth Circuit and for Justice Ruth Bader Ginsburg of the Supreme Court of the United States. He served for two years in the Department of Justice, first as a Bristow Fellow in the Office of the Solicitor General and then as an Attorney–Advisor in the Office of Legal Counsel. In addition, he was in private practice as an associate of Wilmer, Cutler & Pickering in Washington, DC.*

H. Jefferson Powell is the Frederic Cleaveland Professor of Law at Duke University. He was educated at the University of Wales (B.A. 1975), Yale (M.Div. 1979, J.D. 1982) and Duke (Ph.D. 1991). Among his publications are, The Constitution and the Attorneys General (1999), The President's Authority over Foreign Affairs: An Essay in Constitutional Interpretation (2002), Constitutional Conscience (2008), and a modern edition of William Howard Taft's 1916 book on Our Chief Magistrate and His Powers. He has extensive experience in government, and among other positions has served as Principal Deputy Solicitor General in the United States Department of Justice, a deputy assistant attorney general in the Department's Office of Legal Counsel, and as Special Counsel to the Attorney General of North Carolina.

Saikrishna Prakash is Herzog Research Professor of Law at the University of San Diego School of Law, where he teaches constitutional law, administrative law, and securities regulation. He will teach Constitutional Law at the University of Virginia in spring 2008. Prakash was senior editor of the Yale Law Journal and a recipient of the John M. Olin Fellowship in Law, Economics and Public Policy. He clerked for Judge Laurence H. Silberman of the U.S. Court of Appeals for the District of Columbia Circuit from 1993 to 1994, and for Justice Clarence Thomas of the U.S. Supreme Court from 1994 to 1995. After practicing in New York for two years, he served as a visiting professor at the University of Illinois College of Law from 1997 to 1998. He was also an associate professor at Boston University School of Law before joining USD's faculty in 1999. In 2004, he served as a visiting professor at Northwestern University School of Law.

Michael D. Ramsey is a Professor of Law at the University of San Diego School of Law, where he teaches in the areas of Constitutional

Law, Foreign Relations Law and International Law. He is the author of The Constitution's Text in Foreign Affairs (Harvard University Press 2007) and of numerous articles on the President's foreign affairs powers in publications such as the Yale Law Journal, the University of Chicago Law Review, the Georgetown Law Journal and the Cornell Law Review. He received his B.A. magna cum laude from Dartmouth College and his J.D. summa cum laude from Stanford Law School. Prior to teaching, he served as a judicial clerk for Judge J. Clifford Wallace of the United States Court of Appeals for the Ninth Circuit and for Justice Antonin Scalia of the United States Supreme Court, and practiced law with the law firm of Latham & Watkins, where he specialized in international finance and investment. He has taught as a visiting professor at the University of California, San Diego, in the Department of Political Science and at the University of Paris–Sorbonne, in the Department of Comparative Law.

Christopher H. Schroeder is Charles S. Murphy Professor of Law and Professor of Public Policy Studies, Director of the Public Law Program at Duke University. He served as deputy assistant attorney general in the Office of Legal Counsel, U.S. Department of Justice, and in 1996–97 was the acting assistant attorney general in charge of that office. In that capacity he advised the attorney general and the President on issues of presidential authority. In 1992–93, he was chief counsel to the Senate Judiciary Committee. He has written on a variety of questions of presidential authority, including executive privilege, the use of military commissions and national security surveillance authority. Schroeder also writes on environmental law and policy, including co-editing Environmental Regulation: Law, Science and Policy (with Percival, Miller and Leape), currently in its 6th edition. He received his B.A. degree from Princeton University in 1968, a M. Div. from Yale University in 1971, and his J.D. degree from University of California, Berkeley in 1974, where he was editor-in-chief of the law review. Schroeder is of counsel with the firm of O'Melveny & Myers.

Kevin M. Stack is a Professor of Law at Vanderbilt University School of Law, where he now serves as its Associate Dean for Research. Prior to joining the Vanderbilt faculty in 2007, he was an Associate Professor at the Benjamin N. Cardozo School of Law, Yeshiva University. He received his undergraduate degree in philosophy from Brown University, a master's degree in philosophy from Oxford University, supported by a Fulbright Scholarship, and his law degree from Yale Law School. After law school, he served as a law clerk for the Honorable Kimba M. Wood, U.S. District Court in the Southern District of New York, and for the Honorable A. Wallace Tashima of the United States Court of Appeals for the Ninth Circuit. He works in structural constitutional law, administrative law, and legislation. His recent research focuses on the President's statutory powers.

†